EXCEPTIONAL CHILDREN AND YOUTH

An Introduction to Special Education

SIXTH EDITION

EXCEPTIONAL CHILDREN AND YOUTH

An Introduction to Special Education

Merrill
an imprint of Prentice Hall

Englewood Cliffs, New Jersey
Columbus, Ohio

Norris G. Haring
University of Washington

Linda McCormick
University of Hawaii

Thomas G. Haring

Editor: Ann Castel Davis
Developmental Editor: Molly Kyle
Production Editor: Linda Hillis Bayma
Photo Editor: Anne Vega
Text Designer: Anne Flanagan
Cover Designer: Thomas Mack
Production Manager: Patricia A. Tonneman
Electronic Text Management: Marilyn Wilson Phelps,
Matthew Williams, Jane Lopez, Vincent A. Smith

This book was set in Novarese by Macmillan
Publishing Company
Earlier edition(s), copyright © 1990, 1986, 1982,
1978, 1974 by Merrill Publishing Company.
Merrill is an imprint of Prentice Hall.

© 1994 by Prentice-Hall, Inc.
A Simon & Schuster Company
Englewood Cliffs, New Jersey 07632

Printed in the United States of America

10 9 8 7 6 5 4 3 2

ISBN 0-02-350093-X

Prentice-Hall International (UK) Limited, *London*
Prentice-Hall of Australia Pty. Limited, *Sydney*
Prentice-Hall Canada Inc., *Toronto*
Prentice-Hall Hispanoamericana, S.A., *Mexico*
Prentice-Hall of India Private Limited, *New Delhi*
Prentice-Hall of Japan, Inc., *Tokyo*
Simon & Schuster Asia Pte. Ltd., *Singapore*
Editora Prentice-Hall do Brasil, Ltda., *Rio de Janeiro*

Library of Congress Cataloging-in-Publication Data
Exceptional children and youth: an introduction to special
  education
    /[edited by] Norris G. Haring, Linda McCormick, Thomas
G. Haring - 6th ed.
    p.   cm.
    Includes bibliographical references and index.
    ISBN 0-02-350093-X
1. Special education--United States. I. Haring, Norris
G., 1923-. II. McCormick, Linda. III. Haring, Thomas G.
LC398.1E933   1994
371.9--dc20   93-32411

Photo credits: All photos copyrighted by companies or
individuals listed. Nancy Alexander, pp. 106, 484; Andy
Brunk/Macmillan, pp.32, 36, 137, 542, 546; Canine
Companions for Independence, p.333; Paul Conklin, pp.
343, 364, 365, 480, 503, 510, 511, 512; Jim Cronk, p. 469;
Kevin Fitzsimmons/Macmillan, pp. 3, 115; Mary Hagler/
Macmillan, p. 441; Larry Hamill/Macmillan, pp. 12, 30,
128, 146, 167, 415, 549; Marie Hanak, p. 391; Joanne
Kash, p. 328; Koman Spalek/Macmillan, p. 301; KS Studios/
Macmillan, p. 213; Lloyd Lemmerman/Macmillan, p. 252;
Linda McCormick, pp. 71, 289; Gail Meese/Macmillan,
pp. 89, 181; David Napravnik/Macmillan, pp. 79, 151, 159,
183, 192, 200, 218; Harvey Phillips/Phillips Photo
Illustrator, p. 190; Elaine Rebman, p. 285; Sharon Sacks,
pp. 434, 439, 442, 445, 447; Barbara Schwartz/Macmillan,
pp. 87, 98, 233, 259, 366, 379, 527; Marvin L. Silverman/
Macmillan, p. 317; Marie Thompson, pp. 404, 408; Anne Vega/
Macmillan, pp. 65, 73, 101, 273, 457; Luanna Voeltz, p. 293;
Tom Watson/Macmillan, pp. 301, 320, 473; Ulrike Welsch,
p. 467; Todd Yarrington/Macmillan, pp. 109, 230, 277; Gale
Zucker, p. 375.

This book is dedicated to Tom Haring, a precise researcher, a beautiful person, a wonderful father, husband, and son.

mon frere et le sien

When our mutual regard outgrew
the sprawl of primordial friendship,
we by proclamation moved
into the realm of brothers;
Without benefit of common kin,
deserving kith thus may have their due.

We two, better than one,
had his family come as blessing
to make the threefold cord;
His only boy, a father's son,
by dining in due season
swelled the prospects of his genes;
When his purpose in its time
exceeded expectations
of a longer hour's reach,
I thought then of my brother as
the father of his son.

All else, Preacher, many may do
is surely vanity,
but mortals heard
thunder from Olympus
when the gods begot their sons.

A eulogy to Tom Haring, delivered on January 31, 1993,
by Steve Stivers

Preface

The field of education of students with exceptionalities has, from the early years of special instructional planning, been dynamic. Special education is among the newest disciplines, engaged in the comprehensive management of programs for students, who, because of their learning and behavioral characteristics, require individualized education to facilitate achieving their full potential. Since the 1970s, special education has been in rapid transition. Major legislation passed by Congress requiring free, appropriate education for all individuals in the least restricted environment has had the most significant impact on public education since the National Compulsory Education Act. The most important change, at least as it has affected general education, has been the trend toward full inclusion of students with disabilities in regular classrooms. "Inclusive education" means that children with disabilities are to be educated in regular classrooms with their nondisabled peers.

Educators and broad-based education groups such as the National Association of State Boards of Education (NASBE) have also rejected the notion of a dual system for special education and regular education. The 1992 recommendation of NASBE call for "an inclusive system of education that strives to produce better outcomes for all students." Specific goals include training teachers and administrators to work in fully inclusive schools and abandoning labels, separate funding, and separate placement (NASBE, 1992).

In this, the sixth edition of *Exceptional Children and Youth*, we have prepared the most comprehensive, relevant, and current text available for students in higher education who are or will be educating persons with exceptionalities in their regular or special classrooms. This text is a collaborative effort designed to bring to the reader new information based on up-to-date educational practices, research, legislative changes, and administrative considerations. It has become clear that special education, during this period of rapid change, is a moving target. Hitting this target with relevant information is not easy, and the attempt does include conjecture and projections. It is crucial, however, that professionals who are educating students with exceptionalities be knowledgeable about behavioral, sensory, physical, and learning characteristics and categories, as well as the major issues, contemporary practices, and demographic and cultural changes in the field. In planning this edition, we have taken a position of defining realistically the current status, which assumes that special education is in a state of transition from a dual-track, categorical, perhaps even medical model, to a full, inclusive, single-track general curriculum and instructional model committed to educating all students in the regular classroom. For example, even though many educators reject the system of labeling students with regard to category of disability, the categories remain in use and, therefore, are covered in this edition.

We recognize that Public Law 101-476, Individuals with Disabilities Education Act (IDEA) (the 1990 reauthorization of Public Law 94-142), among other changes in the original legislation, added 2 more categories to the 10 categories specified and defined in P. L. 94-142. The 2 categories added were autism and traumatic brain injury. In a real sense, adding categories in the midst of a general trend to fade categorical lines would seem to be paradoxical. In holding to only 8 (which does include a chapter on gifted, an area not included in the IDEA), we combined 5 of the categories in IDEA. The categories are combined as follows:

- Traumatic brain injury is included in the chapter on learning disabilities, chapter 4, because of the changes in learning characteristics that might follow such an injury.
- We include autism in the chapter in behavioral disorders, chapter 5, because the most remarkably different characteristics in persons with autism are behavioral changes.
- Speech or language impairments are included in the chapter on communication disorders, chapter 9. While it can be argued that speech and language impairments constitute a separate category, communication disorders appear across categories, from mild disorders to profound disabilities.
- The multiple disabilities category is included in the chapter on moderate, severe, and profound disabilities (chapter 7). This is particularly appropriate since almost all persons with severe disabilities have multiple disabilities. In addition, deaf-blindness is included in this chapter. Persons with deaf-blindness are, by the nature of the disability, severely disabled.
- Orthopedic impairments and other health impairments are included in the chapter on physical and health impairments, chapter 8. This chapter also includes the instructional adaptations affected by AIDS, fetal alcohol syndrome, and crack and cocaine.

The sixth edition discusses in detail major issues and trends in the education of persons with exceptionalities, including the issue of educational placement of students with disabilities in the face of the major national trend known as inclusive education. According to the Fourteenth Annual Report to Congress (1992), a larger proportion of students with specific learning disabilities, hearing impairments, visual impairments, orthopedic impairments, and other health impairments were educated in regular schools in 1989–90 than previously. Paradoxically, considering the national trend toward full inclusion, a *smaller* proportion of students with speech or language impairments, mental retardation, serious emotional disturbance, multiple disabilities, and deaf-blindness were served in regular schools in 1989–90 than in 1977–78. But societal pressures are having a very significant influence upon educators to provide for full inclusion of students with disabilities in regular classrooms. Strong voices are coming from courts and educational leadership groups. For example, a New Jersey judge in a 1992 decision for full inclusion of a child with severe disabilities stated flatly: "Inclusion is a right, not a privilege for a select few" (*Oberti v. Board of Education of Clementon School District*, 1992.). "Winners All," a 1992 call for inclusion from the National Association of State Boards of Education repeatedly noted, "'All' means ALL" (NASBE, 1992).

In several chapters, the collaborative approach to systems change is discussed as a strategy to achieve balance and enhance the quality of services and education for students with disabilities. Collaborative efforts of professionals extend beyond schools to include adult service agencies, families, and nondisabled peers. This broader, more comprehensive approach has provided enriched Individualized Family Service Plans (IFSPs) for infants as well as Individualized Transition Plans (ITPs) for students leaving high school. This extended "life-span" philosophy of services, along with gains in collaborative professional planning, recognizes the importance of inclusion of the family in education, vocation, career, and social decisions.

Early withdrawal from school of students with disabilities is a major concern in the eyes of professionals engaged in providing services for these students. The dropout rate for students with disabilities is far higher than that of students in the general school population. Specifically, the Department of Education (1992) found that among 15- to 20-year-olds who left school, 43% of students with disabilities had dropped out, compared to 24% in the general population. If education is to respond fully to the call to educate *all* students, we must find answers to why students with disabilities reject the services so essential to their future success in our modern, very diverse society.

Our concern with the disproportionate number of dropouts among students with disabilities is particularly vexing as we examine the outcomes of persons with mental retardation, whether they are integrated or segregated. They often move from job to job and are chronically unemployed. They rarely exceed the semiskilled level of employment, and their salaries, overall, are significantly below the average.

In addition, their social interactions are seriously lacking. For the most part, they are lonely, often rejected, and need assistance in developing meaningful, lasting friendships. The positive side of their socialization, though, is that they are living and experiencing much greater independence in their home communities than in the past. In many more instances than ever before, they are enjoying their own homes, living in supervised apartments for persons with severe disabilities and in completely independent homes for those with moderate and medical disabilities. Their opportunities to express and act according to preferences and the accompanying sense of dignity have increased greatly since the writing of the fifth edition of this text.

As our society is becoming more diverse, many of the same concerns with integrating and demonstrating the full range of civil rights that apply to those from other cultures also apply to persons with disabilities. A growing number of people with disabilities also come from minority and non-English-speaking backgrounds. These individuals are at great risk of being miscategorized and receiving inadequate services.

Even with technological, ideological, and human policy advancements, the quality of life for persons with severe and profound disabilities, with deaf-blindness, and who are medically fragile has been slow to improve. On the positive side, students with deaf-blindness are finally receiving special attention through the nation's educational system. Many exciting demonstration projects are being conducted with particular focus on (1) facilitating communication through a systematically emerging touch sign language and augmented communication, and (2) increasing social interactions through established peer interactions and friendship networks.

Major problems remain in providing high-quality services and effective interventions for persons with multiple-profound disabilities. Their lives have not changed all that much. While there are some opportunities for more experiences with nonhandicapped people, these individuals remain largely with their caregivers and family. Because these persons are just as valuable in every way as anyone else, we must make a major effort to provide greater opportunities for their participation in age-appropriate regular education programs. This means that teachers and support staff must form collaborative teams to become directly involved in administering medication, monitoring services, conducting CPR, caring for students, using machine sectioning following colostomy procedures, and providing gastrostomy feeding.

We still need to identify and specify appropriate rules for teachers of students with exceptionalities. Teacher training must be adequately expanded to include the training and experience required to perform highly specialized roles. There remain crucial, specific responsibilities for special educators in a more inclusive education environment. This means, too, that the role of regular teachers will need to be greatly expanded so that they can provide services to *all* children. Ultimately our response to all children will become natural, and the attitudes that have restricted "easygoing," positive relationships will disappear.

Acknowledgments

We would like to thank Ann Castel Davis and Linda Bayma of Macmillan Publishing and Mary Martin, who assisted Norris Haring.

Contents

Contents

5
Behavior Disorders 166
Douglas Cullinan and Michael H. Epstein

8
Physical and Health Impairments   300
Sherwood J. Best, June L. Bigge, Barbara P. Sirvis

9
Communication Disorders   342
Linda McCormick

✳ 10

Hearing Impairments   378
Sheila Lowenbraun and Marie D. Thompson

✳ 11

Visual Impairment   414
Sharon Zell Sacks and Sandra Rosen

EXCEPTIONAL CHILDREN AND YOUTH

An Introduction to
Special Education

1

Norris G. Haring
University of Washington

Overview of Special Education

 In this chapter you will learn about

- the history of the development of services for exceptional children and youth

- the relevance of *Brown v. the Board of Education* to students with disabilities

- the provisions relating to education for students who are disabled in Public Law 101-476, the Individuals with Disabilities Education Act (IDEA) (formerly Public Law 94–142, the Education of the Handicapped Act)

- the 12 categories of exceptionality as identified by IDEA for purposes of funding and accountability

- the advantages of using systematic instructional procedures in program planning and teaching students with disabilities

- the nature of Individualized Educational Plans (IEP) for preschool, elementary, and secondary students

- the advantages and challenges of inclusive education

- the rationale for social skills programs for students with disabilities

Sarah did not receive a formal diagnosis describing her cognitive and behavioral disabilities, despite many evaluations, until she reached the secondary level. At that time she was diagnosed as "seriously emotionally disturbed." Earlier, when she was 5, one evaluation described her behavior as "autistic-like" and "highly distractible." Since the results of all assessments indicated Sarah to be developmentally disabled, she has been enrolled in special education programs throughout her schooling.

Sarah, now 13 years old, has received all of her education in the same county in rural California. The County Office of Education coordinates nine self-contained special educational programs, scattered throughout the county. Of the nine programs, four for students with severe disabilities are located in the same town: preschool, primary, middle school, and college.

Sarah began her education in an integrated preschool setting that used the High Scope curriculum, a commonly used curriculum designed for preschool and primary grades. During the first few months of school, Sarah would spend the whole day underneath tables screaming, rarely eating or playing with her peers. Gradually, as the school year progressed, Sarah began using words in a meaningful manner with adults, and her inappropriate screaming gradually decreased.

Sarah's next placement was in a self-contained special education classroom, at an elementary school in the same town as the preschool. Sarah's contact with her peers in regular education classes was limited because of two main factors: the location of her room and her daily schedule. Her classroom was located on the periphery of the campus, away from her peers, making integration unlikely, especially during inclement weather. Her daily schedule did not coincide with that of her peers; her arrival and departure times were later, resulting in a different lunchtime.

Sarah was able to be with her peers only during special assemblies and recess times. During these times Sarah appeared to enjoy participating with children her own age. She met a girl, Jenny, who became a peer tutor. Jenny included Sarah in several social activities, such as slumber parties. This was the first time Sarah had stayed overnight at a friend's house.

When Sarah was 9 years old, she was placed in an intermediate, self-contained special education classroom in an elementary school 15 miles from her first two placements. Her schedule was the same as her schoolmates', thus permitting maximum integration time. Sarah began to mix with her peers in more settings than in previous years. In addition to lunch, recess, and assemblies, Sarah participated in fourth-grade P.E., computer, and library classes.

Now Sarah attends a special education class in a middle school in the same town where she began her education. The county office of education is developing policies that favor inclusion, and the middle school that Sarah attends is in a transition phase of this inclusion process. She is now enrolled in a self-contained special education class, where she spends 20% to 30% of her day. She spends the other 70% to 80% of her day with regular education students in academic settings, P.E., exploratory, library, lunch, assemblies, field trips, and community outings. Sarah receives speech and language services both in her self-contained classroom and during community outings. She participates in P.E. and lunch without assistance from any special education staff. Jenny, her friend from the primary classroom, assists Sarah in both settings when needed. Sarah is integrated in exploratory classes, along with two other students from her class, with assistance from a special education paraprofessional. Sarah's educational goals for this class include improved language, functional, and social skills.

Despite the fact that Sarah never attended her neighborhood elementary school, she has established friendships that have remained intact throughout her school years. This is primarily due to Sarah's mother, Jenny's mother, and Sarah's teachers. Sarah also has the advantage of knowing many students in her classes because she has been in the same county educational system for 10 years and in the same school district for 7 years. Sarah went to preschool with several of the students at the middle school she now attends.

Throughout the years Sarah has made tremendous gains in both language and social skills. She is able to communicate her needs effectively to a variety of people in a wide range of settings. She no longer inappropriately screams or cries in public. Her independence has increased in the areas of personal and domestic skills.

Most important, Sarah has developed friendships. Her mother, Kate, remarks that whenever she and Sarah go grocery shopping, at least one person comes over to talk to Sarah. Kate is pleased about this because she feels Sarah is safer in a community where people know her and know her needs. Kate is pleased with Sarah's progress and her friendships.

The authors thank Bridget Kelley, doctoral student in special education at the University of Washington, for this report.

INTRODUCTION

In almost every general education classroom throughout the world there are children with exceptionalities. Many of these children in general education are not formally identified and categorized as having exceptionalities. However, teachers recognize differences and, as much as possible, make programming and management adjustments.

Terminology for children with exceptionalities has changed over the years. Today these general terms apply:

- *Exceptional*: Describes an individual whose intellectual, physical, or social behavior deviates from the norm. Functioning may be higher or lower.
- *Disorder*: General dysfunction.
- *Disability*: Loss of intellectual, social, physical, or educational function.
- *Handicap*: Limitation placed on individual by environmental demands.

Special education has developed as a discipline rapidly since World War II, and, as a result, students with mild, moderate, and severe disabilities have been identified, categorized, and placed in resource rooms, special classes, and special schools. Even though this effort to identify and segregate children with disabilities has been thorough, there are a significant number of students with educational exceptionalities who remain unclassified in general education classrooms. The three categories of exceptionality, whose members to a significant extent remain in regular classrooms, are the gifted, students with learning disabilities, and students with emotional and behavior disorders. These students are often unidentified throughout the elementary grades as long as they do not become hyperaggressive or develop a "high profile" (N. G. Haring, Jewell, Lehning, Williams, & White, 1987).

This lack of complete, accurate identification makes it difficult to specify the incidence of children and youth with exceptionalities precisely. Since the Education for All Handicapped Children legislation was enacted in 1975, records on the numbers of students identified and classified have improved. These records indicate that 10% of the school population have disabilities and are receiving special education services. In addition, at least one child in every typical classroom is an exceptionally accelerated learner or has a very special talent. These are students who are so significantly advanced in their cognitive information-processing, language and communication, and social skills that they, too, require special educational programming and instructional strategies.

5

Whether students have learning and physical disabilities or are accelerated learners, they are like nonexceptional children in all other characteristics. They have similar social, emotional, and physical needs. Yet once they are identified as being very different individuals, we often tend to exaggerate their differences.

It is also characteristic of those who have differences to want to conceal them. At the risk of being seen as different and possibly rejected by the peers, some gifted children hide their rapid conceptualization ability. Conversely, children who cannot associate meaning with printed words sometimes use intricate systems to conceal that they cannot read to avoid being stigmatized as nonreaders.

Differences in individual learning, behavioral, and physical characteristics are often so significant that both general and special educators need to have specialized training in order to reliably identify and skillfully arrange the appropriate resources and technologies, as well as instructional strategies, to create an educational environment that maximizes learning for exceptional children.

Fortunately for persons with exceptionalities, educators have given increased attention to diversity in learning and behavior, which has resulted in the application of technology, adaptations in the instructional environment and programming strategies, and in acquisition of advanced teaching competencies in order to meet their needs. Generally, regular educators are beginning to spend more time with exceptional children; and they are using the results of successful research and practice to improve the teaching of these children in regular classrooms.

Special educators have advanced significantly in their knowledge of individualizing instructional procedures, applying appropriate technical advances, and working in cooperation with supporting disciplines. These kinds of improvements in education have increased the likelihood that children and youth with exceptionalities will be identified and educated appropriately. State and federal legislation has mandated school districts to provide an appropriate education for all children. This legislation is both comprehensive and inclusive, and it requires education for individuals with exceptionalities from the ages of 3 to 21, including systematically finding and identifying preschool children, educating them through young adulthood, and helping them make successful transitions from school to society. This is consistent with the goals of Education 2000, a set of goals for American education established under the administration of President George Bush.[1]

Of course, as with most other disciplines, education has espoused many different theories, philosophies, and methodologies, and the special education field, too, shows a variety of theories about programming theory, classroom placement, and administration policy. The various theoretical trends in special education have given rise to many important issues that provide the basis of curriculum content in many graduate classes in education. In the final analysis, however, it is the classroom educational team's responsibility to educate children and youth with exceptionalities: to help these students complete their education and make the transition to successful vocational placement and life in a very complex society.

---

1 Education 2000 did not specifically address special education. Since the goals do not mention segregated classrooms for children with disabilities, it is assumed that the goals are meant to include children with disabilities in the regular classroom.

No matter how one examines this responsibility, it is formidable. In this book every possible effort has been made to provide: the most recent information available about children with exceptionalities; an introduction to the impact these exceptionalities have on educational requirements; and the special education strategies, technologies, and support services available to assist in educating children with disabilities.

HISTORY OF SPECIAL EDUCATION

Prior to the late 1700s the fate of the exceptional individual was likely to be a cruel one. For example, the Greeks, Romans, and other early cultures routinely killed deformed or unwanted children. Physical deformities were viewed as the result of witchcraft or a curse imposed by the gods. Emotional disturbances were attributed to possession by the devil. In the Middle Ages physical competence was basic to the foundation of feudalism, and people with physical impairments were given little regard. Mentally retarded persons sometimes were kept as "jesters" for the entertainment of the rich and royal.

As time passed, certain religious elements began to maintain that the mentally ill and retarded were "innocents of God" and deserved to be treated with kindness and care. But, if care was given at all, it was often in crowded, unheated asylums where the residents were poorly clothed, underfed, cruelly treated, and often chained. And, in some European cities, people paid to stare at asylum residents, much as we pay to watch the animals in a zoo.

The earliest efforts to teach persons with disabilities were for individuals who were deaf or blind. Special hospices were created for the care, education, and rehabilitation of persons who were blind. In the 4th century Saint Basil founded a hospice for persons who were blind in Palestine. The Nationale des Quinze-vingts Hospice was established in Paris in the mid-13th century by King Louis IX as a refuge for soldiers blinded in the Crusades. Near the end of the Roman Empire, Didymus, a blind philosopher and theologian, devised an alphabet made up of block letters. In 1651 Horsdorffer devised wax tablets that made it possible for blind persons to write (Wright, 1980).

The Age of Enlightenment and the 19th Century

Exceptional individuals faced severe difficulties in the period we now call the Age of Enlightenment, which began in the 18th century. Life expectancy was still rather low; for example, 70% of infants born in London through the 18th century died by the age of 5, and the mortality rate among infants with physical disabilities was significantly higher (Wright, 1980). The age, however, saw the first systematic scientific and humanitarian efforts to teach the deaf and blind.

In 1755, a French abbot, Charles-Michel de l'Épée, opened a school for deaf students in 1755, using manual methods to teach communication. Thomas Braidwood of Scotland and Samuel Heinicke of Germany became known for their work with the oral method of teaching the deaf. Both methods were studied in Europe by the Reverend Thomas Hopkins Gallaudet of Connecticut, who established the first school for the deaf in the United States in 1817.

The history of education of the blind also developed significantly in this period. In 1784 Valentin Häuy, a French educator, established a school in Paris and became the first to use embossed letters as a means of training the blind to read. The school's most famous student was Louis Braille, who developed the tactile reading system most widely used by blind students today. Häuy later founded schools in Russia and Germany, and by 1820 there were schools for the blind in most European countries.

Brilliant philosophers—including Thomas Jefferson, in America, and Jean-Jacques Rousseau, in France—framed new political doctrines at whose heart were the ideals of human liberty and equality. A climate that nurtured such concepts of democracy and individual freedom also encouraged reform in the treatment of individuals with disabling conditions. European physicians were the first to apply the ideas to work with the exceptional. Three names in particular are linked: those of Pinel, Itard, and Séguin.

Philippe Pinel (1745–1826) was a prominent French physician. As director of a Paris institution for the mentally ill, Pinel became famous for releasing his patients from their chains. He also pioneered occupational therapy. Despite a basic belief that children suffering from "idiocy and insanity" were incurable, Pinel fought for more humane treatment (Kauffman, 1982). Though it would not be viewed as such today, Pinel's approach was called "moral treatment." It was, at least, a beginning.

Jean-Marc-Gaspard Itard (1775–1838), Pinel's student, was an authority on diseases of the ear and on the education of the deaf. His beliefs about education were strongly influenced not only by Pinel but also by the Enlightenment philosopher John Locke, who described the human mind as a blank slate awaiting sensory input. Itard put these theories to the test when he was given charge of a young boy found living wild in the forests of central France. The nonverbal and "savage" youth was known as the wild boy of Aveyron. Itard named him Victor. After 5 years of intensive work with Victor in a program based on sensory stimulation, Itard described his efforts as a failure. Although Victor had acquired some language and social skills, he was not "normal." This "failure" is now identified as the first special education program, and Itard is the person to whom most historians attribute the initiation of special education practices as we know them today.

Itard's student, Édouard Séguin (1812–1880) was a famous educator of retarded children. In 1837 he established a school for the mentally retarded and was the first to advocate that *all* mentally retarded individuals were capable of learning. After emigrating to the United States in 1848, Séguin continued his work. His writings (*Idiocy and Its Treatment by the Physiological Method*, 1866) detail the methods that were earlier developed by Itard and that would eventually serve as the foundation of the lifework of Maria Montessori.

The ideas of the Enlightenment were considered revolutionary at the time; however, they addressed only our most general notions of fair treatment and education for those with disabilities. Nevertheless, they offered the first descriptions of concepts that continue to inform the philosophies of special education. These concepts include sensory stimulation, individualized instruction, task analysis, emphasis upon functional skills, careful structuring of the learning environment, positive reinforcement for correct performance, and a belief in the appropriateness of education for every child.

Though much of special education's groundwork was laid in Europe, the reforms and idealism of the Enlightenment were carried into the 19th century by a number of outstanding American educators and activists. The work of Gallaudet has already been mentioned. Samuel Gridley Howe (1801–1876), founder of the Perkins School for the

Blind, not only developed new teaching methods for the blind but also convinced the Massachusetts legislature to fund a program resulting in an experimental school for the mentally retarded. Dorothea Dix, an energetic crusader for institutional reform, called for the creation of new institutions—more humane ones—to accommodate individuals with disabilities.

In later years, reformers would demand an end to the use of institutionalization as a treatment strategy. Despite the efforts of a few farseeing individuals, over the years institutions had become larger, less personal and familial, overcrowded, and sometimes brutally inhumane. In response to these changes was a growing opposition to the principle of institutionalization itself. People came to feel that it was wrong to segregate people with disabilities in separate, isolated environments. Institutions, they argued, should be reserved only for those with the most serious disorders and the least capacity for leading independent lives. But the movement toward deinstitutionalization did not fully mature until recently, after many decades of simmering debate.

Changes in the Early 20th Century

The impetus for special education lost momentum during the last part of the 19th century as the United States struggled to heal massive social, political, and economic wounds suffered during its own Civil War. The pace of change accelerated as the country entered a new period of industrialization and urbanization. Cities began to deal with an influx of immigrants whose differences in habits and appearance were met with suspicion and rejection.

The late 1800s marked an upsurge of interest in heredity. A major source of this interest was Charles Darwin's writing on evolution. Many people seized on Darwin's theories about the survival of the fittest as a reason for eliminating the "undesirable" elements of the population: those with disabilities, the poor, and immigrants. These people, it was said, were responsible for all of society's problems and should be prevented from reproducing. Policies of forced institutionalization and sterilization of those with disabilities became common. Social attitudes toward exceptional populations reached a new low, which lasted until about the time of World War I.

It should be remembered that during these bleak years, children without disabilities often were denied the benefits of education. For centuries, both in this country and in Europe, education had been to a large degree a privilege of the rich. In 1876 less than 5% of American children between ages 5 and 17 were in school. It was common for children to attend classes for only a few years, and for just a few months of the year. In a rural, agricultural economy, schooling was interrupted for planting and harvests or as the result of transportation problems and other obstacles. With industrialization came even greater difficulties. Factory workers were paid so little that all family members had to contribute wages in order for the family to survive. Children as young as 6 were expected to toil 10 to 14 hours a day.

Compulsory education finally became a reality in all states in 1918. During this period, called the Progressive Era, educational reformers joined with organized labor to win the first of many child labor laws and to advance the cause of public education nationwide.

The early decades of this century can be seen as a period of changes in social attitudes toward all children; young people were no longer to be treated as miniature adults but rather as individuals with their own desires and needs. During this period there were developments in psychology, educational theory and practice, and government policy, medicine, and technology that would help lay the groundwork for the tremendous expansion of special education that was to come.

Studies in the field of medicine led to important discoveries about the nature and causes of many disabling conditions. The traumas of World War I ushered in a new era of research and understanding of the brain and its relationship to learning behavior. Much of the superstition, fear, and rejection associated with persons who were disabled had been rooted in lack of understanding. As medical explanations were discovered for epilepsy, cerebral palsy, and other diseases and syndromes, social attitudes changed. With understanding came advances in treatment and prevention—and in some cases cures. Better care for mothers and infants before, during, and just after birth reduced or eliminated many congenital defects, and in the fifties, the Salk and Sabin vaccines eliminated polio as a major cause of physical impairments.

Technological developments were also important. The mass production of automobiles and advances in public transportation made it possible to serve children with disabilities from a large area in centralized day schools. The invention and refinement of such aids as braces, motorized wheelchairs, tape recorders, and hearing aids contributed to improvements in the life-styles of those with disabilities.

Equally significant have been advances in the field of education itself. The development of reliable testing methods provided a way of accurately measuring students' abilities and disabilities. The French professor Alfred Binet (1857–1911) and his student Theodore Simon completed the first draft of a standardized intelligence test in 1905. The test was introduced into the United States in 1908 and refined and adapted. It was followed by increasingly accurate testing procedures in a variety of areas, from audiology to emotional disturbance. Along with medical research, accurate assessment helped educators to understand exceptionalities and to distinguish one from the other. Until these advances in understanding, mental retardation and emotional disturbance, especially, had often been confused.[2]

Tremendous progress was made in educational theory and practice in the early and middle 1900s. Outstanding individuals such as Freud, Piaget, and Skinner, as well

---

2   Binet was commissioned by the minister of public instruction in Paris to develop a way of identifying children who were not performing well in regular education and who might benefit from special education. Although Binet devised a method for discriminating among students by means of an IQ measure, his aim was to identify in order to help improve, not to label for the purpose of limiting instruction.

   American hereditarians, members of a movement animated by H. H. Goddard, ignored Binet's caveats about his test: it provided a score to be used as a practical device, not to define anything innate or permanent; the scale was a rough guide for identifying children who needed help, not for ranking normal students; and it was an empirical guide for finding children who needed improvement. The American application of the Binet test as adapted by the Stanford-Binet has blatantly violated all three of Binet's principles for use of his test (Gould, 1981).

as the many researchers who applied their theories in the classroom, made a profound impact on the field. Psychiatry, speech pathology, and a host of related fields of study were introduced during this time. Contemporary special education owes a sizable debt to the work of individuals in these varied disciplines, as well as to efforts continuing to come out of the field of medicine. Fascinating personal accounts by several leaders in special education, tracing the sources of their involvement and commitment in the field (Blatt & Morris, 1984) reveal that most of them did not receive formal training in "special education." Only in relatively recent years has special education training at a doctoral level become common in American universities.

The diverse roots of the field could not help but shape the direction of growth. For most of its adult life, special education has viewed itself—as it has been viewed from the outside—as sufficiently different from the mainstream of professional education to require special types of training. And yet, one of its major concerns, emerging over time, has been to keep the educational options of exceptional individuals as much in the mainstream as possible. As we shall see, the dichotomy of word and form has not been without tensions.

As special education grew into its own, its leadership naturally tended to emerge from within the discipline itself. Contributions of individuals from other fields remain important, however, especially as delivery of services receives an increasingly interdisciplinary focus. Leadership in the field underwent additional changes as parents and families began to demand increased involvement in the education of their exceptional children.

In addition, our public school systems are becoming increasingly diversified; school and communities are facing new social challenges while fiscal resources are being reduced. Very productive solutions to economic concerns have come from the emerging practices of transdisciplinary teams and support from cooperative arrangements among regular educators, special educators, administrators, and parents. Local community schools are expanding their roles and are assuming greater responsibility than ever before in coordinating social and health services.

Growth of Advocacy

The U.S. government assumed an active role in the development of education at the beginning of this century. Starting with the first White House Conference on Children and Youth, in 1909, and the founding of the Children's Bureau in 1912, federal agencies have taken a leadership role in studying the needs of our nation's youth. It is safe to say, however, that much of the progress made over the years on behalf of exceptional children and youth has been guided by other forces, primarily efforts led by professionals and parents.

The earliest of the advocacy organizations, now known as the American Association on Mental Retardation, was initiated by Édouard Séguin in 1866. The 20th century has seen the creation and expansion of organizations at the local and national levels for nearly every population and disabling condition. Many organizations, such as the Council for Exceptional Children (CEC), founded in 1922, are primarily for advocates without disabilities. From 1941 until 1974 the CEC functioned as an affiliate of the National Education Association. As an independent organization, it launched the

Foundation for Exceptional Children, a nonprofit concern that promotes research, innovation, and efforts to secure the legal, educational, and human rights of exceptional children. The influence of the CEC is great; its national membership exceeds 50,000 individuals, including 10,000 students. Organized at both state and local levels, CEC's 14 overall divisions (e.g., CASE—Council of Administrators of Special Education; TED—Teacher Education Division; TAG—The Association for the Gifted; and DEC—Division for Early Childhood) were created to focus on special areas of membership interest and need.

The Association for Retarded Citizens, founded in 1933, was primarily a result of parents' efforts. Like other parent advocacy organizations, it serves an essential function by providing (1) an informal forum through which parents can share problems and needs, (2) a source of critical information regarding available services and resources, and (3) a structure through which parents can obtain needed services for their children.

Other organizations are made up of people with disabilities themselves: the American Federation for the Blind; United Cerebral Palsy Association; Association for Children and Adults with Learning Disabilities; Association for the Gifted and Talented; National Epilepsy League; American Speech, Language, and Hearing Association; and the Council on Children with Behavior Disorders. Two relative newcomers are the Association for Persons with Severe Handicaps and the National Association for the Education of Autistic Children.

Together, special education and other advocacy communities have produced a growing number of very vocal participants in the ongoing debate over the needs of exceptional individuals for public education. These groups found an especially influential voice for change in President John F. Kennedy, who had a sister with mental retar-

A typical special class.

dation. Kennedy did much to bring the concerns of people with disabilities before the public. In 1961 he commissioned a Presidential Panel on Mental Retardation, which made far-reaching recommendations regarding prevention of retardation, as well as on issues relating to the deinstitutionalization, rights, dignity, and care of individuals who are mentally retarded. Ten years later the United Nations adopted a Declaration of General and Specific Rights of the Mentally Retarded, a symbol of the international recognition and support that had been gained.[3]

Significant achievements in the field of special education accompanied awakening recognition in the sixties of the needs and rights of exceptional individuals. Among these were important developments in educational research. The behavioral principles described in this book that have proven so effective with special populations were identified and refined during this period. One result was the conceptualization of the delivery of special education services as a continuum of services, or cascade, model (Deno, 1970), shown in Figure 1–1. The major characteristic of this model is the sequence of levels of educational placement, distinguished by their relative restrictiveness, that is, distance from regular education programs. Within this framework the regular public school classroom was viewed as the most natural, and therefore least restrictive, option. Nevertheless, until the passage of the Education for All Handicapped Children Act in 1975, few students with disabilities were educated in regular classrooms. Other important models, methods, and curricula were developed; new professional roles emerged; and professional training programs were expanded and improved. In 1948 only 77 colleges and universities provided training programs in educating the exceptional. By 1954, the number had grown to 122; in 1973 it was over 400; and in 1976 it exceeded 600. Accompanying this increase in professionals was a sixfold increase in the number of exceptional students served from 1948 to 1972 (Reynolds & Birch, 1977).

Legislation and Litigation

An important catalyst for change in special education was the civil rights movement. Efforts to integrate racial minorities had both direct and indirect bearing on the movement for integrated education of students with disabilities. In *Brown v. Board of Education*, in 1954, the Supreme Court ruled against so-called "separate but equal" schooling for blacks and whites. The case affirmed education as a right of all Americans, which could not be deprived except by due process of the law.

---

3   The practice of sterilization of the "feeble-minded" was maintained in some states until the 1970s. Even the noted and respected justice Oliver Wendell Holmes, Jr., in a speech given to the Supreme Court in 1927 upholding the Virginia sterilization law, stated: "We have seen more than once that the public welfare may call upon the best citizens for their lives. It would be strange if it could not call upon those who already sap the strength of the state for these lesser sacrifices. . . . Three generations of imbeciles are enough" (cited in Gould, 1981, p. 335).

       The state of Washington, in the 1988 election, passed a referendum to update the language used in the legislation, which referred to the individuals who are mentally retarded as idiots, imbeciles, and morons.

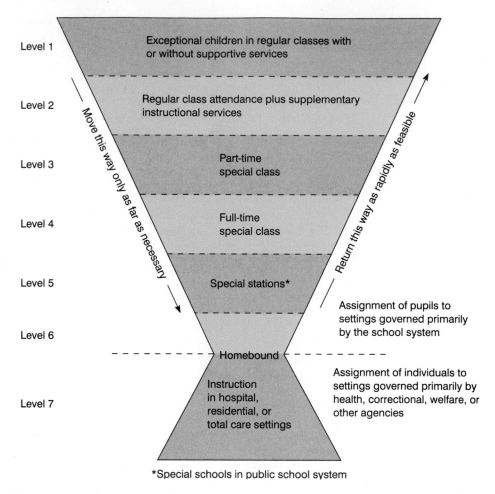

Level 1 — Exceptional children in regular classes with or without supportive services

Level 2 — Regular class attendance plus supplementary instructional services

Level 3 — Part-time special class

Level 4 — Full-time special class

Level 5 — Special stations*

Level 6

Homebound

Level 7 — Instruction in hospital, residential, or total care settings

Move this way only as far as necessary

Return this way as rapidly as feasible

Assignment of pupils to settings governed primarily by the school system

Assignment of individuals to settings governed primarily by health, correctional, welfare, or other agencies

*Special schools in public school system

Figure 1–1
The cascade system of educational placement.
Source: From "Special Education as Developmental Capital" by E. Deno, 1970. *Exceptional Children, 37,* p. 236. Copyright 1970 by the Council for Exceptional Children. Reprinted by permission.

The relevance of *Brown v. Board of Education* to the individuals with disabilities was quickly apparent. Traditionally, the school system had operated on the assumption that its primary role was to provide an education for the majority. All too often, exceptional students had been considered disruptive elements who impaired the school's ability to function for the good of the majority.

Other organizing efforts on the part of minority groups brought some concrete gains for students with disabilities. One of the first laws to provide federal funds for education of those with disabilities (Public Law 89–10, described in Figure 1–2) was directed primarily at meeting minority students' educational needs. Passage of this and other civil rights laws also helped mobilize the parents of children with disabilities to organize themselves. Throughout the postwar decades, parent groups became increasingly active and played a critical role in winning for all citizens with disabilities the educational rights they have today. These parent groups argued that the school must provide a free education to *all* children, no matter what their disabilities. Moreover, the educational program must be appropriate to the child's abilities and needs. Parents took their arguments to the local school boards, to the courts, and eventually to Congress. Special education as it exists today was created essentially by law. Beginning in the early sixties, state and federal legislation began to translate into public mandate what had, up to that point, remained a matter of personal philosophy.

Rather than discuss the complex particulars of each piece of relevant legislation, we have summarized major federal education laws related to services for exceptional children in Figure 1–2. Certain broad trends and implications of this legislation need to be highlighted. The first of these trends is the gradual shift in tone from permissive to mandatory legislation. Initial legislation was essentially permissive in nature, stating that schools *may* provide special education services but assuming also states' rights over control of educational spending. Funds resulting from such legislation served a purely *incentive* purpose, only loosely regulated at the federal level.

As a result of the permissive structuring of early legislation, the Constitution's guarantee of equal protection and compulsory school attendance laws notwithstanding, the system continued to handle exceptional students by segregating them into special classes or by refusing to serve them at all. Although by the middle seventies, about 70% of the states had enacted laws allowing districts to develop programs for students with disabilities, many children were specifically excluded (Weintraub & Ballard, 1982). The estimate of exceptional children and youth in the nation receiving no education was as high as 1 million (Reynolds & Birch, 1977).

Section 504 of the 1973 Rehabilitation Act (Public Law 93–112) marked an important shift from permissive to mandatory legislation in stating that persons with disabilities could not be excluded from any program or activity receiving federal funds simply on the basis of their handicapping condition. *Handicapping* was defined in terms of vocational opportunity, which was the focus of the act.

A legislative landmark was reached with the enactment, on November 29, 1975, of Public Law 94–142. This was the Education for All Handicapped Children Act, whose name was later changed to the Education of the Handicapped Act (EHA). It included a mandatory provision stating that

> in order to receive funds under the Act every school system in the nation must make provision for a free, appropriate public education for every child between the ages of 3 and 21 (unless state law does not provide free public education to children 3 to 5 or 18 to 21 years of age) regardless of how, or how seriously, he may be handicapped.

This law is the most sweeping statement this nation has ever made about rights of children with disabilities to full educational opportunity. Two aspects are especially noteworthy. First, by assuring a "free appropriate public education" to all children with disabilities between the ages of 3 and 21, the law rejects the practice of excluding exceptional children because of their differences from normal learners. Second, because of its highly specific provisions for the kind and quality of education children with disabilities are to receive, the law establishes a new principle: the obligation to offer an individually planned education to meet the unique needs of each eligible child. Because its specific provisions make the act a forceful mandate rather than a mere expression of hope for the exceptional child, it is important that we consider its key requirements and guaranties in some detail:

1. *All children must be provided with a free public education, no matter what their disability.* This provision is based on the principles that all these children can benefit from an education and that all citizens have an equal right to the benefits of their government, which includes education. As defined in P.L. 94–142, the financial responsibility of government extends not only to the educational program itself but also to any services that a child needs in order to benefit from that education (e.g., physical or speech therapy, transportation to school).

2. *All children receiving "special education and related services" must be fairly and accurately evaluated.* In the past, many problems and abuses in special education could be traced to poor evaluation practices. All too often children were inappropriately labeled and placed in programs with no consideration for their real abilities and needs. Most controversial was the tendency to overidentify minority students as mildly mentally retarded, a problem that was found to be largely the result of culturally biased tests. P.L. 94-142 safeguards the evaluation process by requiring that more than one type of evaluation be used, that all tests be free of ethnic/cultural bias, and that the tests be used by trained professionals in a proven and appropriate manner. Further, the child's parents must give their consent before the evaluation process is initiated.

3. *Education of a student with disabilities must be appropriate to his or her individual capacities and needs.* To guarantee that this occurs, P.L. 94-142 requires the development of an Individualized Educational Plan (IEP) for each student. The IEP must be based on the evaluation and prepared at least once a year by a committee that includes the child's teacher, a school district representative, an expert in the child's disability, *and* the child's parents. It must include statements of the child's present level of functioning, long-term educational goals and shorter-term measurable objectives, and support services needed. Although not a binding contract—in the sense that educators cannot be sued if the student fails to meet projected goals—the IEP does represent a serious commitment on the part of the school and should be the most important guide in planning a student's educational program and placement.

4. *Children and youth with disabilities must be educated in the "least restrictive," or most normal, environment feasible.* School districts must offer a continuum of placement options from the most restrictive (residential institutional care) to the least restrictive (full-time placement in a regular classroom). They must not assign a student to a more restrictive setting unless it can be demonstrated that the more restrictive setting will result in greater gains than a less restrictive setting. Placements must be close to the child's home whenever possible and in the company of the student's nondisabled peers as much as possible. When academic integration is not feasible, students with and without disabilities should be brought together for such activities as P.E. classes, lunch, and assemblies.

5. *Students' and parents' rights shall be protected at all stages of the special education process.* In addition to the requirement that parents approve the initial evaluation of their child and play an integral role in developing the IEP, other legal (due process) protections are written into the law. Parents must be notified in advance any time that the school proposes to change a child's placement or evaluate the child. They have the right to review their child's school records and to request—with cause—

that information in the files be changed. They have the right to present complaints with regard to their child's educational program and the right to call for an impartial hearing if disputes cannot be otherwise resolved.

Congress took a further step in 1986 by enacting amendments to EHA that focused on young children. Public Law 99–457, required that 3- to 5-year-olds with disabilities be served even in states that did not provide public education for children that young. This law initiated a new era of federal support for early intervention and preschool services. It established a timetable for providing a free and appropriate education for preschoolers, targeting 1991 as the date by which these services were to be in place nationwide. Its provisions activated a new preschool grant program to assist states in developing a comprehensive system of services aimed at early intervention and added incentives through revised discretionary grant programs. The amendments mandated early identification of children eligible for services, legal reimbursement for families seeking access to services, and a specialized IEP called the Individualized Family Service Plan (IFSP).

In 1990 Congress reauthorized P.L. 94-142 in the form of Public Law 101-476, the Individuals with Disabilities Education Act (IDEA). In changing the law's name, Congress gave notice that the emphasis would now be on individuals rather than on handicapping conditions. This basic philosophical change can also be seen in the writing and amending of other disability-related laws since that time.

IDEA built on EHA by adding these new services or focuses:

- Addition of two new eligibility categories, autism and traumatic brain injury. Advocates for the inclusion of Attention Deficit Disorder (ADD) were disappointed that Congress chose not to include ADD. Congress did, however, create a discretionary research and information program on ADD.
- Addition of rehabilitation counseling to EHA's list of related services.
- Inclusion of transition and assistive technology services in the IEP. Transition was defined as: "a coordinated set of activities for a student . . . (that) promotes movement from school to post-school activities, including post-secondary education, vocational training, integrated employment (including supported employment), continuing and adult education, adult services, independent living, or community participation."
- Placement of the Bureau of Indian Affairs and tribally controlled schools under IDEA's aegis. IDEA further emphasized inclusion of minorities by requiring applicants for grants and contracts to describe how they would address the needs of children with disabilities from minority backgrounds.
- Establishment of new priorities for projects in early childhood education for children with disabilities and developmental risk factors. Areas of emphasis included transition from medical care to intervention services, then to preschool; services for infants with prenatal exposure to maternal substance abuse; technological devices to aid infants and preschoolers; and assistance to parents and service providers in using technological devices.
- Expansion of the concept of least restrictive environment, mandating a "change (in) the delivery of services from segregated to integrated environments" for children and youth with more severe disabilities.
- Expansion of services for and research on children with severe behavior disabilities.

1965	Elementary and Secondary Education Act (ESEA) authorized federal financial assistance to local educational agencies to help meet the special needs of educationally deprived students (P.L. 89–10).
1965	ESEA Amendments granted federal funds to state agencies for educating children and youth with disabilities (P.L. 89–313, Title I).
1966	ESEA Amendments provided assistance to state and local agencies for education of children and youth with disabilities (P.L. 89–750, Title VI).
1967	ESEA Amendments created regional resource centers for evaluation of children and youth with disabilities and services for children and youth with deaf-blindness (P.L. 90–247).
1968	Handicapped Children's Early Education Assistance Act established experimental preschool programs to serve as demonstration projects for children with disabilities (P.L. 90–538).
1969	National Century on Educational Media and Materials for Handicapped Act created national network of educational materials and media for education of children and youth with disabilities (P.L. 91–61).
1970	ESEA Amendments enacted Gifted and Talented Education Assistance Act, authorized federal support for gifted and talented and for children and youth with learning disabilities (P.L. 91–230).
1972	Social Security Act amended to include supplemental security income (SSI) to provide direct financial support for people with disabilities.
1973	Amendments to Vocational Rehabilitation Act (P.L. 93–112) emphasized provision of services for those with the most severe disabilities, included Section 504—the Bill of Rights for the handicapped, and Section 503, defining employment rights for people with disabilities.
1974	Educational amendments increased federal funds for Title VI programs (see P.L. 89–750), set forth procedural safeguards, assured education in the least restrictive environment (P.L. 93–380), and identified the gifted and talented as a part of the Special Projects Act.
1975	Education for All Handicapped Children Act, later renamed Education of the Handicapped Act (EHA), (P.L. 94–142) increased federal commitment to providing a free and appropriate education for all people with disabilities in the least restrictive environment, providing all needed supplementary aids and services, assuring that the rights of children with disabilities and their parents are protected, assessing states and localities to provide for education of children with disabilities, and assessing and assuring the effectiveness of efforts to educate these children. Included were protections of due process procedures for parents and children, Individualized Educational Plans and evaluation, hearing rights, and appeal rights.
1977	Amendments to EHA (P.L. 95–49) included the approved federal definition of learning disabilities.

Figure 1–2
Major federal education laws for exceptional children.

1978   Gifted and Talented Children's Education Act provided money to states for planning as well as grants for personnel training, model programs, and research.

1983   Amendments to EHA (P.L. 98–199) extended a variety of discretionary grants and established new programs for transition of secondary students and evaluation of services as well as financial incentives to expand services for children from birth to 3 years of age.

1984   The Carl D. Perkins Vocational Education Act sought to provide high-quality vocational education to underserved groups and encourage improvement of vocational education programs.

1986   Amendments to EHA (P.L. 99–457) established a further priority requiring that children with handicaps, ages 3 to 5, be served even in states that do not provide public education for children that young.

1986   Amendments to the Rehabilitation Act emphasized importance of transition and post-secondary education programs and added supported employment services for people with severe disabilities to traditional vocational rehabilitation programs.

1988   Technology-Related Assistance for Individuals with Disabilities Act authorized grants to states and required the Office of Special Education and Rehabilitative Services (OSERS) to fund awareness programs, finance assistive technology and services, and deal with other consumer-oriented, technology-related issues.

1989   Reauthorization of Carl D. Perkins Vocational Education Act of 1984 substituted words "applied technology education" for "vocational education," authorized an increase in funding, and aimed at ensuring appropriate vocational education programming for students with disabilities.

1990   Americans with Disabilities Act laid a foundation for full equality for people with disabilities in society as a whole and prohibited discrimination by private employers, government, transportation, telecommunications, and other entities. Obligations for educators are nearly identical to those of Section 504.

1990   Individuals with Disabilities Education Act changed EHA's name; broadened scope of eligible disabilities; placed emphasis on preparing students for life after special education, adding, for example, the areas of assistive technology, transition services, and rehabilitation counseling; enhanced services to younger children and minorities; and changed overall focus from handicapping condition to individual (P.L. 101–476).

1992   Reauthorization of Rehabilitation Act of 1973 replaced "handicap" with "disability" throughout, allowed easier eligibility for vocational rehabilitation services for individuals with severe disabilities, and addressed interagency linkages for transition services.

Undeniably, the trend of the principal legislation of the past two decades has been increasingly specific and mandatory. Running counter to this trend, however, is another, which gained momentum throughout the eighties. Its direction reflected a renewed emphasis on states' rights and local autonomy regarding education, resulting in attempts at federal deregulation, and giving impetus to move to repeal some of the provisions of P.L. 94–142, altering federal rules and regulations related to this law. Despite statements of federal legal and financial commitment to appropriate educational programs for all youngsters with disabilities, the actual level of federal financial commitment is disappointingly small compared to state-spending requirements.

Case Law. Litigation has also played a crucial role in supporting the civil right of individuals with disabilities to education in appropriate, integrated environments. In fact, litigation can be most easily comprehended as the bite that backs up legislation's bark. Once a law is enacted, whether or not it is administered effectively and properly is a question most often decided in the courts. Without this crucial court interpretation, laws might have little or no actual effect on the lives of exceptional children.

What have the courts had to say about the application of law concerning special education activities of state and local education agencies? Figure 1–3 contains a detailed summary of significant judicial decisions, beginning with the 1954 *Brown v. Board of Education* case. This decision marked a turning point in a long judicial trend that had, up to that time, held the view that school attendance was a privilege granted at the discretion of local school officials (Zelder, 1953). Following *Brown v. Board of Education*, school attendance could no longer be considered privilege but must be held as a right of each child.

Another trend in the litigation summarized in the figure is the way in which the cases continually seek to refine the definition of appropriate, integrated education programs, testing and trying the legislation as it applies to each segment of the exceptional population and the ways in which services are delivered to the individuals making up the population as a whole. Generally, suits are filed concerning an individual's *inclusion* or *exclusion* regarding services. Suits for inclusion are most often brought by parents of children whose disabilities are obvious and who are being denied some type of educational service. Suits for exclusion are filed primarily by parents of children with mild disabilities who attended school but whose placement threatens to stigmatize them. Both types of litigation establish precedent that serves to fine-tune the kinds of educational services made available.

As courts are asked to make more and more decisions based on careful consideration of a child's individual characteristics, the importance of accurate assessment and of appropriate placement based upon assessment findings puts more and more demands upon the skills of education specialists.

NUMBERS OF STUDENTS WITH DISABILITIES

As shown in Table 1–1 the total number of children and youth served by special education in the United States was slightly over 4.8 million in 1991, comprising about 10% of the school-age population (U.S. Department of Education, 1992). Overall figures from 1976–77 to 1990–91 show that the number of children diagnosed with disabilities increased steadily in the late seventies, leveled off in the early and middle eighties, and then began to climb. In fact, the percentage of children and youth with disabilities increased 2.8 percent between 1989–90 and 1990–91, the largest one-year increase since the 1980–81 school year (U.S. Department of Education, 1992).

This sudden growth is believed to be the result of several factors, including (1) the addition of new disability categories within the law; (2) the broadening of age ranges and services; and (3) increased societal problems, including maternal drug abuse and childhood poverty.

The largest growth for any one category of disability has been in the category of students with specific learning disabilities. The proportion of such students has more than doubled since 1976–77, and in 1990–91 these students accounted for 49% of the special education population. Proportions of students with other disabilities were 23% with speech or language impairments, 13% with mental retardation, and 9% with serious emotional disturbance.

By far the largest proportion of children and youth served are between the ages of 6 and 17. Statistics suggest that, although law requires service to a population from birth to age 21, traditional school-age children still make up the bulk of the population.

Table 1–1
Students ages 6 to 21 served under IDEA, Part B, and Chapter 1 of ESEA (SOP)—by disability[a]

	IDEA Part B		ESEA (SOP)		Total	
Disability	Number	Percent[b]	Number	Percent[b]	Number	Percent[b]
Specific Learning Disabilities	2,117,087	50.5	27,290	14.9	2,144,377	49.1
Speech or Language Impairments	979,207	23.4	10,979	6.0	990,186	22.7
Mental Retardation	500,877	12.0	51,781	28.1	552,658	12.7
Serious Emotional Disturbance	356,050	8.5	36,509	22.4	392,559	9.0
Multiple Disabilities	80,272	1.9	17,353	11.0	97,625	2.2
Hearing Impairments	42,317	1.0	16,995	9.0	59,312	1.4
Orthopedic Impairments	43,763	1.0	5,630	3.1	49,393	1.1
Other Health Impairments	52,027	1.2	3,285	1.9	56,312	1.3
Visual Impairments	17,783	0.4	5,903	3.2	23,686	0.5
Deaf-Blindness	794	0.0	728	0.4	1,522	0.0
All Conditions	4,191,177[c]	100.0	176,453	100.0	4,367,630	100.0

Source: From Fourteenth Annual Report to Congress on the Implementation of the Individuals with Disabilities Education Act (p. 6) by the U.S. Department of Education, 1992, Washington, DC: U.S. Department of Education.

a   The data in the table are from the school year 1990–91. Note that autism and traumatic brain injuries were added to the eligibility list with the passage of IDEA in 1990. Figures on their proportions were not included in the Fourteenth Annual Report.

b   Percents are within column.

c   If children from birth to age 6 are included, the total number of children served is 4,817,503.

1954 *Brown v. Board of Education.* The U.S. Supreme Court ruled state and local school systems violate black students' rights to equal protection under the Fourteenth Amendment by requiring school segregation; separate education is inherently unequal.

1972 *Pennsylvania Association for Retarded Children v. Pennsylvania.* A district court ruled that state and local school districts are required to provide free appropriate public education for all handicapped children, regardless of the nature or extent of their disability; to educate handicapped children with non-handicapped children to the extent it is appropriate for the handicapped child; to conduct an annual census to locate and serve handicapped children; to stop applying school exclusionary laws; to notify parents before evaluating a child to determine whether the child is handicapped or placing the child in a special education program; to set up a method for impartial hearings if the parents challenge the school's decisions; to periodically reevaluate handicapped children; and to pay private school tuition if they refer the child for private education. In later years, through such cases as *Fialkowski v. Shapp* (1975), the courts further interpreted the original PARC ruling to mean that schools must use proven, state-of-the-art teaching methods to meet the criteria for appropriate education.

1972 *Mills v. Board of Education.* A district court ruled that the District of Columbia is required to provide free and suitable public education to all children with disabilities, regardless of the nature or extent of their liability; to not suspend a handicapped child for more than 3 days without first granting the child the right to a hearing; to continue the child's education in home-based or other nonschool programs during the suspension; to conduct an annual census of handicapped children; to properly evaluate each handicapped child's educational needs; to provide compensatory education to illegally excluded children; to notify parents before evaluating a child to determine whether the child is handicapped and placing the child in a special education program; to set up a method for impartial hearings if the parents challenge the school's decisions; to periodically reevaluate handicapped children; and to give parents the right to see and add to or clarify their children's school records.

1972 *Larry P. v. Riles* (also 1980 and 1992). A district court judge ruled that certain IQ tests discriminate against black children because the tests were not validated as ways to determine those children's intelligence; schools may not use those tests for deciding whether to place black children in classes for mildly retarded children; and other ways of assessing minority children must be used instead of IQ tests. The judge rescinded the ban in 1992, saying it was too broad. At the same time, he ordered the state education department in California to search for other "dead-end" special education programs.

1972 *Frederick L. v. Thomas* (also 1976). Learning disabled children are not educated appropriately, as is their right, when they are not taught by qualified, specially trained teachers.

1975 *Lora v. Board of Education of City of New York.* Emotionally disturbed children must be educated with nonhandicapped children and may not be segregated by race or sex from other children. The court adopted the "mainstreaming" principle.

1979 *Mattie T. v. Holladay.* The state of Mississippi violated Section 504 by failing to include all school-age handicapped children in schools, in the least restrictive settings, and in conformity with nonbiased testing procedures.

1979 *New Mexico Association for Retarded Citizens v. New Mexico.* The state violated Section 504 by failing to include all school-age handicapped children in an appropriate public school program.

Figure 1–3
Significant judicial decisions.

1979   *New York State Association for Retarded Children v. Carey.* Retarded children with hepatitis-B, an infectious disease that can be contained by public health practices, may not be placed in separate, self-contained programs in New York City schools. Such placement violated P.L. 94–142 and Section 504 provisions for least restrictive educational placements.

1980   *Battle v. Commonwealth.* An appeals court established that a policy limiting the school year to 180 days would violate P.L. 94–142 if the policy denied a student free appropriate public education.

1982   *Rowley v. Board of Education of Hendrick Hudson Central School District.* School district does not have to provide an interpreter for a deaf child because the child is making adequate progress in school without such special assistance. In this Supreme Court decision on P.L. 94–142, appropriate education does not require the maximizing of education potential.

1984   *Irving Independent School District v. Tatro.* The Supreme Court ruled that school systems must provide handicapped students with medical services to help them benefit from education unless the services require a physician.

1984   *Smith v. Robinson.* The Supreme Court ruled that parents are not entitled to recover attorney's fees. Also, plaintiffs cannot sue under P.L. 94–142 and Section 504 simultaneously.

1984   *Lunceford v. District of Columbia Board of Education.* When a young man with multiple disabilities was moved from a private hospital to a public hospital, an appeals court ruled the move was not a change of placement, since the change involved no fundamental change in his educational program.

1988   *Lachman v. Illinois State Board of Education.* Appeals court stated that if a school district's methodology for the education of a child involves a restrictive placement, the district need not adopt a different methodology that would permit a less restrictive environment.

1988   *Honig v. Doe.* Supreme Court ruled the expulsion of dangerous students for more than 10 days, when the dangerous behavior is a result of a disability, violates the "stay put" provision and is a "change of placement."

1988   *Cronin v. Board of Education.* A district court in New York held that graduation constitutes a change of placement. Therefore, the school district was precluded from removing a child from school by graduation while review was pending.

1989   *Daniel R. R. v. State Board of Education.* In the case of a boy with Down syndrome, an appeals court framed a two-part test to decide LRE disputes: (1) determining whether education in a regular classroom with supplementary aids can be achieved satisfactorily and (2) if not, determining whether the child has been mainstreamed to the maximum extent appropriate.

1991   *Cocores v. Portsmouth New Hampshire School District.* Parents sought compensatory education services after their son had passed the age of eligibility under IDEA. A district court approved, finding that an action for compensatory education can be brought after a student is no longer eligible if the alleged violation of IDEA occurred while the student was still within the age of entitlement.

1992   *Sacramento School District v. Holland.* A district court ruled that a 9-year-old girl with disabilities must be allowed "full inclusion" in a regular classroom and adopted a definition of that term that reads: "Under full inclusion, the child's primary placement is in the regular education class, and the child has no additional assignment to any special education class for handicapped children."

Much special education research on the teenage-to-adult years has focused on students with disabilities who drop out of school. Results from the National Longitudinal Transition Study of Special Education Students, funded by the Department of Education in 1992, found the dropout rate of students with disabilities was significantly higher than that of students in the general population. The dropout rate was found to be particularly high for students with learning disabilities (23%), emotional disturbance (50%), mental retardation (29%), and speech impairments (28%).

Prevalence Versus Incidence

The task of determining the number of children needing special education services is far from simple. Much depends on whether figures collected represent prevalence or incidence. These two ways of estimating populations are sometimes thought to be interchangeable, yet they are not the same.

Technically, *incidence* means the number of new cases of individuals with an exceptionality over a given period of time (frequently a year). *Prevalence* refers to the total number of existing cases, both old and new, identified in the population at a specific point in time. In this text we confine our discussion to prevalence, using the figures for the categories of disability reported to the U.S. Department of Education for the school year 1990–91 by state agencies as reported in the *Fourteenth Annual Report to Congress* (U.S. Department of Education, 1992). Corresponding figures for the gifted are not available.

Problems in Estimating Prevalence

Even though prevalence figures are generally more reliable than incidence figures, any attempt to accurately assess the prevalence of specific kinds of disabling conditions inevitably encounters several stumbling blocks. First, the definition of any one condition may be open to subjective interpretation and may thus vary widely, even within small geographic areas. Second, a related problem is the question of which criteria and evaluation procedures are employed to determine the existence of a disabling condition. Estimates of prevalence are only as valid as the criteria and evaluating techniques used. Third, funding and professional resources available for services to people with disabilities have a significant impact on prevalence figures. Generally, the more funding and resources available, the higher the prevalence figures. If money and professional help are limited, individuals with disabilities may not be identified or served and thus are not included in statistical analyses. Finally, in reporting prevalence, state and local governments may include only those disabling conditions that fall under federal guidelines for funding rather than using more valid criteria.

In summary, prevalence figures are difficult to obtain, variable, and dependent upon trends in classification and the provision of services.

Defining Categories

Who are the exceptional children and youth being served? IDEA (P.L. 101–476) identifies 12 categories of exceptionality for purposes of funding and accountability:

specific learning disabilities   hearing impairments
speech or language impairments   orthopedic impairments
mental retardation   visual impairments
serious emotional disturbance[4]   deaf-blindness
other health impairments   traumatic brain injury
multiple disabilities   autism

IDEA added traumatic brain injury and autism to EHA's list of disability categories. Traumatic brain injury can be categorized as either general or "closed head," that is, caused by a blunt object, general forceful impact, or a focal, open head wound. In either general or closed head injuries there may be tearing of nerve fibers, bruising of brain tissue against the skull, brain stem damage, and swelling. Posttraumatic symptoms in cases of the most severe trauma may be a comatose state, or, in a milder trauma, drowsiness, disorientation, and nausea. Traumatic brain injury is of special concern to educators because of the permanent effect on learning and behavior characteristics. The most common posttraumatic learning changes are confusion in directionality, marked distractibility, short attention span, and problems in short-term and long-term memory. Changes in behavior are characterized by hyperactivity, impulsivity, and, frequently, aggressiveness. Autism is a severe disorder of childhood, usually appearing by age 2½, characterized by lack of social participation, noncommunication, stereotypic behavior, and lowered cognitive and language abilities.

Although the categories contain a large number of subcategories (e.g., Down syndrome and the chromosomal and metabolic disorders), they provide a functional grouping of disabling conditions.

We provide here an even more comprehensive categorization of disabilities:

1. Sensory disabilities, including hearing and vision impairments.
2. Intellectual deviations, including giftedness as well as mental retardation.
3. Communication disorders, such as speech and language dysfunction.
4. Learning disabilities/minimal brain dysfunction, resulting in learning problems without motor involvement.
5. Behavior disorders, including severe emotional disturbances.

---

4   The Department of Education has considered changing the terminology and definition for this category. The main question is whether to include behavior disorders, thereby broadening the definition of "serious emotional disturbance" and creating a large pool of students who have not been adequately served in the schools but who now would be expected to receive services. The Center for Mental Health Services defines a child with serious emotional disturbance as one "from birth to age 18, who currently or any time during the past year has had a diagnosable mental, behavioral, or emotional disorder of sufficient duration to meet diagnostic criteria specified within DSM-III that resulted in functional impairment which substantially interferes with or limits . . . functioning in family, school, or community activities" (*Federal Register*, 1993). Although this definition is restricted to persons 18 and younger, most states extend the age range through the 21st year, and definitions of serious emotional disturbance differ between the Department of Education and the Center for Mental Health Services, the difference has not, up to this point, caused problems with regard to children's access to services.

6. Physical disabilities and health impairments, including neurological defects, ortho-pedic conditions, diseases such as muscular dystrophy and sickle cell anemia, birth defects, developmental disabilities, and autism.

Within each of these categories, the degree and frequency of difficulties of the exceptional experience vary widely. For example, a person with only slight problems in visual discrimination may require very little special help to function near the norm socially and intellectually. Someone who is blind, on the other hand, may need the help of many specialists over a long period of time to achieve mobility and social adjustment. Similarly, a mild motor impairment might adversely affect an individual's performance in certain games or sports but not in developing other skills.

It should be noted that among the exceptional, the gifted and talented are a sadly neglected group. While the difficulties they experience and the needs they have are often as great as those of other exceptional individuals, little has been done for them. Few laws make special programs available to them, and schools have been slow to meet their educational and social needs. Indeed, all too often the gifted and talented find hostility rather than concern and interest from their teachers and their peers. While throughout the text the term *exceptionality* may be used more or less synony-mously with the term *disability*, we have not lost sight of its broader sense.

Effects of Labeling

Some system for identifying and classifying the exceptional would seem to be a logical first step in providing services to meet their needs. Assigning a label can result in desired increased visibility. For example, parents who were eager to find a more acceptable term for children given such labels as "neurologically handicapped," "mini-mal brain dysfunction," and "educable mentally retarded" adopted the label "learning disabled" and formed the Association for Children with Learning Disabilities (ACLD). This association now has chapters in all 50 states and has proven to be an effective special-interest group in lobbying for legislation, federal funding, and special programs for those with learning disabilities.

Yet there are implicit dangers in the labels that result from such classification. Exceptional individuals display a wide range of differences. No one category can ade-quately describe the social, educational, psychological, and physical advantages or disadvantages of an exceptional person. Many of the labels we use today result from the attempts of medical and psychological researchers to distinguish disabilities; the problems inherent in the medical model for disability are pointed out with increasing regularity.

According to this traditional way of viewing "handicaps," identification procedures locate disabilities in children, just as a physician might diagnose presence of a medical problem in an individual. Clearly, the procedure may be valid for many types of excep-tionality, especially those with an identifiable physical cause. But the appropriateness of the model comes into question for youngsters labeled with "mild disabilities" or "learning disabilities," where it is possible that no disability is noticed until the young-sters enter the school system. In 1968 Lloyd Dunn pointed out that research had not justified the use of certain categories, and current research continues to support this view (Gelheizer, 1987; Reynolds, Wang, & Walberg, 1987).

Studies show learning disabilities to be arguably the least well defined of all special education categories. One noted researcher claims that more than 80% of normal students could be classified as having learning disabilities by one or more definitions now in use (Ysseldyke, 1988). Other evidence of the vague and changing nature of definitions is noted in a peculiar "hydraulic relationship" across categories (Reynolds et al., 1987). In other words, when the number is lowered in one place, it builds up in another. A recent report to Congress, for instance, indicated a decline of 300,000 in the number of students classified as mentally retarded in the period from 1976 to 1983, contrasted to an increase in the same period of 1 million students classified as learning disabled (Reschley, 1988). These statistics are particularly disturbing since, according to government figures, nearly 50% of the children served in 1990–91 were classified as having learning disabilities (U.S. Department of Education, 1992). It is suspected in this "hydraulic relationship," many children who are mildly mentally retarded are being classified as learning disabled.[5]

What are the effects of labeling on the learner? The most obvious is stigmatization. Believing is seeing, according to one theorist. Often it is extremely difficult for "normal" individuals to get beyond labels and the negative perceptions attached to them. The way in which exceptional individuals are viewed may have much more to do with their labels than with their personalities.

Although labels can be used positively to channel individuals toward appropriate services, sometimes they are applied indiscriminantly to exclude individuals from the regular classroom. Further, despite their proliferation among health and education professionals, labels seldom adequately reflect individuals' educational or therapeutic needs. More important, labeling and resultant enrollment in "labeled" programs of instruction may deflate a person's self-concept, actually shaping the individual's limitations and failures and increasing vulnerability to ridicule or isolation. In summary, then, labeling can be a negative experience. Frequent problems are these:

- A tendency may exist for an individual to become what he or she is labeled.
- Expectations for the individual may be the result of preconceived ideas of the label.
- Once labeled, the person has difficulty changing the label.
- A label may affect where an individual is placed in the environment. An environment in which an individual is observed can influence the observer's perception.

In the face of such criticism, one may reasonably ask what is being done to correct or justify the use of systems of classification in special education. There are, on the other hand, practical reasons for labeling persons: (1) in the real world, labels are required by almost all communities in order to acquire medical, social, and educational services; (2) the application of a label can facilitate communication; and (3) the use of labels does distinguish certain populations for research, dissemination, and reporting statistics.

---

5   Two main factors have been considered to be the bases for the dramatic increase in the incidence of learning disabilities. First, general educators are becoming more aware of the characteristics of students with low academic achievement. Second, many students considered to be the "slow learners" now, upon more precise definition, are being categorized as learning disabled.

Trends in Perceptions and Labeling of the Exceptional

IDEA reflected a major change in the way people with disabilities were labeled. In changing the name of the Education of the Handicapped Act to the Individuals with Disabilities Education Act, Congress gave notice that it meant *individuals*, not their disabilities, to be the focus of special education. At the heart of IDEA is the philosophy that the way a person is viewed and treated by others determines how "handicapping" his or her disability might be.

Educators are now more enlightened about the ways in which cultural and historical factors influence our perceptions of exceptional persons. They have grown more sensitive to the dangers inherent in labeling—cultural bias, social stigma, distortion, and oversimplification. The recent focus on the problems inherent in our present system of classification, coupled with stronger demands to protect the civil rights of people with disabilities, has resulted in an active effort to revamp the classification system. Professionals no longer cling to the excuse that labels are necessary for lobbying and obtaining funding. Instead, there is increased interest in changing legislation and funding procedures that require the use of labels.

Some educators are calling for new, quite radical funding strategies, based strictly upon functional, need-defined criteria. In 1986 the National Coalition of Advocates for Students (NCAS) and the National Association of School Psychologists (NASP) issued a joint statement that says, in part,

> We propose the development and piloting of alternatives to the current categorical system. This requires reevaluation of funding mechanisms, and advocacy for policy and funding waivers needed for the piloting of alternative service delivery models. ("Position Statement," 1986, p. 2)

The ultimate goal, of course, is a shift in society's attitudes toward individual differences. This shift in emphasis will mean a relaxation of popular notions of normality. We will view a far wider range of individual differences as normal. More students with disabilities will be allowed in regular classrooms. This move toward full inclusion has been reinforced by recent court decisions. The 3rd Circuit Court of Appeals decision favoring full classroom inclusion for an 8-year-old boy with Down syndrome and severe mental impairment, interpreted IDEA to favor inclusion. In its ruling on the case, *Oberti v. Board of Education of the Clementon School District*, the court noted the apparent tension between IDEA's presumption in favor of mainstreaming and requirement that schools provide individualized programs tailored to specific needs of each child with disabilities. "The key to resolving this tension," the court concluded, "appears to lie in the school's proper use of 'supplementary aids and services' . . ." in the regular class setting, as opposed to schooling in a segregated classroom. Other courts have made similar rulings.

This expanded concept of normality will lead to innovations in classroom instruction to allow for more individualized instruction and to the realization that many people are "exceptional" at some time in their lives—that many need individualized instruction, whether in the form of remedial education, psychotherapy, physical therapy, or advanced training in an area in which they excel. Indeed, we should understand that we all share the same need for special services—some of us more frequently, some less so.

EDUCATION FOR
ALL HANDICAPPED:
A NEW ERA

In her foreword to the *Tenth Annual Report to Congress on the Implementation of the Education of the Handicapped Act*, Madeleine Will noted that the eighties had been one of "extraordinary changes" (U.S. Department of Education, 1988). Her claim is no overstatement. Those "extraordinary changes" continue to characterize special education law and practice.

Although many educators of exceptional children had attempted for years to provide individualized instruction, tailored to individual needs, the Education of the Handicapped Act standardized that process. Two of the act's requirements were profound and controversial statements about how exceptional students should be taught. The first requirement was the mandate that students with disabilities should be placed in "the least restrictive" educational environment in which they could learn successfully. The second was the requirement that every student with a disability be offered an appropriate instructional program to meet his or her specific needs. Further, the law extended the suggested age range served by such instructional programs, and with passage of P.L. 99–457, a mandate for this extension was established to individuals of preschool age. In 1990, IDEA added clout to both these mandates. It further defined least restrictive environment (LRE) by specifying a "change in the delivery of services from segregated to integrated environments;" and it strengthened the Individualized Educational Plan (IEP) provision by requiring that IEPs for students 16 and older must include plans for transition services. These are sometimes called Individualized Transition Plans (ITPs).

The Least Restrictive Setting

In the fifties and sixties, the most widely used public school setting for educating children with mild disabilities was the self-contained day class for the so-called "educable mentally retarded." Teachers in these classes were normally trained to teach one type of exceptionality, but often the classes were filled with students with various disabling conditions. In the sixties and seventies, separate classes for those with learning disabilities became commonplace, and separate classes for students labeled emotionally disturbed began to appear.

Trends in Placement of Those with Mild and Moderate Disabilities.   Even before the passage of P.L. 94–142, schools had begun mainstreaming children with disabilities; that is, integrating them into the regular classroom when it was in their best interest educationally. Two ways of doing this evolved.

One was to employ visual, auditory, learning disabilities specialists and reading or language teachers, as well as speech therapists, to act as consultants (or resource specialists, as some states call them). Some consultants traveled from school to school and worked with students individually or in small groups. Others were available to the classroom teacher to help prepare remedial strategies and special materials and to suggest the best procedures to use. The consultants received special training in diagnosis, continuous evaluation, and individualized and systematic instruction.

The other popular model for teaching those with mild disabilities in regular schools makes use of special "resource rooms" or staffed "instructional materials cen-

The interdisciplinary team.

ters." Under this plan a child is enrolled in a regular classroom for part of the day, and is given special instruction in a separate resource room during another part. Ideally, a resource room has one or more instructional assistants to assist the master teacher or resource teacher and special equipment such as console teaching machines. Both models continue to be used as a means to provide special education in mainstreamed settings.

During the 1989–90 school year, the majority of students with disabilities received special education and related services in settings with non–special education children. According to government statistics for 1989–90, over 32% of students with disabilities were educated in regular classrooms, compared to about 26% in 1985–86. Over 35% were taught in resource rooms (for at least 21% but not more than 60% of the day), compared to 41% in 1985–86. These figures illustrate a move toward increased "main-streaming" of special education students into regular classrooms. The figures have remained stable (about 25%) over the same years for students educated in special classrooms in regular education buildings.

Trends in Placement for Those with More Severe Disabilities.   One of the clearest implications of laws enacted after 1975 was the move to seek more appropriate and less restrictive settings for those with more severe disabilities. Until recently these individuals were usually served in public residential settings. About 8% of those receiving special education in this country were in separate facilities; a little over 5% in separate public or private day schools; and 2.5% in residential schools—variously called training schools, hospital schools, detention homes, or boarding schools. Private boarding schools are still maintained throughout the country, offering services to those with blindness, deafness, emotional disturbances, and learning disabilities. However, increasing awareness of the rights of individuals with severe and multiple disabilities has led to greater scrutiny of public residential facilities in the past few years. Problems with institutionalizing persons with disabilities have consequently been more widely recognized.

> Some of the negative characteristics associated with these institutions are regimentation, lack of privacy, impersonal treatment, limited freedom and independence for the residents, and limited interaction between the residents and the "outside" world. The larger the institution and the larger the geographic area that it must serve, the more difficult it is to normalize that environment for its residents. Activities aimed at improving conditions for residents in institutions can legitimately be called deinstitutionalization (Neufeld, 1977, pp. 15–16).

Instead of noncare, closed-door policies, and isolation of people with severe disabilities in the back wards of institutions, new programs are presently being developed. They emphasize the importance of allowing people with disabilities to remain in their own community and lead as normal a life as possible through the use of hostels, foster homes, group homes, community training centers, day-care facilities, and community-based social services. There are at least two promising alternatives for the education of people who are severely disabled who remain in their home community:

> The "cluster" or self-contained school for special education students offers the advantage of high community visibility, concentrating parents, administrators, and resources—which are apt to be scarce in a community—in one central location. Staff and consultant communication and problem sharing are maximized under this mode. Ancillary professional personnel spend less time in transportation and thus more time in service. Supervised practice teaching and inservice programs are easier to administer, and specialized support services, e.g., medical personnel, can be concentrated in one place.
>
> On the other hand, the "dispersal" model—or the spreading of classes for the severely disabled throughout several, or many, schools in a district—offers the possibility of integration into community life and normalization (Sontag, Burke, & York, 1973). The students are apt to come into contact with the problems of the severely/multiple disabled child, and the possibilities for new approaches for remediation are increased. (Sailor & N. G. Haring, 1977, pp. 70–71)

The dispersal model, emphasizing the importance of the placement in the home neighborhood school, is the preferred option. As students with mild and moderate disabilities spend more time in regular school classrooms, more special educators are learning to work with those with severe disabilities within the context of the public school system.

Including students with severe disabilities in regular education facilities actually goes beyond providing a least restricted environment; and when inclusion is achieved, those with and without disabilities establish very productive instructional relationships. More examples of successful integration appear in the contemporary literature (Gaylord-Ross & Pitts-Conway, 1984; Voeltz, 1984). Among the most interesting and mutually beneficial are those studies that involve people at all levels of ability in meaningful social interactions. The complex problems involved in planned integration are numerous, but the advantages of continuous efforts toward this goal far outweigh them.

Changing Views Toward Placement.   Although the cascade model for providing services predominated for a decade or more (see Figure 1–1), it was later criticized for overemphasizing place, that is, educational setting. It is important to realize that providing a special setting for instruction and providing specialized instruction are not one and the same. By and large, the regular classroom is considered the most appropriate placement for children with mild disabilities, but this placement must be carefully planned with the necessary support services and teacher assistance that provide the individualization necessary for these students. In fact, some special settings have proved to be only diluted versions of regular classrooms. Conversely, the currently popular model of integration into the regular classroom does not necessarily mean better educational opportunities. True, it may remove the stigma of segregated education, but if it fails to meet the individual needs of the exceptional person, it can also, like the segregated classroom, be detrimental to the student. To summarize, educators are becoming increasingly aware

Copying from written page to the blackboard is difficult for many children with learning disabilities.

that effective services for students with disabilities are those that emphasize the quality and individualization of programs with the most integrated settings possible.

A call for increased integration intensified in the mid-eighties, growing recently into a movement for "full inclusion."[6] Some whose ideas have been most influential are Hagerty and Abramson (1987), Gartner and Lipsky (1987), Lilly (1988), Stainback and Stainback (1992), Wang and Walberg (1988), and Will (1986). These educators point out that, although P.L. 94–142 has sought to bring students with disabilities "into the mainstream," the services that support these students are still part of a dual system of education that ultimately perpetuates segregation. "The language and terminology we use in describing our education system is full of the language of separation, of fragmentation, of removal" (Will, 1986). It is argued that maintaining dual systems of education, separate professional organizations, separate personnel-preparation programs, and separate funding patterns may inhibit the integration of the people with disabilities and reduce the effectiveness of their education.

The movement for restructuring, variously called the Regular Education Initiative (REI) or General Education Initiative (GEI), urged a "shared commitment" on the part of special and regular education programs; that is, partnership ". . . to cooperatively assess the education needs of students with learning problems and develop effective education strategies to meet these needs" (Will, 1986). Some have gone so far as to call for an actual merger of special and regular education (Stainback & Stainback, 1987). Others, while not aiming at actual elimination of separate special education services, do question both the practical wisdom and the empirical justification for continuing the existing "second system" approach. The language of the REI and the GEI has been replaced with the newer call for "full inclusion." Educational psychologist Jennifer York wrote of the rewards and challenges of true collaboration:

> Achieving true collaboration among general and special educators necessarily will require mutual adoption of a much broader shared agenda. This shared agenda is the responsibility for *all* students in our school communities. (York, 1991, p. 2)

The proposed reorganization emphasizes expanded decision-making responsibilities for school administrators and teachers, giving those providing actual services more say in how service delivery systems are structured. This would, of course, necessitate change at much higher levels, especially the federal and the state. Change would be required, also, within the professional ranks, on the part of teachers themselves and those responsible for teacher preparation: " . . . General education must develop its capabilities for accommodating a broad spectrum of instructional practices and services . . . [relinquishing] the longstanding assumption that there are two methodologies or psychologies of learning—one for 'special people' and one for 'reg-

---

6 Inclusive education holds that children with disabilities should be placed in regular classrooms in their neighborhood schools. While inclusive education and integrated placement are often used interchangeably, there is a significant difference between the two strategies. In integrated placements, students with disabilities spend part of the day with regular education peers but have a primary or secondary placement in a resource class or special education class. In inclusive education settings, children are most often served in the regular classroom in their home schools by a teacher and an interdisciplinary team.

ular' people" (Wang & Walberg, 1988, p. 129). These proposals are based on the firm belief that a shared educational system would improve the quality of instruction for people at all levels of ability.

Perhaps the most visible ongoing effort to accommodate this partnership exists in the Adaptive Learning Environment program, which evolved from an individualized approach to instruction developed in the seventies at the University of Pittsburgh (Wang & Stiles, 1976). Implemented initially in inner-city schools serving low-income minority pupils, the program is most recently carried out in more varied settings, including rural and suburban schools with middle-class, gifted, and special education students.

Also influential was a set of recommendations by the National Association of State Boards of Education (NASBE), published in 1992, calling for "an inclusive system of education that strives to produce better outcomes for all students." Specific goals include training of teachers and administrators to work in fully inclusive schools and the severing of links among funding, placement, and disability labels (NASBE, 1992).

A 1992 examination of issues and trends by the Federal Resource Center for Special Education listed among its predictions: "Children with mild disabilities will be served in the general classroom as an alternative to pull-out programs such as resource room configurations, and children and youth with severe and low incidence disabilities will be served in inclusive schools." The report cited both philosophical and financial reasons for the increased emphasis on least restrictive environments, and it predicted that a critical shortage of special education personnel would lead to the training of regular education teachers in special education, thus "blurring the borderline between special and regular education" (Hales & Carlson, 1992).

Special educators are united in their concern that exceptional individuals *not* be second-class citizens, relegated to a second-class, segregated school system. They are far from unanimous, however, in their endorsement of the REI/GEI movement or of the current demonstration projects held to be illustrative of the movement's practicability (Fuchs & Fuchs, 1988).

The issue of expanded cooperation between special education and regular education forces is likely to remain a topic for research and debate for some time to come.

Community Integration

The least restrictive environment (LRE) principle has prompted a major national movement among policymakers, selected service delivery specialists, and higher education professionals toward community integration of individual with disabilities. As progress toward integration has taken place, the LRE movement has been put into operation on three continua, involving residential, educational, and vocational services. The expanded arena of service delivery had led to a more comprehensive conceptualization of placement into the community for persons with disabilities. A current outlook suggests strongly that the traditional cascade of services (Figure 1–1) is obsolete and that new continua are needed to represent total community integration in living, school, and work situations. This community-based concept (see Figure 1–4) questions the notion that segregated settings are the most efficient for preparing individuals to function in integrated settings. Taylor (1988) has proposed the following three continua:

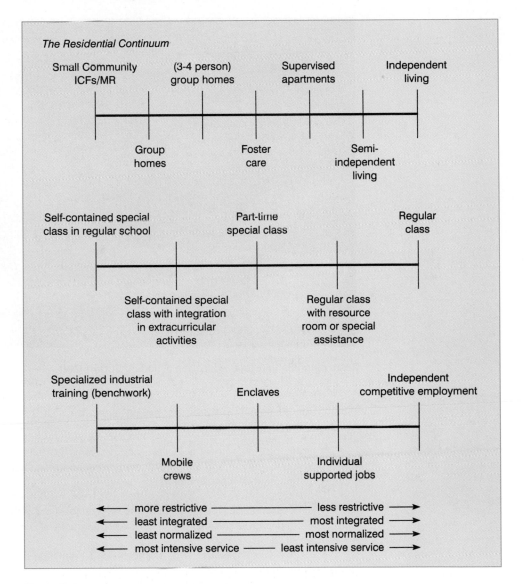

Figure 1–4
Community-based LRE continuum model.
Source: From "Caught in the Continuum: A Critical Analysis of the Principle of the Least Restrictive Environment" by S. J. Taylor, 1988, *Journal of the Association for Persons with Severe Handicaps*, 13, p. 49. Copyright 1988 by the Association for Persons with Severe Handicaps. Reprinted by permission.

1. A community-based continuum of residential services.
2. A community-based special education continuum.
3. A community-based vocational continuum.

Taylor contrasts the LRE principle with the commitment to integration and suggests that integration requires a new stronger focus and direction, which means the

Team planning in regular education includes support staff.

elimination of social, cultural, economic, and administrative barriers to community integration. The focus must shift:

1. From the development of facilities and programs into which people must fit to the provision of services and supports necessary for people with severe disabilities to participate fully in community life;
2. From neighborhoods to typical homes, from regular school buildings to regular classes, and from vocational models to typical jobs and activities;
3. From professional judgment as a basis for determining community involvement to personal choice;
4. From a presumption in favor of integration to a mandate to provide opportunities for integration;
5. From a conditional ("to the extent necessary, appropriate, feasible") to an unconditional commitment to integration;
6. From requiring individuals to change in order to participate in the community to requiring service systems to change;
7. From restrictions applied categorically as a condition for receiving services to opportunities available to nondisabled people;
8. From disability labels as a factor in determining community participation to a recognition of common human needs;
9. From independence to community belonging, and
10. From placing people in the community to helping them become part of the community. (Taylor, 1988, p. 51)

The impact of models such as Taylor's can easily be seen a few years later in IDEA, particularly in its mandate for integrated services.

The Individualized Educational Plan

One of the most specific and most significant provisions of IDEA is the requirement of an Individualized Educational Plan (IEP) for each child in special education. The IEP must be a joint effort of the multidisciplinary child study team, which includes a representative of the local education agency (other than the child's teacher), the child's teachers (regular and special), the parents, any other support staff (e.g., speech therapists, school psychologists, physical therapists), and, whenever appropriate, the child as well. For a preschool child or toddler, IDEA provides parents with an Individualized Family Service Plan (the IFSP); the individual plan for a student leaving high school is the Individualized Transitional Plan (ITP).

According to rules proposed to implement the act, the IEP for each child must include the following:

1. A statement of the child's present levels of educational performance, including academic achievement, social adaptation, prevocational, vocational, psychomotor, and self-help skills.
2. A statement of annual goals describing the educational performance to be achieved by the end of the school year.
3. A statement of short-term instructional objectives (measurable intermediate steps between the present level of educational performance and the annual goals).
4. A statement of specific educational services needed by the child (determined without regard to the availability of services), including a description of:
   a. All special education and related services needed to meet the unique needs of the child, including the appropriate type of physical education program.
   b. Any special instructional media and materials that are needed.
5. The date those services will begin and length of time the services will be given.
6. A description of the extent to which the child will participate in regular education programs.
7. A justification of the type of educational placement the child will have.
8. A list of individuals responsible for implementation of the individualized education program.
9. Objective criteria, evaluation procedures, and schedules of determining, on at least an annual basis, whether the short-term instructional objectives are being achieved (*Federal Register,* 1977).

In essence, the law tells us that we must plan, in advance of placement, how, where, what, and how fast a child will learn. It tells us that the child has the right to be made aware of his or her performance and to be protected so that others will not judge him or her unfairly. It tells us that each exceptional child is to be considered an individual in that he or she receives an individually planned program of instruction. And probably most important of all, it tells us that educational programs must be carried out not only for the traditional school-age child, but also for preschoolers and for those in transition between high school and adult life.

Figures 1–5, 1–6, and 1–7 show examples of a completed IFSP for a preschool child, an IEP for a fifth-grader, and an ITP for a youth making the transition from

---

IFSP PG ___6___

OUTCOMES RELATED TO CHILD DEVELOPMENT: (OVERVIEW)

Child: ____Amy____

Collaborative goals established by the family and team:

Domain	Outcomes
Cognitive	Amy will increase her cognitive skills by sorting objects that are dissimilar, and solve simple problems using tools to assist her.
Communication	Amy will increase her communication skills by learning new requesting and commenting skills, acknowledging others' communications.
Social	Amy will increase her social skills by participating in cleanup activities at home and school and through new peer-play skills.
Gross Motor	Amy will demonstrate improved balance, antigravity strength, and grading of movement as measured by the following objectives
Fine Motor	Amy will demonstrate improved shoulder-girdle stability, bilateral coordination, and fine motor planning as measured by the following objectives
Self-Help	Amy will demonstrate increased oral sensitivity, oral motor control, and independence in feeding and dressing as measured by the following objectives

---

Figure 1–5

A sample from an Individualized Family Service Plan (IFSP).

(A page from Amy's IFSP, written when she was 22 months old. Amy has Down syndrome.)

INDIVIDUAL EDUCATION PROGRAM

Date 11-25-92

(1) Student

Name: Joe S.
School: Adams
Grade: 5
Current Placement: Regular Class/Resource Room
Date of Birth: 10-1-83   Age: 11-1

(2) Committee

		Initials
Mr. Havlichek	Principal	G.H.
Mrs. Snow	Regular Teacher	P.S.
Mr. Bigelow	Counselor	C.B.
Mr. Sheets	Resource Teacher	A.S.
Mrs. S.	Parent	H.R.J.

IEP From 12-1-92 To 12-1-93

(3) Present Level of Educational Functioning	(4) Annual Goal Statements	(5) Instructional Objectives	(6) Objective Criteria and Evaluation
MATH **Strengths** 1. Can successfully compute addition and subtraction problems to two places with regrouping and zeros 2. Know 100 basic multiplication facts **Weaknesses** 1. Frequently makes computational errors on problems with which he has had experience 2. Does not complete seatwork Key Math total score of 2.1 grade equivalent	Joe will apply knowledge of regrouping in addition and renaming in subtraction to 4-digit numbers.	1. When presented with addition problems of 3-digit numbers requiring two renamings, the student will compute the answer at a rate of one problem per minute with 90% accuracy. 2. When presented with subtraction problems of 3-digit numbers requiring two renamings, the student will compute the answer at a rate of one problem per minute with 90% accuracy. 3. When presented with addition problems of 4-digit numbers requiring three renamings, the student will compute the answer at a rate of one problem per minute with 90% accuracy. 4. When presented with subtraction problems of 4-digit numbers requiring three renamings, the student will compute the answer at a rate of one problem per minute with 90% accuracy.	Key Math (after 4 mos.) Teacher-made tests (weekly) Key Math (after 4 mos.) Teacher-made tests (weekly)
	Joe will multiply 2- and 3-digit numbers requiring regrouping.	1. The student will multiply 2, 3, and 4 digits by 1 digit without regrouping with 90% accuracy. 2. The student will multiply 2 and 3 digits by 1 digit with regrouping with 90% accuracy. 3. The student will multiply 2 and 3 digits by 2 digits with no regrouping with 90% accuracy. 4. The student will multiply 2 and 3 digits by 2 digits with regrouping with 90% accuracy.	Key Math (after 4 mos.) Teacher-made tests (weekly) Key Math (after 7 mos.) Teacher-made tests (weekly)
	Joe will use linear, volume, weight, temperature, and money measurements.	1. The student will write dictated money values up to $200.00 with 90% accuracy. 2. The student will identify various weights in pounds and ounces using a scale with 70% accuracy. 3. The student will read a thermometer with 90% accuracy. 4. The student will measure items to the nearest foot, yard, inch, meter, and centimeter.	Teacher observation (daily) Key Math (after 8 mos.)

Figure 1–6

A sample of an Individualized Educational Plan (IEP).

(A page from Joe's IEP—math portion. Joe is a fifth-grade student with mild mental retardation.)

TRANSITION SERVICES COMPONENT OF THE
INDIVIDUAL EDUCATION PLAN (I.E.P.)

Student's Name ___Mark___ I.E.P Date ___12/10/93___

RESULTS OF FUNCTIONAL VOCATIONAL EVALUATION:

	Procedures	Outcomes
Occupational Interests	Observation Student interview Parent/caregiver interview Teacher interview	Likes machines Likes electronics/working alone Likes being alone/working on small things Prefers indoor work
Occupational Aptitudes	Observation CBVA	Good fine motor skills Good fine motor skills Works best in structured environment
Availability of Occupational Opportunities	(Informal) labor market survey	There are 2 electronics assembly shops and several janitorial jobs available.

ANTICIPATED POSTSCHOOL OUTCOMES

Postsecondary Education | Employment | Community Living

Postsecondary Education	Employment	Community Living
___ Vocational Training Program	___ Competitive	___ Independent
___ College Program	✓ Supported	✓ Supported
✓ Not Determined	___ Not Determined	___ Not Determined
___ Other _____		

Comments/additional needs: _____
_____
_____

Note: Included transition goals and objectives are included in the goals and objectives section.

INTERAGENCY RESPONSIBILITIES AND/OR LINKAGES

Involvement of the following organizations/agencies is necessary to meet the student's transition needs. This involvement may range from information gathering to actual initiation of a formal referral. (Written consent is required before any information is released.)

Agency	Purpose	Team Member Responsible to Make Contact	Date Contact Completed
DDD	Tenant support/ongoing support	guardian	12 / 7 /93
DVR	Job training	teacher	10 / 7 /93
People First	Advocacy/recreation	Mark	10 / 20 /93
The ARC	Advocacy/social	Mark	11 / 30 /93

Figure 1–7

A sample of an Individualized Transitional Plan (ITP).

(A page from Mark's ITP. Mark is a 17-year-old high school student who has a developmental disability and lives in a group home.)

school to adult life. Depending upon the needs of teachers and their pupils, as well as upon individual district requirements, IEPs may vary greatly in detail. No IEP is the be-all or end-all in terms of educational prescription, nor should it be an empty paper-work symbol of compliance with law. The hope is that each IEP serves as an integrated, functional element of the entire education program, spelling out needed direction and intent, serving as an ongoing reminder of the direction established, and providing a frame of reference for the ongoing assessment of educational progress.

From Birth to 21: Implications of Expanded Services

Significant strides have been made under IDEA and earlier laws to assure programs with appropriate instruction for school-aged youngsters within the least restrictive environment. Serious efforts also have been made to increase program impact on meeting the specific needs of age groups previously left out of the public school program.

Preschool and Early Intervention. One group targeted for improved services has been infants and preschoolers (birth to age 5) with developmental disabilities. Though many children in this age group were already receiving some type of service, enactment of the 1986 Amendment, P.L. 99-457, extended the assurance of a complete individualized education program to all 3- to 5-year-old children with disabilities. Expansion of these services is a focus in the nineties.

For children aged 2 and younger, attention is directed toward developing interagency service delivery models that address the multiple and complex needs of these children and their families. New policy recognizes the role that the family plays in all early intervention planning and emphasizes the family's decision-making role in drawing up the Individual Family Service Plan (IFSP). The IFSP process is purposely designed to differ from the IEP process, with the recognition that infants change dramatically in their needs and capabilities over very short periods of time. The IFSP process must be flexible and responsive to the family's requirements for assistance. Professionals on service teams are encouraged to help families draft service plans in their own terms, avoiding professional jargon.

In this way, law and policy promote a family-professional partnership, the fundamental theme of which is the empowerment of parents to be educational decision makers, actively involved in the ongoing effort to serve their children (Turnbull, Blue-Banning, Beher, & Kerns, 1986).

Youth in Transition. The second critical challenge has been to meet the needs of secondary students in special education who are making transitions from high school programs to adult life in the community. While previously the goals of transition services were simply to provide some training and perhaps help find the student a place to work, the rallying cry has now become "full community inclusion" (Hayden & Abery, 1993).

In 1984, then Secretary of the Office of Special Education Programs, Madeleine Will, called attention to the need for coordinated planning. The framers of IDEA in

1990 responded by strengthening this area of special education law. They defined transition services as "a coordinated set of activities for a student, designed within an outcome-oriented process," with the goal of moving the student from school to successful postschool activities. Congress expanded postschool activities to include vocational training, integrated employment, continuing and adult education, adult social services, independent living, and community participation. Again stressing IDEA's focus on the person and not the disability, Congress noted that the coordinated set of activities "shall be based upon the individual student's needs."

To facilitate transition services, IDEA added rehabilitation counselors to the list of related services providers. In addition, it required that, beginning at age 16 (in some cases even earlier) and annually thereafter, IEPs must include statements of needed transition services. These statements must specify "interagency responsibilities or linkages before the student leaves the school setting."

Active support of community leaders and parents of the client are now more clearly recognized as critical factors in the success of the adult's integration into the community (Brown & Johnson, 1993). Equally important is training that gives adults with disabilities the social skills necessary to relate successfully to co-workers and other members of the community. Although many students with mild disabilities make the transition to adult life with minimal support from public services, many do not; and students with severe disabilities need explicit transition planning and ongoing public support (Hayden & Abery, 1993). Their success will depend on three factors: preparation in the schools, the transition period, and the quality of adult services.

Recognizing the fact that youth with disabilities require at least as much training as those who are nondisabled, programs providing career training and placement have been initiated. One such program, titled the Career Apprenticeships for Postsecondary Education (CAPE), project is designed to enhance career success for students with disabilities who are completing postsecondary programs. Student career success is promoted through internships and apprenticeships that link the student's interests and program studies with employer needs and job market demands. The program, based at the University of Washington, aims at integrating the efforts of students, employers, career planners, providers of services to students with disabilities, and community support agencies through a five-way partnership model (Stowitschek, 1993). The model includes an awareness campaign, collaborative job development, progressive apprenticeship development, job placement support, and student-directed, cooperative programming. The goal is to provide a guided flexible progression for the student from the postsecondary program to a secure job with natural supports, acceptable starting wages, and a foundation for career advancement.

Job programs must go hand in hand with other provisions for community living, including housing and social life. A program called the Research and Training Center for Residential Services and Community Living at the University of Minnesota was recently organized to enhance the number and quality of opportunities for individuals with mental retardation to live in natural communities (Lakin, 1992). Concern for quality of life of persons with mental retardation sparked a program with the goals of increasing the presence of people with mental retardation in communities, promoting their safety and protection, enhancing their personal growth, fostering independence, and offering opportunities for their social development. Such programs recognize that deinstitutionalization—or even high school completion—can, at worst, throw the person with disabilities into the streets, or, at best, offer the optimum of protection, freedom, success, and community support.

APPROACHES TO
SERVING THE
EXCEPTIONAL

On one level, the history of special education has been characterized by a common effort among educators to expand and improve services to meet the needs of all individuals with disabilities, regardless of their age or the severity of their disabilities. At the level of actual classroom practice, however, the field has seen perhaps more disagreement than agreement. A large part of this controversy no doubt has stemmed from the fact that special education is a kind of hybrid of several older disciplines, particularly medicine, psychology, and education. Thus, special educators over the last several decades have relied on different explanations of what causes a given type of disability and have proposed widely varying strategies for maximizing performance in the face of these disabilities.

Much of present practice in special education, for example, has its roots in the medical model that physicians use to treat their patients: they diagnose an illness or injury in terms of what has caused it and then prescribe medication, surgery, or some other remedy to cure it. In fact, the term "diagnostic prescriptive teaching" is being used in current articles (Gettinger, 1984).

Others in the field of special education use models from psychology to explain how children acquire, retain, and apply information. Developmental theorists, for example, view learning as a prolonged, active, and adaptive process, throughout which the individual seeks, selects, and interprets environmental information. This process is broken out in terms of a series of developmental stages: children are ready to learn certain kinds of information only at certain stages. While the precise ages at which certain types of learning occur may vary from individual to individual, the stages are invariable in their sequence.

Other practitioners may focus particular attention upon sensory modalities as a vehicle to learning—analyzing, for example, whether a child learns better from visual or auditory stimuli. Still others may emphasize the enhancement of various learning processes, such as memory, as prerequisite to progress in acquiring basic skills, such as reading. Some in special education see themselves primarily as scientists. The scientific model seeks to systematically arrange all aspects of the learner's environment and collect information on the learner's progress, in order to identify changes in the environment that result in increased learning.

These examples represent an extremely simplified view of the biases and assumptions informing the many and diverse instructional practices employed by professionals in special education. In spite of these differences in points of view, special educators do share a common, if not universal, conviction about teaching students with disabilities. This common ground is their view that students with disabilites require more detailed assessment of strengths and needs, greater individualization of instruction and curriculum, and more careful and systematic monitoring of performance to prevent them from falling behind on tasks that normal students might be expected to learn almost independently. In other words, it is likely that even two special educators who disagree on the precise causes for a given student's disability, or even on the need to identify the precise causes, might nevertheless work with the student in strikingly similar ways. Both would select materials and activities to develop needed skills and carefully monitor the student's progress or lack of progress. And both would adjust the materials and activities if progress was not satisfactory.

Systematic Instruction

One highly successful and scientifically based approach to teaching learners with disabilities relies on systematic instruction and the application of behavioral principles in the classroom. Systematic instruction is based on the principle that focusing on the behaviors of each individual provides us with the best information about the individual's abilities and needs:

> The specific curricula, materials, and instructional tactics which are required in teaching will vary with the needs of the pupil and the limitations of the situation in which instruction must take place. In order for teaching to be consistently effective, therefore, it must consist in part of procedures designed to determine and monitor the needs of the individual learner. Consistently good teaching is a process of learning—learning how to help others learn. . . . Unless the teacher is prepared to observe the behavior and learning patterns of each student carefully, noting particular needs and reactions to the instructional plan, some of the children will fail. A teacher must have the tools and skills necessary to learn from each child what best facilitates that child's growth. (White & N. G. Haring, 1980, p. 5)

As its name implies, systematic instruction is an organized body of plans and procedures—a technology for teaching. It is based on: (1) gathering objective data regarding the student's performance level at the start of the program, (2) establishing priorities among the functional skills the student needs to learn, (3) identifying the prerequisite behaviors that are necessary to develop these skills, (4) carefully assessing student progress or lack of progress in acquiring new skills, (5) using data from progress assessments to revise instructional procedures before the student fails, and (6) providing opportunities to apply skills in other setting to allow for their generalization. The following elements are especially important to the application of systematic instruction in the classroom.

Task Analysis.   To guide the student from simpler to more complex responses, systematic instruction relies on breaking down a task into a series of small steps. Whenever a student cannot master a specific task, the teacher reduces it to smaller, more manageable units. There must be a careful sequencing of learning tasks. The goal for teaching a student who is severely disabled to feed oneself may be reasonable, for example, but it is hardly precise enough to allow for carefully planned instruction. By dividing the skill into small instructional objectives, the teacher can sequence instruction so that one subskill builds upon another. Thus, if the student has difficulty in chewing food, the teacher knows not to begin mealtime with instruction on how to use a spoon. The first step will be the most fundamental one.

Observation and Measurement.   Systematic instruction might quickly become a rigid set of inflexible procedures were it not for one feature. This highly significant feature is the necessity of continually updating information on how the student is progressing or failing to progress. Take the case of a first-grade student, for example. The teacher specifies a skill that the student must have in order to succeed in the world (for instance, adding simple math facts) and then measures the student's progress in terms of the student's ability to do that task. The information that comes from this direct observation is used to set up an instructional program. The direct measurement of several such target skills tells a teacher what the student can do and what the student still must learn. This information is organized into long-term and short-term objectives that help the teacher place the student in the curriculum and sequence instructional activities.

The teacher continues to collect and use information to make any necessary changes in the instructional plan. By collecting the information frequently—even daily in many cases—the teacher can change a plan before the student actually fails (White & N. G. Haring, 1980). And when the student demonstrates mastery of a skill, the information tells the teacher to advance the student to the next objective in the sequence. This process is called a data-based approach to instructional decisions.

Planned and Individualized Instruction. To carry out such a finely tuned instructional program, the teacher must specify an educational program for each student, the steps within the program, the sequence of learning tasks, preparations and procedures, record of correct and incorrect behavior, and criteria by which change may be measured. Specifying all of this information makes it possible for any person on the teaching staff, and parents, to work with the student on a one-to-one basis.

Thus, by following the simple steps of assessing the student's performance, choosing the exact skills he or she needs to learn now and in the future, and measuring and evaluating the student's mastery of each of those skills, teachers can monitor each student's progress. Plans can be made, and modified, to provide meaningful successes for each individual.

It should be noted that systematic instruction does not end with the simple acquisition of skills and knowledge. Instruction must continue until students achieve consistent and fluent performance in a variety of settings. (The ability to apply a skill learned in one setting, to other situations with other individuals, is called generalization; it is a key focus of instructional programming for students with severe disabilities.)

Systematic instructional procedures are just as applicable to teaching "normal," nondisabled individuals as they are to teaching those with severe disabilities. This point is perhaps the most important of all. It has been our need to be more precise, more careful, and more effective in helping the exceptional child learn that has led to the refinement of teaching skills in special education. Now we face a legal mandate to improve instruction for all students with disabilities, and with it the return of many individuals with mild to severe disabilities to regular classrooms. As these students return to regular classes, perhaps they can bring with them—through consultation from special educators and other, comprehensive inservice training efforts—the systematic instructional approaches that have been developed to help them. Perhaps, in this way, instruction for all students can be made more systematic, and more effective.

Almost all special educators who have experienced success in teaching exceptional children have applied a certain degree of systematic instruction in their approach to instruction. Yet the idea of precise and systematic approaches is still controversial among many practitioners. Those who favor systematic instruction maintain that evidence of changes in academic and social performance cannot be demonstrated without a record of that performance during instruction or before and after an instructional segment. In addition, in order to be able to identify the conditions under which the changes occurred, a detailed description of the instructional plan, including the instructional arrangement, conditions, and materials is necessary. These are considered the technical aspects of teaching (Tawney & Gast, 1984).

On the other hand, Guess and Siegel-Causey (1985) believe the special education teacher must go beyond being systematic.

> It is our position that technicians can be taught to follow carefully prescribed instruction programs. With instruction, technicians can be prepared to systematically and accurately move a severely handicapped learner toward successful completion of an identified educational objective. It is a teacher, however, who can provide a broader approach to the educational process by modifying the instructional environment to enhance untargeted emerging skills that demonstrate movement toward more complex and adaptive levels of functioning. (p. 242)

Social Skills Competence.   The trend toward placing students with disabilities in regular education has been strengthening since the last half of the seventies. While regular educators are generally in favor of this trend, students with social skill deficits can bring additional problems into regular classrooms. As a response to this concern, professionals have given greater attention to social skills assessment and training.

Social competence is significantly related to building positive social interactions between students with disabilities and nondisabled peers (Gustafson & N. G. Haring, 1992). The acquisition of social behavior skills is a major factor in the success of students with disabilities in inclusive education. Social skills can be successfully taught. The majority of the programs for social skills training have focused on behavioral principles emphasizing operant and/or social learning techniques. Behavioral strategies emphasize the systematic arrangement of consequences to increase the frequency of desired behaviors and decrease the frequency of inappropriate behaviors. By contrast, social learning techniques utilize specific training in targeted behaviors, applying modeling, coaching, role playing, and feedback. Employing a systematic combination of behavioral principles and social skills strategies such as self-management, imitation, and immediate feedback has demonstrated rewarding results.

The following offer good examples of published social training programs: *Skillstreaming the Adolescent* (Goldstein, Sprakin, Gershaw, & Klein, 1980); *Skillstreaming the Elementary School Child* (McGinnis & Goldstein, 1984); and A *Curriculum for Children's Effective Peer and Teacher Skills* (ACCEPTS) (Walker & Goldenn, 1983).

Greenberg and colleagues have developed an approach called Providing Alternative Thinking Strategies curriculum (PATHS) (Greenberg, Kusche, Gustafson, & Calderson, 1992). It takes a developmental orientation that accommodates differences in cognitive development, language skills, and affective understanding, and self-control and includes evaluation of goals, steps for overcoming obstacles, and specific activities to enhance generalization.

Larson's Social Thinking Skills Program (Larson, 1988) teaches students to use a problem-solving process with these steps: (1) recognizing that a problem exists, (2) getting ready to think, (3) stating the problem and goals, (4) getting the facts, (5) making plans, (6) picking the best plan, (7) being prepared, and (8) taking action.

Building durable social relationships while trying to accommodate for social skill deficits can be critical to preparing students for inclusive school; but both building meaningful, durable social interaction contexts and supporting friendships are also important in bringing about satisfying social experiences for students as they adjust to regular education classrooms (T. G. Haring & Breen, in press).

For several obvious reasons, social relationships enhance the total experiences of students with disabilities in inclusive contexts. By interacting with age peers, these students can develop and maintain many important skills as a result of the positive consequences they experience. In general, relationships with nondisabled peers help students with disabilities make geometric gains in adapting to the natural environment, which facilitates their independence and full participation in school and neighborhood (T. G. Haring & Breen, in press).

Nonaversive Strategies

Since the Association of Persons with Severe Handicaps passed the Resolution on Intrusive Intervention in October 1981, calling for the cessation of aversive procedures, innovations in the use of nonaversive consequences have been applied in many educational settings. Replacing punishment with nonaversive consequences was probably one of the most important refinements in the strategies for teaching students with disabilities in the eighties. This advancement is particularly significant because individuals with disabilities are more likely than nondisabled to experience aversive treatment in their educational programs (Campbell, 1986). Guess, Helmsetter, Turnbull, and Knowlton (1986) have asserted that aversive procedures continue to be an integral part of behavioral technology. In addition, they charge university programs in special education and behavioral psychology with promoting aversive procedures in many applied settings. Meyer and Evans (1989) have written a helpful manual to use in training professionals who work with students with disabilities in the practical application of nonaversive intervention strategies. It is crucial that research in using nonaversive consequences be increased and that effective models for managing disruptive and harmful behavior in a variety of training and natural settings be developed. In many states, advocates for people with disabilities are working to help pass laws and regulations prohibiting abusive practices.

Positive Behavior Support.   Recently professional educators and behavior managers have realized the functional value of avoiding the use of aversive techniques, and the refinement known as "positive behavior support" has been developed (De Vault & N. G. Haring, 1993). Positive behavior support provides a new way of conceptualizing behaviors and behavior management. Its approach is to understand the structure and function of a specific behavior and then to use that information to teach the student an alternative repertoire of appropriate behaviors. It uses applied behavior analysis, a set of instructional procedures that have become highly developed since their introduction more than 40 years ago and that are implemented regularly by educators and support personnel. While positive behavior support can be applied in any intervention, its most successful applications have been with the acquisition, maintenance, and generalization of functional skills; the development of social competence; and support in managing behavior problems (O'Neill, Albin, Storey, & Sprague, 1990).

Broadly speaking, positive behavior support includes these steps:

- Identifying the current function of the behavior (e.g., crawling rather than walking, inappropriate social behavior).
- Changing the outcomes.
- Applying multiple intervention strategies.

1. *Identifying the current function of behavior.* Before intervening to change a student behavior, the professional needs to identify the function of the behavior for the student, that is, to find out what precedes or follows the behavior and is apparently maintaining it. This identification process, called functional assessment, should provide clues to what environmental events may be important to consider in changing the behavior. By systematically varying the relevant events, the professional needs to establish which events are most closely related to the behavior and then concentrate on those events in designing intervention.

2. *Changing the outcomes.* The next tactic is to increase the repertoire of desired behaviors. When the student knows what is expected and knows an increasing number of appropriate behaviors, these behaviors can come to replace the problem behaviors. Strengthening the student's repertoire of appropriate behaviors increases the likelihood that his or her social interactions will become more positive and frequent. Through positive behavior support, a student can be encouraged to build a social network of peers and thus establish a firm basis for social integration, which is essential for a normal life-style in a fully inclusive environment.

3. *Applying multiple intervention strategies.* Even after the functional assessment has provided substantial information about the student's behaviors and their context, it is critical to continue systematic observations. Such observations can increase knowledge of the student's patterns of behavior and broaden the range of appropriate interventions. Selecting interventions that increase the desired results depends on examining and employing the teaching events over which the teacher has control so that predictable, consistent responses can be planned and carried out.

Positive behavior support procedures assume a practical attitude about interaction. They involve determining the conditions in the environment that can be controlled to increase the probability of the desired behavior. The proactive goal is to teach the desired adaptive behaviors and functional skills; to provide opportunities to perform the skills under conditions different from those in the training settings; and to produce independent, active learners through teaching self-control skills, goal setting, self-recording of progress, self-evaluation, and self-reinforcement.

As part of its philosophy, positive behavior support applies the "dignity standard," which states that the procedures employed and the way in which they are used does not violate the dignity of the student. To achieve this, the intervention used should be the least intrusive strategy needed to produce the desired behavior change.

Consistent with the nonaversive philosophy, the positive behavior support approach includes

- preventive behavior technology, that is, rearranging the context and conditions associated with the problem behavior
- comprehensive systems approach, using teams of support personnel and peers to strengthen positive behaviors
- establishment of emergency procedures, which are distinguished from programming strategies and which are arranged in advance to deal with difficult-to-predict emergency situations

The comprehensive systems approach involves a program-wide effort, including the arrangement of environmental features, such as social interactions, with the support of peers, staff, and family. The approach has clear implications for general policy, funding, staff training, and system change.

In summary, positive behavior support concentrates on proactive behavior programming designed to arrange environmental events and conditions to increase the possibility of desired responses occurring. The strategy necessitates an examination of the environments to ascertain that they are responsive, socially enriched, and positive. It also requires a systematic examination of positive programming features to ensure the maintenance of initial and ongoing assessment, appropriate instructional activities, well-organized environmental events, trained personnel to manage behavioral change, regular feedback to students on appropriate behaviors, and the following sequence for managing behavior problems:

1. Defining the behavior of concern
2. Collecting information on the frequency and patterns of the behavior's occurrence
3. Making a functional assessment
4. Identifying possible interventions
5. Applying interventions, with continuing data collection
6. Evaluating the effectiveness of intervention

A Transdisciplinary Team Model for Special Education Services

The special education teacher, a lone adult in a classroom of children, may all but disappear from the educational scene in time. Recently an impressive array of other professionals have joined the teacher to form teams. In an inclusionary setting, team members often bring their services to the child in the regular education classroom. Ideally two kinds of teams, interagency and on-site, operate to promote the child's educational, health, social, and family well-being. Federal law mandates services in all areas related to a child's education when a child is deemed eligible for special education services.

The Interagency Team.   Exceptional children and their families may have connections with a variety of social, health, vocational, and educational agencies. If professionals from each agency work together for a child's welfare, they are able to avoid redundant services and pursue common goals. And if, in turn, this team stays in communication with the educational team, all can benefit by the holistic approach their efforts provide. The makeup of the interagency team depends on the child's disability, the child's needs at a certain time in life, and the family's situation. It might include professionals from vocational, medical, and rehabilitation services and from welfare, legal, and social agencies. Personnel might change as the child's and family's needs change. These are sometimes called "collaborative teams." Members may not see the child on a daily basis, but are involved in planning and delivering services.

The On-Site Educational Team.   Members of on-site educational teams are those who work with the child day to day. They are concerned with the programmatic needs of particular students, that is, what is being taught, how it is being taught, and how well the child is learning on a continuing basis. Educational teaming differs from the IEP meeting, which is a planning meeting, or a specially called staffing meeting, in that the core team meets on a regular basis, perhaps weekly or biweekly. A member can be anyone who knows the student or provides services to the student or family. Core members often include the special education teacher, the instructional assistant, a social worker, a communication disorders specialist, a nurse, an occupational therapist or physical therapist, and an administrator. Invited members might include general education teachers, parents, a psychologist, the child's school bus driver, doctor, grandparent, or day-care provider. The rationale for the team is that, especially for students with moderate and severe disabilities, the ongoing meetings provide necessary continuity. The child's complex needs require a variety of people working together, with regular planning and feedback sessions. Regular meetings enhance awareness of the role that each team member plays, help to build morale, help prevent the frustration and feelings of isolation that build up without the exchange, encourage continuous evaluation, allow for more efficient use of time for each service provider, and offer opportunities for professional growth.

Establishing teams is an important first step, but educators have also realized that good teamwork does not necessarily follow. Researchers have studied the ingredients of successful transdisciplinary teamwork. For example, a teaming model designed by researchers at the University of Washington, called the Education Teaming Trainer's Kit, is an inservice tool to facilitate the creation and nurturance of effective teams (Lynch & N. G. Haring, 1991). Breaking the process of teamwork down into component parts, the training model encourages the team to establish ground rules, to create effective agendas, to make use of a facilitator, and to remain nonjudgmental. Another step-by-step inservice approach is provided by New SHARE Collaborative Training (De Vault & N. G. Haring, 1992), which teaches such skills as facilitation, positive interdependence, trust building, and dealing with conflict. Some researchers characterize collaboration as a style of interaction; that is, they concentrate on *how* groups work together, not on *what* they do. Friend and Cook (1992) conclude that effective groups are based on mutual goals, voluntary participation, parity among participants, and shared responsibility, accountability, and resources.

The teams are made up of a variety of service providers, which may include any of the professionals whose responsibilities are described in the next sections.

Paraprofessionals.   Trained paraprofessionals are employed in every kind of special education setting, and they work with persons with all levels of disabilities. They may perform any of a wide variety of clerical, instructional, and other tasks—including observing students, writing reports, assisting in preparing instructional materials, reinforcing learning with small groups, and (with students who are severely disabled) performing housekeeping duties (Tucker & Horner, 1977).

Reading Specialists.   These specialists, trained in diagnosis and remediation of reading problems, most frequently work with reading problems in children not specifically labeled with disabilities.

> The reading specialist may be a classroom teacher who has had a well-structured program of advanced preparation, a special resource teacher who assists others in a variety of educational matters, or a remedial reading teacher. . . . The well-prepared reading specialist usually proceeds through a series of diagnostic steps that are sequenced to obtain the largest possible amount of information about a child's problems with the smallest amount of time and testing that can be expended to achieve the desired results. . . . The excellent reading teacher provides a program of developmental instruction as the foundation for remedial work and adds heavy amounts of additional work to fill the gaps in the child's skills that have been identified. (Sartain, 1976, pp. 492–493)

Communication Disorders Specialists.   Although the communication disorder specialist (also called speech pathologist, speech clinician, speech therapist) may work in private practice, hospitals, clinics, rehabilitation centers, or government agencies, 70% of these professionals work in the schools (Stick, 1976). Formerly they had relatively large caseloads—around 50 students, with whom they worked once or twice a week, often requiring them to travel to several different school buildings each day. The majority (probably 80%) of the cases involved articulation problems (Stick, 1976). In recent years, however, more and more emphasis has been placed on the larger problems of language delays and language disabilities evidenced by many children with disabilities (see chapter 4). Because so many individuals with severe disabilities are nonvocal or have serious communication delays and problems, the growth in programs and services for this population must include substantial increases in the numbers of these specialists.

School Psychologists/Educational Diagnosticians.   Traditionally, the school psychologist conducted the psychoeducational diagnosis of each student referred for possible placement. This "workup" usually consisted of administering a battery of standardized tests, including an intelligence test, academic achievement tests, and one or more tests of social or emotional development. The school psychologist's recommendation was frequently the principal basis on which a student was labeled with or without a disability. In recent years the school psychologist's evaluation has included more direct observations of the student's behavior in school. Many school psychologists now act as consultants to regular and special teachers, particularly in such areas as establishing behavior management programs. In most cases the member of the assessment team required by law to be present at the IEP meeting is the school psychologist.

Transition/Vocational Education Teachers. These teachers, with their skills in providing work experiences and job training for students, are essential in special or mainstream programs to prepare students with disabilities for adult careers. Unfortunately, few vocational education teachers have had sufficient training in working with students with disabilities, and several studies report that these teachers have largely negative views toward integrating these students into regular vocational education programs (Comptroller General, 1976; Minner, Knutson, & Aloia, 1979). Perhaps one explanation for this reaction lies in the fact reported by the U.S. Government Accounting Office (GAO) that in 1974 only about 500 vocational education teachers of the 266,000 in the country had received special training in working with individuals with disabilities (Comptroller General, 1976). Although some progress has been made in changing attitudes and providing training for educators (Minner & Knutson, 1980; Regan & Deshler, 1980), far more must be done to fully involve vocational educators in planning and programming for students with disabilities.

Guidance Counselors. Guidance counselors can assist students with disabilities in career planning (Nelson, 1980) and can also play an important role in helping these students adjust to school life—by counseling, offering management suggestions to teachers, and serving as liaisons between home and school (Wallace & McLoughlin, 1988).

Physicians. Physicians play a crucial role in identifying children with potential disabilities, primarily because they are often the first professionals to assess the development of infants and young children. And because serious medical problems threaten many children with severe physical disabilities, physicians' evaluation and guidance are very important. Physicians are frequent sources of support and direction to parents of students with mild disabilities as well. They often prescribe medication to change the behavior of youngsters who are learning disabled, particularly those considered hyperactive. And although many educators criticize the overuse of such medication, teachers and physicians can work together productively. In one instance, when teachers directly measured students' academic performance, they were able to give physicians pertinent, reliable data on how differences in medication affected their students' schoolwork (Scranton, Hajicek, & Wolcott, 1978).

Nurses. Nurses specially trained in working with children with disabilities can assist in early screening and assessment of preschoolers, and they can observe parents' perceptions and needs (Erikson, 1976). They can also advise and assist teachers of students who are severely disabled in the development of nutrition and social skills programs and in the use of medication in classroom management. They can set up guidelines and procedures for emergency and illness care and even help develop programs to teach self-help skills, such as self-menstrual care for girls with retardation (Blackard, Hazel, Livingston, Ryan, Soltman, & Stade, 1977). Nurses may also take responsibility for providing genetic counseling for families of children with disabilities.

Physical and Occupational Therapists. These professionals survey the muscular abilities of persons with disabilities and prescribe and implement appropriate programs. At the earliest stage of intervention with infants, they coach the parents on how to manage their child, and later they work to ensure that the individual with disabilities is handled and placed in normal positions for proper physical development. Therapists also recommend adaptive equipment—wheelchairs, prone board, pillows, scooters, standing tables, walkers—to help individuals with disabilities function more independently. Physical and occupational therapists provide assessment, treatment, and consultation on the development of both gross and fine motor skills, as well as self-help skills (e.g., feeding) where motor problems may interfere with progress. They often administer individual therapy, and many also train classroom teachers and paraprofessionals to work with students in order to free themselves for more specialized, complicated therapy.

Adaptive Physical Education/Recreation Therapy Specialists. These professionals can help students with disabilities participate in physical education programs, an important step in integrating them into the mainstream of school life. Many also work in state and local agencies that provide recreation and leisure programs, most often called therapeutic recreation. Their goal is to help individuals with disabilities experience the same physical, emotional, and social benefits of recreation and leisure activities that people without disabilities enjoy (Heward & Orlansky, 1980).

Social Workers. Caseworkers from social welfare agencies often work with families of children with disabilities from poor socioeconomic areas, families of delinquent youths, and with children with disabilities placed in orphanages and foster care. They can sometimes give educators home environment information relevant in planning for appropriate placement or programs and can also represent the school's decisions to parents or guardians. They can even help monitor the effects of home-based intervention programs with children in preschool and Head Start programs.

School Administrators. The building principal or administrator in charge of special education services can provide IEP team members with support and access to resources, such as special transportation to a special center or a sign language interpreter for a deaf student. The administrator is primarily responsible for making sure that all the requirements for due process and confidentiality have been met, scheduling IEP meetings, making certain that all necessary information is available for the team's decision making, and even making the final recommendation when the team cannot reach a consensus (Pasanella, 1980).

Rehabilitation Counselors.   With the passage of IDEA in 1990, Congress added the rehabilitation counselor to the list of related service providers. IDEA regulations define "career development, employment preparation, achieving independence, and integration in the workplace and community of a student with a disability" as the rehabilitation counselor's job (*Federal Register,* 1990). The task of helping integrate the young adult into the community broadens the rehabilitation counselor's responsibilities from job counseling to helping the youth with overall adjustment to adult life. IDEA's addition of this service is another indicator of the importance Congress places on the period of transition to adult life.

Family.   Because they play a critical role in child development, families are central to the list of those involved in education of the exceptional child. Educators cannot ignore the family's important role, nor can they develop strong, effective programs without family involvement. Central is the concept that all families have strengths. Some families, however, have strengths that are more developed.

Schools and educational teams that operate on this philosophy see parents as an integral part of the comprehensive education team (Shirey & N. G. Haring, 1991). School personnel view the child as a part of a family and consider family needs and perspectives in planning and implementing educational programs. IDEA mandates family involvement in forming the IEP, but effective educational teams involve the family much more closely than simply for a periodic IEP meeting.

Researchers have identified categories of family strengths that include commitment to the family, mental and physical health, communication skills, encouragement, appreciation, time spent together, and ability to handle stress. Educators can improve the IEP process and their day-to-day interactions with families by recognizing and fostering these strengths. Goals of family inclusion are to make parents an integral part of the comprehensive education team and to encourage school personnel to view the child as part of a family.

Teachers as Problem Solvers

In the early 1900s, when immigration, compulsory school attendance, and other Progressive Era reforms brought large numbers of students with special needs into the schools, it became necessary for education professionals to come up with some means of serving the needs of this population. The solution arrived at was to remove these students from regular classrooms and provide them with a special education in separate classrooms and even separate facilities.

By the forties the special class was a standard feature in most urban districts, spreading throughout the country in the years following World War II. This separation of services led to great differences of professional orientation and preparation between special and regular education teachers, which continue today despite revolutionary changes in the sixties and the middle seventies.

What are the implications for both special and regular education teachers, given the far-reaching mandates of special education legislation of the last two decades? And what additional implications result from calls to reform by groups espousing a closer partnership between special and regular education systems?

Certainly, there will be a continued requirement for specialized services from a segment of the education community. Just as certainly, there will be an increasing demand for regular education to become more flexible and to include special education training as a part of preservice and inservice preparation. Some thinkers, however, view the most important changes as those that affect how teachers see themselves, how they view their relationships to other teachers, and how they approach the problems teaching presents them, regardless of the particular methodologies they may favor (Skrtic, 1988).

The present general structure of school organization may be seen, up to the present, as an essentially closed system. Teachers are encouraged to remain within the confines of their own classrooms, to guard their own territory carefully and actively—including the teaching competencies they have mastered. This setup naturally puts teachers in opposition to one another, making it unlikely that they will request assistance from one another or offer unsolicited advice. Teacher relationships are loosely coupled, placing an emphasis upon individual efforts rather than on teamwork. In this adversary arrangement, there is little incentive for cooperation or shared concern. Such a system maintains and strengthens the special/regular education dichotomy.

An alternative to this closed organizational structure is a structure that is adaptable, open, and encourages reciprocal relationships between professionals (and, at another level, between student and teacher). Teachers are encouraged to interact, soliciting and offering one another advice and support. The ultimate goal of such a structure is to encourage teachers to be problem solvers, that is, to seek as many diverse, creative solutions as possible to the questions generated by individuals' learning needs. Rather than pitting teacher against teacher, strategy against strategy, the new emphasis would be upon collaborative efforts among unified teams of education and related service professionals.

Integrated and Inclusive Education

Recent trends have emphasized a move toward providing appropriate education for all students in their neighborhood schools. This trend has obvious advantages for the future adaptation to the home community. Early friendships can be more readily maintained when children and youth with disabilities remain in a familiar environment. Integrated education refers to a plan that provides placement in the regular classrooms for some period of time during the school day. Inclusive education provides full-time placement in the regular classroom. Ultimately, the goal of inclusion is the participation in social relationships across the range of human interaction from casual acquaintance to the maintenance of long-term friendships (T. G. Haring & Breen, in press). Several national agencies, including the Association for Persons with Severe Handicaps, the Association of Supervision and Curriculum Development, and the National Association of State Boards of Education have offered supportive statements for inclusive education. These organizations are promoting the total inclusion of all students in the regular classroom. On the other hand, the Council for Exceptional Children has reservations about totally inclusive education. Many members of this organization are concerned about how regular teachers can provide the full range of educational considerations for children with exceptionality while balancing effective instruction for the diversity represented by these children.

There are many successful inclusive education programs throughout the United States and Canada. In each example that we have examined, several different strategies were applied; however, there were some common practices. All of the inclusive programs we observed used collaborative approaches to providing services. The support services formed comprehensive teams and provided their services directly in the regular classrooms. Each program had a well-planned, systematically arranged administrative organization with a common purpose, complete agreement among the professionals involved, and a completely optimistic attitude about the future success of the plan. We might go as far as to hold that unless the above conditions prevail, the school may not be ready for inclusive education.

Societal Changes

Special educators and their students are caught up in a fast-changing society. Many experts, including educational psychologist Jennifer York, believe that these changes are affecting education dramatically. Dwindling financial resources, an increasingly diverse population, complex world problems, violence in society, and a new explosion of information are having an impact on schools everywhere. Special educators need to be concerned because proportionally, such problems as poverty, racial imbalance, and maternal drug abuse are magnified in the population of exceptional children. Recent figures from the Department of Education show striking connections. In 1991, for example, youth with disabilities were twice as likely to be African-American, substantially less likely to be Hispanic, and only slightly less likely to be white than total population of youth. For all disabilities combined, 65% were white, 24% were African-American, and 8% were Hispanic. (For youth in general, 70% were white, 12% were African-American, and 13% were Hispanic.) Moreover, within the population with disabilities, racial disproportions were especially noticeable. African-American youth were more highly represented in every disability category, but highest in speech and language impairments, mental retardation, serious emotional disturbance, visual impairments, and deaf-blindness (U.S. Department of Education, 1992, p. 15).

Reasons for this disproportionality have been a matter of national concern. Some contend that economics, not race, is the main variable, in that children of color are more likely to be poor and to miss out on prenatal, perinatal, and postnatal care. Some charge that school professionals are more likely to place minority and poor children in special education because of low expectations. And for decades many have argued that the standardized assessment instruments used to decide a student's placement are culturally biased.

CURRENT TRENDS

Special education is a multidisciplinary field, encompassing many areas that include speech, occupational, and physical therapies, as well as behavioral and cognitive psychology. It is reasonable to conceptualize modern special education as a discipline that uses the combined strategies from its own research and from other areas to provide a comprehensive, integrated approach to teaching. Its emphases tend to shift as a result of research findings, changes in society at large, and new legislation. Current trends reflect these influences.

Special educators are giving increased attention to diversity in learning and behavior and are changing instructional practices to accommodate these diversities. This approach signifies less reliance on disability labels and more reliance on adapting instructional strategies to the individual student. Instruction is based on adapting traditional teaching modes to the student's needs, as well as applying successful practices based on current research.

Schools are moving toward full inclusion of students with disabilities in regular classrooms. Education in the least restrictive environment (LRE), mandated by P.L. 94–142, has been interpreted in many ways over the years. If society is to become more accepting of individual differences among its members, full inclusion is sought by many as a necessary course of action and a logical outcome of the LRE mandate. Courts and practitioners see supplementary aids and services within the classroom as the key to successful inclusionary education. Certain regular and special educators, advocacy groups, and broad-based education groups are promoting a single, inclusive system of education to replace the two-tiered special/regular education structure. The trend in placement for students with severe disabilities has followed practices in placement for students who are less disabled. However, the procedures for achieving inclusion for students with severe disabilities have involved more systematic planning, more intensive preparation of personnel involved, and more collaborative team efforts.

A move toward increased communitywide inclusion for people with disabilities has gone hand in hand with the inclusive philosophy for classrooms. The LRE movement has prompted a major national thrust by policymakers, service delivery specialists, and higher education professionals toward full community integration. In fact, law now mandates transition services for secondary students as part of the Individualized Educational Plan (IEP). The overall goal is for people with disabilities to live in typical homes in regular neighborhoods, pursue typical jobs and activities, and receive services adapted to their needs in that natural environment.

At the other end of the age spectrum, services for infants and preschoolers have expanded. IDEA was designed in part to provide improved services for children with developmental disabilities from birth onward. For children aged 2 years and younger, attention is given to developing interagency service delivery models, recognizing the critical role of the family in all early intervention, and emphasizing the family's decision-making role in designing the Individual Family Service Plan (IFSP).

Classroom research and practice have moved toward systematic instruction, a scientific approach based on the application of behavioral principles in the classroom. In addition, systematic instruction provides an organized body of procedures that includes (1) gathering data regarding the student's performance level, (2) establishing priorities among the functional skills the student needs to learn, (3) identifying behaviors necessary for developing these skills, (4) continuously assessing progress toward skill acquisition, (5) using data from progress to revise the instructional program, and (6) providing opportunities for students to apply skills in natural settings to assess generalizability of performance to new situations. A positive behavioral support strategy can refine this approach, providing a way to manage behavior problems.

Sheryl Burgstahler
University of Washington

The computer is one of the most liberating and empowering technologies to come along in a long time for people with a variety of handicaps.

(N. Coombs, a professor who is blind who teaches students who are deaf, cited in Wilson, 1992, p. A18)

Use of Computer Technology by Students with Exceptionalities

As computers and networks become indispensable in the information age, access to these tools is important for all students. Computer technologies have the potential to help children with disabilities become more fully participating and contributing members of society. They can be used by these children as tools for communicating, accessing information, writing, learning, and performing other tasks. They can help ensure equal opportunities in education to individuals with disabilities and facilitate their transition to work and community living. Here are some examples of how computers can be used by children with disabilities.

Compensatory Tool

Participation in school activities can be difficult for individuals who cannot see, speak, hear, or use writing implements. Besides using computers for the same purposes as nondisabled students, children with disabilities can use them as compensatory tools to overcome functional limitations imposed by their disabilities. Technology can be used to increase sensory input, enhance mobility, perform as a prosthesis, and facilitate receptive and expressive communication. For example, a portable computer equipped with speech output can be used as a "voice" in class discussions for a child who cannot speak. A computer with adaptive technology can be used as a writing or drawing instrument by someone who cannot use his or her hands. In short, computers make it possible for students with disabilities to perform

tasks for themselves that they otherwise would be dependent on others to perform. Once students learn satisfactory methods to operate computers, new activities are open to them and the amount of time that it takes to complete their work can be reduced. Application of appropriate technology early in life, because it enables children to control their environment, may even help prevent them from developing feelings of learned helplessness.

Computer-Assisted Instruction

Computers allow students with disabilities to participate in learning activities more independently and thereby reduce the effect of their disabilities on the acquisition and use of skills and concepts. Drill-and-practice, tutorial, simulation, word processing, problem-solving, and other software programs give these students learning opportunities that would not be available in other ways. For example, word processing and tutorial software may help students with hearing, learning, and language disabilities develop language and writing skills. Educational software that provides multisensory experiences, interaction, positive reinforcement, individualized instruction, and repetition can be useful in skill building for children with specific learning disabilities. Special software can even teach children who are severely and multiply disabled the concept of cause-effect by demonstrating that their actions (e.g., hitting a switch) have an impact on their environment (e.g., a picture is created, music is played, or a toy is activated). Computers offer infinite patience, learner control, immediate feedback, branching capabilities, multisensory interaction, and a nonthreatening learning environment. Some of the qualities of computers that teachers of exceptional children have found to be particularly powerful include their ability to hold attention, increase motivation, and enhance a learner's self-concept.

Access to Information

Computers and networks provide new options for accessing information through on-line library catalogs, encyclopedias, dictionaries, journals, books, newspapers, data bases, and other resources. For those with disabilities that make it difficult to visit libraries and/or turn pages, information sources on networks, CD-ROM, and other media provide opportunities to read publications on their computer screens. Computer technology can also assist in the process of media conversion. For example, a student who is blind has the technology to access newspapers and journals on-line and can use adaptive software and hardware to have the materials read aloud or printed in braille. The expansion of networking services around the world gives students with disabilities who are equipped with appropriate technology access to a wealth of resources without assistance and reduces the necessity to move about.

Electronic Communication
Telecommunications is a powerful mode of communication. Those with hearing and speech impairments who have a personal computer, modem, and appropriate software can communicate with others on electronic networks. When teachers use computer-mediated communications for classroom discussions, they allow students who are deaf and speech-impaired to communicate on an equal level with other students. By stimulating and enhancing interactions with nondisabled peers, electronic communication can also facilitate the social and language development of children with disabilities.

Adaptive Technology Providing Computer Access
Some students with disabilities face barriers to giving input to computers, interpreting output, and reading computer documentation. Thousands of commercially-available adaptive hardware and software products have been developed to provide functional alternatives to standard operations. Some computer devices assist individuals with a variety of disabilities. For example, equipment that provides flexibility in the positioning of monitors, keyboards,

and tabletops is useful for many users with disabilities. Adjustable copy holders can also ease accessibility. Similarly, the availability of portable computers can assist students with note taking and communication in classes. Some approaches to removing input, output, and documentation barriers for children with specific disabilities are described below.

Children with Orthopedic Impairments

Input
Plugging all computer components into power outlet strips with accessible on/off switches can make it possible for students who are disabled to turn equipment on and off independently. Adaptive hardware and software can enhance standard keyboard use by children with orthopedic impairments by permitting input with little or no use of the hands. Individuals can control the computer by pressing keys with one finger or with a pointing device, such as a mouth stick or a head stick. Hardware switching devices can be used to lock the SHIFT and CONTROL keys to allow sequential keystrokes to input commands that normally require two or more keys to be pressed simultaneously. Software utilities can also create "sticky keys" that electronically latch the shift, control, and other keys and allow those who are typing with single fingers or pointing devices to press keys sequentially rather than concurrently. The key repeat function can be disabled for those who cannot release a key quickly enough to avoid multiple selections. Keyboard guards (solid templates with holes over each key to assist precise selection) can be used by those who lack fine motor control. Sometimes repositioning the keyboard and monitor can enhance accessibility. For example, mounting keyboards perpendicular to tables or wheelchair trays or at head height can assist children with limited mobility who use pointing devices to press keys.

Some hardware modifications completely replace the keyboard and/or mouse for individuals who cannot operate these standard devices. Expanded keyboards (larger keys, spaced far apart) can replace standard keyboards for those who lack fine motor control. Minikeyboards provide access to those who have fine motor control but lack a range of motion great enough to use a standard keyboard. Keyboards can be modified to have fewer key options to simplify input to special software for children who are severely and multiply disabled. Track balls and specialized input devices can replace mice.

For children with more severe orthopedic impairments keyboard emulation is available, including scanning and Morse code input. In each case, special switches are controlled by the use of at least one muscle over which the individual has voluntary control (e.g., head, finger, knee, mouth). To make selections, individuals use switches activated by movement of the head, finger, foot, breath, etc. Hundreds of switches tailor input devices to individual needs. In Morse code input, users enter Morse code by activating switches (e.g., a sip-and-puff switch registers dots with a sip and dashes with a puff). Special adaptive hardware and software translate Morse code input into a form that computers understand so that standard software can be used.

Voice input provides another option for children with disabilities. Speech recognition systems allow students to control computers by speaking words and letters. A particular system is "trained" to recognize specific voices.

Special software can further aid children with mobility impairments. Abbreviation expansion (macro) and word prediction software can reduce input demands for commonly used text and keyboard commands. For example, word prediction software that anticipates entire words after several keystrokes can increase input speed.

Output

Screen output is often preferred to printed output for children with orthopedic impairments who cannot manipulate objects, such as pages in a book.

Documentation

Standard documentation is difficult to deal with for those who cannot use their hands. On-screen help can provide efficient access to user guides for children who are unable to turn pages in books.

Children with Visual Impairments

Input

Most individuals who are visually impaired can use standard keyboards. However, braille input devices are available as well. Large print or braille key labels can assist with keyboard use.

Output

Special equipment for visually impaired children can modify display and printer output. Computer-generated symbols, both text and graphics, can be enlarged on the monitor or printer, thereby allowing individuals with low vision to use standard word processing, spreadsheet, electronic mail, and other software applications. For individuals with some visual impairments, the ability to adjust the color of the monitor or change the foreground and background colors is also of value. For example, special software can reverse the screen from black on white to white on black for people who are light sensitive. Antiglare screens can also make screens easier to read.

Voice output can be used to read screen text to children who are blind. Special software programs "read" computer screens and speech synthesizers "speak" the text. Refreshable braille displays allow line-by-line translation of the screen into braille on a display area where vertical pins move into braille configurations as screen text is scanned. Braille printers provide more permanent output for users with visual impairments.

Documentation

Scanners with optical character recognition can be used to read printed material and store it electronically on computers, where it can be read using voice synthesis or printed with braille translation software and braille printers. Such systems can provide independent access to journals, texts, and homework assignments for students with visual impairments. Some hardware and software vendors also provide braille, large print, and electronic versions of their documentation to support visually impaired users.

Children with Hearing and/or Speech Impairments

Input
Students with hearing and/or speech disabilities generally do not have special problems inputting information with a standard keyboard and mouse.

Output
Although students with hearing impairments can use computer applications without special adaptive technology, alternatives to audio output can assist the computer user who is hearing impaired. For example, some computer software provides the option of giving visual output whenever audio output is normally used.

Documentation
Students with hearing and/or speech impairments typically do not have difficulty using standard written or on-screen documentation.

Children with Specific Learning Disabilities

Input
Software that aids in efficient and accurate input can assist some students with learning disabilities. Children can compensate for high rates of input errors by using spell checkers, thesauruses, and grammar checkers. In addition, word prediction programs (software that predicts whole words from fragments) have been used successfully by students with learning disabilities. Macro software, which expands abbreviations, can reduce the necessity to memorize keyboard commands and can facilitate the entry of commonly used text.

Output
Some children with learning disabilities find adaptive devices designed for individuals with visual impairments useful. In particular, large print displays, alternative colors on the computer screen, and voice output can compensate for some visual and reading problems. People who have difficulty interpreting visual material can improve comprehension and the ability to identify and correct errors when words are printed in large fonts or spoken.

Documentation
Computer documentation provided in electronic forms can be made more accessible to those with reading difficulties by enlarged character and voice synthesis devices.

Use of Computer Technology by Teachers and Administrators
Computer-based technology indirectly benefits students with exceptionalities when it is used by teachers and administrators for information access, communication with peers, and classroom management. Examples include computer-assisted management for program planning and scheduling, instructional management, information management, data analysis, student evaluation, and materials preparation. In addition, teachers and administrators can use electronic mail and network resources to collaborate with peers and share research results, intervention strategies, and curricular ideas. Computer-based tools can help teachers and administrators use their time more efficiently, gain access to a wider range of expertise, and manage intervention activities more effectively.

Summary
Students with disabilities face barriers to educational opportunities and careers. However, computers are helping to remove some of these barriers. As word processors replace typewriters, electronic spreadsheets replace handwritten books, and on-line services replace telephones and paper communication, individuals with disabilities who have computer access become capable of handling a wider range of activities independently—both in school and the workplace.

An emphasis on teaching social skills competence has accompanied the move toward full inclusion in schools and communities. Its goal is to foster the skills necessary for students with disabilities to develop positive social interactions with nondisabled peers. Several instruction programs have been developed in this area. Most apply behavioral principles, including operant and cognitive theory, along with social learning techniques.

A transdisciplinary model for special education services is replacing the model of the lone teacher in the classroom, especially as inclusive education becomes more prevalent. Teams of specialists in communication disorders, physical and occupational therapy, social services and other areas provide support in classrooms to accommodate students with diverse abilities and needs. These teams differ from IEP teams in that they meet frequently and deal specifically with students' day-to-day programmatic needs. This new organizational structure involves teachers working together as problem solvers and as classroom researchers to find practical strategies to improve teaching. The philosophy provides a structure that is adaptable, open, and encourages relationships. Regular teachers are encouraged to interact with special education teachers and support team members, soliciting help and support.

While these current trends may seem diverse, they are all pointed toward the goal of achieving the best possible learning and social outcomes for individuals with disabilities, leading to their full participation in community life throughout childhood and adulthood. Academic, career, and social skills are all seen as interwoven into a fabric of community inclusion.

SUMMARY   The first special education program is sometimes said to have been Jean-Marc-Gaspard Itard's 5 years of work with the wild boy of Aveyron. Several decades later Édouard Séguin argued that all mentally retarded individuals could learn, paving the way for further development of the field. The early 20th century saw more gains in the education of special individuals: Binet drafted the first intelligence test in 1905, and compulsory education was mandated in 1918, advancing the cause of all public education. Later in the century, in 1954, *Brown v. Board of Education* affirmed education as the right of all Americans, a right that could not be denied except by due process of law.

Since this landmark case, the country has witnessed a gradual growth in concern and services for children with disabilities, culminating in the passage of the Education for All Handicapped Children Act (P.L. 94–142) in 1975. This law marked a victory for people hoping to gain for all exceptional individuals appropriate individualized education programs within the least restrictive, most integrated settings possible. Further legislation, in 1986 (P.L. 99–457), confirmed the extension of such services to preschoolers 3 to 5 years of age. The reauthorization of P.L. 94–142 in 1990, under a new name, the Individuals with Disabilities Act (P.L. 101–476), solidified gains for individuals who are disabled from birth to adulthood and changed the language of the law to place emphasis on the individual, not the disabling condition. Other laws that helped guarantee the right to education for all children were Section 504 of the 1973 Rehabilitation Act (P.L. 93–112), which mandated that persons with disabilities could not be excluded on the basis of the handicapping condition from any program or activity receiving federal funds, and the 1992 reauthorization of the Rehabilitation Act, allowing easier eligibility for vocational rehabilitation services for individuals with severe disabilities and addressing interagency linkages for transition services.

How many children and youth are affected by these laws, and who are they? Figures and categories are difficult to pin down because of differences among statistical methods and approaches. However, recent figures provide a useful snapshot. The total number of students served in special education in the United States was slightly over 4.8 million in 1991. Proportionally, this constituted 10% of the school age population. The percentage of students with disabilities served increased 2.8% between 1989–1990 and 1990–1991. The largest growth within any one category was in students with specific learning disabilities, who accounted for 49% of the special education population. Proportions of students with some other disabilities were 23% with speech or language impairments; 13% with mental retardation; 9% with serious emotional disturbance; and 1% with severe disabilities. Those most likely to go "unclassified" and hence to be overlooked for individualized instruction are gifted students, students with behavior disorders (particularly those who internalize their fears and concerns), and students with learning disabilities.

Even as the field of special education continues to evolve, the concern of all special educators continues to be that each exceptional individual achieves the fullest possible access to autonomy and decision making in his or her own life and full participation across the range of human interactions.

STUDY QUESTIONS

1. Discuss the importance of the 1954 Supreme Court ruling in *Brown v. Board of Education*.

2. List three provisions assured to individuals who are disabled by P.L. 94–142, the Education for All Handicapped Children Act, later renamed the Education of the Handicapped Act.

3. What additions did the Individuals with Disabilities Education Act (IDEA) make to the Education of the Handicapped Act?

4. What additional provision did the amendments to the Education of the Handicapped Act P.L. 99–457 mandate?

5. Contrast prevalence with incidence as they are used to represent the number of persons with disabilities in the United States.

6. List the categories of exceptionality as defined by the Office of Special Education and Rehabilitation Services.

7. What are the dangers involved in labeling exceptional persons?

8. Discuss the advantages and disadvantages of using resource rooms in providing special education for students with disabilities.

9. According to the provisions of IDEA, what specific information must the Individualized Educational Plan include?

10. Discuss the ways in which transition planning can facilitate the preparation of secondary students with disabilities for adult life in the workplace and the community.

11. Define systematic instruction and discuss the advantages of using the procedures in educating persons who are disabled.

12. Discuss the trend in teacher preparation designed to develop teachers as skilled problem solvers.

2

Linda McCormick
University of Hawaii

Cultural and Linguistic Diversity and Exceptionality

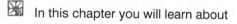 In this chapter you will learn about

- the history of litigation and legislation affecting provision of equal education opportunities for minority students

- issues associated with assessment and appropriate placement of minority students

- the implications of cultural pluralism, cultural assimilation, and cultural competence

- the values and beliefs of different cultural groups and the relevance of these values and beliefs to success in academic and social environments

- the purposes and procedures for prereferral intervention

- procedures and activities for teaching minority students with special education needs

SOONG

Soong is a second-grade student in a school in a large, racially mixed district. She was born in a refugee camp in Thailand while her family was awaiting relocation to the United States. Neither Soong's parents nor her older siblings had any formal schooling before coming to the United States. They have been in this country for almost 7 years now. Like many other refugees, the members of Soong's family continue to have difficulties related to memories of experiences in their native land of Laos and the loss of loved ones. Two of Soong's older siblings were in the program for culturally and linguistically diverse exceptional (CLDE) learners when they were in the early grades. They seem to be doing better in intermediate school.

With observation of Soong, it is not difficult to understand her teacher's concern. Soong doesn't seem to feel part of the class. She keeps her eyes on her desk, her arms circling her open book as if protecting it, and she never raises her hand. In the cafeteria she sits alone, with her eyes on her plate. She eats very little. On the playground she retreats to the corner of a fenced area, where she squats with her elbows on her knees and her chin in her hands. She hums to herself as she watches her peers on the playground equipment.

Soong's problems are similar to those of many students from racial or ethnic minorities who experience problems with the academic and social expectations of school. Soong is receiving help from a prereferral assistance team of teachers for what her teacher describes as "psychological, linguistic, and learning difficulties." The team is working to sort out sociocultural factors from problems associated with learning and behavioral difficulties. In short, the team is trying to determine whether Soong has psychological or learning problems or if her difficulties are related to motivation and the problems inherent in trying to learn in a classroom where the language and values are different from those of the home. The team's goal is to develop a plan and provide resources to help Soong be successful in her second-grade classroom.

HISTORY   If predictions are realized, by the year 2000, one out of every three persons in the United States will belong to a linguistically or ethnically diverse group. Our schools will, of course, mirror these figures. As the number of multicultural and bilingual students in the United States continues to increase, the challenge is to try to narrow the gap between the services they need and the availability of personnel and other resources needed to provide these services. Teachers must be prepared to consider the cultural values and life-styles of each child in their class and to understand each child's socialization and communication styles, as well as his or her motivational system.

In America the two groups who have struggled the most for equal educational opportunity are minorities and persons with disabilities. Today children are more likely than ever before to be members of racial or ethnic minorities and speak a language other than English. As a result, there are more students than ever before who belong to both groups. Whether children are members of a racial or ethnic minority or are disabled or whether they belong to both groups, they bring special and important skills and abilities, as well as valuable experiences, to the class. That they are more similar to their "regular" peers than they are different does not mean that they can necessarily benefit from the same learning experiences. Because they bring very different competencies and attitudes to the learning environment, they may need different instructional experiences.

Educators today are expending a great deal of effort to understand, respect, and provide for cultural and linguistic diversity. This has not always been the case. Before 1954 there was little concern for ensuring equal educational opportunities for minority students. School segregation was defended by reference to an 1895 Supreme Court ruling stating that segregation did not create a badge of inferiority if segregated facilities offered an equal education.

In 1954 the *Brown v. Board of Education* decision held that segregated schools are not, in fact, "equal." Rather, they were described as "inherently unequal." It was argued that segregation of black and white children in separate schools denied black students their right to equal educational opportunity, as guaranteed by the Fourteenth Amendment.

The *Brown v. Board of Education* ruling did not have the immediate effect that was expected. It was fully a decade before there was any significant legislation to end educational inequalities, and it came about then because the Kennedy administration and Johnson's Great Society made a commitment to equal opportunity.

The efforts and struggle of many people, especially African-American leaders, finally reached fruition when in 1964 the Civil Rights Act and the Economic Opportunity Act were passed. These pieces of landmark legislation gave the federal government the power it needed to intervene in cases of discrimination within the individual states. Title VI of the Civil Rights Act established (1) that the federal government could (and would) use its control of money to shape local school policies and (2) that responsibility for determining whether school systems were segregated (and if they were, doing something about the situation) would rest with the U.S. Office of Education. Southern school districts were required to submit specific desegregation plans to the U.S. Office of Education.

The Education of Handicapped Children Amendment (Title VI) was added to the Elementary and Secondary Education Act (ESEA) in 1966, to provide for the needs of children who are disabled, and the Bilingual Education Act (Title VII) was added to the ESEA in 1967. The Bilingual Education Act, which provided financial assistance for local schools to design educational programs for children from environments where the dominant language was other than English, was applauded as the first official acknowledgment that lack of English proficiency impedes access to educational opportunities.

In the late sixties a major concern of educators and parents was the realization that culturally and linguistically diverse students were overrepresented in special education programs. Parents and advocates took action on this concern with three court cases addressing the issue of overrepresentation of minority children in special education.

In 1970 parents of Hispanic students brought a class action suit, *Diana v. State Board of Education*, against the state of California. They charged that classrooms for the educable mentally retarded contained approximately double the number of Hispanic students than would be expected by the proportion of Hispanic children in the general school population. They argued that the Hispanic children were being certified as eligible for special education placement on the basis of English IQ tests, which were not appropriate for use with non-English-speaking children.

Shortly thereafter, in 1972, another class action suit was initiated by parents of six African-American children who had been classified as mentally retarded (on the basis of their performance on standardized intelligence tests). This suit, *Larry P. v. Riles*, was against the San Francisco Unified School District. The parents presented data showing (1) that there was a disproportionate number of African-American students in special classes for the educable mentally retarded (EMR) and (2) that these children scored in the normal range of intelligence when retested. The suit asked for a moratorium on the use of individual intelligence tests for the placement of African-American children and a ceiling on special education placement of these children. The ceiling was to be based on the percentage of African-American children in the total school population. The parents were successful. A preliminary injunction stopped the use of IQ tests as the main criterion for placing African-American students, and it ordered annual reevaluation of children currently in EMR classes.

In 1974, at the height of the concern for discriminatory assessment practices, minority parents initiated yet another class action suit. This suit involved bilingual education rather than special education. Filed on behalf of 1,800 Chinese-American children, the suit, *Lau v. Nichols*, contended that the instruction of these children was provided in a language they did not understand. Once again the parents were successful. The Supreme Court decision held that "there is no equality of treatment merely by providing students with the same facilities, textbooks, teachers, and curriculum; for students who do not understand English are effectively foreclosed from any meaningful education." This ruling meant that all public school systems receiving federal aid must ensure that children from non-English-speaking backgrounds receive some form of special help in learning standard English. As a result, they can obtain equal educational opportunity.

The decisions in these cases in the seventies were among the forces that moved special education theory, research, and practices toward alternative classification schemes and a wider variety of programming options for students with special needs. Many of the points put forth in these decisions were ultimately incorporated into the amendments of the Bilingual Education Act and the mandates of the Education for All Handicapped Children Act (Public Law 94–142), which was signed into law in 1975. These mandates include due process, parental involvement, nondiscriminatory assessment, and placement in the least restrictive environment. (Congress changed the name of this act to the Individuals with Disabilities Education Act, IDEA, in 1990 and the most recent amendments to IDEA are identified as Public Law 102–119 [1991]).

After the enactment of P.L. 94–142, there were two other important class action suits. Both cases, which were filed in New York, dealt with inappropriate identification, assessment, and placement of minority students in special education programs. *Lora v. New York City Board of Education* (1984) was filed on behalf of African-American and Hispanic children assigned to special day schools for the emotionally disturbed. *Dyricia S. v. New York City Board of Education* (1979) was filed on behalf of Puerto Rican and other Hispanic students with disabilities and limited English proficiency who required bilingual special education programs. These cases led to a consolidated judgment calling for the provision of appropriate bilingual programs for all students with disabilities.

Decades have passed since the court decisions and legislation described above, but fundamental assessment and placement issues remain. In 1988 MacMillan, Hendrick, and Watkins examined evidence to determine if the situation had improved in the eighties as compared to the seventies. Specifically MacMillan et al. looked at (1) the extent to which modifications in assessment and programming successfully affected the racial isolation noted in programs for students with mild retardation, (2) the possibility of reverse racism in screening and identification, (3) the availability of new options for serving students with IQ scores in the 70 to 85 range, and (4) instructional arrangements for minority students described as marginally achieving. They found racial isolation, fewer children being served, and generally fewer remedial options for marginal achievers.

Racial Isolation.   In the late sixties and early seventies, the major argument for abolishing self-contained special classes for students labeled as mildly retarded was that these classes were racially segregated (e.g., Dunn, 1968). When MacMillan et al. looked at whether modifications in assessment and programming in the seventies and eighties had effectively altered the ethnic balance in these classes, they found that representation of Hispanic children was more nearly appropriate but that there continued to be a disproportionate number of African-American children in special education classes. Interestingly, they found that when minority children *were* mainstreamed, they were likely to be enrolled in regular classrooms that were disproportionately high in minority students.

Reverse Racism.   MacMillan et al. were interested in finding out whether the learning problems of minority children were more likely to go undetected or be ignored than those of children in the majority group. Said another way, the issue was whether concern for quotas had taken precedence over concern for children's individual needs and whether there was a disproportionately high percentage of minority children in the group of "unserved" children. Unfortunately, this latter result did seem to be occurring (based on the evidence of one study and numerous anecdotal reports from school personnel). Quotas *did* seem to be a concern, and the learning problems of minority children *were* more likely to go undetected or ignored than those of other children.

Children with IQ Scores in the 70 to 85 Range.   Students labeled mildly retarded in the late eighties were more disabled than students with that label in the late sixties and early seventies because of revisions in the definition of *mentally retarded* by the American Association on Mental Deficiency (AAMD) (Grossman, 1983). (Under the new definition, children were not classified as retarded unless IQ scores were below the 70 to 75 range.) Logic suggested that many children with IQ scores in the 70 or 75 to 85 range might subsequently have been reclassified as learning disabled (LD), rather than as mentally retarded. After some investigation it was concluded that this was not the case. The requirement in the definition of LD is that students must demonstrate a substantial difference between intelligence and achievement. As a result, children with low achievement *and* low IQ scores could not be classified as LD. Thus, because they fell into neither category, they were no longer served.

So, overall, the class action suits had both positive and negative results. On the positive side, children functioning at the high end of the retarded range were no longer being labeled as mentally retarded, but, on the other hand, some children with real needs were no longer eligible for special services.

Marginal Achievers.   MacMillan et al. also looked at whether minority children who were marginally achieving were being well served. They found that most students with low achievement and IQ scores in the 70 to 85 range had been removed from special classes and were now being served in remedial classes. They continued to be denied access to mainstream settings because most had difficulty with such requirements as minimum competency tests.

In conclusion, the MacMillan et al. findings suggest that the court decisions of the early seventies and P.L. 94–142 may not have substantially increased educational opportunities for culturally and linguistically diverse students. The disappointing conclusion that there seemed to be an even narrower range of appropriate programs and fewer remedial options was echoed in the data from two minority research institutes. Institutes in Texas and California were funded by the federal government in the eighties to study the special education offered to Hispanic children. With regard to assessment, the institutes found that (1) language proficiency is not seriously taken into account, (2) testing is done primarily in English, (3) language problems typical of second language learners are misinterpreted as disorders, (4) home data are not collected and incorporated as valid information, and (5) the same few tests are used with the majority of children (Figueroa, Fradd, & Correa, 1989). Most depressing was the finding that tests scores decrease after special education placement and that reevaluations typically lead to continued special education placement.

In addition to overreferral, some researchers have noted underreferral of language minority students for special education (Campbell, Gersten, & Kolar, 1992; Gersten,

Morvant, George, & Woodward, 1992). What Macmillan et al. feared seems to be occurring: many students who truly need specialized assistance are not receiving it. There are few support services available for language minority students until they reach some level of proficiency in English. Until that point special education personnel do not seem to feel comfortable assessing and programming for these students (Campbell et al., 1992).

Thus, the assessment needs of culturally and linguistically diverse learners continue to pose a challenge to the American educational system. Educating these students is a complex task that goes beyond awareness and cultural sensitivity: it requires a commitment to developing cross-cultural competence.

DEFINITION   *Culture* is the filter through which we view life and the major influence on what we believe and how we behave. From birth, all experiences that we share with our family, friends, and community contribute in a cumulative fashion to the development of this cultural filter. These shared experiences ultimately guide the way we think, the way we feel, and the way we behave.

Computer experiences can improve school performance of children from culturally diverse backgrounds.

Culture is not a rigidly prescribed set of characteristics, but rather a set of tendencies shared by persons with the same upbringing (Hanson, 1992). The extent to which these tendencies are realized and acted on depends on such factors as socioeconomic status, sex, age, length of residence in a locale, and education. The degree of cultural orientation that children bring to the academic environment depends on the strength of their ethnic identification, which, in turn, is affected by the strength of the family's cultural orientation.

The Council for Exceptional Children defines a *minority group* as "any group which because of racial or ethnic origin constitutes a distinctive and recognizable minority in our society" (Fuchigami, 1980, p. 241). There are two important points to remember about minority cultures: (1) that they are every bit as rich, and significant as, the majority culture; and (2) that their membership is no more homogeneous than members of the majority culture.

The term "culturally disadvantaged" should be avoided. It suggests that economic and environmental poverty and membership in a minority culture are somehow inherently related. Although it is true that minority status and poverty are often among the variables related to lack of success in school, this does not mean that these factors (alone or in combination) *cause* failure. All that can be stated with certainty is that these factors, separate and in combination, pose an enormous challenge to the educational system. Also, the term is a misnomer because it implies that such students lack a "culture," which is not the case.

Cultural pluralism is the belief that society is strengthened and enriched by the contributions of different groups. The opposite of cultural pluralism is *cultural assimilation*, the belief that diverse cultures should be merged into a single, homogeneous society with common life-styles, values, language, and cultural practices. The concept of cultural assimilation is offensive to many because it tends to obscure the unique contributions of different cultural groups to the society as a whole. Cultural pluralism has been called the "salad bowl theory" (Erickson, 1985); cultural assimilation is often referred to as the "melting pot theory."

Other terms that have relevance to the education of culturally and/or linguistically diverse students with special needs are multicultural education and bilingual education. *Multicultural education* is education that teaches the values underlying cultural pluralism. Teaching and learning are based on the premise that all students benefit from exposure to different people, beliefs, and ideas. Multicultural education provides students with opportunities to relate to and evaluate new perspectives. Rodriguez (1982) argues that multicultural concepts should be incorporated into every facet of education: "The concept of multicultural education is not based on the premise that there are ethnic minority students in the classroom, but that there are differences in students within any classroom and that all of those students live in a pluralistic society" (p. 227).

Bilingual education is education that reinforces the student's home language and culture while at the same time teaching the ability to function in another language. Instruction in both skills and content is typically provided in the student's home language *and* in English. Bilingual education attempts to preserve the traditions of non-English cultures while at the same time helping children become functioning members of the English language culture. A program that is sometimes confused with bilingual education is English as a Second Language (ESL). Although an ESL program may be one component of bilingual education, the focus in an ESL program is exclusively on English as both the goal and the medium of instruction.

Multicultural bilingual special education is a combination of the three programs: multicultural education, bilingual education, and special education. As noted earlier in this chapter, the concept of bilingual special education can be traced to two major pieces of legislation: the Bilingual Education Act of 1967 (P.L. 90–247) and the Education for All Handicapped Children Act of 1975 (now named Individuals with Disabilities Education Act [IDEA], P.L. 102–119). These resulted in the provision of an individualized program of special instruction, using the child's home language and the home culture along with English (Baca & Cervantes, 1989). The child's special education needs are primary; language and culture are the means through which the necessary instruction is provided.

At the broadest level, teachers need to know about, and be sensitive, to cultures and languages different from their own, and they need to apply that knowledge and sensitivity in the assessment and teaching processes. Effectiveness in working with students from other cultures depends on complex and subtle interactions between feelings and understanding of cultural and linguistic differences and similarities. Lynch and Hanson (1992) call these qualities *cultural competence*. They emphasize that cultural competence does not mean knowing everything about every culture. Rather, it means "respect for differences, eagerness to learn, and a willingness to accept that there are many ways of viewing the world" (p. 356).

Members of minority cultural groups are no more homogeneous than members of the dominant culture.

CHARACTERISTICS   Membership in a cultural minority should not be predictive of learning and behavior problems in school, but very often it is. Minority children *do* have problems in school, and some of their problems can be traced directly to their different cultural beliefs. A first step toward developing cultural competence is to learn about the values and beliefs generally common to the different cultural and ethnic groups found in American schools. Keep in mind, however, that information such as provided in this section will hamper rather than enhance cultural competence if these descriptions are seen as stereotypes.

Families with Anglo-European Roots.   Among the values and assumptions that are attributed to people with Anglo-European roots is a high regard for individualism, privacy, and equality (Hanson, 1992). Students with an Anglo-European background tend to be more casual and informal than students from other cultural groups. They value promptness, achievement, work, and materialism. Among the strongest child-rearing biases of this group are beliefs in education and in independence. These beliefs lead families to foster self-help and self-reliance skills at an early age.

Families with Native American Roots.   Among the values and assumptions ascribed to people with Native American roots are individual autonomy, the ability to endure deprivation, bravery, a proclivity for practical jokes, and belief in the existence and essence of a supernatural power (DuBray, 1985). There is a strong belief in the value of being in harmony with nature and being part of a group that emphasizes collateral relationships rather than individualism (Joe & Malach, 1992). Where time is concerned, there is a preference for the present (rather than the past or the future) and for viewing time in a rhythmic, circular pattern. In Indian families, family members other than the parents may assume the major child-rearing responsibilities. Grandparents often provide the child's spiritual guidance while the child's uncles may provide discipline (Joe & Malach, 1992).

Families with African-American Roots.   Families with African-American roots place great value on family and kin relationships. An important task of child-rearing is developing the child's knowledge of family members (Willis, 1992). The family is viewed as the source of strength, resilience, and survival. Child-rearing is considered a community responsibility. Setting limits or disciplining children is an important strategy for teaching children to be sensitive and to show them the importance of following rules to avoid confrontation with authorities. In contrast to cultures that push children toward early adulthood, African-American families stress the importance of giving the child an opportunity to be a child and enjoy the care and protection of responsible adults until such time as he or she is ready for adulthood (Willis, 1992). Education and personal competence are major life goals.

Families with Latino Roots.   The term *Latino* is used here because it is one used by Zuniga (1992), whose work we draw heavily from in the next several paragraphs. It is an alternative to the term *Hispanic*, which is used by the U.S. Bureau of Census (U.S.

Bureau of Census, 1991) to identify Americans of Mexican-American, Puerto Rican, Cuban, Central and South American, and Spanish descent. Latino Americans constitute the second-largest minority group in the United States (about 36% of the U.S. minority population). They are among the most diverse population groups in the country, and also the youngest.

Latino families have a collective orientation that supports family and community life. Parents tend to be very nurturing, permissive, and indulgent with young children. Unlike many Anglo-European families, they do not believe in pushing children toward achievement of developmental milestones (Zuniga, 1992). Parents elicit and encourage positive emotions. Fighting among siblings and displays of anger and aggression are not tolerated. Latino children are highly sensitive to nonverbal indicators of feelings, and they are typically warm and responsive in interpersonal interactions. As children get older, they expect (and are expected) to assume work roles within the family (i.e., baby-sitting, helping with chores).

Families with Asian Roots. Asian-Americans are the fastest-growing ethnic minority group in the United States (Chan, 1992). They originate from three geographic areas with strikingly diverse political and economic conditions: East Asia (China, Japan, Korea), Southeast Asia (Cambodia, Laos, Vietnam, Burma, Thailand, Malaysia, Singapore, Indonesia, the Philippines), and South Asia (India, Pakistan, Sri Lanka). Collectivism is the cultural pattern most prevalent in these regions. All values are viewed in the context of a profound loyalty, obligation, and duty to the welfare, harmony, and reputation of the family. Asian countries confer a great deal of status on teachers and put emphasis on scholarship. Children are taught that by excelling in school, they are honoring the family; at the same time they are preparing for future successes that will further enhance the family's status and well-being. Asian parents who advocate traditional child-rearing practices tend to be controlling, restrictive, and protective. Child-rearing practices assume that children have an inherent predilection for good but that proper training is required to develop these positive characteristics (Chan, 1992). Children are taught to maintain harmony by suppressing aggressive behavior, overt expressions of negative emotions, and personal grievances.

Families with Native Hawaiian and Pacific Island Roots. Most emphasized in the native Hawaiian culture are values associated with relationships, particularly the relationship of the individual to the 'ohana (family), the community, the land, and the spiritual world (Mokuau and Tauili'ili, 1992). Hawaiians have an overriding commitment to (1) cooperation (as opposed to confrontation or conflict), (2) children, and (3) communion with the land and with spiritual ancestors.

The culture of the Samoans, the other Pacific Island group with the largest population in the United States, is in some ways similar to the native Hawaiian culture. Life is organized around the aida (family), which is structured hierarchically according to rank or status, as well as age and gender (Mokuau & Tauili'ili, 1992). The matai (village chief) is responsible for the welfare of all related families in a village (each household may have a chief). Very often the chief functions in a parental role, exercising as much authority in child-rearing as the biological parents. In Samoan culture, discipline and control are often overt and direct, very often relying on physical punishment. Older siblings are responsible for the routine care of young children.

Families with Middle Eastern Roots.　　The Middle East includes parts of Asia and Africa (the states of Lebanon, Syria, Israel and the Occupied Territories, Jordan, Iraq, Saudi Arabia, Kuwait, Bahrain, Qatar, the United Arab Emirates, Oman, Yemen, Egypt, Sudan, Turkey, and Iran). There are great variations in language, religion, and social and political systems among these states. There are also many values that they hold in common, particularly values pertaining to family interactions and child-rearing (Sharifzadeh, 1992). In the Middle East, the individuals' first and primary loyalty is to the family in its extended form. Providing many of the services that are performed by formal organizations in Western cultures, the extended family is the source of guidance and support, as well as recreational and entertainment activities. Middle Eastern families emphasize parent-child attachment and bonding. In contrast to Anglo-European Americans, who focus on and encourage independence, they are not particularly concerned with young children learning self-care skills (i.e., toileting, eating, bathing, dressing). Rather, mothers want their young children to develop a dependent role in preparation for the mutual bonding that is valued in adult life. Although fathers spend time playing with young children, they rarely engage in day-to-day care-giving routines (Sharifzadeh, 1992).

This has been only a very brief introduction to some of the cultures represented in American schools and neighborhoods. Cultural competence—the application of knowledge of and sensitivity to cultures and languages different from one's own—begins with the awareness of cultural and linguistic differences and similarities.

Cultural beliefs affect family values, which affect child-rearing practices which, in turn, affect children's cognitive, language, and social development. The home experiences of many minority children do not prepare them for the expectations of schools and teachers. Behaviors that are encouraged and acceptable at home may be considered inappropriate at school, and vice versa.

For young children from minority cultures, going to school for the first time signals the end of insulated security and innocence (Leung, 1990). They become aware of their minority status, and they begin to experience stress, confusion, conflict, and defeat. Not understanding the dynamics involved in the transition from home to school, teachers and parents may fail to intervene. These statements by 5- and 6-year-olds provide some insight into the feelings that young children from minority cultures have when they start school (Leung, 1990):

> "I have no friends. I want to play with them, but I can't . . . I wish I have a friend."

> "Ma, don't speak Chinese: It's embarrassing!"

> "If I am good, when I go to Heaven, will God change me into an American?"

Leung argues that perceived physical, linguistic, and cultural differences threaten the psychosocial and cognitive well-being of young children, placing them at risk when they make the transition from family-focused to family-and-school-focused experiences. Being different is perceived as undesirable. This perception must be addressed

in a sensitive and competent manner, or children from minority cultures are likely candidates for both social and academic failures.

Language Differences

There are countless differences in the way parents from different cultures teach their children how to use language and express themselves verbally. One difference is the emphasis placed on language versus silence. Among some Latinos, for example, silence is considered an admirable quality: it is thought to demonstrate thoughtfulness and self-restraint. Children are expected to be silent, to listen, and to wait before speaking (Coles, 1977).

Some minority children are quite competent in English when entering school; others may have had minimal exposure to it. They may speak Spanish, the second most common language in the Untied States; one of the many Asian languages; one of the native American dialects (e.g., Hawaiian pidgin); or some less common language, such as Arabic or Tongian. Bilingual children and children who speak a dialect share a common problem: they face the challenge of learning a second language while receiving instruction in that language.

It is estimated that 7% to 10% of the general school-age population has some problems related to learning language (American Speech-Language-Hearing Association, 1982). The prevalence among bilingual children may be even greater. Certainly it is more difficult to identify and accurately diagnose their problems. Difficulties with English that are related to lack of knowledge of the language must be distinguished from difficulties that could reflect a language delay or disorder. Complicating the task is a range of general issues associated with language and communication assessment, as well as specific issues related to distinguishing among language differences, delays, and disorders.

IDEA requires that students with limited English proficiency (LEP) be evaluated in their native language. Unfortunately, there is not total compliance with this mandate. A study from the Handicapped Minority Research Institute on Language Proficiency indicates that many districts use the same assessment procedures for LEP students as for English monolingual students (Ortiz, 1986). Ortiz contends that most referrals of LEP students for poor academic performance are not the result of academics at all; rather, they are related to the students' limited English proficiency. Yet language competence receives relatively little attention: only 25% of the LEP students' folders reviewed by Ortiz contained evidence of current language testing, and only a few indicated that children were tested in their native language or bilingually (as the law requires).

Multicultural Giftedness

Children from cultural and linguistic minorities are underrepresented in classes for the gifted. This is because most states use IQ test scores and excellence in academics to identify gifted children. Among the reasons that minority children may not score high enough on IQ tests are cultural or language differences, economic and health factors, attitudinal factors, and cross-cultural stress (Harris, 1991).

Ideally, provisions for new immigrant students who are gifted should include a variety of approaches to identification, service, and evaluation. Harris (1991) notes that many new immigrants live below the poverty line, with an estimated 80% coming from Third World countries. It is particularly difficult to accurately identify and provide appropriate services for children of new immigrant families.

ASSESSMENT

The intent of the assessment requirements included in the Individuals with Disabilities Education Act (IDEA) is to decrease the likelihood that cultural differences will be mistaken for disabilities. State and local education agencies must ensure that

1. assessment procedures are selected and administered in a manner that is not racially or culturally discriminatory
2. tests have been validated for the specific purpose for which they are used and are administered by trained personnel in the child's native language or other mode of communication
3. assessment procedures are administered by a multidisciplinary team
4. no single test or procedure is used as the sole criterion for determining placement

Assessment results should provide educators with reliable and valid information for making decisions about (1) whether there are problems in a student's education, (2) the nature of the problems (if there are problems), and (3) what to do about the problems. Unfortunately, there are few assessment instruments that are able to yield this type of information. In reality, tests are *never* the best way to get an accurate picture of *any* student. Test scores tell us little about what a student knows and even less about how the student learns. This is particularly true where culturally and linguistically diverse students are concerned.

The overrepresentation of minority children in classes for the mentally retarded and emotionally disturbed and their underrepresentation in classes for the gifted attests to the myriad problems surrounding assessment practices. The Council for Children with Behavior Disorders summarized the situation in a thoughtful position paper in 1989. The group argued that assessment practices are generally biased and useless and that current practices tend to misrepresent abilities, as well as disabilities. Rather than improving educational programming, they result in inappropriate labeling and classification.

While the assessment mandates of IDEA have definitely contributed to decreasing discrimination, discriminatory assessment practices continue, as does the search for "culture-free" and "culture-fair" tests. The tests most often judged as culture-fair are (1) the *System of Multicultural Pluralistic Assessment* (SOMPA), developed in 1979 by Mercer; (2) the *Kaufman Assessment Battery for Children* (K-ABC), published in 1983 (Kaufman & Kaufman); and (3) Feuerstein's (1979) *Learning Potential Assessment Device* (LPAD).

Traditional standardized approaches tend to be most discriminatory when used with students who are culturally and/or linguistically diverse. The most promising alternative to traditional standardized assessment instruments is *curriculum-based assessment* (CBA) (Deno, 1985; Howell & Morehead, 1987). Curriculum-based assessment provides a measure of specific skills, as well as information about broad skill level. Curriculum-based measures generate information relevant to the educational decision-making process. They can be used for identification, eligibility determination, program plan-

Referral for special education evaluation may often be a teacher's way of saying that a child's behavior is bothersome.

ning, and monitoring. Students' abilities are tested against the reference of knowledge and skills that the class or school curriculum requires.

The tendency to place all of the blame for special education inequities involving minority students on assessment instruments may not be fair. Some assessment problems may be associated with the way that education decisions are made and the way that personnel responsible for these decisions view children from minority cultures (Ysseldyke, 1979). There is some evidence that teachers (1) expect minority children to have higher incidences of disabilities than other children (Ysseldyke, Algozzine, Regan, Richey, & Thurow, 1980); (2) judge them as less competent than their peers (Kelley, Bullock, & Dykes, 1977; Spring, Blunden, Greenberg, & Yellin, 1977); and (3) disproportionately and erroneously refer them for special education evaluation (Greenleaf, 1980; Tobias, Cole, Zibrin, & Bodlakova, 1981).

Research suggests that referrals for special education evaluation may not indicate true learning or behavior problems so much as a negative interaction between teachers' values and beliefs and students' characteristics that reflect different cultural values and beliefs. Because teachers tend to refer students who bother them, referrals for special education evaluation and placement may be best viewed as the teacher's way of saying that he or she is having problems coping with a student's behavior. This assertion is supported by data showing that newly arrived immigrant children are often referred for special education assessment even before they have had time to learn the demands and expectations of the classroom (Ysseldyke & Algozzine, 1984). There is a high probability that the students, once referred, will be found eligible for special education services (Ysseldyke, Algozzine, & Allen, 1981). Prereferral intervention (described below) is one way to prevent this type of inappropriate referral.

In concluding this analysis of assessment, we reiterate the consensus that our assessment system is severely limited in its ability to identify the true nature of students' learning difficulties, especially when students' cultural experiences predispose them to diverse language and learning styles. The second point we emphasize is that there is no single factor that is responsible for the disproportionate representation of minority students in special education classes. Bias is a complex and poorly understood concept. The educational system can (and does) break down for these students at many points, and there are many factors that contribute to the breakdown.

PREREFERRAL
INTERVENTION

The purpose of prereferral intervention is to prevent inappropriate referrals. It is a formal process in which teachers are assisted to identify and deal with problems related to the influence of students' linguistic and cultural characteristics on learning and academic success—rather than referring them for special education.

Ortiz and Garcia (1988) describe a prereferral intervention program for Hispanic students. The program staff works with teachers to answer these questions:

1. *Is the student experiencing academic difficulty?* The objective is to determine sources of the student's academic problems and provide remediation while the student is in the regular classroom.
2. *Is the curriculum effective for the multicultural student?* The objective is to ensure that the behavioral characteristics related to the student's cultural and linguistic status are not responsible for his/her academic and behavioral problems. This is done by

adapting and supplementing the curriculum and developing and/or validating new materials.

3. *Is there clear evidence that the student did not learn what was taught?* Data are collected to determine the specific nature of the problem, whether it is evident across contexts, whether parents concur there is a problem, and whether the perceived problem is different from the problems of similar students in the class.

4. *Is there evidence of systematic efforts to identify the source of difficulty and take corrective action?* Depending on the problem, corrective action could take the form of professional inservice training, teaching the student prerequisite skills, or redirection of the instructional program.

5. *Do student difficulties persist despite efforts to identify and remediate them?* If difficulties persist, mainstream alternatives (i.e., special incentives, multimedia material) are explored.

6. *Have other program alternatives been identified and tried?* The focus at this level is on identifying alternative program possibilities. Examples would include tutoring, bilingual education, a compensatory education program, or an ESL program (if the student has been incorrectly classified as English-proficient).

7. *Do difficulties continue despite implementation of systematic, high-quality intervention alternatives?* If problems persist despite all prereferral activities, then the student is referred for a comprehensive multidisciplinary evaluation.

CURRICULUM IMPLICATIONS

The two types of curriculum approaches for linguistically diverse minority students are (1) approaches with a native language emphasis and (2) approaches with sheltered English or structured immersion (Gersten & Woodward, 1992).

The basic tenet of native language emphasis approaches is that until students have a reasonably good knowledge of English, instruction should be in their native language. The argument is that premature introduction to English language academic materials is counterproductive and harmful. Thus, students are provided the normal school curriculum in their native language during the years when they are learning English. There are differences of opinion as to how rapidly students should be introduced to English language instruction, which content areas should be emphasized, and how long native language instruction should be maintained.

The basic tenet of the second set of approaches, the sheltered English or structured immersion approaches, is that an understanding of English can be achieved concurrently with instruction in content areas (e.g., reading, history, social studies). However, English must be provided at a controlled and modulated level. Teachers implementing these approaches carefully control their classroom vocabulary, using concrete objects and gestures and other facilitation strategies to enhance understanding. The goal is for students to learn English while at the same time acquiring basic academic skills.

Most research comparing the two types of approaches has produced equivocal findings. Gersten and Woodward (1992) contend that the type of approach may be less important than the quality of instruction provided and its impact on students. Both types of approaches face the same tough challenge: teaching both a second language and traditional subject matter in the time allocated to teach only subject matter.

While there are not yet reliable data supporting a comprehensive set of effective practices for language minority students with learning difficulties, these practices are beginning to emerge as especially promising (Gersten & Woodward, 1992):

1. *Give children reading material that interests them and makes sense to them.* Use of comprehensible, highly motivating books, especially those with predictable story patterns, assists students to make associations between what they already know and new concepts.
2. *Use redundancy, simple declarative sentences, frequent checks for comprehension, and physical gestures and visual cues to enhance understanding of new concepts.* New ideas or concepts should be explained several times, using slightly different terms.
3. *Encourage students to express their ideas in English, using increasingly complex forms.* Students should be encouraged to produce longer sentences and express more complex ideas and feelings.

Figueroa et al. (1989) argue that a major problem in special education for language minority students is the lack of integration between the programs provided by special education teachers and the student's instructional program in the regular classroom. Special education programs tend to emphasize mastery of discrete skills (called the task-analytic approach) while instruction in the regular classroom may emphasize whole language approaches, used with language majority students. Yates and Ortiz (1991) identify the following instructional activities as most effective with culturally and linguistically diverse students with disabilities. They suggest that instruction should include

1. activities that draw heavily upon prior knowledge and encourage expression of the student's experience, language, and interests
2. activities that do not involve rote learning or drill of isolated, decontextualized pieces of information
3. activities that are intrinsically motivating and foster feelings of success and pride
4. activities that can be accomplished with peer collaboration and approval

Evidence for the effectiveness of these activities is the observation that they result in the most intensive and prolonged levels of task engagement.

INNOVATION AND DEVELOPMENT

The duration and the intensity of the debate for more appropriate and effective methods of assessment and instruction for culturally and linguistically diverse students reflect the complexity of the problem. A recent study illustrates this point. Harry (1992) reports findings from an ethnographic study of the views of 12 low-income Puerto Rican parents whose children were classified as learning disabled or mildly mentally retarded. Most of the parents in Harry's study said that their children were fine until they started school. This study reminds us that conceptions of disability and labeling are social constructions: the definitions for deviance that have been established by our society do not represent objective reality or "truth." Rather, they represent a social agreement as to what we will consider deviant. As professionals, we need to continually remind ourselves that certain beliefs—for example, the belief that a child's failure to master certain skills or behave socially in a certain way is indicative of an objectively identifiable intrinsic deficit—are nothing more than theoretical constructs.

This contention echoes the arguments of many researchers and scholars concerned with the educational needs of students from low-status minority groups. Trueba (1989) states this case particularly well. Trueba attributes the disabilities of culturally and linguistically diverse children to our schools, noting that "children's seeming 'unpreparedness' for mainstream schooling is only a measure of the rigidity and ignorance of our school system, which creates handicap out of social and cultural differences" (p. 70).

The Council for Exceptional Children (CEC) has established a Division for Culturally and Linguistically Diverse Exceptional Learners in order to more adequately address the needs of educational professionals interested in becoming more culturally competent. CEC has also formed an Ethnic and Multicultural Concerns Network to address diversity and multicultural issues among the various divisions that constitute the CEC. These organizational efforts are evidence of recognition that school personnel need to change to accommodate the drastically changing student population (more heavily minority, economically poor, speakers of a language other than English, etc.).

Teacher Competencies

In 1982 Ortiz and Yates set forth these competencies as essential basics for special educators who work with culturally and linguistically diverse students. The teacher should

1. comprehend, speak, read, and write a student's native language and provide ESL instruction
2. understand basic concepts of first and second language acquisition and the relationship of the two
3. understand linguistic, cultural, socioeconomic, and related variables and their effects on the teaching-learning process
4. be familiar with recommended assessment practices and methods for adapting these procedures to prevent discrimination
5. use assessment data to plan, select, adapt, and develop curricula
6. provide instruction that is linguistically and culturally relevant *and* appropriate to students' special learning characteristics
7. achieve parental and community involvement in the education process
8. achieve effective communication and collaboration among bilingual education, regular education, special education, and other relevant programs or support personnel

These competencies, like those developed by others in the eighties, were based on review of the literature and expert judgment. Since that time, the importance of these competencies has been validated (Yates & Ortiz, 1991).

MODEL PROGRAM

*E*chevarria-Ratleff and Graf (1988) describe a Bilingual Special Education Model Site (one of six) funded in the early eighties in California by the Programs, Curriculum, and Training Unit of the Special Education Division, California State Department of Education. This program, the Bilingual Special Education Resource Specialist Program (RSP), is located at Paramount Elementary School in the Azusa Unified School District, about 20 miles east of Los Angeles. Median household income in 1985–86 was $16,000 a year, and 89% of the families were employed in skilled, semiskilled, and unskilled occupations. Of the 600 students at Paramount Elementary approximately 70% were Hispanic, and 32% of these were limited-English-proficient (LEP).

The Paramount program involved 24 students certified as learning disabled in grades 1 through 5. Reading, spelling, and math abilities (as measured on the Wide Range Achievement Test) varied widely. When these students were evaluated for English language proficiency, 9 (38%) were identified as LEP and 15 (62%) as fluent-English-proficient (FEP).

The key feature of this program that led to its designation as a model site was the three-level prereferral process. The first level of this process was the requirement that the regular classroom teacher implement and document at least eight of the following academic or behavioral interventions:

1. Conference with the student
2. Parent conferencing, class visits, home assistance
3. Change in seating
4. Provision of study carrel
5. Time-out
6. Reward system
7. Assertive discipline
8. Special recognition of student strengths
9. Special contract and/or behavioral agreement
10. Buddy/tutorial system
11. Modified assignments
12. Academic regrouping
13. Remedial reading
14. Remedial math
15. Classroom change for subject matter
16. After-school help/counseling
17. Different materials
18. Tutoring (cross-age, classroom aide)
19. Reteaching
20. Learner keeping study book
21. Daily rehearsal of expectations for student
22. Classroom management
23. Other learning modalities

The second level of the process (if the first level did not prove successful) was referral to the Student Study Team (SST). The function of this team was to avert inappropriate special education referral (level 3). Parent and student participation was encouraged throughout, and an interpreter/translator was provided for non-English-speaking individuals. All required special education assistance was provided in the student's primary language by both the bilingual psychologists and the bilingual speech and language personnel.

**TIPS FOR
HELPING**

1. Provide activities that draw on each student's prior knowledge and encourage expression of individual experiences and interests.

2. Avoid activities that require rote learning and drill.

3. Provide motivating activities that maximize opportunities for success and pride.

4. Arrange opportunities for peer collaboration and cooperation.

5. Use curriculum-based assessment rather than traditional standardized measures.

6. Encourage and support students to share their culture with others in the class.

7. Learn as much as possible about students' home and community, interests, talents, skills, and potentials.

SUMMARY

This chapter has emphasized the problems surrounding provision of equal and appropriate education opportunities for culturally and linguistically diverse students who need special instruction because of disabilities or giftedness. What culturally and linguistically diverse students need most are teachers with special cultural awareness—teachers who establish an atmosphere of acceptance and appreciation for individual differences.

Programs for these students have evolved slowly over the past three decades. They have been influenced by (1) civil rights legislation, (2) bilingual education efforts, and (3) initiatives on behalf of persons with disabilities (Fradd & Correa, 1989). What gains in behalf of these students that have occurred have come about because of the efforts of parents, advocacy groups, and public-interest organizations. For change to continue, culturally diverse families and professionals must continue to actively advocate for equitable services.

STUDY QUESTIONS

1. Discuss the major legislation and litigation affecting provision of equal educational opportunities for minority students.

2. Define these terms: minority groups, cultural pluralism, cultural assimilation, multicultural education, bilingual education, multicultural bilingual special education, and cultural competence.

3. Contrast and compare the values and child-rearing beliefs of your own family and culture with those of the cultures described in the chapter.

4. Discuss issues related to the assessment and the appropriate placement of minority students.

5. Describe the rationale and typical procedures for prereferral intervention.

6. Describe the types of instructional activities that are generally appropriate for culturally and linguistically diverse students with disabilities.

3

Linda McCormick
University of Hawaii

Infants and Young Children with Special Needs

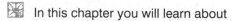 In this chapter you will learn about

- the history of concern and legislation for infants and young children with special needs

- the new provisions of the Individuals with Disabilities Education Act (IDEA) affecting services for infants and young children with disabilities and their families

- the causes of disability in infants and young children

- assessment and evaluation processes appropriate for infants and young children

- the characteristics of effective early intervention services and curriculum models used in early intervention programs

- approaches to inclusion of young children with disabilities in mainstream settings

ROBBY

Robby is a small 4-year-old with sparkling brown eyes and a ready smile. He has cerebral palsy as a result of birth complications. His vision and hearing are within normal limits. Though Robby has little intelligible speech, he communicates very successfully, using gestures and facial expressions to answer questions and indicate wants and needs. He is beginning to learn to use a communication board. Robby moves around independently, either by crawling or with his wheelchair.

Robby's mother began taking him to an early intervention program when he was an infant. Now he goes to the community preschool that his older brother attended. He rides to and from preschool in a specially equipped school bus. Most of the teachers at this preschool have had some general inservice training in special education. Prior to Robby's entering the preschool, there was a special getting-ready-for-Robby inservice training. This was provided by Robby's family (his mother, his brother, and his grandfather) and staff from the special education program at the public school (preschool consultant, physical therapist, speech/language therapist). The preschool consultant and the therapists now come to the preschool several times a week to work with Robby and consult with the staff. Robby's grandfather helped the parent association build a wheelchair ramp at the preschool and widen the door to the bathroom to make it accessible. The physical therapist helped Robby's teacher arrange the furniture and the activity centers in the classroom so that Robby can move around independently. It's a good year for Robby. He has made many new friends.

HISTORY

The history of services for infants and children with special needs is relatively brief. The history of early childhood special education (ECSE) is even shorter—it was not recognized as a separate area in the field of special education until the early seventies. ECSE aligns philosophically with traditions in regular early childhood education, while drawing from the fields of nursing, human development psychology, public health, social work, and sociology. Recent legislation, which will be discussed in this chapter, has led to significant expansion and consolidation of ECSE. It has also stimulated increased demands for qualified early intervention personnel.

Philosophical and Theoretical Roots

The initial impetus for early intervention was the recognition that (1) intelligence and other human capacities are not fixed at birth and (2) early patterns of learning and behavior in infancy and preschool influence and set the pace for later functioning. These ideas were put forth in the forties, fifties, and sixties in two classic research studies and in two books.

    The first research began in 1939, when Skeels and Dye, two researchers at the University of Iowa, transferred 13 children under 3 years of age from an orphanage to a state institution. All but 2 of the children were classified as mentally retarded (average IQ was 64). The children were placed on a ward with adolescent mentally retarded teenage women. The women, who became surrogate mothers, were given some train-

Learning in infancy sets the pace for intellectual functioning.

ing in how to hold, feed, talk to, and play with the children. They were also provided with toys and some educational materials. Twelve other children, only 2 of whom were classified as mentally retarded (average IQ was 86), remained in the orphanage. They received adequate medical and health services, but, because the orphanage was understaffed, they received no individual attention and little, if any, other stimulation.

Some 18 to 36 months later, when data were collected on both groups of children, the results of the experiment were dramatic. The children moved to the adolescent ward showed a mean gain of 27.5 IQ points; all were eventually adopted. The children who remained in the orphanage had a mean loss of 26.2 IQ points. Some of the latter group remained in institutions for the rest of their lives. It is not difficult to see why this study contributed greatly to changing well-entrenched notions about the lack of plasticity of intelligence.

Twenty-five years later Skeels (1966) located all 25 children for a follow-up study, and the results were as remarkable as the findings from the original study. Of the 13 children placed in the ward, 11 had married, and only one marriage had ended in divorce. The marriages had produced 9 children, all of normal intelligence. The median educational level for this group was 12th grade; 4 had attended college. All were either employed or homemakers, with jobs ranging from professional and business work to domestic service. Sadly, the 12 children who had remained in the orphanage did not fare well at all. The median level of education of this group was 3rd grade. One had died, and 4 others were still institutionalized. All but one of the noninstitutionalized adults were employed as unskilled laborers.

A second study added to the growing interest in the effects of early stimulation. This study by Kirk in 1958 measured the effects of 2 years of experience in a preschool program on the social and cognitive development of 43 children (IQs ranging from 40 to 85). Fifteen of these children lived in an institution and attended a nursery school; the other 28 children lived at home and attended a preschool program. The 38 children in the control group—26 lived at home and 12 lived in an institution—did not have the benefit of either a nursery school or a preschool experience. IQ gains for the children who received early intervention ranged from 10 to 30 points, the IQs of control group children declined. The differences between these groups maintained over a period of several years.

Also contributing to changing views about fixed intelligence was the publication in the early sixties of two scholarly books by well-respected authors. The first book, by J. McVicker Hunt, presented an extensive review of research on intellectual development and environmental influences. His book *Intelligence and Experience*, published in 1961, emphasized Piaget's developmental perspectives on intelligence rather than the psychometric approach that was popular at that time. Hunt's two major recommendations to accelerate intellectual development were (1) focus on the early years as the most critical stage of child development and (2) optimize young children's interactions with the environment.

The second book, published in 1964, was Benjamin Bloom's classic work entitled *Stability and Change in Human Characteristics*. This book presented the results of an extensive review of longitudinal studies on human development. The data supported three basic premises regarding the critical nature of early experience: (1) that variations in early experiences shape human characteristics, (2) that environment and early experience are especially important because human development is cumulative, and (3) that initial learning is easier than attempting to replace inappropriate behaviors (once learned) with new ones.

The conclusions of the research and publications of this period regarding the positive impact that early stimulation can have on preventing and reversing developmental deficits may not seem that "earthshaking" now, but they were startling ideas at the time, and they were extremely important catalysts for changes in attitudes.

Evidence building an irrefutable case for early intervention continues to accumulate. The compelling findings of Ramey and Ramey (1992) from three early educational intervention programs designed to prevent mental retardation and improve school readiness are the most recent additions to this research base. These studies further strengthen what are already very strong arguments that early educational intervention can significantly improve children's intellectual performance and academic achievement. The most valuable contribution of the Ramey and Ramey research is the information about what types of children are in greatest need of early intervention and what types of programs are most effective for these children. These statements summarize the significant findings of this research:

- Children of mothers with low IQ scores are particularly at risk for poor intellectual outcomes, but they respond very well to intensive, systematic early intervention.
- Early intervention in center-based programs, supplemented with home visits to educate parents about how to provide good developmental stimulation, is much more effective than only home-based or only center-based services.
- The more actively a family participates in intensive, high-quality early intervention programs, the higher the developmental outcomes for their vulnerable, high-risk children.
- The benefits of continuous educational intervention over the first five years of life last at least until early adolescence.
- Early educational intervention reduces the rate of failing a grade during the elementary school years by almost 50%.

Legislation

The Head Start legislation, funded in 1964, was the first legislative action specifically for young children with special needs. The original Head Start legislation targeted disadvantaged youngsters, with no mention of services for young children with disabilities, but it was a step in the direction of federal support for early intervention.

In 1968 the efforts of many parents of children with disabilities and professionals engaged in working with such children were rewarded with passage of the Handicapped Children's Early Education Assistance Act (Public Law 90–538). This law provided funds for exemplary demonstration programs for infants and preschoolers with disabilities and their families. The initial projects funded under P.L. 90–538—then called the First Chance or HCEEP (Handicapped Children's Early Education Program)—continue to provide a basis for extending services to infants and preschoolers with special needs and to their families. (This program is now called the Early Education Program for Children with Disabilities [EEPCD].)

Following enactment of P.L. 90–538, several events helped establish the new field of early childhood special education (Peterson, 1987). First, there was passage of Public Law 92–424 (the Economic Opportunity Amendments) in 1972, requiring Head Start centers to reserve at least 10% of their enrollments for preschoolers with disabilities. Opening the doors of Head Start centers to children with disabilities gave a tremendous boost to early intervention efforts. Then, in 1973 the Division for Early Childhood (DEC) was established within the Council for Exceptional Children (CEC). The DEC continues to be among the most active of the divisions in the CEC; membership has multiplied many times since its inception. This membership provides an important forum for review of issues related to the education of infants and young children with special needs and to their families. The journal of DEC (*Journal of Early Intervention*) contributes to the strength of the organization and the entire field.

Public Law 94–142 (Education for All Handicapped Children Act) was passed in 1975. This act, now called the Individuals with Disabilities Education Act (IDEA), remains the most important milestone in the history of education for children with special needs. Originally it did not provide substantial monies for services for young children. Most important was what it represented: formal endorsement of early intervention efforts.

In 1986, Public Law 99–457, the first of several "Education of the Handicapped Act Amendments" was passed. P.L. 99–457 contained significant early childhood initiatives to encourage states to provide more comprehensive early intervention services. One initiative, Part B—Section 619, provided increased incentives to states to establish services for preschool children (ages 3 to 5) with disabilities. Another initiative, Part H, established a new program to encourage and assist states to design a comprehensive statewide early intervention system for infants and toddlers with disabilities (or at risk for disabilities) and for their families.

The name of the original legislation was changed to Individuals with Disabilities Education Act (IDEA) in 1990, and in 1991 both Part H and Part B (and other sections) of IDEA were reauthorized (P.L. 102–119). For the most part, the reauthorization did not make significant changes in the early intervention components of IDEA. Most of the changes to Part H and Part B were simply in terminology.

Part H Provisions.   As noted above, Part H, the section dealing with infants and toddlers with special needs, authorizes and appropriates funds for states to implement a statewide comprehensive, coordinated, multidisciplinary service delivery system. States are given some discretion regarding the range of services that will be available. However, the legislation clearly specifies the types of services and the criteria for provision of services to be included in the state's service delivery system. Another requirement for states is the establishment of an Interagency Coordinating Council (ICC) to advise and assist the state agency responsible for the statewide early intervention system.

Part B of IDEA, the section dealing with the educational rights of school-age students with disabilities, has specific procedures to protect the rights of parents and children. (These are discussed in other chapters in this text.) Part H provides similar, and in some cases, greater protections for the rights of infants and toddlers with disabilities and their families. These Part H procedural safeguards are presented in Table 3–1.

Table 3–1
Part H protections for infants and toddlers with disabilities and their families

1. *Parents may examine records.* Parents have the right to examine any records and reports dealing with their child or their family. They may examine records relating to screening, assessment, eligibility determination, development and implementation of the Individual Family Service Plan (IFSP), individual complaints dealing with their child, as well as intervention information.

2. *Prior notice in their native language.* Parents must receive written prior notice in their native language when the state or a service provider proposes (or refuses) to initiate or change the identification, evaluation, placement, or provision of services to the child and the family.

3. *Confidentiality.* The family has the right to confidentiality of personally identifiable information, including names, the family's address, the child's or parent's social security number, and any personal characteristics that would make it possible to identify the child or family. The parents must provide written consent for any exchange of information among agencies.

4. *Parents may accept or decline services.* Parents have the right to decide whether they, their child, or any other family members will accept or decline early intervention services. They may consent to some recommended services and reject others; the state must provide those that the parents want. Whatever they decide does not jeopardize their access to any service.

5. *Written parental consent.* Written consent must be obtained before any assessment of the child and before any services can be provided.

6. *Surrogate parents.* When an eligible child's parent or guardian is not known or cannot be found, a surrogate parent must be assigned to represent the child in all matters related to evaluation and assessment, development of IFSP, and the ongoing provision of services.

7. *Continuity of services.* The child is entitled to continue receiving services while a complaint process is under way unless the parents and the agency agree otherwise.

8. *Prompt and unbiased dispute resolution.* States must appoint an impartial person to carry out hearing procedures for resolving complaints brought by parents.

9. *Relief through the courts.* Parents have the right to bring a civil action in state or federal court if they do not agree with the findings and decisions regarding administrative complaints.

10. *Procedures for resolving systematic complaints.* The state must develop and implement procedures for receiving and resolving any complaints from parents or others regarding violation of the Part H regulations.

Part H requires development of an Individualized Family Service Plan (IFSP) for each family of an infant or toddler eligible for early intervention services. The IFSP is very different from the Individualized Educational Plan (IEP) required for preschoolers and older children. It is an ongoing, interactive process rather than simply a planning document. The IFSP includes a statement of eligibility based on the infant's or toddler's present levels of development (i.e., physical, cognitive, communication, social and emotional, and adaptive development), as well as a statement of the family's resources, priorities, and concerns related to the child's development. The heart of the IFSP is the gathering and the sharing of information between families and early intervention professionals. The major goal of the IFSP process is to provide a supportive context to enable families to make informed choices about what they want and need in the way of services both for their infant or toddler and for themselves.

Another important mandate of Part H is provision of service coordination as part of the services for families. The following are basic service coordination functions: (1) coordinating assessment activities and participating in development of the IFSP, (2) assisting families to identify service providers, (3) coordinating and monitoring services, and (4) facilitating development of a plan for transition to preschool services (where appropriate).

Three instructions regarding service coordination are provided: (1) that the IFSP must include the name of the service coordinator; (2) that the service coordinator may be a professional whose expertise is immediately relevant to the infant's, toddler's, or family's needs or a person qualified to carry out service coordination responsibilities; and (3) that the service coordinator is responsible for the implementation of the IFSP and coordination with other agencies and persons. Parents may be their own service coordinators or co-service coordinators. (Service coordination is not required in Part B—Section 619 for preschoolers. However, recognizing the value of service coordination, some school systems are providing such services for preschoolers with special needs.)

Part H mandates services for two groups of infants and toddlers: (1) those who are developmentally delayed and (2) those with established conditions that typically result in developmental delays (e.g., diagnosed physical or mental conditions that have a high probability of resulting in developmental delay). The states define developmental delay and describe the procedures that will be used to determine the existence of a delay in each of the developmental areas. A third group of infants and toddlers may be served if the state chooses to do so: those who are at risk for significant future developmental problems.

Part B Provisions.   Part B—Section 619 addresses the needs of 3- and 4-year-olds with disabilities. It states that preschoolers eligible for special education and related services are entitled to all the rights and protections that IDEA provides for older students. These rights and protections include free appropriate public education (FAPE), placement in the least restrictive environment, multidisciplinary evaluation, procedural safeguards, due process, and confidentiality of information.

One provision of Part B—Section 619 that is different from provisions for older students is the possibility of using a "noncategorical" eligibility category. States may use the general category "children with developmental disabilities" for 3- to 5-year-olds. The reason for making this option available is that many of the categories used for older school-age children are not appropriate for preschoolers.

Part B—Section 619 also supports efforts to assist parents and strengthen the role of the family in planning for the child's educational program. The Individualized Educational Plan (IEP) for a preschooler may include planning for assistance to parents if necessary to help the child benefit from special education, and parent training activities are among the support services provided.

The preceding part of the chapter has summarized historical and current issues concerning legislation for infants and young children with disabilities and the development of ECSE. A discussion of the special issues and needs of gifted preschoolers is provided in chapter 12. What is currently most important is the recognition by virtually all professionals in special education and related fields, by many lawmakers, and by a substantial percentage of the general population that early intervention makes a difference. More than ever before in this country's history, there are concerted and coordinated national efforts to provide the special resources that will maximize the growth and development of infants, toddlers, and preschoolers with special needs.

DEFINITION

An *exceptional child* is one who is different enough from the "standard" or "average" child to require special methods, materials, services, and possibly equipment in order to attain desired learning objectives. Children may differ in the rate at which they learn (compared to age-peers), or they may learn in different ways. Some parents and professionals prefer using the term *children with special needs* to describe such children.

Decisions related to definition are always controversial because definition is closely related to "labeling." Labeling comes under attack because labels create negative expectations about children while providing little educationally relevant information. Nevertheless, labeling continues as a part of the process of determining children's eligibility for special services.

As noted above, states that participate in the Part H program are required to provide services for infants and toddlers (birth through age 2) who meet eligibility criteria in two categories and, optionally, in an at-risk category.

One required category is labeled "developmentally delayed." Each state must establish a definition of the term *developmental delay*. The definition must specify (1) the levels of functioning or other criteria that will be used in determining a child's eligibility and (2) how the existence of a delay will be determined. The delay may be in one or more of the five areas: cognitive, physical (including vision and hearing), communication, social and emotional, or adaptive development.

The second required category includes children who have a diagnosed physical or mental condition that has a high probability of resulting in developmental delay. Examples are Down syndrome and other chromosomal abnormalities, severe microcephaly, Cornelia de Lange syndrome, sensory impairments, fetal alcohol syndrome, seizure disorders, and inborn errors of metabolism.

The law gives states the option of serving infants and toddlers who are at risk of substantial developmental delays if early intervention services are not provided. As with the term *developmental delay*, each state can adopt its own definition of *at risk*. There is a suggestion that, in defining at risk, states should include well-known biological risk factors and other factors identifiable during the neonatal period that place infants at risk for developmental delay. Examples include low birth weight, respiratory distress, lack of oxygen, brain hemorrhage, and infection. In addition to biological risk factors, states may include environmental risk factors. Examples of environmental risk factors are a potential for child abuse, teenage parents, and poverty. (Prenatal exposure to illicit drugs is a biological risk factor *and* an environmental risk factor.)

As noted above, Part B—Section 619 gives preschoolers (ages 3 to 5) with disabilities the same special education and related services as provided older children (6 through 21). Eligibility criteria for preschool children vary widely across the states and territories. Some have extended the 12 eligibility categories used with older children to preschoolers. Others have chosen to use a generic label such as "developmentally disabled," either in addition to, or in place of, the categories used with older students.

PREVALENCE

Prevalence refers to the current number of children who meet the criteria for exceptionality; incidence refers to the number of children who, at some time in their life, might be considered exceptional. Because states are required by the Office of Special Education and Rehabilitative Services (OSERS) to report the number of children receiving special education services in the different disability categories, there are relatively accurate prevalence figures available for students with disabilities between the ages of 6 and 21.

Prevalence figures are not so easily generated where infants and preschoolers are concerned. In time there will be prevalence figures for infants and toddlers served through Part H efforts, but these data are not yet available (U.S. Department of Education, 1990). An estimate of the number of infants and toddlers with disabilities can be generated by using census figures. According to the U.S. Census Bureau, there were about 11,172,000 children age 2 years and younger in the U.S. in 1988. About 7% of the infants born yearly have congenital abnormalities: one third of the abnormalities are observable at birth and the remaining two thirds likely to be identified by preschool age. On the basis of the above census figure, this suggests that *at the very least* there are 670,000 infants and toddlers needing early intervention services.

Getting accurate figures for the prevalence of 3- to 5-year-olds with disabilities is also a problem. It is estimated that approximately 362,000 preschoolers with disabilities were served in the 1988 school year (U.S. Department of Education, 1990). Since this is only about 3% of the population of 3- to 5-year-olds in the United States, it represents probably less than half of the preschoolers needing special services.

CAUSES

In the majority of cases the cause (or causes) of disability in infants and young children is unknown. In others the disability can be attributed to one or some combination of factors occurring during the prenatal period, the perinatal period, or the postnatal period. Problems occurring during the prenatal period are usually attributable to biological and chemical factors (e.g., mutant genes, radiation, toxic chemicals, harmful drugs, maternal infection, blood incompatibility, fetal malnutrition, and placental insufficiency) or environmental factors (e.g., maternal age, socioeconomic status, and family size). Problems arising during the perinatal period may be caused by trauma during labor or delivery, neonatal medications, prematurity, anoxia, or low birth weight. Problems arising in the postnatal period include illness, chronic disease, accidents, environmental toxins, and other environmental factors, such as poverty, abuse, and family dysfunction.

Infants and children who have a greater possibility than others of experiencing certain adverse biological or environmental conditions that are known to cause defects or that are highly correlated with the onset of later problems are said to be vulnerable or at risk. Tjossem (1976) categorizes infants and young children who are especially vulnerable for developmental disabilities into three at-risk groups. Children who fall into more than one group have an increased probability for developmental delay and other problems. The three at-risk conditions are these:

1. *Established risk.* Included in this group are infants and young children with diagnosed medical disorders, usually of known etiology. The range of symptoms and expectancies for physical and developmental problems is usually well known for these disorders. This category includes children with genetic abnormalities (e.g., Down syndrome) where mental retardation, physical differences, and various growth deviations are predictable. Keep in mind that the assertion that certain physical and mental differences are predictable for these children does not mean we can foresee the ultimate impact of the disorder on a child's development. That will depend upon a range of variables associated with medical, educational, and therapeutic intervention.
2. *Biological risk.* This group includes children whose prenatal, perinatal, or postnatal histories suggest potential biological insult that poses a threat to normal development, though abnormalities may not be detected initially. Prenatal contributors to biological risk include pregnancy complications (injury, diseases, or infections) and maternal dysfunction such as diabetes or labor complications. Perinatal and postnatal risk conditions include prematurity, low birth weight, infections of the nervous system, and ingestion of toxic substances.
3. *Environmental risk.* Included in this category are infants and young children who are biologically and genetically normal at birth but whose early life experiences and environmental surroundings impose a threat to normal development. Conditions known to affect development include quality of maternal care and stimulation, nutrition, medical care, and opportunities for social, sensory, and educational stimulation.

CHARACTERISTICS   The disability categories and descriptions set forth in IDEA and the defining characteristics associated with each of these groups are presented in the other chapters in this text. As noted in the discussion of the legislation, states are not required to use these categorical labels with children under the age of 5. Aware of the limitations of assessment procedures for infants and preschoolers and of the inappropriateness of the categories used with older students for differentiating the service needs of preschool children, many states have chosen to adopt "noncategorical" eligibility options.

Whatever categorization scheme a state uses, however, there are likely to be many children with disabilities—particularly those with learning disabilities, mild mental retardation, or behavior problems—who are not identified until they experience problems in school. This is especially true of children from low income areas, who may be perceived as developing normally until they have to deal with the expectations of school. Another group of children often not identified until they start school are children whose birth conditions (i.e., neurological damage, low birth weight) place them at risk for developmental problems. The only children sure to be identified at birth or shortly thereafter are children with established conditions (i.e., Down syndrome) and infants with severe neurological or sensory impairments.

Early intervention can prevent or significantly decrease the impact of an at-risk condition.

Ideally it would not be necessary to diagnose and label young children in order to serve them. Among the most controversial issues in ECSE are (1) the ability to identify children with special needs and (2) the wisdom of classifying children with social, learning, and behavioral deficits at the preschool level. Reliable identification of young children with learning disabilities is especially difficult because of the lack of valid and reliable assessment procedures. Tests administered in early childhood have not been shown to be highly predictive of later performance. Moreover, assessment results are difficult to interpret: young children present a complex developmental profile (Kennedy, Sheridan, Radlinski, & Beeghly, 1991).

Haring et al. (1992) argue that it should not be necessary to expose preschool children to the possible detrimental effects of labeling. Instead of labeling preschoolers as having learning disabilities, they advocate consideration of clusters of characteristics that might indicate that the child is at risk for later academic difficulties. These characteristics are (1) delayed concept development, (2) speech delays, (3) language delays, (4) attentional problems, (5) hyperactivity, (6) immature reasoning abilities, (7) visual and/or auditory perceptual problems, (8) lack of academic readiness skills, and (9) social and/or affective skills deficits. Young children with these characteristics would be identified as at risk and provided with appropriate early intervention services.

ASSESSMENT   In IDEA, the assessment requirements for preschoolers are the same as those for older school-age populations. Some of the assessment requirements for infants and toddlers are the same; others are different. Part H of IDEA requires assessment, with the parent's written consent, for every infant and toddler who is referred to the program. Each infant or toddler must be assessed to determine eligibility for services and to determine the child's status in five developmental areas: physical development, cognitive development, communication development, social and emotional development, and an adaptive development. This multidisciplinary assessment identifies the unique strengths and needs of the infant or toddler so that services appropriate to meet these needs can be specified.

Unlike Part B (for ages 3 to 5), Part H also requires a family-directed identification of the support and services necessary to enhance the family's ability to meet the developmental needs of their infant or toddler. However, the regulations are clear that this family-focused aspect of the assessment process is voluntary. If family assessment is carried out, it must be conducted by persons trained in appropriate methods and procedures, and it must be based on information provided by the family in a personal interview. In addition, it has to incorporate the family's own description of its resources, priorities, and concerns related to enhancing their child's development. (The statement of family needs may be included in the written Individualized Family Service Plan, or IFSP, but only with the family's consent.)

The regulations for Part H specify that in the selection and administration of assessment procedures, there must be every effort to avoid racial and cultural discrimination. The procedures must be administered in the parents' native language or other mode of communication (i.e., sign language). The assessment and the first IFSP meeting must take place within 45 days of the initial referral (unless there are exceptional circumstances such as illness that make timely assessment impossible).

Precise definition and differentiation of the terms *screening*, *diagnosis*, *assessment* and *evaluation*, and the processes related to each of these measurement procedures are important. Each has a different purpose and unique products.

1. *Screening* is typically the first assessment procedure. The purpose of screening is to determine if the child has a problem requiring more extensive observation. Where infants and young children are concerned the purpose of screening is to determine if the child is a *potential* candidate for early intervention.
2. *Diagnosis* is a more comprehensive procedure than screening. It typically involves observations, testing, and/or interviews by a team of professionals from different disciplines. The purposes of diagnosis are (1) to determine the nature of the problem, (2) to identify and label the problem, and (3) to determine its cause or causes.
3. *Assessment* focuses on collecting the types of data necessary to generate specific intervention objectives and instructional strategies. These data provide baseline information against which to consider the effects of intervention.
4. *Evaluation* is comparison of the child's performance before and after intervention, as well as the monitoring or tracking of the child's progress during the instructional process.

Because the purposes of each of these processes are so different, it is not surprising that each calls for different types of instruments and procedures.

Screening

The question asked at the screening level is, Does the child have a problem that warrants further testing and observation? Screening instruments are not intended to be used for diagnosis or for intervention purposes: they are designed for the purpose of *identification*. The comprehensiveness of screening programs varies, depending on the purposes of the screening and the types of services for which children are being identified.

Comprehensive screening considers all aspects of growth and development. Because of the large number of children involved, however, procedures are kept brief and inexpensive to administer. The National Program for Early and Periodic Screening, Diagnosis, and Treatment (EPSDT) recommends screening children across four areas: biological, psychological, family context, and environmental and social/cultural variables likely to impact development. (EPSDT is a program for children eligible for Medicaid as a result of chronic disabilities.)

Great care must be taken in administering and interpreting all measurement devices used with young children. This is particularly important when it comes to screening infants and very young children. There is always the possibility of false positives and false negatives. (The statistical concept of "false positives" refers to children who are identified as having a problem when in reality none exists. The concept of "false negatives" refers to failure to identify difficulties that really do exist.) The best way to minimize the potential for these problems is to use more than one measure and supplement all assessment data with information from family members and others who know the infant or young child well.

Diagnosis

The purpose of diagnosis is to confirm (or disprove) whether the child has a significant delay, disorder, or impairment and, if so, to determine the nature of the problem. Generally, diagnostic evaluations make no attempt to prescribe specific intervention objectives and strategies.

Many of the instruments used for diagnostic purposes with infants and young children with disabilities conditions were originally designed for normally developing children. Here are two examples:

Bayley Scales of Infant Development (Bayley, 1984): measures cognitive functioning, motor skills, and social behavior (0–30 months)

Peabody Picture Vocabulary Test (PPVT) (Dunn, 1981): measures receptive vocabulary (2½–18 months)

This is an example of a diagnostic instrument developed specifically for infants and young children with disabilities:

The Kent Infant Development Scale (KIDS) (Katoff, Reuter, & Dunn, 1978): measures development in cognitive, motor, social, language, and self-help areas (0–5 months)

Assessment

The key question that guides selection of an instrument or battery of assessment instruments for infants and young children is, Which skills should be the primary focus of early intervention? Many assessment procedures in early intervention are based on surveys of normal child development. They include a wide range of developmental skills sequenced in the order in which they are demonstrated by normal children. Because they use the "typical" behavior of normally developing infants and young children as a reference, developmentally-based assessment procedures are not always the best choice to guide formulation of goals and objectives for intervention.

Ecological inventory procedures, which identify the skills children need in order to participate in activities in present and future environments, are a better source of intervention goals and objectives. This approach is especially popular with professionals concerned with infants and young children with severe or multiple disabilities (Brown et al., 1979; Guess, Sailor, & Baer, 1977). The ecological approach to assessment identifies important skills and breaks them down into small, teachable steps. Instead of assessing and teaching skills in a developmental sequence, teachers identify the skills most needed by children to participate in activities in important natural environments and then assess and teach the skills in the settings.

All types of assessment are more difficult with infants and young children than with older children. The performance of young children tends to vary across time, settings, and people in the surroundings. The person administering the assessment is often in the position of having to rely on inferences because infants and very young children do not have sufficient verbal ability to express their range of intentions, and, of course, infants cannot even point in response to instructions. Another problem in assessment of infants and young children is stranger anxiety. Because young children

Colorful and manipulable materials help to maintain young children's attention.

are wary of unfamiliar adults, there is usually a need to schedule a fairly lengthy "warm up" period for them. Also, because of their shorter attention span and fatigue, it is often necessary to schedule two or three short sessions rather than a single session. Strategies to maintain the young child's attention include (1) use of colorful and manipulative materials, (2) alternating verbal and manipulative items, and (3) using positive reinforcement (including edibles).

Evaluation

Evaluation consists of monitoring performance or of tracking and quantifying the effect of instructional programming. An evaluation measurement involves ongoing data collection (by teachers, paraprofessionals, and therapists) *while* instructional or therapy services are being delivered. There are any number of types of data that can provide useful information: samples of children's work, frequency counts of correct and incorrect responses, brief probes of specific behaviors administered on a regular basis, and anecdotal reports.

The purpose of evaluation is to monitor individual children's progress across instructional areas. The question that evaluation seeks to answer is, Are instructional procedures facilitating attainment of targeted skills?—or, stated in another way, Are teaching strategies working? To be useful, evaluation procedures must closely reflect the objectives of a program.

INTERVENTION

Early intervention services may be home-based, center-based, or a combination of the two. Home-based programs (sometimes called home-visitor programs), where the parent or caregiver is the target of instruction, are commonly used to serve infants and toddlers. The interventionist goes into the home, furnishing special toys, materials, and instruction. One focus of the instruction is parent-child interactions (but there are many others). Center-based models provide direct instruction or therapy for the child at a site other than the home. Children are usually served (individually or as a group) a few hours a day for 3 to 5 days a week. Parents typically meet in groups to support and assist one another. Programs that adopt a combined approach take one of two forms: (1) services may be provided in the home and in the center simultaneously or (2) services may be provided initially in the home and then later, when the child is older, in the center.

Among the variables that seem most important to the success of early intervention programs are these:

1. The skills and experience of the teacher(s) in providing for individual differences.
2. The extent to which training objectives are embedded in ongoing daily/functional activities that are of interest to children.
3. Efficient and effective use of instructional time and natural cues and consequences.
4. Quality and quantity of services to, and involvement of, parents.
5. Frequency of data collection and program updating.

What should the proper goals of early intervention be? Is it reasonable to target "normal functioning" with all children? Bricker (1986) argues that expectations need to be tempered with the reality that less dramatic outcomes than "normal functioning" are the rule, particularly for children with more serious and pervasive disabilities. This does not, however, suggest a need to dilute or reduce intervention efforts. Rather, it suggests focus on alternative goals such as independent functioning and full or partial participation in routine activities in natural environments.

Because the early childhood period is a time of many transitions, *transition* is an important concept in early intervention. Most infants and young children with disabilities and their families make at least three major transitions before the children reach the age of 6: from the neonatal intensive care unit to home and infant services; from infant services to a preschool program; and from a preschool program to kindergarten. The stress inherent in these transitions may not be avoidable, but, with well-conceived advance planning and support, it can be minimized. The parents themselves or the staff of the sending program are typically the ones to initiate the transition process from infant services to preschool and from preschool to kindergarten.

The three tasks inherent in transitions are (1) selecting a program with the family and then preparing children and family members for the new program, (2) supporting children and family members as they adjust to the new program, and (3) helping program staff in the new program support children's participation in activities and routines (Chandler, 1993). The following are steps in the transition planning process as listed by Noonan and McCormick (1993):

1. Establish a transition team that includes family members and staff from current and receiving programs.
2. Schedule meetings to develop an initial transition plan, identify possible placements, determine what tasks will need to be done and by whom, formulate time lines for referral and preplacement activities, decide how records and other information will be transferred, agree to preplacement services, and plan for follow-up activities.
3. Place the child once necessary environmental adaptations have been completed.
4. Provide whatever inservice training, consultation, and therapy services are needed.
5. Follow up and evaluate the transition.

In regard to training the staff of the receiving program, it is essential that exchanges occur between regular early childhood personnel and the special education personnel. Such interaction is most effective when there is a collaborative approach that recognizes and values the knowledge and expertise of both groups. Regular early childhood personnel may have little information about, and experience with, the terminology and techniques for working with children with disabilities and monitoring their progress. Early interventionists, on the other hand, may have little background or experience with children who are developing normally. Initial training and support interactions typically emphasize the similarities between children with disabilities and their nondisabled peers. This is followed by a discussion of the specific strengths and unique needs of the child with a disability and special techniques for managing and supporting the child's learning and adjustment. Subsequent meetings may focus on such topics as feeding, positioning, adapting activities and materials, and assessment.

CURRICULUM
IMPLICATIONS

In the broadest sense, a curriculum is a collection of goals and objectives designed and carried out for instructional purposes. The curriculum, as one element of a service delivery system, is a means of translating early intervention program's philosophy or theory of development, learning, and/or education in action. The curriculum should clearly specify *what* is to be taught—the information and skills to be transmitted and acquired and *how* instruction is to take place.

Curricula in early childhood special education can be categorized according to basic philosophy and practices. Traditionally ECSE curricula have been (1) developmental, (2) behavioral, or (3) cognitive.

1. *Developmental curricula.* Curricula based on developmental tenets stress all aspects of development: physical, emotional, language, social, and cognitive. The content is based on developmental skills derived from surveys of large numbers of normally developing children. The teacher's role is to enhance the natural growth processes by providing learning opportunities in an enriching and nurturing environment.

2. *Behavioral curricula.* Curricula derived from behavioral tenets are directive and skill-based. Sometimes called *functional* or *remedial*, this approach focuses on identification of specific skills to improve the child's current functioning. The teacher's role is to carefully plan and structure the child's experiences to build specific skills critical for success in the child's immediate and subsequent environments. Advocates of this approach argue that the normal sequence of development is not necessarily an appropriate reference for instructional programs for children with disabilities, particularly those with severe impairments (e.g., Guess et al., 1977).

3. *Cognitive curricula.* Curricula derived from cognitive theory draw primarily from the work of Jean Piaget (1971). The focus is on facilitating development of thinking and problem-solving skills. These curricula differ from the developmental curricula described above in that they derive from a specific theory rather than simply observations of normally developing children. Piaget's theory is a stage theory, with sequences of skills described in the order in which they occur within each stage. The most significant characteristic of his theory is that skills are ordinal, meaning that each higher skill in a sequence is more complex than the previous skills and incorporates the less complex, previous skills. Piaget (1952) describes the progression of six sensorimotor sequences (object permanence, means-end behavior, spatial relations, causality, schemes for relating to objects, and imitation) that infants acquire by about the age of 2. These skills and concepts are precursive to later language and communication, concept development, and problem solving. Piaget also offers a theory for the development of preacademic skills in the years between ages 2 and 6.

Over the past decade, as all three of these curriculum models have expanded to include more naturalistic and functional perspectives, their differences have diminished. The developmental curriculum model has expanded to include a focus on infant/child–adult interactions. The behavioral model has expanded to include goals selected from an inventory of expectations in important present and future environments. Rather than being taught in contrived arrangements, skills are facilitated in routine ongoing activities, using natural (rather than contrived) stimuli and consequences. Likewise, the cognitive curriculum model has expanded to incorporate a more social perspective. The focus is on enhancing the social-cognitive skills that will establish and maintain a range of ongoing interactions.

What has emerged as a result of the shift to a naturalistic perspective is a variety of *naturalistic curriculum models*. The primary goal of naturalistic curriculum models is to increase the infant's or young child's control, participation, and interaction in natural environments (Noonan & McCormick, 1993). What distinguishes naturalistic curriculum models from traditional models is the emphasis on context. The natural environment is the source of curriculum content and methods, and it provides the settings, as well as the criteria, for judging child progress.

Differences in theoretical underpinnings and approaches to practice are one of a number of barriers to integration of children with special needs into regular preschool and child-care settings. Naturalistic curriculum models represent a significant step in the direction of resolving differences between regular early childhood education and early childhood special education. The developmentally appropriate practices (DAP) model advocated by the National Association for the Education of Young Children (NAEYC) (Bredekamp, 1987) is a naturalistic curriculum model that includes the dimensions of age appropriateness and individual appropriateness. DAP emphasizes the importance of maximizing opportunities for children to develop social competence in the context of routine activities.

A naturalistic curriculum model may begin with an ecological assessment to identify and describe the child's participation in routine activities at home and in other natural environments. Developmental assessment information is used to supplement the information produced by the ecological assessment. The next step is for parents and professionals to establish intervention priorities and develop an individualized intervention plan. The individualized intervention plan includes a description of the contexts or occasions for instruction, physical positioning and materials arrangement, intervention techniques, expected responses, consequences, and correction procedures. Finally, a functional individualized schedule is developed to identify occasions for teaching the skills, and then intervention begins.

MAINSTREAMING   Social competence and communicative competence are among the most important accomplishments of the preschool years. Natural mainstream environments that maximize opportunities for children with disabilities to interact with normally developing peers are the best places to encourage (1) shared experiences, cooperative learning, and advanced play; (2) opportunities for social and communicative interactions; and (3) observational learning of appropriate social and communicative behaviors.

In the two decades since the first arguments for educating young children with disabilities in mainstream settings began to appear, there have been countless demonstrations of effective mainstreaming (e.g., Odom & Strain, 1984). There is now substantial research demonstrating that even children with the most severe disabili-

With careful planning, children with and without disabilities can make developmental gains.

ties can be successfully and appropriately served in regular preschool and child-care settings (e.g., Strain & Odom, 1986). Young children with disabilities and normally developing children both derive substantial benefits from carefully planned integration. Benefits include

1. opportunities to observe and imitate appropriate developmental and behavioral models
2. more complex and age-appropriate social and communicative interactions
3. natural and adaptive contingencies
4. greater variety of experiences and environments

In the late seventies and early eighties, the implicit assumption seemed to be that these benefits would just occur—that they were somehow inherent in integrated settings. We now realize that this view of integration was naive. Here is a summary of what we have learned over the past years:

1. Simply placing preschoolers with disabilities in the same programs as children who are nondisabled does not ensure social interactions or imitation between children in the two groups (Guralnick, 1990).
2. If structured skills development is carefully planned, both children with disabilities and children who are nondisabled make appropriate developmental gains (Cooke, Ruskus, Apolloni, & Peck, 1981).

3. Teachers in mainstream settings need special training to help children with disabilities receive the full benefits of integration (Cooke et al., 1981).
4. Children who do not have disabilities do not actively reject peers with disabilities or acquire their maladaptive behaviors (Guralnick & Groom, 1988).
5. Children who do not have disabilities are quite proficient in adjusting their communicative attempts to the developmental levels of their peers with disabilities (Guralnick, 1981).

Probably the greatest barrier to achieving more widespread mainstreaming at the preschool level has been the lack of publicly funded regular education preschool settings. Enrolling children with disabilities in private preschools or preschools funded by groups other than state education agencies requires lengthy interagency negotiation that, even under the best of conditions, is tedious and difficult. However, mainstreaming is happening in every community and in every state because arguments like the following are simply too strong to ignore:

1. *Maximum exposure to, and experiences with, peers who are not disabled are the primary means by which children with disabilities can learn the ways of the normal world (normalization).* Young children with disabilities need and have a right to the same experiences as their peers who do not have disabilities. They also have the right to the support and resources that will enable them to benefit from these experiences. Separating young children with disabilities from normal experiences creates distance, misunderstanding, and rejection (peer attitudes that are difficult to correct later). By not removing children from normal settings in the first place, we avoid reentry problems.
2. *Settings that include only children with disabilities cannot provide normal socialization experiences. Mainstreaming seems critical to the acquisition, maintenance, and generalization of important social skills.* Young children with disabilities who interact only with peers with limited behavioral repertoires do not learn normal social skills because there are no opportunities to observe, imitate, or practice normal skills. Young children with disabilities need opportunities to observe peers who exhibit (1) age-appropriate play and exploratory skills, (2) competent communication skills, and (3) constructive and appropriate social interchanges.
3. *Young children with disabilities must have continuous opportunities to observe and imitate same-age peers who are developing at a normal rate.* Children with disabilities who are only around peers with the same or similar disabilities never have the opportunity to observe age-appropriate behaviors.
4. *Early integration encourages positive attitudes and the awareness that children with disabilities are more similar to their peers without disabilities than they are different.* Substantial benefits accrue to teachers, other professionals, parents, and most important, peers who do not have disabilities from opportunities to observe and participate in integrated settings. The best time to initiate planned instruction about individual differences for children who do not have disabilities is during the preschool and primary years. Introducing children who are not disabled to the cognitive and affective aspects of blindness, physical disabilities, deafness, and mental retardation helps them develop an empathic understanding of persons with these disabilities. Both the nature of preschool children and the design of preschool curricula are amenable to teaching about disabilities.

MODEL PROGRAM

The Preschool Preparation and Transition Program (PPT) at the University of Hawaii is funded by Early Education Programs for Children with Disabilities (EEPCD), U.S. Office of Special Education and Rehabilitative Services. PPT was created in response to the need for preparing parents for the transition from infant intervention programs to preschool services. A second goal is to expand opportunities for full inclusion of young children with disabilities in mainstream settings. The development of the program model began in 1986 and continued through 1989. Several demonstration and replication sites participated in model development and field testing, including three infant programs in Hawaii and two infant programs in Virginia.

The PPT model has four main components: parent education, preparatory curriculum, staff development, and systems cooperation. Parents enrolled in an infant program participate in a PPT parents' needs assessment and an interview with a professional to gather transition-related information. They are also helped to develop a Transition Notebook, which is a binder with sections to hold important records and information about local resources. Parent education sessions are held periodically to provide information about legal rights, steps in the transition process, participation in the IEP (Individualized Educational Plan), and selection of appropriate preschool or child-care settings.

PPT uses two strategies to identify target skills: the ecological inventory and the preschool survival skills checklist. The ecological inventory involves an interview with the parents to select and prioritize the skills their children can learn in the context of daily routines. The preschool survival skills checklist and curricula strategies are used to evaluate and strengthen specific skills that have been determined to contribute to success in mainstream preschool and child-care settings.

Staff development is accomplished through regular, informal modeling, consultation, and inservice training for the infant program staff and the staff for early childhood services.

Systems cooperation focuses on interagency collaboration to facilitate smooth transition from infant services to preschool settings. PPT staff then support the inclusion of children with disabilities in regular early childhood settings.

PPT is completing its first outreach phase (1990-1993). The project has been expanded statewide to all infant programs. Activities are now focusing on preschool support activities.

The Americans with Disabilities Act (ADA) passed in 1990 (Public Law 101–336) will have a marked impact on mainstreaming. One of the mandates of this legislation is the requirement that public accommodations, *including early childhood programs and family child-care homes*, ensure access for individuals with disabilities. This means taking *readily achievable* steps to modify existing facilities and practices to accommodate the individuals' disabilities. A child-care center cannot deny services to a child with a disability even if a separate program specifically for children with disabilities is available. Child-care programs must include children with disabilities in all activities (e.g., field trips, playground activities, art projects). Although the new regulations do not apply to religious organizations that operate programs, a center that is located in a religious facility but operates independently must comply with the ADA requirements.

Many of the actions required by ADA are already being implemented by programs throughout the country. As more and more programs implement ADA, opportunities for mainstream placements of children with disabilities will clearly be increased. The admissions policies and procedures of many child-care centers will change. Admissions policies, program brochures, and waiting list procedures will no longer intentionally *or unintentionally* exclude children with disabilities.

INNOVATION AND DEVELOPMENT

The areas where there is the most development and expansion in early childhood special education are (1) the nature of family involvement in services for infants and toddlers with severe disabilities, (2) culturally sensitive family support services, and (3)

Integration of young children with disabilities with nondisabled peers is considered "best educational practice."

integration of technological advances. The number of professionals working with infants and toddlers with special needs and their families continues to increase and undoubtedly will for at least another decade. Demand and funding for services for this population are also increasing, as are opportunities for professional preparation.

Family Involvement.   Early intervention professionals have long recognized that parent involvement in programs for children with severe and multiple disabilities is essential in order for these children to reach their developmental potential. What is new and positive is the significant expansion of the roles of parents and the expanded support for families. In addition to being teachers and advocates for their own children, parents are acknowledged as full partners in the decision-making process.

The newer parent involvement models are multidimensional and flexible (Turnbull & Turnbull, 1986). They are based on the notion of "evolving needs," which maintains that the needs of individual parents change over time and are affected by a variety of factors, including the child's health and developmental status; responses to the child and family by relatives, friends, and professionals; the availability of support services; financial constraints on the family; and so on. Parent services include identifying individual parent needs and providing a variety of training and support options to address those needs.

Recognition of Cultural Diversity.   As services become more family-focused, there has been growing recognition of the need to address the issue of cultural diversity in the United States. Ideally, families would receive services and support from professionals who, in addition to being knowledgeable and competent in their discipline, would speak the same language as members of the family of the children to whom they are providing services and share family values and beliefs. Unfortunately, this is often not the case. Families receive services and support from early interventionists who have attitudes, beliefs, values, customs, and languages different from their own. The burden is on interventionists to develop cross-cultural competence (Lynch & Hanson, 1992).

Integration of Technological Advances.   Computers and other assistive technology are especially critical for children with disabilities. Many of these children depend on assistive technology for mobility, communication, and learning. Familiarity and skills related to the use of assistive technologies is an essential competency area for early interventionists. They must be prepared to participate in team processes and ethical decision making regarding the selection and use of technological devices and equipment, ranging from such simple devices as adapted eating utensils and switch-adapted, battery-operated toys to complex computerized environmental control devices.

The impact of microcomputer technology will continue to be felt in the areas of (1) program management and evaluation, (2) dissemination, (3) augmentative communication (in which, for example, technology allows children who are disabled to supplement or replace inadequate speech capability), and (4) as a medium of instruction

1. Arrange the environment so that children can see each other, share materials, and help one another.

2. Make every effort to maximize positive child-child interactions.

3. Children with disabilities are children first, who will learn and grow in fairly predictable ways if they have opportunities to explore and interact with the environment.

4. To develop independence and confidence, provide children with opportunities to make choices.

5. Be sure that verbal instructions are specific, informative, and at the child's level of language understanding.

6. Take advantage of every opportunity for toddlers and preschoolers with disabilities to observe and imitate same-age peers.

7. When a task seems too difficult, help the child find another way to produce the same effect.

TIPS FOR HELPING

(Odom & Warren, 1988). Project ACTT (Activating Children Through Technology) is an example of a "computer age" program. Project ACTT provides a curriculum and technical assistance to early intervention programs that want to integrate the computer into their educational programming. The objectives of the ACTT curriculum are (1) to foster children's expectation of control over the environment and help them develop a sense of autonomy, (2) to provide children with opportunities and possibilities for communication, and (3) to develop children's problem solving and general thinking (Huntinger, 1986).

SUMMARY

Infants and young children with disabilities and their families face a far better future today than they did a generation ago. However, professionals and parents must guard against complacency; although a great deal has been learned about meeting the special needs of these children, there is still much to be accomplished. Most important as we move toward the year 2000 is the growing consensus that early intervention works. It gives young children with disabilities the impetus they need and deserve to succeed in present and future environments.

Increasingly, infants and young children with disabilities are being afforded opportunities to participate in activities and services in integrated natural environments. Early interventionists must learn to consider each child's total needs when developing and implementing program plans involving assistive technology to ensure its availability and use in all of these settings.

STUDY QUESTIONS

1. Discuss the early research and significant books that contributed to changing views about fixed intelligence.

2. Discuss the history of legislation for infants and young children with special needs.

3. Contrast the provisions of the Individuals with Disabilities Education Act (IDEA) for infants and children with those for older school-age students.

4. Describe the Part H provisions related to service coordination and list service coordination functions.

5. Differentiate established risk, biological risk, and environmental risk.

6. Discuss the problems of labeling as they apply to infants and young children.

7. Differentiate screening, diagnosis, assessment, and evaluation and give an example of an appropriate procedure in each process.

8. List the variables that seem most important to the success of early intervention programs.

9. Contrast these curriculum models: developmental, behavioral, cognitive, naturalistic.

10. Provide reasons for, and the advantages of, inclusion of young children with disabilities in mainstream settings.

4

Cecil D. Mercer
University of Florida

Learning Disabilities

In this chapter you will learn about

- the highlights in the history of the field of learning disabilities

- the meaning of the term *learning disabilities* and identification criteria

- the possible causes of learning disabilities

- the characteristics of learning disabilities

- assessment for identification of a learning disability

- service or placement options for students with learning disabilities

- approaches used in curriculum planning for students with learning disabilities

- integrated programming for students with learning disabilities

Roman Numerals	Our Numerals
I	1
V	5
X	10
L	50
C	100
D	500
M	1,000

Fifteen-year-old Scott is an alert, handsome youngster who plays baseball on his high school junior varsity team. In the classroom his attention is good, he understands explanations well, and his oral answers usually are precise. Scott's class standing, however, is low in almost every subject. Scott reads in a slow, halting manner, and his spelling is atrocious. His spelling problems hinder his progress in classes that require taking notes or responding to essay questions. His written reports and assignments are incomprehensible because his handwriting is difficult to decipher. Fortunately, Scott excels in mathematics and enjoys the recognition he receives for being a good math student.

There is no doubt that Scott is intelligent, and his records consistently indicate intelligence test scores in the high-normal range. In the last few years his parents have become frustrated and have developed a pattern of acceptance-rejection. They have been told throughout Scott's schooling that he is bright, and they cannot understand his lack of performance in school. They tend to think Scott is lazy, although he works hard at baseball and completes his afterschool chores. His parents also are concerned about Scott's tendency to argue and initiate fights. He frequently is reprimanded both at home and at school.

For an hour a day Scott goes to a learning disabilities resource room where a teacher works with him on reading and spelling and uses social skills training to help him control his tendency to fight.

The learning disabilities teacher frequently consults with Scott's other teachers. Recently, Scott's literature and history teachers agreed to allow him to record class lectures on audiotapes. In addition, a classmate is recording the class biology book so that Scott can listen to the tape as he reads the textbook. To improve Scott's reading comprehension, Scott is being taught a paraphrasing learning strategy, and an error-monitoring learning strategy is helping him detect and correct errors in his writing. Also, Scott is responding well to cooperative learning techniques implemented in his classes. Because Scott's attitude and grades are improving, his teachers believe that their collaboration and recent teaching of particular learning strategies have had a beneficial effect.

Although there is some confusion regarding the nature of individuals with learning disabilities, some basic descriptions currently exist. All students with learning disabilities have an academic problem in one or more areas, and this problem is not due primarily to emotional disability, mental retardation, visual or auditory impairment, motor disability, or environmental disadvantage. In their problem area(s), they are not achieving in accordance with their potential ability. Social and emotional problems may or may not be present.

HISTORY By 1960 most public schools provided special education services to some students with disabilities. Programs and services were extended to students with mental disabilities, emotional disabilities, blindness, deafness, speech impairments, and physical disabilities. Still, there remained a group of students who had serious learning problems but did not fit any of the existing categories of exceptionality. Many had average or above-average intelligence and appeared to be physically intact. Because there were no apparent reasons for their learning problems, their parents and teachers sought help from professionals in a variety of fields.

Numerous theories emerged from medicine and psychology to explain the problems of these students. Explanations included laziness, brain damage, perceptual impairments, dyslexia, and neurological impairment. A multitude of terms was introduced to describe the characteristics the students exhibited. Confusion, frustration, and eventually progress resulted. Initially, the medical profession concentrated on identifying students with learning problems. Psychologists joined in the effort, studying characteristics of such students. However, in both these fields, recommendations for treatment were few and limited. In the early sixties it became apparent that educators would have to involve themselves in treating students with complex learning problems.

Local associations of parents formed to organize classes and provide services not offered in public schools. The number of local groups and state organizations increased rapidly, and in 1963 a national conference was held in Chicago to organize a national association. At this conference Samuel Kirk introduced the term *learning disabilities*. Parents, who had been dissatisfied with the then-existing terms, received this new term enthusiastically and formed the Association for Children with Learning Disabilities (ACLD). Kirk's introduction of the term and the formation of ACLD are viewed as the official beginning of the learning disabilities movement, although the stage had been set for this development by previous movements whose interaction has been traced by several authorities (Hallahan & Cruickshank, 1973; Wiederholt, 1974). Seven primary movements influencing the learning disabilities field are identified in Table 4–1: spoken language, written language, perceptual-motor skills, reinforcement theory, cognitive theory, interest groups, and government policy. Significant developments presented in this chapter are charted on the table according to their area or origin.

In 1968 and 1969, several key events occurred. First, the National Advisory Committee on Handicapped Children (NACHC) was established to develop a definition of learning disabilities. Under Kirk's leadership the committee drafted a definition that still is used today. Second, the Council for Exceptional Children (CEC) established the Division for Children with Learning Disabilities (DCLD). Through the efforts of ACLD

Table 4–1

Highlights in the field of learning disabilities

	Spoken Language	Written Language	Perceptual-Motor Skills	Reinforcement Theory	Cognitive Theory	Interest Groups	Government Policy
	Circa 1940s: Osgood, Myklebust, Wepman, Kirk	Circa 1930s: Orton (brain-dominance theory), Monroe, Gillingham, Stillman, Spalding	Circa 1940s: Strauss, Werner, Lehtinen, Cruickshank, Kephart, Doman and Delacato, Frostig	Circa 1950s: Skinner, Haring, Lindsley	Circa 1950s: Bruner, Chomsky	Circa 1950s: Fund for Perceptually Handicapped Children, New York Association for Brain-Injured Children	No direct legislation
	Psycholinguistic teaching	Multisensory remedial reading techniques; phonics	Delineation of characteristics of brain-injured children; reduced stimuli techniques	Operant conditioning; precision teaching	Focus on "inner" thinking processes		
1963	← Kirk's speech to parents suggesting term *learning disabilities* →						
	ITPA and psycholinguistic teaching widespread	Remedial reading emphasis; 3 Rs stressed	Extensive use of P-M tests and training activities	Lovitt's application of precision teaching to LD		ACLD formed	Task forces I, II, and III planned
						ACLD expansion to international organization	Clements' use of term *minimal brain dysfunction*
1968	Growing criticism of psycholinguistic approach—led by Hammill and colleagues	Rapid development of commercial programs (e.g., DISTAR; shift from ability to skill model	Growing criticism of P-M approach—led by Hammill and colleagues	Growing use of precision teaching; direct instruction stressed by Stephens; criticism of ability model	Piaget's developmental stages	DCLD formed; Continuing ACLD multidisciplinary emphasis; DCLD teacher-oriented emphasis	NACHC definition P.L. 91–230, the LD Act
1975							P.L. 94–142 identification of learning disabilities as handicap and request for precise LD definition
1963	← Controversy over definition extensive in 1975–77 period						
	Process tests and treatments minimized in 1977 *Federal Register*; value questioned by researchers	Proliferation of commercial materials spurred on by IEP requirement in P.L. 94–142	Severe criticism of P-M approach; P-M minimized in 1977 *Federal Register*; value questioned by researchers	Appearance of commercial precision teaching programs	Cognitive approach supported by Hammill	Increased attention on process vs. ability; controversy within and between ACLD and DCLD	1977 *Federal Register* federal funding of LD research institutes
1980	Oral language training provided mainly by language specialists	Widespread criterion-oriented commercial programs	P-M widely criticized; some resurgence in occupational therapy; Ayres influential	Directive teaching and precision teaching gaining in use	Cognitive interventions stressed by University of Virginia LD Research Institute	National Joint Committee for LD (NJCLD) formed from 6 organizations	Beginning of federal deemphasis of education

Year							
	Work of Bryan and associates highlights pragmatic language problems of LD individuals; Commercial language tests expanding rapidly; Subgroups of LD—the language learning disabled (LLD)—becoming more prominent	More emphasis in the literature on the LD adolescent-oriented commercial programs; Computer-assisted instruction for LD students available on a large scale; Learning strategies developed at University of Kansas have major impact on teaching LD adolescents	P-M test introduced by Barbe and Swassing	*Journal of Precision Teaching* published; Learning strategies draw from direct instruction research	Publication of Reid and Hresko's text on cognitive approach to LD; Learning strategies draw from cognitive research	LD definition proposed by NJCLD; DCLD withdrawal from CEC (Hammill-led movement) and formation of Council for Learning Disabilities (CLD); New CEC division—Division for Learning Disabilities (DLD)—begun by cadre of former DCLD members	Much support for LD in public hearings; LD category intact at federal level
1984			Detroit Tests of Learning Aptitude revised; Ayres revising sensory integration test; supportive data for P-M still lacking				
1986				Precision teaching content included in majority of college teacher training programs	Metacognition influences identification and treatment of LD		P.L. 99-457 adds services for infants, toddlers, and their families; Will promotes regular education initiative (REI)
1987		Learning strategies being developed for elementary-level LD		Applied behavior analysis becomes popular terminology; Curriculum-based assessment (CBA) emerges as a primary assessment system	Wong's summary of the impact of metacognition in LD and prediction of continuing growth; Cognitive approaches influence teaching practices	CLD publishes position papers opposing discrepancy formulas, inclusion of low achievers in LD programs, and P-M programs	Regular education initiative becomes major issue; many LD experts disagree with REI rational and potential benefits
1990		Whole language approach being tried with LD students		Behavioral theory receives less support; however, CBA and direct instruction maintain influence			P.L. 101-476 changes the title of the law to IDEA; *disabilities* replaces the term *handicapped* across categorical areas; Integrated programming increases

← Eclectic viewpoints becoming more widespread. The learning strategies approach is an example of a major intervention → program that draws from numerous orientations and research bases and DCLD, legislators were made aware of children with learning disabilities and the paucity of educational services available to them. As a result of intense lobbying, the Children with Learning Disabilities Act of 1969 was passed into law (Public Law 91–230). This legislation provided for a 5-year program of teacher training, research, and the establishment of model education centers for children with learning disabilities. In 1975 "learning disabilities" was included as one of the disabling conditions in Public Law 94–142, the Education for All Handicapped Children Act, and a more precise definition was requested. The period from 1975 to 1977 was highlighted by much debate and controversy over the definition of learning abilities and practices for their identification. On December 29, 1977, the U.S. Department of Education released regulations for defining and identifying learning disabilities. These regulations guided P.L. 94–142 practices.

Amendments to P.L. 94–142 have expanded the age range of children who are entitled to special education. For example, Public Law 99–457, adopted in 1986, included incentives for states to implement services for infants, toddlers, and their families. Moreover, Public Law 101–476, adopted in 1990, changed the title of the special education law to the Individuals with Disabilities Education Act (IDEA) and altered the language of the law from "handicapped children" to "children with disabilities." It also provided services for adolescents making the transition from high school to postschool activities, expanded early intervention programs, placed greater emphasis on meeting the needs of ethnically and culturally diverse children with disabilities, and promoted better dissemination of special education information to parents. Thus, IDEA incorporates Public Law 94–142 and its amendments to provide a free, appropriate education for all young people with disabilities through the age of 21. It is important to the field of special education and the area of learning disabilities.

DEFINITION

No other area of special education has expended so much effort in developing a definition as the area of learning disabilities. The major definitions formulated over the years have reflected terminology that can be classified into three primary categories: brain injury, minimal brain dysfunction, and learning disabilities (Mercer, 1992).

The first description of students with learning problems was based on the assumption of brain injury (Strauss & Lehtinen, 1947). However, parents disliked the term *brain injury* and the permanence it implied, and professionals claimed that it was of little use in classifying, describing, or teaching children. During the sixties the term *minimal brain dysfunction* (MBD) emerged. MBD theorists proposed that minimal or minor brain injury was linked with learning problems. However, the MBD definition never was accepted widely either. Educators found the MBD label no more useful in planning education intervention than the brain injury label.

In time the emphasis on medical factors was replaced with concern for psychological and educational variables. Special educators preferred to refer to students with learning problems as "educationally handicapped," "language disordered," or "perceptually handicapped." Finally, both parents and educators endorsed the term *learning disability*.

With the responsibility for funding special education programs for children with learning disabilities came the need for a clear and functional definition. A definition was developed by the National Advisory Committee on Handicapped Children (NACHC) and incorporated into Public Law 91–230, the Learning Disabilities Act of 1969. Acceptance of this definition was widespread. By 1975, 31 states were using the NACHC definition or some variation of it (Mercer, Forgnone, & Wolking, 1976; Murphy, 1976).

Nonetheless, when P.L. 94–142 was passed in November 1975, it required that learning disabilities be defined more precisely, and the U.S. Office of Education was charged with this task. After two years the regulations for defining and identifying students with learning disabilities appeared in the *Federal Register*. These regulations endorse a definition of *specific learning disability* that is almost identical to the earlier NACHC definition:

> "Specific learning disability" means a disorder in one or more of the basic psychological processes involved in understanding or in using language, spoken or written, which may manifest itself in an imperfect ability to listen, think, speak, read, write, spell, or to do mathematical calculations. The term includes such conditions as perceptual handicaps, brain injury, minimal brain dysfunction, dyslexia, and developmental aphasia. The term does not include children who have learning problems which are primarily the result of visual, hearing, or motor handicaps, or mental retardation, or emotional disturbance, or of environmental, cultural, or economic disadvantage. (U.S. Office of Education, 1977, p. 65083)

Although the definition remained virtually the same, the regulations included criteria for identifying students with learning disabilities that helped to clarify the learning disability definition:

Academic Component, Qualified by Discrepancy Factor

1. A team may determine that a child has a specific learning disability if:
   a. the child does not achieve commensurate with his or her age and ability levels in one or more of the following areas when provided with learning experiences appropriate for the child's age and ability levels: oral expression, listening comprehension, written expression, basic reading skill, reading comprehension, mathematics calculation, or mathematics reasoning.
   b. the team finds that a child has a severe discrepancy between achievement and intellectual ability in one or more of the same areas listed in the preceding statement.

Exclusion Component

2. The team may not identify a child as having a specific learning disability if the severe discrepancy between ability and achievement is primarily the result of:
   a. a visual, hearing, or motor handicap
   b. mental retardation
   c. emotional disturbance
   d. environmental, cultural, or economic disadvantage (U.S. Office of Education, 1977, pp. 65082–65085)

The identification criteria focused on academic skills of concern and interpreted academic problems within the context of a *discrepancy factor*. A discrepancy exists when a student's academic performance falls far below his or her estimated ability in one or more subjects. A student may have average intelligence yet function in reading or math several grade levels behind his or her chronological age. Many authorities consider the discrepancy factor to be the common denominator of learning disabilities. However, both the definition and the criteria state that a child cannot be labeled as having a learning disability if the discrepancy between academic achievement and estimated ability is due to physical or sensory handicaps; mental retardation; emotional disturbance; or environmental, cultural, or economic disadvantages. This is known as the *exclusion component*.

The above 1977 U.S. Department of Education definition was incorporated into the Individuals with Disabilities Education Act (IDEA). Mercer, King-Sears, and Mercer (1990) surveyed all the state departments of education concerning the definition and identification criteria used for learning disabilities. Their results show an emerging consensus on most of the components included in the definition. However, an examination of the definition used indicates that compared to a similar survey that was completed 5 years earlier (Mercer, Hughes, & Mercer, 1985), the use of the exact IDEA definition decreased from 72% to 57%. This decrease resulted because many states changed the wording or included the discrepancy component or prereferral conditions in their definitions. Thus, numerous states embrace the major components of the IDEA definition but are not satisfied with its wording or inclusiveness.

Reactions to the federal definition and criteria remain mixed and controversial. Dissatisfaction with the definition resulted in the formation of the National Joint Committee for Learning Disabilities (NJCLD), a group composed of representatives from six professional organizations. NJCLD reached agreement on a definition in 1981 (Hammill, Leigh, McNutt, & Larsen, 1981). In 1986 the ACLD (now the Learning Disabilities Association of America) presented a definition that stresses the lifelong nature of a learning disability and extends a learning disability beyond the academic domain by placing an emphasis on students' socialization and self-esteem. In 1987, the Interagency Committee on Learning Disabilities (ICLD) proposed a definition stressing the inclusion of social skills deficits. Thus, in 1988, the NJCLD slightly modified its earlier definition to reflect current knowledge and react to the definition developed by the ICLD:

> *Learning disabilities* is a general term that refers to a heterogeneous group of disorders manifested by significant difficulties in the acquisition and use of listening, speaking, reading, writing, reasoning, or mathematical abilities. These disorders are intrinsic to the individual, presumed to be due to nervous system dysfunction, and may occur across the life span. Problems in self-regulatory behaviors, social perception, and social interaction may exist with learning disabilities but do not by themselves constitute a learning disability. Although learning disabilities may occur concomitantly with other handicapping conditions (for example, sensory impairment, mental retardation, serious emotional disturbance) or with extrinsic influences (such as cultural differences, insufficient or inappropriate instruction), they are not the result of those conditions or influences. (NJCLD, 1988, p. 1)

This revised definition indicates that learning disabilities may occur across the life span, and it distinguishes between a learning disability and problems in self-regulatory behavior, social perception, and social interaction.

Given the respective definitions proposed by the various organizations, committees, and governmental agencies, it appears that the learning disabilities definition remains in a state of confusion. Closer inspection, however, allows for a more optimistic position. The most influential definitions (i.e., the 1977 *Federal Register*, NJCLD, ACLD, and ICLD definitions) have more similarities than differences. They include many of the same major components, such as discrepancy, academic, exclusion, and neurological factors. Hammill (1990) notes that the most influential definitions are in fundamental agreement on most issues.

PREVALENCE Variations in terminology, definitions, and assessment practices result in different prevalence rates for learning disabilities. The U.S. Department of Education (1991) notes that the percentage of students classified as having learning disabilities ranged from 2.2% to 7.8% for the 1989–1990 school year. These differences are due to variations in identification criteria, actual differences across states in the number of students with learning disabilities, policy variations (e.g., prereferral policies), and aberrations in data-reporting practices.

The U.S. Department of Education (1991) reports that 3.6% of individuals in the United States from the ages of 6 through 21 years were classified as having learning disabilities. This percentage represents a decrease from recent years (i.e., from about 5%) because of a change in the method of its computing. For 1990 the Department of Education computed the percentage by dividing the number of young people with learning disabilities, from the ages of 6 through 21, by the *resident* population of individuals in the same age range. Previously, the percentage was calculated by comparing the group with learning disabilities to individuals within the same age range *enrolled* in school. Because the total number of same-age residents is greater than the total number of same-age students enrolled in school, the proportion of individuals classified as having learning disabilities decreased.

The actual number of students identified as having learning disabilities is increasing—a fact resulting in much concern. The number of students with learning disabilities, from the ages of 6 through 21, has increased from 1.2%, or 797,212, in 1976 to 1977 to 3.6%, or 2,064,892, in 1989 to 1990. This latter figure of over 2 million with learning disabilities represents 48.5% of all students identified for special education. The category of learning disabilities makes up, by far, the largest group of students served by special education.

Because of limited resources for special education, the rapid growth in the number of students classified as learning disabled and the variability of prevalence rates are important concerns of educators and legislators. There are several reasons for the increase in the number of students identified as having learning disabilities:

1. As public awareness of learning disabilities has increased, there are more referrals from parents, teachers, and other professionals.
2. Improved identification procedures have resulted in classifying more children and adolescents with learning disabilities (Lerner, 1993).
3. Instructional services provided in learning disability programs offer viable alternatives to students at risk for educational failure.
4. The learning disability label appears to have higher social acceptance than other categorical labels (Lerner, 1993).

A learning disability is difficult to identify at the preschool level because learning disabilities are considered primarily academic learning problems and they are frequently not detected until children begin formal academic instruction. Also, for a preschool child there is less opportunity to document a discrepancy between ability and achievement. Obviously, the preschool child cannot be far behind in reading or math because little is expected in these areas at this level.

CAUSES

In the majority of cases the precise cause of a student's learning disability is unknown. Nonetheless, numerous causal factors have been proposed. They can be grouped into four basic categories: acquired trauma, genetic/hereditary influences, biochemical abnormalities, and environmental influences.

Acquired Trauma

Insult or injury to the central nervous system that originates outside the individual and results in learning disorders is called in the medical literature *acquired trauma*. Spivak (1986) reports that about 20% of students with learning disabilities have had a prior brain injury. Acquired central nervous system damage can occur during gestation or labor and after birth. Various pre-, peri-, and postnatal traumas have been shown to be correlated with learning problems.

Prenatal Causes.   Complications during pregnancy have been linked empirically with children's learning problems. In a review of the literature, Gold and Sherry (1984) found a correlation between maternal alcohol consumption during pregnancy and later learning disabilities in the child. The effect of maternal drug consumption, both prescribed and nonprescribed, has been a related line of research. As Brackbill, McManus, and Woodward (1985) clearly point out, "Obstetrical drugs cross the placenta easily and quickly. They readily pass through incompletely developed blood/brain barriers. They concentrate in brain structures that are still developing and therefore at high risk to damage" (p. 109). Of all the suspected physiological causes of learning problems, those associated with acquired prenatal trauma (alcohol, obstetrical drugs, illicit drugs such as cocaine, tobacco) are the most preventable. Increased awareness and understanding on the part of parents and physicians about the consumption of certain substances and their potentially adverse effects would lead to better practices and a decrease in the incidence of disability related to their consumption.

Perinatal Causes.   Events that affect the child during birth are called *perinatal traumas* or *perinatal stresses*. Included are prematurity, anoxia, prolonged labor, and injury from medical instruments (e.g., forceps). Birth complications have been associated with later learning disabilities characteristic of minimal brain damage (e.g., language and motor problems, attention deficits). Smith (1983) notes that although perinatal complications are more prevalent in students who later exhibit learning problems, many normally achieving students have experienced similar complications. Thus, predicting later school-related problems on the basis of birth complications alone is risky.

√Postnatal Causes.   Accidents and diseases after birth that are purported to lead to brain damage and concomitant learning problems include strokes, high fever, encephalitis, meningitis, and head trauma (e.g., severe concussion). Bigler (1987) reports that the majority of individuals who suffer head injuries are adolescents or young adults. Telzrow (1987) notes that there is an adverse effect on the educational progress of most students who sustain head injuries.

In the 1990 amendments to P.L. 94–142, it was clarified that students with traumatic brain injury are included as "children with disabilities." These students previously were covered by the law, but now they are identified as a separate and distinct class who are entitled to the law's benefits. Behaviors due to traumatic brain injury vary depending on the extent and location of the injury as well as the age of the victim, and each person with a brain injury exhibits different resulting abilities and deficits and displays a unique pattern of recovery. Several maladaptive behaviors associated with traumatic brain injury are cognitive in nature such as distractibility, irritability, impulsivity, failure to initiate activities, poor decision making, and failure to shift from one activity to another. Other behaviors are deficits in interpersonal skills such as poor anger control, extreme attention-seeking behavior, failure to respond to others' social cues, and failure to self-monitor behavior for appropriateness (Deaton, 1987). Additional areas of residual deficits due to traumatic head injuries include cognitive impairment, language deficiencies, impairment of motor functioning, memory and attention deficits, and behavior and personality changes (Telzrow, 1987). Deaton presents various effective behavioral treatment strategies for improving behavior, and Telzrow provides guidelines for dealing with the academic deficiencies encountered by students with traumatic brain injury.

Despite many years of research and practice, diagnosing children with learning disabilities as neurologically impaired remains a difficult task (Kavale & Forness, 1985). One reason is that the child's neurological system is still maturing, making it difficult to differentiate between a lag in maturity and an actual disorder. In addition, although there are some age-normative data on neurological development (e.g., motor and sensory functions), further work is needed to improve the validity and reliability of the neurological examination. Feagans's perspective (1983) concerning the relationship between learning disabilities and neurology continues to apply:

> Neurological research is a burgeoning area in which new techniques often outstrip our knowledge of how to use them effectively. This is often the case because theories of how measures of brain activity relate to behaviors and how behaviors relate to academic progress and learning remain to be formulated. (p. 489)

√Genetic/Hereditary Influences

Several investigators have examined the relationship between genetics and learning disabilities. Hallgren (1950) studied 276 dyslexic individuals and their families. The prevalence of reading and language problems among the children's relatives led him to conclude that learning problems are inherited. More recently, DeFries and Decker (1982) compared families of 125 children with disabilities and 125 children without disabilities (a total of 1044 subjects) and found greater rates of reading disabilities within the families of the group with disabilities. Coles (1980), however, questions the conclusions of many of the family studies, stating that they offer little evidence of a hereditary basis and do not address the issue of environmental impact on learning.

Although evidence exists to support genetic influences in the etiology of learning disabilities, the extent of this relationship remains unclear. Future studies are needed that include large samples and improved control of variables such as environmental influences. A better understanding of the role of heredity in transmitting learning disabilities eventually may help medical professionals develop and implement preventive measures.

✓ Biochemical Abnormalities

Because some students with learning disabilities have neither diagnosed neurological damage nor a family history of learning problems, it has been hypothesized that biochemical abnormalities may be a causal factor. Imbalances in neurotransmitters are assumed to cause difficulties in neural impulse transmission and consequent learning and behavior problems. For example, some attention deficits have been associated with overrapid neural impulses that do not allow the brain adequate time to process incoming information (Adelman & Taylor, 1983b; Shaywitz, 1987; Silver, 1988). Most research in this area focuses on the possibility of a chemical basis for this condition and involves measuring levels of various chemicals in the blood, urine, and cerebrospinal fluid of individuals with learning disabilities. Results have been inconclusive, however, and specific knowledge about neurotransmitters is in the early stages of development.

The notion of linking allergies to learning disabilities was popularized when Feingold (1975, 1976) linked allergies to hyperactivity. He claimed that learning disabilities could be caused by allergic reactions to salicylates and artificial colors and flavors in food. For treatment he recommended the Kaiser-Permanente (K–P) diet, which eliminates foods that contain natural salicylates (e.g., apples, tomatoes, oranges, peaches, various berries); foods containing artificial colors and flavors; and miscellaneous items that contain salicylates or artificial colors and flavors, such as toothpastes, perfumes, and compounds containing aspirin. Although there are some avid supporters of the K–P diet, well-conducted studies indicate that it helps only a small percentage of hyperactive children (Silver, 1987). Allergic reactions to foods that do not contain salicylates or flavors and colors, such as milk, wheat, sugar, and chocolate, also have been linked to learning disabilities (Rapp, 1978; Silver, 1987).

It also has been suggested that learning disabilities can be caused by the blood's inability to synthesize a normal supply of vitamins (Cott, 1972). Consequently, some individuals recommend megavitamin therapy, in which large daily doses of vitamins are administered. There is, however, no conclusive evidence to support the claims made for this therapy (Silver, 1987). In fact, large doses of vitamins did not improve the performance of children with learning disabilities in one study conducted to test the therapy's effectiveness (Kershner, Hawks, & Grekin, 1977).

✓Environmental Influences

Many educators feel that inadequate or poor learning environments contribute significantly to the learning and behavior problems of many students with learning disabilities (Carnine, 1989; Gersten, Woodward, & Darch, 1986). There is evidence that the problems of most students with learning disabilities are corrected through direct, systematic instruction (Gersten, Carnine, & Woodward, 1987; Kimball & Heron, 1988; Mercer, Peterson, & Ross, 1988). Engelmann, Carnine, Gersten, and their associates at the University of Oregon have conducted research that strongly supports the position that the learning problems of many students with learning disabilities are prevented, corrected, or ameliorated via direct instruction. Moreover, the work of Deshler and Schumaker at the University of Kansas demonstrates that the learning strategy curriculum they have developed is effective in teaching adolescents with learning disabilities to succeed in school. Kirk and Chalfant (1984) discuss a Teacher Assistance Team Model that has proven effective in helping teachers reduce the number of inappropriate referrals and in resolving many students' problems. Research indicates that school-based teachers are able to work with one another to better meet the needs of students with learning problems (Graden, Casey, & Christenson, 1985; Showers, 1990; West & Idol, 1990). It is apparent, then, that effective instructional curricula and strategies exist for teaching students with learning disabilities. However, when they are not put into practice, the inadequate educational environment contributes to the number of students labeled as having learning disabilities.

CHARACTERISTICS

The identification criteria presented in the Individuals with Disabilities Education Act (IDEA) provide an initial framework for examining characteristics of learning disabilities, with the focus on academic and language difficulties. Kirk, Gallagher, and Anastasiow (1993), along with numerous others (Bryan, 1991; Lerner, 1993), broaden the range of difficulties to include perception, motor, social-emotional, metacognitive, memory, and attention problems. The importance of various characteristics is likely to be debated for some time.

In any review of proposed characteristics of learning disabilities, four points should be remembered:

1. Each student is unique and may exhibit a learning problem in one area but not in others.
2. Characteristics used in identifying a student as having a learning disability must persist over time. Many students who do not have a learning disability exhibit characteristics of learning disabilities for brief periods (e.g., hyperactivity surrounding a field trip).
3. In the process of identifying learning disabilities, it is preferable to describe characteristic behaviors rather than to label the student.
4. As noted earlier, learning disabilities are identified in terms of a discrepancy between achievement and estimated ability.

Academic Learning Difficulties

Academic learning problems are the most widely accepted characteristic of individuals with learning disabilities. Mathematics, reading, and written expression are the areas in which these problems occur, with reading problems being the most common.

Reading Problems.   Reading is one of the central difficulties of students with learning disabilities. Carnine, Silbert, and Kameenui (1990) suggest that it is the principal cause of failure in school. Reading experiences strongly influence a student's self-image and feeling of competency. Reading failure can lead to misbehavior, anxiety, and a lack of motivation. Problems in reading are manifested in a variety of ways. Table 4–2 presents selected difficulties related to the reading habits, word recognition, comprehension, and miscellaneous symptoms of students with learning disabilities. In a review of research on reading comprehension and reading/learning disabilities, Weisberg (1988) reports that reading comprehension problems must be viewed from an interactive model. She reports that reading comprehension is multifaceted and that problems of students with learning disabilities are examined best in the context of such variables as the reader's prior knowledge of the topic, the text structure, and situational conditions. She notes that students with learning disabilities need explicit instruction in understanding tasks.

Math Problems.   Many students with learning disabilities have difficulty mastering math skills and concepts. In school settings, difficulties with math often result in school failures and seem to generate high levels of anxiety. Bartel (1990) states that

Reading is one of the central difficulties of students with learning disabilities.

Table 4–2
Selected reading behaviors of children with reading disabilities

Characteristics	Comments
Reading Habits	
Tension movements	Frowning, fidgeting, using a high-pitched voice, and lip biting
Insecurity	Refusing to read, crying, and attempting to distract the teacher
Loses place	Losing place frequently (is often associated with repetitions)
Lateral head movements	Jerking head
Holds material close	Deviating extremely (from 15 to 18 inches)
Word Recognition Errors	
Omissions	Omitting a word (e.g., *Tom saw @cat*)
Insertions	Inserting words (e.g., *The dog ran* [fast] *after the cat)*
Substitutions	Substituting one word for another (e.g., *The house ~~horse~~ was big*)
Reversals	Reversing letters in a word (e.g., *no* for *on, was* for *saw*)
Mispronunciations	Mispronouncing words (e.g., *mister* for *miser*)
Transpositions	Reading words in the wrong order (e.g., *She away ran* for *She ran away*)
Unknown words	Hesitating for 5 seconds at words they cannot pronounce
Slow choppy reading	Not recognizing words quickly enough (e.g., 20 to 30 words per minute)
Comprehension Errors	
Cannot recall basic facts	Unable to answer specific questions about a passage (e.g., *What was the dog's name?*).
Cannot recall sequence	Unable to tell sequence of the story read
Cannot recall main theme	Unable to recall the main topic of the story
Miscellaneous Symptoms	
Word-by-word reading	Reading in a choppy, halting, and laborious manner (e.g., no attempts are made to group words into thought units)
Strained, high-pitched voice	Reading in a pitch higher than a conversational tone
Inadequate phrasing	Inappropriately grouping words (e.g., *The dog ran into* [pause] *the woods*).
Ignored or misinterpreted punctuation	Running together phrases, clauses, or sentences

Source: From *Students with Learning Disabilities* (4th ed., p. 498) by C. D. Mercer, 1992, New York: Merrill/Macmillan. Copyright 1992 by Macmillan Publishing Company. Reprinted by permission.

students with math deficiencies are as disabled as individuals who are unable to read. In a survey of 110 learning disabilities resource room teachers, Carpenter (1985) found that one third of their instructional time was spent teaching math. Difficulties with math are common at all age levels. During the preschool and primary years, many children cannot sort objects by size, match objects, understand the language of mathematics, or grasp the concept of rational counting. During the elementary years, they have trouble with computational skills (Cawley & Miller, 1989). In the middle and upper grades, students experience difficulty with fractions, decimals, percentages, and measurement. Secondary school students with learning disabilities also may make errors like those of younger students—for example, having difficulty with place values and with basic operations. Carpenter's survey found no significant differences between elementary and secondary resource room teachers in the amount of time devoted to teaching math to students with learning disabilities.

In 1989 the National Council of Teachers of Mathematics released a report calling for major reforms in mathematics instruction. Given that traditional mathematics instruction is failing many students, including those with learning disabilities, the reason for concern is apparent. Fortunately, the efforts of several educators have resulted in significant contributions regarding mathematics instruction for students with learning disabilities. The works of Cawley and his associates (Cawley, 1984, 1985; Cawley & Miller, 1989), Carnine and his associates (Engelmann & Carnine, 1982; Kelly, Gersten, & Carnine, 1990; Silbert, Carnine, & Stein, 1990), and Thornton and her associates (Bley & Thornton, 1989; Thornton, 1989; Thornton & Toohey, 1985) represent major efforts to understand and ameliorate the mathematical deficits of students with learning disabilities. Table 4–3 presents selected problem areas and their implied relationship to math performance.

Language Difficulties

Of the students identified as having learning disabilities, a large portion exhibit a language-learning impairment. Estimates of the prevalence of students with a language-learning disability among students with learning disabilities range from 40% to 60%, and from 1.5% to 2% of all school-aged children (McKinney, 1984; Wiig & Semel, 1984). In a study of elementary students, Gibbs and Cooper (1989) found mild to moderate language deficits in 90% of 242 students with learning disabilities. Moreover, Vogel (1975) notes that research indicates that many children who do not read well suffer from underlying language problems. A language disorder is characterized by problems in language comprehension, expression, speech discrimination, and word-finding difficulties. Because language skills and academic functioning are related so closely, it is sometimes difficult to determine the primary disability (i.e., reading or language).

Perceptual Disorders

Perception involves recognizing, discriminating, and interpreting sensation. Specialists in learning disabilities traditionally have given much attention to perceptual problems that affect learning, especially to visual and auditory disabilities. Although several authorities continue to stress perceptual disorders, emphasis on perceptual problems has recently diminished.

Motor Disorders

Students with motor problems may walk with a clumsy gait or have difficulty throwing or catching a ball, skipping, or hopping. Others exhibit difficulties with fine motor skills, such as those needed for cutting with scissors, buttoning, or zipping. Like perceptual disabilities, motor problems received substantial attention in research history but recently have been deemphasized (Myers & Hammill, 1990). For example, the IDEA definition of learning disabilities mentions motor disabilities only to the extent that they relate to basic psychological processes.

Table 4–3
Common difficulties that affect math performance of students with learning disabilities

Learning Difficulty		Math-Related Performance
Motor		writes numbers illegibly, slowly, and inaccurately has difficulty writing numbers in small spaces (i.e., writes large)
Memory	Short-term	is unable to retain math facts or new information forgets steps in an algorithm is unable to retain the meaning of symbols
	Long-term	works slowly on mastering facts over time performs poorly on review lessons or mixed probes forgets steps in algorithms
	Sequential	has difficulty telling time does not complete all steps in a multistep computation problem has difficulty solving multistep word problems
Language	Receptive	has difficulty relating arithmetic terms to meaning (e.g., *minus, addend, dividend, regroup, multiplicand, place value*) has difficulty relating words that have multiple meanings (e.g., *carry, times*)
	Expressive	does not use the vocabulary of arithmetic has difficulty performing oral arithmetic drills has difficulty verbalizing steps in solving a word problem or an algorithm
Abstract Reasoning		has difficulty solving word problems is unable to make comparisons of size and quantity has difficulty understanding symbols in math (e.g., $>$, $<$, $\times$, $=$) has difficulty understanding the abstract level of mathematical concepts and operations
Metacognition		is unable to identify and select appropriate strategies for solving computation and word problems has difficulty monitoring the problem-solving process in word problems and multistep computations is unable to generalize strategies to other situations
Social and Emotional Factors	Impulsive	makes careless mistakes in computation responds incorrectly and rapidly in oral drills corrects responses frequently when asked to look at or listen to a problem again does not attend to detail in solving problems
	Short attention/ Distractibility	does not complete work in assigned time has difficulty doing multistep computation starts a problem and does not finish it but goes on to next problem is off-task

Source: From *Students with Learning Disabilities* (4th ed., pp. 551–552) by C. D. Mercer, 1992, New York: Merrill/Macmillan. Copyright 1992 by Macmillan Publishing Company. Adapted by permission.

Social-Emotional Problems

Frustrated by their learning difficulties, many students with learning disabilities act disruptively and acquire negative feelings of self-worth. Rappaport (1975) notes that emotions of students with learning disabilities develop differently from those of their peers. Rather than learning and developing attitudes about tasks they "can do," children with learning disabilities often learn what they "can't do." This lack of positive self-regard often results in poor self-concept and self-esteem. Licht (1984) reports that because of their repeated failures, students with learning disabilities often develop maladaptive achievement-related beliefs, which, in turn, create problems that go beyond the original disabilities.

Several authorities (Bryan & Bryan, 1986; Gresham & Elliott, 1989; McKinney, 1989) note that children with learning disabilities frequently experience problems in interacting with parents, teachers, peers, or strangers. Bryan (1977) suggests that the social-emotional problems of some children with learning disabilities are due to social imperceptiveness. Specifically, she reports that many children with learning disabilities lack adequate skills in detecting subtle affective cues. The area of social skills deficits in learning disabilities has received recent attention. For example, the Interagency Committee on Learning Disabilities (ICLD) definition of learning disabilities includes social skills deficits as a primary disability; this has generated much discussion about whether social skills deficits are a primary or secondary disability in the overall area of learning disabilities (Hammill, 1990). Although information regarding the social skills deficits of students with learning disabilities is increasing (Gresham, 1988; Hazel & Schumaker, 1988), data still are lacking on the percentage of students with learning disabilities who exhibit social skills deficits. Gresham and Elliott (1989) present a responsible perspective on the social skills deficit issue: "The fact alone that many children classified as learning disabled display social skills deficits, coupled with the evolution of an adequate assessment and remediation technology, is reason enough to target social behaviors for intervention" (p. 123). The following social-emotional areas may be appropriate for organizing intervention with students who have learning disabilities: hyperactivity, distractibility, poor self-concept, adaptive behavior problems, social skills deficits, impulsivity, disruptive behavior, withdrawal, dependency, and perseveration (that is, redundancy in writing or attending, such as repeating "rrr").

Metacognitive Deficits

Literature is accruing that suggests that some students with learning disabilities exhibit metacognitive deficits (Baker, 1982; Wong, 1991). Basically, metacognition consists of two factors: (1) an awareness of the skills, strategies, and resources that are needed to perform a task effectively; and (2) the ability to use self-regulatory mechanisms (e.g., planning moves, evaluating the effectiveness of ongoing activities, checking the outcome of effort, remediating difficulties) to ensure the successful completion of a task (Baker, 1982).

Hresko and Reid (1981) report that the study of metacognitive variables (predicting, planning, checking, monitoring) in students with learning disabilities may lead to a better understanding of how these variables function, resulting in more productive educational interventions. Wong (1991) notes that metacognition research has added significantly to the understanding of the reading problems of students with learning disabilities. Metacognition holds promise for helping practitioners understand and teach students with learning disabilities.

Memory Problems

Memory is crucial to the learning process, and it is well documented that children with learning disabilities have difficulty remembering academic content (e.g., math facts, words, rules). Most authorities recognize several types of memory: short-term memory, long-term memory, sequential memory, rote memory, recall, and recognition. Hallahan and Kauffman (1988) note that students with learning disabilities usually have problems remembering auditory and visual stimuli. Swanson, Cochran, and Ewers (1990) found that measures of memory differentiate students with learning disabilities from slow learners and average students. Specifically, they note that students with learning disabilities exhibit distinct deficiencies in working memory. Teachers frequently report that students with learning disabilities forget spelling words, math facts, and directions. Torgesen and Kail (1980) provide the following conclusions:

1. Students with learning disabilities fail to use strategies that students without disabilities readily use. For example, in learning a list of words, students without disabilities will rehearse the names to themselves or group the words in categories for studying. Generally, students with learning disabilities do not use these strategies spontaneously.
2. Students with learning disabilities may have difficulty remembering because of their poor language skills. Thus, verbal material may be particularly difficult to remember.

Attention Problems and Hyperactivity

To succeed in school, a student must understand and maintain concentration on relevant classroom tasks and must be able to shift attention to new tasks. Students with attention problems are unable to screen out extraneous stimuli and are attracted by irrelevant stimuli. They may exhibit short attention span, distractibility, and hypersensitivity. Many researchers have documented the existence of attention problems and related behaviors (Hallahan, Kauffman, & Lloyd, 1985).

Attention deficits and related behaviors received substantial coverage with the introduction of the term *attention deficit disorder* (ADD) in the 1982 *Diagnostic and Statistical Manual of Mental Disorders* (American Psychiatric Association, 1982). Moreover, increased awareness of attention deficits occurred with the revised publication of the manual in 1987 (American Psychiatric Association, 1987) in which the disorder term was changed to *attention deficit-hyperactivity disorder* (ADHD). Silver (1990) reports that between 15% and 20% of students with learning disabilities have ADHD.

As noted, hyperactivity often is mentioned in conjunction with attention problems. Generally, *hyperactivity* refers to an excess of nonpurposeful motor activity (e.g., finger and foot tapping, asking questions incessantly and often repeating the same question, inability to sit or stand still). As a little league football coach, I had the opportunity to witness this phenomenon outside the classroom. William, one of our 10-year-old players, was classified as having learning disabilities. At football practice he constantly picked fights, generally goofed off, talked back to coaches, and used "tacky" language. After a long practice in which William had been especially difficult to manage, the head coach asked the players to gather in front of him. William obeyed along with the others. In no uncertain terms the coach told them to listen to what he was about to say because he did not want to repeat his instructions. After he was assured everyone was listening, he told them that the next practice was on Monday at 5:30, and they should wear their helmets and pads. Then he asked if there were any questions. William raised his hand. The coach said, "Yes, William?" William asked, "When's the next practice?" The coach, obviously upset with the question, responded, "William! What was the first thing I said?" William thought for a moment and replied, "Listen."

Delinquency and Learning Disabilities

Some researchers link learning disabilities to delinquency because many students with learning disabilities are unable to judge social situations and social consequences. For example, Hazel and Schumaker (1988) report that the performance of social skills such as negotiation and resisting peer pressure is less developed in individuals with learning disabilities than in their peers. In fact, the performance of adolescents with learning disabilities on these skills resembles the performance of juvenile delinquents (Schumaker, Hazel, Sherman, & Sheldon, 1982).

If students with learning disabilities are deficient in cognitive skills related to such areas as resistance, judgment, decision making, goal setting, and social perception, their disability may put them at risk for delinquency. However, some researchers argue that delinquency is a social response to the ongoing problem of general failure across many dimensions of the student's life. In a study of 53 delinquent adolescents, Meltzer, Levine, Karniski, Palfrey, and Clarke (1984) found that many had school problems as early as kindergarten. Moreover, these investigators found that 45% of the delinquents were delayed in reading by the 2nd grade. Some authorities feel that learning problems contribute to an adolescent's sense of failure and frustration, which, in turn, leads to aggressive behavior (Unger, 1978). Preliminary results of a 4-year study of the learning disability/juvenile delinquency link show that the proportion of individuals with learning disabilities is greater among delinquents than among nondelinquents (Keilitz, Zaremba, & Broder, 1979). Keilitz and Dunivant (1986) note that adolescents with learning disabilities are at relatively high risk for delinquency.

While there appears to be a relationship between learning disabilities and juvenile delinquency, no empirical evidence exists to support a theory that learning disabilities cause juvenile delinquency. Many agree with Bachara and Zaba (1978): "It is time to take the question of juvenile delinquency beyond the correlation phase" (p. 245) and provide specialized services to the delinquent. Crawford (1984) found that after a course of academic remediation (55 to 65 hours during a school year), the delinquent behavior of one group significantly decreased. Likewise, Keilitz and Dunivant (1986) note that some rehabilitation programs are effective in remediating academic deficiencies and reducing future delinquency.

Learning Disabilities Across the Life Span

Characteristics of learning disabilities must be viewed within the context of an individual's age. In the past the field of learning disabilities has focused primarily on children of elementary age; however, recent directions support a life-span view. Table 4–4 presents the most prominent characteristics for each age group.

The Young Child with Learning Disabilities.   Two major events have focused attention on serving preschool children who are at high risk for school failure. In 1985

Table 4–4
Life-span view of learning disabilities

	Preschool	Grades K–1	Grades 2–6	Grades 7–12	Adult
Problem Areas	Achievement of developmental milestones (e.g., walking) Receptive language Expressive language Visual perception Auditory perception Short attention span Hyperactivity Self-regulation Social skills Concept formation	Academic readiness skills (e.g., alphabet knowledge, quantitative concepts, directional concepts, etc.) Receptive language Expressive language Visual perception Auditory perception Reasoning Motor development Attention Hyperactivity Social skills	Reading skills Arithmetic skills Written expression Verbal expression Receptive language Attention span Hyperactivity Social-emotional skills Reasoning	Reading skills Arithmetic skills Written expression Verbal expression Listening skills Study skills Metacognition Social-emotional skills Independence	Reading skills Arithmetic skills Written expression Verbal expression Listening skills Study skills Social-emotional skills Metacognition Vocational Assessing community resources
Assessment	Prediction of high risk for later learning problems	Prediction of high risk for later learning problems	Identification of learning disabilities	Identification of learning disabilities	Identification of learning disabilities
Treatment Types	Preventative	Preventative	Remedial Corrective	Remedial Corrective Compensatory Learning strategies	Remedial Corrective Compensatory Learning strategies
Treatments with Most Research and/or Expert Support	Direct instruction in language skills Behavioral management Parent training	Direct instruction in academic and language areas Behavioral management Parent training	Direct instruction in academic areas Behavioral management Parent training Metacognitive training	Direct instruction in academic areas Tutoring in subject areas Direct instruction in learning strategies (study skills) Self-control training Curriculum alternatives Metacognitive training	Direct instruction in academic areas Tutoring in subject (college) or job area Compensatory instruction (i.e., using aids such as tape recorder, calculator, computer) Direct instruction in learning strategies

Source: From *Students with Learning Disabilities* (4th ed., p. 50) by C. D. Mercer, 1992, New York: Merrill/Macmillan. Copyright 1992 by Macmillan Publishing Company. Adapted by permission.

the National Joint Committee on Learning Disabilities and the Preschool Child issued a position paper outlining the needs and issues regarding the identification and treatment of preschool children with learning disabilities. In 1986 the passage of Public Law 99–457 provided legal and economic incentives for serving preschool children with learning or behavior difficulties and established a framework for these services. Table 4–4 indicates that learning disabilities can affect an individual at all ages. Because learning disabilities are primarily an academic learning problem and academic instruction usually does not begin until the 1st grade, diagnosis of learning disabilities for young children is merely predictive. Also, the rapid and unpredictable growth rates of young children complicate the accurate identification of learning disabilities. Educators and diagnosticians must take care not to label a young child prematurely as having a learning disability (National Joint Committee on Learning Disabilities and the Preschool Child, 1985). Thus, professionals and parents must be knowledgeable about and alert for behaviors and characteristics that are associated with later learning problems. Generally, the importance of perceptual skills in diagnosis and treatment reaches its peak during the preschool years and diminishes as the child gets older. Moreover, during the preschool period, developmental milestones and language development are monitored closely. Also, short attention span and hyperactivity represent "warning flags" to many diagnosticians. The positive influence of parent training as a factor in the treatment of young high-risk children is well documented.

The Elementary School Child with Learning Disabilities.   Children of elementary school age have received the most emphasis in learning disabilities. During grades 2 through 6, academic learning problems appear, and ability-achievement discrepancies emerge. Social-emotional problems also become more of a factor during the elementary grades. Diagnosis usually is accomplished through ability and achievement tests. As with individuals of all ages, direct instruction in the skill areas is an important intervention component.

The Adolescent with Learning Disabilities.   Most of the early literature about characteristics of the individuals with learning disabilities focused on children. Because many differences between children and adolescents exist across physical, mental, and emotional areas, it is not appropriate to apply the characteristics of children to young adults. The teenager should be viewed as an adolescent first and then as an exceptional student. Many characteristics of the adolescent period (e.g., puberty, independence, peer-group pressures) interact with learning disabilities and the demands of the high school curriculum to create numerous academic and social-emotional problems. Many professionals recently have made a much-needed effort to understand the characteristics and needs of the adolescent with learning disabilities (Deshler & Lenz, 1989; Deshler & Schumaker, 1983; Schumaker, Deshler, Alley, & Warner, 1983). The following are some of their most pertinent findings:

1. Most adolescents with learning disabilities exhibit severe academic achievement deficits and typically score below the 10th percentile on achievement measures in reading, written language, or mathematics. Moreover, the majority of adolescents with learning disabilities perform poorly in all achievement areas.

Cooperation between parents and the learning disabilities teacher can enhance the student's motivation and achievement.

2. The academic skill development of many adolescents with learning disabilities plateaus during the secondary grades, generally by the 10th grade. For example, the average reading and written language achievement of students with learning disabilities in the 7th grade is at the high 3rd-grade level and plateaus at the 5th-grade level in senior high school.

3. Most adolescents with learning disabilities are deficient in study skills. A majority of the students perform poorly in such areas as test-taking skills, note taking, listening comprehension, monitoring writing errors, and scanning.

4. Many adolescents with learning disabilities exhibit social skills deficiencies. Social skills problem areas include accepting negative feedback, giving feedback, negotiating, and resisting peer pressure.

5. Many adolescents with learning disabilities have deficits related to the demands of settings (e.g., school, work) in which they are required to participate and be successful.

The Adult with Learning Disabilities. Traditionally, the adult with learning disabilities has not received much examination. With the growing realization that individuals with learning disabilities continue to have unique needs as they attend college, enter employment, or begin facing the demands of being self-sufficient citizens, information about these individuals is accruing rapidly. Horn, O'Donnell, and Vitulano (1983) reviewed the literature published since 1960 on the long-term outcome of individuals with learning disabilities. Their analysis uncovers a variety of conflicting results, but some factors contribute to favorable and unfavorable outcomes. Their most pertinent observations include the following:

1. For most individuals with learning disabilities, basic academic skill deficits persist into adulthood. This finding seems to be highly correlated with lower socioeconomic status and severity of initial academic deficits as reflected in achievement and IQ measures.

2. Follow-ups of educational/vocational attainments of individuals with learning disabilities reveal some positive findings. For example, Horn et al. report "convincing evidence that LD persons do attain educational levels and vocational status commensurate with normal learners in the general population" (p. 553). This finding suggests that many adults with learning disabilities compensate for their academic skill deficits. Also, evidence indicates that adults with learning disabilities tend to become involved in education and vocations that do not rely heavily on verbal skills. In addition, these comparable educational/vocational attainments take longer for the person with learning disabilities to achieve than the normal learner.

3. The follow-up studies of the social-emotional adjustments of individuals with learning disabilities yield mixed results. Horn et al. note that additional research is needed to determine definitive directions regarding emotional/behavioral adjustments. To date, some studies support poor adjustment and some indicate good adjustment. In a study of 911 high school graduates with learning disabilities, Sitlington and Frank (1990) report that 54% met the following criteria: (1) employed or "meaningfully engaged," (2) living independently or with a relative, (3) paying a portion of their expenses, and (4) involved in more than one leisure activity.

Heterogeneity of Learning Disabilities

Most special educators agree that students with learning disabilities are a heterogeneous group. Theoretically, a child may qualify as having a learning disability by exhibiting a discrepancy between ability and achievement in one or more of the seven areas listed in the IDEA criteria and by satisfying the conditions of the exclusion clause. Thus, a student who exhibits just one academic discrepancy problem is labeled as having a learning disability, and so is one who has discrepancies in all or any combination of the seven areas. Thus, within the guidelines of the IDEA and other prominent definitions, there are numerous types of learning disabilities (e.g., math group, written expression group). Moreover, many professionals agree that there is a much broader range of learning disability characteristics beyond those included in the IDEA definition. Theoretically, an individual with learning disabilities could have one or all of the many cognitive or social-emotional problems that students with learning disabilities often exhibit. When the severity or degree of each problem area is considered, the possible characteristics are enormous. The heterogeneous nature of learning disabilities does not mean that the category is too nebulous to exist; however, it does remind professionals of the complexity of students with learning disabilities, and it behooves them to follow certain guidelines:

1. Outside the common denominator of having a discrepancy in (an) academic area(s), educators must consider each individual with learning disabilities as having a unique set of cognitive and social-emotional behaviors.

2. Professionals must avoid stereotypic descriptions of individuals with learning disabilities that assign characteristics that may or may not exist.

3. Professionals must delineate the subgroups of learning disabilities. As McKinney (1984) points out, "The emerging literature on LD subtypes supports a multiple syndrome approach to theory in the field and offers a new paradigm for research which seems to accommodate the heterogeneity produced by the complex collection of disorders encompassed" (p. 49).

4. Educators must approach each student with learning disabilities with the viewpoint that "no two are exactly alike" and, thus, educational and behavioral interventions must be tailored to individual needs.

Although results are not conclusive, research of subtyping is yielding some preliminary clusters. Basically, three subtypes are emerging: (1) a language deficit group; (2) a visual deficit group; and (3) a behaviorally impaired group (Bender & Golden, 1990). In addition, several researchers (Lyon, 1985; Swanson, 1988; Swanson et al., 1990; Torgesen, 1988) are examining memory variables in relation to subtypes of students with learning disabilities. Lyon (1985) and Torgesen (1988) suggest remedial reading strategies for a subgroup of students with learning disabilities with serious memory deficits. Kavale and Forness (1987) point out that subtyping research will make meaningful contributions to the degree that it leads to the discovery of educationally relevant subgroups for which effective treatments are identified. Future subtyping research will be followed with guarded optimism to see if it leads to more precise identification and treatment of students with learning disabilities.

The heterogeneity of learning disabilities does not imply that a different treatment is necessary for each individual. Direct and systematic educational and behavioral interventions are effective across a large number of students with all types of characteristics. Intensity of an intervention, as well as the various kinds of interventions, must be considered as important factors in planning instruction.

ASSESSMENT Determination of a learning disability begins by an examination of the parameters that define it, with the heterogeneous nature of the population taken into account. Some investigators focus primarily on the student's academic disabilities, whereas others stress attention, memory, perceptual, social-emotional, or motor problems. The debate over the importance of various parameters of learning disabilities is likely to continue for some time. Meanwhile, the identification criteria in the federal regulations and those noted by authorities in the field should be considered. (See the Model Program box for a description of a comprehensive multidisciplinary diagnostic and training program.)

Assessing Specific Components of a Learning Disability

Mercer et al. (1990) report that learning disability definitions used by state departments of education usually include an exclusion factor and statements about academic and language achievement and process. The Individuals with Disabilities Education Act (IDEA) definition includes the exclusion, academic, and language components but omits the process area (involving the ability to process information). As noted earlier, federal regulations also include a discrepancy factor that many consider to be the common denominator of learning disabilities. Popularized by Bateman (1964), the discrepancy factor refers to the difference between a learner's estimated ability and actual achievement. Mercer et al. report that 86% of the states include the discrepancy component in their identification criteria. Likewise, Frankenberger and Fronzaglio (1991) note that 77% of the states recommend using discrepancy criteria to identify learning disabilities.

Exclusion Component.   The exclusion component is a major component in state criteria for identifying learning disabilities (Chalfant, 1985; Mercer et al., 1990). Factors such as hearing and vision may be checked before undertaking an extensive examination for learning disabilities. The following exclusions are appropriate in view of the IDEA regulations:

1. Mental retardation, as evidenced by a score of not less than minus 2 standard deviations on an individual test of intelligence, with interpretation by a certified psychologist
2. Blindness or partial sight, as evidenced by visual acuity in the better eye with best possible correction of 20/70 or better
3. Deafness or impaired hearing, as evidenced by auditory acuity with no more than a 30-dB loss in the better ear unaided, and speech and language learned through normal channels
4. Physical disabilities, with no evidence of primary physical disabilities directly related to the student's problem areas
5. Emotional disturbance so severe as to require a therapeutic program
6. Environmental or cultural disadvantage

Exclusion factors 2, 3, and 4 require a physical exam or a check of a recent medical record. Factors 1 and 5 require testing by a psychologist. Factor 6 usually is documented by testing and teaching in the student's native language, reviewing anecdotal records, and conducting interviews and obtaining background information (perhaps with a social worker's help) on cultural factors and experiences.

Academic Achievement Component.   Assessment of academic achievement continues to be a major factor in identifying students with learning disabilities. Academic achievement problems usually are interpreted within the ability-achievement discrepancy factor included in the IDEA identification criteria. Common areas of assessment are reading (word recognition and comprehension), math (calculation and reasoning), and written expression.

Although informal measures, curriculum-based assessment, and criterion tests are used extensively in the area of academic achievement, assessment of academic areas for identification purposes involves primarily the use of standardized tests. Scores are reported in a variety of ways (e.g., grade level, age level, percentile, stanine, scaled score). Many authorities (Salvia & Ysseldyke, 1991) discourage the use of grade-level scores in favor of the use of scaled scores.

Language Achievement Component. Language is typically evaluated by standardized tests in listening comprehension and oral expression. In language assessment it is important to distinguish between the production of oral language (i.e., a student's voice quality and articulation) and the linguistic qualities of oral expression (i.e., morphology, semantics, syntax, pragmatics). Moreover, language assessment may focus on receptive abilities (listening comprehension) or expressive abilities (oral expression). The *Goldman-Fristoe Test of Articulation* frequently is used to assess articulation and has excellent psychometric properties (Salvia & Ysseldyke, 1991). The *Test of Language Development–2* and the *Clinical Evaluation of Language Fundamentals—Revised* are used to measure general language functioning. These are only a few of the language tests used in this assessment area.

Process Component. The process component, highly criticized for having nebulous constructs and measurement problems, continues to be considered by many professionals as illusive and difficult to research. Chalfant (1985) reports that the area of students' information processing should be included but that the assessment of it needs to be improved. Mercer et al. (1990) report that although the process factor is included in 92% of the learning disability definitions used by state departments of education, only 22% of the states include it in their identification criteria. Moreover, it is not included in the IDEA procedures on evaluation.

All standardized tests used in the process area are inadequate. Though some tests have acceptable reliability, none exhibits convincing evidence of empirical validity (Arter & Jenkins, 1979). The analysis of subtest scores on tests of intelligence or ability (e.g., WISC–III, K–ABC, *Woodcock-Johnson Psycho-Educational Battery–Revised*) often is used to assess problems. Chalfant (1985) recommends that the results of standardized tests of process abilities be validated by observations of student performances on classroom tasks that require the process being measured. Unless observations are consistent with the test results, the designation of a process deficit should not be made. Finally, Chalfant notes that it is crucial that technically adequate measures be developed in the process area.

Discrepancy Component. The discrepancy component is basic to the identification of learning disabilities. As specified in the identification criteria of IDEA, a severe discrepancy is defined as an individual's failure to achieve in one of the seven areas commensurate with his or her age and ability. Moreover, the gap between achievement and intellectual ability must be large enough to result in a "severe discrepancy." Mercer et al. (1990) and Frankenberger and Fronzaglio (1991) found that most states are attempting to operationalize the discrepancy (that is, establish operational definitions in terms of student performance) as part of their criteria for identifying students with learning disabilities.

Individual tests of intelligence such as the WISC–III, the K–ABC, and the *Stanford-Binet Intelligence Scale* (Form L–M, 1972 norms edition) usually are used to measure intellectual ability. Achievement in one or more of the seven areas is assessed via standardized tests. For determining a severe discrepancy, a multitude of procedures have been reported (Chalfant, 1985; Cone & Wilson, 1981; Keogh, 1987; Mercer et al. 1990). Cone and Wilson discuss several procedures (grade-level deviation, expectancy formula, standard score comparisons, regression analysis) for quantifying a discrepancy and conclude that standard score comparisons and regression equations are potentially viable methods for operationalizing discrepancy. (For a discussion of the controversies and issues of operationalizing the discrepancy component, see Finlan [1992] and Swanson [1991].)

INTERVENTION

The Individuals with Disabilities Education Act (IDEA) identifies a learning disability, accompanied by a severe discrepancy in specific learning areas. as a condition that requires special education. Some educators mistakenly view all learning disabilities as mild learning problems and conclude that learning disabilities should be served entirely within the regular classroom or, at most, in a resource room. Learning disabilities include disabling conditions that range from mild to severe (Weller, 1980), making necessary a full spectrum of service arrangements for students with learning disabilities. The service or placement options for students with learning disabilities include a regular class with a consultant teacher, resource room, a special class, a special day school, and a residential school. The resource room is now the most common service arrangement. Affleck, Madge, Adams, and Lowenbraun (1988) conducted a study comparing an integrated classroom model with the resource room model. Comparing the achievement of students with learning disabilities in both models, they found no differences. The integrated classroom model enabled the students with learning disabilities to remain with normally achieving peers throughout the day and was more cost-effective than the resource room model. Because the integrated classroom model is a less restrictive environment than the resource room and produces similar student gains at a lower cost, Affleck et al. suggest it as a viable placement alternative for students with mild disabilities.

With the numerous placement options available, it often is difficult to select the best one. About 18% of students with learning disabilities receive instruction entirely within regular classrooms, 59% are served in both resource rooms and regular classrooms, and 22% are in self-contained classes (U.S. Department of Education, 1990). Children with learning disabilities have a wide range of needs, and schools vary in the types of resources available. Thus, needs and resources must be examined *student by student* and not be guided by trends or philosophies insensitive to the uniqueness of the student.

CURRICULUM IMPLICATIONS

Curriculum planning for students with learning disabilities is influenced to a large degree by the theories of the curriculum planners regarding learning disabilities. These theories affect program content and teaching strategies. Which skills are emphasized, how they are taught, and how their mastery contributes to the overall education of a student with learning disabilities are issues determined by the curriculum developer's perspective.

Language Programs and Materials

More research needs to be conducted before definitive conclusions can be drawn concerning the effectiveness of language programs with students with learning disabilities. However, numerous commercial language programs and materials are available for teaching students who have language-learning disabilities. Because language is interactive, no single program is appropriate for use alone, and the teacher should select programs based on the language needs of the individual students.

Clinical Language Intervention Program.   This program (Semel & Wiig, 1982) is used to teach semantics, syntax, memory, and pragmatics to students in kindergarten through 8th grade. It includes over 2,000 stimulus pictures, matching verbal stimuli, suggested task formats for intervention, and activities for generalization training to other situations. Strategies for individualization of materials are offered. Also included are a teacher's guide with suggested methods and strategies, a picture manual, an activities manual, and a progress checklist.

DISTAR Language.   Originally developed for culturally disadvantaged children in Head Start programs, DISTAR *Language* (Engelmann & Osborn, 1976) is a highly structured approach to language intervention. It is designed for students in preschool through 3rd grade and focuses on expressive and receptive language and cognitive development. The program uses a didactic approach, with repetitive group drills, to teach higher concepts. Following a script, the teacher models, elicits group and individual responses at a fast pace, and reinforces the appropriate response or corrects the inappropriate response. Various language skills are taught such as identity statements, pronouns, prepositions, and multiple attributes. A teacher's guide and all materials are packaged in a kit.

Let's Talk: Developing Pro-Social Communication Skills.   Wiig (1982) designed this program to develop and strengthen the prosocial communication skills of students from the age of 9 to adult. Practice in functional communication is provided through prescribed training activities and communication card games. Students learn to express positive and negative feelings; present, understand, and respond to information in spoken messages; adapt messages to the needs of others; and approach conversations with expectations of what to say and how to say it.

Multisensory Approaches

Multisensory approaches are based on the premise that learning is facilitated for some students if information is received through several senses rather than just one or two (vision and hearing). Frequently, kinesthetic and tactile stimulation are used along with visual and auditory stimulation. The multisensory programs that feature seeing, hearing, tracing, and writing often are referred to as VAKT (visual-auditory-kinesthetic-tactile) programs. To increase tactile and kinesthetic stimulation, sandpaper letters, finger paint, sand trays, and raised and sunken letters are used.

The Fernald (1943, 1988) method and the Gillingham and Stillman (1970) method are reading approaches based on VAKT instruction. The Fernald method stresses whole-word learning. The Gillingham-Stillman method derives from the work of Orton (1937) and features sound blending, the process of taking isolated sounds and blending them into a word. Slingerland (1971) adapted this approach to develop a multisensory language arts program for students with learning disabilities.

Another multisensory approach, used with individuals who have severe reading problems, is the neurological impress method (Heckelman, 1969; Langford, Slade, & Barnett, 1974). In this approach the student and teacher read together, aloud and rapidly. The student follows by moving a finger along the words. It is reasoned that hearing the words provides stimulation and feedback. The research on this method, however, is inconclusive.

Multisensory approaches feature distinct instructional procedures and may be viewed as independent of specific content. These procedures often are used with individuals who have severe learning problems.

Data-Based Instruction

Data-based instruction is a widely used approach to teaching. It has its roots in applied behavior analysis, direct instruction, and criterion-referenced instruction. It is a direct skill instructional model that focuses on the direct and continuous measurement of student progress toward specific instructional objectives (Blankenship & Lilly, 1981). Many educators (Alberto & Troutman, 1990; Kerr & Nelson, 1989; Tindal & Marston, 1990) agree that it holds much promise for current and future teaching practices. The major features of data-based instruction include selecting a target skill, selecting a measurement system, collecting and graphing data, setting instructional aims, analyzing data, and making instructional decisions. The student's progress toward mastering the targeted behavior is tested regularly—often daily—through the number of correct and incorrect responses given in a specific time period (frequently 1 minute). The rate of performance is emphasized. Teachers record the daily performance of each student and graph the results. Mastery usually is defined in terms of a certain rate of correct responses (e.g., reading 100 to 140 words per minute with 2 or fewer errors).

Basic Guidelines of Data-Based Instruction. Howell, Kaplan, and O'Connell (1979) offer several guidelines for implementing data-based instruction by means of precision teaching:

1. Initially count only priority behaviors.
2. Identify strategies to make the timing and recording of behavior easier.
3. Evaluate the recorded data frequently.
4. Use probes or criterion-referenced tests.
5. Make sure the system remains a tool for teaching rather than a "cause." Use precision teaching only so long as it helps the student.

White (1986) details the salient features of data-based teaching and discusses highly successful programs.

Commentary on Data-Based Instruction. In a national survey of 136 learning disabilities teachers, Wesson, King, and Deno (1984) found that the majority (53.6%) of learning disabilities teachers (N = 110) who knew of direct and frequent measurement used it; those not using it felt it was too time-consuming. Wesson et al. report that the time involved in direct and frequent measurement need not be extensive. Fuchs, Wesson, Tindal, Mirkin, and Deno (1981) report the results of a study in which teachers were trained to reduce by 80% the time they spent in direct measurement (e.g., preparing, directing, scoring, graphing). According to Wesson et al. (1984), "Trained and experienced teachers require only 2 minutes to prepare for, administer, score, and graph student performance" (p. 48). They also report that direct and frequent measurement is no more time-consuming than other evaluation activities.

Direct Instruction

Instructing students on appropriate tasks under conditions that motivate them requires careful planning and monitoring of progress. To deliver this type of individualized programming, the teacher must be highly organized. This highly organized approach to instruction often is called *direct* or *systematic instruction*. Many studies support or encourage the use of direct instruction for students with learning problems (Brophy & Good, 1986; Carnine, 1989; Englert, 1984; Gersten et al., 1987; Stephens, 1977). According to Rosenshine (1978),

> Direct instruction refers to high levels of student engagement within academically focused, teacher-directed classrooms using sequenced, structured materials. . . . [D]irect instruction refers to teaching activities focused on academic matters where goals are clear to students; time allocated for instruction is sufficient and continuous; content coverage is extensive; student performance is monitored; questions are at a low cognitive level and produce many correct responses; and feedback to students is immediate and academically oriented. In direct instruction, the teacher *controls* instructional goals, *chooses* material appropriate for the student's ability level, and *paces* the instructional episode. Interaction is characterized as structured, but not authoritarian; rather, learning takes place in a convivial academic atmosphere. (p. 17)

Gersten et al. (1986) expand Rosenshine's definition of direct instruction to include curriculum design. Gersten et al. (1987) note the key principle of direct instruction: "For all students to learn, both the curriculum materials and teacher presentation of these materials must be clear and unambiguous. While many writers treat curriculum design and effective teaching as separate strands, practitioners play them in concert" (pp. 48–49). Gersten et al. (1987) list six critical features of direct instruction:

1. An explicit step-by-step strategy
2. Development of mastery at each step in the process
3. Strategy (or process) corrections for student errors
4. Gradual fading from teacher-directed activities toward independent work
5. Use of adequate, systematic practice with a range of examples
6. Cumulative review of newly learned concepts (p. 49)

Students with learning disabilities, by definition, exhibit deficits in academic performance. The direct instruction approach concentrates on improving specific academic skills without dealing with inferred process deficits. In a review of the literature, Treiber and Lahey (1983) state, "This is not to say that learning disabled children do not have process deficits; rather that direct treatment of these inferred deficits is neither possible nor necessary for academic improvements to occur. This assertion is not a statement of faith, but rather a conclusion based on empirical evidence" (p. 113). Treiber and Lahey discuss literature that indicates the success of direct instruction with students with learning disabilities across academic areas of reading comprehension, handwriting, letter identification, sight-word vocabulary, math, and oral reading.

One line of direct instruction research that appears encouraging for the nineties involves the teaching of higher-order skills (e.g., literary analysis, chemistry, legal reasoning, problem solving, critical reading, ratio and proportions, social studies, and syllogistic reasoning) to at-risk and special education students at levels comparable to those of their advantaged peers (Carnine, 1989, 1990). Gersten et al. (1987) note that the following principles are emerging for teaching higher-order skills:

1. Before learning cognitively complex skills, students need explicit direct instruction in relevant facts and concepts.
2. The teaching of open-ended processes in which a range of responses is appropriate necessitates clear models of successful solutions; a range of examples; and specific, corrective feedback.

Finally, the teaching of these higher-order skills is being implemented successfully through videodisk instruction. Perhaps today's technology will encourage more systematic use of direct instruction in school districts across the nation.

Many teachers use direct or systematic instruction for students with academic learning difficulties.

Cognitive Instruction

It is apparent that many students with learning disabilities are deficient in numerous aspects of cognitive functioning. They have been described as "inactive learners," "passive learners," and "strategy-deficient learners" across a variety of cognitive processes including attention, memory, comprehension, and problem solving (Hallahan & Reeve, 1980; Lloyd, 1980; Loper, 1980; Torgesen, 1977). These deficiencies of children with learning disabilities underscore the need to develop interventions that facilitate the use of cognitive strategies and improved academic learning.

Turnure (1985, 1986) suggests that research on cognitive development should examine interaction between the following dimensions: (1) the characteristics of the learner (e.g., skills, knowledge, attitudes); (2) the learning activities (e.g., attention, discrimination, rehearsal); (3) the nature of the criterion task (e.g., recognition, recall, transfer); (4) the nature of the materials (e.g., sequencing, structure, appearance, difficulty); and (5) the instructional agent (e.g., how the teacher describes, questions, sequences instruction, models). Turnure suggests that the teacher is the central organizer of the various dimensions of instruction. A model that emphasizes the teacher's role as the primary "learning situation organizer" places great responsibility on the teacher. Inherent in such a model is the assumption that the teacher has sufficient knowledge and experience to enhance learning and successfully make decisions that provide for an appropriate balance among the instructional dimensions.

Lenz, Bulgren, and Hudson (1990) note that the concept of "information-processing sensitive instruction" refers to instruction with the following characteristics:

1. Is fashioned and differentially delivered based on the teacher's knowledge of the range of the information-processing and communication abilities of students (Deshler, Alley, Warner, & Schumaker, 1981)
2. Promotes student attention or reception of incoming information (Lenz, Alley, & Schumaker, 1987; Mayer, 1987)
3. Promotes the activation of strategies that enable the student to access and integrate prior knowledge with to-be-learned information (Ausubel, 1960; Lenz et al., 1987; Mayer, 1983)
4. Promotes the activation of strategies that enable the student to build logical or structural connections between and among incoming ideas and ideas already in memory (Bulgren, Schumaker, & Deshler, 1988; Mayer, 1987)
5. Promotes the active participation of the student in the learning process as a planner, implementor, and evaluator (Hughes, Schumaker, Deshler, & Mercer, 1988; Van Reusen, Bos, Schumaker, & Deshler, 1987)
6. Instructs the student in the "why, when, and where" aspects of information related to the use of knowledge (Brown, Day, & Jones, 1983; Lenz & Hughes, 1990)
7. Informs the student of progress and provides appropriate feedback in a manner that improves learning (Kline, Schumaker, & Deshler, 1991; Palincsar & Brown, 1984)
8. Leads the student in the learning process through expert scaffolding and proleptic teaching (Deshler & Schumaker, 1988; Vygotsky, 1978)
9. Takes advantage of the developmental and social contexts of learning by gradually moving from adult guidance and modeling to peer and student guidance and modeling (Allington, 1984; Lenz, Schumaker, Deshler, & Beals, 1984; Palincsar & Brown, 1984; Vygotsky, 1978)

10. Plans for and promotes the acquisition and integration of semantic, procedural, and strategic knowledge throughout all phases and types of instruction (Mayer, 1987)

Programming for Adolescents with Learning Disabilities

This section on programming for adolescents with learning disabilities features a functionalist cognitive approach to instruction. Specifically, learning strategies that have been successful are highlighted.

The provision of secondary programs for students with learning disabilities is relatively new. Successful demonstration programs have been developed in many states, and the federal government has funded several projects (Riegel & Mathey, 1980). Although few programs have been validated empirically, the recent surge of programs and literature has increased knowledge about secondary programming for learning disabilities.

Analysis of Academic Demands.   Deshler and associates at the University of Kansas Institute for Research in Learning Disabilities have examined the demands placed on students in secondary mainstream classrooms. Schumaker and Deshler (1984) summarize the literature and discuss their findings in three general areas: (1) work habit demands, (2) knowledge acquisition demands, and (3) knowledge expression demands. Work habit demands require that students be able to work independently with minimum feedback or help from the teacher. Students must be able to complete assignments and follow classroom rules. Knowledge acquisition demands are numerous. Students must be able to listen to presentations and take accurate notes. They must gain information from materials written at a secondary level, and they must be able to study. Knowledge expression demands are vital to success at the secondary level. Students must be able to demonstrate their knowledge on classroom tests and on minimum competency tests. They also must be able to express themselves in writing—in both descriptive and narrative prose. In addition, they must participate in classroom discussions.

Motivation.   Motivation to learn or participate is essential to the success of any intervention approach. For the adolescent with learning disabilities, lack of motivation is often a roadblock to school success.

A variety of motivation techniques are available to help low achievers in high school. Deshler, Schumaker, and Lenz (1984) divide the approaches into two broad categories: (1) those using extrinsic controls and (2) those focusing on developing intrinsic motivation. From their review of motivation studies, Deshler et al. report several extrinsic control techniques that have been used successfully to improve the academic skills of adolescents with learning disabilities. The most useful techniques involve token economies, contingency contracting, and verbal feedback. Techniques aimed at facilitating intrinsic motivation also are receiving support. Schumaker et al. (1983) report that the focus on the motivation component at the University of Kansas Institute for Research in Learning Disabilities is to produce independent and active learners. To accomplish this goal, the intervention is aimed at training self-control skills, including one or more of the following: goal setting, self-recording of progress, self-evaluation, and self-reinforcement. Rooney and Hallahan (1988) investigated the effects of self-monitoring instruction on the behavior of middle school students with learning disabilities. They found that self-monitoring enabled the students to work more independently and maintain high levels of attention without adult assistance. Deshler et al. report that self-control training holds much promise for helping students with learning disabilities complete their assignments. They note that the training procedures are implemented easily and do not depend on expensive extrinsic reinforcers.

From their review of the motivation literature, Adelman and Taylor (1983a) list tactics for enhancing intrinsic motivation, including the following:

1. Reinforce the student's perception that learning is worthwhile by providing choices in curriculum content and procedures. Discussions concerning the relevance (real-life applications) of various content also are helpful.
2. Through discussion, obtain a commitment to those options the student values and indicates a desire to pursue. Contractual agreements are helpful.
3. Hold informal and formal conferences with the student to enhance his or her role in making choices and negotiating agreements.
4. Provide feedback that conveys student progress. The student must not perceive the feedback as an effort to entice or control. To this end, self-correcting materials are useful.

One recurring theme in the literature on managing and motivating adolescents with learning disabilities is the need to involve the student. In their discussion of secondary classroom management, Kerr and Nelson (1989) state, "We strongly recommend that you encourage pupils to participate in all aspects of the curriculum. Specifically, they should be involved in selecting and ordering their own academic and social goals, in making decisions about the classroom structure, and in setting consequences and contingencies" (p. 157).

Another dimension that can be included in efforts to promote student motivation relates to the beliefs that students have about themselves. Many students do not believe that they can learn or change. Ellis, Deshler, Lenz, Schumaker, and Clark (1991) present four techniques for teachers to use to help students alter their beliefs about their learning and performance:

1. Engineer instructional arrangements to promote and reinforce student independence.
2. Communicate high expectations for students through words and actions.
3. Help students identify and analyze beliefs that underlie their behavior as ineffective learners.
4. Help students discard unproductive beliefs through a variety of activities and interactions.

Social Skills Training. The social skills deficits of many adolescents with learning disabilities are becoming well documented (Baum, Duffelmeyer, & Geelan, 1988). Numerous authorities (Deshler & Schumaker, 1983; Schumaker & Hazel, 1984; Zigmond & Brownlee, 1980) recommend social skills training for students with learning disabilities. It is felt that social skills development helps the adolescent with learning disabilities in several ways:

1. Social competence helps compensate for academic deficits.
2. Social skills are needed for success in the mainstream and in employment.
3. Social skills training helps adolescents with learning disabilities derive maximum benefit from academic and vocational instruction.
4. Social competence is fundamental to good interpersonal relationships and fosters improved leisure and recreational activities.

Zigmond and her colleagues at the University of Pittsburgh and Deshler and his associates at the University of Kansas are developing social skills curricula for adolescents with learning disabilities. Zigmond's curriculum, the School Survival Skills Curriculum, features three strands: (1) behavior control; (2) teacher-pleasing behaviors; and (3) study skills (Silverman, Zigmond, & Sansone, 1981). The curriculum developed at the University of Kansas Institute for Research in Learning Disabilities, *Social Skills for Daily Living*, focuses on such skills as resisting peer pressure, accepting and giving compliments, asking and answering questions, making friends, responding to teasing, following instructions, apologizing, and joining group activities (Schumaker, Hazel, & Pederson, 1988).

Interpersonal social skills also can be taught through direct instruction. Schumaker and Hazel (1984) discuss four types of instructional interventions that have been used to facilitate the acquisition of social skills:

1. *Description*: Primarily oral techniques in which the teacher describes how to perform a skill appropriately
2. *Modeling*: Demonstrations of the social skill by live models or by film, audiotape, or pictorial models
3. *Rehearsal*: Verbal rehearsal of required skill steps to ensure that the individual has memorized the steps in sequence and can instruct himself or herself in what to do next, and structured practice (e.g., role-play activities) whereby the learner attempts to perform the skill
4. *Feedback*: Verbal feedback following rehearsal to inform the individual on which steps were performed well and which behaviors need improvement

Frequently, combinations of these procedures are included in social skills training interventions.

Another technique that has proven effective in developing the social skills of students with learning disabilities is peer instruction. Strain and Odom (1986) examined the effects of peer trainers on social skills development and found that use of this technique increased social responding, social initiations, and length of exchanges for target students.

Learning Strategies.   To help students with learning disabilities cope with the complex demands of secondary curricula, Alley and Deshler (1979) recommend a learning strategies approach. Learning strategies are defined as techniques, principles,

Peer instruction sometimes helps to develop the social skills of students with learning disabilities.

or rules that enable a student to learn, solve problems, and complete tasks independently. This approach is not designed to teach specific course content but to help students develop and use the skills necessary to acquire, store, and express content. Basically, it focuses on teaching students how to learn and how to demonstrate command of their knowledge in performing academic tasks. For example, a reading strategy may be used by a student with 5th-grade reading skills to obtain relevant information from a textbook chapter written at the 10th-grade level. Deshler and his colleagues at the University of Kansas Institute for Research in Learning Disabilities developed a learning strategies curriculum, and its components have been specified, developed, and validated in classrooms. Field-testing and evaluation data indicate good student progress and a high degree of consumer satisfaction (Schumaker et al., 1983). In addition, Cronin and Currie (1984) provide a comprehensive resource guide on learning strategies and study skills that may be helpful to the secondary teacher in developing a learning strategies curriculum.

The teaching methods used with students exhibiting learning problems are crucial to the success of the instruction. The staff at the University of Kansas Institute for Research in Learning Disabilities developed and validated a teaching sequence that is

Table 4–5

Learning strategies curriculum of the University of Kansas Institute for Research in Learning Disabilities

Acquisition	Storage	Expression and Demonstration of Competence
Word identification	First-letter mnemonic	Sentence writing
Paraphrasing	Paired associates	Paragraph writing
Self-questioning	Listening and note taking	Error monitoring
Visual imagery		Theme writing
Interpreting visuals		Assignment completion
Multipass		Test taking

based on sound learning principles. These acquisition steps provide the student with the knowledge, motivation, and practice required to apply a skill or strategy to materials and situations comparable to those found in regular secondary classrooms (Schumaker et al., 1983).

The learning strategies curriculum organized by Deshler and his colleagues features strategies to help in the acquisition, storage, and expression/demonstration areas (see Table 4–5).[1]

Curriculum Alternatives.   When the adolescent with learning disabilities with his or her complex needs enters the secondary setting with its extensive demands, the need for a diversity of services becomes apparent. At least seven types of program services are required: academic remediation, instruction in learning strategies, content instruction, social development instruction, training in functional living skills, career-related instruction, and transition instruction (Mercer & Mercer, 1993). No one service approach is appropriate for all adolescents with learning disabilities. Deshler, Schumaker, Lenz, and Ellis (1984) report that the real challenge is not in determining which approach is right or wrong but in ascertaining under what conditions and with whom a given service is most effective.

In the planning of programs for adolescents with learning disabilities, many questions arise: Should basic skill instruction continue throughout the high school years? Should the student with learning disabilities take regular content area courses? Should the curriculum emphasize functional living skills? Should vocational training be stressed? Answers to these questions depend, of course, on the individual needs of each student. Some students with learning disabilities are able to complete regular courses. Many continue their education in colleges or trade schools. Others work to acquire vocational and functional living skills to prepare them for productive life after

---

1   Additional information can be obtained by contacting the Coordinator of Training, Institute for Research in Learning Disabilities, 3061 Robert Dole Human Development Center, The University of Kansas, Lawrence, KS 66045–2342 (913/864–4780).

MODEL PROGRAM

The University of Florida Multidisciplinary Diagnostic and Training Program (MDTP) is a team of professionals from neurology, psychology, language, and special education who serve children in kindergarten through 6th grade who have complex medical, behavioral, or learning problems. Although the majority of the children have learning disabilities or emotional disabilities, students from all exceptionalities have been served by MDTP. After a student is referred—from 1 of 12 school districts in north and central Florida—an MDTP liaison teacher visits the student's classroom for observation and consultation with the teachers. Next, the student goes to the University of Florida campus for a medical and language evaluation at J. Hillis Miller Health Center and an educational and psychological evaluation at the College of Education. After the evaluations are completed, a case conference is held with school district personnel and MDTP staff. At this conference a diagnosis is determined and intervention plans for the student are detailed.

It may be decided to return the student to his or her home school and to assign the MDTP liaison teacher to consult with local school personnel to implement the intervention plan, or the decision may be made to enroll the student in the MDTP diagnostic and training classroom. This class is located in the College of Education, and the student may attend it for a period of from 1 to 6 weeks. Students attending the class receive intensive treatment aimed at documenting effective teaching and management strategies for each individual. Data-based instruction is used to determine the effectiveness of instructional programs (e.g., reading, language, math, spelling) and management techniques (e.g., point system, contingency contracts, parent involvement). When effective interventions are documented, the student's local school teacher visits the class to observe and learn the interventions. Then the student is returned to his or her local school, and the MDTP liaison teacher continues to consult with the teacher to implement the intervention plan. To date, over 200 children have attended the diagnostic class, and all have made excellent progress in their problem areas. Much emphasis is placed on designing interventions that are feasible to implement in the school districts. Peer teaching, learning strategies, direct instruction, self-correcting materials, computer-assisted instruction, instructional games, contingency contracts, parent management training, and data-based teaching are some of the techniques that are used extensively.

In addition to serving hundreds of students with complex problems, MDTP is a valuable resource for preservice and inservice training in special education, curriculum and instruction, counselor education, speech and language, educational psychology, and medicine. Moreover, the parent training component offers services to parents and provides university students with the opportunity to be involved with parent training. The program operates at no cost to the families of the children.

Although the advantages of MDTP are numerous, some disadvantages do exist. The expense of the program would prohibit some school districts and universities from implementing it. Also, because the diagnostic classroom is well equipped and has a low pupil-teacher ratio, some teachers think it is impossible to teach these students in their own classroom settings, which may lack these features.

John J. Ross, M.D., is director of the program.

high school. The secondary program should include basic placement options relevant to the student's long-range development and should support those options with a strong counseling program.

Madeleine Will, assistant secretary for the Office of Special Education and Rehabilitative Services in the Reagan administration, and other educators (Reynolds, 1989; Stainback & Stainback, 1987; Wang, Reynolds, & Walberg, 1986) advocate a system of service delivery to special education students referred to as the Regular Education Initiative (REI). The REI includes major revisions in how services are provided to students with learning disabilities. The REI emerged because Will (1986) and several of her colleagues (Wang, Reynolds, & Walberg, 1986) maintain that negative consequences occur when special education students are separated from their normally achieving peers to receive instructional services.

Mainstreaming derives from the least restrictive environment concept implicit in the REI and refers to the practice of integrating students with disabilities socially and instructionally into regular education as much as possible. In school A, the placement of a student with learning disabilities in a full-time mainstream program may be the least restrictive environment, whereas in school B, part-time placement in a resource room would be the least restrictive environment for the same student. The difference in scenario exists because the quality of services varies across districts, schools, teachers, and placements. School A has several regular teachers who are excellent at tailoring instruction to meet the needs of students with learning disabilities. School B has a learning disabilities resource teacher who does an excellent job of teaching students to achieve academic gains and use learning strategies to become more independent learners. Unfortunately, the regular teachers at school B in this student's grade level are not sensitive to the instructional needs of students with learning disabilities. The variations in mainstream settings led Bender and his associates (Bender & Ukeje, 1989) to research why some mainstream teachers receive students with learning disabilities and tailor instruction appropriately, whereas other teachers respond negatively to mainstreaming. This condition is a core issue concerning the REI.

When the instructional and social needs of students with learning disabilities are met in mainstream settings, then mainstreaming is the most appropriate placement. The question of what constitutes an effective mainstream program is becoming increasingly important. Research on the efficacy of mainstreaming has been inconclusive (Carlberg & Kavale, 1980). Several investigators (Gottlieb, 1981; Gresham, 1982) report that mainstreaming has not resulted in significant social and educational growth for learners with disabilities. Others (Haring & Krug, 1975; Macy & Carter, 1978) report that regular class placements have had positive effects on students with disabilities. Coleman, Pullis, and Minnett (1987) state that these mixed findings are in part the result of a lack of precise guidelines for implementing and investigating mainstreaming.

Several researchers (Wang & Baker, 1985, 1986; Waxman, Wang, Anderson, & Walberg, 1985) reviewed empirical studies of adaptive instruction used in mainstream settings. They identified the following instructional features as promoting successful mainstreaming:

1. An instructional match is maintained for each student.
2. Individualized pacing for achieving instructional goals is maintained.
3. Student progress is monitored, and continuous feedback is provided.
4. Students are involved in the planning and monitoring of their learning.
5. A broad range of techniques and materials is used.
6. Students help each other to learn.
7. Students are taught self-management skills.
8. Teachers engage in instructional teaming.

Although the REI has theoretical appeal and promising directions, existing realities remind professionals that the data are lacking for eliminating the special education service alternatives. There is evidence that students with learning disabilities, as well as other students with learning problems, are not making acceptable progress. "Business as usual" is not acceptable in either mainstream or more segregated settings. Changes are needed and must be implemented according to a systematic plan that incorporates what is known about the change process in schools (Gersten & Woodward, 1990; Loucks-Horsley & Roody, 1990; Miller, 1990; Slavin, 1990). Keogh (1990) highlights the needed focus in this process of change in the following passage:

> It is clear that major changes are needed in the delivery of services to problem learners, and that these services need to be the responsibility of regular as well as special educators. It is also clear that teachers are the central players in bringing about change in practice. It follows, then, that our greatest and most pressing challenge in the reform effort is to determine how to improve the quality of instruction at the classroom level. (p. 190)

INNOVATION AND DEVELOPMENT

The area of learning disabilities has accomplished much in its brief existence. Public interest has been generated, litigation initiated, legislation written and passed, educational programs developed, and professional organizations established. Despite continuing controversy several noteworthy trends can be identified:

1. A transition from the medical model to the educational model has occurred, based on research concerning effective interventions and problems in accurately diagnosing information processing and neurological deficits. Lately, the medical model is becoming more influential. It is hoped that this resurgence will be founded on research-based practices and not on unproven theories and diagnostic instruments.
2. Direct instruction has emerged as a research-supported intervention for teaching academic and social skills.
3. Data-based instruction continues to accrue support as a viable instructional approach.
4. Speech and language clinicians are now the key professionals responsible for the oral language of students with learning disabilities. The subgroup of language-learning disabilities is gaining recognition and acceptance as an important area of focus. A variety of language tests is now available.
5. The written language movement shifted to a criterion-oriented academic intervention approach, serving as a catalyst for the proliferation of commercial academic programs. Today, publishers are a major force in instruction of students with learning disabilities.

6. Primarily through the work of Deshler and his colleagues and Zigmond and her colleagues, a promising emphasis on the adolescent with learning disabilities has emerged. Deshler's learning strategies approach is having a widespread effect, and commercial programs in this area are becoming more numerous.

Definition

The field continues to seek a precise and universally accepted definition of learning disabilities (Silver, 1988). Currently, the definition from the Individuals with Disabilities Education Act (IDEA) is used widely, but dissatisfaction remains. The discrepancy factor, a key component in identifying students with learning disabilities, is apt to be included in any forthcoming definition. Operationalizing the discrepancy (that is, defining the discrepancy in performance terms) remains difficult and controversial (see the Fall 1991 issue of *Learning Disability Quarterly*, which is devoted to this topic). A taxonomy of learning disabilities also may be developed in the near future. In view of the heterogeneous nature of students with learning disabilities, many experts agree that such a schema would be helpful in dividing learning disabilities into instructionally relevant subgroups.

Assessment

Ysseldyke and his colleagues at the University of Minnesota Institute for Research in Learning Disabilities initiated criticism of the assessment practices in learning disabilities (Ysseldyke et al., 1983). In essence, they recommended that less time and fewer resources be allocated to assessment and more time and resources to instruction. Too much time is spent on assessment that gathers data of too little use. For example, numerous tests are based on ill-defined psychological constructs presumed to underlie learning problems. Although many commercial standardized tests are available, the need persists for reliable, valid, and instructionally relevant ones. Perhaps some of the recent and forthcoming tests will be beneficial. To help the practitioner, several texts (McLoughlin & Lewis, 1990; Salvia & Ysseldyke, 1991) provide an excellent consumer's guide for evaluating tests. Curriculum-based assessment appears to hold much promise and rapidly is gaining popularity as an assessment procedure.

Teacher Preparation

The concern for quality teacher training has become a national issue. The need for teachers to work collaboratively has become an essential factor in meeting the needs of students with learning disabilities. Thus, training in collaborative consultation is a trend that promises to receive more emphasis. States are initiating competency tests for teachers, introducing merit pay plans, and challenging colleges of education to develop viable teacher education programs. Colleges of education must establish viable partnerships with schools to ensure teacher preparation that is based on situations encountered in real life. Thus, the problem of teacher preparation has been recognized, and this area should see active developments.

Cognitive Approaches

The influence of the cognitive research is apparent in the promotion of a cognitive approach to understanding and treating learning disabilities. Since 1978, at least 60 studies involving more than 1,000 students have demonstrated the appropriateness of various applications of the cognitively based learning strategies and the benefits that can be achieved for many students with learning disabilities (Lenz, 1992). In addition, ongoing research continues to refine and develop the instructional dimensions of the approach, and current research efforts promise to expand its applications. Wong (1987) notes that

> slowly, but surely, a *quiet revolution* in remedial teaching appears to be occurring among learning disabilities teachers. Along with the traditional emphasis on remediating basic reading and math skills, LD teachers have realized the need simultaneously to teach their students how to learn and how to self-regulate their learning. (p. 191)

Minimum Competency Testing

Implicit in the *America* 2000 goals for education is competency testing for America's students (National Governors Association, 1990). In an effort to establish or maintain credibility in the educational system and improve educational services, many states are instituting minimum competency tests. Primarily, these tests are used to ensure that students who are being promoted or graduated possess certain basic skills. The relationship of minimum competency tests and the student with learning disabilities currently is being examined. Some alternatives are being explored, including (1) exempting students with learning disabilities from minimum competency testing; (2) providing test modification for students with learning disabilities (Grise, 1980); (3) including minimum competency skills in the student's individualized educational program; and (4) using minimum competency results to design remediation programs for students with learning disabilities. Minimum competency testing is an educational trend that requires the development of certain policies and procedures for students with learning disabilities.

Life-Span View of Learning Disabilities

Until recently the field of learning disabilities focused primarily on the school-aged child. Professionals now are beginning to gain information about the older individual with learning disabilities. The development of college programs for individuals with learning disabilities currently is receiving much attention. Many recent studies focus on the status of students with learning disabilities at the college level in terms of identification and intervention. In a review of the published work on college learning disabilities programs, Hughes and Smith (1990) note that little empirical data exist on young adults with learning disabilities in the college setting. Some studies focus on procedures for identifying college students who have learning disabilities. For example, Knowles and Knowles (1983) found that the *American College Test*, the *Standard Test of Academic Skills*, and grade-point average identified college freshmen with learning disabilities with 84% accuracy. Mellard (1990), in conjunction with the California community college system, is developing a comprehensive eligibility model for identifying students with learning disabilities. This and other models should lead to the development of improved services for college students with learning disabilities.

It is hoped that in the nineties higher education will respond to the needs of adults with learning disabilities. To meet the needs, Cordoni (1982) suggests providing a director of college programs, support groups, and resources for youth and adults with learning disabilities, and there have been some concrete steps in this area by colleges, universities, and agencies.[2]

The field of learning disabilities began in the sixties as the baby-boom generation was growing into puberty; therefore, many individuals of the baby-boom generation missed being identified as having learning disabilities during their school years. As a result, many adults have undiagnosed learning disabilities that currently may be affecting the quality of their lives. In several studies, social deficits are reported as the major area of concern for adults with learning disabilities. Chelser (1982) reports a rank ordering of areas in which 560 adults with learning disabilities felt a need for assistance:

1. Social relationships and skills
2. Career counseling
3. Developing self-esteem, confidence
4. Overcoming dependence, survival
5. Vocational training
6. Getting and holding a job
7. Reading
8. Spelling
9. Managing personal finances
10. Organizational skills

In response to the needs of adults with learning disabilities, the National Joint Committee on Learning Disabilities (1985) developed a position paper that lists numerous recommendations. Spekman, Goldberg, and Herman (1992) conducted a study of factors that relate to success for young adults with learning disabilities. Their concern for adults with learning disabilities is apparent in the following passage:

> Instead of focusing on areas that differentiate learning disabled from normally achieving peers, we must continue our search for factors that make a difference in terms of ultimate life adjustment *and* seek ways to foster their development. (p. 169)

Single-Subject Research

When group designs are used and individual scores are averaged, it is possible that the mean score is not representative of any individual's performance, because individuals with learning disabilities are a heterogeneous population. Single-subject research is tailored to evaluate the effects of treatments on an individual's performance, and its

---

2   *The FCLD Guide for Parents of Children with Learning Disabilities* (available from FCLD, 99 Park Avenue, New York, NY 10016) provides basic information about learning disabilities (including alternatives beyond high school) and lists sources of information and help. The *Directory of Facilities for Learning Disabled People*, which includes a list of colleges, universities, and agencies providing such facilities, is available from Bosc, P.O. Box 305, Dept. F, Congers, NY 10920.

use has been recommended by numerous authorities (Haring & Schiefelbusch, 1976; Lovitt, 1975). Moreover, the recent guidelines (Council for Learning Disabilities Research Committee, 1992) for selecting and describing subjects with learning disabilities for research, if followed, should help alleviate a major problem of learning disabilities research—the variability of subjects with learning disabilities among studies.

Microcomputers

The influence of microcomputers on the teaching of students with learning disabilities is extensive. The computer can be used as a tool for classroom management, as well as classroom instruction. Hofmeister (1984) suggests that the most appropriate use of the computer is as a supplementary tool to allow teachers more time to teach. Teachers can be partially released from time-consuming tasks through computer-managed instruction, particularly in developing individualized educational programs and in computer-managed record keeping. Computers can store sequences of instructional objectives and student performance information, as well as track student progress, complete proper forms, and provide required record-keeping data (Fuchs, Fuchs, & Hamlett, 1989; Kulik, Kulik, & Bangert-Drowns, 1985).

A computer's animation, sound effects, and game-playing situations can make drill and practice exciting.

Computer-assisted instruction refers to software that is designed to provide instruction. The computer offers some unique advantages in instructing students with learning disabilities. Attributes of computer-assisted instruction that appear useful in helping students achieve include the following (Fitzgerald, Fick, & Milich, 1986; Haynes & Malouf, 1986; Kolich, 1985; Lindsey, 1987):

1. Tasks are analyzed and presented in meaningful sequences.
2. Materials are presented in a manner that allows the student to progress at his or her own rate.
3. Reinforcement of individual student responses is immediate. The computer can provide continuous and positive feedback and praise, thus giving the student a higher sense of self-esteem.
4. Constructive criticism is offered without the human elements of emotion or embarrassment.
5. Software exists that enables the student to increase his or her rate of correct responses.
6. The use of animation, sound effects, and game-playing situations makes drill and practice motivating.
7. The computer is suited to the discovery method of learning. Programs that simulate real-life experiences allow the student to make decisions and see the consequences.
8. Strategies related to problem solving can be adapted for the computer through programs such as adventure games and software that teaches how to program.
9. The computer can be made "user friendly" by programming it to use the student's name when giving lessons. A computer also is nonjudgmental and allows the student to make mistakes in a nonthreatening environment.

Educational software can differ in method or mode of delivery as well as in quality. Watkins and Webb (1981) and Ellis and Sabornie (1986) discuss six modes of delivery: drill and practice, tutorial, educational games, simulations, problem solving, and word processing. Moreover, Shuell and Schueckler (1988) note that to transcend traditional instructional methods, computer programs must (1) use the student's knowledge base, (2) provide guided and independent practice, (3) give corrective feedback, (4) present materials in steps that facilitate learning, (5) provide clear lesson overviews and goals, (6) conduct periodic performance evaluations, and (7) finish with a summary and review of the lesson's main points.

In addition to the many general uses of the computer for students with learning disabilities, several investigators report on specific applications that are suited especially to children with learning disabilities. Grimes (1981) notes that for students who have difficulty maintaining on-task attention, computer programs can promote attention with color cuing, animation, underlining, and varying print sizes. For students who respond impulsively, the computer can provide cues or hints to inhibit impulsive responding. For those who take a lot of time to respond (reflective responders), computer programs can be tailored to allow extra response time.

Research on the use of computer-assisted instruction with students who have learning disabilities appears promising but remains inconclusive. Majsterek and Wilson (1989) reviewed several computer-assisted instruction studies that focused on teach-

*E*llis and Sabornie (1986) reviewed the "promises" for computers as they relate to students with mild disabilities:

1. *Increased motivation.* The most common promise for the computer was that it would increase motivation to learn. This potential generally is acknowledged to be true. Working on the computer seems to be intrinsically motivating to many children.

2. *Increased positive self-concept.* Although there are no studies directly addressing this promise, there is logical support for the contention that the computer has the potential to increase a student's positive self-concept. It is logical to assume that production of a greater number of academically correct responses and better grades contribute to helping students feel better about themselves.

3. *More effective instruction.* The expectation has been that computer-assisted instruction would be more effective than many traditional instructional practices. Although research results have been conflicting up to this point, there is considerable support for this contention. Computer-assisted instruction may be more appropriate for certain content and skill areas than for others and may be most effective when paired with certain other instructional practices.

4. *Better for teaching new skills or knowledge.* Although there is still some debate regarding when to use computer-assisted instruction in problem-solving instruction, it is certainly an effective tutoring device for teaching new concepts.

5. *More effective for skill automaticity.* Computer-assisted drill and practice programs have demonstrated good results. They seem to be effective particularly for decoding, speed, accuracy, and teaching multiplication facts.

6. *Effective instructional engineering.* The hope was that there would be well-designed programs that teachers with limited computer expertise could use effectively. Despite considerable optimism regarding the potential of computers for such instructional techniques as pacing instruction and providing effective and immediate feedback, teachers lack the software and the competencies to be able to use computers at sophisticated levels of instructional engineering.

7. *Improved writing ability.* The hope was that word processors significantly would improve student interest and skills related to writing. Preliminary studies in this area suggest that word processors do not necessarily improve writing skills, but explorations into effective writing instruction using the computer have only just begun.

Other technologies that hold promise for students with learning disabilities include videotape and videodisk players. Either can be attached to the microcomputer to provide interactive video. The combination is interactive in the sense that students can view the material on the screen and respond via the computer.

ing basic skills to students with learning disabilities. They concluded that computer-assisted instruction could produce equivalent—or slightly less than equivalent learn-ing—with less teacher time than traditional instruction. Other reports of computer-assisted instruction used to teach students with learning problems (Ellis & Sabornie, 1986; Hasselbring, Goin, & Bransford, 1988; Woodward & Carnine, 1988) conclude that student achievement usually is greater when computer-assisted instruction supple-ments rather than replaces teacher-directed instruction. Keefe and Candler (1989) report mixed results on the effectiveness of using word processors with students who have learning disabilities. However, several individual studies report good results with the use of computer-assisted instruction in teaching students with learning disabilities (for example, spelling—Fuchs et al., 1989; world geography—Horton, Lovitt, Givens, & Nelson, 1989; reading—Torgesen, Waters, Cohen, & Torgesen, 1988; health—Wood-ward, Carnine, & Gersten, 1988).

Computer-assisted instruction is promising, but limited information exists con-cerning how microcomputers can be applied best in the classroom (Cosden, Gerber, Semmel, Goldman, & Semmel, 1987; Stowitschek & Stowitschek, 1984; Torgesen & Young, 1983). However, it is apparent that through the use of appropriate software, students with learning disabilities can be motivated through individualized instruction to accomplish needed academic practice. (See the Focus on Technology box for a review of the "promises" for computers as they relate to students with mild disabili-ties.)

SUMMARY All students with learning disabilities have an academic problem in one or more areas and are not achieving in accordance with their potential ability. This chapter traced the recent history of the field of learning disabilities and presented the major defini-tions and criteria for identifying students with learning disabilities. Prevalence esti-mates indicate that individuals with learning disabilities are the largest group within the total population of individuals with all kinds of disabilities.

The causes of learning disabilities were discussed in terms of four categories: acquired trauma, genetic/hereditary influences, biochemical abnormalities, and envi-ronmental influences. Each student with learning disabilities is unique, and character-istics of learning disabilities may include one or more problem areas, including acade-mic learning, language, perception, motor use, social-emotional adjustment, metacognition, memory, and attention.

Methods of assessing learning disabilities were discussed in terms of five learning disabilities identification components: exclusion, academic achievement, language achievement, process, and discrepancy. Service and placement options for students with learning disabilities were presented. Five approaches to teaching students with learning disabilities—language programs and materials, multisensory approaches, data-based instruction, direct instruction, and cognitive instruction—were discussed, and programming considerations for the adolescent with learning disabilities were considered. Integrated programming was discussed, and instructional features that promote successful mainstreaming were presented.

Recent innovations and developments in the field of learning disabilities involve such areas as teacher preparation, cognitive approaches, minimum competency test-

1. Provide support; be cheerful, complimentary, and enthusiastic.

2. Provide structure; clearly specify rules, assignments, and duties.

3. Establish situations and tasks that lead to success.

4. Use simple vocabulary in giving directions and in interacting with students.

5. Use self-correcting materials to minimize students' public experiences of failure and to provide immediate feedback.

6. Practice skills frequently; use instructional games and otherwise vary drill formats as much as possible to maintain interest.

7. Allow older students with learning disabilities who have difficulty writing to record answers on tape and provide extra time to complete tasks to students who work slowly.

8. For older students with learning disabilities who have difficulty organizing and understanding material, provide outlines to be filled in as they read or listen to lectures.

9. For older students with learning disabilities, tape lecture material and provide them with class time to listen to tapes to check notes, review, and study.

10. Pair adolescents with learning disabilities with peer helpers and provide class time for these pairs to work on specific assignments, play instructional games, and study materials such as vocabulary and concept cards.

11. Use microcomputers for drill and practice of basic academic skills.

12. Teach self-instruction techniques and learning strategies to help students with learning disabilities learn in varied situations.

TIPS FOR HELPING

ing, life-span view of learning disabilities, and the use of microcomputers. The field is an active and exciting area that is making great strides in facilitating the identification and instruction of persons who have learning disabilities.

STUDY QUESTIONS

1. Discuss the evolution of the term *learning disabilities*.

2. Write a definition of learning disabilities. Compare the components of the definition with the identification criteria.

3. Discuss the prevalence of learning disabilities. Present causal factors related to learning disabilities.

4. Discuss five characteristics of learning disabilities. Explain why individuals with learning disabilities are considered to be a heterogeneous group.

5. Discuss the assessment of specific components of a learning disability.

6. Describe service or placement options for students with learning disabilities.

7. Discuss data-based instruction, direct instruction, and cognitive instruction.

8. Discuss programming for adolescents with learning disabilities.

9. Discuss the Regular Education Initiative (REI) and present instructional features that promote successful mainstreaming of students with learning disabilities.

10. Discuss five innovations or developments in the field of learning disabilities.

Douglas Cullinan
North Carolina State
University

Michael H. Epstein
Northern Illinois University

5

Behavior Disorders

 In this chapter you will learn about

- biological and psychological phenomena and the major theoretical models that explain how children's behavior disorders originate and are perpetuated

- the main behavioral-emotional problem characteristics of children with behavior disorders

- the methods and educational purposes of assessing behavior disorders of students

- the psychoeducational, behavioral, and ecological interventions for students with behavior disorders

- currently emerging issues in the education of students with behavior disorders

Twelve-year-old Michael has long-standing problems in school. He was behind his peers in academic skills when he entered 1st grade, and he has gradually fallen further behind. Nearly every one of his elementary school teachers has noted his inability to remain seated, persist with a task until completion, listen and look appropriately in class, and wait until his turn in learning or play groups. Sometimes Michael is unresponsive to the teacher or peers for several minutes to several hours. Most of his classmates try to avoid Michael, and some ridicule his mistakes. At times he seems to enjoy the resulting attention and disruption, but at other times the ridicule makes him angry and prompts an argument, a tantrum of crying and cursing, a fight, or a period of disobedience and disrespect toward the teacher.

Michael's unhappy situation is not confined to school. He comes from a family that is well known to the city's social service, legal, and education agencies. His father has an arrest record for domestic violence, disorderly conduct, and he also has numerous traffic offenses. Two of Michael's older brothers were adjudicated delinquent and assigned to detention centers for several months, following many community complaints and court appearances related to petty theft, drug use (and perhaps sales), violence to other children, setting fires in the neighborhood, nighttime roaming, and generally being beyond parental control.

At the age of 9, Michael began receiving special education services. Assessment indicated, among other things, that Michael's reading, mathematics, and language arts achievement were no better than the 1st-grade level, even though his intellectual ability was within normal limits (IQ score of 87) and there was no substantial evidence of brain disorder. Michael's parents were doubtful about their ability to control him at home, but they vowed to support whatever the school decided to do (Michael's dad offered to "whip" him at the school's request). The initial placement decision was to provide Michael with counseling and academic tutoring in a resource room for up to 2 hours every school day, along with providing consultation to the boy's teacher about managing his behavior.

However, Michael's learning and social behavior showed no improvement, and within several months he was placed in a self-contained class for pupils with emotional and behavioral disorders. Michael remains enrolled in that class, where he is slowly learning to read and do simple arithmetic. On most days his behavior is tolerable, but it is not uncommon for Michael to argue with classmates or the teacher. About twice a month he is involved in a serious incident of threatening or carrying out aggression toward another pupil before, during, or after school. His special education teacher is concerned about Michael's upcoming transition to middle school, but she sees an opportunity as well. She has been working with colleagues to arrange for Michael's increased participation in regular education and perhaps, as a result, a more successful school experience for him.

Students who do and say things that interfere substantially with the appropriate functioning of both themselves and others are often described as showing behavior disorders. Behavior disorders, sometimes referred to as emotional disturbance or maladjustment, can take a wide variety of forms. Students may exhibit little or no classroom participation, communication, or other interaction at play or in other contexts; excessive physical aggression, threats, disobedience, destructiveness, or moving around; a lack of basic academic and school readiness skills and of organized learning strategies for acquiring them; verbal and other expressions of extreme fear, sadness, guilt, or self-doubt. Children and adolescents with the most severe behavior disorders often exhibit strange movements and postures, profound language limitations, a lack of basic self-care skills, and fundamental cognitive disturbances. No young person with behavior disorders will show all of these problems, but most will show more than one.

HISTORY Special education for students with behavior disorders is a modern development shaped by earlier ideas and practices. Our ancestors believed that supernatural powers controlled all manner of phenomena that were difficult to understand—including seasonal changes, reproduction, and deviant behavior. Behavior disorders were often interpreted as evidence of possession by evil spirits that needed to be exorcised. In addition, very early versions of today's biological and psychological explanations of behavioral and emotional disturbances existed (Achenbach, 1982). Two modern schools of thought—psychodynamic psychology and behavioral psychology—have strongly influenced the field of behavior disorders.

Special Education

Child labor and compulsory schooling laws in the 19th century helped make public education a major social institution that had to deal for the first time with children and adolescents with a variety of physical, sensory, learning, and behavior disorders. By about 1900 provisions for delinquent and hard-to-manage pupils were not uncommon in large cities. In the early years of the 20th century, children with behavior disorders sometimes received education in institutions and special schools, but it was seen as an extra service, often an extension of psychotherapy. Students showing behavior disorders were commonly excluded from school.

As special education college courses and state certification requirements became widespread, some students with behavior disorders began to be placed in special classes for youngsters with mental retardation or brain injury. Only in the fifties and sixties, as psychoeducational and behavioral models became influential, did modern features of special education for students with behavior disorders emerge.

This was a period of innovation. Norris Haring (Haring & Phillips, 1962), adapting methods for children with brain injury, developed a highly structured class for pupils with behavior disorders, focusing on the predictability and consistency of the child's everyday home and school environment. The Council for Children with Behavioral Disorders—a special-interest division of the Council for Exceptional Children—was chartered in 1964. In the three decades since then, education for students with behavior disorders has been broadly affected by the letter and the spirit of public policy developments, including laws such as Public Law 94–142 of 1975 and Public Law 101–476 of 1990 involving educational and other rights of children with disabilities (Heward & Orlansky, 1992). Despite all the positive developments, how far we still have to go has been made distressingly clear by recent evaluations of the needs of and services for children with behavior disorders (e.g., Institute of Medicine, 1989; Knitzer, Steinberg, & Fleisch, 1990).

Psychodynamic Psychology

First developed nearly a century ago by Sigmund Freud and revised by other theorists and therapists, psychodynamic psychology is concerned with the development and interaction of mental processes. Behavior disorders are thought to be outward symptoms of abnormal mental processes.

Psychodynamic psychology has influenced treatment of children and adolescents in two main ways. First, psychoanalysis and other psychodynamic therapies have been used to treat youngsters in clinics, institutions, and schools. In 1950 Bruno Bettelheim relied heavily on psychoanalysis to create his Orthogenic School with its permissive "therapeutic milieu," where young people with behavior disorders could be freed from their mental conflicts and anxiety. Play therapy (Axline, 1969) and transactional analysis (Berne, 1964) are two examples of the many psychodynamic therapies for students with behavior disorders.

Second, psychodynamic principles have been adapted to produce the psychoeducational model, which has deeply influenced special education for students with behavior disorders (Rezmierski, Knoblock, & Bloom, 1982). Its beginnings can be traced to the work of Fritz Redl at a program for highly aggressive boys (Redl & Wineman, 1951). While stressing acceptance of students, Redl expected behavior improvement and enforced limits in the program. His adaptations of psychodynamic treatment included the life-space interview technique for crisis exploration and strategies for managing "surface behavior" problems. William Morse (1965) later conceptualized the crisis-helping teacher, and Nicholas Long (1974) established a program for training teachers to use psychoeducational interventions and developed a curriculum to promote student self-control. Mary M. Wood (Wood, Combs, Gunn, & Weller, 1986) established curricula and programs based on integrating psychoeducational concepts into a developmental view of the needs of children with behavior and learning problems.

Behavioral Psychology

Beginning in the thirties, B. F. Skinner's laboratory research identified important relationships between behaviors and environmental stimuli. His work established the science of behavior known as operant conditioning, which holds that behavior can be predicted accurately and modified substantially through knowledge of, and control over, the appropriate stimuli. Operant conditioning has been applied to complex human behavior patterns such as those involving language and education (Skinner, 1957, 1968).

Behavioral psychology began to be used systematically to help students with behavior and learning problems about 1960. Early reports focused on intervention with individual children, but before long there were organized school and institutional programs based on operant conditioning. In one pioneering application, Frank Hewett (1968) developed and evaluated the Engineered Classroom plan, which used a system of tokens and praise to reinforce task accomplishments within a carefully structured educational environment. Herbert Quay and his colleagues (Quay, Glavin, Annesley, & Werry, 1972) showed how behavioral principles could be used in a resource room program for students with behavior disorders. Under the direction of Hill Walker, the Center at Oregon for Research in Behavioral Education of the Handicapped (CORBEH) developed, evaluated, packaged, and disseminated interventions to correct classroom disruption, poor academic readiness skills, social withdrawal, and aggression outside the classroom (Walker, Hops, & Greenwood, 1984).

To summarize, contemporary special education for students with behavior disorders has been shaped by diverse influences, especially developments in psychodynamic and behavioral psychology (see Cullinan, Epstein, & Lloyd, 1991; Kauffman, 1993). This diverse background is a strength in many ways; at the same time it is one cause of continuing disagreements on fundamental issues.

DEFINITION

Children and youth with behavior disorders are certainly not rare, and most of us have observed or dealt with such young people. Ironically, there is no generally accepted definition of behavior disorders. One of the major stumbling blocks to a universal definition is the varied and sometimes conflicting viewpoints concerning their nature. Another issue is the subjectivity of standards for determining exactly what is a behavior disorder; standards of normality can vary by age, sex, subculture, community, politics, and economic conditions.

Another obstacle involves problems of assessment. Despite promising recent advances, available procedures are still inadequate to measure the social, emotional, and behavioral problems of school children. Thus, an uncomfortable degree of subjectivity is required to identify pupils with behavior disorders and specify their problems (Walker & Fabre, 1987). One further obstacle is the potential harm in labeling students—the lowered self-concept, loss of popularity and acceptability among peers, and decreased teacher expectations (Smith, Wood, & Grimes, 1987).

Figure 5-1 presents key definitions selected from the dozens available. Despite continuing criticism (Executive Committee, 1987; Forness & Knitzer, 1990), the federal definition of *serious emotional disturbance* (SED) continues to be used by the U.S. Office of Special Education as it administers financial support and other federal activities related to research, teacher training, and state programs. Recently a broad-based coalition of advocacy and professional organizations has developed a preferred term (*emotional or behavioral disorder*) and a new definition (Forness & Knitzer, 1990). These advocates have pressed Congress to make the new term and definition official (see the Proposed Federal definition in Figure 5-1).

The first four definitions in Figure 5-1 under the heading "By Perspective" reflect various theoretical perspectives on behavior disorders. The last definition under that heading reflects aspects of behavior disorders that are of particular interest to educators; its key phrases are worth a close examination.

Federal

Children with serious emotional disturbance exhibit one or more of the following characteristics over a long period of time and to a marked degree:

1. An inability to learn which cannot be explained by intellectual, sensory, or health factors
2. An inability to build or maintain satisfactory interpersonal relationships with peers and teachers
3. Inappropriate types of behavior or feelings under normal circumstances
4. General pervasive mood of unhappiness or depression
5. A tendency to develop physical symptoms, pains, or fears associated with personal or school problems

Children who are schizophrenic qualify; children who are socially maladjusted do not qualify, unless it is determined that they show serious emotional disturbance. (adapted from *Federal Register*, 1977, *42*, 42478, as amended *Federal Register*, 1981, *46*, 3866)

Proposed Federal

"Emotional and behavioral disorders" means a disability that is

1. characterized by behavioral or emotional response in school programs so different from appropriate age, culture, or ethnic norms that the responses adversely affect educational performance, including academic, social, vocational or personal skills
2. more than a temporary, expected response to stressful events in the environment
3. consistently exhibited in two different settings, at least one of which is school-related
4. unresponsive to direct intervention applied in general education, or the condition of a child is such that general education interventions would be insufficient

Emotional and behavioral disorders can coexist with other disabilities. Emotional and behavioral disorders include a schizophrenic disorder, affective disorder, anxiety disorder, or other sustained disorder of conduct or adjustment, affecting a child, if the disorder affects educational performance. (adapted from Forness & Knitzer, 1990)

By Perspective

1. *Biological.* A biogenic mental disorder is a severe behavior disorder that results solely from the effects of biological factors, including both gene action and the effects of the physical-chemical environment. (Rimland, 1969, p. 706)
2. *Psychodynamic.* A child suffers emotional conflict whenever anything interferes with the satisfaction of the child's instinctual drives and the resulting frustration produces a state of tension. (Lippman, 1962, p. 3)
3. *Behavioral.* Psychological disorder is said to be present when a child emits behavior that deviates from an arbitrary and relative social norm in that it occurs with a frequency or intensity that authoritative adults in the child's environment judge, under the circumstances, to be either too high or too low. (Ross, 1980, p. 9)
4. *Ecological.* Emotional disturbance [is] a reciprocal condition that exists when intense coping responses are released within a human community by a community member's atypical behavior and responses. The triggering stimulus, the rejoinder of the microcommunity, and the ensuing transaction are all involved in emotional disturbance. (Rhodes, 1970, p. 311)
5. *Educational.* Behavioral disorders of a student are behavior characteristics that (a) deviate from educators' standards of normality and (b) impair the functioning of that student and/or others. These behavior characteristics are manifested as environmental conflicts and/or personal disturbances, and are typically accompanied by learning disorders. (Cullinan et al., 1983, p. 52)

Figure 5–1
Definitions of behavior disorders.

Behavioral Characteristics.   Educators are concerned mainly with their students' behavior—their movements, language, and obvious physiological responses, such as tears or a flushed face—and the effects of this behavior on objects and people in the environment. Even mental or emotional problems are deduced from an observation and interpretation of behavior.

Deviation from Educators' Standards of Normality.   There is, of course, no clear-cut boundary that divides normality from abnormality. We all have expectations about what is typical in school situations, which may take into account age, sex, and other characteristics. Behavior disorders usually involve familiar behaviors that occur with a frequency, duration, and/or intensity that is too great or too small relative to educators' expectations. Teachers are likely to tolerate moderate behavior problems for a while but become concerned if they intensify or persist. Most often, educators' standard of normality involves a range of behavior perceived as typical of some group of students. Behavior that exceeds this range may be identified as disordered.

Impaired Functioning of the Student and/or Others.   Some behavior disorders involve substantial personal distress, as indicated by self-deprecating remarks, unrealistic anxieties, sadness and depression, or an inability to make friends. Other disorders interfere with the young person's personal, emotional, or educational development; examples are a lack of essential academic skills, short attention span, and excessive dependence on the teacher. Still other behavior disorders—including aggression, bizarre statements or actions, and disruptive rule violations—impede the productive performance of others. Of course, not all behavior disorders impair the functioning of *only* the student or *only* others. Behavior that is personally distressing or interferes with self-development often disturbs other people eventually; conversely, the student whose behavior disturbs others is likely to experience social and personal repercussions.

Environmental Conflicts, Personal Disturbances, and Learning Disorders. It is convenient to discuss behavior disorders of children and adolescents in terms of these three general aspects. *Environmental conflict* refers to aggressive-disruptive, hyperactive, and social maladjustment problems; *personal disturbance* includes anxiety-depression and social withdrawal problems (Cullinan, Epstein, & Lloyd, 1983). Many students with these difficulties also have *learning disorders* that must be addressed by teachers (Epstein, Kinder, & Bursuck, 1989).

PREVALENCE   Prevalence information is important to persons responsible for educating students with behavior disorders, affecting funding, personnel development, and other administrative issues. It can also tell us how behavior disorders differ according to age, sex, race, socioeconomic status, or geographic area, and this information has implications for our ideas about causes and interventions.

There have been many prevalence studies of behavior disorders in children and adolescents in schools and communities (see Costello, 1989; Graham, 1979), but for various reasons—especially differences among definitions and research methods—the resulting estimates have varied from less than 1% to more than 30% of the school-age population. The federal accounting of students with disabilities (U.S. Department of Education, 1992) indicates that about 400,000 students in the United States (approximately 1% of the school population) are identified as having serious emotional disturbance (SED). Probably many more students could qualify but are not identified because (1) teachers and parents avoid assigning the SED label whenever possible; (2) in the school, personal disturbances are not as obvious as environmental conflicts, and thus tend to be overlooked; (3) by law, special education must be provided to all students found to have a disability (e.g., SED), so some districts find only as many students with behavior disorders as can be served within existing personnel and budget limitations (Kauffman, 1993; U.S. Department of Education, 1992).

Highly accurate prevalence estimates will probably remain elusive as long as there are problems with definition and assessment. Our own guesstimate, based on individual studies and prevalence reviews, is that behavior disorders among students may follow a "rule of one third"; in any school year about one third of all students show behavior problems that concern their teachers to some extent. One third of this group (about 10% of the total student population) show disorders to a degree that moderate to substantial alterations of ordinary educational procedures are needed. And about one third of these (roughly 3%) exhibit behavior disorders severe enough to justify special education and/or other intervention services. Included in this 3% would be the very small number of children (no more than 1 in 1,000) diagnosed as exhibiting autism or other severe behavioral disorders (Prior & Werry, 1986; Schreibman & Charlop, 1989).

CAUSES

What do we mean by cause in the context of behavior disorders? To scientists trying to understand behavior disorders, a helpful kind of cause is the necessary-and-sufficient condition (Achenbach, 1982). When a necessary-and-sufficient condition operates, the behavior disorder will definitely occur; when it does not, the disorder cannot occur. To remedy the problem, one simply needs to identify and control the necessary-and-sufficient condition. Unfortunately, such powerful and uncomplicated causes of children's behavior disorders have been identified rarely, if ever. Instead, the vast majority of causes are contributory conditions—situations that increase the risk that a behavior disorder will occur. Research indicates that some conditions increase this risk more than others, but in most cases the causes of behavior disorders cannot be pinned down. Given the complex nature of human behavior, necessary-and-sufficient conditions may never be proven for most behavior disorders.

Fortunately, effective intervention is possible even when the initial causes of behavior disorders are not known; in fact, knowing the causes may have little relevance for effective intervention. Many contributory conditions—brain damage or severe child abuse, for instance—involve historical events that cannot be undone, yet effective intervention can reduce or eliminate the impairments.

It would take several pages to list every condition that has been suggested as a cause of behavior disorders. However, the proposed causes can be classified into a few categories. First, research points to a number of biological and psychological conditions that can be important determinants of an individual's development, both normal and abnormal. Second, there are several models of behavior disorders; the psychoeducational, behavioral, and ecological models are particularly relevant. Each of these models involves certain ideas about how behavior disorders are produced and perpetuated, and each provides intervention principles that have been translated into special education practices.

Biological Conditions

Research continues to reveal how human characteristics are influenced by the genetic material inherited from parents (Willis & Walker, 1989). Genes control critical chemical chain reactions in our bodies, so gene defects that produce a broken link in these chains may cause drastically disturbed functioning. Defects of chromosomes (collections of genes) can also cause serious physical and behavioral problems. Certain long-term research strategies have been designed specifically to discriminate the effects of nature and nurture of human adjustment, and results increasingly point to heredity as a contributory condition in some behavior disorders.

Many events operating before, during, and after birth can produce brain disorders (structural damage to the brain or dysfunctions such as abnormal electric activity). The relationships between brain disorders and behavior disorders continue to intrigue and baffle researchers (Gray & Raymond, 1990). Ingestion of various toxic substances by a child or pregnant mother may produce negative effects on the child's behavior, including learning disorders (Willis & Walker, 1989). The list of such toxins includes legal and illegal drugs, tobacco, alcohol, and pollutants and other environmental chemicals. Severe, chronic deprivation of either general nutritional needs or certain specific dietary substances can cause not only physical and mental retardation but behavior disorders as well (Kopp, 1983). However, popular theories about children's hyperactivity being caused by excess food additives or sugar in the diet are not backed by much scientific evidence (Werry, 1986).

One major obstacle to a clearer understanding is the technical inadequacy of widely used assessment procedures for brain disorders (Werry, 1986). Nevertheless, reviews of the available evidence (Schreibman & Charlop, 1989; Werry, 1986) suggest several important conclusions: (1) severe-profound behavior disorders, especially autism, are often associated with brain disorders; (2) mild-moderate behavior disorders can be caused in various ways, one of which is brain disorder; but (3) in most instances behavior disorders are not caused by brain disorders, and most children with brain disorders do not show behavior disorders.

Psychological Conditions

The family is universally recognized as a fundamental influence on the socialization and development of children and adolescents, and much research has focused on family structure and functioning as possible causes of behavior disorders. Major family variables related to behavior disorders include (1) absence of father or mother; (2) conflict between parents; (3) sibling relations; (4) a parent with behavior disorders (especially psychotic or severely antisocial); (5) parental hostility, neglect, or abuse;

and 6 inconsistent or extremely lax discipline (Cullinan, Sabornie, & Epstein, 1992; Hetherington & Martin, 1986; Ramsey & Walker, 1988; U.S. Department of Education, 1992). However, it is uncertain whether any of these family variables are necessary-and-sufficient conditions for behavior disorders. The influence of each varies according to the child or adolescent's sex, age, and socioeconomic status, for example. Evidence does indicate that these and other family variables often operate as contributory conditions, with each additional one in a child's experience increasing his or her risk for a behavior disorder.

Normal and abnormal socialization can also be shaped by peers, the school, the media, socioeconomic disadvantage, and other influences beyond the family. Peer interaction is a central aspect of child development, providing opportunities for companionship, social status, self-understanding, personal maturity, and adjustment to society. Behavior disorders seem to cause poor peer relations, and vice versa; in either case children and youth with poor peer relationships are not likely to be happy or effective students (Gresham, 1988). Further, even satisfying peer relationships can contribute to some disorders, because peer groups often encourage behaviors that deviate from the standards of teachers, parents, and others.

Schools can also contribute to behavior disorders (Kauffman, 1993; Kozol, 1992) through insensitivity to students' individuality, inappropriate expectations for students that become self-fulfilling prophecies of failure, teacher ineptitude in providing management and instruction, and preoccupation with irrelevant tasks and routines. On the other hand, schools can be important in preventing and correcting behavior disorders (Peacock Hill Working Group, 1991).

Socioeconomic disadvantage refers to a collection of circumstances so intertwined that it usually is not feasible to isolate the effects of any one. These factors include poverty, minority status, family breakdown, inadequate educational and other services, and frequent exposure to deviant persons. Socioeconomically disadvantaged children are at increased risk for problems at school (Patterson, Kupersmidt, & Vaden, 1990), including identification as SED (Cullinan et al., 1992; U.S. Department of Education, 1992). They often enter school without all the skills and behaviors that primary grade teachers commonly expect of students, making them educationally disadvantaged from the very beginning (Chan & Rueda 1979). A majority of students with behavior disorders are socioeconomically disadvantaged (Cullinan et al., 1992; U.S. Department of Education, 1992).

Television and other mass communication media play an ever greater role in the socialization of children and adolescents. Concerned individuals and organizations have protested the frequency with which sexual and aggressive programming appears on television. Research on televised violence indicates that a large percentage of the programs watched by children contain violence (Gadow & Sprafkin, 1993) and that televised aggression can promote aggression in viewers. However, it is not clear that, in real life, televised aggression increases aggression among children with behavior disorders (Gadow & Sprafkin, 1993).

Stress refers to a situation in which the adaptive resources of a person are strained or exceeded by demands in the environment or within that person (Johnson, 1986). Physical, social, or psychological events that initiate stress (e.g., injury, loss of a loved one, frustrated attempts to reach a goal) are called stressors. Stressors can produce physiological changes (e.g., breathing, circulation, or blood chemistry); disrupt attention, problem solving, language, and performance; and prompt fear, anger, or other strong emotions. Many observers in the classroom and clinic are convinced that stress is a principal cause of disorders of thought, feeling, and behavior. Stress is a key feature of a major psychoeducational concept of behavior disorders called the conflict cycle (Wood & Long, 1991), to be described later.

Interaction of Biological and Psychological Conditions

Although biological and psychological conditions have been discussed separately here, most theorists conclude that they operate together to produce behavior disorders (Garrison & Earls, 1987). One conception of how biological and psychological conditions interact to produce children's behavior disorders appears in the research of Thomas and Chess (1977) on temperaments—styles of behaving that are probably determined by biological conditions prior to birth. Thomas and Chess found that a child's particular pattern of temperament usually influences which child-rearing practices his or her parents adopt; in turn, these parental practices influence the child's behavioral development. Young children whose temperament results in any of the following sets of behaviors are especially difficult for parents to manage and are more likely to experience school problems: (1) irregularity in feeding, sleeping, and other biological functions; (2) avoidance of, and poor adaptation to, new situations; and (3) frequent intensely negative moods and behavior. Thus, temperaments could eventually influence teachers' reactions as well as parents', with important continuing repercussions for the child's behavior and development.

Models

The psychoeducational, behavioral, and ecological models provide different explanations of the causes of behavior disorders and offer different recommendations about appropriate intervention. This section considers the views about causes of behavior disorders associated with each of the models.

Psychoeducational Model.   The psychoeducational model adapts ideas and practices of psychodynamic psychology for use in schools, institutions, camps, and other education-therapeutic settings for children and adolescents with behavior disorders. Wood and Long (1991) have described a psychoeducational perspective on behavior disorders called the conflict cycle. In this view, if parental or societal expectations interfere with the child's attempts to satisfy his or her own basic needs, an improper self-image will develop. The child will also view the world as hostile or restrictive and will behave according to this negative view. The young person will also view typical academic and social demands in school negatively, creating stress; as a result, the young person will feel anxious and behave defensively and immaturely. These behavior patterns ordinarily provoke negative reactions in teachers and peers that perpetuate the individual's maladaptive feelings and behaviors, creating a self-fulfilling cycle of conflict and failure. Wood and Long believe that teachers who conceptualize a student's behavior disorders in terms of the conflict cycle will better understand how these behaviors are tied to disturbed emotions and how the student can be supported and helped to modify his or her view of the world, leading to more adaptive behavior.

Behavioral Model.   Originating mainly in Skinner's principles of operant conditioning, the behavioral model has profoundly influenced special education. A fundamental concept is that most human behavior is learned. Drives, emotions, thoughts, and feelings are not believed to be major causes of behavior. Instead, principles of operant conditioning explain the origin, perpetuation, and modification of behavior—both normal and abnormal. For example, if family members, teachers, or peers reinforce a child for dependent, aggressive, withdrawn, incompetent, or other undesirable behavior, such behavior will occur more frequently or more intensively. And if prosocial, skillful, or other desirable behavior is not reinforced, it will decrease (Cooper, Heron, & Heward, 1987).

When students engage in disruption, aggression, withdrawal, dependence, hyperactivity, and other maladaptive behavior patterns, teachers often react in ways that reinforce these patterns. They may give a reminder about a broken rule, console the students with hugs, reprimand or publicly ridicule them, or engage them in a discussion about the necessity of being good citizens. Though different in some ways, these reactions have one important element in common: they provide attention from an adult as a consequence of inappropriate behavior. Such attention can reinforce disordered behavior, and classroom research has demonstrated that teachers do tend to pay much more attention to problem behavior while ignoring task-oriented or prosocial behavior (Morgan & Jenson, 1988). Behaviorists point to this process as one major way in which behavior disorders arise and are perpetuated.

Many behavior disorders involve coercing people through arguing, withdrawing, threatening, crying, fighting, or other behaviors (Patterson, DeBarsyshe, & Ramsey, 1989). When the adult or child to whom such behaviors are directed gives in to the coercer's demand, coercion is reinforced. Further, the youngster readily learns that intense and persistent coercion is more likely to succeed than mild coercion.

Children can also learn inappropriate behavior through models (Bandura, 1986). Modeling can be a particularly powerful source of problem behavior if the student's home, school, or community contains many peers or adults who demonstrate aggression, delinquency, anxiety, nonparticipation, or otherwise maladjusted behavior and who fail to demonstrate cooperative, achievement-oriented, and other prosocial behavior. As noted earlier, television and other popular media provide numerous models of deviant behavior.

Ecological Model.   Based on ecological concepts used in anthropology, ethology, psychology, sociology, and other disciplines, the ecological model of behavior disorders emphasizes overall patterns of interaction among the individual's behaviors and the social and physical environments in which these behaviors take place. Expectations, restrictions, and demands are present in every behavior ecology system (ecosystem), and when the person's behavior is in harmony with these, there is a "goodness-of-fit." In the ecological model a behavior disorder is a lack of goodness-of-fit; it is a disturbance in patterns of interaction between an individual and the ecosystem, not a property of either the student or the ecosystem alone (Rhodes,

1970). Unfortunately, people involved in the disturbed ecosystem do not usually see it this way. When ecological goodness-of-fit is disturbed, the student tends to blame peers or teacher, and teachers, administrators, and others often initiate a labeling process that locates the source of disturbance in the student.

The ecological model has influenced both the psychoeducational (Swap, Prieto, & Harth, 1982) and behavioral (Cantrell & Cantrell, 1985; Rogers-Warren, 1984) models of children's behavior disorders. One major effect has been increased recognition of the need to consider the many ecological systems in and out of school that may affect the student. The school yard, school bus, home, community, peer groups, church, social agencies, and other ecological systems may contribute to classroom disturbance as well as present opportunities to reduce disturbance. Thus, important systems should be identified, their physical and behavioral aspects should be assessed, and intervention plans should be made based on this information. New developments in community-based, multidisciplinary service to children with behavior disorders (Algarin & Friedman, 1991; Algarin et al., 1990) are compatible with the ecological model.

CHARACTERISTICS

In the most general sense, the characteristics of students with behavior disorders include all behavior patterns that prompt others (especially educators) to identify the student as showing behavior disorders. Most teachers of students with behavior disorders will eventually deal with a wide variety of maladaptive functioning. However, research and teacher observations indicate that certain behavior problem characteristics are more likely to be identified than others, and educators should be especially aware of, and skilled in, these areas.

Evidence from various sources, especially research on prevalence and classification of the problems of students with behavior disorders (Achenbach & Edelbrock, 1989; Epstein, Kauffman, & Cullinan, 1985; Quay, 1986), shows that the major characteristics exhibited by students with behavior disorders fall under two general headings that can be called *environment conflict* and *personal disturbance.* The evidence further suggests that environmental conflict includes at least three specific varieties: aggression-disruption, hyperactivity, and social maladjustment. Personal disturbance appears to include at least two specific varieties: anxiety-depression and withdrawal. Further, students with behavior disorders often show learning disorders that may appear as cognitive disabilities or academic skill deficits. These patterns of learning disorders vary somewhat by age and sex (Epstein et al., 1985; Epstein et al., 1989).

Table 5–1 summarizes the characteristics and representative behaviors for the more common mild-moderate behavior disorders and the infrequent severe-profound disorders. The severe disorders involve some behavior problems that appear to be extreme expressions of the characteristics in mild-moderate behavior disorders. However, the behavioral similarities do not necessarily mean similar causes, outcomes, or appropriate treatments.

Mild-Moderate Behavior Disorders

Aggression-Disruption.   Aggression, broadly defined, is commonplace, and under some circumstances is important for survival and encouraged by society. However,

Table 5–1
Major characteristics of children and youth with behavior disorders

Disorder	Representative Behaviors	
	Mild-Moderate Disorder	**Severe-Profound Disorder**
Environmental Conflict Aggression-Disruption	Fighting; cruelty; bullying; tantrums; rule violations; disrespect; negativism; threats; destructiveness	Self-injury; primitive assaults; destructiveness; negativism
Hyperactivity	Attention deficits; impulsivity; over-activity; accompanied by aggression-disruption	Repetitive, bizarre motor and verbal acts that appear to provide self-stimulation; other overactivity
Social Maladjustment	Peer group-oriented stealing, fighting, vandalism, other illegal acts; substance abuse; sexual irresponsibility; truancy	Indifference to peers and classmates; extreme lack of social interactions
Personal Disturbance Anxiety-Inferiority	Low self-confidence; situation-specific avoidance; crying; physiological over-arousal; statements of worry; skill disorganization	Extreme upset over minor changes in a familiar situation
Social Incompetence	Failure to initiate verbal or motor behavior toward peers and others; failure to reciprocate initiations of others; incompetent or aggressive social initiations resulting in peer rejection	Same, but in more severe degrees; apparent indifference to interpersonal activity, even toward parents and siblings; play skills usually lacking
Learning Disorders	Low-normal intellectual performance; substantial deficits in basic academic skills and general educational achievement	Often moderate to profound mental retardation; substantial deficits in language, attention, memory, other abilities; deficient self-help skills

behaviors that produce destruction, pain, or disadvantage to others usually disturb both adults and children and may produce counteraggression. Typical instances of the aggression-disruption characteristics are cruelty, bullying, threats, fighting, screaming, tantrums, hostile resistance, disobedience, and disrespect to the teacher.

Aggression-disruption is a common characteristic of children in special education and mental health treatment (Baum, 1989; Kazdin, 1989; Mattison, Morales, & Bauer, 1992). Boys are three to six times as likely as girls to show this characteristic, and it concerns teachers of the behaviorally disordered substantially more than other problems. This concern with aggression-disruption is probably well placed, because follow-up research on children and adolescents has consistently indicated that, no matter what their age when first identified, highly aggressive children are much more likely than nonaggressive youngsters to remain in conflict with persons in their environment. In fact, such behavior puts the child at high risk for juvenile and adult delinquency and other forms of maladjustment (Baum, 1989; Kazdin, 1991).

Hyperactivity. Extensive interest has been focused on the nature and treatment of the clinical disorder category called attention-deficit hyperactivity disorder (ADHD) (American Psychiatric Association, 1987), also commonly referred to as hyperactivity. ADHD is marked by attention deficits (not persisting on a task, easy distractibility), impulsivity (hasty and mistaken decision-making processes, disorganized work strategies, interrupting others), and inappropriate overactivity (restless moving about, fidgeting). Many children with ADHD also show deficits in rule-governed behavior, aggression, learning disorders, "soft" neurological signs (some evidence of brain dysfunctioning, such as minor disabilities in coordination, reflexes, and visual-motor per-

Verbal or physical aggression is often a characteristic of students with behavior disorders.

ception), and social incompetence (Campbell & Werry, 1986; DuPaul, Guevremont, & Barkley, 1991). The problems of ADHD are often exhibited by students in special education. Logically, an ADHD student whose aggression, impulsivity, overactivity, social incompetence, and other behavior problems are especially severe would be more likely identified as exhibiting behavior disorders, whereas one whose learning and attention problem dominate might be identified as showing learning disabilities.

The reported prevalence of hyperactivity has varied widely, with more careful recent studies ranging from about 1% to 5% of elementary-age pupils and identifying 4 to 7 boys for each girl. Approximately half of the referrals to child guidance clinics are for hyperactivity (Paternite & Loney, 1980). Officially, ADHD must have been evident by about 7 years of age, and adolescents are not usually identified as hyperactive. However, hyperactive children, especially those who also show aggression, are at increased risk for various kinds of maladjustment in adolescence and beyond (DuPaul et al., 1991; Whalen, 1989).

Social Maladjustment.   The term *social maladjustment* refers to behavior that violates laws or conventional standards of the school or community but conforms to the standards of some social subgroup. Social maladjustment may include gang- or group-related vandalism, stealing, fighting, truancy, sexual precocity, and substance abuse (Moore & Arthur, 1989; Quay, 1986). These behavior patterns are often motivated by economic gain and/or the need to achieve the approval and admiration of subgroup peers. Males are five to six times as likely to show this type of disorder as females.

Social maladjustment provides an especially clear illustration of the difficulties of conceptualizing and defining behavior disorders (Center, 1990) because some socially maladjusted behaviors are commonly performed by many adolescents (Feldman, Caplinger, & Wodarski, 1983; Nye, Short, & Olson, 1958) and because the norms and expectations for some of the behavior patterns involved (e.g., sexual activity, alcohol and drug use) can vary sharply across age groups, places, and periods of time. Further, socially maladjusted behaviors do not necessarily result in personal distress for the performer; in fact, interpersonal functioning, at least with subgroup peers, is often enhanced rather than impaired.

On the other hand, social maladjustment clearly impairs the functioning of other persons, as is obvious from official statistics, media reports, personal experiences of teachers, students, and victims. Even the grim statistics cannot fully portray the actual consequences in terms of unreported crimes, lost instructional time, a school climate of fear and discouragement, and so on (Baker, 1985). Research indicates that socially maladjusted adolescents are at high risk for many kinds of adult disorders (Quay, 1986), especially those youth identified as juvenile delinquents and placed in correctional facilities (Moore & Arthur, 1989).

Anxiety-Depression.   Students with this behavior pattern may refuse to speak up when in class, show pessimism and disinterest in key aspects of their lives, be visibly nervous when presented with an assignment, become ill when it is time to go to school, and show a lack of self-confidence in performing common school and social behaviors. The anxious child or adolescent is likely to experience a strong anticipation of danger, feel physiological arousal and discomfort, become disorganized in thinking, and avoid the feared situations (Morris & Kratochwill, 1991).

Surveys indicate that about 2% to 4% of children and adolescents show clinically diagnosable (very severe) anxiety disorders and depression; perhaps 20% show, at some time, moderate degrees of these problems (Quay & LaGreca, 1986; Siegel & Ridley-Johnson, 1985). The sex ratio is approximately equal through early adolescence, but older adolescents with anxiety-depression are more likely to be female. Children and young adolescents who exhibit anxiety-depression are less likely to experience continuing serious maladjustment than older adolescents with anxiety-depression (Kaslow & Rehm, 1991; Last, 1989).

Social Incompetence. This characteristic is evidenced by students who rarely take part in play and other informal peer interactions and resist joining educational activities. They often appear uncommunicative, extremely shy, self-conscious, and moody. Greenwood, Walker, and Hops (1977) described two variations: (1) noninteractive students, who have poorly developed social skills and may fear interactions with others; and (2) rejected students, who do initiate social interactions but in such aggressive, immature, or otherwise inappropriate ways that their interactions are avoided or ignored by other children. Similarly, Gresham (1988) discriminated important differences between students with inadequate social skills and those with behavior problems that interfere with their social interactions.

Students with behavior disorders evidence environmental conflict, personal disturbance, and/or learning disorders.

It seems self-evident that social incompetence reduces the developing individual's opportunities for friendships and other important chances for profiting from classroom and informal learning activities. Research shows that unpopular children tend to remain unpopular over time. Surprisingly, however, mild to moderate social interaction difficulty, in and of itself, does not seem to be a strong predictor of continuing psychological maladjustment (Gersten, Langner, Eisenberg, Simcha-Fagen, & McCarthy, 1976).

Learning Disorders.   In our society a young person's adjustment is closely linked to how well he or she acquires and applies information presented at school. Failure to learn basic academic skills, poor performance in the various subject areas, and a lack of vocational preparedness are severe obstacles to proper adjustment. Among students in general, behavior problems are clearly associated with lower achievement and ability (Cullinan et al., 1992; Kauffman, 1993). Students with behavior disorders are usually substantially behind in reading, arithmetic, and spelling achievement (Kauffman, Cullinan, & Epstein, 1987); these deficits seem to grow larger as the student passes through school (Epstein et al., 1989).

Although the measured intelligence of these students can range from 70 (or even below) up to high levels of intellectual giftedness, IQs usually fall in the 80 to 100 range (Cullinan et al., 1992; U.S. Department of Education, 1992). Some students with behavior disorders display the specific ability problems commonly associated with learning disability, such as impulsivity, attention deficits, and learning strategy deficits (Denton & McIntyre, 1978; Firestone & Martin, 1979; Foley, Cullinan, & Epstein, 1990). Other cognitive problem areas may account for some behavior disorders, such as deficits in social perception that predispose the youngster to aggression (Dozier, 1988).

Neither mild achievement deficit nor slightly below-normal intelligence is a strong predictor of maladjustment in adulthood (Kohlberg, LaCrosse, & Ricks, 1972). However, children who show poor achievement together with a significant degree of environmental conflict are at substantial risk for a wide variety of adult maladjustments (Kazdin, 1989; Whalen, 1989).

Severe Behavior Disorders

Children with severe-profound behavior disorders (psychoses) have been assigned a confusing variety of labels, reflecting the fact that these disorders are still largely a mystery. Some authorities believe that different varieties of child psychosis exist, others say these are only different manifestations of essentially the same disorder(s), and many assert that this issue is irrelevant to effective treatment. The bulk of the evidence indicates that there are at least two distinguishable psychoses of childhood: autism and childhood schizophrenia (Cantor, 1989; Ornitz, 1989; Prior & Werry, 1986). Psychoses are found in less than one tenth of 1% of children, about 75% of them boys. Psychotic children rarely become well-functioning adults, and most continue to require extensive supervision and care. However, some treatment developments offer hope for changing this prognosis (e.g., Lovaas, 1987). The best predictor of eventual functioning seems to be childhood intellectual level (Prior & Werry, 1986).

There has been considerably more research in autism than on childhood schizophrenia. The best evidence to date links autism to brain disorders that interfere with the individual's social and cognitive development (Ornitz, 1989; Prior & Werry, 1986). Children with autism commonly bite, scratch, and pick at themselves, bang their heads, and otherwise inflict grievous self-injury; they may assault others in primitive ways and destroy furnishings, toys, and other objects. They often show activity disorders that seem to be linked to attention and perception disturbances, including excessive locomotion, extended periods of virtually motionless staring, and various repetitive, stereotyped vocalizations and body movements that seem intended to provide self-stimulation. Many autistic children show reactions resembling extreme anxiety when they detect minor changes in their surroundings and routines. Frequently they are grossly incompetent socially, rarely initiating interactions toward peers and having few appropriate play or social skills; they often seem totally indifferent to friendship or love, even from family members. Typically, autistic children exhibit serious learning disorders. Normal or higher IQ levels are possible, but most affected individuals are mentally retarded (many severely). Language, if present at all, is fundamentally abnormal. Attention, perception, and memory disorders are common, as are deficits in feeding, dressing, toileting, and other self-help skills (Schreibman & Charlop, 1989).

Federal education regulations originally included autism as a variety of serious emotional disturbance. At the urging of autism advocates, the U.S. Department of Education separated the two and placed autism into "Other Health Impaired" category in 1980. The Individuals with Disabilities Education Act of 1990 established an "autism" category, defining the term as follows:

> "Autism" means a developmental disability significantly affecting verbal and nonverbal communication and social interaction, generally evident before age 3, that adversely affects a child's educational performance. Other characteristics often associated with autism are engagement in repetitive activities and stereotyped movements, resistance to environmental change or change in daily routines, and unusual responses to sensory experiences. The term does not apply if a child's educational performance is adversely affected primarily because the child has a serious educational disturbance . . . (*Federal Register*, 1992, p. 44801)

This definition reflects one trend in the field that views the central problem of autism as a brain disorder affecting language and related mental functions.

Scientific evidence on childhood schizophrenia is sketchy. In some cases it may be an early form of adult schizophrenia, perhaps caused by genetic defects in the brain chemistry that make the individual highly vulnerable to various stressors. The name of this disorder may be misleading, because few cases become apparent before early adolescence. Many characteristics of the problem include tantrums, repetitive or otherwise bizarre movements and postures, withdrawal and social rejection, and unpredictable emotional changes such as an extreme display of fear (Cantor, 1989). Intellectual functioning is generally higher than in autism, but there can be cognitive disturbances like those found in adult schizophrenia, including delusions (unfounded beliefs), hallucinations, and disjointed, confused language and reasoning (Prior & Werry, 1986).

ASSESSMENT

Assessment involves the gathering and use of information pertaining to a behavior disorder. Often it is most useful to gather this information in the form of numbers (e.g., test scores) that represent the student's status or functioning on some behavior characteristic or other area of interest to the educator. The appropriate assessment procedure can provide usable data on educational strengths and problems, medical disorders, family and community situations, and other important information. The numbers can then be used in such activities as classifying and researching. Assessment can be used to classify or to complete scientific research; more important, assessment is crucial to educators in screening for behavior disorders, placing a student in an appropriate program, designing an intervention plan, and monitoring the student's progress under the plan (Tindal & Marston, 1990).

Assessment Methods

Most methods of assessing a child's school problems are of three types (Cullinan & Root, 1985). They may focus on (1) actual functioning in a natural situation, (2) actual functioning in a contrived situation, or (3) reported functioning.

1. *Actual functioning in a natural situation.* It is often important to assess the student as he or she engages in classroom activities. In the direct observation method (Cooper et al., 1987; Shapiro & Kratochwill, 1988), carefully defined behaviors are observed by the teacher or other recorder, and the number of times each behavior occurs is recorded. For example, a student's aggression might be assessed each day for several weeks by counting how many times he or she hits, pushes, and argues with classmates. The resulting daily totals provide a concrete representation of important aspects of aggression. The totals can be checked for a trend or compared to other students' totals to help decide just how different this student's aggression is. A variation of this assessment method involves scoring products of the student's behavior, such as daily performance on academic assignments that demonstrate a skill.

2. *Actual functioning in a contrived situation.* It is sometimes more convenient to set up a standardized testing situation in which the behaviors assessed are intended to represent what the child does in natural situations. For example, a standardized test of intelligence comprises numerous tasks intended to call for the intellectual ability needed in real-world situations. There are also standardized tests of specific psychological abilities (e.g., auditory perception, fine motor coordination), knowledge and achievement (e.g., reading and language development), adaptive behaviors (e.g., social interaction skills), and other important characteristics (Hammill, Brown, & Bryant, 1989).

3. *Reported functioning.* Many characteristics are assessed by using reports of the student's functioning, which may come from the student, peers, teachers, parents, or some other informed source. Important information can obtained through an interview with the student or other informant. Interviews with a structured format (standard questions about specific problems, situations, and behaviors) are more useful for educational purposes than unstructured interviews.

Another measure of reported functioning is the behavior rating scale, which usually contains a standard group of items, each describing a behavioral asset or problem. For each item there is a scale of 2 or more points indicating the extent to which a student shows that behavior. For example, an item about social withdrawal might have to be marked by the teacher as "no problem," "mild problem," or "severe problem," reflecting a judgment of how much the student shows social withdrawal. Sociometric techniques require each member of a social group to identify desirable and undesirable members of their group. For example, each student might privately identify one peer with whom he or she likes to interact and one who is disliked or avoided. In analysis of the responses of all group members, it is possible to identify a few students who are generally admired, some who are actively rejected, and others who are simply ignored.

Uses of Assessment

Screening is designed to sort pupils who definitely do not need special education now from those who may, and to do so with relatively little time and effort. For instance, the Systematic Screening for Behavior Disorders assessment procedure (Walker et al., 1988) uses data on a student's social and emotional functioning as reported by the teacher and from direct observation of the student. These data are combined to suggest, among other things, who should be considered for special education.

For each student thus screened, further assessments may be made of school behavior, academic achievement, cognitive abilities, teacher and classroom variables, home and community situations, neurological and other medical status, feelings, and so on. Such diverse information is considered at a conference that often includes the child's regular teacher(s), principal, special educators, psychological diagnosticians, and other professionals, as well as the student's parent(s) and (less often) the student. The purpose of the conference is to decide whether special education is needed and if so, to begin to develop an Individualized Educational Plan (IEP).

Once the student is placed, teachers usually perform further assessment to translate educational objectives into effective intervention. Teachers usually need to know about the student's problems in detail (e.g., how many arguments and fights, how many positive interactions with classmates, percentages of assignments completed per day) in order to select appropriate teaching techniques and set realistic goals for improvement. Direct observation is particularly useful for these purposes and for monitoring the student's progress toward IEP goals (Howell & Morehead, 1987; Walker & Fabre, 1987).

Unfortunately, many educational assessment practices have little relevance to designing and monitoring interventions for students with behavior disorders. Although assessment of medical, mental, home, community, and other conditions may be important in a multisystemic, multidisciplinary effort, such a multifaceted assessment effort will seldom indicate appropriate educational goals or teaching procedures for an individual (Walker & Fabre, 1987). Because assessment consumes critical time and talent, educators must be especially careful in selecting assessment methods to match the information needs.

Age-Level Distinctions

Each assessment method has been used at various student levels, but different ages often call for differences in the complexity and content of assessment. For example, a sociometric procedure for preschool and early elementary students is included in the *Test of Early Socioemotional Development* (Hresko & Brown, 1984). The names of three friends are solicited privately from each student in a class, and a group tabulation can identify unpopular youngsters who may need assistance. In contrast, Bower's (1969) *Student Survey* sociometric for secondary school students presents a list of positive and negative behavior descriptions (e.g., "a student who gets into fights or quarrels with other students"). Each student writes the name of a classmate who best fits the description, and a tabulation may reveal a consensus of peer perceptions. It can be important to identify a student perceived negatively by many peers, as well as a student not suggested for either positive or negative descriptions. In similar ways, the objectives and content for other assessment methods for behavior disorders vary by the age of the student.

INTERVENTION The psychoeducational, behavioral, and ecological models involve intervention principles and techniques compatible with their different views of behavior disorders. How each of these models looks at the nature of behavior disorders and the role of education in helping youngsters is reviewed briefly in Table 5-2.

Psychoeducational Interventions

Surface behavior management (Long & Newman, 1976) includes practices designed to prevent or minimize the unfortunate results of disordered behavior on the student himself or herself, fellow students, or the ongoing program. Management techniques include (1) designing the structure, schedule, and other program aspects so as to avoid behavior problems; (2) letting students know which behaviors are permitted or at least temporarily tolerated; and (3) interfering with behaviors that cannot be tolerated by giving verbal or physical expressions of support, changing tasks, or separating the student from a provocative situation. The *life-space interview* (Wood & Long, 1991) is an on-the-spot verbal exploration of a crisis situation in which the teacher's goal is (1) to help the young person overcome strong emotions and return to ongoing activities (emotional first aid); and/or (2) to promote the student's insight into environmental, emotional, and other factors that lie behind his or her maladaptive behaviors (clinical exploitation of events). *Reality therapy* (Glasser, 1969) and *transactional analysis* (Harris, 1976) are examples of here-and-now psychodynamic therapies that have been adapted for use in special education situations; their emphasis is on personal responsibility for one's own life and a commitment to reasonable and specific behavior changes.

Psychoeducational curricula are collections of activities intended to provide students with understanding and greater control of feelings and thoughts. For example, the Self-Control Curriculum (Fagen, Long, & Stevens, 1975) shows how to assess and teach eight personal skills believed necessary for a student to control his or her own

Table 5–2
Comparison of psychoeducational, behavioral, and ecological models

Model	Nature of Behavior Disorder	Appropriate Educational Intervention
Psychoeducational	Biological energies and parental action together influence the child's personality development for better or for worse. Maladaptive behavior and emotions are signs of improper personality development. Though not always apparent, these personality weaknesses can be activated by stress created by home, school, or other problems; the result often is behavior disorders.	The teacher must help students understand their problems and effectively cope with them. This is best accomplished when the teacher develops a trusting and respectful relationship with students, teaches them to recognize and manage stressful situations, and helps them to develop appropriate personal strengths for dealing with future life challenges. School activities often need to be individualized for the student. Games, simulations, art, and other nontraditional activities are favored.
Behavioral	Psychologists have discovered key principles of learning that describe how behavior is learned and maintained. These principles apply even to behavior disorders. For instance, students can learn maladaptive behaviors and emotions by observing them in a peer or parent. Also, when teachers pay attention to disruptive, strange, or self-defeating behavior, they may be reinforcing these maladaptive behaviors unintentionally but effectively.	The teacher must identify deficient behaviors to increase and excessive behaviors to decrease. Identified behaviors are measured often so that the teacher remains aware of behavior changes. The teacher teaches and reinforces adaptive social, academic, or other behaviors to increase them. Maladaptive behaviors must not be reinforced. Students can be taught to take control of their own education by learning to identify, measure, and reinforce behaviors needing improvement.
Ecological	Each student operates as part of various social systems, including school systems. The student's behavior may fit harmoniously with the other parts of the system; if it does not, the system may become disturbed and not function smoothly. Other persons in the system (e.g., teacher, classmates, principal) react by identifying the child as disordered when, in fact, the system—not any one part of it— is what is disordered.	The teacher must understand all parts of the disturbed system so that a variety of changes can be tried to eliminate disturbance. The student may be taught new competencies or helped to give up maladaptive behavior patterns. Just as important, however, are other changes: modifying the expectations and attitudes of teachers, classmates, parents, and others; obtaining resources needed to provide a more supportive educational situation; and helping to mobilize psychological, health, or other services that impact systems outside the school.

A life-space interview explores what's involved in a crisis, leading to an attempt to foster self-control.

emotional impulses (attention, memory, sequencing, anticipating, understanding feelings, coping with frustration, delaying actions, relaxing).

Behavioral Interventions

Behavior modification interventions (Kerr & Nelson, 1989; Wolery, Bailey, & Sugai, 1988) rely on a relatively few basic teaching strategies.

1. *Positive reinforcement* is a procedure in which a particular behavior is followed by a reward, with the result that the behavior is more likely to be performed in the future. For example, if a student shares academic or play materials with a peer and is then positively reinforced by the teacher's compliments and praise, he or she is more likely to share in the future.

2. *Negative reinforcement* is also a procedure for making a behavior more likely to occur; it involves the removal of unpleasant stimuli after a specific behavior is performed. For instance, a teacher might tell students that the arithmetic assignment is in two parts and that anyone completing the first part with perfect accuracy will not be required to do the second part. The behavior of a student who completes the first

part perfectly will be negatively reinforced by removal of the requirement to complete the second part, and the student will be more likely to complete such assignments accurately in the future.

3. _Punishment_ is a process in which a behavior is made less likely to occur in the future because it is presently followed by some aversive consequence. If whenever a student exhibits aggression against peers, he or she is required, as a consequence, to engage in brief physical exercise, his or her aggressive behavior is punished and may be made less likely to recur. Alternatively, behavior can be punished by consequences that either (1) withdraw a specific amount of reward (response cost procedure) or (2) prevent access to rewards for a certain period of time (time-out procedure). For example, the teacher can discourage unauthorized moving about the classroom by either removing a specified privilege or withdrawing a few minutes of recess.

4. _Extinction_ is a procedure to decrease the likelihood of behavior that formerly has been reinforced. For example, some teachers attend to and thereby unintentionally reinforce excessively dependent behaviors, such as repetitious requests for clarification or approval. Teachers who recognize that they have been encouraging dependency in this way may decide to ignore unnecessary requests. This procedure is extinction if it succeeds in reducing the dependent behavior. For details of these and related operant conditioning principles, see Cooper et al. (1987) and Ferster and Culbertson (1982).

These basic behavior modification procedures can be combined in various ways to yield other useful teaching techniques. A _token economy_ is a simulated economic system based on a token reinforcer, such as check marks, stickers, points, or play money (see Kazdin, 1985). Individual students or groups may earn tokens for some specified behaviors and lose them for others. Tokens can be redeemed for desirable items and privileges. Teachers can even simulate economic features of society such as saving, layaway, interest, inflation, and price reductions. Educational programs based on token reinforcement have been used to improve academic skills, conduct, and other behaviors relevant to the normalization of students with behavior disorders.

A _behavioral contract_ is a written description of the relationships between a person's behaviors and the consequences of performing those behaviors. A contract should specify (1) responsibilities (target behaviors), (2) monitoring procedures (ways in which the student's performance is to be observed and recorded), and (3) privileges (reinforcers earned by the student on completion of the responsibilities). All aspects of the contract should be agreed to by both teacher and student; some negotiation may be required.

Behavior modification procedures have been developed for groups of students, even entire classrooms. Two advantages of group contingencies are that (1) the power of the peer group is used to encourage appropriate behavior and (2) teacher time and effort are saved compared to individual contingencies for each group member (Litow & Pumroy, 1975). The two main group contingency types are _interdependent and dependent group contingencies._ In an interdependent contingency the performance of the group as a whole determines the consequences for each group member. In a dependent contingency the performance of one member of the group can determine the consequences for each member of the group.

Behavioral group contingencies are designed to use the peer group's considerable influence to encourage prosocial goals.

Various differential reinforcement strategies can be used as "positive" alternatives to punishment for reducing maladaptive behavior (Deitz & Repp, 1983). For instance, differential reinforcement of low rates of behavior can encourage a student to perform a behavior less frequently. The target behavior might be reinforced only if it has occurred no more than some preset number of times that day. This limit can be reduced gradually as the behavior comes under control.

Although many behavior modification procedures feature the teacher as planner, recorder, and implementer of behavior change, a student can also serve in these roles. Though many aspects of behavioral self-management are poorly understood and remain controversial (Bornstein, 1985), there clearly are self-management techniques relevant to the needs of students with behavior disorders (Nelson, Smith, Young, & Dodd, 1991; Olinger & Epstein, 1991). These techniques generally involve students in observing, recording, instructing, rewarding, and/or punishing their own behaviors.

Behavior Modification for Children with Severe Disorders.   Children with autism and other severe disorders have received extensive attention from behavioral researchers (see Schreibman & Mills, 1983). The work of Ivar Lovaas and his colleagues (Lovaas & Newsom, 1976) was pivotal in establishing behavioral techniques for teaching important skills to autistic youngsters individually. Intensive and long-term application of these techniques has reportedly resulted in substantial improvements in life adjustment for many autistic children (Lovaas, 1987).

The techniques have been extended to groups of autistic students. Koegel, Russo, and Rincover (1977) have identified five crucial teaching skills: (1) giving clear, concise instructions; (2) providing sufficient physical guidance, demonstrations, and other prompts for the desired behaviors and knowing how to remove the prompts gradually as the student begins to respond properly; (3) providing immediate, effective consequences (primarily edibles and praise for correct behaviors, extinction or time-out for inappropriate behaviors); (4) presenting each instruction as a separate response opportunity so that the student will not become distracted or confused; and (5) knowing how to shape a desired final behavior by reinforcing responses that are each one step nearer the goal.

In addition to how students with autism should be taught, it is important to consider what they should be taught. Most behavior goals must be approached in a step-by-step fashion, and so teachers need task analysis and instructional programming skills to specify the steps (Howell & Morehead, 1987; Sailor & Guess, 1983). Fortunately, carefully specified, stepwise instructional programs for many important skills are now available (Lovaas et al., 1980). Guidelines for teaching students with autism are provided by Koegel (1981), Koegel and Schreibman (1981), Lovaas et al. (1980), Sailor and Guess (1983), and others.

Ecological Interventions

Proponents of the ecological viewpoint have provided some general recommendations for education of students with behavior disorders (Apter, 1982). First, they suggest that the educational system (indeed, society as a whole) should become more accepting of deviant behavior so that fewer students are labeled as behaviorally disordered. Further, when treatment is needed, changes in the educational environment should be targeted as carefully as modifications in the student's behavior (Rhodes, 1970). In addition, it is emphasized that a localized ecosystem, such as the classroom, is subtly but significantly interrelated with other ecosystems, such as the home and community; therefore, the most effective intervention is one that goes beyond the local problem to bring about changes on a larger scale. Thus, ecological special educators argue for a redefinition and expansion of teaching practices to include work with other teachers, involvement with parents and the community, and active child advocacy to help others recognize the needs and rights of children.

The ecological-behavioral approach (Cantrell & Cantrell, 1985) has stimulated recent work on generalization of behavior change to new situations so as to help in mainstreaming. For instance, transenvironmental programming (Anderson-Inman, Walker, & Purcell, 1984; Anderson-Inman, 1986) is a mainstreaming technology that calls for (1) assessment of key expectations of the regular classroom; (2) preparing students for mainstreaming by making certain they can meet the social, academic, and other demands of regular education; (3) implementing a variety of behavior generalization strategies (Stokes & Baer, 1977) to help the student use, in the mainstream setting, skills taught by the special educator; and (4) assessing the student's performance in the mainstream setting after placement to evaluate progress and identify any further needs.

Similar in concept to transenvironmental programming is the functional skill curriculum for students with autism (Donnellan & Neel, 1986; Neel, Billingsley, & Lambert, 1983). This curriculum teaches skills that do or will contribute to the student's ability to operate independently in school, at home, and in the community. Several key assumptions are at the heart of this concept:

1. Community and other natural environments are carefully assessed with regard to skill and other demands, and the student's current ability to meet those demands is also assessed.
2. The skills and behaviors to be taught are carefully selected to be those most likely to help the student meet critical present and/or future environmental demands.
3. These critical skills and behaviors are taught in the natural environment. A major rationale for this approach is that most students identified as autistic have substantial difficulty generalizing skills taught in one situation (e.g., a special classroom) to other settings (e.g., a store).

A large-scale ecological intervention for children with behavioral, emotional, and other problems is the Willie M. program (Behar, 1984; Fernandez, 1987), administered by the North Carolina Department of Human Resources. This program screens, diagnoses, and provides and evaluates professional services for children and adolescents with emotional, mental, or neurological disabilities who are highly violent or assaultive. Since 1981 more than 2,000 North Carolina boys and girls have been certified as Willie M. class members; about 1,000 are served at any one time. The vast majority are males 10 to 18 years old, and about half live in foster or institutional care. Most have a juvenile court record, with about 4% convicted of murder, rape, robbery, or assault; about half have histories of assault against parents or siblings. The majority have educational achievement deficits in comparison to their ability; about 70% of Willie M. class members are in special education for students with behavior disorders.

Obviously these young people's needs include but go far beyond education. The Willie M. program's response requires coordination of treatment in multiple ecological systems by various helping professionals, including special educators. To avoid conflicts between agencies and to reduce the chance of children "falling through the cracks" of agency jurisdictions, each Willie M. client is assigned a case manager to coordinate educational, psychological, medical, social work, housing, legal, and other needed professional services.

Age-Level Distinctions

Each intervention technique can be used with any student with behavior disorders, but age may need to be considered in determining the objectives and application of an intervention. For example, behavioral self-management techniques have been used with students of all ages. In the Think Aloud program (Camp & Bash, 1981; Camp & Ray, 1984) aggressive male primary-grade students have been taught to give themselves appropriate instructions, use new skills to avoid problems in social situations, and evaluate their decisions, resulting in beneficial effects on their behavior and thinking. Self-management has also been used with older adolescent girls in a correctional institution (Seymour & Stokes, 1976). These young people were taught to record their own productive educational and vocational training behaviors, and the self-recorded behaviors clearly improved. Like behavioral self-management, other intervention techniques must be applied in ways that take into account the age level of the student.

CURRICULUM IMPLICATIONS
Recent curriculum developments have begun to address some of the educational needs of students with behavior disorders. For instance, numerous curricula are now available for training in social skills, defined as "those behaviors which involve interaction between the child and his peers or adults, where the primary intent is the achievement of the child's or adult's goals through positive interactions" (Cartledge & Milburn, 1986, p. 8). Because students with behavior disorders often have significant social skill deficits, curricula designed to enhance competence in this area are of special interest to their teachers.

Age-Level Distinctions

Elementary.   The ACCEPTS (A Curriculum for Children's Effective Peer and Teacher Skills) social skills curriculum (Walker et al., 1983) was designed to teach crucial social behavior skills for successful adjustment to the behavioral demands of mainstream settings. Its primary goal is to prepare children with disabilities from kindergarten through 6th grade to enter and succeed in less restrictive settings. A related goal is to teach skills that enhance classroom adjustment and contribute to peer acceptance. ACCEPTS includes 28 skills grouped into five major content areas: (1) classroom skills, (2) basic interaction skills, (3) getting along, (4) making friends, and (5) coping skills. The classroom skills area focuses on competencies essential for successful classroom adjustment as defined by teachers (e.g., listening to instructions, following directions). The other four areas focus on skills needed for competent interaction with others.

The ACCEPTS curriculum is based on a direct instruction model that emphasizes defining and sequencing the skills to be taught, providing examples and nonexamples to communicate the skills clearly, utilizing a variety of practice activities during instruction, and using systematic correction procedures. The instructional format allows for one-to-one, small group, or large-group presentation. Depending on the rate of student progress, the program can be completed in 5 to 10 weeks. In controlled evaluations the ACCEPTS program not only taught social behavior skills but also led to behavioral changes for children with disabilities in classroom and playground settings.

Secondary.   One secondary school social skills curriculum is Structured Learning (Goldstein, Sprafkin, Gershaw, & Klein, 1980). This curriculum includes four major components: modeling, role playing, feedback, and transfer training. Modeling refers to presenting a group of students with a demonstration of the skill behaviors they are to learn. Following the demonstration, students are given an opportunity to role-play and practice the skills demonstrated. In the feedback component the teacher and other students provide the role-player with encouragement and suggestions for improvement as the behavior becomes more like the model. Transfer of training involves several procedures designed to increase the likelihood that the behavior will be performed in real-life situations.

The Structured Learning curriculum includes 50 skills that fall into six content areas: (1) beginning social skills, (2) advanced social skills, (3) skills for dealing with feelings, (4) skill alternatives to aggression, (5) skills for dealing with stress, and (6) planning skills. To be placed at the appropriate position in the curriculum, the student is rated for competence on each of the 50 skills by a teacher or other individual familiar with the student's behavior. Students with similar skill deficits should be grouped together, and the curriculum is presented in a small-group format of 5 to 8 pupils and 2 adults. For each of the 50 skills, the developers have provided a behavioral description, tips to facilitate training, suggestions for the demonstration content, and other helpful recommendations. Several studies have evaluated the use of Structured Learning with aggressive, antisocial adolescents. Findings showed that the program successfully trained such social skills as empathy, negotiating, assertiveness, following instructions, self-control, and perspective taking (Goldstein et al., 1980).

Evaluations of the ACCEPTS, Structured Learning, and other social skill curricula indicate that these programs can bring about important changes in the social competence and adjustment of treated students. Further work is needed to determine how such behavior changes can be better maintained over time and extended to other settings. Also, as Walker et al. (1983) point out, social skills training alone is not likely to remediate all the problems of students with behavior disorders. They recommend the use of powerful behavior modification procedures to control inappropriate behavior, combined with social skills training to provide the student with adaptive, socially acceptable ways of dealing with people.

MAINSTREAMING

Mainstreaming students with behavior disorders successfully is a complex task. Once students are removed from the regular classroom and placed in educationally segregated settings, regular classroom teachers and administrators sometimes feel less responsible for the students' education, and regular teachers may not look forward to the students' return. Thus, prior to removing a student from a regular class, every effort should be made to provide consultation and other help to the regular teacher to maintain that student in the regular class setting.

At present, many questions exist about how best to mainstream students with behavior disorders (Braaten, Kauffman, Braaten, Polsgrove, & Nelson, 1988). Unfortunately, research on the methods and outcomes of mainstreaming these students is not common, so that sound, evaluated methods such as that presented in the Model Program box are especially important. Two other well-developed ideas that hold promise for integrating students with behavior problems into regular education are discussed next.

Madison School Plan

The Madison School Plan provides special education support according to students' readiness for regular classroom functioning. Four levels of programming are offered, based on students' competence. The lowest level, Preacademic I, emphasizes basic skills of attending, following directions, and being on task. It is essentially a special class with extensive behavior modification, remedial work, and other highly structured features. Preacademic II stresses taking part in classroom activities and getting along with others. Here there are fewer students and more natural reinforcers (e.g., praise instead of treats), assignments resemble regular class work, and there is some regular education participation. As students develop competencies, they move to levels that emphasize development of academic skills. At the third level, Academic I, there is a simulation of the regular classroom, with grades given on a daily or hourly basis and natural reinforcers only. Also, there is substantial regular class participation and regular class work. The Academic II level is full participation in a regular classroom with close cooperation of regular and special teachers.

The Madison School Plan uses two average-size classrooms that are subdivided into the three special or transitional settings. Pupils can begin at the lowest level (self-contained) and gradually move into the regular classroom as they develop the necessary skills. Also, students may be placed originally at a higher level, as appropriate. Although the Madison plan was not originally designed exclusively for students with behavior disorders, it has great logical appeal for use with these students.

CLASS Program

The CLASS (Contingencies for Learning and Social Skills) program enables regular classroom teachers to control the aggressive and disruptive behavior of a student. It integrates several separate behavioral interventions into a teaching package. Prior to intervention, baseline data are collected on disruptive behaviors in the regular class. This information is compared with other referral information to clarify selection decisions and intervention goals. The student's teacher, principal, and the targeted student are then presented with the CLASS package.

The CLASS program itself contains several elements (Walker et al., 1984). First, there is a group-oriented contingency reward. The targeted student earns points for displaying appropriate classroom behavior and following the teacher's rules. The teacher praises the student each time a point is earned. Second, if enough points are earned during the day, the entire class shares in a preselected reward (e.g., extra recess, playing a game). Third, arrangements are made with the parents to provide a home reward such as extra TV time or treats when the student brings home a satisfactory daily report card, which occurs only if the student has earned a sufficient number of points.

CLASS is initially carried out and demonstrated by the consultant, but the classroom teacher soon begins to assume an active role and within several days is implementing CLASS with little or no help. As the program moves to completion, the use of points is phased out as teacher praise begins to maintain the student's appropriate behaviors. The CLASS program is designed to be completed in about 2 months.

Research supports the efficacy and replicability of CLASS for elementary school students with behavior problems (Walker et al., 1984). CLASS has usually been implemented to prevent the need for additional special services. However, it appears to be quite suitable as an aid to reintegrating a student with behavior disorders into regular education.

A resource room program for mainstreaming students with behavior disorders has been developed and evaluated by Rhode and her colleagues (Morgan & Jenson, 1988; Rhode, Morgan, & Young, 1983; Smith, Young, West, Morgan, & Rhode, 1988) for use in elementary and secondary schools. The general procedure for this resource room involves individualized instruction in regular and remedial academic areas and simple behavior modification procedures (praising, ignoring, reprimanding). In addition, a special mainstreaming procedure is implemented, initially in the resource room for about 3 hours per week for approximately 4 months (self-evaluation training phase). Subsequently, the procedure continues under the control of the regular classroom teacher, with training, consultation, and other support from the resource teacher (transfer phase).

Self-Evaluation Training Components (Resource Room)

1. First, resource room rules are taught through discussion, modeling, and role playing.
2. Next, the teacher rates each student's conduct and academic work on a scale of 0 to 5, with 0 designating extensive rule breaking and 5 designating all rules followed and work 100% correct. Ratings are initially made at 10- to 15-minute intervals during the training session.
3. Each student has a point card on which he or she receives points equal to the teacher's rating. These points can be exchanged for privileges or other small rewards at the end of the session.
4. Then, students are taught to rate their own academic and behavior performance on the same scale. At the end of each interval the student explains his or her self-rating and the teacher explains his or her rating of the student.
5. Accuracy of self-evaluation is encouraged by awarding points for "matching": the student is awarded his or her self-rating in points if it is within 1 point of the teacher's rating. For example, if the teacher's rating is 3 and the student's self-rating is 4, the student gets 4 points. The teacher also gives bonus points for exact matches. If the self-rating and the teacher rating differ by more than 1 point, the student earns no points.
6. As training proceeds, the matching contingency is faded (gradually eliminated) in two ways. First, the number of students called on to match declines over sessions; eventually there is only an occasional "surprise" rating comparison, once or twice a week. Because the students who will match are selected at random, they must all self-rate accurately in case they are selected. Second, the time interval that is self-rated is gradually increased. Throughout the period in which matching is faded, students who are not called on to match the teacher's rating continue to receive points according to their self-ratings.

The success of programs such as the Madison School Plan and CLASS depends on many factors; for instance, it may be necessary to implement the entire program. Several less extensive, commonsense strategies for regular teachers to use in integrating students with behavior disorders are included in the Tips for Helping section at the end of the chapter.

Age-Level Distinctions

Mainstreaming students with behavior disorders is not an exact science, and many factors must be weighed to ensure its success (Lloyd, Kauffman, & Kupersmidt, 1990).

Transfer Components (Regular Classroom)

1. The transfer phase begins when a student's behavior meets a selected criterion (e.g., 80% or more appropriate behavior for a 4-day period).

2. As the student's behavior approaches the criterion, the resource teacher prepares the regular teacher to assume a major role in the transfer plan. The procedure is explained, with emphasis on following the plan consistently and using the rules, praise, and the ignoring style of behavior management. The resource teacher also visits occasionally to observe and provide feedback about the regular teacher's implementation of the transfer plan.

3. At the beginning of the transfer phase, the mainstreamed student uses the 0 to 5 scale to rate his or her own academic and conduct performance every 30 minutes. The regular teacher also rates the student and gives feedback on self-rating accuracy. The regular teacher conducts surprise matches every 2 or 3 days and the student earns points according to his or her own self-ratings and exchanges points for rewards each day by briefly visiting the resource room.

4. As the student's behavior and academics continue to be highly appropriate, the interval for self-evaluation is extended from 30 minutes to 60 minutes.

5. Likewise, the student begins to exchange points less frequently; the days that points can be exchanged for rewards are determined at random and therefore cannot be predicted by the student. Eventually, the student is no longer allowed to exchange points for rewards. Surprise matches and teacher feedback on accuracy of self-rating continue to occur, however.

6. In the final step of transfer, the student begins to self-evaluate verbally rather than by marking a self-rating card. Soon, even this verbal self-evaluation is faded to two randomly selected days a week. Teacher feedback on accuracy of self-evaluation is discontinued, and in the end the student no longer gives verbal self-evaluations but is encouraged to evaluate his or her performance privately.

7. Some students require a booster session. If appropriate behavior in the classroom falls below a certain criterion, the resource teacher meets with the student privately for a review. Rules and rule violations, feedback from the regular classroom teacher, and positive behavior alternatives to rule violations may be discussed.

This mainstreaming program reliably teaches students with behavior disorders to evaluate and control their own performance. In some cases, improvements in the resource room carried over to the regular education setting (Rhode et al., 1983; Smith et al., 1988). This partial success is encouraging because students with behavior disorders are difficult to mainstream successfully. Further study of this promising program may reveal how to increase mainstreaming success rates.

These factors include the attitudes and behavior of students, teachers, and others involved; the similarity of the student's functioning to the performance expected in the regular classroom; the range and quality of support for the mainstream effort; and the personal characteristics, such as age, of the mainstreamed student. For instance, some plans for educating students with behavior disorders in regular classes rely extensively on parents' ability to present or withhold reinforcers at home. But as children grow older, parents seem to control fewer and fewer powerful reinforcers, so home-based reinforcement practices may be more appropriate for use with younger students. On the other hand, mainstreaming older students with behavior disorders requires more careful consideration of vocational and community independence issues.

Meeting the needs of a student with behavior disorders requires skill and commitment of the regular and special education teachers.

PREVENTION   The large number of students with serious emotional disturbance (about 400,000 identified, up to 3 million suspected) and the continuing shortage of special teachers and other professionals trained to educate these children emphasize the need for prevention of emotional and behavioral disorders. *Primary prevention* addresses a population or subgroup that currently does not show the problem of concern, but whose members are determined to be at risk to develop the problem. Action is taken to preempt development of the problem in the first place. *Secondary prevention* addresses individuals who show mild indicators of developing a serious problem. Early identification of and intervention for the problem may reduce its intensity, duration, and development. In other words, primary and secondary prevention differ in terms of time (before vs. early in the problem) and target (at risk groups vs. individuals who seem to be developing problem behaviors) (Hightower & Braden, 1991).

Primary Mental Health Project

Cowen and others developed an early intervention project for young students at risk of developing significant learning and behavior disorders (Cowen & Hightower, 1990). Begun more than 30 years ago, the Primary Mental Health Project (PMHP) is intended to prevent the development of major adjustment problems among preschool and primary grades (grades 1 to 3) students at risk for such problems.

To identify the students at risk, screening and referral activities continue throughout the school year. Utilizing multiple sources of information and different assessment methods, the screening and referral process selects youngsters whose presently minor behavior and learning problems indicate a high danger that they will develop behavioral, emotional, and other school maladjustments.

Selected children receive direct service from a "child associate"—a paraprofessional carefully chosen for nurturance, desire to help, and "benevolent firmness" (Hightower & Braden, 1991, p. 420). Supervised by a professional, the child associate meets with the child 1 to 3 hours per week for building a relationship, talk, play, academic skill tutoring, behavior contracting, and other activities as needed. Supervising professionals are also responsible for improving communication between home and school and within the school regarding the program, and delivering training in PMHP practices to educators, parents, and other persons who may need to be involved (Cowen & Hightower, 1990; Hightower & Braden, 1991).

Life Skills Training

Life Skills Training (LST) is principally a substance abuse prevention program. Its creators (Botvin, 1986; Botvin & Tortu, 1988) view students in grades 7 to 9 as highly prone to take potentially dangerous challenges, ignore established rules, and please the peer group. Therefore, they are at high risk for experimentation with drugs and health-damaging substances (as well as nontraditional values, behaviors, and lifestyles). The LST program is designed to teach resistance to social pressures, reduce the desire to use substances, and increase personal skills, as well as feelings of competence.

LST first presents information about the short-term consequences of using tobacco, alcohol, and marijuana, because young adolescents who use these can be taking the first step toward serious substance abuse. LST participants are taught how they may be pressured to use substances and how to decide what to do for themselves, responsibly. The teens are also taught how to relax in order to reduce anxiety in social situations. Decision making, relaxation, refusal, and other social skills are demonstrated and practiced within the group, and further practice in different situations is encouraged (Botvin & Tortu, 1988; Hightower & Braden, 1991).

INNOVATION AND DEVELOPMENT

Assessment Innovations

It is widely recognized that educational assessment of those with behavior disorders needs to be improved in various ways (Council for Children with Behavioral Disorders, 1987; Walker & Fabre, 1987). For example, assessment ideally should (1) be based primarily on objective criteria; (2) use assessment methods and results in a more consistent way across screening, identification, intervention design, and progress-monitoring phases; and (3) use effort and other resources efficiently and effectively. These needs have guided several innovative assessment procedures for behavior disorders (Canter, 1991; Tindal, Wesson, Deno, German, & Mirkin, 1985; Walker et al., 1988).

For instance, the Standardized Screening for Behavior Disorders (SSBD) procedure (Walker et al., 1988) uses multiple, objective assessment methods to screen a broad variety of behavior disorders of elementary school students. The SSBD is sequential in that there are three "gates," or screening steps. At gate 1 classroom teachers identify students who show externalizing (environment conflict) or internalizing (personal disturbance) problems; externalizers and internalizers are then rank-ordered. At gate 2 teachers provide more detailed information on the three-highest externalizers and internalizers to determine their behavior problems and whether they exhibit these problems more frequently than normal. If any students exceed criteria at gate 2, they are evaluated more intensively at gate 3. Key target behaviors are directly observed and recorded in the classroom and elsewhere. These data and norms on the behaviors observed are used to decide whether the student needs to be evaluated for official identification and special education.

Even if a student is screened out of special education at gate 1, 2, or 3, the SSBD model supports and provides opportunities for preidentification intervention for students' problems. Although the SSBD is a screening procedure, its assessment methods and data can be used in later stages (identification, designing intervention, monitoring progress), providing better consistency and efficiency of assessment. Initial research and demonstration results support the value of the SSBD (Walker et al., 1988).

Comprehensive Community-Based Services

Many students with behavior disorders—seemingly more so than ever before—experience severe personal, economic, mental health, and social problems, as well as educational ones. There is a growing consensus that the scope and depth of such problems must be addressed by multiple disciplines and agencies in a coordinated way (Knitzer, 1993). Too often, the range and intensity of needed services is available through placement in settings away from the regular school, often even away from the home community. Recently, models of comprehensive, community-based services for children with behavior disorders and their families have been developed and implemented to deliver multidisciplinary, multiagency services without resorting to unnecessarily restrictive or faraway placements.

These models owe much of their impetus to significant government and foundation support, especially the Child and Adolescent Service System Program (CASSP) of the National Institute of Mental Health, and the Robert Wood Johnson Foundation (Beachler, 1990). The model programs of services for students with behavior disorders developed include statewide ones (Behar, 1985; Burchard et al., 1991; Nelson & Pearson, 1991; VanDenBerg, 1989) and local ones (Jordan & Hernandez, 1990). Although these innovative projects involve a variety of features, several general components appear to be essential to developing a comprehensive, community-based "system of care" (Stroul & Friedman, 1986): (1) interagency collaboration, (2) target population definition, (3) principles of care, (4) comprehensive needs assessment, and (5) individualized services.

Interagency collaboration involves a clearly defined arrangement among the primary child-care agencies that addresses such critical issues as agency responsibilities, financing of services, joint planning, and collaborative programming (Duchnowski & Friedman, 1990). Within this framework, specific agencies or sources of services are designated to deliver services such as special education, social welfare, mental health, court system, vocational training, and recreation.

A _definition of the target population_ helps develop eligibility criteria for identifying those children and youth most in need of services, determining who will provide the services, and assigning responsibility for the costs of services (Jordan & Hernandez, 1990; Magrab, Young, & Waddell, 1985). Care must be taken that the definition meets the needs of the local community.

Policymakers must then agree on the _principles of care_ that will establish a direction and purpose for the community-based program. These principles should address the comprehensiveness, individualization, coordination, integration, and evaluation of services in the desired system, as well as program goals, accessibility, family involvement, and other principles that help determine the context or climate in which services will be delivered (Jordan & Hernandez, 1990; Stroul & Friedman, 1986).

A _comprehensive needs assessment_ is essential in order to specify the multiple, diverse needs of children and families, as well as the complex capabilities and limitations of agencies and other service providers (Arizona Department of Health Services, 1991; Friedman, 1988; Illback, 1991; Magrab et al., 1985). At the same time, a needs assessment must not itself become an expensive, time-consuming barrier to system change. A thorough yet efficient needs assessment should secure both quantitative data (e.g., archival) and qualitative data (e.g., interview).

Another key component is commitment to _individualized services_ to the child and family—basically, tailoring the program to the child's needs rather than fitting the child into existing patterns of service (Burchard & Clarke, 1990; Burns & Friedman, 1990). Flexibility in applying resources is essential, yet accountability is just as important—clients, service providers, and the public must have a way to verify that services are delivered in accordance with the treatment plan. Model programs such as Kaleidoscope (K. Dennis, personal communication, 1989), the Alaska Youth Initiative (VanDenBerg, 1989), and Project Wraparound (Burchard & Clarke, 1990) have developed and evaluated concepts related to individualized services, such as _unconditional care, intensive case management, family involvement,_ and _cultural competence_ (Stroul & Friedman, 1986).

Comprehensive community-based services require careful consideration and evaluation. Although there are still many unanswered questions, these approaches appear to hold substantial promise for students with behavior disorders.

New Populations of Students

Educators of students with behavior disorders have always been challenged by their problems, but the students being referred for services today show even more difficult and complex problems. Homelessness, substance abuse, delinquency, and child abuse and neglect have all added to the worsening mental health status of children and youth. Students experiencing these problems are more frequently found to be in need of special education and related services.

The prevalence of homelessness has increased dramatically in recent years among children (Kozol, 1988), as well as adults; families with young children are the fastest-growing segment of homeless people in the U.S. (Wirt, 1989). Homeless children present a myriad of medical, mental health, and learning problems (Khanna, Singh, Nemil, Best, & Ellis, 1992), such as developmental difficulties, anxiety, acute depression, abuse and neglect, hospital emergency treatment and admission, and pervasive health problems—problems that often go beyond the capabilities of educational and social agencies.

Over the past 25 years, illicit substance use and abuse has increased dramatically among American youth (Schinke, Botvin, & Orlandi, 1991), along with evidence of the dangers of alcohol, tobacco, and drugs (Leone, 1991). Informal reports from their teachers suggest that students with behavior disorders abuse substances more than peers without disorders. Although research is not definitive on this topic (Morgan, 1992), many of the factors that generally increase youths' risk for substance abuse, such as low self-esteem, poor educational performance, peer pressure, antisocial behaviors, and family breakdown, occur quite frequently among students with behavior disorders.

Everyone is aware that law violations in the U.S., especially violent ones, have been increasing for some time. Between 1965 and 1985, arrests of juveniles more than doubled (Select Committee on Children, Youth, and Family, 1989). Early onset of delinquent behavior predicts high rates of serious offenses in later adolescence (Tolan, 1987) and beyond. Juvenile delinquency is related to lower verbal IQ, delayed moral reasoning, and low self-worth (Henggeler, 1989). Students with gang affiliations and those who engage in antisocial acts and/or illegal activities are more and more frequently served by special educators of students with behavior disorders.

Reports of child abuse and neglect have risen sharply in the past two decades; 90% of the American public views child abuse as a serious national issue. More than 1 million children are physically abused each year by their caregivers, and the number at risk for abuse may be increasing (Wolfe, 1987). While certain child development problems, sociocultural issues, and family status factors have been offered as explanations of abuse, there does not appear to be any single cause of child abuse. According to Wolfe (1987), "Child abuse can best be explained as the *result of an interaction* between the parent and child within a system that seldom provides alternative solutions (e.g., through exposure to appropriate parental models, education, and supports), or clear-cut restraints (e.g., laws, sanctions, and consequences) for the use of excessive force to resolve common child-rearing conflicts" (p. 51).

Teachers of students with behavior disorders have always been on the front lines of society's responses to its problems. Homelessness, juvenile delinquency, substance abuse, and child abuse are alarming, desperate problems that have escalated in recent years, and special education is now serving many of the children involved. Exactly what to do is certainly not understood right now, but numerous promising models of intervention and prevention are now being developed, implemented, and evaluated (Morgan, 1992; Schinke et al., 1991; Wolfe, 1987). Most of these models feature family involvement, multiple locations for action (e.g., home, school, and community), peer interventions, and coordination of two or more professions or agencies of assistance.

Research Needs

Until recently there was little data-based research on students with behavior disorders, and much more still needs to be done to improve our knowledge of characteristics, assessment, educational treatment, and other issues. A few of the more pressing research questions are discussed here.

1. *How can special educators better educate students with behavior disorders?* Many widely used and commonly recommended teaching procedures have not yet been objectively evaluated with students with behavior disorders (Cullinan, Epstein, & Kauffman, 1982). Also, educational procedures often consist of several components, and even if a certain procedure has been shown to work, it is not known whether some of the components can be omitted without a loss of effectiveness. In cases where some components are expensive, time-consuming, or dependent on extensive teacher training, component analysis research may show how the intervention procedure can be streamlined. In addition, when two or more well-developed intervention procedures or programs exist, they can be directly compared in a study. For example, direct comparisons have shown the feasibility of using behavior modification interventions as an alternative to drug therapy in some children with hyperactivity (Kazdin & Wilson, 1978). If research shows that one procedure produces superior results, there may be implications for school program changes, teaching competencies, and the like.

2. *How can we determine whether behavior changes are of real value?* A wide variety of areas of student functioning can be selected for intervention; changes in functioning can be great or small. Recently, researchers have begun to focus on ways to evaluate whether changes produced by an intervention result in practical, personally and socially worthwhile improvements. Such evaluation, often called social validation (Kazdin, 1977), may involve (1) determining whether the changes have brought the student's performance within acceptable levels (social comparison technique); and/or (2) having teachers, parents, and other important individuals in the student's social environment judge their level of satisfaction with the behavior change (subjective evaluation technique). Social validation deals with how closely the student's functioning fits expectations of appropriate performance, which is a major consideration in the ecological approach and in any reasonable definition of behavior disorders.

3. *Are behavior improvements generalized to other settings and maintained over time?* Most behavior changes that are not durable are of limited importance to special educators. In addition, an intervention capable of improving student functioning in the classroom would be of far greater practical value if it also led to similar improvements in other settings without the need to apply the intervention in each setting. To date, there is too little research on the generalized effects of educational treatments for students with behavior disorders. Both the generalized and enduring effects of educational procedures demand attention. Of particular importance is the related issue of transition from secondary school to work, community, and other nonschool environments. Many youths with behavior disorders are unemployed and unprepared for work (Neel, Meadows, Levine, & Edgar, 1988). Effective career preparation methods need to be developed and evaluated for these young people.

4. *Can students with behavior disorders be taught self-control?* Teachers of students with behavior disorders have become increasingly interested in the training of self-control skills. The very nature of self-control is debated from a number of viewpoints

Although the causes of their problems may be different, students with behavior disorders experience many of the same learning difficulties as other students with mild disabilities. Thus, they can profit from many of the same instructional strategies, including computer-assisted instruction (CAI). The major computer instructional formats used with students with mild disabilities are (1) drill and practice, (2) tutorials, (3) simulations, (4) problem-solving programs, and (5) word processing. Each uses a somewhat different delivery method, matching the type of learning strategies involved.

Drill-and-practice programs present material in a repetitive fashion until the student reaches some prespecified criterion. The computer is ideal for drill and practice. In addition to being more palatable to students than workbooks or flashcards, drill-and-practice programs save teachers (and parents) considerable time and patience. The computer can generate a large number of individualized problems or examples of a given type, present them at a pace commensurate with the student's ability, provide correct or reinforcing feedback, keep records, and determine when a satisfactory performance level has been reached.

Tutorials are designed to help students acquire new information and/or skills. Ideally, the level of sophistication and the direction of the dialog are determined by the student's responses. Effective tutorial programs impart new information, quiz the learner on understanding of the new information, and provide branching responses that depend on the student's answers. A typical format is the presentation of paragraphs of material interspersed with a succession of carefully planned questions. Tutorials can be as much fun as games, or as boring as worksheets, depending on how the material is presented.

Simulations are teaching games that provide a realistic context for problem solving. Some simulations model real social and physical phenomena and associated decision making, whereas others use fictional situations. These programs can provide students with exposure to such adventures as piloting an airplane, running a nuclear reactor, or crossing America's wilderness with the pioneers. Students are required to make decisions regarding what data to collect, how to alter the environment, and when to seek the advice of authorities. In most situations there is more than one path to successful problem resolution, each with specific consequences. The graphics and multisensory mode used in simulation programs make them particularly attractive for students with special needs. The effect of reading deficiencies can be minimized by presenting information graphically or with a speech synthesizer.

Problem-solving programs teach students to apply step-by-step decision-making procedures to translate data into a useful informational format and develop conclusions. Taking a somewhat more direct approach to teaching problem-solving skills than simulations, they focus on helping students learn (1) to structure problems in a logical form, (2) to express ideas as algorithms (procedural rules for problem solving), (3) to use computer models to simulate real systems, and (4) to analyze data.

Word processing programs are used to help students improve writing, grammar, spelling, and sometimes, even reading skills. With simple keyboard commands, the user can make changes in text; paragraphs can be rearranged, spelling corrected, and new words or phrases inserted. Word processing programs give students a product they can be proud of when they finish an assignment. How motivating word processing is depends on the student's proficiency in using the program, the student's typing ability, and the teacher's creativity in assigning interesting activities.

(Bandura, 1978; Bornstein, 1985; Catania, 1975). Behaviorists view self-control training as the teaching of specific self-management behaviors (self-observation, self-recording, self-instruction, punishment) so that students can use these behaviors to modify their functioning in other areas (Mace & Kratochwill, 1988). Psychoeducationists see self-control training as developing the student's inner capacity to monitor and regulate personal behavior flexibly and adaptively (Fagen et al., 1975). Both behavioral and psychoeducational teaching procedures and curricula are available for teaching self-control (e.g., Bornstein, 1985; Fagen et al., 1975). Ironically, there is relatively little scientific research on self-control among students with behavior disorders, and existing results are equivocal (Bornstein, 1985). Researchers need to identify the variables associated with effective self-control training for students with behavior disorders and evaluate the efficacy of these training programs (Baer & Fowler, 1984).

Those who teach students with behavior disorders cannot be expected to make major research contributions, but they must keep abreast of the issues, be critical consumers of research findings, and demand reasonable evidence of the value of any assessment or intervention recommended by an expert. Perhaps more than any other factor, the movement toward better research holds the key to advances in special education for students with behavior disorders.

SUMMARY   Contemporary special education for students with behavior disorders is a recent development that has been diversely influenced by many factors, including developments in education, medicine, law, and psychodynamic and behavioral psychology, as well as social and economic trends. Although many attempts have been made to define behavior disorders, no definition is universally accepted. Nevertheless, there are two broad areas common to most authoritative definitions. Children with behavior disorders (1) deviate from standard expectations of behavior and (2) impair the functioning of others and/or themselves. Federal data indicate that about 1% of the school-age population is identified as behaviorally disordered, although scientific prevalence surveys suggest that several times this many students probably are experiencing behavior disorders.

Many factors contribute to normal and atypical development. Heredity, brain disorder, family conflict and breakdown, improper discipline, peer influence, schools, socioeconomic disadvantage, and stress are some of the factors that can contribute to behavior disorders. Many behavior disorders arise from the interaction of biological and psychological conditions. Three major models have evolved to explain behavior disorders. The psychoeducational model is based on mental conflicts, especially those set in motion by stress. The behavioral model explains disorders in terms of the effects of specific environmental events. The ecological perspective views a behavior disorder as a disharmonious interaction within an ecosystem.

The major characteristics of behavior disorders fall under the general categories of environmental conflict, personal disturbance, and learning disorders. Environmental conflict is characterized by aggression-disruption, hyperactivity, and social maladjustment. Anxiety-depression and social incompetence are subcategories of personal

1. Provide a carefully structured environment with regard to physical features of the room, scheduling and routines, and rules of conduct. If there are to be unstructured activities, clearly distinguish them from structured activities in terms of time, place, and expectations.

2. Let students know the expectations you have, the objectives that have been established for them, and the help you will give them in achieving those objectives. When appropriate, seek input from them about their strengths, weaknesses, preferences, and goals.

3. Reinforce appropriate behavior and ignore or mildly punish inappropriate behavior. Generally, try reinforcement procedures before using mild punishment strategies such as response cost or time-out. When beginning a behavior modification program, reinforce the target behavior as frequently as possible; eventually provide reinforcers on a more intermittent schedule.

4. Children and adolescents acquire and modify much of their behavior by observing the actions of others. Modeling can be a potent part of any educational program. Model appropriate behavior and refrain from words and actions you do not wish students to imitate.

*TIPS FOR
HELPING*

5. Do not expect students with behavior disorders to have immediate success; work for improvement on a long-term basis. Plan for gradual, step-by-step change. Reinforce approximations to or attempts at the desired behavior. Continue with the intervention strategy being used when a student is making progress toward an objective; try another way if there is no progress.

6. Initiate a home-school communication system. Contact parents consistently via letters, telephone calls, and scheduled meetings. Do not wait for problems to arise; point out to parents the positive aspects of their child's behavior and school experiences.

7. Motivate students to learn by actively engaging them in and challenging them by the curriculum. Vary the presentation format; combine group instruction, experiential learning, independent exercises, and other teaching practices in your instructional program.

8. Be fair: be consistent but temper your consistency with flexibility.

9. Be sensitive to students as individuals and as a class; balance individual needs with group requirements.

10. Try to understand the frustrations, hopes, and fears of students and their parents. It is a true accomplishment to feel sympathy for a student's plight while tenaciously refusing to discontinue an intervention that you believe will help the student.

disturbance. Typically, students with behavior disorders exhibit learning disorders, including below-average academic achievement and intellectual abilities.

Severe to profound behavior disorders are mainly of two types: autism and childhood schizophrenia. Biological factors seem to figure prominently in the causation of these disorders. Students with severe behavior disorders may show cognitive and language disorders, aggression, over- and underactivity, self-stimulation, social incompetence, and lack of adaptive behaviors.

Psychoeducational, behavioral, and ecological models involve intervention principles and techniques compatible with their different views of behavior disorders. Psychoeducational techniques use surface behavior management, the life-space interview, and several brief forms of psychotherapy. Behavior modification strategies are positive and negative reinforcement, punishment, extinction, token economies, behavioral contracts, group contingencies, and self-management to alter behavior. Ecological techniques call for modification in the total environment and focus on improving the child's functioning in natural environments such as the regular classroom and community.

Useful curricula have been developed for students with behavior disorders, especially in the area of social skills. These students often possess significant social skill deficits that limit their chances to succeed in regular education settings. Social skill curricula teach adaptive, socially acceptable ways of interacting with peers and adults, which can improve students' chances of being successfully mainstreamed and making the transition to community living after completion of schooling.

Although long neglected, educational assessment of behavior disorders has begun to benefit from innovative approaches such as the Standardized Screening for Behavior Disorders (SSBD) procedure. Cognitive perspectives on causes and treatment of behavior and emotional problems are beginning to affect special education for students with behavior disorders. Although some exemplary educational programs are available for these young people, much remains to be learned through research.

STUDY QUESTIONS

1. Research has identified several biological and psychological phenomena that can be important determinants of behavior disorders. Discuss these phenomena and their educational implications, particularly as they relate to teachers of students with behavior disorders.

2. The psychoeducational, behavioral, and ecological models provide different explanations of the behavior disorders of children and adolescents. Describe how each model would explain the disordered behavior of Michael in the opening vignette.

3. List six general kinds of social, personal, and learning problems experienced by students with behavior disorders. Describe each of these problems as typically exhibited by individuals with mild-moderate behavior disorders.

4. Name the two main kinds of severe-profound behavior disorders. Describe the social, personal, and learning problems that may be exhibited by these students.

5. Describe and give examples of the three main kinds of assessment methods. What purpose does each method serve?

6. Describe the rationale, methods, and purposes of the SSBD assessment procedure.

7. Describe an intervention that illustrates the psychoeducational model, the behavioral model, and the ecological model. Explain why each selected intervention illustrates the particular model.

8. Students with behavior disorders often have significant social skill deficits. Identify curriculum programs designed to enhance competence in this area and the components of these curricula that make them effective.

9. If you had recently been hired as a mainstreaming consultant for a local school district, what would your recommendation be to the staff for establishing a mainstreaming program for pupils with behavior disorders?

10. Discuss several emerging issues of concern to professionals in the field of education for students with behavior disorders.

6

Mild Mental Retardation

James R. Patton
University of Texas at
Austin

Edward A. Polloway
Lynchburg College

 In this chapter you will learn about

- historical developments in the field of mental retardation

- various issues related to definition of mental retardation, including various perspectives on it; the most frequently used classification and systems; eligibility criteria and approaches to assess mild mental retardation based on these criteria

- the most common characteristics of individuals with mild retardation and recent changes in understanding them

- the major components associated with providing services to individuals with mild retardation (i.e., curriculum, integration, transition planning)

*F*or years the field of mental retardation has grappled with the issue of where best to educate students who are mildly retarded. Most recently, emphasis has been given to their inclusion into regular classes. Including students with mild mental retardation in general education classes is certainly desirable philosophically and attainable practically. However, successful inclusion requires that changes be made in the way programs are typically organized. The following scenario about Ryan points out some of the possible rewards of inclusive arrangements for individuals with mild retardation (e.g., liking school and teachers, having friends), as well as some of the areas that must be addressed (e.g., liking social studies because of less work, not being fond of reading, hating math) if this arrangement is to work to the benefit of students. As Ryan gets older, educators will particularly need to focus on how to ensure that his curriculum prepares him for work (e.g., his current career choice of fireman) and adult life in general.

Ryan is a 13-year-old 7th grade student who is classified as mildly retarded. He spends most of his day in general education classrooms and receives tutoring 2 hours a week from a volunteer. Ryan related to his tutor how he feels about school, his teachers, and what he would like to be when he grows up. His words and ideas provide a brief glimpse into his life.

"I feel good and fun about school. My favorite thing to do is to play games. I like playing games because I can beat people when I play. This makes me feel good. My favorite game to play is Monopoly. I can spend lots of other people's money.

My teachers are nice. I go to four different teachers. My favorite class is social studies because I don't have a lot of work and I don't have to do any math in social studies. I don't like reading and I hate fill-in-the-blanks kind of reading sheets. I never have anyone help me when I do reading sheets. In science, I work by myself. That's why I am in this new book. I write down any ole thing I want to. I work real fast. I hate to do math because I hate to do subtracting. Math is not fun.

I have lots of friends. They are nice to me. They teach me how to play kickball and play sports. I don't really like sports much, though.

When I grow up, I want to be a fireman. Want to know why? Firemen don't have to use math."

The authors thank Leticia Rose-Farrow for her report on her work with Ryan.

Mental retardation is a condition that historically has been susceptible to confusion and misunderstanding. In great part the confusion has arisen from an uncertainty and naivete about the characteristics, needs, and capabilities of persons with mild mental retardation. Because the population of individuals with milder forms of retardation has changed over the course of the last few years, there is evidence today of even more confusion.

Mental retardation is also influenced by sociopolitical factors (i.e., social conditions that lead to governmental action). Some professionals (Blatt, 1987; Sarason, 1985) suggest that mental retardation is basically a social phenomenon. Mental retardation is never a thing or a characteristic of an individual but rather a social invention stemming from time-bound societal values that makes diagnosis and management seem both necessary and socially desirable (Sarason, 1985, p. 223).

This chapter discusses the topic of mild mental retardation, presenting issues related to sociopolitical context, definition, assessment, prevalence, causes, characteristics, intervention, and current and future developments.

HISTORY

Throughout history various types of services have been provided to people with mental retardation. Even though many of these services derive from the efforts of specific individuals or groups, powerful sociopolitical influences have also been involved.

> Many people . . . think that the issues facing special education today are new. But if you read the historical literature of special education, you will see that today's issues and problems are remarkably similar to those of long ago. Issues, problems, and ideas arise, flower, go to seed, and reappear when the conditions are again right for their growth. (Patton, Kauffman, Blackbourn, & Brown, 1991, p. 236)

With this in mind we can examine briefly how people with retardation have been treated in times past.

So far as persons with retardation are concerned, the time prior to the 18th century can be considered antiquity. For centuries there was much misunderstanding of retardation and much inconsistency in its treatment. In some societies those with retardation were given the role of buffoons or jesters. In others they were viewed as capable of divine revelations or condemned as demons. People who received some type of special treatment were more severely impaired. During this period the concept of mild mental retardation essentially did not exist. Because physical and motor skills were stressed over the ability to read, write, and calculate, most of these people probably blended into society reasonably well and were not recognized as having significant difficulties.

During the 1700s a social climate characterized by humanism and openness began to develop. To a great extent this climate evolved from the Renaissance of the 14th, 15th, and 16th centuries. For the first time sincere and dedicated attempts were made to intervene in the lives of people with retardation (e.g., Itard's work with Victor). A resounding optimism dominated the early part of the 1800s and lasted for well over half of the century. As the 19th century progressed, optimism turned to pessimism. The Civil War and the dramatic transition from an agrarian society to an urbanized, industrial one were accompanied by many internal problems in the United States. An attitude arose toward people with retardation that can best be described as disillusionment.

Many factors contributed to this change. People had soured on the grandiose and overzealous claims of early optimists such as Guggenbuhl who predicted that individuals with retardation could be cured. In addition, a eugenics movement arose, aiming to control the proliferation of "feeblemindedness" through segregation, sterilization, and selective breeding (Smith, 1985, 1989; Smith & Polloway, 1993). Also, through the efforts of Binet at the turn of the century, the first mental measurement scale was born, providing the ability to identify mild forms of retardation and resulting in increased diagnoses of retardation. Attention to the issue of mental abilities was intensified as the result of the large number of immigrants entering the country who were incorrectly assumed to be intellectually subaverage (i.e., they performed poorly on English language tests). This population explosion added fuel to the fire: suddenly mental retardation seemed a problem of enormous proportions. Repression and mistreatment of people with mental retardation became commonplace.

In the fifties, treatment of individuals with retardation underwent noticeable changes. Most important was the development of a national policy to combat retardation. A renewed climate of encouragement was created, in which "parents, professionals, and the federal government initiated new developments" (Hewett & Forness, 1977). The sixties gave special education the spotlight. Federal funding became available, and with it came the expansion of services for many persons with disabilities. Chief among the changes was the recognition of their legal rights, affirmed by landmark litigation and legislation in the seventies.

The period also witnessed the first major challenge to the prolific growth of special education classes and to the procedures by which they were being run. In his often-cited article Dunn (1968) noted that many culturally diverse students who were not mentally retarded were being incorrectly placed in these settings. With the passage of the Education for All Handicapped Children Act (Public Law 94–142) of 1975, a federal mandate to provide an appropriate education to those with disabilities was established. The implementation of this law resulted in a major effort to integrate students with disabilities into regular education whenever possible. The implications of this practice for students identified as mildly mentally retarded are still being realized and have been further enhanced by the Individuals with Disabilities Education Act (IDEA) (Public Law 101–476).

The late seventies and early eighties witnessed several significant trends. One was the heavy reliance on the resource room model to provide educational services to many students with mild disabilities. Also, with much professional attention being given to the needs of the previously unserved population of students with severe retardation, there was a marked shift in interest away from individuals with mild retardation (Strichart & Gottlieb, 1982). Haywood (1979) acknowledged a related "shift of resources away from mildly and moderately retarded persons" (p. 429).

A recent development is the changing nature of this population (MacMillan, 1989; Polloway & Smith, 1988). There has been a decrease in the number of students who are classified as mildly retarded (i.e., educable mentally retarded). A related consequence is that this group is now "a more patently disabled group" (MacMillan & Borthwick, 1980, p. 155). One is inclined to ask where all these students have gone. Some have been reclassified and placed in programs for students who are learning disabled; others have been decertified and have joined the ranks of the "slow learners" in regular classrooms, for whom there are limited services. And many other students who previously would have been identified are simply not being identified now, largely because of a reluctance to classify students as mentally retarded.

Other major trends occurred during the eighties. The emphasis on what happens to students with mild mental retardation after they leave school resulted in major developments in transition planning and new employment options. Systematic studies of efforts to prepare students for "life after high school" have been conducted and disseminated. The movement away from sheltered employment to more competitive and supported employment is clearly in evidence.

The theme of integration of individuals into the school and community now dominates the field. Related to the idea of normalization or social valorization (Wolfensberger, 1983), integrative efforts can be seen in school settings (i.e., inclusive education, where students are taught in regular classes) and in community settings (e.g., community living arrangements). Much professional effort is being directed to the achievement of more inclusive outcomes.

A number of pressing questions have been raised in recent times: What are the characteristics of this new population of students with mild retardation? How successful are individuals who were formerly classified as mildly retarded and are now in general education? How can the high dropout rates, low employment, and disappointing figures on independent living for this population as reported in studies be reversed (Affleck, Edgar, Levine, & Kortering, 1990; U.S. Department of Education, 1992)? Are alternative curricular options needed for this group of students? Can this new group of students with mild retardation be successfully educated in integrated settings? What accommodative practices are needed to assist students in inclusive environments?

DEFINITION   Generally speaking, mental retardation refers to a condition characterized by restricted intellectual ability and difficulty in coping with the social demands of the environment. Although there is much variability in this population, all individuals with mental retardation demonstrate some degree of impaired mental abilities, most often apparent in academic areas. Moreover, a person with retardation displays an intelligence quotient (IQ) significantly below average and a mental age (MA) appreciably lower than the chronological age (CA). In addition, persons with retardation demonstrate more inappropriate and less mature social behavior than their peers. In the case of mild retardation this discrepancy in social competence can be subtle. This group is challenged most dramatically by the school setting, thus between the ages of 6 and 21; their inability to cope may be seen in problems with peer relationships or noncompliance with teacher-initiated directions.

The 1983 AAMR Definition

The most widely accepted definition of mental retardation is the one developed by the American Association on Mental Retardation (AAMR). Its earlier form (Grossman, 1973) was incorporated into the Education for All Handicapped Children Act (Public Law 94–142), thus becoming the accepted federal definition. The 1983 revision (Grossman, 1983) differs somewhat in wording and meaning and is as follows:

> Mental retardation refers to significantly subaverage general intellectual functioning resulting in or associated with concurrent impairments in adaptive behavior and manifested during the developmental period. (p. 11)

Limited intellectual abilities are most noticeable in language development.

As is evident from this definition, mental retardation is defined in terms of three important factors: (1) intellectual functioning, (2) adaptive behavior, and (3) age of onset.

Intellectual functioning can be conceptualized as a cluster of abilities, such as the capacities to learn, solve problems, accumulate knowledge, adapt to new situations, and think abstractly. Operationally, it is typically determined by performance on an intelligence test, an instrument used to evaluate intellectual functioning that yields an IQ. Significantly below average is defined as an IQ of approximately below 70. The 1983 AAMR definition suggested using a flexible upper IQ range of 70 to 75 rather than an exact cutoff of 70.

Figure 6–1 graphically demonstrates the relationship of IQ and retardation.

An individual's level of _adaptive behavior_ is determined by the degree to, and efficiency with, which the individual meets "the standards of maturation, learning, personal independence, and/or social responsibility that are expected for his or her age level and cultural group" (Grossman, 1983, p. 11). In other words, the term refers to how well people cope with the demands of their immediate environment. As the definition indicates, there can be a close relationship between intellectual functioning and adaptive behavior. Two major components of adaptive behavior are the level of skill development and the relationship of acquired skills to developmental and chronological age. Particularly important are the skills necessary to function independently in a range of situations and to maintain responsible social relationships (Coulter & Morrow, 1978).

Criteria for assessing adaptive behavior vary according to developmental age and situational context. It is important to be aware that people function in a number of different roles, in a variety of social contexts, and within a multicultural and pluralistic society (Mercer & Lewis, 1977). Accordingly, behavior is strongly influenced by situational and cultural factors. A good example of cultural influence can be found in the area of eating skills. In many cultures it is quite acceptable to use one's fingers extensively while eating; this same behavior is usually considered inappropriate in Anglo-Saxon cultures.

The *developmental period* is the period of time between conception and 18 years of age. Below-average intellectual functioning and deficits in adaptive behavior must appear during this time frame to be considered indicative of mental retardation. "Developmental deficits may be manifested by slow, arrested, or incomplete development resulting from brain damage, degenerative processes in the central nervous system, or regression from previously normal states due to psychosocial factors" (Grossman, 1983, p. 11).

According to the 1983 definition, deficits in intellectual functioning and adaptive behavior must exist concurrently. This requirement is important because, only if and when both of these conditions are met, would a person be classified as mentally retarded. In reality, the intellectual functioning dimension has often been superordinate to adaptive behavior in determining whether a person is considered mentally retarded or not. Issues related to assessment will be discussed later.

In an effort to allow for exceptions to the general rule, the concept of *clinical judgment* was introduced in AAMR's 1977 revision of the definition and retained in the 1983 definition. This concept permits diagnostic teams to classify as mentally retarded certain individuals who display severe problems in adaptive behavior even though their IQ scores are above the 70 to 75 upper range. On the other hand, it is possible that certain students with lower IQs may not be considered mentally retarded because of their demonstrated competence in adaptive behavior. Any classification of an individual as mentally retarded should be based on current functioning and should not indicate an ultimate or perma-

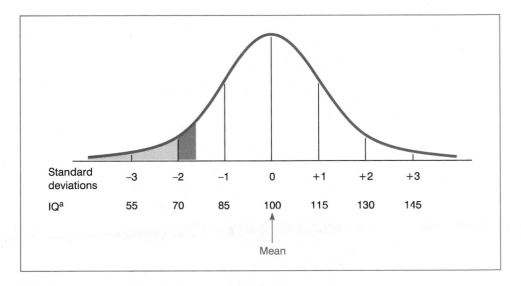

Figure 6–1
Assumed normal distribution of intelligence
Note: Shaded areas indicate the possible range for mental retardation based on IQ score alone.

a   Based on Wechsler scales.

nent status. Diagnostic teams must exercise sound professional judgment and assume responsibility for misdiagnosis. The present trend—in many cases where clinical judgment has been applied—has been to define mental retardation more conservatively, reflecting a reluctance to mislabel students. The result has been a sharp reduction in the number of students being classified as mentally retarded in many states.

The 1992 AAMR Definition

In 1992 the AAMR presented its most recent revision of the definitions. According to the AAMR (1992) manual, mental retardation is defined as follows:

> Mental retardation refers to substantial limitations in present functioning. It is characterized by significantly subaverage intellectual functioning, existing concurrently with related limitations in two or more of the following applicable adaptive skill areas: communication, self-care, home living, social skills, community use, self-direction, health and safety, functional academics, leisure, and work. Mental retardation manifests before age 18. (American Association on Mental Retardation, 1992, p. 5)

Four assumptions are considered to be essential to the application of the AAMR's revised definition.

1. Valid assessment considers cultural and linguistic diversity, as well as differences in communication and behavioral factors.
2. The existence of limitations in adaptive skills occurs within the context of community environments typical of the individual's age peers and is indexed to the person's individual needs for supports.
3. Specific adaptive limitations often coexist with strengths in other adaptive skills or other personal capabilities.
4. With appropriate supports over a sustained period, the life functioning of the person with mental retardation will generally improve (AAMR, 1992, p. 5).

Here is an analysis of some key phrases in the definition:

1. *Mental retardation refers to substantial limitations in present functioning . . .* Mental retardation is defined as fundamental difficulty in learning and performing certain daily life skills. There must be a substantial limitation in conceptual, practical, and social intelligence. Some personal capabilities are specifically affected while others (e.g., health and temperament) may not be.
2. *It is characterized by significantly subaverage intellectual functioning . . .* This is defined as an IQ score of approximately 70 to 75 or below, based on assessment that includes one or more individually administered general intelligence tests. These tests, along with other available test scores and information, should be reviewed by a multidisciplinary team.
3. *Existing concurrently . . .* Intellectual limitations occur at the same time as adaptive skill limitations.
4. *With related limitations . . .* The limitations in adaptive skills are more closely related to the intellectual limitations than to some other circumstances such as cultural or linguistic diversity or sensory limitation.
5. *In two or more of the following adaptive skills areas . . .* Evidence of adaptive skill limitations is necessary since intellectual functioning alone is insufficient for a diagnosis of men-

tal retardation. Functional limitations must exist in at least two adaptive skill areas, showing a generalized limitation and reducing the probability of measurement error.

6. *Communication, self-care, home living, social skills, community use, self-direction, health and safety, functional academics, leisure, and work* . . . These skill areas are central to successful life functioning and frequently relate to the need that people with mental retardation have for support. Assessment of functioning must be referenced to the individual's chronological age.

7. *Mental retardation manifests before age 18* . . . The 18th birthday approximates the age when individuals in this society typically assume adult roles. In other societies, a different age criterion might be more appropriate (AAMR, 1992, p. 5–6).

The 1992 revision of the definition reflects a continued movement in the field in the direction of functional perspective on the disability. While the two primary dimensions (i.e., IQ and adaptive behavior) remain the same, the context for mental retardation has been further developed (Adams, 1984).

Developmental Disabilities Definition

The relationship of mental retardation to developmental disabilities is one of significant overlap. The definition of developmental disabilities being used today is defined in the Developmental Disabilities Assistance and Bill of Rights Act of 1984 (Public Law 98–527):

> A severe chronic disability of a person which (a) is attributable to a mental or physical impairment or combination of mental or physical impairment; (b) is manifested before the person attains age twenty-two; (c) is likely to continue indefinitely; (d) results in substantial functional limitations in three or more of the following areas of major life activity: (i) self-care, (ii) receptive and expressive language, (iii) learning, (iv) mobility, (v) self-direction, (vi) capacity for independent living, (vii) economic self-sufficiency; and (e) reflects the person's need for a combination and sequence of special, interdisciplinary, or generic care, treatment, or other services which are of lifelong or extended duration and are individually planned and coordinated.

It is safe to say that developmental disabilities imply significant limitations and thus apply to people who are more severely disabled. Although the term may be appropriate for certain individuals who are mildly retarded, it does not refer directly to this group.

Classification of Retardation

Mental retardation can be classified in numerous ways; traditionally the two most common methods have been by etiology and by severity. Although etiological (causal) classification provides little in the way of practical instructional information to educators, it is essential that professionals in the field have at least some working knowledge of this area. When professionals from different disciplines work together, they need to be able to communicate with one another, which means they need to be familiar with various etiologies and their implications for programs. These are discussed below in the section on *Causes*.

A wide range of disciplines classify retardation by severity. The classification system cited most often is the 1983 AAMR system, which used the terms mild, moderate, severe, and profound. The four levels were intended to describe subcategories of retardation on the basis of IQ and adaptive behavior, although in reality IQ dominated delineations of these levels (e.g., mild retardation = IQ 70/75 to 55/50).

In school settings, however, different systems are often used. As Utley, Lowitzer, and Baumeister (1987) found, states vary in the terminology and classification they use to describe this population. Only 56% of the states use the term *mental retardation*, and only 14% use the precise 1983 AAMR classification system. For instance, Iowa has used the term *mental disabilities* and sets the upper IQ limit of 85 in its guidelines for defining mild mental disabilities.

Historically, terms such as educable and trainable (corresponding in general to mild and moderate/severe, respectively) have often been used in school environments and in the literature. Although prejudicial and problematic, these terms remain in use today in many places. As a result, it will not be uncommon to hear of students referred to as EMR (educable mentally retarded) and TMR (trainable mentally retarded).

The use of EMR and TMR designations in the schools has been waning in recent years and given way to a more informal system of classification using the two terms mild and severe. Loosely based on the Grossman (1983) system, such designations simplify the awkward system of four levels, which was originally based largely on IQ scores and on standard deviations (SDs) below the mean (i.e., mild = 2–3 SDs, moderate = 3–4 SDs). Frequently in the literature, the mild and severe terms have been used somewhat loosely to refer to broadly conceptualized groups.

In the revised AAMR classification system (AAMR, 1992), however, levels of disability have been removed and their use has been discouraged. Instead, the manual recommends a system based on intensity of needed supports. Definitions of the four levels of supports are provided in Table 6–1.

Table 6–1
Definition and examples of intensities of supports

Intermittent

Supports on an "as needed basis." Characterized by episodic nature, person not always needing the support(s), or short-term supports needed during life-span transitions (e.g., job loss or an acute medical crisis). Intermittent supports may be high or low intensity when provided.

Limited

An intensity of supports characterized by consistency over time, time-limited but not of an intermittent nature, may require fewer staff members and less cost than more intense levels of support (e.g., time-limited employment training or transitional supports during the school to adult period).

Extensive

Supports characterized by regular involvement (e.g., daily) in at least some environments (such as work or home) and not time-limited (e.g., long-term support and long-term home living support).

Pervasive

Supports characterized by their constancy, high intensity; provided across environments; potential life-sustaining nature. Pervasive supports typically involve more staff members and intrusiveness than do extensive or time-limited supports.

The complete three-step process for diagnosis, classification, and systems of supports is provided in Table 6–2. The reader should consult the manual (AAMR, 1992) or the workbook (Seiter, 1992) for further information.

Relationship of Mild Retardation to Other Conditions

Relationships between mild mental retardation and other conditions are not clear-cut or straightforward. Many used to believe there was much similarity among students who were mildly retarded and students who were learning disabled, behaviorally disordered, or low achieving. Now, however, the belief is beginning to be reexamined. Changes within the population of students identified as mildly retarded indicate that this group may be more disabled than before, resulting in more distinct differences. Only limited research exists to validate this observation; therefore, final conclusions

Table 6–2
The three-step process: Diagnosis, classification, and systems of supports

	Step 1. Diagnosis of Mental Retardation *Determines Eligibility for Supports*
Dimension I: *Intellectual Functioning* *and Adaptive Skills*	Mental retardation is diagnosed if: 1. The individual's intellectual functioning is approximately 70 to 75 or below. 2. There are significant disabilities in two or more adaptive skill areas. 3. The age on onset is below 18.
	Step 2. Classification and Description *Identifies Strengths and Weaknesses and the Need for Supports*
Dimension II: *Psychological/* *Emotional* *Considerations* *Dimension III:* *Physical Health/* *Etiology Considerations* *Dimension IV:* *Environmental* *Considerations*	1. Describe the individual's strengths and weaknesses in reference to psychological/emotional considerations 2. Describe the individual's overall physical health and indicate the condition's etiology 3. Describe the individual's current environmental placement and the optimal environment that would facilitate his or her continued growth and development
	Step 3. Profile and Intensities of Needed Supports *Identifies Needed Supports*
	Identify the kind and intensities of supports needed for each of the four dimensions. 1. Dimension I: Intellectual Functioning and Adaptive Skills 2. Dimension II: Psychological/Emotional Considerations 3. Dimension III: Physical Health/Etiology Considerations 4. Dimension IV: Environmental Considerations

must wait further verification. Nevertheless, some general statements about relation-ships of mild mental retardation to other conditions are possible.

The relationship of mild mental retardation to learning disabilities remains some-what confusing because the identification of students with learning disabilities has been fraught with problems. On a conceptual level there is a clear distinction between these two categories, based on the level of measured intellectual ability. However, stu-dents in the two categories may share many learning, social, and emotional character-istics. As mentioned earlier, this distinction is distorted by the fact that some students initially classified as mildly retarded have been reclassified as learning disabled (Gott-lieb, Gottlieb, Schmelkin, & Curci, 1982; Patrick & Reschly, 1982; Tucker, 1980).

There is evidence that individuals with mild mental retardation exhibit behavioral disorders at a higher rate than does the general population (Forness & Polloway, 1987; Polloway, Epstein, & Cullinan, 1985). The problem of differential diagnosis (i.e., are these students primarily mentally retarded or primarily behaviorally disordered?) adds to the confusion. By virtue of the fact that problems in adaptive skills areas is a major part of the 1992 AAMR definition, it is not surprising that this relationship will con-tinue to be marked by confusion. As has been the case in the past, behavioral prob-lems are likely to continue to be contributing factors in decisions to refer individuals with mild mental retardation for services. There is an increasing need to address the requirements of students who are both mentally retarded and behaviorally disordered.

The relationship of students with mild retardation to low-achieving students is also fraught with confusion. By a process of elimination, low achievers are neither mildly retarded nor learning disabled. Yet they can present problems in learning, acad-emic performance, social skills, and emotional maturity very similar to those of the other two groups. Some receive services through entitlement programs such as Chap-ter 1. On a practical level it is difficult to distinguish a student who functions near the upper borderline of the mentally retarded range from a low-achieving student. Again, many students formerly classified as mildly retarded are now part of this group, which does not qualify for special education, and are functioning as "marginal achievers" (MacMillan, 1988). The problems presented by this low-achieving group are a major concern for school systems.

Two important conclusions can be drawn regarding the relationship of mild men-tal retardation to other conditions. First, it is not always clear how these different con-ditions relate to one another, usually due to factors relating to definition and eligibility. Second, some individuals with mild mental retardation are truly multiply disabled and require the services of professionals from a variety of disciplines (Forness & Polloway, 1987).

PREVALENCE

Estimates of the size of the total population of Americans who are mentally retarded have ranged up to 3%. In recent years the validity of any figure near 3% (the equivalent of more than 7 million individuals) has been challenged, and a more conservative esti-mate of 1% or less has been suggested (Ramey & Finkelstein, 1981). This lower figure more accurately reflects the number of individuals who meet both criteria of subaver-age general intellectual functioning and deficits in adaptive behavior. Tarjan, Wright, Eyman, and Kerran (1973) provide some additional insights regarding a lower figure:

Many preschool children and adults, however, do not show major impairment in general adaptation even with relatively low IQs. As a consequence, the clinical diagnosis of mental retardation, particularly when it is of mild degree, is age-dependent. It is usually not established before school age and often disappears during late adolescence or young adulthood. (p. 370)

Analysis of federal data reporting the number of students aged 6 to 21 identified as having mental retardation reveals some interesting developments. A significant decrease has occurred nationwide in the number of students classified as mentally retarded in the public schools—from approximately 820,000 in 1976-77 to approximately 500,000 in 1990–91 (U.S. Department of Education, 1992).

Although no large epidemiological studies have been conducted in the United States to address this phenomenon, two studies outside the country (Baird & Sadovnick, 1985; Rantalkallio & Von Wendt, 1986) suggest that the group of students with mild retardation no longer can be considered to constitute the overwhelming majority of all cases of mental retardation (Forness & Polloway, 1987) as previously thought. Historically, figures of 70% to 80% have been posited; today the percentage of students who are mildly retarded is considerably less.

There are a number of plausible reasons for this change. As Polloway and Smith (1983) indicated, the factors most responsible for the change are (1) definitional changes implicit in the Grossman (1973, 1983) manuals, leading especially to increased concern for adaptive behavior; (2) the rippling effects of litigation (e.g., *Diana v. State Board of Education*, 1970; *Larry P. v. Riles*, 1972) challenging the use of the label *mentally retarded* and the special class placement for minority children that followed; (3) the encouragement of a more restrictive concept of retardation as a comprehensive disorder rather than as one based solely on current status; and (4) the successes of early intervention programs with disadvantaged children. Perhaps the most significant reason for the change in prevalence is the reluctance of school professionals to identify students as mentally retarded.

CAUSES   We can talk definitively about the causative factors of retardation in perhaps fewer than 50% of all cases (Polloway & Smith, 1994). In fact, the less severe the retardation, the less likely it is that we can determine a single cause with any certainty. Implicit in this statement is the assumption that for many people who are mildly retarded, the causes of their condition are closely related to environmental factors or perhaps to biophysical factors of unknown or unspecifiable origin. Table 6–3 lists the AAMR etiological categories.

Essentially two major groups of causes exist: biological and psychosocial. Biological causes, frequently easier to identify than psychosocial causes, have traditionally been associated with moderate, severe, or profound forms of retardation. According to a recent review by McLaren and Bryson (1987), pathological factors can be identified in 60% to 75% of the cases in which an individual has an IQ below 50. Psychosocial causes play a significant role in many cases of mild retardation and are hypothesized to interact with inherited traits. In approximately 60% to 75% of the cases of mild retardation, the cause cannot be specified (McLaren & Bryson, 1987) and can probably be assumed to involve an interaction of polygenic transmit (multiple genes) and negative environmental influences (Polloway & Smith, 1994).

Table 6–3

Various causes of retardation according to the 1983 AAMR medical classification (Grossman, 1983)

Type	Examples
Infections and Intoxicants	Rubella, syphilis, toxoplasmosis, bacterial and viral infections, drugs, smoking, caffeine, alcohol, lead
Trauma or Physical Agent	Hypoxia, irradiation, trauma
Metabolism or Nutrition	Lipid storage diseases (Tay-Sachs), carbohydrate disorders (galactosemia, hypoglycemia), amino acid disorders (phenylketonuria), endocrine disorders (hypothyroidism), other (Prader-Willi syndrome)
Gross Brain Disease (postnatal)	Neurofibromatosis, Sturge-Weber, tuberous sclerosis, Huntington's chorea
Unknown Prenatal Influence	Anencephaly, microcephaly, meningomyelocele, hydrocephalus
Chromosomal Abnormality	Cri-du-chat; Down syndrome, Klinefelter syndrome, fragile X
Conditions Originating in the Prenatal Period	Prematurity, postmaturity, low birth weight
Psychiatric Disorder	Psychosis
Environmental Influences	Psychosocial disadvantage

There has long been controversy over the degree to which environmental and genetic factors operate to cause deficits in intellectual functioning. Most researchers now agree that there is some interaction between both kinds of factors in the majority of cases. In effect, genetic endowment may impose a range of intellectual potential; however, this potential is greatly influenced by many environmental variables. Ramey and Finkelstein (1981) compiled a list of the environmental factors that have been associated with psychosocial causes:

- Maternal factors (IQ below 80, limited education, little positive involvement with the child)
- Poverty (low socioeconomic status)
- Family factors (disorganization, large numbers of children)
- Poor prenatal care
- Spoken language patterns of lower complexity

Often, when the environment seems to be a major factor in retardation, attention to the individual's physical needs is warranted as well. It is possible that some of these physical and/or psychosocial factors cause subtle neurological deficits that are not easily identified (Ramey & Finkelstein, 1981).

Prevention

In 1976 the President's Committee on Mental Retardation set two goals regarding prevention:

Goal: At least 50% reduction in the incidence of mental retardation from biomedical causes by the year 2000

Goal: Reduction of the incidence and prevalence of mental retardation associated with social disadvantages to the lowest level possible by the end of this century (pp. 135, 137)

The first goal is constantly being addressed through medical and technological advances; however, more progress is needed as certain conditions that cause neurological damage such as lead poisoning continue to be found. Although educators interested in mild retardation recognize the importance of biological factors, they tend to be more engaged in dealing with the ramifications arising from social disadvantage, as targeted in the latter goal.

At the very root of the problem is poverty. To effectively prevent the negative outcomes associated with poverty, major social changes are required. Data indicating the alarmingly high rates of poverty in this country coupled with federal budget cuts in social programs experienced in the eighties do not portend an optimistic future. It is interesting to note, as Begab (1981) did, that few prevention efforts are primary in nature (i.e., directed toward eliminating the root causes of retardation); most are better classified as secondary or tertiary efforts. In other words, most programs have been designed to deal with mild mental retardation after the fact.

To be effective, prevention efforts have to be focused on two areas. The first area of prevention involves provision of services at the preschool level for children who have been identified as mildly retarded or at risk. This may seem more like intervention; however, its purpose is to prevent school failure later on. The second area of prevention primarily involves education in a more pervasive sense. The thrust is more effectively to prepare those youngsters who come from lower socioeconomic settings for the demands of living. This means (1) reducing the number of individuals who are unemployed, (2) curbing the staggering number of teenage pregnancies, and (3) controlling the school dropout rate. The underlying idea is simple: to improve the quality of lives, to give hope, to provide a more stable future.

CHARACTERISTICS

Individuals who have mild mental retardation are typically capable of functioning adequately in a number of domains in a variety of contexts. However, there are times when they have difficulty coping with environmental demands. As a group they may encounter their greatest difficulties in school and in making the transition to community living.

Three important considerations need to be understood before characteristics are examined. First, persons with mild retardation have the same basic physiological, social, and emotional needs as their peers. Second, these individuals differ greatly among themselves in many ways. Not every person who is mildly retarded has all of the characteristics discussed here. Nonetheless, we can certainly make some generalizations solely to provide a framework for our understanding of mild retardation. Third, few current data exist on the characteristics of students with mild retardation. This dearth stems from the relative absence of recent research activity in the area (Haywood, 1979; Prehm, 1985) and from the fact that population changes in mild retardation have outdated the rich research foundation developed in the sixties and seventies (Gottlieb, 1982; MacMillan, Meyers, & Morrison, 1980; Polloway & Smith, 1988).

To provide a generalized picture of the characteristics that may be common to individuals with mild retardation, the following discussion focuses on a series of general areas, including learning-related characteristics, language development, sociobehavioral characteristics, physical traits, and life adjustment variables.

Learning-Related Characteristics

To educators, learning characteristics—including cognitive and motivational traits of people who are mentally retarded—are critically important. Learning has been defined as "the process whereby practice or experience results in a change in behavior which is not due to maturation, growth, or aging." The learning process is complex, and a significant amount of research has been conducted on how individuals with retardation learn. Although recently there has been a decrease in attention to this topic, a number of generalizations can be made. Table 6–4 provides a summary of critical learning-related characteristics, a brief explanation of their meaning, and references.

While the importance of cognitive and other learning characteristics is well recognized, the critical value of motivational factors has often been overlooked (Baumeister & Brooks, 1981). Learning characteristics are intimately related to the functional disparity between ability and performance in persons who are mentally retarded. Several related specific motivational areas need to be briefly discussed. The reader is referred to Zigler (1973) for further discussion about research on motivation.

Often individuals who are mentally retarded exhibit an external locus of control, because they perceive the consequences of their own behavior, both positive and negative, to be the result of fate, chance, or other forces beyond their control. This perception is similar to the concept of learned helplessness, the "psychological state that frequently results when events are uncontrollable" (Seligman, 1975, p. 9). Although it is developmentally appropriate for very young children to feel this way, as they mature, most children shift to an internal locus of control (Lawrence & Winschel, 1975). Because students who are mildly retarded may experience failure in their early school careers, they are likely to develop an experience of failure (Logan & Rose, 1982; MacMillan, 1982). To escape the unpleasant experience of failing, they tend to avoid failure-producing situations and consequently may have reduced aspirations and set lower goals for themselves (Zigler, 1973). Individuals who are seldom successful in their academic pursuits will soon want to avoid such situations. As a result, motivation is negatively affected.

A related characteristic of some students who are retarded is an outer-directed learning style, associated with a reliance on other people for solving problems. This style may be a result of their distrust of their own abilities (Zigler, 1966) and of past failure. Many teachers have heard their student say, "I can't do this" or "This is too hard." Usually, this type of verbal expression is routine, and the task is still attempted despite the statement. However, some students continuously require or demand the assistance of teachers, aides, or fellow students.

Balla and Zigler (1979) identified three determinants of the outer-directed motivational style just described: (1) general level of cognitive development, whereby persons functioning at a low intellectual level are most likely to be imitative; (2) attach-

Table 6–4
Learning-related characteristics

Characteristic	Description	Reference
Attention Variables	• Difficulty in the three major components of attention: attention span (length of time on task), focus (inhibition of distracting stimuli), and selective attention (discrimination of important stimulus characteristics).	Alabiso (1977) Zeamon & House (1963, 1979)
	• Key concern is to train students to be aware of the importance of attention and to learn how to actively monitor its occurrence.	Connis (1979) Howell, Rueda, & Rutherford (1983) Kneedler & Hallahan (1981)
Mediational Strategies	• Less likely than normal learners to employ effective techniques for organizing information for later recall.	Spitz (1966)
	• Typical techniques of mature learners include verbal rehearsal and repetition, labeling, classification, association, and imagery.	
	• Research indicates that students who are retarded have difficulty producing mediational strategies.	Bray (1979) Robinson & Robinson (1976) Strichart & Gottlieb (1983)
	• Tend to be "inactive learners."	
Memory	• Difficulty in the area of short-term memory (STM) but retain information over the long term.	
	• Long-term memory (LTM) is usually similar to that of persons who are not handicapped.	Belmont (1966)
	• Certain STM problems involving nonsensical tasks have been associated with deficits in the spontaneous use of mediational strategies.	Cohen (1982)
	• As noted above, strategy production is difficult for students with mild retardation, but improvements in recall can be achieved when they are shown how to proceed in an organized, well-planned fashion.	Baumeister & Brooks (1981) Borkowski & Cavanaugh (1979)
Transfer/ Generalization	• Tend to show deficiencies in the ability to apply knowledge or skills to new tasks, problems, or stimulus situations.	Stephens (1972)
	• Such difficulties relate to the inability to form learning sets.	Stevenson (1972) Robinson & Robinson (1976)
	• In particular, they may fail to use previous experience to formulate rules that will help solve future problems of a similar nature.	
Cognitive Development and Abstraction	• Ability to engage in abstract thinking or to work with abstract materials is usually limited.	
	• Symbolic thought, as exemplified by introspection and hypothesizing, is restricted. Such problems clearly relate to the individual's cognitive development.	Dunn (1973) Kolstoe (1976)
	• Common assumption that individuals who are mildly retarded will not reach Piaget's (1970, 1971) level of formal thought and thus even as adults will be limited to engaging in concrete skills consistent with the stage of concrete operations.	Polloway & Patton (1993)

Students with mild mental retardation can learn to engage in on-task, self-directed behavior.

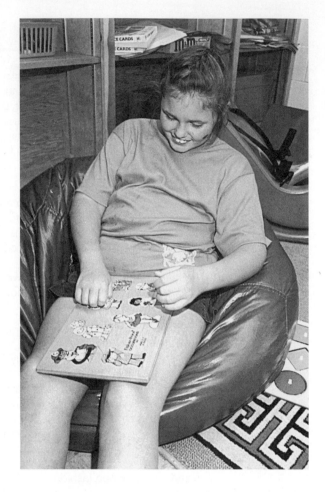

ment to adults, in which a strong dependence predicts a greater degree of outer-direction; and (3) degree of past success, because experiences of failure are most significant in producing external orientation. It will be important to reevaluate assumptions of failure set and the outer-directed style because it appears that the majority of such students enter school-based special education programs directly from preschool programs or at the beginning of their school careers rather than being referred for placement after having failed in school over a period of time (Polloway, Epstein, Patton, Cullinan, & Luebke, 1986).

Language Development

Because the development of speech and language is closely associated with intellectual development, it is not surprising that persons who are mentally retarded display problems in these areas. Specifically, there is a high prevalence of speech problems (MacMillan, 1982; Spradlin, 1963), with difficulties in articulation (e.g., substitution and omission of sounds) occurring most often. In addition, language deficiencies are common, including delayed oral language development (Dunn, 1973) and restricted vocabulary and incorrect grammatical usage (Spradlin, 1968). Language skills can be one of the greatest obstacles that individuals with mild retardation must overcome if they are to be fully integrated into society (Polloway & Smith, 1982).

With the gradual change in the population of students identified as mildly retarded, it is likely that teachers will be faced with problems beyond the dialectical variance that might be expected for an individual from a minority culture. Polloway and Smith (1988) have indicated that the change in the population would likely result in more evidence of language delay in this group, rather than just the problem of dialectical and linguistic differences.

A list of specific characteristics will help illustrate the possible language difficulties experienced by persons with mild retardation. The following list, adapted from a review by Wallace, Cohen, and Polloway (1987) and Smith, Polloway, Patton, & Dowdy (in press), is a set of characteristics that may be found in students identified as mildly/moderately disabled:

- Has difficulty with verbal expression
- Experiences problems with various aspects of verbal receptive language
- Finds it difficult to carry on a coherent conversation
- Does not respond to complete thoughts or gets lost in sentences or in expression in general
- Attends inefficiently when attempting to process verbal directions
- Gives inappropriate responses to verbal questions
- Prefers visual tasks that require little listening
- Cannot determine the main idea from orally presented material
- Experiences difficulty in discriminating between similar-sounding words (e.g., *tap* and *top*, *pen* and *pin*)
- Cannot accurately retell a story that was previously read aloud
- Has difficulty identifying and producing rhyming words
- Omits common prefixes and suffixes
- Cannot accurately repeat a series of words or digits that were orally presented

Sociobehavior Characteristics

By definition, deficits in adaptive skill areas must exist for an individual to be classified as mentally retarded and, in fact, the literature has frequently acknowledged the increased occurrence of emotional and behavioral problems in individuals with mental retardation. However, there is a relatively limited data base on the prevalence of specific problems in children and youth with mental retardation (e.g., Matson & Breuning, 1983). The primary research base in this area developed from comparisons between students identified as mildly retarded who were placed in special versus regular class programs (e.g., Kehle & Guidubaldi, 1978; Luftig, 1980; for reviews, see Cegelka & Tyler, 1970; Corman & Gottlieb, 1978); the focus of these studies was, therefore, primarily on the effects of educational placements rather than on an analysis of specific behaviors.

What generalizations can be made about sociobehavioral characteristics? It can probably be concluded that students with mild retardation have more adjustment problems than do their peers. The differences reported by Polloway et al. (1985) to be most pronounced at the elementary level included self-concept, attentional problems (as discussed earlier), and anxiety.

The relevant literature on self-concept has generally indicated that students who are mildly retarded report lower levels of self-efficacy than do their peers (Simeonsson, 1978). Other findings support the existence of low self-concept as evaluated from the perspective of teachers on items that encourage a focus on specific skill deficiencies (Polloway et al., 1985). It can be concluded that students who are mildly retarded do not hold strong, positive feelings about their own abilities and potential. Obviously, there is considerable correlation between negative self-concept and chronic failure.

Another common assumption stated in previous research reviews (e.g., Logan & Rose, 1982; MacMillan, 1982) is that children who are mentally retarded exhibit higher levels of anxiety than their peers. More recent data also offer some support for the existence of higher anxiety levels, especially for specific items on a rating scale most directly related to general anxiety (e.g., nervousness, inability to relax) (Polloway et al., 1985).

Individuals who are mildly retarded also often have poor interpersonal relationships. For example, they are more frequently rejected than accepted by their peers (Polloway et al., 1986). Gottlieb and Budoff (1973) found that the more inappropriate their behaviors, the more likely they were to be rejected. Subsequent research (Gottlieb, Semmel, & Veldman, 1978) indicated that this rejection results from the nondisabled students' perception of behavioral inappropriateness rather than of academic incompetence. These findings have important implications for the integration of students with mild retardation into general education settings.

Physical Traits

The physical, motor, and health characteristics of individuals with mild retardation have not traditionally differed dramatically from those of nonretarded comparison groups. The individuals with mild retardation often display no distinctive physical or health characteristics. As Dunn (1973) pointed out, performance of those with mild retardation, particularly in motor skills, is significantly better than that of other students identified as mildly retarded who are neurologically impaired or multiply disabled. With these latter groups, the very nature of their conditions causes them to differ physically from individuals who are not mentally retarded. However, as the mild retardation population becomes increasingly a group with more disabilities, the variance from their peers in physical, motor, and health domains is likely to increase as well.

Several observations can be made about physical traits. Individuals who are mildly retarded are below comparative standards for body measurements of persons not mentally retarded (equated by age) in height, weight, and skeletal maturity (Bruininks, Warfield, & Stealey, 1978). Some individuals—principally the emerging population of students who are classed as mentally retarded—display concomitant physical problems such as cerebral palsy, convulsive disorder, and sensory impairments (Epstein, Polloway, Patton, & Foley, 1989; Forness & Polloway, 1987). Unfortunately there is also an increased likelihood of injuries resulting from child abuse (Zirpoli, 1986).

Related health problems are commonly noted in this group as well. In particular, inappropriate and unbalanced diets, susceptibility to disease and illness, inadequate

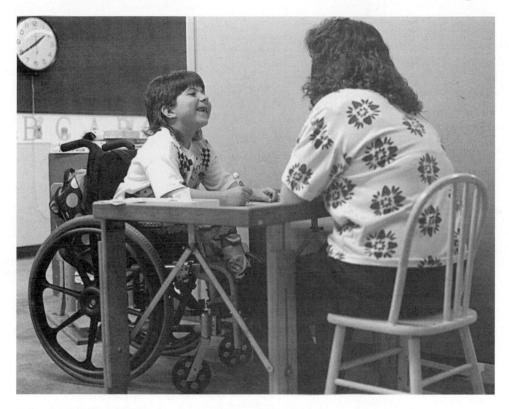

Various related services such as speech therapy are often required as part of an appropriate education.

health care, and dental problems have been found to be characteristic of many persons with mild retardation, obviously reflecting psychosocial correlates of retardation.

Research on the motor development of children who are mentally retarded has traditionally indicated parallels between them and students who are not disabled. Both groups follow the same developmental sequence, although the former may experience certain specific motor delays (e.g., Chasey & Wyrick, 1971; Edgar, Ball, McIntyre, & Shotwell, 1969; Kral, 1972). At the same time, however, a gap has been noted in coordination and fitness (Dunn, 1973; Francis & Rarick, 1959) and overall motor performance (Bruininks, 1977), which is likely to be more pronounced at increasing levels of severity. A study reported by Reschly and his colleagues (Reschly, Robinson, Volmer, & Wilson, 1988) illustrates this relationship between severity of retardation and motor skill deficits (see Table 6–5).

Life Adjustment Variables

Included among life adjustment variables are characteristics related to occupational success and community living skills. Crain (1980) studied the postschool economic and vocational status of graduates with mild retardation. She found that most were in

Table 6–5

Motor skill means and weaknesses by IQ

IQ	N	$\bar{X}$[a]	s.d.	Total with Weaknesses[b]	
				N	%
<50	39	2.10	1.07	29	74
50–54	33	2.18	1.10	23	70
55–59	35	2.46	1.07	17	49
60–64	52	2.48	0.96	25	48
65–69	59	2.53	0.95	24	41
70–74	121	3.08	0.91	26	21
75–79	155	2.95	0.88	40	26
80–84	118	2.97	0.85	30	25

Source: From *Iowa Mental Disabilities Research: Final Report and Executive Summary* by D. Reschly, G. Robinson, L. Volmer, and L. Wilson, 1988. Des Moines, IA: State of Iowa: Department of Education. Adapted by permission.

a   Mean scores were derived from a Likert rating scale that used the anchor points 1 = Significant Weakness, 2 = Weakness, 4 = Strength, 5 = Significant Strength.

b   Total was formed from the sum of the Significant Weakness and Weakness ratings.

the civilian labor force (68%), but that the majority held unskilled (e.g., dishwasher, maid) and semiskilled (e.g., nurse's aide) positions.

Edgar (1987) conducted a comprehensive follow-up on individuals who left secondary school special education programs. He reported that students who were mildly retarded infrequently dropped out of school, and yet of those who graduated, only 43% were employed, 44% had never been employed, and only 4% were making at least minimum wage.

These latter data reflect the fact that, increasingly, students who are mildly retarded are likely to be lower functioning and have greater need for training in life skills. It is unfortunate that, despite recent advances in the training of individuals with severe disabilities, less attention has been devoted to the same goal for students with mild disabilities.

In general, adults who are mildly retarded can obtain and maintain gainful employment, although a critical factor is their ability to demonstrate personal and social behaviors appropriate to the workplace. Furthermore, this population can deal successfully with the demands of adulthood if prepared to do so. For many, successful adjustment is achieved through the assistance of families, benefactors, and/or various adult service providers.

ASSESSMENT   Assessment in the area of mild mental retardation requires the comprehensive collection of information through various techniques, including formal and informal testing, curriculum-based measures, interviews, observations, and cumulative records. The process requires examination of intellectual functioning, academic achievement, social and emotional dimensions, adaptive behavior, medical factors, and language development. Specific areas focused on differ depending on the purpose of assessment and the age of the individual.

The two primary focuses in the identification of mental retardation are the measurement of intellectual functioning and the assessment of adaptive behavior. Although other areas (e.g., medical factors) are typically examined, classification of students as mentally retarded primarily requires confirmation of problems on these two dimensions.

Intellectual Functioning

Intelligence tests sample a cluster of behaviors from which to infer levels of intellectual functioning. The resulting score—the IQ—is simply an index of how well an individual performed these behaviors on the test. Most intelligence tests currently being used to make eligibility decisions in school systems are individually administered and are scored with reference to age norms, providing a comparison of a student's tested mental age and chronological age.

The most commonly used instruments in the schools have been the Wechsler Intelligence Scale for Children, 3rd Edition (WISC-III) (Wechsler, 1992) and the Stanford/Binet Intelligence Scale (Thorndike, Hagan, & Sattler, 1986). Other instruments such as the Kaufman Assessment Battery for Children (K-ABC) (Kaufman & Kaufman, 1983), the Woodcock-Johnson Psychoeducational Battery—Revised (Woodcock & Johnson, 1989), and the System of Multicultural Pluralistic Assessment (SOMPA) (Mercer & Lewis, 1977) are also used regularly in various parts of the country.

Much controversy exists over the use of intelligence tests in the schools, centered on these basic issues:

- *Definition of intelligence.* There is considerable disagreement as to what intelligence is and how to measure it.
- *Overemphasis on the intelligence component.* Deficits in intellectual functioning are often more heavily weighted than deficits in adaptive behavior.
- *Stability of IQ scores.* If intelligence is a basic, unchanging attribute, why do IQ scores fluctuate?
- *Cultural bias.* Critics emphasize that the verbal nature and middle-class standards of the commonly used tests discriminate against ethnic minorities, as well as linguistically different and economically disadvantaged students.

Adaptive Behavior

Assessing adaptive behavior is as significant for the diagnosis of mental retardation as is assessing intelligence. However, although there is some agreement on general components of adaptive behavior, its role in assessment of mild retardation has suffered from imprecise definition and lack of psychometric sophistication. Criticism of the use of measures assessing adaptive behavior has also resulted in part from practical problems (e.g., administration of the instruments). Nevertheless, assessment of adaptive behavior should be supported and encouraged.

Several formal scales have been developed and are commercially available. Some of the most frequently used instruments are the AAMR Adaptive Behavior Scales, the

Vineland Adaptive Behavior Scales, and the Comprehensive Test of Adaptive Behavior. Two versions of the AAMR scales exist: a residential and community version (ABS-RC:2) (Nihira, Leland, & Lambert, 1993b) and a school version (ABS-S:2) (Nihira, Lambert, & Leland, 1993a). The domains assessed by the two versions are depicted in Figure 6–2.

The Vineland scales are a revision of the original scale widely used throughout much of this century. These new scales assess adaptive behavior in four domains: communication, daily living skills, socialization, and motor skills. A survey form, an expanded form (Sparrow, Balla, & Cicchetti, 1985b), and a classroom edition (Sparrow, Balla, & Cicchetti, 1985a) are available. The survey and expanded forms also include a maladaptive behavior scale.

The Comprehensive Test of Adaptive Behavior measures behavior in six areas: self-help skills, home-living skills, independent living skills, social skills, sensory and motor skills, and language concept and academic skills. This scale differs from others in that, for each item, a follow-up testing procedure is provided, to be used if the behavior has not been confirmed through previous observation.

The key controversy regarding adaptive behavior measurement does not concern disagreement about its importance in the definition of mental retardation. Instead, it concerns disagreement about what behaviors to measure and the relationship of these behaviors to school-related criteria.

Approaches that assess adaptive behavior only in environments out of school produce a measure that is predictive of a limited scope of behaviors and may downplay the significant needs of students within the school setting. Similarly, school-based assessment ignores a great range of behavior and situations that are part of the child's life. Comprehensive assessment approaches that take into account the full range of interaction show promise and represent more appropriate alternatives to traditional assessment (Reschly, 1988).

INTERVENTION

A variety of programming alternatives are available for individuals who are mentally retarded. Three major issues dominate the topic of intervention: (1) lack of services, (2) appropriateness of existing services, and (3) efficacy of services.

1. Because programs have for some time been available to school-age children under federal and state laws, gaps in service most often have affected young children and adults. The needs of infants, toddlers, and preschool age children are now being addressed, as in 1986, Public Law 99–457 greatly expanded services and incentives for serving this group. Older individuals frequently have found that when formal school ended, so did most educational services.
2. The second issue, of appropriateness of education offered, remains one of debate, and it is a question that is not answered easily. However, it must ultimately be considered in terms of the immediate and future needs of the student.
3. The third concern involves what Turnbull and Barber (1984) call the cost-yield issue. They suggest that the efficacy of special education be approached from two perspectives: a cost-benefit basis (i.e., economic perspective—does it save money?) and a cost-effectiveness basis (i.e., personal perspective—do individuals prosper and progress?).

To provide an overview of intervention programs for children, adolescents, and adults who are mildly retarded, this section focuses on a series of closely related topics including service delivery, inclusion, curricular options, and transition planning.

Service Delivery

Early Childhood.   Appropriate services are required by federal law for preschool-age youngsters who are disabled, and incentives are available to states to develop programs for the birth to 3-year-old group as well. All children identified are entitled to an Individualized Family Service Plan (IFSP). Clearly, the emphasis of intervention is twofold: with the child and with the family.

For a substantial percentage of youngsters with mild retardation, these special education programs may not be relevant, because many in this group are not identified until they enter school and begin having difficulties. Those who are identified early may be served in preschool special education classes and classified in some generic fashion (e.g., learning impaired, developmentally disabled, or preschool disabled). A larger number of youngsters who potentially may be considered mildly retarded are likely to be identified as at risk at this age. Consequently, they will probably receive services in various early intervention programs, which may or may not be classified as special education. At-risk youngsters can be divided into three types (Keogh & Daley, 1983):

1. *Established risk:* Children with known medical conditions that affect their lives
2. *Suspect risk:* Children with developmental histories suggestive of biological problems
3. *Environmental risk:* Children with no known medical or biological problems but whose life situations are associated with potential problems

Many young children who have the greatest chance of later being identified as mildly retarded fall into the last category.

Considerable research has pointed to the positive effect of early intervention on the later growth and development of children who are mildly retarded (Rogers-Warren & Poulson, 1984). Lazar and Darlington (1982), in their review of early education efforts, found a number of positive outcomes—one of which was that fewer of these children were assigned to special education classes. Various options exist as to which type of program orientation is most effective. Evaluation of the Follow Through Project, established to sustain the early gains of children enrolled in Head Start programs, indicated that a teacher-directed, or direct instruction, orientation produced significant student gains (Stebbins, St. Pierre, Proper, Anderson, & Cerva, 1977). Even though the importance of early intervention has been validated (Ramey & Campbell, 1984; Schweinhart, Berrueta-Clement, Barnett, Epstein, & Weikart, 1985), the delivery of such services is often inadequately coordinated (Johnson & Chamberlin, 1983).

School Age.   Public school systems offer a number of program options for students who are mildly retarded and eligible for special education. The three most common special education arrangements are (1) full inclusion in regular education classes; (2)

ABS—School (2nd ed.)

Part One:

Independent Functioning. This domain pertains to eating, toileting, maintaining a clean and neat appearance, taking care of clothing, dressing and undressing, and utilizing transportation and other public facilities.

Physical Development. This domain assesses a person's sensory and motor abilities.

Economic Activity. People's ability to manage their financial affairs and be consumers is examined by this domain.

Language Development. This domain examines receptive and expressive abilities and how people utilize those skills to effectively deal with others in social situations.

Numbers and Time. Basic mathematical competencies are examined by this domain.

Prevocational/Vocational Activity. Because there are certain skills that relate to successful job or school performance, items within this domain examine a person's ability to function in these settings.

Responsibility. Examines the extent to which people can be held accountable for their actions, belongings, and duties.

Self-direction. This domain examines whether people maintain an active life-style or choose to remain passive.

Socialization. The socialization domain examines an individual's ability to interact with others.

Part Two:

Violent and Antisocial Behavior. This domain relates to personal behaviors that are physically or emotionally abusive.

Rebellious Behaviors. This domain examines several aspects of rebelliousness, including impudence, tardiness, and misbehavior in groups.

Untrustworthy Behaviors. This domain looks at behavior related to stealing, lying, cheating, and showing disrespect for public and private property.

Stereotyped and Hyperactive Behavior. These behaviors include making inappropriate physical contact, behaving in a manner considered stereotypical of developmental disorders, and being overly active.

Eccentric Behavior. Behaviors that are deemed as bizarre work against normalization. This domain examines several such behaviors.

Withdrawal. This domain is helpful in determining the degree to which a person withdraws from activities or fails to respond to others.

Disturbed Behavior. Several personal behaviors are bothersome to others, and this domain addresses a few of those annoyances.

Figure 6–2
AAMR Adaptive Behavior Scales—Components

ABS—Residential and Community (2nd ed.)

Independent Functioning. This domain pertains to eating, toileting, maintaining a clean and neat appearance, taking care of clothing, dressing and undressing, and utilizing transportation and other public facilities.

Physical Development. This domain assesses a person's sensory and motor abilities. Visual and auditory abilities are examined, as are both fine-motor and gross-motor skills.

Economic Activity. People's ability to manage their financial affairs and be consumers are examined by this domain.

Language Development. This domain examines receptive and expressive abilities and how people utilize those skills to effectively deal with others.

Numbers and Time. Basic mathematical competencies are examined by this domain.

Domestic Activity. People's ability to take care of their living quarters is examined by this domain.

Prevocational/Vocational Activity. Because certain skills relate to successful job or school performance, items within this domain examine a person's ability to function in these settings.

Self-Direction. This domain examines whether people maintain an active life-style or choose to remain passive.

Responsibility. Examines the extent to which people can be held accountable for their actions, belongings, and duties.

Socialization. The socialization domain examines the ability of an individual to interact with others.

Violent and Antisocial Behavior. This domain relates to personal behaviors that are physically or emotionally abusive.

Rebellious Behaviors. This domain examines several aspects of rebelliousness, including impudence, tardiness, and misbehavior in groups.

Untrustworthy Behaviors. This domain looks at behaviors related to stealing, lying, cheating, and showing disrespect for public and private property.

Stereotyped and Hyperactive Behavior. Examines behaviors that include making inappropriate physical contact, behaving in a manner considered stereotypical of developmental disorders, and being overly active.

Inappropriate Body Exposure. Relates to behaviors of a sexual nature.

Eccentric and Self-Abusive Behavior. Examines behaviors that cause harm to oneself or that are deemed as bizarre and work against normalization.

Withdrawal. This domain is helpful in determining the degree to which a person withdraws from activities or fails to respond to others.

Disturbed Behavior. Several personal behaviors are bothersome to others, and this domain addresses a few of those annoyances.

resource services, with students spending a limited time in special education settings (usually for reading, language arts, and/or math instruction); and (3) self-contained classes, with students spending most or all of the school day in special education. Although other settings are possible, the majority of students are in one of these three settings. The educational placement of students with mental retardation (all levels of functioning) for the school year 1989-90 is provided in Table 6–6. Interestingly, the most likely setting remains the self-contained classroom.

The guiding principle that schools should follow is to educate students with retardation in integrated, regular education settings wherever possible and appropriate. Although this issue will be addressed in more detail in the next section, it is instructive to note here that this goal must be examined in light of the emerging data suggesting that the needs of this group may be more significantly at variance with those of their peers. Regular education placement implies that these students are capable of handling the instructional and behavioral/classroom demands of a given setting and that this setting is able to accommodate these students. It also suggests that the nature of the curriculum meets the current and future needs of these students (Polloway, Patton, Epstein, & Smith, 1989). If these prerequisites are fulfilled, then the regular classroom is the placement of choice.

When appropriate, a resource service model has the advantage of addressing significant areas of need, while allowing students to spend considerable time with their peers. The major drawback of this model is the possible splintered nature of instruction.

The self-contained setting offers a more sustained program of specialized instruction, because students are in these settings for longer periods. Yet its clear disadvantage is that it severely limits the amount of interaction a student has with regular education students. In addition, the curricular focus may be inappropriate for some students with mental retardation.

The nature of programs for students with mild retardation varies from one locality to another. Further, there is a limited data base from which to draw any firm conclusions. One study (Epstein, Polloway, Foley, & Patton, 1989) analyzed Individualized Educational Plans (IEPs) for elementary-age students who were classified as mildly retarded and served in self-contained settings. It provides an overview of annual goals developed for these students. Academic goals in the subject areas of reading and math were found in the IEPs of 80% of the students. Interestingly, relatively few students had IEP goals concerned with social-emotional development. The absence of

Table 6-6
Percentage of students from ages 6–21 identified as mentally retarded serviced in different educational environments

Educational Environment	Percentage of Students
Regular Classroom	6.7
Resource Room	20.1
Separate Class	61.1
Separate School	10.3
Residential Facility	1.4
Homebound/Hospital	0.4

academic goals in subject areas of science and social studies and in the area of career education is also worth noting. The data collected in this study are, however, only illustrative, and they may not reflect the status of all such programs.

Many students who are mildly retarded may also receive one or more related services, such as speech/language intervention, physical therapy, occupational therapy, mental health counseling, or special transportation. Epstein et al. (1989) studied this area as well and found that speech/language therapy was the most frequently delivered related service (to 71% of the students).

It is important to consider some of the implications of the large decrease nationally in the number of students identified as mentally retarded. Some higher-functioning students with mild retardation have been reclassified and are now being served in classes for students with learning disabilities (Mascari & Forgnone, 1982; Polloway & Smith, 1988). Others, including those who have been declassified and those who would have been identified as mildly retarded in the past but are not being so identified now, are found in regular education. They have joined the group of students known as slow learners, low achievers, or at risk for school failure, who have typically been underserved.

Many of the educational arrangements available to elementary-age students are also available to adolescents with mild retardation, including regular education placement, resource services, and self-contained classes. However, the instructional emphases are—or at least should be—quite different from those at the elementary level. Intermediate and high school programs are usually characterized by predominantly instructional orientations, which vary considerably. These orientations are discussed later in the chapter.

One trend in the delivery of instruction to adolescents who have retardation is the increased use of community-based instruction (CBI). Many skills essential to independence in the community are best taught in the community, such as using a laundromat or vending machines. The value of the community-based design is that it provides instruction in natural settings, eliminating many of the problems students encounter attempting to generalize what they have learned in a classroom situation to the real world. Programs that highlight functional skills are particularly well suited to this delivery method.

Appropriateness of placement and program design can be determined only on an individual basis. With the alarmingly high rates of students dropping out of school, it becomes more important to develop programs sensitive to students' current needs and relevant to their future lives. Although we have chosen to separate them in this discussion, all of the topics in this section are interrelated and must be considered together. Thus, placement cannot be examined apart from the curricular emphasis inherent in that placement. Furthermore, any placement should be perceived as a tentative commitment, subject to review and change as needed.

Adulthood.   The adult lives of persons with disabilities have been given increased attention in recent years. Studies continue to suggest that these adults are employed significantly less often than the general population and, when employed, they typically are in less skilled jobs. Many have only part-time jobs. As the result of this situation and the federal initiatives to address it, there has been a proliferation of programs dedicated to enhancing the *transition* of students from school to community, with a primary focus on employment.

Not all young adults who have retardation adjust successfully to the demands that life and society make on them after they leave school; some require additional services. They may need continuing education to adjust to everyday living or to develop vocational training skills. In a society that is constantly changing and becoming more technologically complex and that is increasingly in need of service-oriented workers, many adults will need retraining. Adults with retardation may also require regular assistance in finding and using community resources and services. Other major areas of everyday life that cause problems include making a living, managing personal finances, and using leisure time well. Adults with retardation also frequently have difficulty obtaining and maintaining housing, gaining public acceptance, and establishing meaningful relationships.

Continuing education for this group is largely restricted to what is available to the general public. Just as regular education causes problems for some members of this group, adult offerings may pose difficulties as well. Some adults who need assistance can qualify for vocational rehabilitation services. Adult services and training opportunities do exist in most communities, but they are too few and may have long waiting lists.

Inclusion

Continuing attention has been given to integration efforts at all age levels. Our ultimate goal is to have individuals with mild mental retardation fully included in their adult lives. Social integration implies more than mere proximity; it also suggests a reasonable degree of social acceptance, relative freedom from restrictive practices, and a certain display of social valorization (Wolfensberger, 1983). Integration helps individuals with mental retardation to build increased levels of competence while presumably calling on them to achieve a certain degree of independence and personal responsibility.

Integrating individuals with mild retardation into alternative settings means different things depending on age level. During early childhood the issue is moot for those children who are not identified at this age. However, for those who are labeled as mildly retarded or learning impaired or with some other category name and who may be receiving some type of services, the issue of integration becomes real. Because most public schools do not provide early childhood programs for students who are not disabled, potential sites for integrating young children are more limited. Some school systems have found ways to include preschoolers with retardation in private child-care and preschool programs.

For the school-age level, much attention is being directed at including students with mild retardation in regular education. However, a cautionary note is warranted. As noted earlier, the emerging, lower-functioning group of students with mild mental retardation, where found, requires better-planned efforts to be integrated successfully into regular education.

In a descriptive study of the demographic and sociobehavioral characteristics of students who were classified as mildly retarded, Polloway et al. (1986) found that few of these students spent the greater part of their school day in regular education. The investigation examined the integration of younger students (i.e., those who would have been identified more recently) and older students (i.e., those who have been identified some time ago). Although younger students spent less time in regular education than the older students, neither group could be characterized as enjoying inclusive education. Even less encouraging was the finding that a significant number of younger students (50% of the boys and 42% of the girls) spent no time in regular settings.

It can be concluded that more comprehensive efforts at integration are needed to achieve success with this group of students. Such efforts are particularly critical at the elementary level where, as will be discussed, there is the greatest degree of curricular concordance used with students who are not disabled. The findings reported above should not forestall continuing efforts to provide services in integrated settings; however, they do suggest that these settings may not be appropriate for some members of the mild retardation group.

Although integration of secondary-level students who are mildly retarded can occur, there may be some significant barriers on the types of integration possible. Foremost is the reality that some of these students have a history of low academic achievement and may find the academic demands of regular education to be an overwhelming challenge. Nonacademic classes (e.g., art, drafting) and extracurricular activities may provide more viable forums for integration, as well as do areas where individual students can perform well.

When formal schooling ends, most individuals with mild retardation are naturally integrated into the community. However, inclusion in the ongoing activities and events of the general population of adults is not guaranteed. The success of this transition depends on how well prepared these individuals are for the demands of young adulthood. As noted earlier, some persons may require continued assistance to accomplish the goal of full inclusion in life.

If we can agree that integration in its broad connotation is, in fact, central to much of what we are trying to accomplish in special education, then we must shift our attention from the goal in itself to the processes needed to achieve it. While there seems to be universal acceptance of the former, there is less consensus about the latter. As a starting point from which to examine the process of integration, we should

- identify and analyze successful inclusionary efforts (Mascari & Forgnone, 1982)
- closely examine the demands for successful functioning in a person's subsequent environment
- give sufficient time to preparatory efforts—helping the individuals with retardation to develop appropriate social skills and preparing individuals in the recipient setting for interaction with the new population (Polloway & Patton, 1986)
- structure situations in which the person who has retardation can work cooperatively with those who are not disabled on tasks that this person can perform reasonably well (Gottlieb & Leyser, 1981)
- investigate the daily interactions of individuals who are mildly retarded and their classmates or co-workers
- continually reassess the performance of individuals and the quality of the programs into which they have been placed (MacMillan, Meyers, & Yoshida, 1978)

It is also important to recognize that integration should be conceptualized as more than the placement of students into academically focused classes. There are many ways to provide opportunities for those with mild mental retardation to interact with those who are not disabled (e.g., extracurricular activities, schoolwide projects). The foremost requirement is a commitment to the concept.

Curricular Options

Before considering the curricular needs of students with mild retardation, we need to establish a few basic guidelines.

- All curricular issues should be examined with a view toward providing students with programs that are sensitive to their current and future needs. Consideration of both school level transitions and integrative transitions into the community must be considered (Polloway, Patton, Smith, & Roderique, 1991).
- Curricula and instructional procedures should challenge students to maximum growth and development. Situations where students experience excessive frustration or have no opportunities to learn from mistakes should be avoided.
- Programs should strive to address not only students' deficits but also their strengths. We often fail to notice students' strengths and to provide opportunities for students to excel.
- As students get older, emphasis on vocational and life skills development should be part of the students' programs. As highlighted earlier, the overriding goal is for these students to function successfully and be fully included in their communities.
- Instructional programs should be teacher-directed and based on carefully selected and well-designed instructional techniques (cf. Becker & Carnine, 1980).
- Curricular modification may be necessary to accommodate lower-functioning students: content, sequence, and pace of instruction may have to be adjusted.

The curricular focus at the early childhood level is on providing children with experiences that develop their cognitive, communication, psychomotor, and social-affective skills—those readiness skills requisite for successful performance in kindergarten and the primary grades. The concept of transition applies to this level as well, particularly at two key points: from infant to preschool programs and from preschool to kindergarten programs. Certain nonacademic skills such as the ability to get along with other students in group activities or the ability to pay attention for a given period of time become important instructional areas.

From the time that students enter elementary school until the time they leave, much attention is focused on basic academic skill development in areas such as reading, mathematics, and language arts. Certainly no one would argue against the importance of these basic areas. Unfortunately, other critical content areas such as science and social studies are sometimes relegated to secondary status. A strong case for the inclusion of these areas has been made (Polloway et al., 1989), using the arguments that these subjects (1) present the type of information that broadens students' knowledge and experiential base and (2) are necessary for success in regular education settings. If we are to identify student strengths, we should also explore students' interests and abilities in the areas of music, art, drama, and movement.

Another important skill area in great need of attention is social skills. By definition, students with mild retardation have difficulty in adaptive skill areas, which include social skills. Students' specific problems in the sociobehavioral area were detailed earlier. It is likely that many students will require approaches that directly teach a variety of specific social skills.

One area of the curriculum that receives much attention in print and professional discussion but not in practice is career development. To maximize the success of transition efforts, which will occur later in students' schooling, career development must be initiated at the elementary level (Clark, Carlson, Fisher, Cook, & D'Alonzo, 1991).

As one might expect, there is a shift in curricular emphasis at the secondary level. Important curricular decisions must be made, and they must be based on individual educational goals and probable subsequent life-styles of the students. In general, a number of different curricular orientations can be identified in most secondary programs. They differ in emphasis and the degree in which they vary from the general education curriculum. Table 6–7 highlights these orientations.

The curricular option chosen depends on the needs of students. For many secondary students with mild retardation, an academic-oriented program may be appropriate; for others the focus must be a functional one, which emphasizes vocational and everyday living skills. A way of conceptualizing program orientation has been proposed by the Division on Mental Retardation (1992) of the Council for Exceptional Children:

> The Board of Directors of the Division on Mental Retardation (CEC-MR) affirms the importance of what students need to learn within and outside the school setting as the basis for determining curriculum and instruction for the individual. Given the importance of interaction with peers, initial consideration should be given to meeting students' needs within the regular classroom. However, the individual needs of students in general education will differ sometimes from those of students with mental retardation. Therefore specialized programs, such as community-based instruction, may take precedence from time to time, particularly at the secondary level. When the individual needs of students with mental retardation vary significantly from those of other students in the regular classroom, meeting their needs must not be constrained by philosophical concerns. Professionals should strive for helping students function in environments in which they will find themselves on leaving school. An increased commitment to life skills and vocational training in both general and special education may present an appropriate opportunity for achieving both curriculum and integration objectives desired for students with mild mental retardation.

A number of everyday life skills need to be taught if students with mild mental retardation are to adjust successfully to adulthood. Cronin and Patton (1993) organize the major demands of adulthood into six areas: employment/education, home and family, leisure pursuits, community involvement, physical/emotional health, and personal responsibility and relationships. Specific skills required in each of these areas are intricately tied to where individuals live and the demands placed on them there. There is another reason why it is crucial to incorporate such topics into the curriculum of students with mild retardation: these students have difficulty learning about these skills on their own.

The need for curricular innovation at the secondary level has been identified as a top priority by teachers (Halpern & Benz, 1987). Polloway and Patton (1993) argue for

Table 6–7
Overview of curricular options in secondary programs

Curricular Theme	Specific Curricular Orientation	Major Features	Functional Relevance
I. Academic Content Coverage		• General education content taught in special settings • Materials can be those used in general education or alternative ones • Concern about special teacher's background to teach some content areas	• Need for similar content acquisition as nondisabled peers • Precursor to integration into general education classes
II. Remedial	Basic Skills	• Goal is to increase academic performance to desired levels • Intensive programming in reading, math, language arts • Generalization of skills needs to be programmed • Some programs that focus too much on this orientation may neglect other areas	• Increase literacy levels • Can address deficit areas so that students can be integrated into general education classes
	Social Skills	• Relates to social skill development, affective needs, and behavior change needs • Generalization of acquired behaviors can be a concern	• Increase one's social competence • Potential benefits for inclusive settings • Importance of developing one's self-concept
III. Regular Class Support	Tutorial Assistance	• Teacher works with student on instructional topics that have immediate relevance in the general classroom • Provides a short-term emphasis on needs but may not have long-term value	• Addresses immediate needs (e.g., test) for the student • Serves a diplomatic function—it helps the general education teacher with students who need ongoing assistance

Compensatory Tactics	• Idea is to circumvent areas of difficulty (e.g., using a calculator when significant problems in this area) • Techniques may not be available for all situations • Typically used in conjunction with other orientations	• Provides an alternate way to achieve desired goals in spite of problems
Learning Strategies	• Cognitive-based techniques that teach students how to use their abilities and knowledge to solve problems, acquire information, deal with given situations • May not be useful with all students • Must be used in conjunction with other orientations—if students are not in general education • Important to program for transfer of skills from the training setting to others	• Provides long-term tactics for dealing with similar situations • Allows students to compete with peers who do not have disabilities
Cooperative Teaching	• Team approach to addressing the needs of students • Special education teacher works in the general education classroom	• Provides content learning and inclusion
Vocational Training	• Focus in on the acquisition of requisite skills in a specific vocational area • Variety of vocational training options are available • Addresses a major component transition service requirement of IDEA	• Students acquire a specific vocation skill or skills before leaving school • Motivates students by providing relevance to the curriculum • Shifts focus away from past failure in academic domains
Life Skill Preparation	• Acquisition of specific life skills to deal with the typical challenges of everyday life • Content emphases should be based on a realistic appraisal of what students will face when school is over • Life skills can be taught in educational placement	• Competency in dealing with major life demands is required of all individuals • Motivates students and shift focus away from previous failure experiences

IV. Adult Outcomes

247

the development of comprehensive curricula that attend to the diverse requirements of students with special needs. Comprehensiveness implies that programs for students with mild retardation should be

- responsive to the present needs of an individual
- consistent with the objectives of maximum interaction with peers who are not disabled while balanced with critical curricular needs
- integrally related to service delivery options (i.e., resource programs, self-contained settings)
- derived from a realistic appraisal of potential adult outcomes
- focused on transitional needs across the life span
- sensitive to graduation goals and specific diploma track requirements

These features suggest that a greater degree of curricular freedom be afforded at this level.

Transition Planning

Of the many vertical transitions that occur throughout the schooling of students, none has received more attention than the one from school to community. The need to plan for events that occur as students leave school and for those situations that they will encounter after leaving has already been emphasized. The importance of this planning for students with mild retardation stems from the fact that few from this group will find themselves in higher education. For most, the task is to move from the known environment of school to a life-style in which they will face new challenges on a daily basis. Adulthood is likely to be a time when formal assistance is limited and when they need to find natural support systems. With this in mind, we need to take action while these students are still in school and assist them in making the transition to adulthood and establishing some sense of stability in their lives.

Although many different transition goals could be enumerated, the following three embody the thrust of the transition movement:

- To arrange for opportunities and services that support quality living
- To prevent the interruption of needed services
- To maximize community participation, independence, and productivity as young adults

These goals can be accomplished if the following conditions are met: (1) attention to the curriculum and planning process at the secondary level, (2) involving appropriate professionals who can help link students/families with adult services or employment possibilities, and (3) through development of options and opportunities in the community.

To facilitate the movement from school to community, it is essential that effective and timely planning occur. This can be done by recognizing that certain activities should happen before students leave school. One time line for planning such activities is presented in Table 6–8. This table also suggests who should be responsible for a given transition activity.

MODEL PROGRAM

*P*arents and professionals alike are genuinely concerned that adults who have mental retardation become productive and reliable members of the work force. One effort designed to achieve this result is the Community Training and Employment Program (COMTEP). COMTEP is a community-based vocational training and placement program that serves adults with mild or moderate retardation. It has some unique features. Funded in 1983 and administered through the Association for Retarded Citizens of Hawaii, COMTEP is structured around three primary phases of operation: (1) vocational assessment, job matching, and prevocational training; (2) COMTEP–employer training partnership; and (3) supported employment.

The first phase is concerned with identifying vocational areas in which clients are interested and for which they possess the requisite skills. Assessment activities include formal vocational evaluations and situational assessments. One month of prevocational training may also be necessary for some clients; it can address appropriate interaction and communication skills as well as work responsibility and career planning.

The second phase of the program requires the participation of both COMTEP and the employer. After a suitable employment site is found by program staff, both parties agree to certain provisions. The employer provides (1) direction and supervision to the new employee, (2) reasonable accommodation, and (3) wages. COMTEP provides (1) a training facilitator (job coach) for up to 3 months to maximize the success of the placement by providing individualized training to the new employee and by minimizing the disruption to the business; (2) liability coverage for the new employee and the trainer during this on-site training period; (3) access for the employer to the Targeted Jobs Tax Credit Program in which the employer receives substantial tax benefits; and (4) work-related support (e.g., employment counseling, job club) to the employee with retardation.

During the third phase COMTEP provides ongoing support for a full year to the employer and the client by troubleshooting, upgrading certain skills, and/or retraining.

The value of the COMTEP model is that it focuses on individual needs and trains individuals on the job, in contrast to the typical classroom setting from which clients who have retardation must generalize to real situations. The program is attractive to employers for two major reasons. It eases the responsibility and the extra time required to assist employees with retardation in adapting to their new setting. In addition, the employment of such individuals entitles employers to certain tax advantages. Thus, COMTEP provides positive outcomes to all parties involved.

Table 6–8
Time line for transition planning

Year(s) in High School	Transition Activity	Responsibility
First year	Initial transition planning	
	• Identify potential services and placements after high school in transition areas	School representatives, parents, student
	• Begin to match needs of student with available knowledge of local community resources	School representatives
	Appropriate communication	
	• Provide information of community agencies regarding transition needs of student	School representatives
Middle Years	Active transition planning	
	• Conduct formal vocational assessment	School representatives
	• Determine appropriateness of referrals to specific community agencies	Transition team
	• Begin enrollment where appropriate (e.g., SSI, waitlists)	Parents/guardians, student
	• Review programming implications for school	School representatives
	• Initiate IEP planning to support transition plan	Transition team
Last Year	Facilitate transition to community	
	• Arrange cooperative programming	School representatives
	• Identify responsibility for continuing transition coordination	School representatives, parents, adult service providers
	• Finalize enrollment in postsecondary education or employment	Parents/guardians, student, school representatives, adult service providers
	• Assist families to enroll students in service programs as needed	School representatives

Inherent in the planning process is the development of an Individualized Transition Plan (ITP). The Individuals with Disabilities Education Act (IDEA) requires that transition services be part of every student's Individualized Educational Plan (IEP). Although the format and emphases of ITPs vary from one school district to another, most ITPs are noticeably similar. They usually include the following information: the different transition areas being addressed, action steps required to meet the student's needs in these different areas, person(s) responsible for achieving the listed activities, and a time frame for accomplishing the task. The major areas to be considered should relate closely to those identified by Cronin and Patton (1993) and discussed in the previous section on curricular considerations. In reality, however, if any area is preeminent, it is the employment area. An example of an individualized transition plan is provided in Figure 6–3.

Transition planning must be guided by principles that tend to increase the probability that students will successfully adjust to adulthood. Five of the most important guidelines are (1) families must be involved; (2) planning must be comprehensive; (3) secondary-level curricula must address transitional needs and adult outcomes; (4) planning should involve interagency collaboration; and (5) planning should be flexible and responsive to individual values, goals, and experiences (Patton & Browder, 1988).

Intervention/Education/Training

Many issues relevant to the education of individuals with mild retardation require further investigation and discussion. The cost-yield issue noted earlier will continue to be worth stressing, especially in times of fiscal restraint and program reevaluation.

Improvements in the decision-making process of identifying individuals with mild retardation are needed, especially in relation to culturally different students. The concept of adaptive behavior and its role in the eligibility process must be clarified. Most

Transition Service Areas	Person/Agency Responsible	Timeline
Employment/Education Goal:		
Home and Family Goal:		
Leisure Pursuits Goal:		
Community Involvement Goal:		
Physical/Emotional Health Goal:		
Personal Responsibility and Relationship Goal:		

Figure 6–3
Individualized Transition Plan

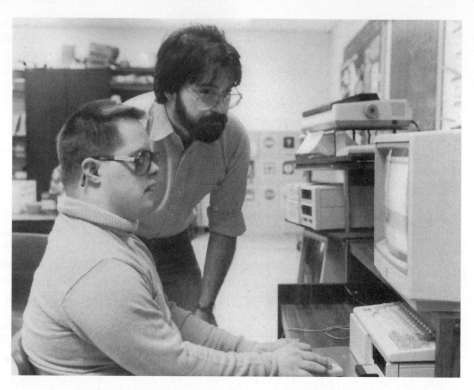

It is essential to provide experiences that will help young adults deal with an increasingly technologically complex world.

important, professionals who make eligibility decisions must be sensitive to what is ultimately best for the student, taking into consideration curricular, inclusionary, and efficacy variables.

Instructional/curricular changes may be necessary in many programs for students with mild retardation, particularly in programs that have experienced the population changes noted in this discussion. More attention must be given to the needs of students who are considered "dual diagnosed"—mildly retarded and behaviorally disordered. Few programs are adequately meeting the needs of this growing group.

Innovative efforts to develop comprehensive curricula are warranted. Emphasis on directive teaching, community-based instruction, and maximizing the time students are actively engaged in learning should also be sustained. Regardless of the characteristics of the student population, the focus must be on preparation for young adulthood and successful transition to living in the community.

Over the last few years there has been a decided shift from segregated sheltered employment (i.e., workshops) to supported and competitive employment. The advantages of supported and competitive employment options include greater integration, better wages (at least minimum wage), and less supervision over the long term. These models have been found to be effective with more severe groups and are certainly appropriate for individuals with mild retardation (see Bellamy, Rhodes, Mank, & Albin, 1988; Wehman, 1992; Wehman & Kregel, 1985).

A major problem about which school systems have long known but have done little involves students with significant learning-related problems who may not qualify for special education services. As students who are mildly retarded and learning disabled continue to be decertified in many school districts, there is an even greater need to provide services to this group of problem learners. Meyen and Moran (1979) have suggested that special services may need to be available to all students who need special assistance, regardless of how briefly the services are needed. One suggestion is to move to a system that is more concerned with labeling *services* than *students*, thereby allowing students who are experiencing problems to obtain the needed services without determining eligibility (Polloway & Smith, 1988). Leinhardt, Bickel, and Pallay (1982) offer the idea that compensatory education and special education for students with mild disabilities be merged into a single system.

The need to acquaint students with technology is threefold. First, it can be an effective, highly motivating way of providing instruction. Second, from an adult outcomes perspective, a cursory level of computer competence is an unavoidable requirement of the future. Third, computer competence may lead to certain types of employment. If we are to prepare students for adulthood, we must introduce them to the technology that will be used in many facets of their lives.

Criminal Justice System

Limited attention has been directed toward issues surrounding the adjudication and incarceration of individuals with mild retardation. The relationship of mental retardation and delinquency/criminality is not precisely known; nevertheless, mental retardation seems to be more a contributing factor than a cause.

Morgan (1979) studied national prevalence data indicating the number of individuals in juvenile correctional facilities who are disabled. He found that approximately 7.7% of the incarcerated population was mildly retarded. Although this figure was probably inflated, the magnitude of the situation is alarming. Even a more conservative figure somewhat lower than 7.7% differs significantly from the less than 1% of mental retardation found in the general population.

Plausible explanations for the high rates of retardation among juvenile offenders are much like those describing the relationship of learning disabilities and juvenile delinquency (Keilitz & Miller, 1980): (1) these individuals experience sufficient school failure to precipitate delinquent behavior, (2) they have certain behavioral characteristics that make them more susceptible to delinquency, and (3) they are treated differently by the juvenile justice system. There is still much debate as to which of these factors are responsible.

It has been estimated that the prevalence of adult offenders who are mentally retarded is approximately 10% of the prison population. Like the figure for younger offenders, this is probably inflated; nevertheless, an inordinate percentage of the prison population has retardation. The reasons that individuals enter the criminal justice and correctional systems have been discussed elsewhere (Beirne-Smith, Patton, Ittenbach, 1994). Most attempts to explain their overrepresentation revolve around two hypotheses: (1) that certain characteristics of individuals with retardation make them more likely to enter these systems and (2) that the nature and functions of the legal/correctional system tend to facilitate entry of this group into the system.

The issues surrounding this adult group are similar to those surrounding the juvenile group. The major difference is that there is no legal mandate to provide an appropriate special education to adult offenders. Although some correctional facilities have established distinct units or special programs within the institution for providing specialized education and training, these initiatives continue to receive low funding priority. The reality is that prisons are not designed to treat (i.e., educate, habilitate, or train) persons who have retardation (Marsh, Friel, & Eissler, 1975).

Quality of Life

Issues pertaining to the adjustment of adults with mild retardation in community settings are wide ranging. One difficulty in judging community adjustment is identifying criteria that indicate such adjustment. An intriguing technique for gathering information about the lives of adults with mild retardation is to obtain it from these individuals themselves. It is interesting that far too often programs are designed and, more important, decisions are made for these adults based on what we think they want rather than what they actually want. It is important that we respect the dignity inherent in making choices and therefore respect their desires, feelings, and attitudes.

Major areas of continuing need for persons with mild retardation include

- creating public acceptance of this group
- supporting them in gaining and maintaining full-time employment in jobs that are equal to their individual competencies
- locating appropriate living arrangements
- developing the skills and knowledge to use community resources effectively
- providing integrated leisure and recreational outlets
- helping them deal with sexuality, marriage, and parenthood
- assisting them in developing meaningful and lasting relationships
- advocating for their needs as well as encouraging them to become self-advocates and to find natural supports within their daily settings
- recognizing the host of needs that come with growing older and providing appropriate services
- encouraging them to pursue lifelong learning, because change is inevitable and adapting to it is essential

Many young adults who are mildly retarded readily blend into the community or, as Grossman and Tarjan (1987) note, they "may again become asymptomatic in adulthood" (p. v). Others do not and continue to struggle with the demands of adulthood each and every day. It will be important to monitor the population of students who are now identified as mildly retarded to ensure that they are being provided services that will maximize the probability of their living with dignity and respect.

The field of mental retardation is an exciting one: it always has been and will continue to be. Like most fields it is not static, and for this reason we must continually reexamine what is happening and how it is affecting those about whom we are concerned.

*A*mong the factors contributing to the lack of academic success of students with mild disabilities—including mild mental retardation—are attention problems, memory deficits, and lack of motivation. Computer-assisted instruction (CAI) has several capabilities that make it well suited to the special educational needs of these youngsters.

1. *Reduction of distraction and irrelevant stimuli.* Relevant stimuli can be highlighted with verbal cues, animation, sound effects, and/or external prompts such as arrows. Also, text presentation can be delayed so that the student sees only one letter, word, or phrase at a time.
2. *Simplification and repetition of task directions.* Task directions can be presented in a printed format and/or with a speech synthesizer at a level appropriate to the student's reading ability or receptive vocabulary. Repetitions can be provided as often as necessary at whatever pace the learner can handle.
3. *Practice for overlearning.* Drill and practice programs are ideal for skills and concepts such as math facts, spelling, and sight words that require repetitive presentation. An added advantage is the possibility of giving the student control of the presentation pace.
4. *Modeling and demonstrations.* Technology provides ways to have simultaneous audio and visual presentation, which can make modeling and demonstrations more effective.
5. *Prompts and cues.* The availability of so many ways to prompt and/or cue responses (i.e., sound, color, animation) with CAI facilitates errorless performance.
6. *Instruction in small, manageable steps.* CAI is especially well suited to delivering instruction in small steps with frequent responses.
7. *Immediate and frequent reinforcement and feedback.* Students with mild disabilities need motivators powerful enough to overcome their dislike for school. In addition to providing immediate corrective feedback in a nonthreatening manner, the computer has numerous reinforcement possibilities. The ability of microcomputer instruction to provide continuous feedback and positive reinforcement when deserved contributes to a sense of self-esteem. Students can be reinforced for a correct response with a personalized praise statement, graphic displays, or brief game segments. Moreover, because feedback on correct and incorrect answers is immediate, the student does not have to wait until a teacher can grade the work.

As emphasized in this chapter, although they are an extremely diverse group, students with mild disabilities share some common problems (in addition to academic failure). One area where many experience significant difficulties is the acquisition, development, and use of language and communication skills. The emphasis in most language intervention efforts with these students is on the importance of establishing a shared context for communication—one that is both functional and mutually satisfying for both conversation partners. The nonportable computer does not lend itself particularly well to development of this type of communication skill per se. However, this situation is changing as computers become increasingly more portable. Language and communication skills can be taught with portable computers and, more important, practiced in the school, at home, and in community settings.

1. Set academic learning and life skill goals that are realistic for the individual and relevant to the community in which the individual lives.

2. Assign learning tasks that (1) are personally important, (2) are carefully sequenced from easy to difficult, (3) allow the learner to be successful, and (4) have implications for success in subsequent environments.

3. Recognize the individual's strengths and weaknesses, provide incentives for performance, establish necessary rules for appropriate behavior, and use consistent consequences.

4. Explain required learning tasks in terms of concrete concepts. Stress real-life applications.

5. Encourage the individual to take part as fully as possible in everyday events, even when participation involves a reasonable degree of risk. Promote independence.

6. Train the individual who cannot achieve total self-reliance (who is not able to generalize problem-solving skills) how to obtain reasonable support services.

7. As your position permits, create learning, living, or work opportunities that will enhance the quality of the individuals' lives.

8. Include individuals who have retardation in decision-making processes that affect them. Stress the importance of their freedom of choice.

9. Remember that people who have mental retardation are much more like than unlike their peers.

10. Consciously seek ways that promote social integration in learning, living, working, and recreational activities.

TIPS FOR HELPING

SUMMARY   Mental retardation is a condition subject to confusion and professional and public debate. It is a broad field, encompassing individuals whose abilities and disabilities are widely divergent. *Mild retardation* is a complex and highly variable concept.

Historically, the treatment of persons with retardation has been a function of social and political influences and the efforts of certain individuals and groups. Within the last 40 years persons with retardation have gained many rights and services through legislation and policy changes. Nonetheless, many more advances in education, vocational training, and socialization are still to come. One current development is the changing nature of the population of persons with mild retardation. Significantly fewer students are being classified as mildly retarded, and the current group tends to be lower functioning. These changes pose immediate challenges for providing appropriate services to this group.

The definition of retardation has regularly changed over time, generally under the auspices of the American Association on Mental Retardation (AAMR). The 1992 revision (AAMR, 1992) retains the three major components of the earlier definitions: (1) significant subaverage general intellectual functioning, (2) deficits in adaptive behavior, and (3) manifestation during the developmental period. The concept of clinical judgment was also retained.

Individuals who are mildly retarded can function adequately in various environmental contexts. However, they encounter problems in certain settings, particularly educational ones. They have common human needs and differ greatly among themselves in many ways. The major areas of difficulty include personal-social development, learning, language, physical/health, and life adjustment.

The positive effects of early intervention for children who are educationally at risk or mildly retarded are clear. It is important not only to teach preacademic skills but also to address specific nonacademic skills needed for survival in educational settings. At the elementary level, curricula and methodology for students with mild retardation may be somewhat similar to those selected for students in regular education. However, some specialized materials may be used, and the pace may be different. When students who are mildly retarded progress to the secondary level, major curricular decisions must be made. All students will benefit from some level of instruction in the areas of functional life skills and vocational training. Furthermore, all students must be prepared for the transition to life after high school. Programs should be designed to be both appropriate to individual needs and balanced with an emphasis on integration.

STUDY QUESTIONS

1. Evaluate the treatment of people with mental retardation today as compared to that 30 years ago and 80 years ago.

2. Explain the major components of the latest AAMR definition of mental retardation. How are these criteria assessed? How does the definition differ from Grossman (1983)?

3. How has the population of students with mild retardation changed over the last 15 years? What are some plausible explanations of this phenomenon?

4. How can personal-social characteristics of individuals with mental retardation affect their learning?

5. Defend continued funding of early intervention programs for children who are not disabled but are at risk for subsequent difficulties.

6. What are the implications on curricula and integration posed by the differences in the population of students with mild retardation?

7. Based on the information presented in this chapter, what are the requisite components of successful integration efforts?

8. What postsecondary options are available to students who are mildly retarded? How can schools facilitate the transition to these postschool environments?

9. Why is technology both a boon and possible barrier to individuals with mental retardation?

10. What does quality of life mean?

7

Mark Wolery
Allegheny-Singer Research
Institute

Thomas G. Haring

Moderate, Severe, and Profound Disabilities

In this chapter you will learn about

- the causes of severe mental retardation

- the nature of mental retardation and the implications of the characteristics of students with severe disabilities

- the steps in the assessment process for instructional program planning for such students

- major curricular domains (content areas) and current practices in teaching students with severe disabilities

- issues and considerations related to the placement of students with severe disabilities in general education classrooms

- current issues faced by educators of students with severe disabilities

This chapter was completed after the untimely death of Dr. Thomas G. Haring. However, his keen intellect and sound expertise are reflected in many of the ideas described and the research that is cited in this chapter. The field of severe developmental disabilities will greatly miss the brilliance and significance of his prolific research contributions, as will the new investigators and teachers whom he trained. I greatly miss his critique of my work and I miss his friendship. I take responsibility for any weaknesses or shortcomings found in this chapter.

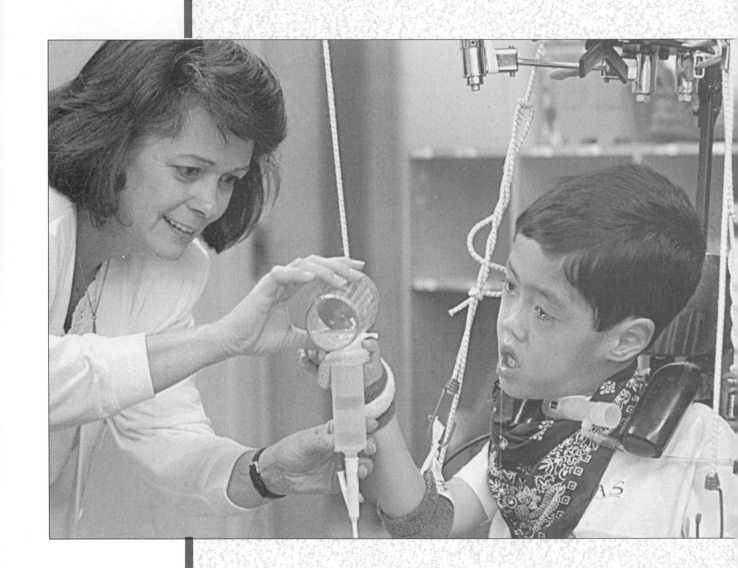

*J*uanita is a 9-year-old girl of average height and is rather thin. She dresses similarly to her peers, and if one were looking at a class photograph, she would not stand out from them. However, a short period of observation would indicate that she is not the usual 9-year-old child. She has been diagnosed as having severe mental retardation with an IQ score of 37 and adaptive behavior scores indicating that she has substantial deficits in communication, social, and academic areas. The cause of her mental retardation is not known. She is nearsighted, but wears glasses that correct her vision to 20/20. Physically, she is more awkward than her age-mates, but she is able to move around her home and school and is quite active. She speaks in short sentences, but individuals who are not familiar with her may have difficulty understanding what she says. While she usually does not engage in problem behavior, she will have a tantrum or withdraw when she is faced with repeated failure. She has a seizure disorder, which is currently controlled by medication.

Juanita has three siblings who are not disabled and lives at home with both parents and an older brother and sister; her favorite sister is currently away at college. Juanita has been in early intervention programs since she was 12 months of age—when her parents were disturbed by her lack of alertness, failure to crawl, and lack of attempts to speak. Her parents are well informed about her condition and hope that someday she will be able to live in a sheltered apartment or a group home and work full-time. However, they worry a great deal about what will happen to her as they get older and are less able to care for her. They do not want to burden her siblings with her care, but at the same time they realize she will likely need someone to help her throughout her life.

Juanita attends the public school in her neighborhood with her brother and some friends from her street and church. She is enrolled in a special education classroom at the school, but she does not spend all of her time there. Her teacher, Ms. Laird, is responsible for seven children with moderate and severe disabilities and she has two teaching assistants. However, each child spends some time each day outside of the classroom in community-based instruction and in general education classrooms.

When Juanita arrives at school, she goes to a homeroom class with two of her friends from her neighborhood. She stays there for the lunch count, attendance, and a brief socialization time. When the students in the class break up to go to different classrooms, she goes to the special education classroom. The next hour is spent on learning functional academic skills in a group led by Ms. Laird. Then she joins a language group that is led by the speech-language pathologist and that includes three of her friends who do not have disabilities. The goal of this group is to increase her conversational behavior. She then goes to the prekindergarten class where she works as a teacher's helper getting snacks ready and cleaning up after snack time (washing the tables, emptying the trash, etc.). She says she is going to be a teacher. She then goes with Anthony (a boy from the special education class) and a teaching assistant for community-based training. This focuses on learning to ride the bus, crossing the street carefully, using a public telephone, asking for directions to given locations, behaving appropriately in public (e.g., not talking with strangers, staying near Anthony, waiting in line, not handling things on shelves), and securing services from the community (ordering in fast-food restaurants, making purchases, manipulating money, learning to select the cheapest item, etc.). She returns to school for lunch and eats with her friends from the homeroom class. After lunch she goes to physical education with her friends. She returns to the special education classroom to work on a variety of skills including learning to play games her friends who are not disabled have chosen, calculator use, snack preparation, and janitorial skills (sweeping, using a vacuum cleaner, washing windows). An occupational therapist has worked with Ms. Laird to devise activities that will improve Juanita's fine motor control.

Her parents are quite pleased with the educational services provided to Juanita, and they have regular contact with Ms. Laird. Over the years they have taught her many domestic (toileting, self-feeding, dressing), communication, play, and social skills. Because they value work, they ensure that she has regular chores just like her siblings do. She is responsible for feeding the pet dog, and she helps load and unload the dishwasher. She enjoys participating in family activities such as going out to eat, going to movies, taking part in events at church, and visiting friends.

The focus of this chapter is on a small percentage of students who have the label of "mental retardation." It addresses students with moderate, severe, and profound mental retardation. Many individuals given these labels also will have other disabilities (e.g., vision, hearing, health, and physical impairments) that complicate their lives and education. Although they all have severe disabilities, they are quite different from one another. A student such as Juanita will need very different instruction from a student with severe cerebral palsy or a student with dual sensory (hearing and vision) impairments. Despite these differences, the goals of education and the general principles that guide assessment and instructional activities for those with severe disabilities are similar. The goals are to promote maximum self-sufficiency of these individuals; to facilitate their independent or partial participation in activities associated with living, working, and recreating in the community; and to enhance their social relationships with their families and others. Assessment activities involve ecological evaluations and other methods to understand students' behaviors *and* the contexts in which they function (T. G. Haring, 1992; Rainforth, York, & Macdonald, 1992). The instructional strategies involve direct instruction using behavioral principles and procedures that are embedded into ongoing routines and activities of the day.

HISTORY   Many descriptions of the history of people with severe disabilities imply that there was minimal history prior to 1975, when the passage of Public Law 94–142, the Education for All Handicapped Children Act, mandated a free and appropriate public education for all children, including those with severe disabilities. Historical descriptions typically indicate that many infants and children with severe disabilities died because the medical technology needed to preserve their lives was undeveloped. Although the limited survival of persons with severe disabilities in history is true, the stories of those who survived help us understand the relationships between disability and society. They help us realize how social roles and expectations continue to define the opportunities for people with severe disabilities.

Early Historical Context

Throughout history people have attempted to understand, provide for, and—in some notable instances—educate children who differed markedly from the norm. This history sheds light on how a culture views disability and human variation and leads to a major conclusion: the treatment and dignity accorded people who differ is more a product of prevailing social theories and cultural practices than of an inherent property of persons with disabilities. Societies historically create social roles for people with disabilities that tell more about the society than about such persons. A clear example occurred during the eugenics hysteria of the twenties (Gould, 1981; Wolfensberger, 1972). During the 19th century in the United States, the prevailing attitude toward persons with disabilities and mental retardation was one of optimism. New schools and residential facilities were developed with the view that students and residents could be taught to work productively and enter society. During the early 20th century, a change in immigration patterns—fewer immigrants from Great Britain and northern Europe and many more from southern Europe and Mediterranean countries—fed an irrational fear that new immigrants were genetically inferior and that action was needed to prevent the genetic slide of the country into idiocy. In this climate of hysteria, the treatment, quality of residential services, and opportunities for integration into the community for persons with disabilities noticeably worsened. Instead of promoting integration into communities in a productive manner, schools and institutions became facilitators in removing people from society. Individuals with severe disabilities were viewed as inevitable products of inferior genetics with no hope for meaningful learning or productive work. The important point is that this view had little or nothing to do with the characteristics of people with disabilities; rather, it was a reflection of the role created for them within the context of a larger cultural trend—that is, the irrational fear of large numbers of immigrants who were viewed as inferior.

A history of one child with severe disabilities, who is unusually important because of his appearance at a unique point in history, is provided by Lane (1979). Lane's history is actually a biography of two people, Victor, the wild boy of Aveyron, and Jean-Marc-Gaspard Itard, a 26-year-old physician who was sponsored by the French government to educate Victor.

Between 1798 and 1800 farmers and hunters in the Aveyron district reported sighting an unclothed boy running wildly through the woods. The winter of 1800 was one of the coldest in history. Early in the year, driven by hunger and cold, the wild boy entered a shop in a town. From that point, he became a *cause célèbre* throughout France, and a major test of some fundamental principles in philosophic discourse on the nature of human beings.

The discussion of the nature of humans was viewed as important to the formation of new, more benevolent forms of government during this period, known as the Enlightenment. At that time, Rousseau was developing a philosophy based on humans as "noble savages." He proposed that government and cultural institutions inhibited the natural dignity of people. In contrast, other philosophers, notably Locke, argued that the fulfillment of humanity can be achieved only through the development of civilization, culture, and education. To the age, a scientific "proof" of the importance of civilization and an active role of government in shaping society for the betterment of people would be critically important. The discovery of a "wild boy," totally unexposed to society, offered an opportunity to establish the true nature of humanity and present proof of the role of instruction and experience in creating civilization. The wild boy became an international sensation that attracted the attention of the greatest philosophers and natural scientists of the time. These individuals were confronted by a boy who, by all current standards, would be classified as severely disabled. He was approximately 15 years old, entirely mute, and had autistic behaviors such as repetitively rocking back and forth and appearing to be unaware of, or uninterested in, human contact. His primary interests were in food and in escaping to the woods. For almost a year his most minute behavioral patterns and reactions to situations were observed and recorded. He did not, as some would have hoped, instantly learn language and become a civilized young man. Instead, after a year of intense study, "after the natural philosophers stopped coming to see the *enfant sauvage*, after the boy had shown no progress that would allow some hope for his instruction" (Lane, 1979, p. 53), Sicard (the director of the Institute for Deaf-Mutes, where the wild boy was living) concluded that he was a "congenital idiot," and thus, no hope from education or treatment could be expected.

This was the situation as Itard came upon it in 1801. Everyone was giving up hope for the wild boy (who still had no name). In contrast, Itard viewed the situation with optimism. He saw the wild boy, whom he named Victor, not as a hopeless defective but as a child who lacked language and therefore was cut off from all socializing influences. Itard had been trained in a theoretical approach for understanding and teaching language and was eager to test it in practice. He lived with Victor for 5 years and devoted every day to systematically teaching him the cognitive skills that underlay language as Itard understood them. From this experience Itard discovered some fundamental principles of behavioral theory and developed procedures and concepts that would later guide the development of sign language and oral approaches for instruction of children who are deaf. Although Victor failed to learn oral language, perhaps due to injuries sustained to his voice box (his throat may have been slit when he was abandoned as a young child), he learned sophisticated systems for classifying objects and understood many complex and abstract concepts. He lived a life that was free from many of society's obligations with the aid of Itard's former housekeeper who remained devoted to him throughout his life.

The history of Itard and Victor symbolizes the history of treatment for people with disabilities and illustrates two fundamental misconceptions about disability. The first misconception is that people with disabilities play a given role in a culture because of the nature of their disability or the characteristics of their condition. The treatment and opportunities that were accorded Victor were a function of where he "fit" into society's considerations and debates at the time; they were not defining characteristics of Victor. Victor was viewed as fitting a role that would decide an important philosophic debate. Thus, in his treatment, his environment was structured to resolve this debate. The conclusion for us is, When new, more facilitative roles for individuals with disabilities are accepted and the individuals are given opportunities to achieve those roles, their life-styles become fundamentally different.

The second misconception about disability is that learning difficulties are a characteristic of the learner rather than of the instruction. Under Itard's instruction, the gains and developmental progress (as well as the failures) evidenced by Victor were not inherent characteristics of Victor, but rather inherent characteristics of the instructional procedures that Itard developed and used. Thus, if a student fails to learn, instead of defining that failure as a property of the student and his or her abilities, it should be defined as an inadequacy in the instruction, and more effective procedures should be developed as a consequence.

Modern History

What we now accept as current practice in the United States began to be shaped during the sixties. In 1961 President John F. Kennedy, who had a sister with severe disabilities, began to focus national attention on improving services. He created the President's Panel on Mental Retardation, which was instrumental in creating new services and increasing funding for research and training. It was not, however, the executive branch of government that led the way in establishing new rights to educational opportunities. In the seventies the courts were the most important force in shaping services. The first major case, *Pennsylvania Association for Retarded Citizens* (PARC) *v. Commonwealth of Pennsylvania* (1972), was brought as a class action suit. Pennsylvania operated a large institution for individuals with disabilities (Pennhurst) that was found guilty of numerous violations of individuals' rights and of failure to provide appropriate educational services. The court ordered the Commonwealth to develop individualized educational plans that were appropriate for each student, find children in Pennsylvania who were disabled and who were not yet receiving education services, develop formal systems for protecting the due process rights of children, develop appropriate curriculum guidelines, and conduct assessments in an unbiased manner. All of the features of the PARC decision, which applied only to the Commonwealth of Pennsylvania, were later elaborated in Public Law 94–142, the Education for All Handicapped Children Act of 1975. P.L. 94–142 was, of course, a major piece of legislation that applied to all school-aged children with disabilities in the United States and mandated, among other provisions, that they receive a free and appropriate public education (Turnbull, 1990).

The more recent history continues to be shaped by active efforts to focus judicial and legislative action to secure appropriate education and the civil rights of students with severe disabilities. The 1986 amendments (Public Law 99–457) to the act provided increased incentives to states to deliver services to infants, toddlers, and preschoolers with disabilities (Turnbull, 1990). As a result, all states currently provide a free appropriate public education to children 3 to 5 years of age who have disabilities, including severe disabilities. Most states are developing statewide comprehensive service systems for infants and toddlers with disabilities (Gallagher, Trohanis, & Clifford, 1989). These amendments also promoted what was already considered best practice—devising intervention programs more directly in line with families' goals, priorities, and concerns (Dunst, Trivette, & Deal, 1988).

In 1990, the act became the Individuals with Disabilities Education Act (IDEA) (Public Law 101–476). The 1990 act added two categories of disabilities (autism and traumatic brain injury) through which students may be eligible for special education and related services. Also, assistive technology was designated as a related service, and Individualized Transition Plans (ITPs) to employment or postsecondary education were required by the time students are 16 years of age.

Another legislative initiative passed in 1990, the Americans with Disabilities Act (Public Law 101–336), has substantial provisions for all individuals with disabilities, including those with severe disabilities. This legislation, described as sweeping civil rights legislation, extends Section 504 for individuals with disabilities. It specifies that they should have equal access and reasonable accommodations in employment and in other areas of public and private services.

These recent advances are a substantial tribute to the effectiveness of the advocacy efforts of families of children with disabilities; of individuals with disabilities themselves; of professionals who work with the population; and of professional/advocacy organizations such as the Association for Retarded Citizens (ARC), Council for Exceptional Children (CEC), and the American Association on Mental Retardation (AAMR) (Cutler, 1993). Of particular importance to individuals with severe disabilities is the Association for Persons with Severe Handicaps (TASH) that was founded in 1974 with Norris G. Haring as its first president. TASH now includes thousands of parents, teachers, university researchers, teacher trainers, and individuals with disabilities. TASH has been quite effective in influencing legislation and public policy and publishes a professional journal (*Journal of the Association for Persons with Severe Handicaps*) and a newsletter.

DEFINITION

The population described as severely disabled is quite broad. It includes students with autism; with moderate, severe, or profound retardation; with dual sensory impairments (i.e., those who are simultaneously deaf and blind); and with moderate to profound retardation who also have physical or sensory impairments. The term is not generally used for students with physical disabilities who are free of mental retardation or for those with mild mental retardation.

Traditionally, the most widely accepted definitions of mental retardation were those of the American Association on Mental Retardation (AAMR). Specifically, "mental retardation refers to significantly subaverage general intellectual functioning existing concurrently with deficits in adaptive behavior and manifested during the developmental period" (Grossman, 1983, p. 1). Three criteria were required: (1) performance on measures of intellectual functioning (IQ tests); (2) performance on measures of adaptive functioning (i.e., usually assessments of skills related to functioning in the natural and social environment); and (3) difficulties arising during childhood. The degree of mental retardation (i.e., mild, moderate, severe, and profound) was assigned based on specific scores on intelligence tests with concomitantly similar scores on measures of adaptive performance.

Recently the AAMR has published a new classification system that is similar to, and builds upon, the previous definitions. Specifically, it states:

> *Mental retardation* refers to substantial limitations in present functioning. It is characterized by significantly subaverage intellectual function, existing concurrently with related limitations in two or more of the following applicable adaptive skill areas: communication, self-care, home living, social skills, community use, self-direction, health and safety, functional academics, leisure and work. Mental retardation manifests before age 18. (American Association on Mental Retardation, 1992)

This definition specifies the domains of adaptive behavior and states that there must be two or more deficits. The definition assumes that (1) the deficits are not a result of cultural or linguistic diversity; (2) adaptive performance must be compared to that of chronological age mates in community settings and there should also be identification of the supports needed; (3) students have strengths in addition to deficits; and (4) in most cases improvements will be noted when appropriate supports are provided over time (American Association on Mental Retardation, 1992).

Despite long-standing attempts to define mental retardation and to establish precise classifications of it, two points are pertinent. First, under IDEA and previous legislation, each state separately specifies the criteria by which students become eligible for special education services. However, the states do not necessarily use the AAMR classification system, and the same criteria are not necessarily used across different states (Frankenberger & Fronzagilo, 1991). Thus, a student classified in one state as having a given level of mental retardation may be classified differently in another state. Second, a student's precise classification does not necessarily reflect the educational needs of the student. For example, two students, one with moderate mental retardation and one with severe mental retardation, may appropriately have similar educational programs, while two students with severe mental retardation may appropriately have educational programs that are very different from one another.

PREVALENCE

In 1975 Abramowicz and Richardson reviewed 19 studies and found the rate of persons with IQ scores of 40 or below to be about 4 per 1,000 persons. A recent review of over 20 additional studies using an IQ of 50 or below found the rate to be about 3 to 4 per 1,000 persons (McLaren & Bryson, 1987). They also found that the number varied by age. From birth to 5 years, the rate tended to be from 1.2 to 2.5 per 1,000; higher rates occurred between 10 to 20 years of age, and rates tended to be stable (3 to 4 per 1,000) after 20 years of age. This variation by age, however, appears to be due to the number of cases identified rather than to the number of cases that actually exist. More males than females are diagnosed as having severe mental retardation, and this may be a result of biological differences (e.g., X-linked cases) and gender role expectations. The 3 or 4 per 1,000 rate is substantially higher than would be expected from the normal distribution curve for intelligence. This higher rate is probably due to the large number of factors that can cause mental retardation before, during, and after birth. Interestingly, the figures reported by state departments of education show a decline in the number of individuals with mental retardation over time (Ysseldyke, Algozzine, & Thurlow, 1992); however, this is likely due to increasing numbers of students being labeled as having learning disabilities rather than as having mild mental retardation.

CAUSES

Although the precise cause of a severe disability is not possible to identify in some cases, disabilities often result from genetic, chromosomal, or medical difficulties surrounding development, birth, or early infancy. The causes are generally related to randomly occurring genetic or medical conditions and not to cultural factors. These conditions affect all social, economic, racial, and linguistic groups equally. The cause of severe disabilities frequently is inferred rather than documented by indisputable evidence, and in about 40% of the cases none is known (McLaren & Bryson, 1987). Jones (1988) describes and illustrates most syndromes associated with mental retardation.

Genetic and chromosomal causes account for about 60% of the known causes of severe disabilities. More than 80 specifically identified syndromes are associated with either single-gene or chromosomal conditions. Conditions that result from the alteration of a single-gene are (1) tuberous sclerosis—severe mental retardation with autistic behaviors, (2) phenylketonuria (PKU)—mild to severe retardation, (3) Lesch-Nyhan syndrome—severe retardation accompanied by self-injury, and (4) cystic fibrosis—normal intelligence with progressive lung damage.

Chromosomal abnormalities result when there is either too much or too little genetic information. Because of problems during cell division in the production of eggs or sperm, some cells may end up with an extra chromosome, a missing chromosome, or extra pieces of chromosomes. Perhaps a fifth of the individuals classified as having severe disabilities have Down syndrome, which is produced by an extra 21st chromosome (trisomy 21). A major factor in the formation of this extra chromosome is maternal age (although some cases of Down syndrome are unrelated to maternal age and are due to defective sperm) (Holmes, 1987). The average age of mothers with Down syndrome babies is about 40 years. Mothers who are 30 years or younger account for only about 10% of the persons with Down syndrome. The risk factor of having a child with trisomy 21 increases most rapidly after 30 or 35 years of age (Holmes, 1987). The distribution of abilities within the group of those with Down syndrome is broad: many have moderate mental retardation, some have measured intelligence in the normal range, and others have severe mental retardation. There also are persons with disabilities who have trisomy 18 and trisomy 13.

Many medical complications increase the probability of mental retardation and severe disabilities. Complications in the birth process resulting from the use of forceps, multiple births, and lack of oxygen to the baby can increase the chances of mental retardation or other disabilities. In addition, a variety of infections such as meningitis can directly cause brain damage. One of the most prevalent infections associated with a variety of disabling conditions (sensory impairments, autism, and severe mental retardation) occurs when a pregnant woman contracts rubella (German measles). Fortunately, if public attention comes to be focused on proper programs of immunization, this cause of severe disabilities could be eliminated. This is an example of how prevention can save tremendous human suffering and substantial fiscal resources. A number of environmental events and conditions increase the probability of mental retardation, including injury as a result of auto accidents during pregnancy or after birth, maternal malnutrition, and contact with environmental toxins. Additionally, maternal alcohol consumption is recognized as a major prenatal cause of retardation (Crocker, 1992a).

Thus, many factors can cause severe disabilities, and three statements about causes should be made. First, some—but not all—causes of severe disabilities are preventable given our current knowledge and technology. Much is known about prevention of mental retardation, and for some conditions a considerable amount of progress has been made in preventing their occurrence (Baumeister, Kupstas, & Klindworth, 1990; Crocker, 1992a, 1992b). However, much remains to be learned, and unfortunately, much of what is already known remains to be put in action. For example, many factors that put children at risk for mental retardation (e.g., lack of prenatal care, poverty, teenage pregnancy, alcohol consumption, child abuse) interact together to increase the risk of disability and require major changes in life-styles of individuals and in how public agencies provide services to them. Second, with rare exceptions (e.g., PKU), identification of the condition and/or its cause does not result in precise prescriptions for treatment. For example, knowing that a student has Down syndrome, does not necessarily provide useful information in planning an appropriate education.

Nonetheless, knowledge of causes may be important in helping families understand the condition and in dealing with it. Third, in the case of genetic conditions, genetic counseling for families is often necessary. This is particularly true if they desire to have additional children or already have children who are unaffected by the disorder. The remainder of this chapter focuses on the notion that the diagnosis of severe disabilities does not prevent us from attempting to improve the lives of those who are affected, as well as the lives of their families.

CHARACTERISTICS

Individuals with severe disabilities are relatively few in number (3 to 4 per 1,000), but are not a homogenous group. They are, in fact, so different from one another that it is virtually impossible to list characteristics that apply to all. In attempting to define students as severely disabled, the U.S. Department of Education listed behavioral characteristics of this group:

> The term "severely handicapped children and youth" refers to handicapped children who, because of the intensity of their physical, mental, or emotional problems, need high specialized educational, social, psychological, and medical services in order to maximize their full potential for useful and meaningful participation in society and for self-fulfillment.
>
> The term includes those children and youth who are classified as seriously emotionally disturbed (including children and youth who are schizophrenic), autistic, profoundly and severely mentally retarded, and those with two or more serious handicapping conditions such as deaf-blind, mentally retarded-blind, and cerebral-palsied deaf.
>
> Severely handicapped children and youth may experience severe speech, language, and/or perceptual-cognitive deprivations, and evidence abnormal behavior such as failure to respond to pronounced social stimuli; self-mutilation; self-stimulation; manifestation of intense and prolonged temper tantrums; absence of rudimentary forms of verbal control; and may also have extremely fragile physiological conditions. (*Federal Register*, 1988, p. 118)

Not all students with severe disabilities have all of these characteristics. Despite their heterogeneity, five statements can characterize most individuals with severe disabilities.

First, all individuals with severe disabilities are human beings—human beings who happen to have substantial disabilities. This may appear to state the obvious, but such a view was not always accepted—or put into practice. Substandard living conditions of many residential institutions in the early and middle part of this century attest to the fact that persons with severe disabilities were not perceived as humans, or, taken in best light, not accorded the value placed on other humans. Further evidence of their second-class status is evidenced in the fact that federal legislation (Americans with Disabilities Act) was required to ensure that they were not discriminated against in employment and public and private accommodations and services. To support the "personness" of individuals who have disabilities, the words we use to refer to them have undergone dramatic change. In the past, individuals with mental retardation were called retardates, retarded students, severely handicapped students, and so on. Currently, professionals and families alike use phrases such as "children with . . . ," "students with . . . ," or "persons who have . . ." Such phrases are more respectful of their person and deemphasize the disability. This subtle but important change in terminology was primarily brought about by advocates within the Association for Persons with Severe Handicaps (TASH).

Second, nearly all students with severe disabilities will require instruction across many curricular domains and life skill areas (Falvey, 1989). The influence of their disabilities on their development and learning is pervasive; it is not restricted to selected areas. They will "require intensive, ongoing support in several major life areas in order to participate in the mainstream of community life, and [will be] expected to require such support throughout life" (Bellamy, 1986, p. 6). The intensity and longevity of the effects of severe disabilities on students' development require that (1) a team of professionals from various disciplines be involved in planning, implementing, and evaluating their educational programs (Orelove & Sobsey, 1991); (2) instruction should focus on skills different from those commonly taught in schools (Meyer, 1991); and (3) instruction may need to be implemented in contexts other than a classroom (Falvey, 1989). Students with severe disabilities will not benefit from placement in general education classrooms unless systematic and substantial efforts occur to ensure that they are socially integrated and their educational needs are addressed (Hilton & Liberty, 1992).

Third, nearly all persons with severe disabilities can benefit meaningfully from educational services. One of the major accomplishments of the field of special education is the significant advances in understanding how to help students with severe disabilities live and work in their communities. Although substantial information has accumulated, much remains to be learned. A particular need exists to develop strategies for those with the most substantial and complex combinations of profound disabilities. Despite slow and steady progress in this area (Sailor, Gee, Goetz, & Graham, 1988), debates have occurred about whether such persons could benefit from education (e.g., Baer, 1981; Kauffman & Krouse, 1981). Nonetheless, all students clearly have a legal right to educational services. As Baer (1981) indicated, the appropriate task for the field is not to debate whether students benefit, but to find ways to ensure that they do.

Fourth, to be meaningful, educational services for students with severe disabilities must be purposeful and tied to the contexts in which they live, work, and recreate (T. G. Haring, 1992; Meyer, 1991). Although nearly all educational activities regardless of the students involved should be purposeful, this need is particularly apparent for students with severe disabilities; they have, by definition, greater skill deficits than other students. Thus, to receive the maximum benefit from their education, their years of schooling should not be wasted by purposeless instruction. Failure to consider contextual factors in providing instruction will lead to lack of skill maintenance and generalization (T. G. Haring, 1992). The context in which skills are used and needed by students with severe disabilities should influence how assessments are conducted, which goals are established, where and how instruction is provided, and how the value of educational services is judged.

Fifth, many persons with severe disabilities will have other disabling conditions, and as the severity of mental retardation increases, so does the likelihood that additional handicaps will be seen (McLaren & Bryson, 1987). Some of the other conditions are seizure disorders (15% to 30% of the cases); cerebral palsy or other motor disabilities (20% to 30%); sensory impairments including vision, hearing, and combinations of the two (10% and 20%); and communication, behavior, and/or psychiatric disorders (30% to 40%) (McLaren & Bryson, 1987). In many cases the associated disorders alone are substantial enough to qualify students for services. In some cases the debilitating effects of these disorders can be essentially eliminated, as in the case of some visual impairments. Ellis (1986), for example, maintains that about 50% of the individuals with mental retardation need eyeglasses and that most will benefit from them. In other cases ongoing intervention is possible for some health, communication, motor, and behavioral disorders. Such intervention can reduce the disorder's severity or can prevent negative outcomes from occurring (Pope, 1992).

ASSESSMENT

Purposes of Assessment

Students with disabilities are assessed for several reasons (Browder, 1991; Salvia & Ysseldyke, 1991). These include (1) screening—to determine whether they should be referred for further assessment; (2) diagnosis—to determine whether a given disorder exists, the nature of the condition, and the extent to which it is evidenced; (3) program eligibility—to determine whether the student meets the criteria for special education services (this is often done on the basis of the diagnosis); (4) placement—to identify the best placement given the student's needs and the ability of various placements to meet them; (5) instructional program planning—to identify the behaviors that the students does independently, does with support/assistance, and does not perform, as well as the contexts in which those behaviors occur, and to identify appropriate teaching procedures; (6) monitoring—to determine whether students are making progress and if not what needs to be changed; and (7) program evaluation—to determine the extent to which program goals are met.

Several comments about purposes of assessment for students with severe disabilities are warranted. First, students with severe disabilities are rarely screened for diagnosis or program eligibility. However, screening to assess their sensory function (i.e., vision and hearing) are important activities and are often conducted by teachers (Kinney, Ouellette, & Wolery, 1989; Sobsey & Wolf-Schein, 1991). Second, diagnostic assessments usually are conducted by professionals such as neurologists, pediatricians, psychologists, and others rather than by teachers. Third, program eligibility varies from state to state (Frankenberger & Fronzagilo, 1991) and often is based on the presence of a diagnosis and other measures. Fourth, diagnostic and program eligibility assessments often are of little use in planning relevant, contextually based instructional programs because of the measures used. Fifth, placement decisions are often made on information that is irrelevant to the instructional strategies or settings. For example, students with diagnoses of moderate mental retardation, autism, or severe mental retardation may be placed in separate classes based on their diagnoses rather than their behavioral or learning characteristics. Appropriate placement assessment requires attention to the physical, behavioral, and social dimensions of potential placements (Brown et al., 1991). Finally, teachers are intimately involved in assessment to plan instructional programs and monitor their effects.

Instructional Programming and Monitoring Assessments

After students have been diagnosed, declared eligible for special education services, and placed in a given classroom, team members must assess them to develop educational plans. Such assessments require careful planning, data collection from a variety of sources using multiple measurement strategies, and a systematic process (Rainforth et al., 1992). The steps of the process are shown in Figure 7–1. The steps should be

Step 1

Plan the assessment activities. This step involves identifying the individuals who will be involved, the contexts, activities, and routines that will be assessed, the measures that will be used, and the schedule for completing each assessment activity.

Step 2

Collect background information. This step involves identifying the family's concerns and priorities about the student's future; securing information about the student's previous educational and medical history; and determining which instructional strategies have been effective with the student in the past.

Step 3

Identify the student's contexts. This step involves identifying the environments (places) where the student currently functions and will be expected to function in the near future, identifying the activities and routines that occur in those environments, and identifying the skills and expectations for participation that occur in those activities and routines.

Step 4

Collect performance information. This step involves collecting information on the student's performance in current environments across domains using direct testing, interviews, observations, ecological inventories, and curriculum catalogs.

Step 5

Analyze data and establish priorities. This step involves making decisions about which environments, activities, routines, and skills are most important for immediate intervention.

Step 6

Write an instructional plan. This step involves specifying the long-term objectives (goals), instructional objectives, teaching procedures, instructional settings, measurement plan, and schedule of instruction.

Step 7

Implement and monitor. This step involves implementing the instructional and measurement plan and monitoring the student's performance by collecting frequent performance data, frequent implementation data, analyzing that data, making decisions based on the data, and adjusting the instructional procedures as appropriate.

Step 8

Evaluate the program at regular intervals. This step involves evaluating the effectiveness of the program in meeting the goals that were identified and making adjustments to identify new goals and to increase the effectiveness of the program.

Figure 7–1
Steps in identifying and monitoring educational goals.

completed by a team of individuals from various disciplines, should involve substantial and sustained input from families, should be ongoing, and should employ an investigative approach for determining what is relevant for each student given his or her unique context and abilities.

1.   *Plan the assessment activities.* Since quite a few people are involved in the assessment process and because the process is ongoing, assessment activities must be carefully planned to increase their efficiency and usefulness. This planning should address issues such as who will be involved, which measures will be used, who will be responsible for conducting each measure, which settings will be involved, and when each activity should be conducted and completed. At a minimum, those who should participate in planning are family members, the student's teacher (or teachers if more than one is involved), and representatives from related disciplines (Orelove & Sobsey, 1991; Rainforth et al., 1992). To ensure contextual or ecological relevance, the assessment must solicit the views of primary caregivers (within and outside of the school) and investigate all settings in which the student spends time and will likely spend time in the future. Thus, part of the planning involves identifying the settings that constitute the student's environment and the activities and routines that occur within those settings. Finally, the team should specify a schedule of the assessment activities and of the responsibilities of each member. Usually, such planning can occur through a meeting and a series of telephone contacts.

2.   *Collect background information.* This step of the process is designed to understand the family members' desires and fears relating to the student's future and to secure information that will be useful in implementing the assessment and subsequently the educational services. Rainforth et al. (1992) provide excellent suggestions concerning procedures and questions related to obtaining information about family members' perceptions of the student's future. Such interviews, of course, should involve professionals who listen to families, who ask questions sensitively, and who are responsive to family members' statements (Winton, 1988; Winton & Bailey, 1993). This task is important in establishing the priorities for the student's education.

Securing background information also involves reviewing records and interviewing individuals who are familiar with the student. Records contain a variety of information that may be useful, such as recent assessments, previous Individualized Educational Plans (IEPs), descriptions of progress, and descriptions of previous interventions. This information allows the team to form initial judgments about the student; for example, whether the student's sensory function is in question and whether given medical conditions and precautions exist (e.g., seizure disorder, heart defect). Information from records should be interpreted cautiously because it may be incomplete, inaccurate, or out of date. Interviewing past teachers, previous therapists, and other caregivers also is useful, and such interviews should focus on the effectiveness of instructional strategies for the student and the student's interests and preferences.

3.   *Identify the student's contexts.* The purpose of this step is to increase the relevance of the assessment and subsequently the instruction. To ensure that the goals that are identified will improve the student's ability to function in life, the assessment activities must be conducted in the settings in which the student spends time and will

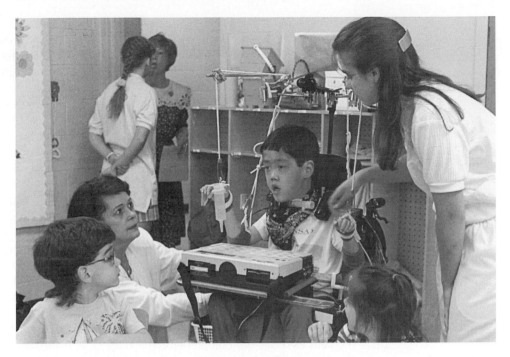

Assessment of students with severe disabilities requires a team effort by competent professionals from different disciplines.

be expected to spend time in the future (Rainforth et al., 1992). Once a setting is identified, the team, through observation and interviews, should decide what occurs within that setting and what is expected of the student in terms of participation and performance. This information will form the base for determining the student's current performance and goals to increase the student's participation, independence, and social relationships. Ideally, the team will identify common expectations that occur across different activities and settings so that these skills can form the core of the student's educational plan.

    4. *Collect performance information.* The three previous steps involve planning the assessment; this step involves implementing that plan. Several measurement strategies can be used in collecting performance information, including direct testing, informal testing, observation, interviews, curriculum catalogs, and ecological inventories. These measurement strategies are used to collect information about the skills and routines that the student can do independently, those that the student can do with support or adaptation, and those that the student needs to learn to be more self-sufficient and more socially integrated. Direct testing with achievement and norm-referenced tests is rarely done to determine instructional goals for students with severe disabilities. The administration procedures, narrow range of acceptable responses, timed response intervals, and lack of adaptations for sensory and physical disabilities frequently make the use of these standardized measures invalid. Some adaptive behavior scales such as the AAMD Adaptive Behavior Scales (Lambert, Windmiller,

Tharinger, & Cole, 1981), Scales of Independent Behavior (Bruininks, Woodcock, Weatherman, & Hill, 1984), and Vineland Adaptive Behavior Scales (Sparrow, Balla, & Cicchetti, 1984) may be useful guides for establishing general parameters of the student's skills. Criterion- and curriculum-referenced tests are used more frequently, and many examples exist, such as the Uniform Performance Assessment System (N. G. Haring, White, Edgar, Affleck, & Hayden, 1982), Adaptive Performance Instrument (Consortium on Adaptive Performance Evaluation, 1980), Brigance Inventory of Early Development (Brigance, 1978), and many others. These measures may provide a general record of the student's skills but are most appropriately used as "sources of assessment ideas rather than scorable items that translate into instructional objectives" (Sailor & Guess, 1983, p. 120). Also, teams often use ecological inventories that involve identifying the curriculum domains (areas), identifying current and immediate future environments in which the student lives and functions, identifying subenvironments in each major environment, listing all activities and routines that individuals without disabilities do in each subenvironment, identifying high-priority activities and routines, identifying all the skills needed for engaging in each activity or routine, determining whether the student can perform the identified skills, identifying any needed adaptations, and developing programs to teach needed skills (Nietupski & Hamre-Nietupski, 1987).

Teams also frequently use curriculum catalogs to identify educational goals. Curriculum catalogs are comprehensive listings of activities individuals do in their living, working, and recreating environments (Wilcox & Bellamy, 1987). From these listings, teams select activities needed by students and assess them to determine whether to teach the required skills. Ecological inventories and curriculum catalogs require direct observation of the student in the natural environments over several occasions. The observations allow the team to assess whether adaptations of the routines/activities and the use of adaptive equipment and devices would be appropriate for the student (Ferguson & Baumgart, 1991; Orelove & Sobsey, 1991).

In addition to identifying skills to be taught, teams should attempt to identify reinforcers and effective instructional procedures. Reinforcers can be identified by (1) asking family members and others about the student's preferences and previously successful reinforcers; (2) observing the student in the natural environment and noting reinforcing events and behaviors performed frequently; (3) providing the student with choices and noting which choices are consistently selected; and (4) allowing the student to experience potential reinforcers and noting the effects of that experience (Bailey & Wolery, 1992). However, the value of reinforcers changes over time, and so frequent and ongoing assessment of reinforcers is necessary (Mason, McGee, Farmer-Dougan, & Risley, 1989). Identification of teaching strategies also is important. Frequently, this is done by asking previous teachers or therapists about strategies effective for the student and by trying out various strategies and collecting data on their effects.

Many of the important skills (e.g., social interactions, use of communicative signals, self-care skills, play/recreation activities, problem-solving skills) must be assessed in their natural context. Thus, the use of direct observation is a primary information-gathering technique. A variety of observational procedures exist (Wolery, 1989), as do prepared systems for collecting observational data on important skills

(Browder, 1991; Neel & Billingsley, 1989). In order to understand students' performance, the effect of environmental variables is important information, and assessment of these factors is called eco-behavioral analysis (Barnett, Macmann, & Carey, 1992; Carta, Sainato, & Greenwood, 1988). Sample variables include the time of day, the individuals who are present, the nature of materials, the arrangement and use of the physical space, the sequence of activities in the day, and the demands and responses of individuals during interactions with the student. Such variables are important in understanding the problem behavior of students and in devising interventions for it (Dunlap, Kern-Dunlap, Clarke, & Robbins, 1991; O'Neill, Horner, Albin, Storey, & Sprague, 1990). This information, however, is also important in devising instructional programs because it assists the team in understanding the influences of context on students' performance (T. G. Haring & Kennedy, 1990). The student's behavioral states (levels of alertness) also should be assessed (Guess et al., 1991). This allows the team to analyze the student's performance in the context of given environmental events (e.g., instructional strategies, peer initiations) and the student's level of awareness.

5.   *Analyze data and establish priorities.* As the assessment information is collected, the team must make sense out of it by summarizing the data and placing the findings in context. The summary should provide a clear picture of what the student can do, with and without support, the situations under which that performance occurs, the variables (e.g., reinforcers, environmental events, instructional strategies) that influence the performance, and the situations in which the student needs to be more independent. From this information and from the priorities of the family for the student's future, decisions can be made about which skills are most important in which contexts and about how those situations can be changed to increase positive outcomes. Establishing priorities is a team decision, but the family members clearly hold the major stakes in the outcomes of such decisions. Thus, their views should have a considerable amount of influence about which skills and routines are targeted for instruction.

6.   *Write an instructional plan.* The instructional plan should include a precise description of what is to be taught, who will teach it, which methods will be used, where the instruction will occur, and how and when progress will be measured and reviewed. This description involves writing instructional objectives, performing task analyses for those objectives, and preparing detailed plans for implementing the instruction during daily routines across environments. This is the student's IEP, and it should contain objectives related to generalization of skills to various contexts, as well as their acquisition (Billingsley, Burgess, Lynch, & Matlock, 1991). The plan should also describe the adaptive equipment and devices that will be used and any modifications in current routines or activities. Further, the plan should specify how related services (e.g., therapy) will be integrated into the student's day and who will deliver and be responsible for such services.

7.   *Implement and monitor.* Once a plan has been developed, it should be implemented, and the results need to be monitored. Monitoring is frequently done using direct observation of the student's performance during instruction or in situations where the skills should be applied. Observations are usually conducted daily, or at

least weekly. Data collection is only the first part of monitoring, however. The team must also analyze the data and make decisions about what changes are needed (Farlow & Snell, 1989; Grigg, Snell, & Loyd, 1989; N. G. Haring, Liberty, & White, 1980). Specific rules can be applied to make such decisions about students' acquisition of skills (N. G. Haring et al., 1980) and the application and use of skills (N. G. Haring, 1988). If the data indicate changes are needed, then adjustments should be devised (Belfiore & Browder, 1992).

8. *Evaluate the program at regular intervals.* In addition to frequent monitoring, the program should be evaluated at regular intervals. Although IEPs must be reviewed annually, more frequent evaluation (e.g., quarterly) is preferred. The purpose of evaluation is to determine whether major changes in the focus of the instructional program are needed. As with other decisions, teams, including the family, should be involved in making any changes.

INTERVENTION

Several factors are important for planning and implementing intervention (educational) programs for students with severe disabilities. First, professionals from several disciplines should be involved because of the vast array and complexity of students' problems (Orelove & Sobsey, 1991). Representatives from physical and occupational therapy, speech and language therapy, nursing, nutrition, social work, psychology, and general and special education will be involved on teams. These professionals must be competent in their own fields, communicate unique information from their fields to others, learn the language of other disciplines and work effectively with members of these disciplines, and integrate information from other disciplines into their practice (Bruder, in press; Rainforth et al., 1992). As students with severe disabilities are included in general education classrooms, special educators' roles change from having their own classrooms to team-teaching with general educators and/or providing extensive consultation and support to them (Harris, 1990; Pugach & Johnson, 1990; Thousand & Villa, 1990).

Second, the needs and perceptions of students' families must be addressed (Bailey, McWilliam, Winton, & Simeonsson, 1992; Covert, 1992). Caring and providing for students with severe disabilities may place stressful demands on families. The effects of the student on the family life cycle and on the relationships within and outside the family system are important issues to consider. Parents' concerns and goals for the student, their perceptions of the student's functioning, and their resources and needs will influence how effective the educational program will be. Families are quite different from one another, and their priorities and concerns change with time; thus, family involvement with professionals and with programs must be individualized (Bailey, in press; Dunst et al., 1988).

Third, much of the instruction should be embedded into ongoing routines and activities and in many cases should be community-based (occur in the community and involve functioning in it) (Falvey, 1989; Rainforth et al., 1992). In the past, skills were taught in isolated sessions, for example, communication skills during language time and social skills during social skills time. This format, however, does not reflect reality. Communication skills involve social skills, and vice versa. Thus, instruction frequently

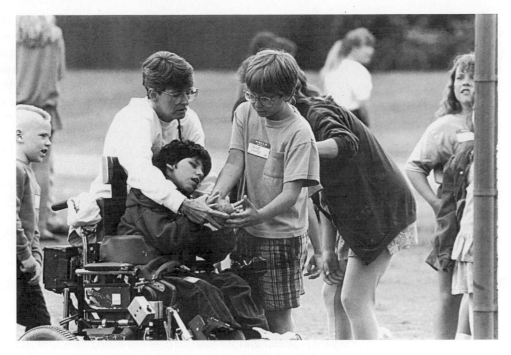

As much as possible, skills should be taught in a natural setting.

is now provided in routines where students need to use a variety of skills. Communication and social skills should be taught as students enter the classroom in the morning, greet the teacher and peers, and engage in social interactions with them. Instruction requires use of many naturalistic teaching strategies, such as incidental teaching and naturalistic time delay, e.g., taking advantage of teaching dressing after swimming (T. G. Haring, Neetz, Lovinger, Peck, & Semmel, 1987; Kaiser, Yoder, & Keetz, 1992). Likewise, many community living, recreational, and vocational skills are taught in settings where they occur. Students learn to cross streets, order in restaurants, purchase groceries, and do their laundry in the community rather than in the school building. Because of practical considerations in implementing such community-based instruction, simulations (Nietupski, Hamre-Nietupski, Clancy, & Veerhusen, 1986) and videotaped modeling may be used (T. G. Haring, Breen, Weiner, Kennedy, & Bednersh, in press).

Fourth, learning involves acquiring, becoming fluent in, maintaining, and generalizing skills to new situations (Wolery, Ault, & Doyle, 1992). Too frequently students learn a skill but do not use it. Students need to learn (1) how to do skills, (2) how to do them at rapid or natural rates, (3) to retain them or perform them over time after instruction has stopped, and (4) to do them when and wherever they are needed. Each of these phases requires different instructional practices. To promote acquisition, teachers use identified reinforcers, apply task analyses carefully, secure students' attention, and use and fade prompts effectively. To promote fluency building, teachers provide practice and ensure that students are motivated to practice. To promote skill maintenance and generalization, teachers teach functional skills in natural contexts; select teaching examples carefully; use naturally occurring reinforcers and schedules; and vary the teaching context by using multiple trainers, settings, and materials (N. G. Haring, 1987; Horner, Dunlap, & Koegel, 1988). In each case, performance is monitored regularly and adjustments are made as needed (N. G. Haring, 1988).

Fifth, the instructional procedures that are used to establish skill acquisition and generalization should be effective and efficient. Research indicates that relatively few procedures have been used to teach a wide variety of skills to students with moderate and severe disabilities (Wolery, Ault, et al., 1992). These procedures use prompts (teacher assistance), which may come in the form of verbal cues, gestural cues, models of correct responses, and partial and full physical assistance. Some of the procedures produce learning without errors. By minimizing errors, teachers increase the speed with which students learn, increase opportunities for positive interactions with students, increase their levels of success, decrease the probability that problem behaviors related to failure occur, and decrease the opportunities for students to practice incorrect or ineffective responses. These instructional strategies employ systematic means of reducing teacher assistance as students learn to perform the skill correctly.

CURRICULUM IMPLICATIONS

Teachers working with those with severe disabilities should (1) organize the curriculum in accordance with life skill domains, (2) teach functional and contextually based skills, (3) teach skills appropriate to students' age, and (4) plan the daily schedule to use resources efficiently.

Organizing the Curriculum by Life Skill Domains

About 15 years ago, Brown et al. (1979) identified weaknesses in prevailing practice of teaching those with severe disabilities and recommended an alternative. The prevailing practice was the use of the developmental model. This approach assumed students with severe disabilities (1) acquired the same skills in a similar sequence of steps as students without disabilities but at a slower rate and (2) needed to learn basic skills before more advanced developmental skills could be acquired. Although the first assumption, known as the similar sequence hypothesis, is consistent with research findings (Weisz & Zigler, 1979), it is more useful in explaining what happens under nonintervention conditions than in describing what is possible with effective instruction. Brown et al. (1979) suggested that this *bottom-up* approach was ineffective for students with severe disabilities and recommended using a *top-down* approach. The curriculum content in the top-down approach comes from an analysis of the final outcome of instruction rather than from students' developmental skills. This approach has been called a functional curriculum, a community-referenced curriculum, and an ecological curriculum. This change in approach influenced what was taught, how teaching occurred, and where it was provided. The traditional development or academic domains of motor, social, cognitive/academic, communication, and self-care skills changed to domains more closely related to the outcomes of learning and the contexts in which that learning was used. Here are some domains in the ecological curriculum (cf. Rainforth et al., 1992):

- *Domestic skills*: Self-care skills (toileting, eating, dressing), home management skills (food preparation, laundry, housecleaning), and related skills needed to function within a home (e.g., communication and social skills)
- *School skills*: Those abilities related to functioning in schools such as interacting with peers, working in groups, participating in regular routines, communicating, complying with schedules and adult requests, and many others
- *Community skills*: Skills related to mobility within the community (e.g., transportation) and use of community facilities (e.g., making purchases)
- *Recreation and leisure skills*: Skills related to occupying time in socially acceptable and enjoyable ways
- *Vocational skills*: Abilities related to securing and maintaining employment that is not demeaning

Teaching Functional, Contextually Based Skills

In each curriculum domain, students should be taught functional skills—meaning the skills that are useful in accomplishing some activity in important environments. For example, learning to dress independently and rapidly is useful in getting ready to go to school, work, outside to play, or for a walk. Some skills will be functional for some students but not for others; for example, putting on overshoes is more useful in wet, cold climates than in dry, hot climates. Skill usefulness is a hallmark of the ecological curriculum. Each behavior must be evaluated as to whether it is useful or leads directly to useful skills. In general, the usefulness of skills can be determined by analyzing their effects. If skills help students be more independent, more acceptable to their peers, and more easily cared for, then those skills are useful and relevant.

Including Chronological Age-Appropriate Skills and Instruction

Closely related to the function of skills is the idea of teaching chronological age-appropriate behaviors in an age-appropriate manner. Such an approach has two basic implications. First, students should be placed in settings with same-age peers. High school-aged students with moderate and severe disabilities should not be placed in elementary school programs but in high schools. Placement with age-mates increases the likelihood that students with disabilities will be included in regular activities such as attending sporting events, school dances, and other extracurricular activities. Second, the skills taught and materials used should be age-appropriate. If sorting is functional for a middle school student, then it should be taught with age-appropriate materials such as plates and utensils rather than with geometric shapes as may be appropriate for preschoolers. Similarly, if listening to music is an appropriate leisure skill for high school students, students with disabilities should listen to music similar to that favored by their peers rather than to nursery rhymes.

Using Resources Appropriately by Having a Detailed Daily Schedule

To teach as efficiently and economically as possible, teachers must use all of the resources available to them, including resources such as teaching assistants, community volunteers, and peers. It also involves using the time available for instruction effectively (Brown, 1991). A widely accepted process for developing the daily schedule is the *individualized curriculum sequencing* (ICS) model (Sailor & Guess, 1983). This process includes at least three steps: (1) completing an event/skill matrix; (2) writing the individualized curriculum sequence; and (3) developing instructional programs (Guess & Helmstetter, 1986; Helmstetter & Guess, 1987). Completing an event or skill matrix involves several distinct steps:

1. *List the events.* List all the activities the student is likely to encounter during the day on the left side of the matrix. These events/activities should include those within and outside the classroom. Examples are "arrival time at the beginning of the day," "going to physical education class," "going grocery shopping," and so on.
2. *List locations.* List all the locations where the events/activities are planned to occur.
3. *Identify times.* List the time the event/activity is planned to occur.
4. *Identify the instructor.* Specify who is responsible for conducting the training or supervising the event/activity.
5. *List skills.* Write the skills that are to be taught across the top of the matrix. These may include behaviors the student needs to learn and problem behaviors that need to be eliminated.
6. *Complete each cell of the matrix.* The intent of this step is to embed instruction on as many behaviors as possible in each event/activity.
7. *Analyze the matrix for instruction on generalization and choice.* "After the matrix is completed, check that each behavior will be taught by two or more instructors, with at least two different materials or activities, and in multiple settings" (Helmstetter & Guess, 1987, p. 265). Also, review the matrix to ensure that there are opportunities for the student to make choices. An example of a completed matrix appears in Figure 7–2.

The second step of the model is to write the individualized curriculum sequence. This involves providing opportunities for a student to respond and planning how those trials are organized. In some cases, several trials on the same behavior are repeated closely in time; in others, clusters of trials are performed on different behaviors fitting into a broader skill or routine. The curriculum sequences also should include behavior checks—times when the teacher observes and reinforces students for appropriate social and classroom behaviors. In some instances important behaviors do not logically fit into some ongoing routine or event, and instruction on them must be scheduled separately. Finally, the individualized curricula sequences should include task analyses that guide the instruction of complex skills.

The third step of the model is to develop the instructional program. It should include a rationale for teaching the skill, the materials, natural cues, instructional prompts, prompt fading procedures, consequences, and data collection sheets.

Several important strategies are effective in teaching a variety of skills to students who have moderate to severe disabilities (Wolery, Ault, et al., 1992). These procedures include response prompting strategies such as the system of least prompts (Doyle, Wolery, Ault, & Gast, 1988), progressive and constant time delay (Wolery, Holcombe, et al., 1992), demonstration/model strategy (Karsh & Repp, 1992), most-to-least prompting, and graduated guidance (Wolery, Ault, et al., 1992).

The individualized curriculum sequencing model is appropriate because it allows instruction to occur in nonschool environments. Further, functional and chronological age-appropriate materials and activities can be used. Natural cues and consequences are part of the learning context, and instruction is provided when the behaviors are needed. The model also allows teachers to plan for learner-initiated and teacher-initiated activities/behavior (Helmstetter & Guess, 1987).

Programs of Skill Development

As noted earlier, the educational program for students with severe disabilities teaches behaviors that promote life skills development and full and partial participation in community activities (Ferguson & Baumgart, 1991). Considerable work by teachers and researchers has been devoted to understanding and teaching such skills.

Domestic Living Skills. Domestic living skills are self-care, home management, and related skills needed for independent living in society. These abilities are central to self-sufficiency and may influence students' residential placement (e.g., institution, group home, remaining with family members, supervised apartment). They include personal hygiene, toileting, dressing, undressing, grooming, eating, self-feeding, laundry and clothing care, housecleaning and maintenance, meal preparation and cleanup, and many others. These skills share several characteristics. They often involve a number of responses chained together to form a more complex skill; are used regularly but in some cases only a few times per day or week; and the result is often more important than the way in which the skill is performed (e.g., shoes can be tied in several ways, but what is important is that they stay tied). These skills are best taught when they are needed—are contextually appropriate (e.g., teaching eating during meals, housecleaning when the house is dirty)—and as entire routines. Students should be taught to prepare a meal, clean the food preparation area, set the table, eat the meal while socializing with others, clean up the table, and wash the dishes as an organized routine rather than as separate tasks in isolation. Although the goal of instruction is independence, adapted, assisted, or partial participation is preferred over total dependence (York & Rainforth, 1991).

When teaching eating and feeding skills, teachers should attend to students' nutritional needs (Crump, 1987; Venn, Holcombe, & Wolery, 1992); the social atmosphere of mealtime routines (Venn et al., 1992); students' muscle tone and movements of the lips, tongue, and jaw; seating position and arm movements; and students' utensil use (Orelove & Sobsey, 1991). Teaching feeding and eating requires consultation with physical and occupational therapists, particularly if students have physical disabilities (Orelove & Sobsey, 1991). Systematic instruction (prompting, fading, and reinforcement) is successful for teaching self-feeding skills (Taras & Matese, 1990). Toilet training should occur when students have the prerequisite skills. These include the ability to retain bodily wastes for consistent periods of time and release them in "large amounts." Also, establishing instructional control and identifying an appropriate sitting position are important (Wolery & Smith, 1989). Several procedures exist for toilet training individuals with retardation (Bailey & Wolery, 1992; McCartney,

This schedule was designed for Heidi who is 17 years old and has Down syndrome, moderate mental retardation, and visual impairments. Heidi's class of 8 students is located in the main building of a regular junior high school. Heidi has many challenging behaviors including noncompliance with directions and inappropriate social behaviors with peers and strangers. She lives in a medium-sized residential facility that has a growing list of community living skills including identifying dollar amounts up to $3, matching picture cues to actual items to be purchased, and following two-step directions from her job coach.

	Activity	Students	Adult[a]	Setting
6:45	Wake up, bathing, grooming, and dressing	Heidi	Ms. Belco	Dorm Room
7:30	Breakfast	Heidi and 5 other girls	Ms. Belco	Kitchen in cottage
8:00	Put on coat, get things for school and walk to school	Heidi and 3 other girls	Ms. Belco	Community
8:30	Morning group—social skills training and conversation training	Heidi, Joni, Cori, and Toi	Ms. Graham	Classroom
9:00	Dress in McDonald's uniform	Heidi	Independently	Bathroom
9:15	Walk to bus stop	Heidi and Ben	Mr. Bates	Community
9:30	Ride bus to McDonald's	Heidi and Ben	Mr. Bates	
9:45	Start work (wipe tables and wash windows)	Heidi	Mr. Bates	McDonald's
10:15	Break—buy soda and drink it and talk with co-worker	Heidi and co-worker	Mr. Bates	McDonald's
10:30	Return to work	Heidi	Independently	McDonald's
11:00	Change clothes	Heidi	Independently	McDonald's bathroom
11:00	Choose which store to shop in	Heidi and Ben	Mr. Bates	Community mall

Figure 7–2

Sample instructional program for a student with a severe disability.

a   Ms. Belco is the cottage mother, Ms. Graham is the classroom teacher, Mr. Bates is the job coach, Mr. Tandy is the general education PE teacher, Ms. Harris is an instructional assistant, and Ms. Wilson is the general education home economics teacher.

1990). Foxx and Azrin's (1973) rapid method is one of the most famous. It involves intense, day-long training with increased liquid intake. Less intensive procedures also can be used (Fredericks, Baldwin, Grove, & Moore, 1975). Dressing, undressing, grooming, bathing, and other personal hygiene skills require students to perform a number of behaviors sequenced together to form a complex task. Prerequisite skills for teaching these skills frequently include purposeful arm movements, maintenance

	Activity	Students	Adult[a]	Setting
11:15	Shopping, purchasing, and list reading at stores	Heidi and Ben	Mr. Bates	Store
11:45	Ride bus to school	Heidi and Ben	Mr. Bates	
12:00	PAL Club and lunch	Heidi	Tina, Sophia, and Carla (friends without disabilities)	Courtyard
11:45	Group discussion (teacher feedback, modeling, and simulation of appropriate lunch and conversational behaviors)	Entire Class	Ms. Graham (3 students without disabilities)	Classroom
1:00	Conversation training	Heidi and Cori	Student teacher	Computer area
1:15	Recreation/leisure (listen to music or play games)	Heidi, Joni, and Jerry	Angie (from PAL club)	Classroom or library
1:40	Mainstreamed PE	Heidi, Gloria, Toni, and Sylvia	Mr. Tandy Ms. Harris	Gym
2:20	Shower and dressing	Heidi and PE Class	Ms. Harris	Locker room
2:40	Mainstream home economics (mending and care of clothing)	Heidi	Ms. Wilson Ms. Harris	Home economics room
3:30	Walk home	Heidi and 3 other girls	Ms. Belco	
4:00	Free time (watch TV, play games)	Heidi and others in cottage	Ms. Belco	Game room
5:30	Dinner preparation, eating dinner, and cleaning up after dinner	Heidi	Ms. Belco	Kitchen
7:00	Laundry, room cleaning, or going out in the community on some evenings	Heidi and roommate	Ms. Belco	Bedroom or community

of a grasp pattern while the arms move, and trunk stability. Also, instruction is more efficient if the student is under instructional control and is imitative. Procedures used to teach these skills frequently involve direct prompts (e.g., physical assistance), reinforcement, and prompt fading (Wolery, Ault, Gast, Doyle, & Griffen, 1991). Many adaptations in the sequences, actual clothing, or utensils have been used (York & Rainforth, 1991).

Numerous domestic skills have been taught including mending clothing (Cronin & Cuvo, 1979), cooking (Schuster, Gast, Wolery, & Guiltinan, 1988), bed making (Swenson-Pierce, Kohl, & Egel, 1987), snack preparation (Griffen, Wolery, & Schuster, 1992), cleaning up of broken glass during dish washing (Winterling, Gast, Wolery, & Farmer,

1992), and use of appliances (Alberto, Sharpton, Briggs, & Straight, 1986). This research has produced a growing body of evidence that students with moderate and severe disabilities can learn self-sufficiency skills. Likewise, it is producing a useful instructional technology.

School Skills.   The ecological curriculum is designed for promoting independence and participation in natural environments (home, work, community). Although schools are, in large part, artificial environments—ones that are used for specific purposes but are not lifelong settings, children spend a great deal of time in them. Thus, instruction on school-related behaviors is important. School behaviors include learning to receive instruction in groups (Collins, Gast, Ault, & Wolery, 1991), complying with adult requests (Cooper, Heron, & Heward, 1987), transitioning between activities, and other classroom deportment skills (Strain & Sainato, 1987). Also, functional skills such as reading signs, menus, and recipe books, writing a grocery list, counting, money exchange, and basic computation have been taught in school settings (Schuster & Griffen, 1991). Decisions about teaching these skills should be made carefully with attention given to whether students will use them.

Schools are inherently social settings. Thus, two interrelated skills are important in schools: communication skills and social skills. These skills are important life skills; are needed in nearly all settings; and are valued by families, professionals, and peers (Baumgart, Filler, & Askvig, 1991; Hamre-Nietupski, Nietupski, & Strathe, 1992).

Instruction of communication skills should be integrated into the teaching of all other domains. Nearly all students with severe disabilities require some intervention in communication skills. As students learn about the world through interactions with objects and other people, they begin to learn to send and receive messages intentionally (Prizant & Bailey, 1992). Through experience, certain meanings, objects, events, and activities are coded by words (or other symbols such as manual signs), signifying the presence of language. Rules for turn taking and other social interaction rules are applied to communicative exchanges, and the student learns to carry on conversations. To make this progression a reality, several instructional strategies have been used. Communication instruction should be embedded in ongoing interactions and should be responsive to students' communicative needs and intents (Kaiser et al., 1992).

Many students with moderate and severe disabilities can learn to understand and use speech; others will require alternative methods of conveying language symbols. Manual sign language and picture system (Bliss or Rebus Symbols) are used (Baumgart, Johnson, & Helmstetter, 1990). Speech-language pathologists should take the lead in deciding whether and which alternative communication system should be used. Several factors influence the selection of an alternative system such as students' motor abilities, their communicative needs, their ability to send and receive messages, their ability to discriminate between symbols, and others' ability to use the system. Technological advances have made it likely that useful alternative communication systems can be designed that will greatly enhance students' communicative abilities. Several strategies such as incidental teaching (Kaiser et al., 1992), the mandmodel procedure (Venn, Wolery, Fleming, et al., 1993), naturalistic time delay

Instruction in communication skills is best done during the interactions between the student and others.

(Schwartz, Anderson, & Halle, 1989), the interrupted chain procedure with time delay (Gee, Graham, Goetz, Oshima, & Yoshioka, 1991), peer-mediated strategies (Goldstein & Ferrell, 1987), and conversational training programs (Hunt, Alwell, & Goetz, 1991) are often used in the teaching of communication skills. Warren and Reichle (1992) present a comprehensive analysis of intervention strategies and issues.

Social skills instruction also should occur in naturalistic contexts (T. G. Haring, 1992). Social competence is one of the primary outcomes of education for all students, including those with severe disabilities (Odom, McConnell, & McEvoy, 1992). Although the skills that make up social competence are varied, they often involve the "child's *effectiveness* in influencing a peer's social behavior and *appropriateness* given a specific setting, context, and/or culture" (Odom et al., 1992, p. 7). Social competence includes, among others, initiating, responding, and maintaining interactions with peers; playing cooperatively; sharing; recognizing and responding to another's perspective; and solving problems jointly.

Nearly all students with severe disabilities will need assistance in acquiring and using such skills. The primary intent of teaching social skills is to promote social relationships that are accepting, responsive, caring, and endure over time; in other words, to promote friendships among students with and without severe disabilities (Strully & Strully, 1992). The roots of such behaviors, of course, are in the student's interactions and relationships with other family members, including parents and siblings. Intervention with social skills has attracted considerable research attention on parent-child interactions (Marfo, 1988; Rosenberg & Robinson, 1988) and child-child interactions (Odom et al., 1992). Specific intervention strategies for child-child interactions include peer initiation training (Strain & Odom, 1986), affection training (McEvoy, Twardosz, & Bishop, 1990), promoting social-communicative competence (Goldstein & Gallagher, 1992), use of cooperative learning strategies (Cosden & T. G. Haring, 1992), teaching play in social contexts (T. G. Haring & Lovinger, 1989), structuring interactive contexts and using materials that promote interactions (Sainato & Carta, 1992), and using self-management procedures (Hughes, 1992).

Community Skills.   Community living skills include skills designed to increase students' independence in functioning in a variety of community environments, including community mobility and the use of community services. Community mobility includes crossing streets, walking to a given destination, and using mass transit systems. Use of community services involves procuring goods and services from community facilities; for example, shopping, going to the hairdresser, or going to a dentist. Frequently community living skills are taught in the actual community settings; for example, learning to buy groceries is done at the grocery store or learning to ride the bus is done on the local mass transit system. This is called community-based or community-referenced instruction. The advantage of this type of instruction is that natural cues, natural materials, natural consequences, and opportunities for interactions with persons who do not have disabilities are available (Falvey, 1989).

A variety of community skills have been taught to students with moderate and severe disabilities. Community mobility skills include street crossing (Marchetti, McCartney, Drain, Hooper, & Dix, 1983) and bus riding (Robinson, Griffith, McComish, & Swasbrook, 1984). For using community facilities, students have been taught to purchase items from grocery stores (Horner, Albin, & Ralph, 1986), convenience stores (McDonnell, 1987), fast-food restaurants (McDonnell & Ferguson, 1988), vending machines (Nietupski, Clancey, & Christiansen, 1984), and a variety of different stores (T. G. Haring et al., in press; T. G. Haring, Kennedy, Adams, & Pitts-Conway, 1987). Students also have been taught to select the lowest-priced item (Sandknop, Schuster, Wolery, & Cross, 1992). Also, safety skills have been taught such as avoiding abduction by strangers (Gast, Collins, Wolery, & Jones, 1993; Haseltine & Miltenberger, 1990) and applying first aid (Gast, Winterling, Wolery, & Farmer, 1992).

Recreation and Leisure Skills.   "Leisure skills give us something enjoyable to do with our free time, and participation in those activities gives us something enjoyable to do with family and friends" (Meyer, 1991, p. 290). Preschool- and elementary-aged students with severe disabilities should be taught toy and social play skills, and older students should be taught chronological age-appropriate leisure and recreational activities.

Assessing and teaching play is an issue that has been the focus of considerable debate. However, it is clear that (1) play behaviors can be categorized and measured consistently; (2) students can be taught to play with toys and with peers; (3) toys can be adapted to make them more accessible; and (4) other skills such as communication and social interactions can be assessed and taught in play contexts (Musselwhite, 1986; Bailey & Wolery, 1992). Also, increasing toy play may help decrease problem behavior (Santarcangelo, Dyer, & Luce, 1987). For older students and adults, a variety of leisure and recreational skills have been taught (Vandercook, 1991). Home-based leisure skills are using the television and radio, playing table games, playing cards, hosting parties or having friends visit, and hobbies. Activities that are available in communities include going out to eat; taking walks; visiting friends; going to museums or historic sites; using community facilities for activities such as bowling, swimming, or billiards or even video arcades; and attending church/synagogue, movies, the theater, and sporting events.

Several characteristics of appropriate leisure and recreational training programs have been identified (Falvey, 1989). Chronological age-appropriate materials and environments should be used in instruction. Leisure skills should be accessible and possible in the student's community. The targeted leisure and recreational skills should result in interaction with peers who are not disabled (Vandercook, 1991). It is recommended that the skills be consistent with the preferences of the student and family to increase the probability that they will be used. In many cases, leisure activities might be adapted to promote at least partial participation by the student. Some adaptations involve using special equipment, changing the steps in the activity, changing the materials involved, modifying the activity's rules, providing additional time for some steps, and providing assistance on specific steps (Banks & Aveno, 1986). Finding and adapting appropriate leisure skills improves the quality of life for many students with severe disabilities.

Vocational Skills. The purpose of instruction for students with severe disabilities is to prepare them to live as normally as possible, including having meaningful work after leaving school. Because their rate of learning is slow, vocational preparation begins at a younger age than is typical for students without disabilities or with mild disabilities. As the students progress through junior high school and high school, increasingly more time should be spent in job sites in the community. Early preparation in job skills is critical, because less prepared students are likely to be placed in more restrictive (less normalized) adult programs, particularly in communities with fewer postschool placement options. Adult programs for learners with severe disabilities fall along the continuum and restrictiveness shown in Figure 7–3.

Day activities programs are generally for persons with the most profound disabilities. The programs' focus typically is to promote sensory awareness and communicative abilities.

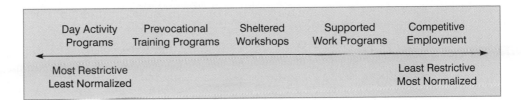

Figure 7–3
Continuum of vocational services and placements for students with moderate and severe disabilities.

Prevocational training programs teach individuals to perform tasks that correspond to jobs available in sheltered workshops or other settings. The focus is typically on increasing production rates such as packaging or assembling items. Students in these programs also typically have instructional objectives such as complying with instructions from supervisors and taking breaks with co-workers. A critical distinction between prevocational training programs and other more normalized work situations is that participants are generally not paid for their work in prevocational programs.

Sheltered workshops were once the highest career alternative for workers with severe disabilities. In these settings, workers with severe disabilities engage in a variety of jobs, including assembling and packaging items for sale. Although sheltered employment is widely used, it has come under increasing criticism; Brown et al. (1983; 1984) discuss several drawbacks of sheltered employment.

Work crew programs are operated by social service agencies to employ workers with severe disabilities. Once set up, the work crew operates like other small businesses. Generally workers are paid at least the minimum wage. Examples of work by such crews are lawn care, window cleaning, painting, housecleaning, and building maintenance.

In *supported work programs*, a school or adult agency engages in several steps to locate jobs, train workers, and provide ongoing follow-up for workers with severe disabilities (Rusch & Hughes, 1989). Supported work placements are generally developed by following several steps:

1. Family members and teachers are interviewed to obtain initial ideas for jobs that would be interesting to the person with severe disabilities and that fit the values of the family.
2. Once a list of potential jobs is made, the local community is surveyed to find existing job opportunities. Frequently, jobs in high-turnover fields such as fast-food chains and manufacturing plants are targeted. However, many programs have been successful in placing workers in higher-status settings such as high-technology industries (Gaylord-Ross, Forte, Storey, Gaylord-Ross, & Jameson, 1987).
3. After a job is located, the staff contacts the potential employer to determine the suitability of the job and whether the employer would be willing to serve as a job site for a worker with severe disabilities. Employers may receive a direct tax credit for employing workers with disabilities.
4. After a contract has been negotiated, a job coach accompanies the worker to the site for training in all aspects of the job. Workers often require training not only in the job but also in the social skills of the workplace (Breen, T. G. Haring, Pitts-Conway, & Gaylord-Ross, 1985; Park & Gaylord-Ross, 1989).
5. As the workers become more proficient, the job coach continues to accompany them to the job but gradually provides less training so that they become accustomed to working independently under the supervision of the existing supervisors.
6. As a final step, the job coach no longer accompanies the worker to the job, but continues to conduct follow-up training and support as needed.

Supported employment has been shown to have many benefits for workers with severe disabilities. These include increased opportunities to participate in social interactions with co-workers, higher earnings than in sheltered employment, and better perceptions by workers who are not disabled (Bellamy et al., 1984). Also, the taxpayer benefits because increases in taxes paid by the disabled worker coupled with reductions in social security payments to the worker who is disabled, more than make up for the wages of the job coach and the tax credits given the employer (Hill, Wehman, Kregel, Banks, & Metzler, 1987).

Competitive employment for individuals with severe disabilities was unheard of 10 years ago. Currently some workers with severe disabilities, including those with severe mental retardation, have successful histories of placement in normal competitive employment (Rusch, 1986). These placements are usually the result of successful supported employment.

MAINSTREAMING The term *mainstreaming* has been used for 20 years to refer to enrolling students with disabilities in classrooms designed for students who are not disabled and where the majority of students do not have disabilities (Odom & McEvoy, 1988). More recently, the term *inclusion* has been used to refer to enrolling students with severe disabilities in general (regular) education classrooms at their home schools (i.e., the ones they would attend if they did not have disabilities). This is done so that the proportion of students with disabilities in each school approximates their proportion of the student population. Among others, the primary distinction between the terms is that mainstreaming implies a practice where students with disabilities enter a system that is really not designed for them, but with inclusion, the entire program is designed to meet the needs of all students regardless of functioning level. In the past, nearly all students with severe disabilities were enrolled in separate schools or separate classrooms that were clustered in one or two school buildings of a local school district (i.e., not proportional to the student population). However, since two goals of education for students with severe disabilities are

Development of friendships is important in ensuring adequate integration of children with severe disabilities into everyday life.

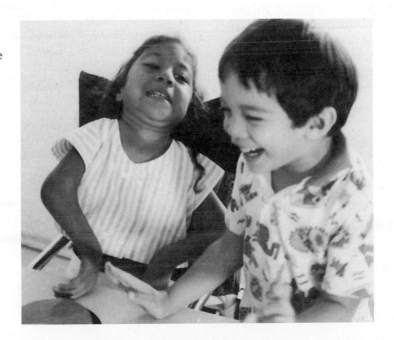

MODEL PROGRAM
Christine L. Salisbury

The Collaborative Education Project was funded by the U.S. Department of Education to develop and validate a collaborative problem-solving strategy for promoting the inclusion of students with severe disabilities in general education classrooms (Salisbury, 1989). A variety of process and outcome data were gathered within the context of the project—data that have helped the field better understand the evolution and characteristics of an inclusive elementary environment.

Overview of an Inclusive Elementary School
Since 1985 students with disabilities in the Johnson City Center School District in Johnson City, New York, have moved from segregated, out-of-district special education programs into district-based, general education classrooms. While substantial progress toward the goal of full inclusion is apparent at the middle and high school levels, the most significant gains have occurred at the elementary level. At Harry L. Johnson Elementary School, where the Collaborative Education Project was based, students with mild to profound disabilities are enrolled full-time in the age-appropriate, regular education classrooms they would attend if they did not have a disability. Is there something unique about this district that makes this level of reform possible? What happens at this particular elementary school that enables teachers to include students with mild to profound disabilities in general education classrooms?

A Typical, Yet Unique District
The development of an inclusive school program is not dependent upon the wealth, geographic location, or size of the school district. The Johnson City Central School District is comparatively small, serving approximately 1,200 students, 100 of whom are classified as having a disability. The dis-

trict operates two elementary schools, one middle school, and one high school. It is among the poorest in per capita income in south central New York. The community has seen a dramatic increase in Amerasian families whose first language is not English. In many ways, the Johnson city district is typical of programs across the country in its composition and the issues it faces.

However, the district is also unique. Nationally recognized for its validated Outcomes Driven Development Model (ODDM) (Joint Dissemination Review Panel–validated, 1985; National Dissemination Network, 1986), the district incorporates many practices endorsed in the effective schools literature within an organizational framework of outcomes-based education (Blum, 1985; Purkey & Smith, 1983). This model has been used across the country by over 300 school districts to initiate educational reform and improve the quality of educational services to students.

Essential Characteristics
There are four characteristics of the school environment at Harry L. Johnson Elementary School that enable the staff to achieve reasonable success in moving toward the development of an inclusive school. These factors directly affect the quality of services delivered to students with and without disabilities enrolled in the school (Salisbury, Palombaro, & Hollowood, 1993). They are vision-based decisions, an explicit value base, an "intentional" environment, and teaming.

Vision-based decisions
Decisions about educational reform and systems change occur within a well-defined, vision-based, decision-making process that teachers and administrators use on a frequent basis. The process requires that all decisions be reached by consensus and that the component decision-making models be "aligned" (internally consistent). Grounded as a series of questions, the process begins by asking, "Is what we're doing getting us what we want?" To answer this question, staff must identify

what it is they wanted to achieve (a goal/vision). Then they must analyze whether what they believe (philosophical base), know (information based on best available research and experience), and are doing (current policies and practices) can lead to attaining that goal. Insofar as the staff identified an inclusive school as one of their "wants," decisions about instructional practices and supports are made in light of what is needed to ensure that all students, including those with severe and profound disabilities, are successful as learners and as members of the school community.

Explicit value base

In the early seventies, the district reached consensus on a core of 10 beliefs related to teaching and learning; among those were mastery, trust, success, inclusion, and cooperation. Conscious efforts were made to put these beliefs in operation, most notably through teaming, mastery learning, and cooperative teaching and learning practices. In practice, the staff's notion of "inclusion" means that all members of the school and neighborhood community should be "connected" and have a sense of "belonging." When teachers model these values through their actions and language, students without disabilities begin to see their peers with severe disabilities as integral members of the community (Salisbury, Mangino, et al., 1993). These core values affect policy and instructional decisions at the classroom, building, and district level.

Intentional environment

When entering this school, one encounters carpeted hallways lined with plants, and esteem-building phrases lettered over each arched hallway that read: "Through these hallways pass the best kids anywhere" or "Harry L. kids are great!" Peering into classrooms one sees no desks; only tables around which groups of children engage in a variety of cooperative learning activities. The school climate reflects the espoused value base of the school.

Teachers in this school use mastery learning principles as the core of their instructional process. They assume that learning should be fun, students

should be successful, decision-making power should be shared, teachers should be flexible, and that individual needs and interests are of paramount concern in the design of instructional activities. These assumptions are most evident when instructional teams meet to write curriculum and plan activities for the students on their team. Because students with severe disabilities are members of these classrooms, team members need to work together to embed IEP objectives into scheduled activities. The staff at this school use a process of curricular adaptation (Salisbury, Mangino, et al., 1993). Adaptations increase the likelihood that students remain a part of the instructional activity and that they feel successful as learners.

Teaming

The commitment to the value of cooperation is apparent in the grade- and/or cross-grade level teams that form the infrastructure of this school. These configurations create natural opportunities for general education staff to share ideas, knowledge, and expertise during daily team planning meetings—opportunities that have direct application for supporting students with disabilities and for resolving issues about their inclusion in general education classes. Curriculum development and instruction, hiring, staff development, and distribution of students to teams are among the areas where staff share decision-making power with the administration. Teams in this school function as sources of support for students and staff, and as catalysts for reform of instructional practices and policies.

Summary

Systemic challenges can be viewed as opportunities for reform. Outcome data from the past three years indicate that an inclusive school environment creates positive learning experiences and outcomes for students with and without disabilities. As more programs merge their strategies and findings, high-quality, inclusive programs will become the rule rather than the exception.

to promote their participation in the community and promote their relationships with others, many persons have advocated full inclusion (Stainback & Stainback, 1990).

Issues of Placement

In terms of placement, two questions are pertinent: Should students be educated in their home school?, and How much time should students spend in the general education classroom? (Brown, Long, Udvari-Solner, Davis, et al., 1989; Brown, Long, Udvari-Solner, Schwartz, et al., 1989; Brown et al., 1991). Brown, Long, Udvari-Solner, Davis, et al. (1989) argue that four reasons exist for placing students in home schools: (1) "to engender a pluralistic society," (2) "to use the most meaningful instructional environments," (3) "to enhance family access," and (4) "to develop a wide range of social relationships with nondisabled peers" (pp. 2–3). Placement in home schools is thought to promote both community integration and social relationships. Although segregated schools and clusters of segregated classrooms persist, many school systems are attempting to enroll students with severe disabilities in their home schools.

Less consensus exists on the amount of time students should spend in general education classrooms. Brown et al. (1991) argue that all students should be *based* in general education classrooms, but not *confined* to them. Other authors argue that students should be fully included—placed full-time in general education classrooms. In theory, but not necessarily in practice, the student's IEP should determine the nature of the placement, including the amount of time spent in general education classrooms. Brown et al. (1991) describe several factors that should be considered in placement decisions. For example, the student's age may be a major factor. Preschoolers with disabilities benefit socially and are not harmed in other developmental areas from full inclusion in programs designed for typically developing children (Buysse & Bailey, 1993). However, high school students with disabilities may need to spend a good bit of their day in job sites learning work skills; thus, full inclusion in general education classrooms is less important. Other factors that should be considered in making placement decisions include the student's need for specific therapy and specialized services; the number of settings in which the student spends time; the skills and attitudes of the general educators; the potential for developing social relationships; the concerns and priorities of families; the likelihood that skills needed for independence will be learned and used; the need for functional skills that can and cannot be acquired in general education classrooms; and the likelihood of learning the skills needed after transition from school (Brown et al., 1991).

Currently, it is difficult to determine the extent to which most students with severe disabilities are educated with their peers who are not disabled. Many schools are committed to serving all students with disabilities in their home schools and in general education classrooms (see the Model Program description).

However, current mechanisms for reporting enrollment data do not provide sufficient or accurate information about placements in home schools or general education classrooms (K. Haring et al., 1992). Thus, it is difficult to determine whether most students with severe disabilities have contact with their nondisabled peers in their school settings. However, at the preschool level, it is clear that the majority of the programs of various types enroll children with disabilities in their programs (Wolery et al., in press).

Promoting Inclusion

Regardless of the site or extent of mainstreaming/inclusion, several issues appear to influence the quality of such experiences. For example, the extent to which the school develops and implements a philosophy that governs how decisions are made relative to educating all students influences the amount and nature of inclusion (Salisbury, 1991). Similarly, the extent to which the team members are committed to inclusion and learn to collaborate with one another are important factors in the quality of such experiences (Rainforth et al., 1992). Also, the goals that are set for students with severe disabilities and the way in which institutional practices are implemented are major factors in determining the benefit of inclusion (Hilton & Liberty, 1992).

Clearly, promoting social relationships with nondisabled peers requires contact with them. The strategies on promoting social interactions (discussed in the Curriculum section of this chapter) should be used as should specialized programs for promoting friendships (e.g., Voeltz, 1982). The context in which friendships are promoted also are important (Forest & Pearpoint, 1992). In addition to promoting social interactions and friendships, peers without disabilities can serve important functions such as acting as peer tutors (T. G. Haring, Breen, Pitts-Conway, Lee, & Gaylord-Ross, 1987) and as partners in cooperative learning groups (Cosden & T. G. Haring, 1992). Such peer tutoring programs often are associated with skill acquisition on the part of the

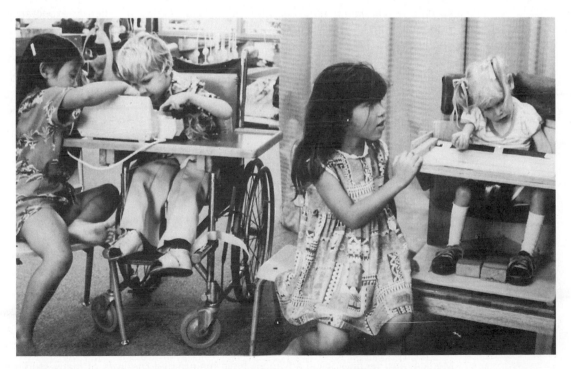

Mainstreaming is facilitated by purposeful contact between students with and without severe disabilities.

student with severe disabilities and increased positive attitudes toward them by their nondisabled peers. Further, inclusive placements provide students with opportunities to learn peer imitation (Venn, Wolery, Werts, et al., 1993) and to use imitation to acquire new skills.

INNOVATION AND DEVELOPMENT

Educating students with severe disabilities is complex, given the pervasiveness of their disabilities. Serious attempts to educate them on a broad scale have occurred only in the past two decades. As a result, several important questions about educational practices and about policy exist.

Issue: The Relationship Between Schools and Families

IDEA requires parents' consent on issues such as assessment, placement, and the Individualized Educational Plan (IEP) for students with disabilities, including those with severe disabilities. As described throughout this chapter, the interactions between family members and professionals should be extensive, ongoing, and collaborative. Unfortunately, many university training programs in most disciplines do not adequately prepare their students to collaborate with families (Bailey, Simeonsson, Yoder, & Huntington, 1990). A number of difficulties can arise in the parent-professional interactions. For example, professionals may (1) not be sensitive to the differences within and across families; (2) develop adversarial relationships with families; (3) view parents as less competent than professionals; and (4) have different expectations and priorities from those of families (Salisbury, 1992). In addition, some very real constraints may exist on the professionals that keep them from interacting with families appropriately. For example, the schools may not provide teachers with flexible schedules for visiting and meeting with families, may not provide time to devote to family issues, and may not support professionals' efforts in advocacy. Thus, both the college-university training programs and the organizational structures of schools must change to promote professional-family collaboration.

Issue: Assessing and Teaching Students

Substantial improvements in our assessment and instructional practices have occurred. Assessment activities involve analyzing students' performance under natural situations in settings where they learn, live, work, and recreate. Further, a number of instructional strategies for promoting students' acquisition (Wolery, Ault, et al., 1992) and generalization of skills (Horner et al., 1988) have been developed. However, much remains to be learned about teaching students with the most profound disabilities (Sailor et al., 1988). Also, much remains to be learned about getting most teachers in most schools to use the latest in assessment and instructional practices.

Issue: Medically Fragile and Chronically Ill Students

Medical and technological advances have maintained the lives of many students who would have died in the past. As a result, students with serious medical problems may participate in educational programs but may require a variety of health-related procedures (Hayden & DePaepe, 1991). Teachers are frequently asked to administer medication, monitor seizures, conduct CPR, care for shunts, treat skin breakdowns, use colostomy and ileostomy procedures, complete gastrostomy feeding, and carry out many other procedures (Izen & Brown, 1991; Mulligan-Ault, Guess, Struth, & Thompson, 1988). Identifying appropriate roles for teachers and implementing adequate training are important and urgent considerations. Also, developing and implementing policies that simultaneously protect the health of teachers and other students and secure the rights to treatment of the affected student are particularly demanding tasks.

Issue: Technology and Students with Severe Disabilities

Advances in technology not only have promoted longer life for some students, but can be used to enhance their education in several ways. For example, the video game technology has been used as a context for teaching social interactions (Gaylord-Ross, T. G. Haring, Breen, & Pitts-Conway, 1984) and teaching skills needed for using certain communication systems (Horn, Jones, & Hamlett, 1991); videotaping has been used to simulate community-based instruction (T. G. Haring et al., in press); and microcomputers have been used in motor skills training programs (Horn, Warren, & Reith, 1992). Students have been taught to use microcomputer communication systems as a means of providing alternatives or replacements to problem behavior (Horner, Sprague, O'Brien, & Heathfield, 1990). Teachers can use technology for administrative tasks and potentially to help in decision making (Hofmeister & Ferrara, 1986). Finally, a number of augmentative communication devices can be used successfully to enhance students' ability to communicate (Baumgart et al., 1990). Several issues remain unresolved, such as assessing the effects of specific technological applications, ensuring that applications keep pace with technological developments, preparing new and existing teachers in technological applications, and identifying and purchasing reliable hardware and software.

Issue: Responding to Students' Problem or Challenging Behaviors

Some students with severe disabilities will engage in problem behaviors that interfere with their learning and the learning of others, is harmful to themselves, and on occasion is life-threatening. Substantial improvements have occurred in our ability to devise acceptable and effective intervention strategies (Repp & Singh, 1990). Best practice now suggests that the functions that the problem behavior serves for the student be identified (O'Neill et al., 1990). Common functions are (1) to escape from demanding tasks or aversive situations; (2) to secure objects, activities, and attention; (3) to secure stimulation; and (4) to avoid aversive internal states or discomfort. Many problem behaviors can be treated by teaching students to perform more efficient replacement behaviors (Horner & Day, 1991). However, conducting assessments to identify the functions of problem behaviors and devise interventions requires highly

*A*s noted in this chapter, technology has a number of potential applications in providing education to students with severe disabilities. Below is a description of an investigation conducted by Horn, Warren, and Reith (1992). This investigation is particularly noteworthy because it illustrates multiple technological applications. The study was designed to evaluate the use of a microcomputer-mediated teaching package with small groups of children. Six young children participated. Each child had severe disabilities including cerebral palsy and other impairments; three were preschoolers and three were toddlers. The study occurred within their respective classrooms and paraprofessionals implemented the experimental sessions. The sessions were designed to give the children practice on performing individually determined motor skills. The children's goals were selected through consultation between the teacher and physical therapist. The target behaviors involved the children maintaining desirable body positions and body alignment. The experimental sessions were delivered in small groups (2 to 4 children) at once.

The equipment included an Apple IIe computer and an "Omnibox was attached to an interface board" in the computer (p. 134). This allowed connections between switches indicating the children were performing their target behaviors and activation of adapted battery-operated toys. As a result, when the children performed the target behavior an individually selected toy was activated; if the child stopped doing the target behavior, the toy would be turned off. In addition, the microcomputer collected data on the children's performance, and it prompted the teaching assistant when to deliver verbal or physical prompts. If one of the children in the group was not doing the target behavior, the microcomputer would signal the teaching assistant to deliver a prompt. Thus, the microcomputer completed several important functions at once. It controlled the children's access to reinforcing toys contingent upon their performance of the target behaviors, it collected performance data, it summarized performance data by printing out a report of each session, and it cued the teacher when to provide each child with assistance.

The use of the package was compared to a condition where the same behaviors were expected of the children, but the microcomputer was not used. The results indicate that the microcomputer-mediated teaching package was effective on a number of levels. First, the children had higher percentages of performance on their target behaviors when the package was used. Second, the children were more engaged in the activity when the microcomputer system was used; engagement was defined as "actively occupied as demonstrated by visual orientation, scrutinizing, manipulating, vocalizing, or otherwise directly interacting with a specific material and/or teacher" (p. 137). Third, the teacher delivered more frequent prompts when the microcomputer package was used. Finally, the teachers in the classroom and the teaching assistants rated the system as allowing them to be more effective and as promoting more desirable changes in children's behavior.

trained professionals and substantial time. Also, much of this research has occurred in clinical not school settings, although a few have (e.g., Dunlap et al., 1991). Thus, substantially more professionals who work with students who have severe disabilities need to be trained in these procedures, and the procedures need to be refined so that they are more applicable in schools.

Issue: Promoting Friendships Between Students With and Without Severe Disabilities

Many families of students with severe disabilities value friendship formation between their child and nondisabled peers more than skill development in other areas (Hamre-Nietupski et al., 1992). The past few years have witnessed the development of a number of effective strategies for promoting positive interactions between students with and without disabilities (Odom et al., 1992) and the conditions under which those interactions are more likely to occur (Breen & T. G. Haring, 1991). However, much remains to be learned about how those interactions can lead to the formation of friendships. Among the questions that illustrate the difficulties in this area are these: How long must a relationship last to be considered a friendship? How can the value of friendships be measured for students with and without disabilities? What conditions appear to increase the probability of friendship formation? How should classrooms be structured and what should teachers do to facilitate friendships? How does forming a friendship with a student who has severe disabilities influence the typical student's friendships with other peers?

Issue: Professionals and Collaborative Teams

The quality of students' educational experiences undoubtedly is tied directly to the competence of the professionals on their educational teams. These teams are composed of representatives from many disciplines. Some of these disciplines (e.g., general education, speech and language pathology, physical and occupational therapy) do not prepare their members to work exclusively with students who have severe disabilities; in fact, some may have no training in working with students who have severe disabilities (Bruder, in press). Further, they may have little training in working on collaborative teams, despite the necessity of doing so to serve students with severe disabilities (Rainforth et al., 1992). Most disciplines will not change their training programs in major ways to provide more training in serving students with severe disabilities (Bailey et al., 1990). Thus, much remains to be learned about how to help professionals gain expertise and competence after they graduate from their training programs and how to teach them to work collaboratively with one another and with families of children with disabilities.

SUMMARY   Individuals with severe disabilities make up a small proportion of the general population (about 3 or 4 per 1,000), and a small percentage of the population of individuals with disabilities. A number of causes exist for severe disabilities including genetic and chromosomal abnormalities and insults prior to, during, and after birth. For many stu-

1. Consult with representatives from other disciplines before starting an instructional program.

2. Identify goals for teaching by collecting information through interviews and direct observation.

3. Select teaching goals that will promote student self-sufficiency.

4. Involve family members in determining what goals are most important for instruction.

5. Ensure that students have multiple opportunities to be with and interact with peers who do not have disabilities.

6. Use an events/skill matrix to plan when and by whom important skills will be taught and embed instruction on priority goals in ongoing routines and activities.

7. Use prompting procedures that are effective and efficient, minimize errors, and involve a systematic means of reducing teacher assistance.

8. Carefully select the training materials, use multiple trainers, employ multiple settings, and ensure that students learn to apply skills when needed.

9. Use simulations and community-based instruction whenever possible to increase the likelihood of students using skills.

10. Monitor student progress during instruction to determine whether and what changes need to be made.

dents with severe disabilities, no cause can be identified; for others, if a cause is identified, it is not helpful in planning instructional programs. A large percentage of students with severe disabilities will have more than one disabling condition, including seizure disorders, sensory impairments, physical impairments, and communicative and behavior disorders.

Assessment of students with severe disabilities can serve many functions, and two that are particularly relevant to teachers are assessment for planning instructional programs and for monitoring the effects of those programs. Assessment for instructional planning involves the use of a systematic process for gathering and analyzing information about how students function and the conditions under which they function. This information is collected from direct testing, informal testing, observations, interviews, and other sources. Intervention requires a team process, collaboration with families, embedding instruction in ongoing activities, conceptualizing and addressing students' performance on multiple levels, and using effective and efficient instructional procedures. The curriculum should be organized by life skills and designed to promote students' independence, participation in community life, and social relationships.

Several important issues exist in the education of students with severe disabilities. Some of these deal with the educational program broadly such as defining relationships between school personnel and families and identifying roles and responsibilities related to serving chronically ill students. Other issues deal directly with traditional teacher roles such as using efficient strategies, using technology, dealing with problem behavior, and promoting friendships among students.

STUDY QUESTIONS

1. How many persons per 1,000 are likely to have severe disabilities, and will they be evenly distributed across gender and age?

2. What are some of the causes of severe mental retardation?

3. What influence do societal and cultural perspectives have on the roles assumed by individuals with severe disabilities?

4. What steps are involved in assessing students for the purpose of planning instructional programs?

5. What measurement strategies other than direct testing should be used in assessing students with severe disabilities?

6. Why does planning interventions for individuals with severe disabilities require participation of the student's family and representatives from multiple disciplines?

7. What major skill areas are often included in the curriculum?

8. Why is it important to conceptualize students' performance in terms of acquisition, fluency, maintenance, and generalization?

9. What are functional skills, and why is it important to teach them to students with severe disabilities?

10. Where are community living and vocational skills best taught?

11. What is full inclusion and what are some of the issues surrounding it?

12. Describe two issues that face educators of students with severe disabilities.

8

Sherwood J. Best
California State University,
Los Angeles

June L. Bigge
San Francisco State
University

Barbara P. Sirvis
State University of New
York, Brockport

Physical and Health Impairments

  In this chapter you will learn about

- the characteristics of individuals who have physical and/or health impairments

- prenatal, perinatal, and postnatal causes of physical and/or health impairments

- assessing students with physical and/or health impairments, as well as the role of the transdisciplinary assessment team in this effort

- physical, psychosocial, and instructional intervention strategies for students with physical and/or health impairments

- curricula for students with physical and/or health impairments at the preschool, elementary, secondary, and postsecondary levels

- the application of technology for students with physical and/or health impairments

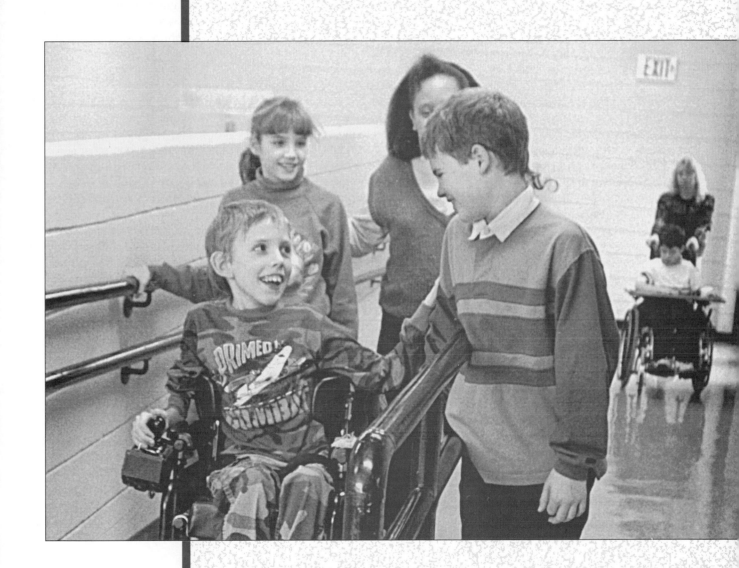

Alfonso is a 12-year-old student with cerebral palsy. When he was born, labor was protracted and he suffered "anoxia," or lack of oxygen, for several minutes. Although his intellect is unimpaired, Alfonso's motor and speech abilities were affected. He cannot walk or control many fine motor activities, and he requires assistance with self-care activities such as dressing and feeding. Writing with a pencil or pen results in scribbles and much frustration for Alfonso. His speech is intelligible only to family, teachers, and others who have known him for at least several months.

It would appear from this description that Alfonso is limited to only a few activities—that his quality of life is perhaps less than other children his age. The reality is that Alfonso is a happy, hard-working student who is assisted toward maximum independence with sophisticated equipment—and with the dedication of many people. Alfonso's parents, teacher, therapist, speech-language specialist, and Alfonso himself—all provided information regarding his motor and communication needs. After careful assessment, Alfonso was provided with an augmentative communication device called a Light Talker. This device is programmed with words and phrases customized to Alfonso's school and home environment. There are switches attached to the lapboard on Alfonso's wheelchair and near the side of his face, which he presses with his hand or head to direct the scanning mode of the Light Talker and select what he wants to say. Then he activates the "voice". Previous augmentative communication devices had relied on a robotic-sounding voice. Alfonso is glad that the voice output of the Light Talker approximates that of a young boy. One of the greatest benefits of a synthesized voice for Alfonso is his ability to talk with friends during recess. Since the programming capacity of the Light Talker is great, this device can "grow" with Alfonso as he becomes increasingly sophisticated regarding its use.

Augmentative communication is not the only form of "high technology" support Alfonso uses. He is making the transition from a manual wheelchair to an electric wheelchair. He gets regular "driving lessons" from his physical therapist. Independent mobility is now a reachable goal, and it will certainly support Alfonso's wish to have a paid job in his neighborhood when he is older.

Technology also assists Alfonso in his schoolwork. An adaptation on his computer allows Alfonso to access word processing programs with his switch devices. When other students turn in written assignments, so can he. The scribbles he once produced have been replaced by printing that is neat and conveys exactly what Alfonso wants to say.

Alfonso attends a class where there is a reverse mainstreaming program: students from an adjacent 3rd-4th grade class join Alfonso's class each day. Activities include reading, spelling, writing, and readers' theater. Alfonso will soon leave this class and move to an integrated 5th-grade classroom. To be successful, this transition must include the support necessary for Alfonso to continue to use his support equipment and to feel good about himself. Alfonso is excited by this prospect and a little frightened, too.

Individuals with physical and health impairments are members of your community and perhaps your class. Like Alfonso many use wheelchairs for mobility or electronic devices for communication, but they can be active members of the community. Many are enrolled in college and university programs while others receive technical training. Individuals with physical and health impairments have interests and opinions as far-ranging and as diverse as those of their peers who are not disabled.

HISTORY

Physical disabilities have been documented through the ages, and responses to individuals with disabilities have grown from extermination, ridicule, and isolation to acceptance, education, and treatment. Isolation of persons with physical and health impairments was once justified for medical and social reasons (Connor, Scandary, & Tulloch, 1988). It was not until the late 19th century that isolation gave way to inclusion, and educational programs began to emerge for children with physical and health impairments.

Early programs emphasized physical care and surgery for persons with cerebral palsy. Educational programming began with children hospitalized for disabilities resulting from such diseases as polio and tuberculosis. Gradually there was recognition that children with more severe disabilities should also have school-based opportunities (Best, 1992).

The first public school class in the United States for children with physical disabilities was established in 1899 in Chicago. Most classes were in hospitals, day camps, and convalescent and residential homes. Many facilities were designed as open-air schools for "delicate" children—those with pretuberculosis, cardiac problems, diabetes, and poliomyclitis. Schools for children with cerebral palsy came later because many of these children had multiple physical and learning problems and were more difficult to teach. In 1913 in New York City, the first public school teachers were assigned to teach children with physical impairments in their homes, and by the thirties such children were benefitting from legislation to reimburse local school districts for the added costs of educating children with disabilities. A team approach to intervention gradually evolved, giving educational programming equal status with medical services. Although a variety of disciplines contributed to the development of such programming, its roots lay in medicine and related fields (Best, 1992; Mullins, 1985).

Volunteer groups of parents and concerned professionals emerged during the first quarter of the 20th century. Their lobbying efforts greatly influenced the establishment of early education programs for students with physical impairments. Many of these groups have evolved into agencies that now function as advocates for those with disabilities at the local and national levels (e.g., National Easter Seal Society and United Cerebral Palsy Association).

World Wars I and II contributed to advancements in complicated orthopedic and rehabilitation procedures for persons with amputations, traumatic spinal cord injuries, and communication and motor coordination impairments as the result of brain injury. The need for rehabilitation led to intensive collaboration of professionals in medicine, therapy, counseling, education, and engineering. Individuals with physical impairments benefitted from advances in artificial limbs, lifesaving health care, physical therapy, methods of improving physical independence, posture and movement improvement, and self-care and communication aids.

Henry Viscardi, Jr., was one of the first Americans to demonstrate that people with physical impairments can learn to work and earn a living (Viscardi, 1972). In early 1950 he collaborated with a small group of individuals to set up a shop in Albertson, Long Island. In this shop, Abilities Incorporated, persons with disabilities found real jobs, not contrived work or charity. This pioneering crew of 5 persons became the nucleus of the nationally prominent Human Resources Center and its school for students with severe physical impairments.

Education and services for persons with physical disabilities are now supported by legislation. Legislation includes Public Law 100–407 (The Technology-Related Assistance for Individuals with Disabilities Act); Public Law 94–142, reauthorized as Public Law 101–476 (Individuals with Disabilities Education Act, or IDEA); and Public Law 101–336 (The Americans with Disabilities Act) (Carney, 1990; Morrissey & Silverstein, 1989; National Information Center for Children and Youth with Disabilities, 1991). These laws have moved students from the isolation of hospitals and custodial institutions to integrated public school classes.

Education is now characterized by placements in less restrictive environments, with options for a full continuum of educational services (Doyle, 1989; Johnsen & Corn, 1989). Removal of architectural barriers and a decrease in attitudinal barriers have led to acceptance of students with physical and health impairments in regular classes where they compete with their nondisabled peers for academic honors and enjoy the benefits of social integration in nonacademic situations.

DEFINITION

We refer to individuals with disabling physical conditions with such terms as *physically challenged* and *physically disabled*. The terms are used more or less interchangeably by professionals, parents, and individuals with disabilities.

The guidelines established in 1975 by Public Law 94–142 (Education for All Handicapped Children Act) and restated by IDEA in 1990 attempt to resolve definitional questions by dividing physical impairments into two broad categories: orthopedic impairments and health impairments.

Severe orthopedic impairments adversely affect a child's educational performance, and include

> impairments caused by congenital anomaly (e.g., clubfoot, absence of some member, etc.), impairments caused by disease (e.g., poliomyelitis, bone tuberculosis, etc.), and impairments from other causes (e.g., cerebral palsy, amputations, and fractures and burns which cause contractures). (IDEA, section 300.5 [6])

The second category, health impairments, comprises physical conditions that affect educational performance, including

> limited strength, vitality, or alertness, due to chronic health problems such as a heart condition, tuberculosis, rheumatic fever, nephritis, asthma, sickle cell anemia, hemophilia, or diabetes. (IDEA, section 300.5 [7])

Physical impairments are frequently accompanied by one or more additional disabilities—communication and/or speech disorders, vision and/or hearing impairments (Hart, 1988; Yuker, 1988). Some individuals with physical or health impairments have conditions resulting in dependency on technology to sustain health or even survival.

These students are said to have specialized health care needs (Sirvis, 1988). Their technology needs might include ventilator use or procedures such as bladder catheterization or suctioning.

Many diseases that once characterized this population (e.g., polio, tuberculosis, rheumatic fever) have been curtailed by advances in medicine. That same medical technology has contributed to the survival of persons with disabilities resulting from traumatic head and spinal cord injury, anoxia, injuries related to physical abuse, and the effects of prematurity and low birth weight. The medical amelioration or resolution of such conditions and the increased incidence of others (such as acquired immune deficiency syndrome) contribute to the continuing clinical diversity of persons with orthopedic and health impairments (Best, 1992).

PREVALENCE

Physical and health impairments often occur in combination with other disabilities. Some students, particularly those with health impairments, have a primary disability in another category. Others have a dual diagnosis: for example, a learning disability or hearing impairment. This makes it difficult to determine a valid prevalence rate for physical and health impairments (Gortmacher & Sappenfield, 1984).

Nonetheless, we can make some prevalence estimates from the data collected by the federal government. A total of 41,514 children of all those who receive special education services in the United States are labeled as orthopedically impaired, while 46,639 are labeled as health impaired. This accounts for approximately 1 percent and 1.2 percent, respectively, of the school-age population who receive special services (U.S. Department of Education, 1990). Others estimate the total number of children with orthopedic or health impairments as only .5 percent of the population of all school-age children (National Institute on Disability and Rehabilitation Research, 1989).

CAUSES

Causes of physical disabilities and health impairments are as varied as the disabilities themselves. The factors involved may be *prenatal* (before birth), *perinatal* (during the birth process), or *postnatal* (after birth). There are two general groups of causes that play a role before birth: genetic factors and factors outside the fetus. Genetic defects in one or both parents may be transmitted to a child. These defects may not be evident in the parents, and in some cases several children in the family may also carry the defective genetic trait without having the disability themselves (recessive genes). For instance, muscular dystrophy, a hereditary disorder rarely found in females, is generally caused by a sex-linked recessive gene transmitted through unaffected mothers to their sons. Hemophilia is also a sex-linked genetic disorder passed from an unaffected mother to her son.

While developing in the womb, the fetus may be adversely affected by external influences called teratogens. A mother's inadequate prenatal medical care and diet, smoking, excessive consumption of alcoholic beverages, or use of drugs such as cocaine, PCP, marijuana, or heroin during pregnancy are potentially harmful to the fetus and may result in physical disability for the child. Another cause of physical disability is prenatal trauma, injury to the fetus resulting from injury to the mother, as might occur in a serious fall (Crain, 1984).

The perinatal period begins with the first labor pain and ends with the infant's first normal breath. It is a time during which there is great risk of trauma or anoxia (lack of oxygen). If a child is not in the appropriate position for delivery, attempts to change the position can cause physical impairments. In addition, any obstruction of the oxygen supply to the fetus—for instance, strangulation by the umbilical cord—can result in physical disabilities. Cerebral palsy is often the result of a severe reduction in the oxygen supply to the fetus during the birth process (Batshaw & Perret, 1986; Fraser, Hensinger, & Phelps, 1990).

Postnatal time periods technically encompass the neonatal period (1st to 28th day), infancy (28th day to 1 year), early childhood (first 2 years), and childhood (after 2 years), as well as adolescent and adult problems. More commonly, "postnatal" refers to the period from birth to 2 years. Physical impairments can result from accidents, the most common being bicycle and car accidents. Accident-related spinal cord and head injuries are frequent postnatal, or acquired, causes of lasting physical impairment. Some accidents result in only temporary disablement. Infection is another primary cause of postnatal physical and health impairment; bacterial and viral infections that attack the central nervous system can result in permanent damage. Infantile encephalitis, a viral inflammation of the brain, can cause muscular weakness. Meningitis (inflammation of the membrane covering the brain and spinal cord) is caused by microorganisms and can result in symptoms similar to those of cerebral palsy. These two infections may occur any time, but they most often occur in the first 2 years of life.

CHARACTERISTICS   This section describes some common physical disabilities found in children and adolescents. We also identify some syndromes and birth defects that warrant consideration on the part of educators, even though they occur infrequently.

Orthopedic and Muscular Impairments

Cerebral Palsy.   This condition accounts for the largest percentage of students with physical impairments. Alfonso, whom you met at the beginning of this chapter, has cerebral palsy. It involves motor impairments that affect the coordination of muscle action and ability to maintain normal postures and balance. Cerebral palsy is nonprogressive, that is, the condition does not worsen. However, the potential for skill development is lost without intervention. Although typically resulting from damage to the brain during the birth process, cerebral palsy can also result from trauma during the prenatal development or after birth. Prematurity, difficult labor, lack of oxygen at birth, and childhood trauma are problems that increase the risk for cerebral palsy (Blackburn, 1987; Bobath, 1980; Holm, 1982).

The amount of physical ability of an individual with cerebral palsy varies greatly. Some youngsters have only slight fine motor coordination problems, some walk with extreme difficulty, and others depend on wheelchairs for mobility (Campbell, 1989).

There are two ways of classifying cerebral palsy: one is based on the limbs affected and the other on the nature of the abnormal movement (Alexander & Bauer, 1988; Bleck, 1982a). The following terms reflect the affected limbs (topography):

- *monoplegia*—one limb
- *paraplegia*—both lower limbs
- *hemiplegia*—both limbs on the same side
- *diplegia*—all four limbs with the greater disability in the legs
- *quadriplegia*—all four limbs with approximately equal disability

Classification based on the nature of abnormal movement uses any of these categories (Bleck, 1982a; Bobath, 1980; Inge, 1987; Thompson, Rubin, & Bilenker, 1983):

1. *Spasticity.* Muscle tone is increased (hypertonia), and muscles are tight and overactive. Unable to contract normally, they resist movement, which is slow and jerky if it occurs at all. Rigidity is a severe form of hypertonia.
2. *Dyskinesia.* Fluctuating muscle tone causes uncontrolled and irregular movement patterns. Flailing limbs may be difficult to control even for gross movements. The severity of the abnormal movement increases when the individuals are excited or under stress or when they try to perform particular movement or skills.
3. *Ataxia.* Lack of coordination is related to poor control of balance and movement. It is difficult to maintain upright posture and to control balance reactions.
4. *Mixed.* The movements described here commonly occur in combination.

Cerebral palsy often affects maturation of the reflexes. The result is inhibition of normal movement, which can interfere with walking, eating, and manipulation of objects (Inge, 1987).

A number of secondary disabilities are associated with cerebral palsy, including sensory impairments, speech difficulties, oral/dental impairments, and behavioral and social-emotional problems. Learning disabilities are common as well. However, there is considerable confusion as to the type and extent of secondary problems because deprivation of experience arising from the disability makes valid assessment difficult (Thompson, Rubin, & Bilenker, 1983).

Muscular Dystrophy.   In muscular dystrophy the muscles suffer from loss of protein. Muscle tissue is gradually replaced by fatty and other tissue until the voluntary muscle system becomes virtually useless. Although muscular dystrophy has several adult forms, in childhood it usually appears in the Duchenne, or pseudohypertrophic, form. This form of the disability is typically evident by the time a child is 3 years old and causes progressive weakness of the skeletal muscles, often in conjunction with a seeming overdevelopment (pseudohypertrophy) of the calf muscles. Initial symptoms may include difficulty in running or climbing stairs; later the child becomes unable to maintain balance even on a level surface. A characteristic waddling gait, giving the impression of awkwardness or slowness, usually appears before muscle weakness becomes so severe that the child needs to use a wheelchair. Weakness in the upper extremities may appear with the awkward gait or somewhat later (Chutorian & Engel, 1982; Lyle & Obringer, 1983).

Individuals with muscular dystrophy tire easily. Even those who can still walk may need wheelchairs for extended trips. With their weakened muscles these individuals fall easily and may have trouble performing simple tasks, such as opening doors. Therapy delays the development of muscle contractures (shortening of muscles), but the disease progresses fairly rapidly toward death, usually in the late teens or early adult years. As their disease progresses, most students with muscular dystrophy require increased physical assistance and adaptations to be successful with schoolwork (Bigge, 1991).

Spina Bifida.   Spina bifida literally means "cleft spine." The three forms of this birth defect are *meningocele, encephalocele,* and *myelomeningocele* depending on the location and extent of the birth defect. A portion of the spinal cord is not enclosed by the vertebral arches. The cord itself protrudes where the vertebrae fail to enclose it, necessitating surgical intervention within the first few days of life. In myelomeningocele, the most complex and common form of the disability, damage to the nerve roots results in a neurological disorder and related deformities. Neurological impairment increases with the degree of malformation of the spinal cord, varying from minor sensory and/or motor loss to paraplegia with incontinence (lack of bladder control). Urinary tract disorders, orthopedic deformities, and problems related to skin sensitivity may also be involved. In many children a blockage causes fluid to accumulate in the brain. This condition, referred to as hydrocephalus, can cause mental retardation if not corrected by surgical implantation of a shunt. Children whose hydrocephalus is not treated are also at risk for language deficiencies, particularly in the area of semantics and pragmatics (Byrne, Abbeduto, & Brooks, 1990). Children with spina bifida require considerable medical attention, often including physical therapy to assist them to develop walking, usually with braces and crutches, and/or to become skilled wheelchair users (Bleck, 1982b; Williamson, 1987).

Spinal Cord Injury.   Injury to the spinal cord usually occurs from trauma such as automobile, diving, or motorcycle accidents. The level of injury determines the extent of paralysis, because different portions of the spinal cord control different areas of bodily sensation and movement. Disability may range from weakness in one extremity to complete paralysis (Jubala & Brenes, 1988). Spinal cord injuries have ramifications beyond the limitations they place on mobility. Potential problem areas include urinary tract infections, respiratory infections, decubitus ulcers (pressure sores) that occur when lack of movement slows circulation, and muscle contractures. Although better medical management has resulted in improved survival rates for persons with spinal cord injuries, rehabilitation procedures rarely result in total return of lost function (DeVivo, Rutt, Black, Go, & Stover, 1992). Emotional problems may develop, requiring psychological intervention. Adaptive aids help the child recover various functions—for example, wheelchairs for mobility, hand controls for driving, electric typewriters for writing, buttonhooks for dressing, and utensils with large handles for eating. Another procedure is to develop alternate muscle groups to perform activities normally done by the nonfunctioning muscles.

Spinal Muscular Atrophy.   Spinal muscular atrophy is a hereditary, progressive disorder that causes muscular wasting. It has a variable course, ranging from slow and chronic to rapid, ending in early death. Usually, atrophy first affects the legs and then progresses to the muscles of the shoulder girdle, upper arms, and neck. Often when individuals with the slower form lose their physical independence, they experience a renewal of previously felt feelings of resentment and frustration (Koehler, 1982).

Osteogenesis Imperfecta. Defective development in the quantity and quality of bone causes osteogenesis imperfecta, sometimes called "brittle bones." Bones are imperfectly formed and do not grow normally in length and thickness. Consequently, they are so fragile that even simple activities such as the ordinary stresses of walking or position changes may cause fractures. Dwarfism and dental defects are commonly associated secondary disabilities. Of particular concern to teachers is the students' potential for development of a severe hearing impairment due to damage to the bones of the middle ear. Academic ability is not affected; however, absence due to hospitalization for treatment of multiple fractures may affect students' performance (Molnar, 1983).

Limb Deficiency. Whether congenital or acquired, limb deficiency (the absence of one or more limbs) may present a major obstacle to physical activity and normal functioning. The extent of the limb deficiency (level of functional loss) affects physical ability. The nature or severity of associated psychological problems depends on the age of onset, severity of the deficiency, and attitudes of parents and other significant people who work with the child. Children may choose to use a prosthetic device (artificial limb), rely on the remaining portion of the limb, or develop compensating abilities in the remaining limbs (e.g., foot skills). Child and parent perceptions of the functional value of the artificial limb are major considerations in this decision. Parent participation in rehabilitation and early intervention processes are crucial to help the child achieve maximum functioning, whether with a prosthetic device or not (Marquardt, 1983). Motivation may be a primary factor in the extent to which a child learns to use a prosthetic device. During the teenage years, preoccupation with body image may lead to rejection of the prosthesis (Wright & Nicholas, 1988). For adolescents and adults who suffer a limb amputation, rehabilitation that focuses on acceptable and appropriate alternative recreation and daily living skills assists in the adjustment process (Nissen & Newman, 1992).

Juvenile Rheumatoid Arthritis. Juvenile rheumatoid arthritis is a chronic, painful, inflammatory disease of the joints and the tissue around them. It has many forms, all of which usually develop in early childhood. Fever spikes (quick, abnormal, extreme increases in temperature), rash, and morning stiffness are characteristic symptoms that often cause absence from school. Because sitting for long periods of time may cause the joints to "gel," children with this disease need freedom to move about at home and in school. Casts, splints, braces, and a variety of assistive devices may be necessary as medical intervention and/or to facilitate independent functioning. Many children show improvement and remission of major symptoms by the age of 18. Residual effects are individualized and vary greatly (Hanson, 1983).

The supportive attitude of friends, family, and teachers is crucial in adjusting to an artificial limb.

Health Impairments

The physical impairments described above are usually visible; the physical problems that we refer to as health impairments are less visible. This lack of visibility causes problems for persons with these disabilities because other people may not understand that their unique behavior patterns are a result of, or an adaptation to, a disability. In addition, the "invisibility" of many health impairments may allow the individual to disguise the condition until the onset of symptoms is life threatening (Best, 1991).

Asthma.   Asthma is the most common childhood pulmonary disease. Characterized by inflammation and resultant blockage of the airways, attacks are triggered by allergens, infections, irritants, exercise, and emotional responses. Symptoms vary widely; treatment includes identification of provoking factors (e.g., pets, chalk dust, certain foods), environmental controls, and appropriate medications. An individual's participation in physical education may be limited if exercise is a major cause of asthma attacks. Asthma is a disorder whose origin is physical, not psychological. Methods of coping include compliance with medication regimens and self-management during episodes, rather than seeking a psychological cure (Creer, Marion, & Harm, 1988). Absence from school may cause problems with peer relations and affect academic performance.

Allergies. Allergies are physical reactions resulting from exposure to specific allergens. These reactions may include coughing, sneezing, hives, inflammation of the eye area, and life-threatening anaphylactic shock. Allergies are caused by pollen, food reactions, animal hair or fur, insect sensitivity, dust, or other irritants. As with asthma, treatment includes removal of the offending source and medical intervention. Although not usually as serious as an asthma attack, the presence of allergy should be noted.

Epilepsy. Epilepsy is not a specific disease, but a symptom of underlying brain abnormality. It is manifested in seizures that may or may not be associated with another physical problem, such as cerebral palsy or a brain tumor. There are several types of seizures. All are caused by abnormal, excessive electrical brain function resulting from a group of conditions that overstimulate the brain's nerve cells (Hermann, Desai, & Whitman, 1988). However, the alteration in brain function associated with seizures does not imply learning problems or mental retardation. Academic ability varies among individuals with epilepsy as it does among persons who are not disabled. Not all seizures are readily visible; only some involve a change in state of consciousness or obvious physical movement. Two categories of seizures have been identified by the International League against Epilepsy: generalized and partial (Low, 1982).

1. *Generalized seizures* include grand mal, petit mal, myoclonic, and akinetic seizures. All usually occur without warning and involve a loss of consciousness. The most striking—grand mal—involves extraneous, uncontrolled movement of all portions of the body symmetrically (equally on both sides). Salivation increases, and bladder and bowel control may be lost. Grand mal seizures typically last only a minute or two, after which the individual may sleep for hours. Petit mal seizures often go unnoticed. Sometimes the only clue that there has been a momentary loss of consciousness may be a slight disorientation in the midst of an activity—for example, a word missed during a dictation assignment. Myoclonic seizures are characterized by sudden, brief, involuntary muscular contractions that may or may not be symmetrical and recurring. The myoclonic jerk—a quick upward movement of the arms and bending of the trunk of the body (flexion)—can cause an individual to fall from a chair. Akinetic seizures are characterized by a sudden loss of muscle tone and posture control and sudden dropping to the ground. Individuals have no ability to break their fall, and unless they wear a protective helmet at all times, the danger of head injury is great.
2. *Partial seizures* may affect both motor function and behavior. They occur in many patterns, ranging from brief loss of consciousness to extended periods of purposeless activity. During a psychomotor seizure, individuals may appear to be conscious when, in fact, they are not at all aware of their abnormal behavior—even, for example, if they are running around the room (Jacobs, 1983; Low, 1982).

Controversy exists about appropriate medical intervention for epilepsy. Although mental retardation is not necessarily associated with epilepsy, the use of medication can lead to problems with academic performance. Teachers should monitor changes in student performance and/or behavior (e.g., drowsiness, inattentiveness) and report these to medical personnel for possible reevaluation of students' medication programs. Teachers must also be aware of the proper steps to take in the event that a student experiences a seizure at school.

Juvenile Diabetes Mellitus.   Often hereditary, juvenile diabetes mellitus is a metabolic disorder characterized by the body's inability to use sugars and starches (carbohydrates) to create energy needed for normal functioning. The pancreas does not make enough insulin, causing the glucose level in the blood to rise because glucose cannot get into the cells without insulin. Without glucose in the cells, the body has no energy and cannot function (Christiansen & Hintz, 1982).

Youngsters with this disorder must take insulin. Teachers should be alert for two different types of reactions. Hypoglycemia occurs when individuals have too much insulin in their systems. It is indicated by rapid onset of headaches, nausea, vomiting, palpitations, irritability, shallow breathing, and/or cold, moist skin. The recommended treatment is to give orange juice, a candy bar, a sugar cube, or other sugar on which the insulin can act. Symptoms of ketoacidosis, the condition that results from an inadequate supply of insulin, are gradual onset of fatigue, increased water consumption, frequent urination, excessive hunger, deep breathing, and/or warm, dry skin. The treatment, of course, is to give insulin (Christiansen & Hintz, 1982).

Children can be taught at a relatively young age to monitor their insulin levels. Regularity in diet and exercise patterns is crucial to maintenance of insulin balance. Generally, there will be no impact on classroom functioning unless there is significant change in routine related to physical exercise or excessive amounts of foods containing sugar.

Hemophilia.   Hemophilia typically appears in males and is characterized by poor blood clotting. Although massive blood loss due to external injury is very dangerous, internal hemorrhaging is a more common and most difficult problem for hemophiliacs. Bumps that would merely cause bruising in the normal child may cause massive internal bleeding in an individual with hemophilia. Blood may pour into joints, destroying surrounding tissue, and causing temporary immobility and pain and possibly permanent disability from joint degeneration. Treatment once involved massive transfusions of whole blood, but modern technology has isolated Factor VIII and Factor IX (clotting factors), which are missing in hemophiliacs. These factors are prepared in a substance called cryoprecipitate, which may be given when needed (Corrigan & Damiano, 1983).

Although learning problems are not directly related to hemophilia, frequent short absences from school because of internal bleeding may retard a student's academic progress. Participation in physical activity and noncontact sports should be encouraged to facilitate healthy physical development (Hilgartner, 1990).

Cystic Fibrosis.   A recessive hereditary disorder found more often in Caucasians, cystic fibrosis is characterized by abnormal mucus secretion by all secreting glands except those that secrete into the bloodstream. The disease begins in the pancreas and soon impacts the normal functioning of the intestine. There is an abnormally high salt level in the sweat of children with cystic fibrosis. Respiratory symptoms—including a dry, nonproductive cough; susceptibility to acute infection; and bronchial obstruction by abnormal mucus secretions—are a major problem. Cystic fibrosis may not be obvious for several months after birth, or it may cause intestinal problems in a newborn child. Recent medical advances have improved what was once a poor prognosis. Early diagnosis may extend life expectancy into adulthood. Treatment may include taking antibiotics, replacing deficient pancreatic enzymes, modifying diet, and breathing exercises (Mangos, 1983).

Children with cystic fibrosis are encouraged to cough to loosen the thick coating on their bronchial passages. In addition, diet, toileting, and medication needs may require allowances to be made for the student during the school day. Participation in physical activity should be encouraged as much as possible. Learning potential is not directly affected by the disease, although psychological adjustment may periodically interrupt attention to academic performance (Harvey, 1982).

Sickle Cell Anemia. Sickle cell anemia is a hereditary disorder more prevalent among, but not limited to, African-Americans. It is a blood condition in which abnormal hemoglobin in the red blood cell is distorted into a rigid, sickle (crescent) shape to create a cell that does not pass easily through blood vessels. As a result, blood supply to some tissues may be blocked (vaso-occlusive episode), causing severe pains in the abdomen, legs, and arms; swollen joints; fatigue; and high fever. Blockage of blood supply can cause a stroke or damage tissues and result in degeneration of joints and related orthopedic problems, including paralysis. Other outcomes can include headache, convulsions, and possible progressive renal (kidney) damage. The symptoms are chronic and recur at irregular intervals. They tend to be more likely in situations of emotional stress, strenuous exercise, chilling, or infection. Although learning potential is not directly affected by sickle cell anemia, frequent absence from school may affect a student's academic performance (Corrigan & Damiano, 1983).

Cardiac (Heart) Conditions. Cardiac conditions may be either congenital or acquired. If acquired, they usually result from some type of infectious disease, such as rheumatic fever. Some congenital heart defects are not detected until later in childhood, making their impact essentially the same as that of an acquired disability. Most students with cardiac problems can attend regular schools and need only minor restrictions on physical activity, depending on the severity of the condition. Inappropriate severe limitations on physical activity can reduce motivation to perform academically.

Cancer. The causes and cures of the uncontrolled irregular cell growth known as cancer are still largely unknown. In children, leukemia (a disease in the blood-forming organs) and tumors of the eye, brain, bone, and kidneys are the most common forms. The prognosis depends on the type of cancer and the time of intervention. Treatment may involve radiation, chemotherapy, and/or surgery. Emotional problems, fatigue, extreme weight loss or gain, nausea, susceptibility to upper respiratory infection, headaches, and baldness are possible side effects of the disease or treatment (Link, 1982). Physical discomfort, irritability, and hospitalization may mean lost time from school or other instructional programs. The teacher's understanding of the progress of the disease and the resultant periods of emotional difficulty will help the child continue to participate in school and interact with peers. Focus should be on qualitative aspects of life, not on negative aspects of death.

AIDS.   AIDS (acquired immune deficiency syndrome) is a term that was defined in 1982 by the Centers for Disease Control (Carr & Gee, 1986). AIDS is the result of infection with HIV (human immune deficiency virus), which attacks and weakens the body's immune system. Transmission occurs via blood-to-blood contact, including various sexual practices, intravenous drug use, blood transfusions, and transmission to babies by infected mothers before or during birth (U.S. Department of Health and Human Services, 1988). The AIDS virus is not spread by insects, kissing, tears, or casual contact (U.S. Department of Labor/Department of Health and Human Services, 1987). There is no known cure. Death occurs, not from the virus itself, but from various opportunistic infections and other conditions. Although there are fewer cases of AIDS in children than in adults, the incidence of AIDS in children now approximates that of Down syndrome and myelomeningocele in the general population (Anderson, Hinojosa, Bedell, & Kaplan, 1990). Therefore, accommodation for the physical and psychosocial welfare of these children in school cannot be ignored (McInerney, 1989).

Although children with AIDS are highly susceptible to colds and infections, they have periods of good health and should therefore be encouraged to participate as fully as possible in school activities. Certain measures should be taken by those who provide care to these students, including correct hand washing, wearing disposable gloves when handling bodily secretions, and cleaning soiled surfaces with a solution of bleach and water. Because these precautions constitute good hygiene for anyone who requires physical care, their universal adoption allows protection for care providers while preserving the privacy of the student with AIDS.

Other Syndromes and Conditions

We have noted here only some of the most common or recently identified physical and health impairments found in children and adolescents. Our list is not comprehensive; there are many syndromes and conditions that occur infrequently but nonetheless warrant major consideration in educational programming. Two conditions—autism and traumatic brain injury—are now recognized as separate disability categories (P.L. 101–119). Earlier classification of autism as a health impairment was based on research reflecting biochemical etiology. Research with persons who have suffered traumatic brain injury (TBI) suggests that many who survive severe trauma have lasting impairments in intellect, language, visual-motor skills, and motor speed (Jaffe, Fay, Polissar, Martin, Shurtleff, Rivara, & Winn, 1992). Even children with mild TBI show subtle disturbances in memory and motor skills. Educational service delivery to children with autism or TBI should continue to reflect least restrictive, most appropriate considerations (Mira, Tucker, & Tyler, 1992).

ASSESSMENT

Self-help, daily living, academic, social, and personal skills all have a role in making independence possible for students with physical or health impairments. The greatest challenge for educators lies in finding ways to help these individuals achieve optimum, age-appropriate independence. Assessment is vital to this process.

The Assessment Team

Medical personnel are frequently the first people involved in diagnosis and follow-up assessments of children with physical and health impairments. Their role is to determine the child's physical limitations and needs and explain them to parents and educational professionals. Physicians evaluate and then prescribe needed medication, surgery, special therapy, or equipment (e.g., catheters and wheelchairs). Medical personnel, with the cooperation of teachers, also assess the effects of medication on students.

Traditionally, the role of the physical therapist (PT) has been to evaluate the individual's quality of movement and use special techniques to alter motor patterns. The role of the occupational therapist (OT) overlaps and complements that of physical therapists (Bleck, 1982a). Occupational therapists focus on upper-body rehabilitation, fine motor activities, and activities of daily living (ADL). Both types of therapists evaluate positioning for various school activities and ADL. They assess students' physical characteristics and match them with adaptive equipment and devices. Ideally, therapy activities should be incorporated into classroom activities to strengthen the transdisciplinary effort (Holvoet & Helmstetter, 1989). The roles of therapists are varied and continually changing. They are aided by rehabilitation engineers, who recommend and construct special mobility and seating systems and design controls for devices such as tape recorders and wheelchairs (Jewell, 1989). The school nurse is a critical member of the transdisciplinary team, attending to students' physical health care needs and contributing to their successful school experience.

Special education teachers and resource personnel provide methods and materials for systematic and ongoing assessment. They also demonstrate how learning environments and teaching techniques can be adapted to individual needs, suggesting such strategies as alternatives to handwriting for students with severe dexterity problems or reconfiguring or repositioning materials for students with a limited range of motion. School principals and classroom teachers also have important perspectives to share.

In addition, parental input is crucial to the assessment process. Parents provide information regarding (1) a student's particular response mode; (2) typical or most adaptive patterns of interaction; (3) communication idiosyncrasies; and (4) resources for access, mobility, and independence training.

Special Emphases

Continual assessment of self-help skills and ADL—including feeding, dressing, maintaining personal hygiene, and managing special health needs—is crucial to the developing child. Determination of specialized techniques for accurate educational assessment are also important. To help develop an appropriate individualized program, assessment should focus on certain major areas.

Performance of Self-Help Skills.

What self-help skills a student has, what skills should be acquired, and what assistance is needed when certain self-help skills cannot be performed independently are vital pieces of information for planning instruction. What a student can currently do and is expected to do in the future in taking responsibility for special health needs is especially important. Most often overlooked is assessment of how well individuals with disabilities can indicate to others how, when, and where help is needed. Most important is to improve each child's current functioning and to plan for improvement in future environments (Orelove & Sobsey, 1987).

Extent of Mobility.

Those involved in educating students with physical impairments need to know the extent of students' mobility, how they move from place to place, and what assistance they might require. Although it is reasonable to assume that walking would be the preferred way to ambulate, the energy expended in walking may have a negative effect on school performance due to fatigue (Franks, Palisano, & Darbee, 1991; O'Connell, Barnhart, & Park, 1992).

Accommodations Required for Physical Differences.

A teacher must know what adaptations or assistance will facilitate a student's participation in educational and leisure activities; what positions, postures, and other physical behavior should be encouraged or discouraged; and what special procedures (medical or emergency) may be necessary (Hulme, Gallacher, Walsh, Nielson, & Waldron, 1987; Hulme, Bain, Hardin, McKinnon, & Waldron, 1989). This information is provided by the child's physical therapist, occupational therapist, and parents. Particularly important is a clear understanding of the physical support necessary for children with specialized health care needs.

Level, Clarity, and Speed of Communication.

Communication skills of individuals with physical and health impairment range from just a few words to body movements or signals, to the use of communication boards or electronic communication devices or the use of typing or handwriting, to highly intelligible speech. For students with unintelligible speech or illegible handwriting, assessment determines discrepancies between levels of understanding and expressive ability. Five questions need to be answered:

1. In what ways and how clearly can the student communicate with (a) intelligible speech, (b) gesture language, (c) consistent body movement or signals for yes and no, (d) pointing at symbols on a communication board, (e) handwriting, and (f) typing and using an electronic communication device?
2. Does the student need extended time to respond?
3. What is the discrepancy between communication skills required to participate in the student's environment and the student's actual skills?
4. How can the student's understanding and skill levels be assessed?
5. How can the student mark answers and record ideas?

Liz is able to indicate to her classmates how to help her set up her work station.

Strategies and Special Devices to Facilitate Learning.   It is essential to determine (1) what arrangements would enable the student to manage classroom equipment, such as pencils, papers, and books; (2) what behavior management techniques are needed; (3) how the student learns most quickly, through hearing or seeing, for instance; (4) how the student can conserve energy at school; (5) what special procedures or materials would aid learning; and (6) what the top-priority objectives are for learning outcomes.

Academic Achievement.   Academic assessment provides information about a student's strengths and weaknesses in different curriculum areas. Assessment information should also provide information about instructional strategies to help the student learn.

- How does the student compare to others his or her age on grade-level proficiency tests?
- What can the student do (and not do) in each basic academic area?
- What is the student's potential in each academic and extracurricular subject studied at his or her grade level?

Assessment techniques used with students who are not disabled can be used with some students with physical impairments, although the techniques may need to use adapted equipment, such as special pencil holders. In some situations, students are given the same test content but in a different mode, perhaps on a tape instead of in print. Some students with disabilities need to use alternative methods to respond to test items: they may type or tell their answers to a scribe, look at one of four choices, or kick when they hear their choice.

Assessment of physical and communicative self-sufficiency is important. Functional skills are measured to determine what the student needs to learn to be independent. If a student is not able to complete functional skills independently, the assessment process should evaluate the student's ability to communicate the need for assistance.

Special Help Required.   Assessment also indicates what specialists are needed to work with a student or consult with the teacher and how their efforts can best be coordinated. It is imperative that assessment of the student's environment in school, at home, and in the community, and both at the present time and in the future, be addressed. The teacher's primary responsibility is to "note what environment it is and what discrepancies are present between skills required by the environment and skills acquired" (Mills & Higgins, 1984, p. 37).

Analyzing and defining components of those discrepancies reflect a major application of an assessment technique called *task analysis*. Task analysis is one of the most frequently used assessment methods with students with physical disabilities (Bigge, 1991). Task analysis is "slicing" a skill in teachable steps. It is the process of isolating sequences needed to perform a skill and describing the component steps toward mastery of the skill. It can be used to analyze performance in every area of the curriculum, as well as to prepare students to interact in different kinds of daily life situations. After initial assessment, task analysis continues to be of value as an instructional strategy.

Age-Level Distinctions

Early Childhood.   Observations of children with physical and health impairments in routine activities is one of the most effective assessment procedures. Observers record how children communicate their desires and what kinds of behaviors they respond to. Do they ignore someone until the person moves directly in front of them? Do they respond to simple verbal requests and warnings? Do they find some way to move themselves? What prompts them to move and to participate in an activity? Interviews with parents can provide additional helpful information.

School Age.   Academic achievement is a major assessment focus for school-age students following a regular or modified education curriculum. The purpose of this assessment is to determine the relative effectiveness of alternative methods of doing schoolwork and taking tests, perhaps using standard keyboards on typewriters and computers, perhaps finding other alternatives for students who cannot use keyboards. Students with severe problems of physical dexterity may try different styles of switches and eventually select one that allows them to stop an electrically controlled scanner on desired letters, pictures, or words on a grid (Angelo, 1992).

Secondary/Transition.   Parents frequently become more intensely interested in assessment at the secondary level. Each student's Individualized Educational Plan (IEP) must contain a statement of transition services that will be provided to help students to prepare for adult life outside of school, no later than age 16. The student's transition plan identifies the linkages among agencies and the responsibilities of each prior to the student's leaving school. Vocational rehabilitation personnel from state departments of rehabilitation and other agencies become team members. Potential employers and supervisors of work/study programs may provide samples of their companies products and give students opportunities to try jobs.

INTERVENTION

Physical and educational programming are the two areas in which intervention usually begins for children with confirmed or suspected physical or health impairments. (See the Model Program box for a description of a comprehensive program for students with physical and health impairments.)

Physical Management and Intervention

From the moment that it is suspected or detected that an individual has a physical problem, intervention is crucial. Initial concerns include positioning and seating, mobility, accessibility, and special equipment.

Positioning and Seating. Sitting may be difficult for a child with physical disabilities. Positions should be found that will "enable him to use his hands to the best advantage, that will be easiest for eye-hand coordination and will present the least difficulties for balance" (Finnie, 1975, p. 229). Several seating positions—including cross-legged sitting, side sitting, and regular chair sitting—provide security and comfort, reinforce proper balance and posture, and counteract uncontrollable movements. Straps and other supports are sometimes provided to improve posture. Medical personnel and therapists should be asked to recommend positions for each child that aid in the development of desired posture and movements or discourage undesirable ones.

Positioning a child properly at a table or desk is another important consideration. Some students use trays attached to their wheelchairs and do not need any other work surface. When students do need some kind of table to work on, the height of the tabletop should permit the student to rest the elbows on it comfortably and view materials on it easily. Tabletop height may also be used as a form of management: the height of the tabletop can be adjusted to encourage more functional body positions. For example, it might be appropriate to raise a desk so that a student who is a wheelchair user can roll under it for ready access of materials. For some who use wheelchairs or other devices that place them in a seated position high relative to the work surface, a podium can be placed in such a way as to bring materials close for easy viewing without compromising good posture.

Whether students use a wheelchair tray or some other surface, they should be able to obtain and put away their books and materials. Thus, placement of these objects needs to accommodate the student's range of arm motion, strength, and manipulative skills. If the student does not have a desk with usable drawers and compartments, organizers such as those used in offices may serve the purpose.

Mobility. A priority for individuals with disabilities is to move from place to place as independently as possible. Brown and Gordon (1987) note that the activity of young children provides the context for their social development. Through physical activities children learn skills and evaluate situations. When mobility is affected by impairment, children may fail to develop competencies necessary to function in the home, community, and society. Medical personnel and therapists can recommend appropriate procedures to help a child achieve independent mobility without negatively affecting the child's physical functions. Young children who cannot walk alone are often taught to roll, crawl, or use crutches, walkers, or wheelchairs. For those who have not achieved even this level of mobility, it will be necessary for the teacher or other personnel to assist in lifting, carrying, or transferring the student. Individuals who help must be aware of the proper techniques (see Finnie, 1975, and Ward, 1984, for a complete explanation of safe and appropriate procedures).

Architectural Accessibility.   The Americans with Disabilities Act (ADA) of 1990 mandates access to public services for those with disabilities, including those operated by private entities (Kalscher, 1991; Reed, 1991). Ramps enable children in wheelchairs or on crutches to enter buildings easily. Toilet facilities, play areas, and drinking fountains must be located so that individuals with physical limitations can have access to them. Grab bars or support railings should be installed beside drinking fountains, in toilet stalls, and near chalkboard sections.

    In the classroom, furniture may be removed to make room for wheelchairs. Footrests and adjustable, swivel seats may be required. Special height-adjustable tables and cut-out or stand-up tables can provide additional help for students with special problems in sitting or standing. Special support devices can facilitate participation in activities that require sitting on the floor.

Special Equipment and Adaptations.   As we have already noted, adaptive devices can improve an individual's ability to function. These range from artificial

With his specially adapted desktop, this student can work comfortably with his peers.

limbs, wheelchairs, and crutches to typewriters and feeding, dressing, and toileting aids. The sooner that needed devices are provided, the greater the child's chance to develop some measure of independence and self-respect. Training with these aids is usually necessary. Teachers, therapists, and parents should all know how to help the individual who is disabled with the devices and should consult with each other regularly on the student's progress and changing needs.

Students should be taught early to manage common classroom materials, such as pencils and papers. They may, however, need to use adapted materials—special tabletops, clipboards, cups with handles, or special pencil holders—to prevent common inconveniences, such as dropping of pencils and other tools, slipping or torn and wrinkled papers, and illegible writing (see Figures 8–1 through 8–3). Solutions can often be simple and inexpensive; the challenge is to find them.

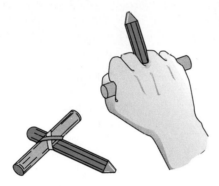

Crayon holder to accommodate grasp

Large crayon made from melted smaller crayons and attached to hand

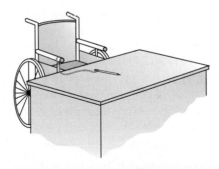

Elastic attached to writing utensil and to desk or wheelchair

Partial glove with pencil holder

Figure 8–1
Sample solutions for dropping.

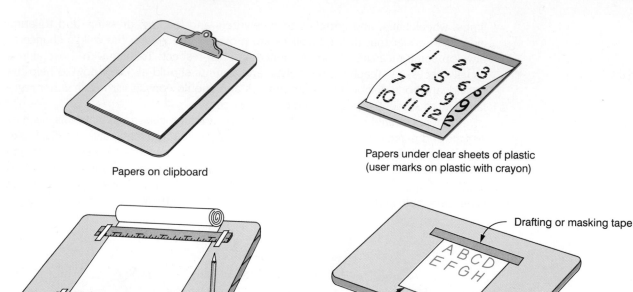

Papers on clipboard

Papers under clear sheets of plastic
(user marks on plastic with crayon)

Rulers taped over continuous roll of paper

Drafting or masking tape

Desk top

Heavyweight paper

Figure 8–2
Sample solutions for slipping, tearing, and wrinkling.

Provision for Individuals with Multiple Disabilities. Individuals with physical impairments often have one or more associated disabilities. A person with cerebral palsy, for example, may have problems related to learning, vision, hearing, speech, emotional adjustment, perceptual-motor involvement, or mental development (Hall, 1984; Hart, 1988). Any combination of disabilities places complex demands on intervention. Specialists and parents must work as a team to decide how best to help each student.

Some youngsters who have the type of cerebral palsy that causes excessive involuntary movements and who also have a severe visual disability may not obtain the maximum benefit from wearing glasses because they are unable to hold their heads still to focus carefully. Ordinarily, children who cannot read print because of visual impairment learn to depend on braille. However, children with cerebral palsy may not be able to read braille because they cannot control the gross movement of their hands or because they lack fine sensory discrimination in their fingertips. In addition, these children have difficulties using hearing aids because their uncoordinated movements cause an excess noise that is amplified by hearing aids.

Health and Disability Management. In addition to managing the students' physical environment, teachers oversee the health needs of their students with disabilities. They must understand the characteristics of various diseases and disabilities and the precise care necessary to deal with them. For example, teachers should be aware that students with muscular dystrophy and cardiac conditions tire easily. Thus, they should encourage those students to take wheelchairs when they visit potential

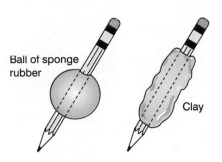

Ball of sponge rubber

Clay

Tape recorder with paddle extensions

Pencils with large shafts

Head-mounted wand for writing or typing

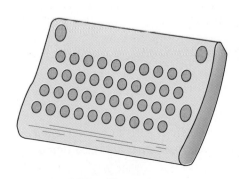

Typewriter with a commercial
or homemade key guard

Agree

Disagree

I should have an allowance.

I need a haircut.

Masking tape

Manipulative activities to
replace writing

Figure 8—3
Sample solutions for illegible writing.

job sites or go to school events, even though students may ordinarily walk around the classroom. They should also be aware that the medical aspects of cystic fibrosis necessitate students' frequent coughing and trips to the bathroom and therefore should encourage these behaviors rather than view them as interruptions.

Because some disabling conditions change—either worsen or improve—teachers have a responsibility to help students and families maintain close contact with medical personnel. For example, they should record and report information on behavior changes that seem related to changes in medication to help physicians find and maintain proper levels of medication to control seizures. Students with spina bifida need instruction on personal hygiene and must be helped to develop awareness of increased odor, which can indicate infection related to bladder control problems.

The reaction of others to students with physical disabilities can be of critical importance, from both a physical and a psychological standpoint. The teacher must make sure that everyone involved understands that a student with recent brain trauma from a motorcycle accident can be knocked over easily, sometimes just by brushing against him or her; or that a jovial punch can cause life-threatening internal bleeding to a student with hemophilia.

Specialized Instruction Intervention

Much depends on what students write and say in class. When students cannot write or talk because of movement problems, adaptations to physical arrangements, equipment, and curriculum may be necessary. Teachers can promote optimal participation on the part of students by following certain guidelines:

1. Assume that students with unintelligible speech understand at a higher level than their expressive language indicates; treat and teach them accordingly.
2. Invite students who cannot talk to show you how they communicate *yes*, *no*, I *don't know*, and *maybe* or *perhaps*.
3. Invite students to demonstrate for you all the ways they can let other people know what they want to say.
4. Respond constructively to students who cannot be understood.
   a. "Please repeat that again."
   b. "Please say that another way."
   c. "Show me by gesture."
   d. "Write, type, or point to the letters or words."
5. Repeat what you think students have tried to communicate, in order to clarify.
6. Find ways for students who cannot write or speak intelligibly to demonstrate increasingly difficult thinking skills.
7. Include all students in group learning experiences; phrase some questions so that students with disabilities can give yes/no answers, provide access to pictures and vocabulary boards, and assist students physically when necessary.
8. Give students time to respond.

Use of Task Analysis.   As noted earlier, task analysis is important in assessing physical abilities. It is also important as a strategy for *instructing* students with physical disabilities. Task analysis is based on the assumption that an individual's failure to perform a task is due to a lack of one or more of the skills involved. The performance of a student with a physical impairment may follow one of several patterns: it may be adequate, incomplete, too slow, uncoordinated, or accomplished only through adaptive techniques or devices. Task analysis is necessary in order to decide the instructional orientation to take in each case.

In many instances students with disabling conditions are able to perform tasks adequately because the tasks require only those body parts that are unaffected by disability. Teachers should emphasize such tasks. Some individuals with physical disabilities can proceed through a curriculum with no adaptations in materials or processes. When a student does not complete a task (*incomplete task completion*), we assume that the student is unable to accomplish one or more parts of the task. Figure 8–4 demonstrates one model for studying and assessing tasks tried but not accomplished. The unaccomplished subtask then becomes a temporary target task. Task analysis may suggest one of three instructional approaches:

1. Teach the unperformed skills so that the individual can finish the entire task in a usual manner.
2. Devise an alternative method of performing the uncompleted parts of the task.
3. Select a different task or goal to be accomplished.

Sometimes it is possible to teach parts of a task without revising the method or using special equipment or materials. It might be possible, for instance, to teach the child whose performance is described in Figure 8–4 to use her unreleased crutch as a door stop so that she can grasp her released crutch before the door closes and then move through the doorway.

10. Keep door open while walking through doorway	✗	
9. Grasp released crutch and held door open	✗	Temporary Target Task
8. Released door knob	✔	
7. Pulled door open	✔	
6. Turned knob	✔	
5. Grasped knob	✔	
4. Reached door knob	✔	
3. Released hand from crutch to reach for knob	✔	
2. Stood in position to open the door	✔	
1. Walked to the door	✔	

Figure 8–4

Sample task analysis: Subtasks for walking through a door while using crutches.

Source: From *Teaching Individuals with Physical and Multiple Disabilities* (3rd ed., p. 251) by June L. Bigge, 1991, New York: Macmillan. Copyright 1991 by Macmillan Publishing Company. Reprinted by permission.

Note: Subtask 9 is now the temporary target task.

For students who cannot perform some parts of a task in the usual manner, the teacher must find an alternative method or adaptive equipment. For example, a child who has control of only one hand cannot both grasp and turn the lid of a thermos. Perhaps the child can be taught to hold the thermos between his legs while he unscrews the lid with his one usable hand. If completion of certain tasks is not a realistic goal, the teacher must set new goals. Some people with severe physical disabilities may never be able to feed themselves. An appropriate objective in such cases might be for them to indicate food preferences, to open their mouths voluntarily at the appropriate time, or to signal on a communication board that they need help. When a person is unable to perform a task, a different functional task should be found.

With *slow task completion*, the pace must quicken. Children who require an hour or more to feed themselves an entire meal may be able to eat faster; others may need adaptive equipment—a plate with sides to keep food from falling off the edge or a spoon bent in a certain way to prevent spilling. In some tasks speed can be increased by eliminating unnecessary movements. The 6th-grade student who can complete math problems on a 1st-grade level but takes several minutes to do just one problem is another example of how slowness impedes functioning. Instruction may stress increasing speed, but it might also help the student learn to use a calculator for tasks of daily life, such as shopping and banking.

Uncoordinated task completion occurs when students with physical disabilities complete a task but with such uncoordinated movements that the results are not effective. Involuntary athetoid movements can cause a child to spill most of her milk as she picks up her glass or moves it jerkily to her mouth. When task analysis identifies this problem, instruction should focus on decreasing the effects of uncoordinated movements, with or without adaptations. The child might be taught to use a holder to stabilize the glass on the table and then drink with a straw. Her handwriting might be improved if she sits on the unused hand to keep it from flailing; she can then focus attention on controlling the movement of the writing hand. Another child who might have trouble typing because he keeps hitting two keys at once could be given practice in localizing his stroke.

Adapted task completion may be the goal for individuals who are weak, lack coordination, or have missing or dysfunctional limbs. The goal of instruction then is to devise whatever alternative methods and support are needed. In the case of a young child who is paralyzed and can barely move her arms, removable, ball bearing armrests attached to her wheelchair may help her feed herself. A spoon might be sewn into a mitt that fits over her hand. For individuals with cerebral palsy who cannot use their hands and arms, painting pictures becomes possible with headpointer brushes attached to headbands. The challenge is always to devise additional adaptations that will permit the performance of even more complex tasks.

Psychosocial Development.   Students with physical disabilities may also have problems of social and emotional adjustment. Disabling physical conditions frequently give rise to anxiety, frustration, and resentment. A supportive environment at home and in school can help relieve these feelings (Best, Carpignano, Sirvis, & Bigge, 1991). Psychological support services may be indicated. However, the response to the student's emotional stress must be balanced to avoid the tendency to be overprotective (Drotar, 1981).

Different psychological and emotional problems have been associated with disabilities present at birth and those that are acquired later. Individuals with congenital disabilities may have a sense of difference—of not being like other people—whereas those with acquired disabilities typically experience a sense of loss. In her classic text on the psychosocial aspects of disability, Wright (1983) suggests that numerous social, psychological, and environmental factors affect the psychosocial development of individuals with disabilities. Some individuals develop coping mechanisms and strategies that assist in acceptance and successful adjustment, while others have negative experiences and succumb to the negative impacts of disability, "giving scant attention to the challenge for change and meaningful adaptation" (p. 194).

The emphasis in instruction is always on creating independence. Through independence many psychosocial problems related to self-esteem, self-confidence, and social interaction can be resolved or at least reduced. Even children whose conditions make them medically fragile and susceptible to injury can be taught to take responsibility for self-protection. Physical activities must often be modified, but the student can succeed socially and academically in an otherwise normal educational program. Educational programming should include preparation for sedentary but mentally active vocational training and leisure.

The psychological problems manifested in youngsters with terminal illnesses are more difficult to cope with. The affected students, their peers, families, and teachers all need the perspectives that can be gained from death education programs. These programs can be incorporated into the curriculum so that younger children can learn from stories about the life cycle of plants and animals, and, eventually, of people. Curricula should reflect age-related conceptualizations of death, because the child's knowledge of change, disappearance, and finality must be established before death is fully understood. Children and their families may experience emotions of denial, anger, bargaining, depression, and acceptance toward death (Kübler-Ross, 1969), although not necessarily in easily identified, nonrecurring stages. Teachers must be sensitive toward these emotions and the ways in which families communicate their feelings about death. The teacher's task is to help the student with a terminal illness develop a concept of quality in a limited life span; the value of educational programming can be in its stabilizing effect on the student's life (Rando, 1984). Thus, curricula for students with muscular dystrophy, cystic fibrosis, and terminal cancer should stress development and achievement of attainable short-term goals.

Age-Level Distinctions

Early Childhood. Intervention for young children with physical and health impairments requires interdisciplinary planning and assistance (Decker, 1992; Krauss, 1990). Activities focus on increasing children's ability to help themselves and teaching them to attend to different situations. Most important is to find ways for young children to communicate to others when they need assistance. They also need help and support learning the processes of eating, using a toilet, undressing, and dressing. Self-help training should begin very early, even though many children can do little for themselves at first and may even lack cognitive understanding.

In addition, young children should be taught to look at other people and attend to what those people are saying and doing; these are the rudimentary skills of attention education. After they learn to attend, the hope is that they will respond to cues from other people. As children learn to give their attention to situations, they can be taught to imitate what they see. They can begin to explore, perhaps with physical assistance from someone. In short, they increase their own awareness of their environment. Many adapted toys exist that can be successfully manipulated by young children with disabilities (Hanline, Hanson, Veltman, & Spaeth, 1986). These toys facilitate children's making choices and gaining control over the environment.

School Age.   School-age intervention continues the efforts of early childhood but adds the academic subjects. Because of the time demands of different specialists and the students' slow work pace, the curriculum of students who are physically disabled is usually confined to basic subjects. However, students should also be exposed to such

Involvement in a fine arts program supports and complements basic subjects.

subjects as career education, social studies, science, fine arts, and physical education. Computer technology can help to expedite the learning processes. It can expand and diversify the approaches to reading, spelling, vocabulary, and other language arts skills. Word processing capabilities can save time and effort in written work (Male, 1988).

Microcomputers offer many advantages to students with poor hand coordination or low energy (Smith, Thurston, Light, Parnes, & O'Keefe, 1989). Pressing keys is easier and quicker than writing by hand, and special adaptations are available for students with problems in physically accessing the keyboards (Foulds, 1982). Key guards reduce the accidental pressing of unintended keys; expanded keyboards use a special connection that allows the user to bypass the computer keys; and special interfaces allow students with severe motor involvement to use a switch to duplicate selection of characters on the keyboard (Burkhead, Sampson, & McMahon, 1986) (see Figure 8–5). Switch interface is used by Alfonso, whose achievements were described in the chapter vignette.

Secondary/Transition.   Ideally, interventions with older students are based on successful interventions from earlier years. Like younger students, secondary students may want help in finding alternatives to the usual ways of doing schoolwork. Use of hand-held computers for note taking may replace writing by hand. Tape recordings of speeches produced on home computers with speech synthesizers may give nonspeaking students an opportunity to make oral reports. Students at this level devise many of these alternatives with help from special education teachers and their peers.

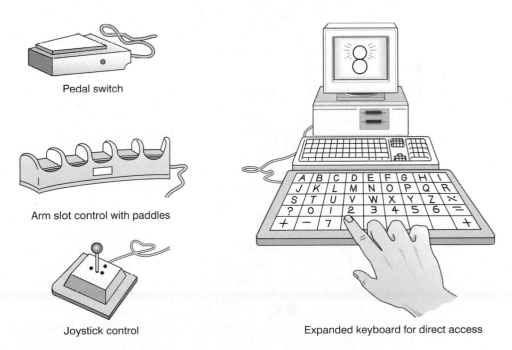

Pedal switch

Arm slot control with paddles

Joystick control

Expanded keyboard for direct access

Figure 8–5
Technology aids for expediting learning.

When students with physical and health impairments have difficulty with the secondary curriculum, other strategies may have to be employed. Sometimes they continue in regular classes and try to gain as much as they can. Others take less challenging classes. Still others take part of their coursework with a special education teacher, who can present the content in a way that meets their learning needs and styles.

Extended work evaluations (vocational opportunities) give students and other significant persons a chance to devise creative approaches to work samples (that is, outcomes of their labor or other work products) so that students may join the work force. Effective adaptations include the use of a speaker phone so that dialing is not needed, special design of file drawers for wheelchair access, and a special lever to hold down a power switch on an electrical tool for an extended length of time. Senior citizen volunteers and retired engineers or other experts may be able to help design, build, or modify adaptive equipment or devices. Here again, task analysis is useful in determining helpful interventions.

Transdisciplinary Efforts

Professionals who provide services for students with physical and health impairments have traditionally worked in semi-isolation. In the last two decades significant changes have occurred, involving increased interdisciplinary cooperation. With the advent of P.L. 101-476 and P.L. 102-119, professionals have had an opportunity to break down even further rigid professional boundaries. The transdisciplinary approach facilitates collaboration among team members by encouraging a process of teaching and learning among them. As a result, the staff should be able to function with increased unity in goals and intervention strategies (Sirvis, 1978; Williamson, 1978).

Programs for young children with physical and multiple impairments tend to employ personnel from medical and allied health, educational, and social service disciplines. A transdisciplinary approach promotes the carryover of intervention techniques across the student's environments. In this approach the entire team participates with parents for implementation of home programs that supplement organized school programs. Most often, all team personnel are involved in providing services on an ongoing basis. Therapy and related interventions are provided by a group to ensure maximum use of time within a usually shortened day. In-class provision of therapy also increases the likelihood of generalization of skills to use in new situations (Hanson, 1984).

During the school-age program, transdisciplinary interaction between health care and educational personnel is critical to pragmatic success (i.e., student functioning effectively in social contexts) and skill generalization. Therapy goals for physical positioning and management can be incorporated into classroom programs (Finnie, 1975; MacNeela, 1987). Educational goals for academic skill development can often be incorporated into therapy—for example, reinforcing knowledge of colors by color-coding stairs used in development of mobility skills.

The emphasis at the secondary level may require that different personnel be included on the transdisciplinary team. As the need for therapy decreases, personnel who focus on postschool opportunities—rehabilitation counselors, vocational instructors, and therapeutic recreation personnel—should become more involved in the program. The Individualized Transition Plan (ITP) mandated by P.L. 101-476 assists this interagency linkage. Whenever possible, all personnel should provide opportunities for interaction within the classroom (Brolin, 1982; Sirvis, 1980).

CURRICULUM IMPLICATIONS

Planning curricula for students with physical disabilities and health impairments is a complex undertaking that should involve a number of people: board of education members, administrators, classroom aides, educators, therapists, vocational counselors, pupil service personnel, community agencies, medical personnel, parents, and the students themselves when appropriate. Suitable educational goals for students of similar ages may range from the most basic components of self-care tasks to academic content leading to advanced degrees.

Although curriculum should be individually determined, Collins, Wolery, and Gast (1992) stress certain common outcomes. These include socialization into society, support for a happy life, self-sufficiency, normalized work and leisure, and meaningful membership in family and communities.

Communications

Communications, as described by Bigge (1988), is a curriculum area that should be included in the course of study of students with physical impairments. Objectives for most of these students are to learn to communicate what they want to say in a way that others can understand, whether in casual conversation or classroom discussion and testing. Research indicates that communication must also be efficient to be optimally successful (Buzolich & Wiemann, 1988; Calculator, 1988). For the first time in history it is possible for persons with unintelligible speech to say all that they want to say and to have others understand them, as the result of advances in technology (Blackstone, 1986; Kannenberg, Marquardt, & Larson, 1988; Mirenda & Iacono, 1990; Zangari, Kangas, & Lloyd, 1988). Intensive and ongoing instruction is necessary to teach language usage, as well as use of speech-synthesizing devices (Burkhart, 1987).

Also difficult for some children is writing because of poor motor control or muscle weakness. Through a communications curriculum they can be taught efficient alternative ways to record answers and express ideas. Tape recorders can be used by many students. In addition, problems can be written on large sheets of paper and placed on an easel so that a child can record his or her answers with a large crayon attached to an extension from a helmet. For some, a communication board is most functional (McEwen & Karlan, 1989).

A communications curriculum should also include instruction in keyboarding; typewriters and microcomputers can be used functionally even when a disability limits typing to one hand (May & Marozas, 1989). Electric typewriters are the easiest for most students with disabilities to handle. Metal or plastic guards placed over the keyboard prevent students from hitting more than one key at a time. The keys can be struck with fingers or in alternative ways—for example, with the eraser end of a pencil held in a student's hand, with a dowel stick attached to headgear, or with a mouth stick. With selected kinds of microcomputers, a special interface card and a single pedal switch can avoid the need to press keys altogether. Microcomputers can even permit individuals with disabilities to draw and paint (Male, 1988).

Chapter 8

Life Experience

Developing physical self-help skills is a priority in curriculum planning for individuals with physical and health impairments across the life span. Program goals should focus on basic functional needs: eating and drinking, toileting, dressing, undressing, bathing, and managing nasal and oral hygiene. Poor coordination, muscular weakness, paralysis, loss of sensation, low vitality, and limb deficiency often prevent children and youth from completing tasks without aids. Special educators, therapists, rehabilitation specialists, and parents need to work together in assessing the physical problems the child faces in managing self-care tasks and in devising needed equipment to simplify those tasks—wheelchairs for one-handed operation, hand splints with spoons attached, or remote controls for electronic appliances and learning aids.

Career/Vocational Education

Throughout any curriculum there should be opportunities for developing task completion skills and other good work habits. Knowing how to perform even the simplest task reduces dependence. The more established that work skills and behaviors become during the school years, the more prepared students will be for their futures—whether they involve volunteer jobs, home employment, sheltered or competitive work, or professional training. Vocational preparation may be the most important part of the curriculum at the secondary level (Sowers & Powers, 1991).

Curricula must include structured preparation for the upcoming transition from school to community, from student to self-sufficient community participant, worker, and leader. For any task, students must learn to compare their skills with those needed. If they find their skills inadequate, they should be taught to seek help to improve them. If improvement is not a realistic goal, even with specialized equipment and procedures, they must learn to explore alternative goals.

Many career education programs follow models that integrate the instruction of skills in several areas, emphasizing the interrelationships of skills needed for independence and responsible behavior as a worker at school, in the family, in a community, and on a job. This approach is believed to develop most fully each individual's potential for economic, social, and personal fulfillment (Brolin, 1982; Kokaska & Brolin, 1985) and to prepare students to function in a variety of least restrictive current and subsequent school and nonschool environments.

Recreation and Leisure Education

Like persons in every community, individuals with physical disabilities and health impairments have a right to develop individual leisure life-styles using community resources. Leisure education is critical to the development of attitudes and skills that will influence overall satisfaction during school years and in later life (Peterson & Gunn, 1984). Leisure concepts, values, and use of resources can be incorporated into existing curricula in social studies, reading, math, and career education; it is important that the concepts be introduced early and continued throughout the curricula. Students should also be exposed to a variety of recreational activities in which they can engage, with or without adaptation for their physical disabilities (Ballard & Calhoun, 1991; Raschke, Dedrick, & Hanus, 1991; Lian & Goyette, 1988; Platt & Janeczko, 1991).

Students should be taught the importance and relevance of leisure to a satisfying life and be introduced to the concepts of choice and decision making in activities that provide enjoyment. In the later elementary years children should be given ample opportunities to explore their environment and to identify leisure-related activities and resources. The focus should be on the integration of leisure into a satisfying, well-rounded existence (Turner, Snart, & McCarthy, 1992).

School Subjects

Individuals with physical and health impairments should progress as far in the range and difficulty of regular school subjects as they are able. Those who can benefit from a curriculum for gifted students should be provided the opportunity to do so. When mental retardation or learning problems accompany a physical impairment, the curriculum may need to focus on functional academics. Sometimes students are not taught to their potential simply because they have limited hand use or unintelligible speech; adaptive devices should be used in such cases. We must not let the presence of a physical or health impairment cause us to underestimate a student's ability to participate in school subjects.

No longer alone, Chris and his canine companion, Imperial, visit with friends at school.

Age-Level Distinctions

Early Childhood.   Motor, social, and communication education are central in any early childhood curriculum. Certain children with severe motor problems must be taught to relax certain muscles to actively assist in being toileted and fed. Promoting optimal postures and movement patterns for functional activities is an early objective (Smith & Nwaobi, 1985). Another challenge for the educator is to locate or develop adaptive devices and adaptive methodology to counteract or accommodate the results of the child's physical disability. Other challenges lie in physical independence education: finding ways to teach young children with disabilities to start to manage their own physical needs.

Motor education does more than improve the quality of children's posture and movement and self-help skills. It also provides an opportunity for students to acquire the experiential learning upon which much other learning is based. It helps children perform a variety of activities—move to a toy they want, put a piece into a puzzle, go down a slide. Thus, it provides the foundations for more difficult, complex skills, and it provides basic experiences upon which language and cognitive concepts can develop. Most important, it reduces dependence on others for what the child wants to do.

Many children with physical impairments also have communication difficulties as a result of language delay and oral-motor incoordination. To prepare these students to function socially and academically in a variety of situations, teachers must collaborate with speech pathologists and parents to teach communication skills as aggressively as they teach academic readiness skills. Curriculum guidelines and related assessment are available to assist educators (California State Department of Education, 1990; Hanson, 1984).

School Age.   Differences exist in curricula for school-age students with disabilities and those for their nondisabled peers, including different kinds of curriculum components and different emphases on social skills education. The total course of study for a student with a physical disability may include some of the regular curriculum components. However, it may also include components taught by a special education teacher or therapist. It will certainly focus on specific special education objectives based on each student's Individualized Educational Plan (IEP). In most cases special education teachers provide direct instruction, as well as coordination of the many facets of a student's curriculum.

Many students with disabilities have had limited interaction with groups of nondisabled persons. Thus, social skills education becomes important (Nelson, 1988). In addition to the more obvious skills needed to make and keep friends, social skills education focuses on developing self-advocacy. Self-advocacy teaches students to assert themselves comfortably and appropriately—to seek permission to tape lessons instead of writing them, for example, or to inquire about staying after school for Boy Scouts one afternoon a week instead of going home every day on the special education bus.

Self-care is one aspect of self-advocacy. Increasingly, students with exceptional learning needs face the complexity of caring for themselves in the world outside the school system, which may place them at physical risk (Rowland & Robinson, 1991; Coleman & Apts, 1991). It is critical that self-care skills be taught to address this possible "home alone" situation (Koblinsky & Todd, 1991).

Collins, Wolery, and Gast (1992) note that specific safety skill training should result from assessment of the student's performance and potential dangers in the individual's current and subsequent environments. Research as to most effective methods for incorporating safety skill training into the curriculum is needed.

Secondary/Transition. Meeting all or part of graduation requirements is the goal of many secondary students with physical disabilities. These students need to pursue subjects and activities that are particularly motivating to them or that move them toward a specific role after graduation.

As mentioned earlier, vocational training is a critical aspect of the secondary curriculum. Successful vocational training programs are characterized by: (1) training that reflects the current job market; (2) training in work-related skills; (3) community-based training, in which instruction covers skills needed to function in the community and takes place in the community; (4) systematic instructional procedures; (5) adaptive strategies to heighten independence; (6) flexibility of staff roles and organizational structure; (7) parental involvement; (8) early paid employment; and (9) collaboration and coordination with postschool service systems (Sowers & Powers, 1991).

MAINSTREAMING   Successful transition of a student from a special education setting to a regular classroom or school depends on many factors, including (1) the amount and kind of support services needed and available, (2) the responsibility for orientation taken by educational personnel, (3) the willingness of professionals to collaborate on programming, (4) the availability of transportation and aides or volunteers, and (5) architectural accessibility inside and outside the new school.

Age-Level Distinctions

Early Childhood. With the advent of federal legislation (including ADA), an increasing number of public programs have become available for infants and preschoolers with physical impairments. Interdisciplinary efforts focus on physical skills and independence, as well as socialization, self-help, and language development. Research supports the need for intervention prior to age 3 for children with physical and multiple disabilities. In response, federal legislation has opened the door for an increased number of public programs to provide services as soon as a physical problem is identified. In addition, private, usually nonprofit, organizations such as the United Cerebral Palsy Association, The National Easter Seal Society, and local agencies provide services for infants and very young children with specific disabilities. Typically, these early intervention programs offer centralized instruction to children and their parents, as well as home instruction and visitation. Physical, occupational, and speech therapy is emphasized and coordinated with educational programming. The thrust at this age level is to *prepare* for mainstreaming.

School Age. As mentioned earlier, some youngsters with physical and health impairments are able to function in regular classes with no supportive help—for example, the child who has mastered the use of an artificial limb. Others may be able

B yron E. Thompson School in the El Monte City School District of California provides educational services for students with physical and health impairments within the West San Gabriel Valley Special Education Local Plan Area (SELPA). Students who reside within 15 school districts east of Los Angeles can attend this program. Placement at Byron Thompson is based on determination of least restrictive and most appropriate educational service delivery mandated by public law. For many students in SELPA, Byron Thompson is not considered least restrictive. They attend their neighborhood schools and may receive only therapy services through the outpatient program at Byron Thompson.

Eighty children ranging in age from 3 to 15 years currently attend Byron Thompson School. Class composition is based on age, not specific disability or developmental level. Children are taught by teachers credentialed in the area of physical disabilities, who are assisted by trained instructional assistants. Students are involved in academic coursework and supported by specialized equipment and computer technology to facilitate their communication, mobility, and academic achievement.

Many of the students who attend Byron Thompson have specialized health care needs, which are met by trained personnel. In addition to health care, therapy services are provided by the medical therapy unit (MTU) housed at Byron Thompson. Efforts are made to integrate therapy goals into classroom activities. This strategy supports transdisciplinary service delivery and enhances academic learning time.

Great concern exists for integration of students who attend Byron Thompson School with students at the adjacent Durfee School. To encourage social integration, adapted equipment is scattered throughout the playground areas of both schools, and there is no separation of play areas by fences or curbs. Teachers schedule recesses to promote opportunities for social integration.

Integration is important in academics, as well. Individuals and class groups at both schools participate in academic programs and/or special events. Students are integrated from all classes at Byron

to succeed in the regular classroom if they receive special services, such as supplementary instruction; physical, occupational, or speech therapy; or counseling. Students with more severe or multiple disabilities may benefit from the socialization experiences and related classroom activities. Each student's individual needs must determine placement, to ensure the most appropriate education in the least restrictive and most natural setting.

Secondary/Transition. Secondary instruction focuses on academic and career education, and on preparation for postsecondary training, school, employment, or

Thompson School for at least part of their school day at Durfee School. In addition to this plan of "forward mainstreaming," "reverse mainstreaming" occurs when classes from Durfee School go to Byron Thompson School for daily integrated language arts instruction. There, groups work on reading, speaking, writing, and listening skills together at tables. Adaptations in the integrated language arts program that are successful for students with physical impairments are available for their nondisabled friends. The success of this integrated language arts program prompted the production of a professional video that has been presented to educational groups at the state and national level.

Byron Thompson School has approached the area of aesthetic development through its handbell choir, which is now in its 16th year. Students at Byron Thompson learn to play English hand bells, which they purchased through various fund-raising events. This experience allows students to affirm their self-worth by their ability to make music. The Byron Thompson Hand Bell Choir has performed at Disneyland, national conventions, and community and civic functions.

Byron Thompson School has served as a university training site for laboratory students and student teachers in special education. School staff and parents whose children attend Byron Thompson are represented on the university's Community Advisory Committee, providing input on current educational and social needs of students with physical and health impairments. Because they are always supportive of student progress, parents and teachers at Byron Thompson have chosen another target for change. This year they plan to raise sufficient funds to install an elevator at Durfee School, because no one should be in education at only the "ground floor."

Because of the implications of their disabilities, many students require intensive training in such areas as life experience and career/vocational education. Students with physical impairments must be prepared with appropriate strategies for transition from public school: using public transportation; finding and maintaining a home for themselves; finding and using personal attendants; maintaining or improving their own physical condition; finding ways to obtain rehabilitation aids and social services; and directing any needed adaptations for their daily life, leisure, and employment.

other life situations. Of concern to educators is the students' ability to participate fully in an appropriate secondary school experience. Teachers and students can explore numerous program options, ranging from full participation in a regular high school program to limited participation and regular attendance at a vocational training program. Implementation of the Americans with Disabilities Act (ADA) addresses issues such as accessibility and transportation (Bowman & Marzouk, 1991). Even a student who is physically dependent on others, does not possess many daily living skills, and is unable to speak or write to communicate may be served in a regular class on a full-time basis. That same student may be able to communicate with yes/no head movements and meaningful facial expressions, to demonstrate on a typewriter a grade-level proficiency in reading and spelling, and to reveal in other ways interests and academic skills similar to those of nondisabled peers. Students can receive physical therapy treatments after school and obtain training in basic living needs during summer school. Every student deserves a program aimed at attainment of critical skills and independent functioning.

INNOVATION AND
DEVELOPMENT

As we better recognize the unique needs of individuals with physical and health impairments, medical, technological, and societal advances should foster continued progress in treatment, intervention, and educational programming for them. Major advances and research efforts are focusing on developments in medicine, genetics, rehabilitation engineering, computer technology, and psychosocial development and growth.

Current medical research efforts include the examination of neurophysiological aspects, surgical therapy, and adaptation resulting from exercise, drug intervention, and assistive devices. Research focused on the neuromuscular aspects of disability is looking at the use of biofeedback, for example, as well as the physical problems caused by traumatic brain injury (Fenton, 1981). Additional research has examined such unique procedures as spinal cord regeneration and the use of a computer to stimulate walking in individuals with paraplegia due to spinal cord injury.

Medical research continues to focus on identifying the origin of *idiopathic* (cause unknown) disabilities such as epilepsy and ways to prevent or alter the course of other disabilities such as muscular dystrophy. Genetic research has identified over 1,500 diseases with a genetic origin. The ability to identify carriers of such disabilities as muscular dystrophy, sickle cell anemia, and hemophilia will continue to have a significant effect on genetic counseling. In addition, it is recognized that children with rare disorders are as deserving of research and attention as those whose disabilities have greater name recognition ("Annual Directory," 1993).

Rehabilitation engineering has emerged as a leading technological field. It encompasses the development of adaptive equipment and systems for seating mobility, communication, and environmental control. The Lainey System is just one example. It is a technical system that integrates components of communication, mobility, and computer access. The system incorporates a commercially available powered wheelchair, a microprocessor-based communication aid mounted on the back of the chair, and a computer system. The interconnecting units can be operated with a single-control interface—the optical headpointer directed toward a clear selection panel mounted in front of the user. The communication aid controls the computer by wireless telemetry. The Lainey System can also provide remote control of appliances in the home or hospital—lamps, televisions, radios, page turners, and more. Another current focus of rehabilitation engineering—robotics (computer control of an external device, such as a mechanical arm)—has been used experimentally with young children with severe physical impairments. The children were taught to control a robot to pour milk and do other chores they could not do for themselves (Behrmann, 1984; Behrmann & Lahm, 1984). Other microcomputer-based devices are described in the Focus on Technology box.

A cost-effective solution offered to enhance independence for persons with physical impairments is the use of trained animal companions. Service animals (usually

A physical impairment can affect a student's range of motion, physical strength, coordination, communication—all of which affect interaction with instructional materials. Perhaps more than any other disability group, it is crucial for students with physical impairments to have access to a computer. Their motor problems may preclude keyboard input, but there are many other ways to input to the computer so that it can be used for a vast range of applications, including communication (oral and written), environmental control, and learning. Often, a single switch device is used. Once computer access has been established with an alternative input method, the student can use the computer for the same applications as nondisabled peers.

Single-switch input requires developing and implementing procedures for proper positioning of the student, selecting the type of switch that will be most appropriate and the way in which it will be stabilized, and establishing switch activation responses. Switches are now available that can be controlled by an eye blink, a knee or foot movement, a puff of air, or whatever muscle can be controlled, no matter how limited that control. In addition to single-switch input devices to access the computer, there are other input possibilities such as speech recognition systems. These systems are designed to be trained to recognize the unique voice patterns of the user, permitting control of standard software packages through the production of speech sounds.

Other technological devices are effective for mobility and independent living. One computer-based innovation for mobility is the electronically controlled wheelchair. Controlling these chairs is similar to, and as easy as changing, a TV station with a remote control. Computer hardware, software, and peripherals make it possible for individuals with severe physical impairments to operate appliances, control environmental devices such as lights and door locks, and perform such tasks as writing checks. Robotics are one means of extending functioning capabilities. For example, a robotic arm can be used to locate, manipulate, and position a typewriter, typing paper, reading materials, a telephone, or self-feeding equipment.

Hooper and Hasselbring (1985) have listed some advantages of electronic communication devices compared to nonelectronic aids:

1. Easier access to larger vocabulary
2. Greater independence because messages can be formulated in advance and stored for later use
3. Increased rate of communication
4. Potential to express more complex word combinations
5. Possibility to communicate with a broader audience and those who are not immediately present (i.e., with printer output or telecommunications)

The computer is also potentially important as a postschool vocational tool. Ability to use special input devices, ability to work with standard office technology, and knowledge about the working environment are essential skills developed through high school and postsecondary programs. Important software systems for prevocational students include word processing, bookkeeping, and accounting.

The new lap-sized portable computers when used in conjunction with larger personal computers hold particular promise for students with physical impairments. For example, the student might use the lap-sized computer in class to take notes and then later interface and expand the notes with the larger personal computer.

These systems are representative of "high technology." Students can also profit from "low technology," simple devices without written or spoken output and without programming capabilities (Church & Glennen, 1992). Simple communication boards based on pictures and letters may be the best initial equipment for some students. In all situations, an individualized match should be made between the user and technology support system.

dogs or monkeys) assist in performing tasks such as picking up dropped items, accessing light switches and elevator buttons, moving a wheelchair, or even feeding their owners. Animal companions provide an opportunity for those with a physical impairment to focus conversation with new acquaintances on enablement rather than on disability and thus are a means for socialization for their owners.

Research and development efforts continue in new and expanding areas. Medical and technological advances create new options for independence and participation for individuals with physical and multiple disabilities. Nonetheless, the need exists for continued improvement in educational intervention so that technological and medical advances will support the growth and development of each individual, thus enhancing the quality of life.

SUMMARY The federal government has identified two categories of physical disabilities: orthopedic impairments and other health impairments. The causes of these disabilities are varied and include prenatal, perinatal, and postnatal factors. Characteristics of these disabilities are diverse but include coordination problems, muscular weakness, paralysis, bone and joint problems affecting movement, and health impairments.

Transdisciplinary cooperation is vital to developing comprehensive programs that facilitate maximum development of each student. The process usually begins with interdisciplinary assessment of (1) performance of self-help skills, (2) mobility, (3) accommodation required for physical differences, (4) communication strategies and systems, (5) strategies and special devices that can make learning easier, (6) modes and styles of learning, and (7) special help required. Task analysis and behavioral observation are the assessment techniques most used.

Intervention focuses on numerous areas, including (1) physical management and intervention, (2) health and disability management, and (3) psychosocial development, again using task analysis as an instruction tool.

Curricular areas for students with physical and health impairments vary according to students' age and disability characteristics. Of general concern are self-help and physical independence, communication, academics, computer applications, career education, and recreation and leisure education. A shift in both management and educational focus has been away from a deficit-amelioration position to one that is functional and outcome-based.

Students with physical and health impairments in regular classrooms may pose unique management challenges. Teachers need to be thoroughly familiar with their students' disabilities in order to adapt the room, equipment, activities, or assignments. Service delivery systems at the elementary and secondary levels range from full integration in regular classes, to integration with support services, to special classes or special schools. Postsecondary arrangements include colleges, regional occupational centers, continuing education programs, and sheltered or competitive employment, depending on the severity of the disability and an individual's academic ability.

Research in medicine, rehabilitation engineering, and computer technology has contributed to the potential for increased independent functioning and a higher quality of life for individuals with physical and health impairments.

1. Listen attentively when you are talking to a person who has difficulty speaking. Persons with unintelligible speech understand more than their expressions may indicate; treat and teach them accordingly.

2. Parents and therapists are excellent resources about special devices and techniques for assisting students. Do not assume that students themselves are uninformed about what adaptations work best for them.

3. A wheelchair is part of the personal property of the person who uses it. Therefore, do not lean or hang on anyone's wheelchair.

4. When speaking to a person who uses a wheelchair, place yourself at the eye level of that person to facilitate conversation.

5. Unless otherwise advised, give students who are disabled the same opportunities to do what their same-age peers do, including field trips, special events, and projects.

6. Openly discuss uncertainties about when or how to assist a person with a disability. Offer to help, and respect the answer you get—even if it is no.

7. Help students and adults who are not disabled understand that behaviors such as drooling, unusual ways of talking, and physical awkwardness cannot be helped and should not be ridiculed.

8. Treat students with disabilities as normally as possible. Do not overprotect them; encourage them to take responsibility for themselves.

9. Persons are not "confined" to wheelchairs, they are enabled by them. Avoid negative and disempowering terms like "victim", "sufferer", etc.

10. Focus on the person, not the disability.

TIPS FOR HELPING

STUDY QUESTIONS

1. Describe several physical and health impairments experienced by schoolchildren. Why is it important to be aware of the presence of a physical or health impairment?

2. Describe prenatal, perinatal, and postnatal causes of physical and health impairments.

3. Describe some possible psychological and social effects of disabilities. Are the effects different when the disability is visible rather than invisible?

4. Discuss intervention strategies for children or adolescents who are physically disabled.

5. In what ways can the teacher modify schoolwork for the student with a physical impairment? Briefly describe several situations requiring modification and the strategies involved.

6. Compare the emphases in curriculum content for preschool, school-age, and secondary/transition educational programs for students who have physical impairments.

7. What are the special considerations in assessment of students with physical disabilities?

8. What technological advances have affected the self-reliance of persons with physical impairments? Describe and explain.

9. Describe uses of task analysis for students with physical and health impairments.

10. What is meant by transdisciplinary service to students with physical and health impairments? What are the roles of the different personnel involved with such students?

Linda McCormick
University of Hawaii

9

Communication Disorders

   In this chapter you will learn about

- the history of the study of language acquisition and practices related to intervention for speech, language, and communication disorders

- new views concerning assessment and intervention for students with language and communication disorders

- the causes and characteristics of speech disorders, language disorders, and communication disorders

- approaches to the assessment of speech, language, and communication disorders

- the nature and practices associated with naturalistic intervention procedures for students with communication disorders

*B*rendyn is 5½ years old. His cognitive functioning is near age level, and his hearing is within the normal range. Brendyn's favorite activities are similar to those of his peers. He likes watching Teenage Mutant Ninja Turtles tapes, playing baseball with his dad, collecting and trading baseball cards, and skating with his new roller blades. The major difference between Brendyn and his peers is his language abilities: he isn't able to express himself as well as his peers.

Brendyn's parents have been concerned for some time about his speech and language development. Except for the words *mommy*, *daddy,* and *no*, he did not talk at all until around the time of his third birthday. Brendyn's preschool teachers described him as "very shy and quiet," "prefers to play alone," and "uses language only to communicate basic needs."

Brendyn gained some language and communication skills in preschool. He learned to express his basic wants and needs with short sentences. Now the mean length of his utterances is about 3 words, and he is beginning to use some inflectional morphemes correctly (e.g., *-ing, -ed*). He follows through on 2-step commands now and even produces some simple 2-step commands. Brendyn is able to answer questions that begin with *what, who, where,* and *when*, but he asks only *what* and *who* questions. He has not yet learned to initiate interactions with peers, and it is unusual for him to take more than two turns in a conversation (with either peers or adults).

Brendyn has recently been evaluated and found eligible for special education services as speech/language impaired. He will remain in the regular kindergarten classroom that he is presently attending. The speech-language pathologist (SLP) will come right into the classroom and work with him there.

Recognizing the strong relationship between poor language development and learning disabilities, Brendyn's teacher and the SLP are concerned that he is at risk for reading and general academic failure. They have developed an intervention plan that will help Brendyn develop the mental operations and thinking skills critical to the development of literacy skills. The SLP is showing Brendyn's teacher some strategies to maximize his opportunities to learn and use language and communication in the classroom and in other school settings (e.g., playground, cafeteria). The SLP is also working with Brendyn's parents and the staff of the after-school program Brendyn attends.

Ironically, the fundamental role of language and communication in human functioning is most evident when language and communication skills fail to develop normally or are impaired in some way as in Brendyn's case. What does it mean to be able to use language? Why is Brendyn having so much trouble learning what his peers seem to acquire so effortlessly? Can language and communication really be that difficult when the overwhelming majority of babies begin talking before they are out of diapers?

The ease with which most young children learn to talk and understand language is misleading. It obscures the enormous complexity of language and the language learning process. If you have any doubts about the complexity of language and language learning, consider the fact that, even after many decades of study, there is not yet complete agreement among researchers about the process of how language is acquired.

In order to produce oral language, children must learn the speech sounds (phonemes) of their language and the ways that sounds are combined to form words. Babies spend much of their first years of life figuring this out. Not only do they learn and practice sounds, they also learn how to modulate voice quality and use appropriate intonation and rate. By the age of 2, they begin producing words and phrases to represent what they know about the world, and shortly thereafter they learn the rules for sequencing words to form grammatically correct and meaningful sentences. By the time they start school, most children are very competent communicators. In addition to a rich and intricate linguistic system, they have learned a range of nonlinguistic devices such as eye contact, gestures, facial expressions, and intonation to ensure that their messages are conveyed and understood. In the early school years, language learning continues; children acquire full structural knowledge of constructions such as passives, coordinators, and relative clauses.

Problems related to language and communication development affect several million children in this country. The primary focus of this chapter will be those students for whom speech, language, and/or communication problems constitute a primary disability. Students with a primary diagnosis of communication disorders represent a substantial percentage of the special education population. The majority of these students demonstrate normal cognitive, sensory, and motor functioning. Most are educated in regular classes.

It is important to recognize that a majority of students with other primary disabilities such as mental retardation, hearing impairment, and physical impairment, also demonstrate speech, language, and communicative problems (Abbeduto, 1991; Ceci, 1986; Frith, 1989). This chapter will only touch upon language and communication disorders associated with or resulting from these primary disabilities.

HISTORY   The history of the study of language acquisition is as tangled as it is rich. Unraveling this history is especially challenging because there are so many disparate threads.

The nature of language and language development has long fascinated professionals from many disciplines. However, there was little effort directed to synthesis of the contributions among disciplines because the basic philosophies and concerns of the different professions were very often at odds with one another. Among those professionals whose disciplines have a primary interest in language are linguists, psycholinguists, sociolinguists, behavioral psychologists, and speech-language pathologists. Owens (1988) describes the interests of some of these disciplines:

- *Linguists* are primarily concerned with describing linguistic symbols and cataloging the rules for forming sentences with these symbols.
- *Psycholinguists* are interested in the psychological processes and concepts underlying language—the cognitive mechanisms that make it possible for language users to produce and comprehend language.
- *Sociolinguists* study dialectic differences and communicative interactions: they are particularly concerned with understanding the implicit rules for language use in diverse socioeconomic, linguistic, and cultural contexts.
- *Behavioral psychologists* are specifically concerned with application of behavioral principles to increase the quality and quantity of language use.
- *Speech-language pathologists* (SLPs) concentrate on assessment and intervention to facilitate and promote development of normal language processes.

Other professional disciplines with an interest in language development and/or language disorders include anthropology and special education. In addition to somewhat diverse theoretical and applied interests, each of the disciplines mentioned above has its own research methods, discipline-specific terminology, and separate technical journals. What follows barely skims the highlights of the contributions these disciplines have made to understanding of, and intervention for, children with language and communication disorders.

Research

In the fifties there were two major theories concerning the nature of language and language acquisition. Noam Chomsky (1957) was the primary spokesperson for one of these theoretical camps—psycholinguistic theory. His writings presented descriptions of the elaborate linguistic processes that language users employ in order to understand and generate language. Chomsky's early theory, called generative transformational grammar, was concerned with describing the nature of a language learner's underlying knowledge. Of particular interest were the views of Chomsky and his colleagues about the source of language knowledge. They reasoned, based on what appears to be some universality or commonality of the principles underlying human languages, that language must be specific to humans and biologically based. The early psycholinguists concluded that the biological basis for language, its universality, and the developmental similarities across children (in the same and different language cultures) pointed to an innate language acquisition mechanism. Chomsky called this "preprogramming" the Language Acquisition Device, or LAD. Although Chomsky has revised his theory (Chomsky, 1981), it retains its basic assumption that language is due to a special linguistic development and that grammar is the essence of language.

In contrast to the psycholinguistic emphasis on syntactic structures (language form) and underlying mental processes, advocates of behavior theory stressed the function or use of language and the active role of the environment in language development. The leading spokesman for this camp was, of course, B. F. Skinner. In his classic 1957 book, *Verbal Behavior*, Skinner described language as learned behavior that is subject to the rules of operant conditions and can thus be studied with behavioral research procedures. Simple units are acquired through parent modeling and selective reinforcement. More complex responses are acquired through chaining and word association. Rather than analyzing language into structural units (morphemes and words), Skinner studied what he considered the functional units of verbal behavior. Functional units are groups of verbal responses that are produced under similar circumstances and result in similar consequences.

The debate during the fifties between Chomsky and Skinner was essentially a variation of the nature vs. nurture controversy. The issue was, Do children come equipped with innate knowledge of language principles and structure that is somehow activated by linguistic input (the psycholinguistic position) or is language acquired through selective reinforcement of imitation, word-referent associations, and chaining (the behaviorist position)?

In the fifties, children demonstrating language delays and/or disorders were not a particular concern for either the psycholinguists or the behaviorists. Fortunately, researchers in neurology, psychiatry, pediatrics, and deaf educators *were* interested in children who, for one reason or another, were not developing language at an expected rate. They were beginning to develop some theoretical formulations concerning etiology and prognosis, but they did not provide practical guidelines that clinicians could apply in intervention activities.

In the late sixties, there were two events that redirected the attention of professionals interested in language acquisition *and* language intervention: researchers in speech pathology began to explore questions related to language disorders, and Lois Bloom (1970) reported data that revolutionized thinking about child language learning. Bloom's data suggested that the emergence of language is heavily dependent on the infant's cognitive attainments. Analysis of children's meanings emerged as a more accurate and powerful way to explain language acquisition than analysis of language structures.

Almost simultaneously, three other researchers (Brown, 1973; Schlesinger, 1971; Slobin, 1970) arrived at the same conclusions as Bloom. They provided three almost identical lists of the concepts underlying children's earliest utterances. What came to be called the semantic revolution had begun. The basic tenet of this new perspective was simple and logical: children talk when they have something to talk about, and they talk about what they understand (Cromer, 1974). The paradigm shift was from concentration on the syntactic structure of children's utterances to semantic analysis. While weakening the notion of innate knowledge of language rules, the semantic revolution awakened new interest in cognitive development. Closest scrutiny centered on Piaget's (1952, 1954, 1962) notions concerning a general symbolic capability that must be achieved before language can be used meaningfully.

The semantic revolution lasted slightly less than a decade. By the mid-seventies some researchers had begun to question the premise that cognitive development *alone* is sufficient to account for early language acquisition (e.g., Bates, 1976; Bruner, 1975). They noted that semantic analysis, like syntactic analysis, removed language from its purpose or function—namely communication. Thus, the paradigm shifted again—this time to the *why* of language. The major tenet of what was called the pragmatic revolution was that effective communication is the overriding motivation for language. The basic premise is that children learn language in order to affect the behavior of others. Research shifted to analysis of the functional and interpersonal characteristics of language and language learning (Bloom & Lahey, 1978).

Changing Paradigms

Although the psycholinguistic and the behavioral perspectives of the sixties had their devotees, both perspectives posed problems for clinicians. The biggest problem was that neither theory provided any clear direction as to precisely *what* to teach, the appropriate order in which to teach targeted skills, or effective teaching techniques. The perceived inadequacy of the dominant theories to address practical issues explains, at least in part, the appeal of the specific abilities approach (also called information-processing theory), which came on the scene in the late sixties. There was widespread acceptance of specific abilities tests such as the Illinois Test of Psycholinguistic Abilities (ITPA) (Kirk, McCarthy, & Kirk, 1968) and the Detroit Test of Learning Aptitude (Baker & Leland, 1967) because they were viewed as taking the guesswork out of assessment. They were touted as capable of identifying the perceptual and processing deficits underlying language deficits. The focus of assessment and intervention shifted dramatically, from targeting developmental abilities or knowledge of linguistic rules to the processes associated with input and output and central processing of information.

The effects of teaching methods aimed at improving processing skills were disappointing. Intervention often involved practice with the same sort of tasks as were on the tests, which did not result in the anticipated improvements in language functioning. Evidence substantiating the validity of the tests and/or the effectiveness of the intervention procedures never materialized (e.g., Hammill & Larsen, 1974; Hammill & Wiederholt, 1973).

Another paradigm shift began to take shape in the early eighties. There was a shift toward viewing language and communication disorders from an interactional perspective. A major tenet of the interactionist perspective, which merges and extends the semantic and pragmatic explanations of language acquisition, is that semantic-cognitive, syntactic, and pragmatic processes are interrelated. The interactionist perspective provides language pathologists (SLPs) and others concerned with language intervention with a theoretically and rationally sound base for the design of assessment and intervention activities.

The field continues to change. Among the most evident shifts in the nineties are new views about (1) assessment, (2) the proper focus of intervention efforts, and (3) how intervention is provided. As described by Westby and Erickson (1992), there are shifts from

- standardized testing to naturalistic assessment
- student-centered intervention strategies to a family systems orientation
- focus on spoken language to focus on literacy
- working in a therapy room to working in the classroom and other natural environments
- viewing children as much alike to an awareness of cultural and linguistic diversity

The shift from standardized testing to naturalistic assessment was precipitated by recognition that language is more than the sum of its parts. A child's mastery of the specific skills needed to understand and express the individual elements of phonology, syntax, morphology, and pragmatics does not guarantee meaningful communication. Standardized tests have limited usefulness to interventionists. While they permit comparison of the performance of students on some language-related skills, they do not tell us what we need to know and do in order to help the student. They tell us little about the student's use of language in natural environments or why a student is not developing language at the expected rate. For intervention-relevant information, we need to assess the student in natural settings, in the context of routine tasks.

The shift from student-centered intervention to concern for the family system has come about with recognition that many language and communication problems reside not within the individual, but rather in the social context—in the student's interactions with peers and others in his or her daily activities. Thus, it has come to be widely acknowledged that successful intervention requires attention to the social systems in which the student operates, including the family system (Westby & Erickson, 1992).

The shift from an exclusive focus on *spoken* language to inclusion of reading and writing has come about with recognition of the interdependency of literacy and overall language abilities. Literacy is not a separate ability: it is a fundamental dimension of normal language development in our culture. Success with reading and writing requires interactions with people, contexts, and language. Thus, facilitation of language and literacy have become shared goals, and teachers and speech-language pathologists are working collaboratively as consultants in the process of language development.

The shift from working with individual students and small groups in a therapy setting to working in the classroom environment has been gradual. It has come about with recognition that because language is inherent in all aspects of a child's daily life, language instruction cannot be removed from the ongoing stream of activities.

The shift from a focus on student similarities to a focus on student diversity recognizes changing population demographics in the United States. By the beginning of the 21st century, the population that has provided the most developmental and intervention data—Caucasian, mainstream children from middle class, two-parent families—will be in the minority in our schools. There is a growing recognition of the need for new approaches to collect meaningful data concerning intervention-relevant cultural and linguistic differences.

Terminology

The terms *speech*, *language*, and *communication* need be defined because, although the three terms are certainly related, each refers to a unique cluster of concepts and behavior.

Speech is verbal expression of the language code. It is a complex motor behavior that requires precise control and manipulation of the vocal tract and oral musculature. To produce speech, a child must learn to coordinate respiration (breathing), phonation (production of sound with the larynx and vocal folds), resonation (the vibratory response controlling the pitch, intensity, and quality of sound), and articulation (sound formation with the lips, tongue, teeth, and hard and soft palates).

Language is knowledge and use of a set of symbols to represent ideas and intentions. Use of language enables us to "represent an object, event or relationship without reproducing it" (Bloom & Lahey, 1978, p. 5). A language is a set of symbols and rules for combining them in order to convey meaning. Both the symbols and the rules have been agreed upon by members of the language culture.

Some descriptions of language included five components: *phonology, morphology, syntax, semantics,* and *pragmatics. Phonology* is the system of speech sounds and rules for how they can be combined. *Morphology* is concerned about how units of meaning (morphemes) are organized within words to express intended concepts (e.g., tense, plurality). *Syntax* refers to the rules governing the form or structure of a sentence. These rules govern word order, sentence organization, and the relationships between words, word classes, and other sentence elements. *Semantics* refers to the system of rules governing meaning or understanding. It is concerned with the meanings of morphemes and words and word combinations. *Pragmatics* refers to a set of rules for using language in socially appropriate ways to affect the behavior of others. Hymes (1971) defined pragmatics as "tacit knowledge of who can say what, in what way, where and when, by what means and to whom" (p. 12).

Bloom and Lahey (1978) collapse the five components into three: *form, content,* and *use. Form* includes the surface or structure aspects of language that connect to and express meaning (phonology, morphology, and syntax). *Content* is the meaning or semantic aspect of language. Something like a mental dictionary, content includes cognitive information (concepts about the physical and social world) and linguistic information (concepts about how to express cognitive knowledge). *Use* is the pragmatic or social interaction aspect of language.

The relationship between form and the rules governing language use is similar to the relationship between the rules of a game and actual playing strategies (McCormick, 1990). Take backgammon, for example. The rules of backgammon are straightforward and relatively easy to learn. However, the key to winning is learning to use certain playing strategies (and, of course, some luck with the dice). More difficult to explain and learn, playing strategies depend on such variables as the stage of the game and the positions and skills of the other player. The same is true of language use strategies. Mastery of these strategies, called communicative competence, requires considerable practice. It is heavily dependent on awareness of, and selection among, a range of linguistic alternatives (many of which are very subtle) to express communicative intent. How infants learn these communication strategies (e.g., turn taking, code switching, establishing and maintaining a topic) while at the same time learning speech and language skills is one of the many wonders of language acquisition.

Communication is much broader than speech or language. It refers to the act of sharing experiences and perceptions. Communication is the exchange of ideas, feelings, and information. The key word is *exchange.* There are three elements in the exchange, and all must be present for an interaction to qualify as communication. There must be (1) a message, (2) that message must be expressed, and (3) it must be accurately received (understood).

Language is the most efficient and useful communication device. It is considerably more effective for conveying abstract concepts than other communication devices such as gestures, facial expressions, body movements, or pictures. For example, an English-speaking person may succeed in ordering a meal in a restaurant where the waiter does not speak English by using gestures (pointing to items on the menu or on the plates of other diners), but it is difficult to imagine conveying concepts related to politics or religion without language. Communicating abstract concepts without language is extremely difficult, if not impossible.

Communication is not unique to humans. There is communication within and across species. While the communication skills of other species are not as well understood as those of humans, they are universally recognized. All that is necessary to confirm this assertion is to ask a pet owner. The meaningful exchanges between pet owners and their animals are particularly good examples of cross-species communication. Pets are skilled at using such devices as tail wagging, growling, jumping, and purring to convey messages, and there is little question that they can also understand many messages.

DEFINITION

The 1990 reauthorization of Public Law 94–142 as Public Law 101–476 replaced the word *handicapped* with *disabilities* (as reflected in the change of the act's name to the Individuals with Disabilities Education Act, or IDEA). It also expanded the general definition of children with disabilities to include separate categories for children with autism and traumatic brain injury.

When Public Law 94–142 was first passed (in 1975) the category label for students whose primary disability was a speech, language, and/or communication problem was *speech impaired*. In 1983, the Education of the Handicapped Amendments (P.L. 98–199) changed the label for this category to *speech or language impaired*. The definition for this category has not changed since 1983. It is defined as "a communication disorder, such as stuttering, impaired articulation, a language impairment, or voice impairment which adversely affects a child's educational performance" (IDEA Rules and Regulations, 1992, p. 44802). When language disorders were officially included in the above definition, a task force of the American Speech-Language-Hearing Association (ASHA) (American Speech-Language-Hearing Association, 1980) formulated the definitions presented in Figure 9–1.

Definitions for determining language disorders vary across the states, but most specify that children must show language deficits in one or more of the systems of language—phonology, morphology, syntax, semantics, or pragmatics. Deficits may be defined in psychometric terms (e.g., more than 1.5 standard deviations from the mean on at least two tests or subtests designed to measure language ability). Definitions may require specific assessment processes such as a language sample or observations in natural environments.

Many professionals use the label *specific language impairment* (SLI) for children who "exhibit significant limitations in language functioning that cannot be attributed to deficits in hearing, oral structure and function, or general intelligence" (Leonard, 1987, p. 1). Leonard (1990) points out that the diagnosis of SLI is one of exclusion; that is, alternate explanations for the child's failure to learn language have been sought and systemically ruled out. Very often children with SLI are referred to simply as *language delayed* or *language disordered*. The definition of SLI assumes that a relatively isolated impairment can affect language development without affecting general cognitive developmental and peripheral sensory and motor functions.

Communicative Disorders

A. A *speech disorder* is an impairment of voice, articulation of speech sounds, and/or fluency. These impairments are observed in the transmission and use of the oral symbol system.

    1. A *voice disorder* is defined as the absence or abnormal production of vocal quality, pitch, loudness, resonance, and/or duration.

    2. An *articulation disorder* is defined as the abnormal flow of verbal expression, characterized by impaired rate and rhythm which may be accompanied by struggle behavior.

B. A *language disorder* is the impairment or deviant development of comprehension and/or use of a spoken, written, and/or other symbol system. The disorder may involve (1) the form of language (phonologic, morphologic, and syntactic systems), (2) the content of language (semantic system), and/or (3) the function of language in communication (pragmatic system) in any combination.

    1. Form of Language

        a. *Phonology* is the sound system of a language and the linguistic rules that govern the sound combinations.

        b. *Morphology* is the linguistic rule system that governs the structure of words and the construction of word forms from the basic elements of meaning.

        c. *Syntax* is the linguistic rule governing the order and combination of words to form sentences, and the relationships among the elements within a sentence.

    2. Content of Language

        a. *Semantics* is the psycholinguistic system that patterns the content of an utterance, intent and meanings of words and sentences.

    3. Function of Language

        a. *Pragmatics* is the sociolinguistic system that patterns the use of language in communication which may be expressed motorically, vocally, or verbally.

Communicative Variations

A. *Communicative difference/dialect* is a variation of a symbol system used by a group of individuals which reflects and is determined by shared regional, social, or cultural/ethnic factors. Variations or alterations in the use of a symbol system may be indicative of primary language interferences. A regional, social, or cultural, ethnic variation of a symbol system should not be considered a disorder of speech or language.

B. *Augmentative communication* is a system used to supplement the communicative skills of individuals for whom speech is temporarily or permanently inadequate to meet communicative needs. Both prosthetic devices and/or nonprosthetic techniques may be designed for individual use as an augmentative communication system.

Figure 9–1

Definitions of the American Speech-Language-Hearing Association.

Source: From "Definitions: Communicative Disorders and Variations" by the American Speech-Language-Hearing Association, 1980, *Asha*, 22, 949–950.

Subcategory Labels

Speech disorders are problems associated with production of oral language. There are three key factors determining whether an individual's speech is defective (Van Riper, 1978). First, it must be sufficiently atypical to be *conspicuous* (call attention to itself). Second, it must *interfere* with the individual's ability to communicate. Finally, it must be so *unpleasant* that it causes distress for the speaker and the listener. There are three types of speech disorders: voice disorders, articulation disorders, and fluency disorders.

Language disorders are problems related to development of understanding and/or use of the phonologic, morphologic, semantic, syntactic, or pragmatic components of the language system. The problem may be a delay (language seems to be normal but not age-appropriate), or it may be different (deficient). If the problem is a deficiency, the language disorder may be described as receptive or expressive, or the term *aphasic* may be used. *Acquired aphasia* is the common term for a condition involving loss of linguistic ability resulting from some demonstrable brain damage caused by serious illness or trauma to the head (Leonard, 1990).

Like a speech disorder or a language disorder, a *communication disorder* may be the student's only disability, or it may be secondary to other disabilities. Communication disorders are impairments in the ability to formulate, transmit, and understand messages using a conventional symbol system.

The strong relationship between language and/or communication disorders and learning disabilities makes these two categories difficult to separate. Longitudinal studies of preschool children identified as language disordered indicated persistent and chronic problems with academic experiences, particularly reading and writing (Aram & Nation, 1980). There is some evidence that children who exhibit reading disorders but not overt language disorders and children who exhibit reading disorders and language disorders share a set of common features (Kamhi, Catts, Mauer, Apel, & Gentry, 1988). The findings, which are based on multiple measures of phonological, lexical, syntactical, and spatial processing, show that children in these two groups perform many tasks similarly to each other but differently from normal learners. Recall from chapter 4 that spoken and written language problems constitute an important part of the definition of "learning disabilities." The question is whether language problems are a contributor to learning problems, or vice versa. A third possibility, of course, is that the two are interactive (language skills affect reading and reading skills affect language development).

In each of the three subcategories of *speech disorders*, *language disorders*, and *communication disorders*, it is possible to differentiate specific disorders (i.e., voice disorders, syntax problems). These will be presented in the section addressing characteristics.

PREVALENCE

Prevalence and incidence of speech, language, and communication disorders are difficult to determine because deviations in the development and use of speech, language, and communication have a pervasive effect on development and performance in other areas. The proportion of students with speech and language problems seems to decrease over time, as students progress through school. However, the substantial changes across the four age levels (preschool, primary, secondary, postsecondary) in patterns of occurrence of the conditions learning disabilities, speech and language impairments, mental retardation, and emotional disturbance would appear to be one element of a more complex problem (U.S. Department of Education, 1992). In some cases the problems of children with mild difficulties are successfully remediated, and they are no longer labeled and served as having a disability. Equally likely is that students diagnosed as having a primary speech, language, or communication disorder are shifted to another category as they get older.

Of the children receiving special services in the 1990–1991 school year, 23.4% were served as speech and language impaired (U.S. Department of Education, 1992). There is considerable variability in the number of students served across states. Possible explanations for this variability are (1) different category definitions, (2) the tests used for determining eligibility, (3) variables related to test administration, and (4) decision-making related to diagnosis and placement. Some states count only those students for whom speech and/or language disorders are a primary (and only) disability, while others include children who have other problems in addition to speech and/or language disorders.

CAUSES

Identification of the etiology of a speech, language, and/or communication disorder is most likely when that disorder is secondary to another disability such as mental retardation, physical disability, brain damage, visual impairment, or hearing impairment. Even then, however, when a presumed cause of the disorder can be specified, it is rarely possible to predict the precise nature and severity of the disorder. Children with similar disabilities sometimes demonstrate different language disorders.

Figure 9–2 lists factors necessary for the normal development of speech, language, and communication abilities. Miller (1983) groups these variables into three broad categories: (1) neurological factors, (2) structural and physiological factors, and (3) environment factors. Just as the factors that influence normal language development are complex, multifaceted and interactive, disruptions in these factors play complex contributory roles in language disorders. Delay or dysfunction in any one (or any combination) of these factors can present a problem. For example, delayed cognitive development, regardless of whether it is mild or severe, means that the child is not acquiring knowledge of the world at a rate commensurate with his or her peers. This delay will affect acquisition of morphological and syntactic rules, as well as semantic knowledge and pragmatic skills. There will be a direct relationship between the extent of the cognitive delay and the rate of language development. Delay or dysfunction in more than one area compounds the problem. Most devastating is the interrelatedness of these factors. For example, a young child with a visual impairment may experience delayed social development (because the young child is not able to see and interpret many social cues) and has the potential for delayed physical development (because of restricted mobility). The consequence is an experiential deficit that can be expected to affect the rate and course of early language development.

Attempts to assign blame for language disorders are not generally productive because causality is complex and multifaceted. What is productive is to look for circular causative factors and patterns such as presented in Figure 9–2. Keep in mind as you review Figure 9–2 that the effect of these factors on development of speech, language, and communication will be proportional to (1) the degree of the deficit; (2) the

Neuropsychological Factors
1. Cognitive development
2. Information-processing strategies (selective attention, discrimination, concept formation, memory)
3. Motor, output capabilities (neuromuscular control/coordination)
4. Social-emotional development and motivation

Structural and Physiological Factors
5. Sensory acuity (auditory, visual, tactile, gustatory, olfactory)
6. Oromuscular capabilities
7. Speech transmission mechanisms

Environmental Factors
8. Social-cultural variables (socioeconomic level, language culture, dialect)
9. Experiences (care-giver child interactions, linguistic input, caregiver responsiveness)
10. Physical context (availability of toys, pictures, manipulable objects)

Figure 9–2
Factors affecting speech, language, and communication acquisition.
Source: Adapted from "Identifying Children with Language Disorders and Describing Their Language Performance" by I. F. Miller in *Contemporary Issues in Language Intervention* (p. 63) by I. F. Miller, E. D. Yoder, and R. Schiefelbusch (Eds.). 1983. Rockville, MD: American Speech-Language-Hearing Association.

type of deficit (e.g., structural and physiological factors may have more detrimental effects than environmental factors); (3) the age at which the problem occurred; (4) when the problem was identified; and (5) the quality of intervention efforts.

Severe problems in the neuropsychological, structural, and physiological areas presented in Figure 9–2 can be identified at birth or shortly thereafter. Children with one or more of these problems should be provided with early intervention services to replace negative cycles with positive ones.

Speech Disorders

The three major types of speech disorders are articulation disorders, voice disorders, and fluency disorders. *Articulation disorders* are characterized by defective or nonstandard speech sounds. They may be due to a variety of causes. One possible cause is hearing impairment. Other causes include structural defects or neuromotor deficits. Structural defects include gross abnormalities of the oral structures, such as clefts of the lip or palate. These occur during the first trimester of pregnancy and are probably due to some combination of genetic factors coming together under adverse environmental conditions (McWilliams, 1990). *Dysarthria* is a group of articulation disorders resulting from neuromuscular deficits—damage to the central and/or peripheral nervous system. The child's misarticulations are a consequence of lack of precise control over the muscles used in breathing, the larynx, the soft palate and pharynx, the tongue, the jaw, and/or the lips. *Apraxia* is another articulation disorder that is caused by injury to the central nervous system. There is no paralysis or weakness of the muscles of speech (because peripheral nerves that supply these muscles are not damaged). There is an impaired ability to organize the necessary *motor commands* to the speech musculature. Consequently, the individual is not able to properly sequence sounds in words.

Voice disorders are deviations of voice pitch, loudness, or quality. They may be caused by structural differences in the larynx or neurological damage to the brain or nerves controlling the oral cavity. Physiological causes of disordered voice include growths within the larynx (nodules, polyps, or cancerous tissue), infections of the larynx, damage to the nerves supplying the larynx, or accidental bruises or scratches on the larynx. Another cause of voice problems is vocal abuse, such as excessive yelling at ball games or, for preschoolers, excessive crying. Hearing impairment can also cause voice disorders because the child does not learn to speak with an appropriately resonant voice.

The most common *fluency disorder* is stuttering. Many fluency problems are associated with neurogenic disorders, but the cause or causes of stuttering have not been established. It probably has multiple causes with both organic and environmental factors playing a role in its origin and its maintenance.

Language and Communication Disorders

As noted earlier, etiology is more straightforward when language and communication problems are *not* the child's primary disability, but rather secondary to another condition. One exception to this statement is language disorders associated with autism. Though there are numerous hypotheses, the cause of the language problems exhibited by autistic children remains as much a mystery as the cause (or causes) of autism. Another exception is learning disabilities. As noted earlier, the relationship between language disorders and learning disabilities is complex.

A cause (or causes) for the language difficulties of children who appear to perform within normal limits in all *areas other than language* is difficult to specify. The factors most often associated with (if not responsible for) the language problems experienced by children with a primary diagnosis of language disordered are (1) limitations in perceptual ability (particularly auditory discrimination), (2) limitations in cognitive development (particularly in some sensorimotor attainments), (3) nature of interactions with others (particularly linguistic input), and (4) brain damage (Leonard, 1990). Leonard notes that evidence for the latter, brain damage, as a cause for the language problems of children with no other obvious disability is not convincing. However, this may change as technological advances make possible more precise assessment of brain functioning.

CHARACTERISTICS   Speech, language, and communication disorders appear singly and in clusters. They may result from input problems (hearing impairment, visual impairment), processing disorders (problems related to central nervous system dysfunction), or output disorders (e.g., cleft palate).

As noted above, the three major types of speech disorders are (1) articulation disorders, (2) voice disorders, and (3) fluency disorders. Articulation disorders are the most common. Children with articulation disorders demonstrate one or more of the following types of errors: (1) omission, (2) substitution, (3) distortion, and (4) addition. Omission is the failure to pronounce all of the expected sounds in a word. It constitutes the most serious misarticulation because the resultant speech is often unintelligible. Omissions occur most frequently among young children. Children who experience articulation disorders may omit final consonants in words. In substitution errors the substituted sound is generally somewhat similar to the replaced sound. For example, "thilly" might be substituted for *silly* or "wed" for *red*. Third are distortions. There are many types of distortions; the most common example is the lisp. The child may approximate the phoneme but not produce it precisely. The fourth type of error is the insertion or addition of an extra sound into a word. Addition occurs most often in the speech of young children, especially in the context of consonant blends.

There are two types of voice disorders: resonance disorders and phonation disorders. Children with resonance disorders demonstrate either hypernasality (excessive nasal quality) or hyponasality (abnormally reduced nasal quality). Hypernasality is very often a characteristic of the speech of children with cerebral palsy or an unrepaired cleft palate. Phonation disorders may be characterized by speech that is harsh, breathy, hoarse, or husky. In some severe cases there is no voice at all. Voice disorders are less common in children than in adults.

In fluency disorders the natural, smooth flow of speech is interrupted with inappropriate hesitations, pauses, and/or repetitions. Some fluency problems are considered normal because they do not call undue attention to the speaker. For example, repetitions of words and phrases and hesitations usually indicate that the speaker is reflecting on what to say. Listeners expect and accept this lack of fluency. What distinguishes a true fluency disorder from a normal fluency problem is muscular tensions and the fact that the stutterer's lack of fluency is with speech sounds, not words and phrases. A fluency problem that is sometimes confused with stuttering is cluttering. Van Riper (1978) compares the clutterer's speech to the pileup of keys when a beginning typist's speech exceeds control. It is rapid, garbled speech with extra sounds or mispronounced sounds and sometimes mixed-up sentence structure.

There are any number of ways to characterize language disorders. One method is in terms of the aspects of language that the child has not mastered at an age-appropriate level. Any one (or some combination) of the following language dimensions may pose problems for the child: (1) phonology, (2) morphology, (3) syntax, (4) semantics, or (5) pragmatics. The child's knowledge and skills in one (or some combination) of these dimensions may be either deficient (atypical) or delayed (like that of a younger normal language learner).

During the preschool years, children have three major goals in the area of phonological development. They must learn (1) a phonetic inventory, (2) a phonological system, and (3) to determine which speech sounds are used to signal differences in meaning. Children with a phonological disorder may have problems related to learning the sound system of their language and the linguistic rules governing how sounds can be combined.

Other children have difficulty understanding word meanings and word relationships. Problems with plurals (both regular and irregular forms), verb tenses, and the third-person-singular form are examples of morphological problems (*if* same-age peers are using these forms). Young elementary school children may omit inflectional endings altogether. For example, they may omit the third person -*s* on verbs (e.g., "My puppy like popcorn"), the possessive 's on nouns (e.g., "Not Susannah notebook"), and the *-er* on adjectives (e.g., "My box is small than yours"). The morphological problems of older students are most often associated with irregular past verb tenses and irregular plurals.

Some children identified as having a language disorder experience difficulty with the grammatical rules of their language. They cannot organize and order words to form sentences. Examples of syntax difficulties include problems understanding and producing structurally complex sentences, *wh-* questions, sentences with demonstrative pronouns (*this, that, those*), passive sentences, and sentences that express relationships with direct and indirect objects.

Other children labeled as language disordered have a problem acquiring their initial lexicon (mental dictionary). Later they may demonstrate word-finding difficulties (retrieving an appropriate known word when that word is required in a particular situation) and problems with figurative language. Very often there is evidence that the meanings they have assigned to words and word relationships are much narrower than those of same-age peers.

A substantial percentage of children with language disorders lack skills in pragmatics or language use. They do not use language as an effective tool for learning about their world and/or socializing. They produce syntactically well formed and semantically accurate utterances but have problems with communicative interaction strategies such as turn taking and initiating and maintaining a dialogue. They may introduce topics out of context and string together ideas tangentially without regard for the listener's perspective. Subtle cues present a problem. They often fail to adjust their language to the social context or employ even the most common nonlinguistic communication devices such as establishing and maintaining eye contact.

ASSESSMENT   Each of the three aspects of language disorder—speech, language, and communication—requires a different type of assessment. Assessment of articulation, voice, and fluency are the exclusive province of the speech-language pathologist (SLP). A number of factors are considered in the assessment of articulation. These include (1) the extent to which poor articulation is affecting the student's communication; and (2) the frequency, type, and consistency of the student's errors. To assess voice disorders, SLPs rely primarily on clinical judgment—their knowledge and experience—to determine whether a student needs therapy. To assess fluency, SLPs take samples of the student's oral language in various situations. These data are then analyzed to determine the frequency and type of involuntary dysfluencies.

Language skills may be assessed in either a receptive or an expressive task format. Expressive tasks require the child to name or describe something (e.g., "Tell me about _____.") Another commonly used task for assessing expressive language skills is the elicited imitation task. The examiner produces a sentence and asks the child to repeat it. The assumption behind this task is that a child will not imitate a particular linguistic feature properly unless he or she actually uses that feature productively in spontaneous utterances. For example, a child who does not ordinarily use the article *the* in spontaneous language is very likely to omit it in when asked to repeat this sentence: *Mommy put my cookies in the box*. A similar assessment procedure employs delayed imitation. In this approach, the child's response is further removed in time from the examiner's production. For example, the examiner might place two pictures in front of the child and say "The father feeds the dog," "The man feeds the dogs." Then, pointing to the first picture the examiner asks, "Which one is this?" Receptive tasks require the child to respond nonverbally (e.g., "Point to _____."). An example of this type of task would be presentation of several pictures depicting actions with the direction "Show me 'eating.'" Another type of receptive task requires presentation of toys or objects that the child can manipulate. Then the examiner produces a sentence and asks the child to act upon the objects as the sentence indicates (e.g., "Put the baby in the bed.")

The SLP systematically varies tasks, contexts, and the mode of response to observe where the child's performance specifically breaks down (Wiig, 1990). Ways to do this include (1) reducing the complexity of task directions; (2) reducing the numbers of words, phrases, or clauses in sentences the child is asked to produce; (3) ensuring that word choices in spoken sentences are familiar to the child; (4) varying sentence structure; (5) requiring a pointing response rather than a spoken response; and (6) providing printed input rather than spoken input.

Over the past 20 years, the awareness of language disorders and their close relationship to academic learning problems have produced a plethora of assessment measures. However, the traditional assessment measures have some problems. One problem is that many are not practical for either SLPs or teachers because they require a great deal of time to administer. Another problem with traditional assessment instruments is that they are not designed to be used across settings, people, and activities. Finally, a third problem is they do not generate the type of information that is needed to develop intervention content and strategies.

As noted in an earlier section of this chapter, there is a definite trend away from traditional standardized testing toward naturalistic assessment. Rather than assessing fragmented skills in a separate and unfamiliar setting such as a clinic room, assessment procedures are conducted in the context of routine activities in the child's natural environments. In practice this means that when assessing vocabulary, for example, rather than asking a child to label a predetermined set of objects or pictures that the SLP has selected, the examiner observes the child acting with different people in various settings. The examiner then ascertains what words the child uses and where and how those words are used in the natural course of everyday tasks and activities. This analysis would be a type of language sample. In addition to establishing a baseline for student performance, this type of assessment also helps identify the instructional adaptations that will be required to enhance the student's classroom performance.

Age-Level Distinctions

Early Childhood. Procedures to identify and intervene with infants at risk for speech, language, or communication problems should begin at birth. A first step is to identify children with any of the risk factors presented in Figure 9–2—neuropsychological factors, structural and physiological factors, and environmental factors. There are numerous screening tests to use in this early identification process.

The preschool period can be divided into five stages according to the average, or mean, length of children's utterances. Table 9–1 provides an overview of attainments in each of the five stages and the approximate ages when the child can be expected to produce the different length utterances. The *mean length of utterance* (MLU) is a good predictor of language complexity until the child attains an MLU of 4.0 (Brown, 1973).

Table 9–1
Five developmental stages during the preschool period

Stage	Attainments
I (MLU: 1.0–2.0) (Approx. age: 12–26 months)	*Speech.* Produces some words consistently but varies others greatly; limits initial words in number and type of syllables: gradually comes to be governed by phonological rules *Language.* Uses single-word utterances naming specific objects and classes of objects (animate and inanimate) or expressing a relational meaning (existence, nonexistence, disappearance, recurrence); uses successive single-word utterances; uses 2-word combinations to express existence, negation, recurrence, attribution, possession, location, agent-action, action-object, agent-object *Communication.* Uses gestures to express intentions; uses gestures plus vocalization to communicate desires and direct the behavior of others; uses multiword utterances to perform a range of functions
II (MLU: 2.0–2.5) (Approx. age: 27–30 months)	*Speech.* Begins to follow phonological rules that provide for consistent speech performance *Language.* Begins producing morphemes: *in, on,* present progressive (*-ing*), regular plural (*-s*), irregular past tense, possessive (*'s*) uncontractible copula, articles, regular past (*-ed*), irregular third person, uncontractible auxiliary, contractible copula, contractible auxiliary; produces some pronouns (*I, you, them, they, he/she, we, it*) *Communication.* Responds to a conversational partner and engages in short dialogue; uses terms such as *here* and *there* to direct attention or to reference
III (MLU: 2.5–3.0) (Approx. age: 31–34 months)	*Speech.* Articulates all English vowels and the majority of consonants *Language.* Continues to experiment with and modify simple declarative sentences; begins to produce negative, interrogative, and imperative sentence forms *Communication.* Learns to become a better conversational partner, taking turns and using contingent queries and questions; uses a greater variety of forms to attain desired objects and services; can take the perspective of the conversational partner
IV (MLU: 3.0–3.75) (Approx. age: 35–40 months)	*Speech.* May reduce or simplify words and consonant clusters *Language.* Produces questions in the adult form; produces embedded sentences and other complex constructions; uses negative contractions including *isn't, aren't, doesn't, and didn't;* uses the modal auxiliaries *could, would, must,* and *might* in negatives and questions *Communication.* Seems to have a better awareness of the social aspects of conversation; uses some indirect requests
V (MLU: 3.75–4.5) (Approx. age: 41–46 months)	*Speech.* Produces a few consonant clusters and blends *Language.* Has mastered regular and irregular past tense in most contexts; uses the third person singular and the contractible copula; inverts auxiliary verbs appropriately in questions; uses *and* and, later, *if* to conjoin clauses *Communication.* Switches codes (produces simplified utterances) for younger children; uses most deictic terms correctly; can talk about feelings and emotions; produces indirect requests in which the goal is embedded in a question or statement

MLU is computed by counting the number of words or morphemes in a sample of 50 (or 100) consecutive utterances and then dividing the total number of words or morphemes by 50 (or 100). When the MLU has been computed, it is possible to determine whether the child demonstrates a significant delay or deviation from normal expectations by comparing his or her vocabulary, semantic knowledge, syntax, and pragmatic skills with those of normal learners, as presented in Table 9–1.

With preschool as well as with older students, observations in natural environments are critical to assess language use and communication skills. Table 9–2 suggests some contexts for observations of preschoolers; it also suggests specific variables to consider in these contexts. Naturalistic observations should provide at least the following data: (1) how the child gains the attention of another, (2) how he or she initiates play with caregivers and peers, (3) whether he or she anticipates and takes turns, (4) the nature of routine communication events (verbal and nonverbal), (5) when and with whom interactions occur. Standardized tests may be administered to determine how much the child lags behind his or her peers of the same age in the use of language. These tests sample both expressive language skills and receptive language skills.

School Age.   In general, students with language disorders show a later onset of language skills and a slower rate of language acquisition. Assessment of school-age students focuses on identifying the student's specific language impairments and specifying objectives for language intervention. The SLP applies many of the same procedures used with younger children. Most important is to explore language production in its natural habitat, using tasks as similar as possible to those actually faced by students, such as initiating and maintaining a conversation.

SLPs also rely heavily on spontaneous language samples as the best source of information about expressive language skills. Computer programs are also available to analyze language samples and quantify various aspects of language production.

Secondary/Transition.   There is substantial evidence of an increasingly widening gap between the academic achievement of students with language learning disabilities and their peers, and adolescents with language and communication disorders are acutely aware of this gap (Wiig, 1990). Academic and social failures and the feeling of being different are very painful. Some emotional reactions reflecting the pain and negative self-perception include aggression, anxiety, compulsiveness, frustration, rigidity, lack of motivation, and withdrawal. Problems may initially go unnoticed by parents, teachers, and others, but eventually such overt behaviors as fighting, stealing, obesity, anorexia, or depression make it impossible for adults not to respond.

The assumption that children will outgrow their language and learning disabilities and become "normal" adolescents and young adults has turned out to be wishful thinking. These problems do not go away. Most children who experience language learning problems in the elementary grades continue to have difficulties as adolescents and young adults (and later in life). Problems include being understood and lack of ability in using higher-level language such as jokes, sarcasm, metaphoric expressions, and complex communicative intents such as negotiating and persuading. Moreover, students with language learning disabilities seem to differ from their peers in three other aspects

Table 9–2
Suggestions for classroom observations

Context	What to Observe
Group Activities	Amount/extent of participation Appropriateness of interactive behaviors Attention and control strategies Response to directions (individual and group)
Task-Oriented Situations	Material and object preferences Duration of material/object manipulations Appropriateness of material/object manipulations
Social Interactions (with Adults and Peers)	Type of communication devices used to secure desired objects and events Proportion of initiations versus responses Variations in the frequency of communicative behaviors with different adults and peers Agreement between verbal and nonverbal communicative efforts Amount/extent of turn taking (in verbal and nonverbal exchanges)
Free Play	Context of play (isolate, parallel, or interactive) Basis of play (actual or vicarious experiences) Substitution of one object for another in pretend play Appropriateness of pretend activity sequencing

of communicative competence: (1) adapting communicative intentions to the listener and the situation, (2) conveying and comprehending information, and (3) initiating and maintaining cooperative conversational interactions (Donahue, Pearl, & Bryan, 1983). All of these difficulties plus problems learning slang undoubtedly affect how the adolescent with a language learning disability is accepted by peers, which in turn affects development of age-appropriate social skills (Donahue & Bryan, 1984). Sometimes adolescents and young adults may refer themselves to a speech-language pathologist if their speech, language, or communication abilities are causing them social embarrassment or interfering with their academic or vocational pursuits.

There are relatively few standardized instruments designed specifically for students 11 to 18 years of age. The Let's Talk Inventory for Adolescents (Wiig, 1982) considers some aspects of interpersonal communication. The Test of Adolescent Language (TOAL) (Hammill, Brown, Larsen, & Wiederholt, 1980) assesses spoken and written semantics and syntax, both receptively and expressively. The second section of the Clinical Evaluation of Language Functions (CELF) (Semel & Wiig, 1980) was designed for students in grades 5 to 12. It probes aspects of language comprehension and expression. The Communicative Activities of Daily Living (CADL) (Holland, 1980) was developed to be used with adults, but it provides useful guidelines for measuring adolescents' communication.

In conclusion, what is most important to keep in mind concerning speech, language, and communication assessment is the need to consider all aspects of verbal and nonverbal communicative functioning. Fortunately, the federal guidelines for IDEA do not restrict professionals to standardized instruments. As a result, informal naturalistic procedures, particularly important in analysis and description of language and communication disorders, are accepted. Formulation of a clear picture of what students can do, what they are ready to learn, and what is the best way to teach them requires a multidisciplinary approach and a variety of formal and informal procedures.

INTERVENTION Speech pathology services are one type of "related services" provided for by the IDEA. Most SLPs in the United States—an estimated 50%—are members of the American Speech-Language-Hearing Association (ASHA). An estimated 41% of these professionals are employed in the schools. In school settings, SLPs typically assume responsibility for assessment (particularly screening and eligibility determination) and remediation of speech disorders. They rarely have sufficient time to provide direct services for all children with language and communication disorders. Rather than trying to carry out all intervention and remedial programming themselves, they collaborate with teachers and other specialists to design programs to be implemented in the natural environments of the school, the home, and the community. They serve as consultants, program monitors, and peer trainers for teachers. The remainder of this chapter will discuss intervention for language and communication disorders (rather than speech disorders) because this is the information most needed by teachers.

Language intervention is application of procedures to expand (1) the scope and variety of an individual's language knowledge and skills, (2) the functions and uses that language serves for the individual, and (3) the number of social and physical contexts where he or she uses language spontaneously (McCormick & Schiefelbusch, 1990). The broad purpose of language intervention is to bring about certain outcomes judged necessary for successful academic, social, and vocational functioning. Specific intervention goals vary according to the ages and needs of the individuals, but the key intervention issues are the same for all students:

- *What* do we want the student to be able to do that he or she presently cannot do?
- *How* can we teach these new skills and get the student to perform them in the contexts where they are called for?
- *Where* and *when* should we teach the new skills?

Goals

The first and most crucial intervention question is, What do we want the student to be able to do that he or she presently cannot do? At the broadest level, the answer is, To understand and use language appropriately and effectively in present and future social, academic, and vocational contexts. A more specific answer to this question requires information from the assessment process concerning (1) the student's abilities and disabilities, (2) characteristics of environments relevant to the student, and (3) interactional variables. This is present performance information.

The next task is to develop and prioritize instructional objectives. Asking questions like these will generate the type of information necessary to this process:

1. What do same-age peers know about language?
2. How do same-age peers use language?
3. What does the student need to learn to be successful in academic and social situations?
4. What skills/abilities does the student need to be viewed more favorably by peers and adults?

Speech-language pathologists design programs to be carried out by teachers and other specialists.

5. What does the student need to learn in order to succeed in vocational pursuits?
6. What strategies does the student need to acquire in order to use language to learn other age-appropriate skills?

Procedures and Strategies

The key word in current language intervention programming is *natural*. The key concept is social interaction. Intervention procedures are characterized by training in the natural environment, by natural consequences, and by more attention to communication functions and conversational skills. Teaching target responses in the context of daily routines and ongoing activities increases the probability of generalization to new situations. The "natural intervention" trend is an effective alternative to repetitive presentation of training trials until some level of proficiency is achieved. Such highly structured practice formats (called massed trial formats) have not been altogether eliminated, but they are now most often limited to initial acquisition and practice of specific structures.

Naturalistic intervention procedures are drawn from language acquisition research that indicates that the normal language learner's communicative efforts are acknowledged with attention, followed by an immediate confirming response, or rewarded by compliance (Bowerman, 1976; Nelson, 1977). The basic assumption underlying naturalistic approaches is that repeated exposure to targeted forms in multiple natural settings will teach the child to make proper associations between utterances and the environmental stimuli they relate to (McCormick & Schiefelbusch, 1990).

Naturalistic teaching is characterized by more natural social discourse. There is an emphasis on responding to the intention of the child's utterances (rather than the form). The goal is to teach the child that language is an extremely effective tool for (1) regulating the behavior of others, (2) obtaining desired objects and events, and (3) maintaining pleasurable social interactions.

While naturalistic language training approaches incorporate behavioral procedures like shaping, prompting, and differential reinforcement, such procedures are not applied as systematically or consistently as they were in the highly structured training formats of the past. Sometimes generalization training procedures are implemented to ensure the carryover of skills into new situations, but the more likely case is that there

Teaching in the context of ongoing activities increases the probability of generalization.

is no special planning for generalization. Generalization enhancement techniques are inherent in naturalistic approaches.

In summary, naturalistic teaching approaches take advantage of ongoing interactions in daily activities where the teacher (or another adult) and the child encounter objects, people, and events of mutual interest. These naturalistic teaching interactions in familiar routines and activities provide the student with something to talk about and the motivation for communication. Naturalistic approaches have broadest application with children whose language and/or communication problems are less severe. For those with more severe disorders, the naturalistic approaches are a second-level technique, used after the child has acquired a particular language skill—when the concern is with response fluency and generalization.

Instructional Contexts

The term *context*, broadly defined, means environment or surroundings. Traditionally, the therapy room was the primary context for language training. The assumption was that the child would somehow figure out where, when, and with whom to use whatever was learned in the therapy room. The basic assumptions were that (1) language skills learned in the therapy room would be used in all of the child's natural environments (e.g., home, classroom, playground); (2) talking to the speech-language pathologist would generalize to talking with others; and (3) there would be application of what was learned from pictures to real objects and activities. Sometimes these desired outcomes occurred. More often they did not.

Most language skills are best taught and practiced in natural environments.

Appropriate and effective language and communication skills can be taught, practiced, and maintained in natural environments. All these are required in the process: (1) interesting materials, objects, and events; (2) opportunities and consequences for language use; and (3) judicious use of scheduling and routines. Children learn language by using it. The challenge for adults is to maximize their opportunities for successful communicative interactions.

Age-Level Distinctions

Early Childhood. Early intervention programs train the primary caregiver to provide language stimulation in the context of play and routine care-giving activities (e.g., feeding, diapering). Communication functions such as requesting, greeting, giving, and showing are among the most important initial goals. Caregivers are taught to shape primitive communication signals such as smiling, touching, whining, and pointing into more sophisticated communicative behaviors. Also critical for infants and very young children is manipulation of objects and events that will lead to construction of sensorimotor concepts.

Objectives for preschoolers with language delay/disorder include

1. participation (verbal and nonverbal) in group activities
2. initiation of communicative interactions
3. responding to the communication of others
4. requests for desired objects, events, and services
5. compliance with individual and group directions
6. use of conversational strategies such as turn taking

Programming for children who understand and use some multiword utterances focuses on shaping more complex forms and establishing a greater variety of communication functions. Also taught at this stage are semantic-syntactic concepts such as location, possession, and action-object relations.

Ensuring that children experience the rewards of their communicative efforts is a high priority of early communication training. Questions, commands, praise statements (e.g., "Good talking"), and corrections tend to constrain and inhibit communicative interactions so they are avoided. Instead, adults follow the child's lead in play and in talking. Among the techniques most often used in these settings are (1) parallel talking (talking about what the child is playing with), (2) expansion (expanding the topic, syntax, or semantic truth of the child's utterances), and (3) labeling (naming objects and events that attract the child's attention and interest).

Many of the intervention strategies for infants and preschoolers derive from a naturalistic intervention approach called "incidental teaching" or "milieu therapy" (Hart & Risley, 1975, 1982; Hart & Rogers-Warren, 1978). *Incidental teaching* is an umbrella term for a set of language facilitation strategies that derive from observations of naturally occurring parent-child interactions. Data from these observations suggest that caregivers apply the following language facilitation strategies, which are sometimes referred to as "motherese":

1. Talking about shared perceptions when these perceptions (objects, events, and/or relations) attract the child's attention
2. Modeling, imitating, and expanding desired and actual communication efforts on the part of the child
3. Repeating and clarifying words, statements, and requests that the child does not seem to understand
4. Using higher speech frequencies and stress to call the child's attention to important sentence elements

The incidental teaching approach was first described by Hart and Risley in a 1968 article. Since that time there has been substantial research documenting its effectiveness with many different populations of children who are language-delayed and language-disordered. The primary goal of incidental teaching is skill building and elaboration of language forms. Two learning strategies—imitation and cross-modal transfer—are promoted. Cross-modal transfer refers to changes across modalities, for example, changes in receptive language skills as a result of instruction in expressive language skills. The child is prompted and reinforced for imitation because imitation is viewed as a means of encouraging the child's attention to new words and promoting association of new words with objects and events. There are repeated presentations of appropriate language models when the child's attention is focused on the immediate context. This is to teach the child to attend to the words that others use to refer to objects and events. Later the child is encouraged to spontaneously produce these utterances.

Incidental teaching is used in a variety of unstructured and structured classroom settings—free play, snacks and meals, transition periods, art and music periods, and instructional sessions. The only requirements are a variety of attractive and interesting materials, toys, and events and interaction with one or more adults.

School Age.   As the child gets older, it becomes increasingly more difficult to separate language disorders and learning disabilities. Because the two seem to be on the same continuum, many professionals have begun to use the term language learning disabilities to describe the problems these children experience (e.g., Wiig, 1990). Figure 9–2 presented a list of factors that affect the development of speech, language, and communication. Recall that delay or dysfunction in any single factor or any combination of factors can cause speech, language, or communication problems. In turn, these speech, language, and/or communication problems can cause a broad array of academic and social problems. It is difficult to deal with the language and communication problems without attention to effects. In fact, when children start school, the criterion for judging the severity of their language problems and the type of intervention needed is the degree to which academic and social functioning is affected.

The preferred intervention approach with school-age children is to teach targeted skills in the context of ongoing academic instruction and normal social interactions—to approximate "real-life" transactions as much as possible. Remediation of significant expressive language delay requires more than a few hours a week with a speech-language pathologist. It requires continuous intervention in all naturally occurring activities and settings. Language and communication objectives can be embedded within all kinds of classroom activities and study units. For example, an alternative to drill-

and-practice routines (a massed trial training format) is to introduce meanings and functions of new words and concepts into discussions and activities associated with a topic the student is particularly interested in. Children are much more likely to apply their learning strategies (selective attention, concept formation, memory) when they have selected the topic for discussion.

Probably the most important accomplishment of the early school years is learning to read. Advocates of keeping language "whole" in early literacy instruction argue that the best explanation for early reading acquisition lies in children's motivations to make sense of their world as the driving force leading them to begin to derive meaning from print (e.g., Schory, 1990). Advocates of whole language methods argue that children fail to become good readers and writers because reading and writing have traditionally been taught as discrete skills separate from language.

Children with language learning difficulties may not make necessary sound-symbol associations and learn how to sequence sounds as they learn to read in whole-language contexts. As a result, they may need more "code emphasis" (Liberman & Liberman, 1990). Working together, SLPs, teachers, and parents can devise a wide range of interesting and age-appropriate activities and strategies to expand children's opportunities for both language learning and literacy.

Secondary/Transition.   Secondary settings place complex demands on students. Secondary school students are expected to be able to (Schumaker & Deshler, 1984)

1. gain information from materials written at secondary reading levels
2. complete homework and other assignments independently
3. gain information from auditory presentation such as lectures, discussions, and student reports
4. participate in discussions
5. express themselves in writing
6. pass minimal competency examinations

Available data indicate that the above skills are precisely the areas that constitute problems for adolescents with learning disabilities (Schumaker & Deshler, 1984). They read very poorly, often failing to apply whatever learning strategies they have. They rarely ask for help despite having difficulty working independently, and they experience pervasive oral and written language problems in addition to poor spelling. These problems are compounded by significant deficits in social skills, which are particularly devastating because of the importance of the peer group to adolescents.

The major intervention approaches for adolescents are (1) structuring social and academic experiences to increase their opportunities to learn language and communication skills and (2) training in use of specific learning strategies. In other words, the emphasis is on teaching strategies rather than academic content. One method is to develop performance strategies for the phonological, morphologic, semantic, syntactic, and pragmatic systems of language and bring these systems to the meta-level of consciousness (e.g., Schumaker & Deshler, 1984).

Students with severe language and cognitive impairments should be taught the words and international symbols they will need for daily living and personal safety. An especially promising new approach for students with severe developmental disabilities and autism is called facilitated communication (Biklen, 1992). With facilitated communication an adult facilitator provides a keyboard writing system with print output, supporting the child's forearm, wrist, and index finger (if necessary). The adult then uses systematic steps to introduce the child to sound-letter correspondences, to teach simple words, to request simple words in response to fill-in tasks, and ultimately, to converse with the student in writing. In many cases when facilitated communication was introduced, children have typed written messages that far exceeded expectations based on the student's oral communication abilities.

CURRICULUM IMPLICATIONS

A curriculum is a composite of objectives and activities designed to result in attainment of long-term goals. Some commercially produced language curricula include what to teach and how to teach it: others specify only the instructional content (what to teach).

Table 9–3 presents a sample of important goals for infants, preschoolers, and elementary-age students in the three language areas (form, content, and use). The suggestions for teachers (facilitator behaviors) follow from the discussion on intervention. The focus is on implementing naturalistic teaching strategies across the range of physical, social, and temporal contexts. Seven of the most commonly used language teaching strategies were recently summarized by Raver (1987):

1. *Repeats*. Appropriate language is restated or rehearsed to assist learning new vocabulary and reinforce emerging forms.
2. *Imitation/modeling*. The adult provides a model of an appropriate response and tells the child to imitate it.
3. *Indirect commands*. The adult provides suggestions to help children handle problem situations (where language may be an obstacle) alone.
4. *Questions*. Questioning is used to elicit the child's maximum participation in an activity.
5. *Paraphrases*. Paraphrasing provides an abbreviated form of a child's language back to the child to encourage reciprocal language usage.
6. *Sentence completion*. Eliciting expressive language by requesting one- to two-word responses to complete the adult's sentences.
7. *Feedback skills*. Child is encouraged to become a critical listener to his or her own language and the language of others.

Goals for adolescents are not included in Table 9–3 because curricula focuses on teaching learning strategies rather than language or communication strategies, per se. Schumaker and Deshler's (1984) curriculum focuses on teaching strategies for gaining information from written and oral materials, strategies for expressing information in permanent products, memory strategies, and social-communication skills. It is designed to be used in academic settings to overcome the major learning and performance problems of adolescents who are language learning disabled. It is appropriate for students with a reading level as low as 4th grade. All strategies are taught in a structured, systematic fashion using a nine-step teaching methodology:

1. Make the student aware of current learning habits.
2. Describe the new learning strategy.
3. Model the new strategy.

4. Have the student verbally rehearse the strategy.
5. Have the student practice the strategy with controlled materials.
6. Provide feedback.
7. Have the student practice with grade-level materials.
8. Provide feedback.
9. Test.

After students demonstrate skill mastery, a three-phase generalization procedure is begun: (1) an orientation phase in which students are made aware of the different settings and contexts where a particular learning strategy can be used, (2) an activation phase in which students are given practice with the strategy with a variety of materials and contexts, and (3) a maintenance phase with periodic probes to ensure continued application of the strategy.

MAINSTREAMING
Students with speech and language impairments are the most highly integrated of all students with disabilities. According to the most recent federal data available (U.S. Department of Education, 1992), 76.8 percent of students in this category were served in regular classroom placements in the 1989–1990 school year, and another 17.7 percent were served in resource rooms. The small proportion served in separate classes represents, in general, students with very severe language disabilities.

Students with speech disorders are likely to have individual sessions with the speech-language pathologist to improve articulation, voice quality, or fluency. The therapist works with (and through) the classroom staff to serve students with language and/or communication disorders, assisting in the adaptation of materials and procedures, monitoring progress toward specified goals and objectives, and helping the teacher learn to recognize and use routine instructional and social interactions as the context for facilitating language and communication skills.

Though the social and academic requirements of the regular curriculum may have to be modified somewhat to accommodate the needs of a child with a language learning disability, the benefits from keeping that child with normal peers far outweigh the costs in time and effort. For this approach to be successful, collaboration among teachers, speech-language pathologists, and parents must begin with assessment and continue throughout intervention.

INNOVATION AND DEVELOPMENT
Historically, intervention with children experiencing speech, language, and/or communication difficulties relied heavily on presentation of pictured stimuli in highly structured training contexts to elicit desired forms and syntactic structures. Although training in highly structured settings produced successful skill acquisition, students rarely generalized skills to everyday situations because there was little attention to either the meaningfulness of the material learned or the communicative usefulness of the skills. The most notable change over the past decade has been the increasing concern for teaching language through naturally occurring routines and social activities. This trend has accompanied the theoretical shift toward pragmatic-interactive perspectives and acknowledgement of the significant role that peer interactions play in children's language development.

Table 9–3
Selected curriculum goals and teacher behaviors

Age	Form Goals	Content Goals
Infant (birth to age 3)	React to sounds Vocalize single vowel sounds in play and in response Attend/respond to tone of voice Babble repetitive syllable sequences Imitate nonspeech sounds and speech sounds Say "da-da" and "ma-ma" and respond to "no-no" Respond to own name and simple action requests Point to familiar persons, toys, and animals on request Use 2-word sequences Point to body parts (on self and doll) Produce expanded noun phrases Use present progressive inflection (-ing) Use more and different words to encode semantic relations Use intelligible speech (at least 75% of the time)	Look at, manipulate, and search for objects Understand functional relationships Understand functions and social meanings of a large number of objects Understand that an object can exist, cease to exist, and then reappear Understand the location of 2 objects in relation to each other Understand possession and attribution Recognize and name colors Match 2 identical items Group objects by a single dimension Apply previous experiences to new problems Remember objects and events
Preschool (ages 3–5)	Produce expanded noun phrases (demonstrative + article + adjective + noun) Use to be as copula, on, possessive 's & some contractions Imitate sentences up to 6 words Begin to use past tense Achieve MLU of 55 words Use intelligible speech (at least 95% of the time)	Remember daily routines Know shapes, sizes, positions, and colors Know time (day/night) and seasons Know number symbols (1–10) Understand most prepositions Understand most adjectives Follow 3-action commands Ask and answer wh- questions
Elementary (ages 5–12)	Use verb tense (present possessive, simple past, third person present, irregular past and future) Use 5–6 words per utterance Begin complex structural distinctions Extend and modify word meaning with prefixes Use the five basic sentence patterns competently	Understand all prepositions and adjectives Understand basic linguistic concepts (coordination, class exclusion and inclusion, spatial sequences, temporal sequences, cause-effect, instrumental, revision) Understand spatial, temporal, and kinship relations Use word definitions (lexicon) resembling those of an adult

Use Goals	Facilitator Behaviors
Smile, coo in response to voice and adult smiling Show anticipation if about to be picked up or fed Discriminate strangers Vocalize to initiate interpersonal interactions Use gestures to direct adult attention Gesture and vocalize to request desired objects and events Vocalize immediately following the utterance of another person Add information to the prior utterance of communicative partner Ask an increasing number of questions Use utterances to call attention, regulate others, request, participate in social routines, comment, and play	1. Imitate child's utterances in the course of exploratory activities 2. Provide a variety of interesting materials, objects, and events that invite sensory exploration 3. Encourage exploration and manipulation of the physical environment 4. Talk about the child's activities and object and event preferences 5. Draw attention to physical, temporal, spatial and social relationships 6. Acknowledge and respond to the intent of the child's communicative efforts 7. Encourage nonverbal and verbal turn taking 8. Encourage all types of interactive play 9. Model and encourage such social rituals as greetings, polite requests, and responses 10. Teach to heterogeneous groups and plan activities that promote group interaction 11. Provide comments that preserve the child's semantic intent 12. Allow the child to select conversational topics
Change tone of voice and sentence structure to adapt to listener's level of understanding Use alternative forms that take context differences into account Demonstrate some ability to assume another perspective temporarily Show some ability to think about and comment on language Metalinguistic awareness	
Initiate and maintain conversations Consider listener's perspective when encoding messages Respond to listener feedback by altering the message if necessary Understand direct and indirect speech acts	1. Begin with what students can do and build on their strengths 2. Avoid language exercises in favor of training in the natural context 3. Design instructional activities around student interests and topics being studied by peers 4. Focus on functional communication skills that will contribute to social and academic competencies 5. Use games and self-correcting materials as needed to target specific linguistic structures 6. Modify the language of instruction (e.g., verbal and written directions) and adapt reading materials to maximize student chances of succeeding

373

C arol Westby and Geraldine Rouse (1985) describe a unique program for bicultural children with language learning disabilities in Albuquerque, New Mexico: they have drawn from ethnographic research methods to compare, contrast, and understand the nature of interactions among and within cultures. A class, serving eight Hispanic children, ages 6 to 9 years, was team-taught by a Hispanic speech-language pathologist and an Anglo teacher. The children knew the Spanish words for common household items and some Spanish slang, but they relied more on Chicano English for communication. Results of formal tests and interviews with their families indicated that the students were not competent in either English or Spanish.

Goals
The goal of the program was to increase the children's communicative competence in informal social language and school language. An overriding goal of all activities was to develop language to be used for "planning" purposes. Planning requires knowing and thinking about the future and metacognition (thinking about knowing and thinking), which children from high-context cultures are less likely to demonstrate. High-context cultures draw heavily and depend on the immediate context for meaning. The children in this program had not acquired many familiar routines of Hispanic culture, so planning was especially important for them—even in activities that might not have required planning by others.

Activities
Activities varied along a continuum from high to low context. Characteristics of high-context activities were (1) no competition among children and no attempt by adults to determine correct or incorrect responses, (2) student negotiation and control of discussion and conversation, (3) flexible time limits, and (4) use of highly context-dependent language. High-context activities included field trips, cooking activities, weaving (and other art projects), construction of an adobe pueblo, and pretend play with props. Some activities had both high-context and low-context characteristics. They were high context because of the nature of their organization and because the topic of the communication was familiar. However, the lack of contextual cues made them low context. Other activities were at the low-context end of the continuum. These activities had an adult-structured, prescribed format. An example of a low-context activity is calendar time during morning circle. The children routinely respond to the teacher's questions about the month, day of the week, year, season, weather, what they did yesterday, or the day before, and what they would do tomorrow. Minimal or no contextual cues were available to assist comprehension and memory, and responses were judged (gently) as either correct or incorrect.

This program assisted the children in learning how to use aspects of their high-context culture in the low-context environment of the classroom. At the same time, they learned to cope with the school culture.

Because children help one another learn language and communication skills (in play, peer tutoring, conversations, and collaborative work), considerable attention is now directed to increasing interactions among students, particularly interactions between students with disabling conditions and their peers who are not disabled. Computer activities are ideal for this purpose.

There have also been significant technological advances in the field of augmentative communication (see chapters 7 and 8), affecting availability of an array of very powerful and versatile (albeit expensive) computer-based communication devices. These communication systems make it possible to take advantage of whatever motor capabilities a nonverbal student demonstrates to generate spoken and/or written messages. For example, puffs and sucks on a mouthpiece may be used as a switch to control input of information.

Another area where innovations and developments are noteworthy is concern for nonnative English speakers. The numbers of students whose native language is not English are increasing at an unprecedented rate. Of the 34.6 million people in the United States who do not use English as their primary language, 3.5 million are estimated to have speech, language, or hearing disorders (American Speech-Language-Hearing Association, 1985). The educational and therapeutic management of these children is complex and controversial. It is just now beginning to be grappled with in a

Educational and therapeutic management of non-native-English speakers is complex and controversial.

1. Provide materials, objects, and activities that encourage high levels of engagement, cooperative interactions, and communication.

2. Structure the environment to encourage the child to anticipate and to initiate communicative behavior.

3. Provide maximum opportunities for interactions with normal language learning peers.

4. Give your attention, a confirming response, and/or desired objects or activities to encourage and reward communicative efforts.

5. Be sure that verbal messages match the attitudes, feelings, or intentions expressed by tone of voice, facial expressions, and body language.

6. Modify the language of instruction and instructional materials, and provide repetitions to maximize understanding.

7. Encourage children to ask questions when they do not understand the meaning of a word or instruction.

8. Talk about shared perceptions at the time the objects or events are the focus of the child's attention.

manner that may lead to some solutions in the foreseeable future (American Speech-Language-Hearing Association, 1985).

SUMMARY

This chapter has provided an introduction to the complex problems surrounding assessment and intervention for students experiencing speech, language, and communication disorders. In addition to some practical suggestions related to naturalistic intervention strategies, this chapter emphasizes the importance of teachers, speech-language pathologists, and parents working as a team to ensure a generalized approach across environments. Other important themes of this chapter include (1) the importance of focusing on effective interpersonal communication as a primary intervention goal, (2) the need to integrate planning in cognitive, social, and linguistic domains, (3) the importance of assessing and teaching language and communication in the context of routine activities in the natural environment.

STUDY QUESTIONS

1. Discuss the history of the study of the nature of language and language acquisition.

2. Describe new views concerning assessment, the proper focus of intervention, and how intervention is provided for students with language and communication disorders.

3. Differentiate speech disorders, language disorders, and communication disorders, and describe causes and characteristics of each.

4. Describe procedures to assess speech, language, or communication disorders at the three different age levels: early childhood, school age, and secondary/transition.

5. State the important questions to ask when developing intervention objectives.

6. Contrast natural and contrived/artificial language intervention procedures.

7. Discuss how different contexts affect language learning and language use.

8. State broad objectives for preschoolers with language delay/disorder.

9. State broad objectives for school-age children with language and communication difficulties.

10. State broad objectives for secondary students with language and communication problems.

10

Hearing Impairments

Sheila Lowenbraun
University of Washington

Marie D. Thompson
University of Washington

  In this chapter you will learn about

- the normal functioning of the auditory system and the types and causes of hearing loss

- the variables that affect the ability of a child with a hearing impairment to acquire communication skills

- some methods used to evaluate students who are hearing impaired at different age levels

- the various communication modes and language systems used by students with hearing impairments and the benefits and drawbacks of each

- the least restrictive environment controversy as it affects the education of children who are hearing impaired

*H*ow exciting it was to run into John, his mother, and sister at the coffee shop! I worked with John and his family for several years when he was in an early intervention program. John is now 8 years old, and I had not seen him since he was 6. John signs and talks simultaneously, using more speech than sign. He is very excited because he has decided to return to the school near his home next fall, and he will be attending classes with normally hearing children. He will have a sign interpreter to assist him in all his classes.

While we sat and drank pop and coffee, John talked about what he will be doing during the summer: swimming, fishing with his dad, playing with his friends, and watching video movies. John's family has a closed-caption decoder that prints on the screen what is being said in the movie. John's mother signs the movies to him at times, but when mom is not available, he reads the captions, and he informs me that the printed words are helping his younger sister learn to read.

When he was 8 months old, John's mother suspected he had a hearing loss and took him to a pediatrician. She was told that John would likely "outgrow" the problem, a not uncommon response! After many months of frustration, John's mother was able to have his hearing tested and was told that he did indeed have a severe-to-profound sensorineural hearing loss. After obtaining hearing aids, John was enrolled in an early intervention program where he was introduced to auditory training and sign language.

When John turned 3, he entered an integrated preschool program. During his first years at the school, John spent most of the time with peers with hearing impairments learning speech and language and the use of his hearing aids. In kindergarten and 1st grade, he attended classes with normally hearing peers and continues to demonstrate age-appropriate learning skills.

Our perception of the world is based entirely on the information we derive through our five senses: touch, smell, taste, vision, and hearing. If any one of them is faulty, our understanding of the environment is changed; this may lead to changes in cognitive and affective functioning. Of the five senses, hearing and vision best allow us to perceive events with which we are not in direct physical contact. Hearing is particularly valuable as a warning sense. We can hear in the dark, around corners, through closed doors, and above and below ourselves. Through hearing we receive the first indications of trouble in the environment.

Hearing has an additional vital function: it is the sense that normally developing children use to learn the language and speech skills requisite to social interaction and to the acquisition of academic skills. Through language, children gain access to the accumulated knowledge, customs, and mores of their family, culture, and world. Even babies actively take in, process, and organize the language they hear. Like miniature linguists they re-create for themselves the language of their culture.

Children who are hearing impaired and have intact central nervous systems have the same potential to learn language as other children. The usual channel for language learning, however, is the auditory system. Damage to this system may cause the child who is hearing impaired to receive speech information that is limited in quantity and degraded in quality. The challenge is for parents and teachers to provide input to these children in a variety of ways so that they acquire, as quickly as possible, the communication skills necessary to function independently in social and academic contexts.

HISTORY

Hearing impairment has been identified as a human problem almost since the beginning of recorded history. We know of no efforts to educate those with profound hearing impairments prior to the 15th century, but both Hebrew and Roman law included primitive classification systems for deafness. Hebrew law established three categories of hearing and communication disorders and regulated the involvement of people with these disorders in society: (1) people who were deaf and could speak were allowed to transact business but not to own property; (2) people who could hear but were unable to speak were allowed to participate in society with no legal restrictions placed on them; and (3) persons who were deaf and unable to speak were not allowed to own property, engage in business, or act as witnesses. Roman law had similar regulations: (1) those who were deaf and unable to speak from birth were without legal rights or obligations, (2) those who became deaf and lost their speech after learning to read and write were allowed to transact business, and (3) those who were deaf but could speak were not restricted in any way.

The first recorded effort to teach persons who were deaf occurred in Spain in the 16th century when a monk, Pablo Ponce de Leon, taught the firstborn son of a nobleman to speak in order that the son might be legally able to inherit his father's property under the laws of primogeniture. Slowly, education of children with hearing impairment extended to common people. By the 18th century two opposing philosophies had arisen in Europe. The Abbé de l'Épée in France used sign language to instruct persons who could not hear and believed this to be their natural language. However, Samuel Heinicke in Germany and Thomas Braidwood in Great Britain used speech to educate persons who were deaf.

The controversy over the better method began to be felt in the United States in the 19th century. Sent to Europe by concerned citizens of Hartford, Connecticut, to learn how to teach persons with severe hearing impairment, Thomas Gallaudet was rejected in England by the clannish Braidwood family and ended up studying the manual method in France. In 1817 he established the first school for persons who were deaf in America, which is still in existence. The first schools founded on the principle of aural-oral communication were not established until 1867—Clarke School in Northampton, Massachusetts, and Lexington School in New York City.

At the International Convention held in Milan, Italy, in 1880, amid considerable controversy, educators of those with hearing impairments resolved to favor the oral method. Subsequently many schools in the United States stopped using any form of sign language or fingerspelling for classroom instruction. In some residential schools, however, sign language continued to be used in extracurricular activities and in the dormitories. In the adult society of persons with hearing impairments, American Sign Language continued to evolve.

It was not until as recently as the sixties that people again questioned the efficacy of the exclusively oral approach. By the seventies, there was some consensus that the use of fingerspelling and sign language does not negatively affect speech or lipreading ability and that it seems to have a positive effect on academic achievement. Since that time, the majority of programs for students with hearing impairments use *total communication* for classroom instruction. Total communication uses all possible expressive and receptive modes—manual language, fingerspelling, residual hearing with amplification, speech and lipreading, and written language.

Education for persons with hearing impairments became universal in the United States through a system of state-supported residential schools, locally run day schools, and private schools. With the passage of the Education for All Handicapped Children Act (Public Law 94–142) in 1975, the population of the residential schools declined. Smaller, decentralized programs on public school campuses are now available in most communities, and children with hearing impairments are being integrated into regular classroom activities.

The first college program began in 1864, when Abraham Lincoln signed a bill creating Gallaudet College in Washington, DC, as a liberal arts college for persons with hearing impairments. Gallaudet remained the only college program exclusively for the population until the sixties when the National Technical Institute for the Deaf and a demonstration network of regional community college programs were established. Gallaudet is now a university, and it accepts normally hearing students, as well as those who are hearing impaired. However, it is still a bastion of the culture of those who are deaf and others with hearing impairments and in the forefront of research on all aspects of hearing loss. In 1988, amid enormous controversy, Gallaudet students and their supporters helped overturn the appointment of a normally hearing, nonsigning president. Gallaudet is the first and only university in the world to have a deaf president.

DEFINITION   Sound waves are produced by the to-and-fro movement of molecules. One complete movement back and forth constitutes a cycle. The number of cycles occurring per second determines the frequency of a sound. The term used to designate cycles per second is *hertz* (Hz); 1000 Hz means that the frequency of the sound is 1,000 cycles per second. The human ear hears varying frequencies as different pitches. As frequencies decrease, pitch is lowered. As frequencies increase, pitch becomes higher. Although the human ear is sensitive to frequencies between 20 Hz and 20,000 Hz, the most important frequencies are those between 500 Hz and 3000 Hz—the speech range. An increase or decrease of energy at any given frequency will cause a change in the intensity of the sound. Sound intensity is measured in *decibels* (dB) and is perceived as loudness. Normal hearing sensitivity begins at 0 dB for each frequency; that level represents the softest sound that an average person can hear and is called the hearing threshold. Higher numbers indicate louder sounds. For example, a quiet conversation would occur at about 40 dB.

Historically, definitions of hearing loss were based on the decibel levels at which humans responded to pure tone signals at different frequencies. A person was considered deaf if he or she had a hearing loss of at least 90 dBHL (hearing level) at frequencies of 500, 1000, and 2000 Hz; such a person could hear nothing below the 90-dB level in this important frequency range. Anyone with a lesser hearing loss was identified as being hard-of-hearing; these persons could have a hearing loss ranging from 20 dBHL to 90 dBHL. However, because the ability to understand and process speech is of far greater significance than simply responding to pure tones, new definitions were adopted by the Conference of Executives of American Schools for the Deaf (CEAD) in June 1975. These definitions are more functional because they emphasize the impact of the hearing loss on the development of language.

- *Hearing impairment*. This generic term indicates a hearing disability that can range in severity from mild to profound. It includes the subsets of deaf and hard-of-hearing.
- *Deaf*. A person who is deaf is one whose hearing disability precludes successful processing of linguistic information through audition, with or without a hearing aid.
- *Hard-of-hearing*. A hard-of-hearing person has residual hearing sufficient for successful processing of linguistic information through audition, generally with the use of a hearing aid.

Some members of the deaf culture propose alternate definitions.

- *Deaf*. A person whose hearing disability precludes successful auditory processing of linguistic information.
- *Deaf*. A person regardless of degree of hearing loss, who identifies with the deaf culture.

PREVALENCE   According to the 1992 Report to Congress, there were 59,000 children between the ages of 6 years and 21 years who were served under the category "hearing impaired." This number was 1.4% of the total population of school-age children with handicapping conditions (U.S. Department of Education, 1992). Unfortunately these data do not provide information on the type or degree of hearing loss. Northern and Downs (1991) report that one child in every thousand will be born with an irreversible hearing loss, and two in every thousand will acquire a hearing impairment in early childhood. Nearly all children will have some degree of conductive hearing loss (due to ear infection) during the period from birth through 11 years of age.

CAUSES   In the normally functioning ear, sound waves enter through the auditory canal and move through the middle ear into the inner ear, which contains the cochlea (the organ of hearing) and the semicircular canals (the center of balance) (see Figure 10–1). In the process, sound is changed into neural impulses that travel along neural pathways to the brain. The brain then creates meaning from the impulses. Interference with any part of the transmission system can result in impaired hearing. It may involve a restriction in the range of frequencies received, distortion along the frequency spectrum, or an increase in the intensity needed to perceive a sound.

Types of Hearing Loss

Impairment in the mechanical transmission of sound waves (sound conduction) through the outer and middle ear produces conductive hearing losses. The outer ear, as illustrated in Figure 10–1, consists of the external ear (pinna) and a passage about 1 inch long and 1/4 inch in diameter (auditory canal), which terminates at the eardrum (tympanic membrane). Frequently, young children have an excess accumulation of wax in the external ear or fluid in the middle ear; these conditions interfere with sound conduction and produce a conductive hearing loss. Such problems may be corrected through medical attention or surgery.

The middle ear is a small cavity connected to the back part of the throat (nasopharynx) by the eustachian tube. The eustachian tube allows oxygen to enter the middle ear, which helps the middle ear stay healthy. Within the middle ear there are three tiny bones: the malleus (hammer), which is attached to the tympanic membrane;

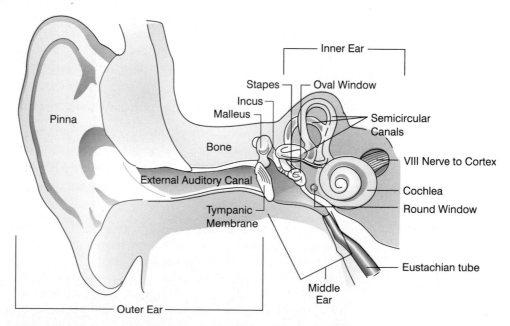

Figure 10–1
Diagram of the ear.

the incus (anvil), attached to the malleus; and the stapes (stirrup), attached to the oval window. Sound waves are carried by this ossicular chain to the inner ear. The most common cause of conductive hearing loss is inflammation or infection of the middle ear, called otitis media. It can usually be alleviated medically through the use of antibiotics or the insertion of a tube through the tympanic membrane to drain fluid from the middle ear (Martin, 1991).

Impairment in the inner ear that interferes with the conversion of sound waves to neural impulses is called sensorineural hearing loss. The intensity of the signal is reduced and the sound is distorted. Most students enrolled in special education programs for those with hearing impairments have this type of hearing loss. Unlike conductive losses, sensorineural losses cannot be reversed through medical intervention. It is not uncommon for persons with sensorineural loss to have a concurrent middle ear problem that requires medical attention and that may cause them to have an additional amount of hearing loss.

Most people with sensorineural loss can obtain some benefit from hearing aids. However, because hearing aids make airborne sounds louder but not clearer, it takes practice to learn to wear and use them well. In recent years some children and adults have received cochlear implants. A cochlear implant is a tiny electronic device that is surgically implanted in the inner ear or cochlea and attached to a receiver-stimulator implanted just behind the ear in the base of the skull. The individual wears a microphone and a speech transmitter attached to a tiny electrical wire leading to an electrical transmitter placed near the implant site.

Sensorineural hearing loss may be genetic in origin, or it may be caused by disease or injury. The loss can occur before, during, or after birth.

Genetic Losses

A hearing loss may be inherited as a single genetic trait or as part of a syndrome. Examples of syndromes that include hearing loss are (1) Waardenburg syndrome, which combines sensorineural hearing loss with abnormal pigmentation and other problems; (2) Usher syndrome, in which sensorineural hearing loss is accompanied by progressive loss of vision; or (3) Treacher Collins syndrome, in which a conductive hearing loss is accompanied by facial anomalies. Deafness can be inherited as a dominant trait, a recessive trait, or rarely, a sex-linked disorder.

At the present time more than 50 genetic syndromes have been identified in which hearing loss may occur, and genetic causes are thought to account for approximately 50% of all cases of deafness in children (Northern & Downs, 1991). In residential schools, it is common to find students who are the second or third generation of their families to attend. The high incidence of marriage between people with hearing impairments is a factor in the high incidence of genetic hearing loss; however, most children who are genetically deaf have normally hearing parents who carry undetectable recessive genes for the condition. Children whose deafness is caused by a single dominant gene are usually born into families that already have experiences with deafness. There is rarely additional injury to the central nervous system before birth, and the incidence of secondary disabilities in this population is no greater than in the population at large.

Nongenetic Losses

As noted, sensorineural hearing losses that are not genetic in origin may be caused by disease or injury. Rubella, commonly called German measles, is a mild viral infection when it occurs in children or adults; however, when it is contracted by a woman during pregnancy, especially during the first 3 months, the developing fetus may be infected. The infection, which attacks the rapidly growing central nervous system, may cause the baby to be born with a hearing loss, defective vision, and/or irregularities of the heart and nervous system such as those associated with mental retardation and cerebral palsy. In 1968 a rubella vaccine was approved and is now routinely given to all preschool children. It has prevented rubella from reaching the epidemic proportions that had previously existed.

A more recently identified problem, for which there is presently no vaccine, is congenital cytomegalovirus infection (CMV). CMV is the most frequent viral infection in newborns (Williams et al., 1982). The virus is transmitted through the placenta or picked up during passage through the birth canal. It is estimated to cause a hearing loss in one third of affected infants (Adler, 1988; Johnson, Daniel, & Chmiel, 1991). Some children affected by this virus develop hearing losses several years after birth. CMV can also cause mental retardation.

Hearing impairment can occur at or near the time of birth as a result of complications in the birth process, such as prolonged labor, premature or abrupt birth (usually due to an accident), or difficulties that necessitate the use of obstetric instruments. Failure to breathe rapidly during or immediately after birth (apnea) is another commonly reported cause of hearing loss. Children whose hearing loss is caused by apnea or by difficult birth are at high risk for other problem conditions, including mental retardation and cerebral palsy. Hearing impairment can be caused after birth by viral infections, such as mumps, measles, and meningitis. Otitis media, the inflammation of the middle ear mentioned earlier, can produce permanent hearing loss if it is a chronic condition. Trauma, accidents, high fevers, and drugs prescribed for other medical conditions are factors in only a small percentage of cases.

There is increasing concern over the incidence of hearing loss caused by excessive exposure to loud noises, specifically amplified sounds generated by rock bands and extensive use of portable headphone sets at high volume. Prolonged exposure to noisy environments such as living close to an airport also places a child at risk. Although the losses thus induced generally will not require students to have special education, they may be sufficient to reduce the quality of life for adolescents and adults.

CHARACTERISTICS   Degree of Impairment

Hearing losses can range from mild to profound. The severity of loss is described in terms of decibels; the larger the number of decibels, the more severe the loss, because the individual can hear nothing below the identified level. The impact on speech and language depends on (1) the frequencies involved—the greater the loss in the main speech frequencies (500 Hz to 3000 Hz), the more severe the impairment; and (2) how well the cochlea and auditory pathways to the brain perceive speech input. A hearing loss may be present in only one ear (unilateral) or in both ears (bilateral). Persons with unilateral hearing losses usually function normally and have problems only with locating the direction of sounds. Those with mild to moderate bilateral hearing losses (20 dB to 60 dB) can usually benefit from amplification. Those with a severe bilateral loss (60 dB to 90 dB) can often be trained to use their residual hearing with amplification and with support from speechreading and sign language. People with profound hearing impairment—those with bilateral losses of more than 90 dB—often derive benefit from amplification but usually rely more on manual communication and speechreading for input. Figure 10–2 shows the different levels of hearing loss and their probable consequences for understanding speech and language in the classroom.

It is important to remember that individuals are affected in different ways by seemingly similar hearing losses. Nonetheless, we can identify some characteristics common to most children with severe and profound losses. The degree to which these children differ from their peers with normal hearing varies with age and other factors. Unless other disabilities are present, developmental differences in infants and toddlers with hearing impairment from their normally hearing peers are minimal. As children who are hearing impaired grow older, however, they often fall behind in language comprehension as they are unable to keep up with the increased complexity and abstraction of the language system. Consequently, their academic, social, and emotional development may also be affected. These effects can be lessened or eliminated by good educational programs, family involvement, and early intervention.

Variables Affecting Education

Even a minimal hearing loss can affect language learning and influence educational progress. The extent of the effect will depend on (1) the type of loss (conductive or sensorineural), (2) the degree of loss, (3) the age of onset, (4) the time of detection, (5) the time of intervention, (6) the age at which hearing aids are fitted and consistently worn, (7) the home environment, and (8) the presence of other disabilities. Several variables of primary importance will be discussed here; type and degree of hearing loss are discussed elsewhere.

Age of Onset.   Hearing losses that occur at birth or prior to language learning are called prelingual. Those that occur after a child has acquired at least the rudiments of a language system are termed postlingual. The age at which a hearing loss occurs is critical, because the usual channel for normal language learning is the auditory system.

From birth, parents constantly provide verbal input, and infants analyze and store this information for future use. Research has demonstrated that an unborn fetus responds to sound and that infants only a few days or weeks old use their hearing to discriminate between sounds (Eimas, Miller, & Jusczyk, 1987; Kuhl, 1987). A longitudinal study of 9- to 18-month-old babies demonstrated how older infants use the auditory system (Friedlander & Cyrulik, 1970). A toy that presented various auditory stimuli, such as music and the voices of different people reading and speaking, was placed in the crib. The babies selected the preferred presentation by pushing a button. A 12-month-old consistently chose to listen to a bright, cheery voice rather than his mother's monotonous one. A 14-month-old followed this pattern but after a few days listened to his mother's voice very carefully and never returned to the other voice.

Characteristics

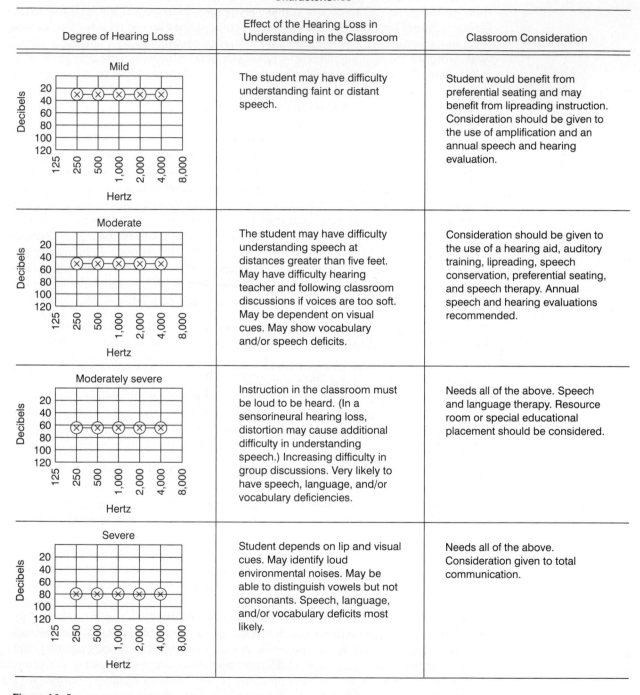

Degree of Hearing Loss	Effect of the Hearing Loss in Understanding in the Classroom	Classroom Consideration
Mild	The student may have difficulty understanding faint or distant speech.	Student would benefit from preferential seating and may benefit from lipreading instruction. Consideration should be given to the use of amplification and an annual speech and hearing evaluation.
Moderate	The student may have difficulty understanding speech at distances greater than five feet. May have difficulty hearing teacher and following classroom discussions if voices are too soft. May be dependent on visual cues. May show vocabulary and/or speech deficits.	Consideration should be given to the use of a hearing aid, auditory training, lipreading, speech conservation, preferential seating, and speech therapy. Annual speech and hearing evaluations recommended.
Moderately severe	Instruction in the classroom must be loud to be heard. (In a sensorineural hearing loss, distortion may cause additional difficulty in understanding speech.) Increasing difficulty in group discussions. Very likely to have speech, language, and/or vocabulary deficiencies.	Needs all of the above. Speech and language therapy. Resource room or special educational placement should be considered.
Severe	Student depends on lip and visual cues. May identify loud environmental noises. May be able to distinguish vowels but not consonants. Speech, language, and/or vocabulary deficits most likely.	Needs all of the above. Consideration given to total communication.

Figure 10–2

Degree of hearing loss and its effect on understanding speech and language in the classroom.

At least 80% of language development has occurred by 3 years of age (McFarland & Simmons, 1980). A hearing loss that occurs after this age (postlingual loss) is less likely to cause as severe an educational problem as a prelingual loss. Children who experience a postlingual loss have had an opportunity to use the auditory system and practice their listening, speech, and language skills; however, they will need help to maintain their speech and language abilities. Children who experience a prelingual hearing loss do not have an opportunity to develop language normally. They require explicit teaching rather than simple exposure to ordinary language input. Speechreading will be of only limited usefulness because only about 60% of English speech sounds are visible as lip movements and many of these look the same as others. For example, /p/ and /b/ and /m/, though clearly visible, cannot be discriminated visually. Learning language through speechreading is therefore a very difficult task because of the incompleteness of the visual reception. Children with prelingual loss require a combination of teaching modes such as speechreading, the written word, and manual signing to supplement the imperfect auditory input.

Time of Identification and Intervention.   It is essential to identify hearing impairment as soon as possible so that both child and parents can participate in an intervention program. The further children move past the critical stage for language learning, the more difficult it becomes for them to learn language, especially the finer nuances of auditory discrimination and the complexities of the total linguistic system. The earlier children are identified and taught to use their residual hearing, the greater their chance to acquire the building blocks essential for more complex skills and to learn language in the same sequence as hearing children.

Another important goal of early intervention is helping parents adjust to their child's hearing loss. Parents who are themselves hearing impaired seem to be more accepting and more able to provide the support and communication essential for the children to develop a positive self-concept and cognitive skills. Like all parents of infants and young children with disabilities, parents of children with hearing impairments need support and understanding as they adjust to their children's special needs. Early interventionists assist families to learn the skills to communicate with their children, provide information as requested, and facilitate contacts with community resources.

Social Development

Normally, young children learn appropriate social interaction skills—such as turn taking, sharing, and the use of *please* and *thank you*—through language. Because children with hearing impairments often get a late start in learning their language and their cultural system, they are generally less socially mature than hearing children. Social immaturity may be manifested in impulsiveness and a lack of responsibility and independence. They may not be sensitive to the feelings of others and thus have difficulty interacting with peers and establishing friendships (Davis, Elfenbein, Schum, & Bentler, 1986).

Intelligence

As would be expected because of the nature of the tests, children who are hearing impaired score considerably lower than normally hearing children on verbal IQ tests.

Traditional intelligence tests are not suited for children with hearing impairments and should never be used as a measure of intelligence for this population. A 1968 review (Vernon) of 50 independent studies indicated that there is essentially the same distribution of intelligence among those who are hearing impaired and populations who are not disabled when they are tested with performance tests rather than verbal intelligence scales. Hearing loss of any severity does not appear to affect intelligence as measured by nonverbal IQ scales (Evans, 1980; Phelps & Branyan, 1990).

Academic Achievement

The academic achievement of children who are hearing impaired contrasts poorly with their documented potential (Phelps & Branyan, 1990). Reading, which is based on language knowledge, is a major deficit area. One major longitudinal study of those with hearing impairments (Trybus & Karchmer, 1977) showed national results of less than 0.3 of a grade improvement in reading per year for a 3-year period. When data were analyzed for subgroups, it was found that students making the greatest gains in reading were those with more hearing, those with no additional disabilities, those who entered school early, and those who had two parents who were deaf. Although some improvement has been noted in some children with severe hearing impairment over the past decade (Brown & Karchmer, 1987), most students remain delayed in school achievement (Berko-Gleason, 1985; Harkins, 1985).

Language

Current data suggest that early introduction to, and consistent use of, total communication in home and school programs provides an improved language base for students with hearing impairments and enhances their social and emotional growth as well. (Matkin & Matkin, 1985; Shafer & Lynch, 1981; Watkins, 1987). The language differences traditionally viewed as an inevitable consequence of having a severe hearing loss may now be seen instead as the consequence of not having appropriate language input at a very early age.

Children who are deaf with parents who are deaf are signed to from birth. Thus, they generally acquire language easily and become fluent with manual language when very young. They learn the language of the deaf culture, American Sign Language (ASL), a visual-gestural language with its own unique syntax, semantics, and pragmatics. ASL does not resemble English or any other oral language, and it is not interchangeable with other sign systems such as British Sign Language or German Sign Language.

Speech

A common assumption is that the speech of children who are severely and profoundly hearing impaired is unclear because these children do not articulate sounds correctly. But articulation is only part of the problem. Other factors, such as poor timing and rhythm, are involved. There is a tendency to prolong both stressed and unstressed syllables and to insert more and longer pauses than necessary, resulting in relatively slow speech. Variation of pitch is typically abnormal and tends to lack linguistic content. Thus, individuals with hearing impairments often do not use the rising pitch we expect to hear at the end of a question or the falling pitch that indicates the conclusion of a declarative sentence. Nasality is also frequently a problem. Sounds such as *m*, *n*, and *ng*, which should be nasalized, are not, while other sounds, such as vowels, which should not be nasalized, may be. Substituting one sound for another and prolonging the voicing of a single sound are other behaviors that contribute to unintelligibility in the speech of those who are hearing impaired.

ASSESSMENT   Audiological Assessment

The professional responsible for audiological assessment is the *audiologist*. This person usually holds a master's degree or doctorate from a department of speech and hearing sciences and is certified by the American Speech-Language-Hearing Association (ASHA). The instrument used to measure hearing is called an *audiometer*. The audiometer presents a series of carefully calibrated tones that vary in frequency (pitch) and intensity (loudness). Testing is done in a specially designed, soundproof booth or room. The results are charted on a graph called an *audiogram* (see Figure 10–3).

Speech audiometry refers to the various methods used to determine at what level children hear speech and how well the speech is understood. Testing of speech comprehension requires that the child have language; therefore, the usual clinical test procedures cannot be used with infants or young children who have not developed language. Speech testing can be done using loudspeakers or headphones; the materials can be prerecorded or presented live.

This young child is learning to take a hearing test using play audiometry.

The *speech reception threshold* (SRT) is the decibel level at which an individual can identify a speech stimulus 50% of the time. SRT is measured by presenting words at different intensity levels until a level is found at which the child can identify 50% of the words correctly. Children respond by looking toward the source of the speech (the loudspeaker), pointing to pictures, or repeating the words they hear. Once an SRT has been determined, the next task is to assess the ability of the student to understand speech under optimal listening conditions. Usually, lists of one-syllable words are presented through earphones or loudspeakers in the testing room. Test results are expressed in terms of the percentage of the words that the child identifies correctly. Children with severe to profound hearing losses often have difficulty discriminating one word from another, and discrimination testing is often a difficult task for them.

Objective audiometry provides additional information about an individual's auditory system without requiring behavioral responses. Tympanometry, one form of acoustic impedance (or immittance) measurement, can identify a middle ear problem by measuring the extent of stiffness or resistance of the eardrum to energy generated by the different sound pressure levels of an auditory stimulus.

Another objective test, administered when children cannot be tested behaviorally because of chronological age or developmental delay, uses electrodes placed on the scalp and at the ear to pick up responses to auditory stimuli. Results obtained in the short latency auditory brainstem response (ABR) tests are averaged and recorded on a chart to show how the peripheral auditory system perceives high-frequency sound. ABR is a reliable measure in the mid- to high-frequency range. Behavioral observation audiometry (BOA) is the behavioral assessment procedure used with infants under 6 months of age who cannot be conditioned to respond to auditory stimuli. Sounds are introduced through loudspeakers into a soundproof room and an examiner observes changes in the infant's behavior. Responses range from subtle ones (eye movements, increased activity, decreased activity) to a whole body startle (Moro reflex). Extensive training and practice are necessary to be able to make accurate judgments about infant responses, and precise information about hearing thresholds cannot be provided. BOA can provide general information about a child's hearing but cannot rule out a mild-to-moderate loss. Because of these limitations BOA is usually used in combination with ABR.

In order to test the hearing of infants 5 to 24 months old, sounds are often introduced through loudspeakers as for younger infants; however, some young children will accept headphones, which makes it possible to evaluate each ear individually. Responses are evaluated according to the normal head turns that infants make in response to sound at this age. Visual reinforcement audiometry (VRA) encourages the infant to continue responding to a sound by using visual reinforcers such as animated toy animals paired with the various sounds. Speech testing with this age group is limited to speech awareness for very young infants and possibly object identification for 24-month-olds. Speech awareness refers to a technique whereby the examiner says the child's name and says "hi!" and marks the decibel level at which the child responds. At the age of 24 months most children know the names of objects such as ball, bear, cup, and shoes. The examiner establishes the names of several objects the individual child understands. Four or five of these objects are placed in front of the child, and he or she is asked to point to each one until the lowest decibel level at which the child can do this is identified.

More precise measurement is possible after age 2 if the child will tolerate wearing headphones or the placement of bone conduction oscillators. Earphones or a bone conduction oscillator (an instrument placed on the bony structure behind the ear or on the forehead) can be used to evaluate hearing in each ear. Some 2-year-olds and most 3-year-olds are taught simple play procedures, such as placing a ring on a stick or dropping a block in a box, to use as responses to the auditory signal. At this age audiologists may begin to evaluate speech discrimination by having the child repeat words and point to pictures. However, these tasks may again be impossible for young children with severe or profound hearing impairments. Since children in the United States are often not identified as having a hearing loss until they are 18 to 22 months of age (Thompson & Thompson, 1991), VRA is often used for a longer period of time. ABR is paired with behavioral testing for more conclusive results.

School Age and Beyond.   School-age children and adults can understand the request to respond by raising a hand each time they hear a signal. Stimuli are usually pure tones of known intensity and frequency presented to each ear individually through earphones or a bone oscillator. A threshold—the intensity at which each frequency is heard 50% of the time—is obtained for each ear. The results of testing are plotted on an audiogram (Figure 10–3). The 0–dB level is the norm against which the individual's threshold is measured; it is the median threshold for a group of adults

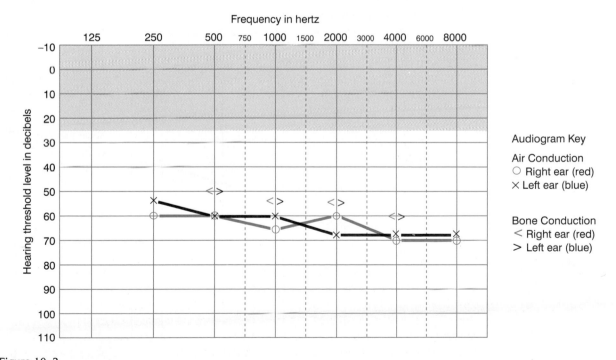

Figure 10–3
Audiogram depicting a bilateral sensorineural hearing loss.
Note: Shading indicates acceptable range. Note that bone conduction results (<>) are approximately the same as air conduction results (OX).

with normal hearing. Deviations from the 0–dB line indicate the additional intensity needed for an individual to hear a sound at a given frequency.

Testing results can show a sensorineural hearing loss (as shown in Figure 10–3) or a conductive hearing loss (as shown in Figure 10–4). One can see that the degree of sensorineural loss in the individual tested on the audiogram in Figure 10–3 might be called moderately severe and will certainly interfere with normal conversation. The conductive loss shown in Figure 10–4 might be termed moderate and will not cause as much difficulty. Regular monitoring of the middle ear as well as effectiveness of the hearing aids should continue to be part of the assessment process throughout the life span. Although not currently used clinically, there is potential for oto-acoustic emissions (OAEs) to provide information about the status of the cochlea and whether it is functioning normally or not. As with the ABR, OAEs can be recorded without the active participation of the infant or child (Decker, 1992).

Cognitive Assessment

The assessment of intelligence in children who are hearing impaired is complicated by the fact that standard IQ tests rely heavily on linguistic competence. Such tests tend to confuse linguistic deprivation with intellectual impairment and thus erroneously identify the child who is hearing impaired as retarded. It is critical that tests be

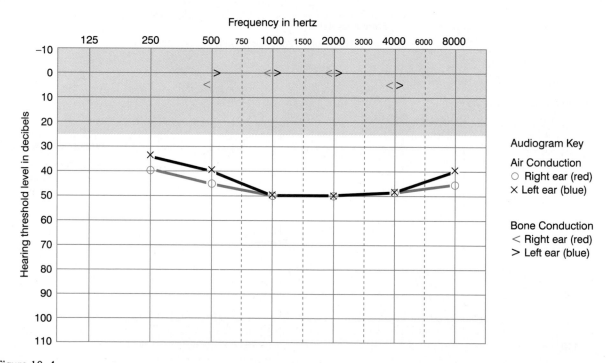

Figure 10–4
Audiogram depicting a bilateral conductive loss.
Note: The bone conduction results are quite different from air conduction results.

selected that minimize the need for verbal language, are not timed, and are presented in a communication mode familiar to the student. A minimum of two tests should be used, and they should be administered individually. The cognitive assessment should be only one part of a team effort. It is also important to (1) have tests administered by professionals who are familiar with hearing impairment, (2) create a nonthreatening environment while testing, and (3) ensure availability of adequate supportive data. All directions should be given in the language and communication mode the child uses daily.

Early Childhood.   The Bayley Scales of Infant Development, which are currently being restandardized, are developmental scales for children 2 to 30 months old with normal hearing (Bayley, 1969). As noted above, it is important to corroborate results of this test and all other tests intended for nondisabled children with other testing. Otherwise, normally developing infants with hearing impairments may be inappropriately identified as cognitively delayed. Although some items on this instrument require auditory and/or language skills and thus necessitate a scoring adjustment, there are a sufficient number of other items that are of value. The Uzgiris-Hunt Ordinal Scales of Psychological Development (Uzgiris & Hunt, 1978), which are based on Piagetian theory and tasks, are also extremely helpful in evaluating certain cognitive skills of children with hearing impairments up to 2 years of age.

The Smith-Johnson Nonverbal Performance Scale for 2- to 4-year-olds (Smith & Johnson, 1977) was designed for both hearing children and children with hearing impairment. Subtest directions are presented in pantomime, and the performance levels (below average, average, and above average) are age- and sex-referenced.

School Age.   One of the most widely used tests for school-age children is the performance scale of the Wechsler Intelligence Scale for Children, Revised (WISC-R) (Wechsler, 1974). The performance scale was standardized using a sample of individuals who are hearing impaired (Anderson & Sisco, 1977) and, according to Sullivan and McCay (1979), was designed to evaluate the cognitive abilities of the population who is hearing impaired, from the age of 6 through 17. Instructions may be given orally or modified by pantomime, visual aids, or total communication, as necessary. IQ scores are derived from performance on six nonverbal subtests: block design, picture arrangement, picture design, object assembly, mazes, and coding. The WISC-R performance subtests are often used in conjunction with the Hiskey-Nebraska Test of Learning Aptitude (Hiskey, 1966). The Hiskey-Nebraska Test of Learning Aptitude contains 12 nonverbal subtests, such as bead pattern memory, memory for color, spatial reasoning, and picture identification. Norms are provided for those who are hearing impaired, as are standardized pantomime instructions.

The Leiter International Performance Scale (Leiter, 1948) has been an extremely popular test for use with children who are hearing impaired because it is administered by pantomime and requires only nonverbal responses. However, questions have been raised about its standardization, reliability, and validity (Salvia & Ysseldyke, 1991). Another appropriate test is the Nonverbal Test of Cognitive Skills (Johnson & Boyd, 1981).

Nonverbal tests such as the Kaufman Assessment Battery for Children (Kaufman & Kaufman, 1982), designed for normally hearing children, can be adapted for those with hearing impairments by modifying the communication mode. Modifying procedures for administration means that the scores are not valid; however, the results can provide useful information for instructional purposes. Only licensed psychologists, experienced and knowledgeable in the assessment of individuals with hearing impairments, should conduct intelligence assessments.

Secondary/Transition.   As students with hearing impairments become older, the availability of tests and materials decreases. The Hiskey-Nebraska Test of Learning Aptitude can only be used until 17 years of age; the WISC-R, until 16; and the Leiter, until 18. An obvious problem is that after age 18, limitations of test materials preclude the development of a test battery.

Communication Assessment

Communication involves the use of language, speech, and the auditory system. Development of a communication system is essential in order to transmit needs and desires and to establish important social-emotional bonds. Because comparatively few language tests have been developed for children with hearing impairments, language tests developed for hearing children and youth are used. However, caution must be exercised when comparing results to hearing norms. Information concerning several language tests developed specifically for children who are hearing impaired is provided in Table 10–1.

Nonstandardized Testing.   The most accurate information about the language of children who are hearing impaired is usually obtained by skillfully using portions of many standardized and informal tests. A language sample often provides the most helpful information about language, including how the student *uses* language.

Early Childhood.   It is important to evaluate all aspects of development in the very young child who is hearing impaired. Of particular importance is assessment of communicative events such as pointing and indicating a need, as well as first words, ability to listen and discriminate among sounds, ability to produce multiword utterances, development of gross and fine motor skills, and development of social, adaptive skills.

School Age.   Although some aspects of language of school-age students who are hearing impaired can be measured with the language portions of standardized achievement tests, such as the Stanford Achievement Test (SAT) (Madden, Gardner, Rudman, Karlsen, & Merwin, 1972), such tests do not evaluate all aspects of the linguistic system or provide information for language goals and objectives. As is true for the preschool population, relatively few language tests are specifically designed and standardized for school-age students who are hearing impaired. However, because language is developmental and children with hearing impairments seem to follow the

Table 10–1
Characteristics of selected language tests for students with hearing impairments

Test	Age Range (years)	Mode		Area Tested				Norm Group
		Receptive	Expressive	Vocabulary	Morphology	Syntax	Semantic Relationships	
SKI-HI Receptive Language Test (SKI-HI RLT)	3–6½	X		X			X	None
Test of Expressive Language Ability (TEXLA)	7–12		X		X	X		65 children with HI, 17 hearing children
Test of Receptive Language Ability (TERLA)	7–12	X			X	X		92 children with HI, 27 hearing children
Test of Syntactic Ability (TSA)	10–19	X				X		450 children with HI
Total Communication Receptive Vocabulary Test (TCRVT)	3–12	X		X				77 hearing children, 95 hard-of-hearing children, 251 deaf children
Grammatical Analysis of Elicited Language (GAEL)	5–9		X		X	X		200 children with HI, 200 hearing children
Maryland Syntax Evaluation Instrument (MSEI)	6–12		X			X		220 children with HI
Carolina Picture Vocabulary Test (CPVT)	4–11	X		X				767 deaf and hard-of-hearing children
Rhode Island Test of Language Structure (RITLS)	5–17	X			X	X		513 children with HI, 304 hearing children

Note: HI = hearing impairment

developmental sequencing of their hearing peers, good language tests developed for school-age children can provide valuable information regarding intervention. The results of such tests will provide the teacher with specific information about the functional language level of a child and about how and where to begin instruction.

Secondary/Transition. Standardized tests designed to evaluate specific areas of language deficit are not readily available for students with hearing impairments who are older than 19. Those that can be used were identified previously—the Total Communication Receptive Vocabulary Test (to 17 years of age) and the Test of Syntactic Abilities (to 19 years of age). For this age group, it may be more appropriate to directly evaluate the skills and knowledge in question. For example, if the concern is whether the students has the necessary skills for job interviews, the best source of information may be a videotape of his or her performance at an actual or simulated interview.

INTERVENTION As soon as a hearing loss has been diagnosed and treated medically or surgically to whatever extent possible, the provision of hearing aids is the next priority. All hearing aids perform the same function and have the same basic components. A microphone picks up sound waves and changes them to electrical energy, an amplifier intensifies the energy, and a receiver changes the electrical energy back into a louder sound. The energy source for the hearing aid is a battery. (See Figure 10–5.) Hearing aids may be selected or modified to amplify certain frequencies more than others in order to mirror the child's hearing loss.

Group hearing aids are often used in classrooms to enable the teacher to eliminate background noise and speak directly to the students. The teacher wears a microphone around the neck. The room may be encircled by a loop of wire that functions as a receiver, or radio-frequency inserts may be fit directly into each child's hearing aid. Auditory information received through the loop or the insert is transmitted to each student by the hearing aid. The newer FM systems can be connected directly to the student's personal hearing aid.

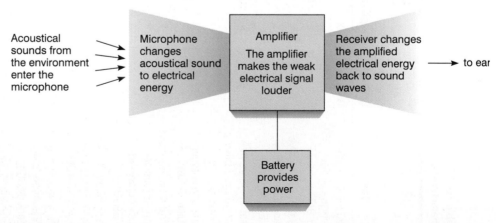

Figure 10–5
How a hearing aid amplifies sound.

Personal hearing aids are of no use unless they are maintained in good working condition. Students need to learn to assume responsibility for the care and maintenance of their hearing aids as soon as possible, with the support of teachers, parents, and audiologists. Maintenance checks should occur daily and include (1) checking the battery using a battery tester, (2) listening to the aid through a stethoscope while saying the sounds /a/, /u/, /ee/, /f/, /sh/, or (3) when the child is able, having the child raise a hand each time he or she hears one of the above sounds. If the hearing aid is not functioning properly, it should be repaired as quickly as possible. Semiannual checks of the hearing aid by the audiologist should be routine.

Modes of Communication

Educators agree that students who are hearing impaired require exacting instruction in all three aspects of language—content, syntax, and function. What they cannot agree on is how this instruction should be provided: two approaches have been proposed and disputed. One approach maintains that individuals with hearing impairments should be educated to become as much like people who hear normally as possible. The goal of education in this view is to enable children and adults with hearing impairments to live and participate in "normal" society. To attain this goal, persons with hearing impairments must learn to speak and read lips and use their residual hearing to whatever extent they can. They must not use alternative communication methods such as sign language. Proponents of aural-oral communication believe that children should not be taught a manual form of communication because they will prefer it (because it is easier) and never develop auditory or oral skills. Thus, they will not be able to reach the goal of total integration.

Proponents of the second approach, using manual communication alone or in combination with oral training, oppose this point of view. They believe that individuals with hearing impairments should not be expected to achieve the impossible goal of becoming "normal" but should be given the communication skills they need in any form possible—oral, manual, and written. With these skills, they assert, such people can be integrated into the world of work, can lead independent lives, and can choose to socialize with other persons who are hearing impaired, as well as with hearing individuals.

In manual communication, messages are sent by meaningful movements of the fingers, arms, and upper torso and are received visually. Thus, the defective auditory-vocal channel is bypassed in communication in favor of the intact visual-motor system.

One type of manual communication is fingerspelling. Fingerspelling in the United States is based on a code of one-handed symbols for each letter of the English alphabet, the ordinal numbers, and some punctuation (see Figure 10–6). Finger positions are discrete and easily learned, and after the code is mastered, any message that can be written can be sent and received. Fingerspelling, then, is a variety of written English. An expert in fingerspelling can send and receive spelled messages at almost the speed of normal oral communication. Fingerspelling eliminates the ambiguities that plague speechreading but is hard for young children to master. An interesting aside is that different countries have developed different fingerspelling codes for the same alphabet. As an example, Great Britain's code requires two hands to form each letter and bears no resemblance to the code used in the United States.

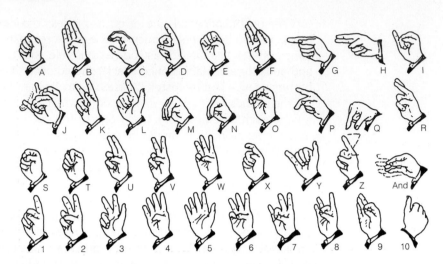

Figure 10–6
Fingerspelling code.

American Sign Language (ASL) is a manual language with no relationship to English or any other auditory-oral language. The fingers, hands, arms, and upper torso are used to communicate ideas rapidly. It has several thousand signs and a unique syntax. ASL is the communication system most often used in the adult deaf community and is, in its own right, a rich and beautiful language; however, it does not convey meaning in the same way as the English language and does not have a commonly recognized written form.

Within the past 20 years, as interest has increased in sign language systems, a number of new, modified sign systems have been created to convey the English language in a manual mode. One of these, Manual English, uses many ASL signs but adds signs for inflectional endings, pronouns, articles, and other structural elements and puts the signs in English word order. Like ASL, however, it communicates by ideas rather than by morphemes (word parts that carry meaning). Other forms of sign language, such as Signing Exact English (SEE II), sign by morphemes rather than by ideas (Gustason, Pfetzing, & Zawolkow, 1972), providing an even closer approximation of oral English.

Some concern has arisen over the ability of teachers and others to use Manual English or SEE II to represent the English language accurately (Kluwin, 1981; Marmor & Petitto, 1979; Swisher & Thompson, 1985). More recent studies have shown that it is *possible* for teachers to correctly convey English manually, but that the extent to which they actually do so is extremely variable and depends on such factors as consistent school policy, frequent monitoring, and self-motivation.

Total Communication. A third approach, *total communication* combines the aural-oral and manual communication approaches. This method originated in the late sixties with Roy Holcomb, a teacher of those with hearing impairments who is himself deaf and a parent of two children who are hearing impaired (Garretson, 1976). Advocates of this approach believe that all means of communicating with a person with hearing impairment should be used and they should be used as early as possible. The goal is not to establish a specific language system but to establish basic communication pathways as quickly and efficiently as possible. If taught and used correctly, total communication uses all the components of an aural-oral program plus sign language.

Methods of Teaching Language

Language is the means for expressing thoughts, feelings, emotions, and concerns. Language is communicated through speech, writing, and signs. There are many different parts to language: the vocabulary we use, how we put words together to form sentences, endings that we add to the words (e.g., 's, -s, -ing) that change their meaning, and the way in which we use language. Any method of teaching the child who is hearing impaired must consider all parts of the language system and must include language teaching as an integral part of all academic subjects. Specific language such as idiomatic expressions, which make up two thirds of the English language, must be taught along with social language useful in personal interactions. In other words, language must be "taught" all day every day, no matter what the student with a hearing impairment is doing.

Traditionally, educators of those with hearing impairments attempted to teach language through intensive programs of formal language instruction. Two primary methods have been used: (1) the grammatical method, which teaches specific grammatical rules to guide the construction of sentences; and (2) the natural method, which helps children learn language by formulating and testing linguistic hypotheses. In programs based on the natural method, language constructions and new vocabulary are introduced in natural, meaningful situations.

Most often, a combined approach is used. Students discuss daily experiences and read and write about them; then the teacher notes specific language needs for each child and works on them systematically. A combined approach encourages the use of students' daily experiences to develop language and at the same time identifies vocabulary and grammatical rules specific to the activity and the functional level of the child.

Age-Level Distinctions

Early Childhood.   The importance of early intervention with young children (birth to 3 years) who are hearing impaired and their families cannot be overemphasized. This principle of early intervention was embodied in Public Law 99–457, passed in 1986. A major focus of Part H of P.L. 99–457 is on working with the entire family. Professionals, in concert with the family, develop an Individualized Family Service Plan (IFSP). Early intervention is crucial to help families identify and use community resources and to assist them in learning to communicate with and enjoy their child. Most states have established home-based and center-based early intervention programs. A major goal is to support the family as it adjusts to meeting the needs of the child. Later, the programs provide children with auditory training on hearing aids and with initial instruction in speech and language, by means of an oral or a total communication approach. Visits to the home are scheduled so that the child receives training in his or her own environment, using meaningful, familiar objects. Meetings of parents' groups, monthly newsletters, and counseling services are other elements of early intervention programs.

Center-based programming varies, depending on the center. In some programs, several parents and children attend together, while in others only one child and parent are scheduled at a time. Meetings of parents' groups may be a regular feature, and counseling services are often provided. The requirement of center-based programs that someone from the home accompany the child can present a problem. Family schedules may be disrupted, and some families may not be able to afford the cost of transportation. Thus, attendance may not be good. A combination home- and center-based program is often the best solution.

School Age.   School-age children who are hearing impaired (3 to 21 years) may be served in private residential schools or state-maintained boarding facilities, private or public day schools, or segregated classes on public school campuses. Many children who formerly would have been served in self-contained classes or separate schools are now included in general education age-appropriate classes for all or most of the day. They may be aided in the regular classroom by amplification, notetakers, and/or manual or oral interpreters, as necessary.

Secondary/Transition.   For students who expect to go on to a 4-year college, the high school experience parallels that of youth who are not disabled. They take a full range of academic subjects to earn an academic diploma. For students who are in integrated programs, much of the academic work may be taken in mainstreamed settings, often with the support of interpreters. Interpreters translate the oral lecture or discussion into sign language; if the student's speech is not readily intelligible, they reverse the process, translating the student's signed comments into oral language so he or she can fully participate in class discussions. Where students elect not to use sign language but still need help with comprehension in lecture settings, interpreters can orally interpret the lecture or discussion so that it is easier to speechread. Support of classroom notetakers is essential, because it is virtually impossible to watch an interpreter or to speechread while taking notes.

At the conclusion of the high school program some students elect to go to regular 4-year colleges, using the support services of interpreters and/or notetakers. Many 4-year colleges have developed formal support systems for students who are hearing impaired and actively encourage them to apply. Some colleges now accept ASL as fulfilling the foreign language requirement for admission and/or graduation. There are also two special 4-year institutions, Gallaudet University and the National Technical Institute for the Deaf, where instruction is given in sign language or total communication.

Postsecondary education for students with hearing impairments takes several forms. At Gallaudet University classes are taught using sign language along with speech. The university offers a range of majors approximating that of many small liberal arts colleges. It also offers master's and doctoral degrees in fields related to deafness. Gallaudet's programs are open to both students who are hearing impaired and those who are not. The National Technical Institute for the Deaf, associated with the Rochester (NY) Institute of Technology, offers a wide variety of vocational and technical degree programs. Some classes are segregated, but for technical classes students with hearing impairments are integrated with nondisabled students and are supported by notetakers, interpreters, and tutors. There is also a network of regional community college programs that offer support services to students who are hearing impaired. Students are mainstreamed into a wide variety of vocational and technical classes, again with the support of interpreters, notetakers, and tutors. Gallaudet University also sponsors continuing education classes in the Washington, DC, area and in other areas of the country where there are large concentrations of adults who are hearing impaired.

For students going on to vocational, 2-year postsecondary schools, high school is largely devoted to improving reading and written language skills, teaching independent living skills, and developing prevocational skills. Again, students typically participate in regular high school classes with support services.

Many students with multiple disabilities do not plan to attend college or vocational school. Secondary education for these students focuses on life skills training for independent living and on preparation for competitive employment. It is especially important for these students to practice the skills necessary for independent community living—such as filling out application forms, managing money, and cooking and home maintenance.

Social development is an essential aspect of education for secondary students. At the high school level and beyond, when fluent verbal communication facilitates socialization, individuals with hearing impairments are at a disadvantage. In the United States there is a strong deaf culture with its own norms, its own shared history and "oral" literature, its own heroes and villains (among the villains are hearing teachers who oppose ASL), and its own language. As noted earlier, the language used in this culture is usually ASL. High school students become part of this culture by socializing with other individuals who are hearing impaired through school, church activities, junior National Association of the Deaf clubs, and athletic events. For the normally hearing parents of an adolescent who is deaf, this is often a traumatic period. They begin to realize that their son or daughter is building a social life in a culture that is not theirs and using a language in which they are usually not fluent. They also realize that their son or daughter has a high probability of marrying another person with a hearing impairment and building a family within the deaf community.

CURRICULUM IMPLICATIONS

Research during the past 25 years has provided substantial information regarding normal linguistic development, which has important implications for instructing those who are hearing impaired. The development of language begins at birth and proceeds very systematically. Initially, children's language is highly dependent on contextual cues. Children learn language in an open, natural environment where there are numerous nonlinguistic cues; and they communicate with gestures and combinations of gestures, vocalizations, and intonation patterns before they are capable of producing single-word utterances (Owens, 1988). At the single-word stage the relationship between language and cognitive development is apparent. For example, as children develop the notion of object constancy, their vocabulary enlarges to include functional terms such as *all gone*, *more*, and *no more*. From 2-word sentences they progress to expanding vocabulary and gradually perfecting complex sentences.

Children who are deaf with parents who are deaf are provided with language input from birth. Thus, they proceed through similar developmental steps at approximately the same age (Schlesinger & Meadow, 1972). Children with hearing impairments who have normally hearing parents are often delayed in development, but they proceed through the same steps as hearing children.

Age-Level Distinctions

Early Childhood.　Ideally, an early intervention program should provide

1. an enriched linguistic environment full of contextual cues, gestures, sign language, and auditory-verbal input
2. systematic auditory training and assistance with selecting and learning to wear hearing aids
3. special training in the *use* or functions of communication, such as requesting and agreeing
4. training in developing object concepts and semantic relations
5. an environment that encourages vocalization

Children with hearing impairments can play and learn natural language using total communication.

Item 4 requires some explanation. Toddlers who are hearing impaired must be taught to notice the features relevant to discriminating and classifying objects. As they perfect their knowledge of features, they expand their cognitive field, develop finger categories, and acquire new vocabulary. To learn 2-word utterances that express a functional relationship, children must understand the significant differences between "this cookie" (a state of existence), "no cookie" (nonexistence), and "more cookie" (recurrence). This type of teaching at an early age is appropriately accomplished in natural environments, where it can become a part of daily routines such as diapering, bathing, dressing, and playing games. The Model Program box describes a home-based early intervention program.

School Age.   A number of curricula have been developed specifically for students with hearing impairments. Many curricula include areas of need specific to these students, such as auditory training and speech development. Although formats may differ, these curricula are generally based on normal developmental processes and provide a good framework within which to develop or find appropriate materials. Standard curricula and texts may be used, but subject matter in content area texts—social studies, science, reading—is often presented through linguistic structures that are too complex for some students who are hearing impaired. Teachers must rewrite these materials or work with students on specific language skills prior to introducing what is supposed to be the content of a course. Frequently, even materials specifically created for students who are hearing impaired must be modified to meet individual student needs.

Secondary/Transition.   At the secondary and postsecondary levels, the main challenge facing students with hearing impairments is the required rapid assimilation of large quantities of written material. Many students with hearing impairments, even those who are college bound, read at a level considerably below that of normally hearing peers. Unfortunately, students who are hearing impaired are also more dependent than their nondisabled peers on the written word as their source of information, because they have less access to auditory media, such as audiotapes, telephones, television, and radio. Consequently, secondary school curricula must give considerable attention to improving the reading and writing abilities of students who are hearing impaired; teachers simplify text material and supplement it with study guides, computer-assisted instruction, and other visual media such as captioned films and film strips.

Because of their lack of access to informal sources of information and because of the language barrier that often exists between students who are hearing impaired and their families, secondary students also need specific information on sexuality and sexual conduct, family life, legal rights and responsibilities, dealing with bureaucracies such as Social Security, and effective use of leisure time.

MAINSTREAMING   The Least Restrictive Environment Controversy

Perhaps for no other group of people with disabilities is there so much controversy over what constitutes the least restrictive educational environment mandated by the

*T*he Early Childhood Home Instruction Program for Infants with Hearing Impairment and Their Families provides service to 45 to 60 families yearly. The families live in large and small communities throughout western Washington state. Most services are provided in the home because it is difficult for many families to bring their children to a distant center. They may lack transportation, funds for gasoline, or baby-sitters to care for their other children during such visits. Another reason is the belief that an infant's home, with all of the naturally occurring events of family life and with the family's own equipment, toys, and household objects, offers the most advantageous environment for teaching and learning. Families feel most comfortable implementing a program designed to meet their children's unique needs in this family environment, and as many people in the family (or neighbors and friends) who wish to participate in the program can do so. It has been possible to serve so many families each year precisely because the program is primarily home-based.

Most of the educational program is conducted in weekly visits to the home. Families are visited by a parent trainer for 1½ to 2 hours each week for the entire year. Parent trainers have a master's degree in education of those with hearing impairments or in the speech and hearing sciences or are parents of children with hearing impairments who have received additional training in working with infants and families.

The purpose of the weekly home visit is twofold: (1) parents learn the skills necessary to provide good auditory stimulation and language for their children; and (2) parents have an opportunity to express their feelings, concerns, and questions regarding their child with hearing impairment and about hearing impairment generally. After an Individualized Family Service Plan (IFSP) is developed, the family and parent trainer discuss activities that will help achieve objectives. Usually, the target skills are first described and then demonstrated by the parent trainer. Then, during the visit, the parents practice the skill to ensure that they fully understand it. An assignment is left so that the parents can practice the skill with the child during the week. Parents usually work on two skills a week—one in the auditory area and one involving communication or language. Siblings and other family members are included as much as possible. The "important others" who participate in the task of instruction usually prove to be apt and interested learners and help the family work as a team rather than leaving the responsibility to one or two family members.

A supervisor visits each family with the parent trainer once a month to make sure that appropriate standards and consistency are maintained. These visits also provide one-to-one inservice training for the parent trainer. The supervisor also receives weekly and quarterly reports from the parent trainers and manages all data regarding both parents and child. Data are reviewed on a regular basis, and changes in the child's program are made as necessary.

For parents who have transportation and are able to bring their children, a play group is offered several times a week. This program provides an opportunity for the children who are hearing impaired and their hearing siblings and/or friends to interact with each other and enjoy experiences they may not have at home. It also provides an opportunity for parents to see other children who are hearing impaired and to discuss problems with other parents.

Parents meet as a group to talk to the program counselor, work on sign language skills, or hear presentations they have requested by audiologists, pediatricians, and other professionals. Information is provided to all parents regarding their rights and the issues related to transitioning to a school setting. All families visit the school their child will attend accompanied by personnel from the program. Often, families return after "graduation" at age 3 to the play group, especially during the summer months.

Individuals with Disabilities Education Act (IDEA), the 1990 reauthorization of Public Law 94–142. The environment that offers maximum opportunity for interaction with peers who are not disabled may also provide drastically inferior opportunities for communication and socialization with other students and adults who are hearing impaired and may offer less-than-adequate support services. Indeed, some adults insist that the least restrictive environment for students who are severely hearing impaired is a segregated residential school, because only within such an environment can they communicate freely. The Commission on Education of the Deaf (1988), in its report to the president and Congress, viewed the least restrictive environment issue as central to appropriate education of students who are hearing impaired and concluded that "Center Schools, including those programs with a sufficient number of children who are deaf on a particular age and grade level, are the least restrictive environment appropriate for many children who are deaf" (p. 33).

Many professionals, however, believe that placing students who are hearing impaired in carefully chosen regular education classes is academically and socially beneficial. This position is strongest when certain conditions hold. Students with hearing impairments should be approximately the same chronological age, mental age, social age, and grade level as the students in the class they are entering. There should be an Individualized Educational Plan and appropriate support services, such as notetakers, interpreters, and tutors. The receiving teacher should welcome the opportunity of having a student who is hearing impaired in the classroom, and there should be constant monitoring. Some center-based programs (such as the one described in the Model Program box) invite hearing children to participate in program activities. Children with a mild hearing loss and good language skills may spend a major part of every day in regular classes, perhaps receiving additional help through speech therapy or academic tutoring. Others may be integrated for specific academic subjects and for social contact during nonacademic periods.

Age-Level Distinctions

Early Childhood.   It is important to remember that hearing infants spend much of their time at home and, unless in day care, do not often play with many other children. The situation for children with hearing impairments is much the same. The hearing loss is often not identified until an infant is 18 to 22 months of age so the child's language development will be delayed. Family life is complicated by the newness of dealing with a child with hearing loss and by visits to professionals, and so finding a way to mainstream with hearing children may be difficult initially. When parents are ready, they can begin the integration process in a natural fashion. At the age of 2½ to 3 years some children enjoy a morning or two each week playing with peers in a regular preschool.

School Age.   As a child with hearing impairment reaches age 3 and moves into an academic setting, it may still be difficult to provide an inclusive setting within the public school system because in most states, hearing children do not start public school until they are kindergarten age or older. Many public schools do provide the possibility of some interaction because they house early childhood programs such as Head Start.

Mainstreaming in private preschools or day-care facilities is an option for children with hearing impairments at the age of 4 or 5, or they have opportunities to interact with hearing children in kindergarten. Results of research regarding the success of integration in promoting academic and/or social growth are equivocal for this age group.

As children with hearing impairments become older, there are increased opportunities for inclusion. Students with hearing impairments who use total communication can be accompanied to regular classes by notetakers and interpreters or classroom aides who sign proficiently. The well-organized resource teacher will plan ahead with the regular classroom teacher and provide tutoring in particular content areas. Coordinating efforts of this type increase the student's probability of success.

For students who rely on the auditory system to receive information, it is important that the regular classroom provide good acoustics. Teachers should be willing to wear a microphone in order to speak directly to the student through an FM amplification system and bypass the extraneous classroom noise. It can also be helpful to use the buddy system and have a peer assist the target student by making sure he or she is on the right page and by taking notes to help fill in what might have been missed.

Secondary/Transition. Academic inclusion for students most severely or profoundly hearing impaired at the secondary and postsecondary levels is dependent on the availability of someone to translate (from English to ASL) or transliterate (from oral English to another mode, such as fingerspelling or Manual English). Information at the secondary and postsecondary levels is usually presented in oral lecture or discussion formats. Even the best speechreader or a student who receives maximum benefit from amplification will have considerable trouble understanding oral communication

Hearing children can learn alongside their siblings who have hearing impairments.

in a large group, and the task becomes virtually impossible when, for example, the lecturer walks around the room, turns around to write on the board, or digresses to a different topic without warning.

Interpreters, who are professionally certified by the National Registry of Interpreters for the Deaf, mediate between the student and the oral information presented. Unless specifically hired for that purpose, interpreters are not tutors or student advocates; they are professional translators such as one might find at the United Nations. Mainstream teachers need to become accustomed to dealing with a student through an interpreter. Etiquette dictates that the teacher look at the student rather than at the interpreter when asking a question or receiving a response. The interpreter should not be addressed directly (e.g., "Do you think Diane understood that?"), because the interpreter will simply convey those exact words to the student. Interpreters must know the communication level of their clients and modify syntax and vocabulary accordingly. In technical fields, interpreters need to be familiar with specialized vocabulary in order to fingerspell accurately and/or invent appropriate signs for frequently used technical terms. Interpreters are bound by a strict code of ethics, including rigid standards to ensure confidentiality of translated material.

INNOVATION AND DEVELOPMENT

Computer-Assisted Instruction

The use of microcomputers offers one of the most promising areas for upgrading the education of children and youth who are hearing impaired and for promoting inclusion of people with hearing impairments of all ages. The characteristics of computer instruction lend themselves to educating children who are hearing impaired. Computers are a basically visual medium, providing a communication modality in which students with hearing impairments usually are not disabled. Other advantages include the fact that (1) they are interactive, requiring frequent active participation in the learning process; (2) the software can be self-paced; (3) reinforcement and error correction are immediate; and (4) branching is possible (in response to error analysis).

By means of computers, people with hearing impairments can access the fast-growing world of electronic mail, data bases, bulletin boards, consumer services, and other benefits available to the hearing population. Equally important, they can communicate readily with other members of the deaf community. Computers are also aids to assessment and individualized instruction.

A major challenge to educators in the future will be to enable students with hearing impairments to take full advantage of this new and increasingly popular tool. Although computers are a visual medium, their educational uses depend heavily on the ability to use language, and consequently on the ability to read and write. Thus, we return again to the major job confronting all who deal with individuals who are hearing impaired—the development of adequate communication skills.

Cochlear Implants

As discussed earlier in the chapter, a cochlear implant is a single or multichannel device that is surgically placed in the ear. One part, a magnetic coil, is placed under the skin behind the ear. An external coil is held in place by the implanted magnet. A wire extends from the implanted coil and ends in an electrode that is placed in the fluid within the cochlea (inner ear). The external coil is connected to an electrical pack that looks much like a body-type hearing aid and that houses the battery power for the system. This pack can be worn in a variety of ways—in a pocket, on a vest, or in a pouch. A tiny microphone that can be hooked over the ear, clipped to a shirt collar, or worn on a barrette is also attached to the pack. The microphone picks up sounds that are carried to this pack or signal processor. The processor converts the sounds to electrical signals, which are transmitted through the implanted coils to the electrode in the cochlea, thereby stimulating electrical impulses in the auditory nerve. The impulses are then carried up through the auditory pathways to the brain.

The cochlear implant, unlike a hearing aid, does not change electrical impulses back to acoustical sounds. Rather, electrical impulses are carried directly through the system to the brain. Implant users have stated that sounds heard through an implant are different from sounds heard through a hearing aid. Evaluation for implant surgery involves many tests and a general physical examination. The surgery to place the implant is usually performed under general anesthesia and involves opening the mastoid (the bony structure within the skull that leads to the middle ear) and the middle ear. Cochlear implants may be particularly helpful to those children and youth who are unable to use hearing aids successfully. There is continued controversy about cochlear implants, such as at what age the implant should be done and how many channels are necessary. Care should be taken to ensure that each child has sufficient practice with a hearing aid and auditory training prior to a decision being made.

Tactile Aids

Tactile aids are devices that use the sense of touch to assist a person who is profoundly deaf to "feel" sounds they cannot hear. They essentially convert sounds into a stimulus that can be felt. The tactile aid is not meant to substitute for a hearing aid; some children wear both. Tactile devices include a vibrator that is often placed on the collarbone and held in place by a vibrator strap. The vibrator is connected to an electrical pack that looks like a body-type hearing aid and contains a charger, an internal microphone, an intensity control, and an input jack for the external mike. The pack can be clipped to a belt or, for young children, placed in a carrier case that the child can wear. The final part is an external tie-clip microphone, which must be attached to the clothing in order to pick up auditory information. The hope is that these tactile aids will assist people who are profoundly deaf to be aware of environmental and speech sounds and, to varying degrees, to be able to discriminate among these sounds. It is also hoped that they will promote better speech production.

SUMMARY   Sound waves move through the outer, middle, and inner ear and are changed into neural impulses, which are given meaning in the brain. Hearing loss comes about when there is interference with the transmission process. A conductive hearing loss results from impairment in the transmission of the sound waves through the outer and middle ear and can usually be corrected. A sensorineural hearing loss results from impairment in the inner ear in the conversion of sound waves into neural impulses; it

1. Seat the students where they can see your lip movements easily.

2. Do not speak too loudly, especially if the students are wearing hearing aids.

3. Avoid visual distractions, such as wearing jewelry, that draw attention away from your lips.

4. Avoid standing with your back to a window or bright light source; it throws your face in a shadow and makes speechreading difficult.

5. Avoid moving around the room or writing on the board while speaking. If possible, use an overhead projector, which allows you to speak and write while maintaining eye contact with the class.

6. During class discussions, encourage the students to face the speaker even if this requires their moving about the room.

7. When a manual interpreter is present, allow the interpreter and the students to select the most favorable seating arrangements.

8. Write assignments and directions on the chalkboard, distribute mimeographed directions, or have a hearing student take notes on oral directions for students who are hearing impaired.

9. Ask the students who are hearing impaired to repeat or explain class material to make sure they have understood it.

10. If a student has a hearing aid, familiarize yourself with its operation, but expect the student to assume responsibility for its care.

TIPS FOR HELPING

cannot be corrected. Hearing losses can be genetic or nongenetic (i.e., caused by disease or injury). Even a mild hearing loss affects learning; the impact of the loss depends on a variety of variables. The individual's social development is also affected.

Audiological assessment uses various methods to measure the extent of a hearing loss. Cognitive assessment of children who are hearing impaired must avoid a linguistic emphasis, since such children are often delayed in their language development. Intervention begins with a hearing aid, as early as possible. Home-based programs, center-based programs, or a combination of the two may be the most effective during early childhood. More and more school-age students with hearing impairments are choosing regular education settings. Debate continues over the best mode of communication for students with hearing impairments. Total communication features both the aural-oral and the manual approach.

Children with hearing impairments who receive good quality linguistic input from birth develop language much like their hearing peers. Thus, early input is critical. As the children grow, attention must be directed toward improving their reading and writing skills and the providing practical, life skills information. Mainstreamed educational placement must be carefully considered so that the needs of students with hearing impairments are met. Computer technology and computer-assisted instruction offer great promise.

STUDY QUESTIONS

1. Differentiate conductive hearing loss and sensorineural hearing loss.

2. Describe how hearing is measured in adults and older children, in preschool children, and in infants and individuals with severe developmental delays.

3. List the major causes of sensorineural hearing loss.

4. Discuss general characteristics of children with severe to profound hearing impairments.

5. Provide a general description of the types of tests available for assessing the cognitive, academic, and communication skills of children with hearing impairments.

6. Differentiate the effects of a postlingual hearing loss and a prelingual hearing loss.

7. Compare the theoretical arguments supporting manual communication, the aural-oral approach, and total communication.

8. Describe the characteristics of early intervention for infants and preschoolers with hearing impairments.

11

Visual Impairment

Sharon Zell Sacks
San Jose State University

Sandra Rosen
San Francisco State
University

 In this chapter you will learn about

- the historical aspects that have shaped the structure of current educational programs for students with visual impairments

- the developmental differences between students who are visually impaired and sighted students and the impact on assessment and educational placement of those who are visually impaired

- the adaptations and methods used to educate students with visual impairments in a variety of educational settings including the mainstreamed classroom

- the importance of incorporating disability-specific skills (e.g., activities of daily living, social skills training, utilization of technology, career and vocational education, efficient use of residual vision) into the daily educational curriculum for students with visual impairments

- strategies used in educating students with multiple disabilities and visual impairments

Four-year-old Lindsay was born 2½ months premature. As a result, she developed retinopathy of prematurity (ROP), which left her with limited residual vision. Another side effect of Lindsay's prematurity, hypoxia ischemia (lack of oxygen), affected her motor function.

Almost immediately after birth, when Lindsay was still in the hospital, her family began to meet with an early intervention educator who had specialized training in serving infants and young children with visual impairments. Her parents began to take an active role in the Development Visual Team Process at the hospital. In addition to Lindsay's parents, the team included a pediatric ophthalmologist, a developmental pediatrician, a neurologist, and the early intervention specialist.

When Lindsay became stronger and gained weight, she was able to go home. A specialist in visual impairment made home visits twice a week, providing the family with strategies to facilitate Lindsay's development and independence around the house and the community. This specialist also accompanied the family to ophthalmological visits and acted as a liaison for the family regarding educational issues.

When she was 18 months old, Lindsay began to attend a toddler program 3 mornings per week. The program emphasized hands-on experiences, interaction with peers, play activities to promote language acquisition, and acquisition of self-help skills. Lindsay's parents took her to a weekly play group where she had opportunities to interact with sighted toddlers.

Lindsay entered a preschool program at the age of 3. The preschool teacher teamed with a prekindergarten teacher for 3 mornings a week to provide Lindsay and her peers with disabilities with opportunities for interactions with nondisabled peers. In addition to prebraille, computer, and preacademic activities, Lindsay receives orientation and mobility instruction, as well as adaptive physical education to strengthen her motor skills. The preschool classroom also stresses self-help skills, decision making, and problem solving. Lindsay is learning to use a white cane to help her travel independently at school and in her neighborhood.

At their last Individualized Educational Plan (IEP) meeting, Lindsay's parents began to discuss transition from preschool to kindergarten with the educational team. They recognize the importance of giving Lindsay experiences interacting with sighted children. Lindsay's parents and the teacher will explore a number of placement options. These include placement in Lindsay's local neighborhood school, which has a resource room program where she could receive itinerant services from a teacher who works with individuals who are visually impaired, or placement in a private school where she would receive services from a vision specialist.

Vision is taken largely for granted by those of us with this sensory system intact. It is difficult to realize all of the ways that serious visual impairment affects the various aspects of a person's life. This chapter provides information about individuals with visual impairments, including current definitions; causes; the various types of impairment; the anatomical structures affected; problems in adapting to visual disabilities; and environmental, technological, and instructional strategies that facilitate learning for those who are visually impaired.

HISTORY   The education of children with visual impairments began in Paris in 1784 when Valentin Haüy, an educator and philanthropist, created the first school for persons who were blind. Haüy's goal was to create a reading system for persons with visual impairment. His student, Louis Braille, actually accomplished this goal by developing and refining the braille code (a series of raised dots), which is still used today by persons who are blind.

Samuel Gridley Howe established the first residential school for persons who were blind in United States in 1829, which continues to operate today. The New England Asylum for the Blind in Boston (known today as Perkins School for the Blind) provides lifelong support for its residents. Two other residential schools, the New York Institute for the Blind and the Pennsylvania Institution for the Instruction of the Blind, began educating children who were blind in the 1830s. These programs provided instruction to all individuals with visual impairments. No distinctions were made with respect to visual functioning. During the middle of the 19th century, all persons with visual disabilities were considered tactile learners. It was not until 1879 and the inception of the American Printing House for the Blind (APH) that books and materials appeared in both braille and large print.

Education of children who were blind and visually impaired in public school programs began in the early 1900s. Frank Hall and John Curtis established the first day school program for children with visual impairments in Chicago. In a moving presentation Hall stated:

> I think the method of segregating the blind, keeping them not with the class with whom they will live after they leave school, cutting them off from society, is the greatest mistake that was ever made. The public school is the place to educate a blind boy, associating him with the people with whom he will associate when he leaves school. (Irwin, 1955, p. 149)

This was a radical perspective well into the fifties, when most disability groups and many professionals were working to establish and fund segregated educational services for those with disabilities. Only approximately 15% of school-age children with visual impairments were enrolled in public school programs throughout the first half of the 20th century.

The impact of retinopathy of prematurity (ROP) in the late forties and early fifties strongly influenced the direction of education of students with visual impairments. Almost 10,000 premature infants were affected by ROP. Many were left with little or no vision.

Some decades later, in the sixties and early seventies, a devastating outbreak of the rubella virus caused serious visual impairments along with multiple impairments in almost 30,000 children. This also influenced the direction of services for children with visual impairments. The focus of educational programming in residential schools changed from an academic perspective to more functionally based curricula. It was not until 1975, with the passage of Public Law 94–142, the Education for All Handicapped Children Act, that a wider range of placement options for students with visual impairments became available.

Today, educational programs for students who are blind and visually impaired have grown to include services for infants and preschoolers, as well as students in transition from school to adult life. (See the Model Program box for a description of a program that provides comprehensive services from infancy through adulthood.) However, the extent and quality of services provided to students with visual impairments continue to be challenged by changing philosophical perspectives among leaders in special education and by fiscal constraints. Future trends for the education of students with visual impairments must embrace the advancements of technology and innovative curricula while ensuring a strong educational program to assist each student in future life endeavors.

DEFINITION   Many people today think that all persons who are blind live in a world of total darkness (Schulz, 1980). In reality, only a small percentage (approximately 15%) of people who are labeled as legally blind or visually impaired are completely without vision (Bailey & Hall, 1990; O'Donnell & Livingston, 1991); the vast majority of people have some degree of usable vision. The terms blindness and visual impairment have been defined in a number of ways by different disciplines to establish eligibility for special services and funding support. There are basically three types of definitions: medical, legal and rehabilitative, and educational.

Medical Definitions

Eye care specialists (ophthalmologists and optometrists) evaluate an individual's visual abilities through ophthalmic examination. Generally two criteria are used in determining quality of vision: visual acuity and visual field. *Visual acuity* refers to the clarity with which a person can see. It is most often measured using the Snellen chart (Figure 11–1). The chart consists of eight rows of letters (or Es for very young children or those who are illiterate) of varying size, each corresponding to the size of a standard print sample at distances from 15 feet to 200 feet. Acuity is measured as the person sits 20 feet from the chart and reads aloud the smallest line of print he or she can visually distinguish (or states which way the "legs" of the Es are facing on the smallest line that can be read). Normal acuity is 20/20. The first number refers to the distance at which the person can see a specified line on an eye chart. The second number refers to the distance at which a person with normal vision could stand and still see the same line. A person with 20/200 vision, therefore, would have to stand no more than 20 feet from the chart to see the same line that a normally sighted person could see from a distance of 200 feet.

A second method of measuring acuity that is becoming more common is contrast sensitivity. A significant factor in how "clearly" a person can see something is the contrast of an object with its background rather than the size of the object alone. As an example, it is easier to see a small piece of white chalk against a black background

Figure 11–1
Snellen scale symbol chart.
Source: National Society for the Prevention of Blindness, 79 Madison Avenue, New York, NY 10016. Reprinted by permission.

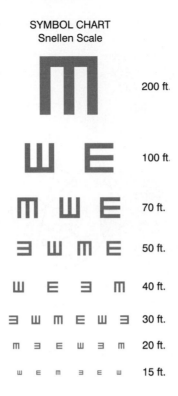

than a dark telephone pole against a dark brown background. Contrast sensitivity is measured by displaying a variety of patterns consisting of alternating black and white bands of varying widths. The narrower the widths become, the more the pattern takes on the appearance of a solid gray color rather than black and white bands. The point at which a person is no longer able to distinguish between the black and white bands identifies the amount of contrast a person needs to see an object. The lower the requirement for contrast, the higher a person's acuity.

Visual field refers to the area seen by the eye at a given moment. Using peripheral, or side, vision, a person can normally see an area of about 180 degrees from left to right while keeping his or her eyes straight ahead. There are a number of tests for visual field such as perimetry in which a person looks ahead at a target while the examiner flashes small lights in varying spots in the peripheral field. By determining to which lights a person responds or does not respond, the ophthalmologist or optometrist is able to draw a "map" of the person's visual field, showing where the person may or may not see (see Figure 11–2).

Legal and Rehabilitative Definitions

The term "legal blindness" is used by governmental and rehabilitation agencies to determine whether or not a person qualifies for legal benefits such as tax advantages and services (e.g., instruction in nonvisual methods of travel and daily life skills, assistance in job training and in obtaining employment).

Figure 11–2
Visual field diagram showing areas
of field loss in a patient's right eye.

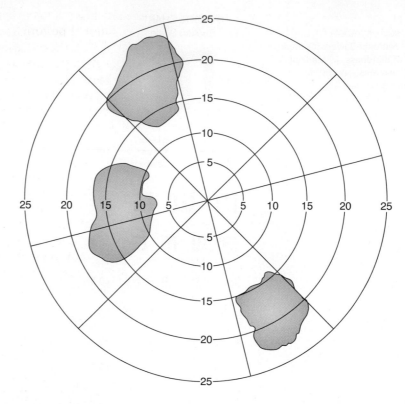

A person with visual acuity of 20/200 in the better eye after correction (e.g., glasses) is considered *legally blind*. Legal blindness may also mean that a person, regardless of visual acuity, can see no more than an angular distance of 20 degrees out of 180 degrees without shifting his or her head or eyes. This means that the person would see only about 1/9 of the area seen by a person who does not have visual impairment (Figure 11–3). A person with 180 degrees of field (normal) can see all of the items in this scene. A person with 20 degrees of field can see only the items that lie within the shaded area.

Visual impairment signifies a visual field loss that leaves no more than 20 degrees of visual field or a visual acuity in the better eye after correction ranging from 20/70 to total blindness.

Low vision refers to a visual impairment that is severe enough to impact the performance of learning and everyday tasks, but which still allows some useful visual functioning.

A person is considered eligible for services from state departments of rehabilitation if his or her vision in the better eye following correction is less than 20/60 or if the field of vision is no greater than 20 degrees.

Educational Definitions

Educational definitions of visual impairments rely on more functional criteria. The Individual with Disabilities Education Act (IDEA; Public Law 101–476) defines children with visual handicaps as those who have "a visual impairment which even with correction, adversely affects . . . educational performance." Educationally, children with visual impairments are considered "functionally blind," "low vision," or "visually limited," depending on their ability to use their vision to learn (see Table 11–1).

A child is considered *blind* if he or she can only learn through tactile or auditory channels (Caton, 1981). A child who is blind might use braille as a reading medium, as well as a computer with voice output and/or auditory tapes as part of the educational program. A child is considered *low vision* (formerly referred to as partially sighted) if he or she is severely visually impaired after correction but has increased visual functioning through the use of optical aids, nonoptical aids, and environmental modifications and/or techniques (Corn, 1980). A child who has low vision can use his or her residual vision functionally for learning and may use it as a primary means of acquiring information. The child may combine the use of remaining vision with tactile and auditory methods, depending on the amount of usable vision. A child is considered *visually limited* if his or her use of vision is limited under average circumstances, but he or she is considered sighted for educational purposes and in all other situations (Barraga, 1983). A child who is visually limited may benefit from adaptations such as special lighting, corrective lenses, or modified teaching materials.

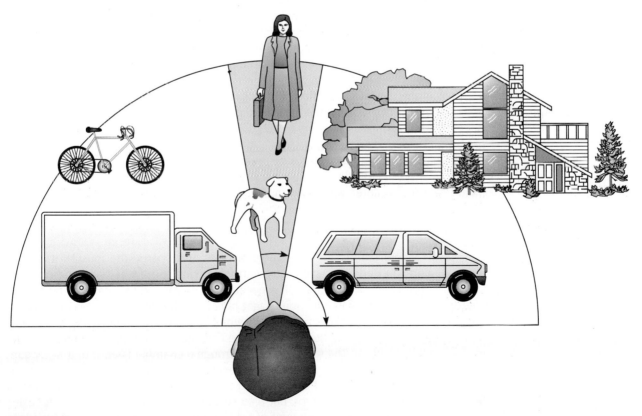

Figure 11–3
Visual field.

Table 11–1
Educational definitions of visual impairment

Term	Definition
Blind	Child learns through tactile or auditory channels.
Low Vision	Child is severely visually impaired after correction but can increase visual functioning through the use of optical aids, nonoptical aids, and environmental modifications and/or techniques.
Visually Limited	Child's vision is limited under average circumstances, but he or she is considered sighted for educational purposes and in all other situations.

PREVALENCE

Visual disability is considered a low-incidence disability; it affects only approximately 0.1% of school-age children. Accurate data on numbers and demographic characteristics of children with visual impairments are difficult to obtain because the majority of children with visual impairments have multiple handicaps (Kirchner, 1990). Many are enrolled in programs for students who have intellectual impairments, physical disabilities, or multiple disabilities and are reported by their primary diagnosis. Probably the most accurate statistics on the number of children who are visually impaired are those compiled annually by the American Printing House for the Blind (APH). Each year APH compiles a registry of legally blind children being served in school programs. In 1992 it reported more than 42,431 children enrolled in these programs.

There has been a steady increase in the number of children who are visually impaired since the late seventies (Kirchner, 1990). Data compiled by APH indicate a 9% increase in children who are visually impaired between 1987 and 1991. The number of children in infant programs increased by 25% and the number in preschool programs increased by 41% (APH, 1987; APH 1992). This rise is due in part to the improved ability of physicians to save premature infants and to sustain lives of those born with severe medical problems. It is perhaps also due in part to better and earlier identification of children with impairments.

CAUSES

Structure and Function of the Visual System

The visual system consists of the eyeball and its inner parts, the muscles that surround it, and the nervous system connections linking the eyeball and the occipital lobe, or vision center, in the brain. The eyeball can be likened to a camera, both in its anatomy and in many of its functions. Light rays pass through the cornea (a transparent cover in front of the iris and pupil), which performs a major role in bending (refracting) the rays so that they will be focused clearly on the retina and provide optimal vision (Figure 11–4). The rays then pass through a chamber filled with a water substance known as the aqueous humor. From there they pass through the pupil, which is an opening surrounded by a structure called the iris. The iris not only gives eyes their brown, blue, green, or hazel color, but also serves an important function in focusing light rays and in regulating the amount of light entering the eye. The work of the iris in light regulation can be compared to the function of the F-stop on a camera. After passing through the pupil, the light rays pass through the lens of the eye. Slight changes in the shape of the lens serve to additionally focus the light rays as they travel to the retina. Behind the lens, the light rays pass through a transparent gelatinous substance known as the vitreous humor which gives the eyeball its round shape. Finally, the light rays reach the retina, which is analogous to the film in a camera.

The macula is the small central portion of the retina responsible for fine, detailed vision such as reading print; the remainder of the retina provides peripheral vision, enabling a person to see large objects and movement. The retina itself is made up of neural cells, mainly photoreceptor cells called rods and cones. The rods serve primarily to enable the eye to see dim light and to detect movement. The cones enable the eye to see fine detail; they are responsible for color vision. Attached to the sides and back of the eyeball are six extraocular muscles, which also attach to the bony structures of the skull. These muscles control the movement of the eyes upward, downward, and to the sides.

Visual Impairment

Visual impairment can take several functional forms. In addition to acuity impairment and field loss, problems occur in refraction, accommodation, muscle balance, and color vision. Each of these problems can have a specific effect on the child's ability to function in the school, home, and community.

Refractive Errors.   Myopia (nearsightedness), hyperopia (farsightedness), and astigmatism (blurred vision) are the most common types of refractive errors. Normally, light rays pass through the cornea and lens where they are refracted and then come to a focus directly on the retina. Myopia occurs when the eyeball is not spherical but is elongated from front to back, causing the light rays to focus in front of the retina instead of on the retina (Figure 11–5). Hyperopia occurs when the eyeball is shorter

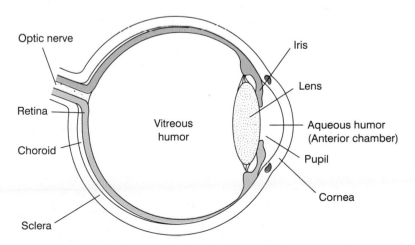

Figure 11–4
Cross section of the human eye.

than normal from front to back, which causes the light rays to focus behind the retina (Figure 11–5). Astigmatism occurs when the cornea, which is relatively spherical in shape, becomes distorted and assumes a football shape, or develops a wavy surface instead of a smooth surface. In each of these cases the result is blurred vision due to improper focusing of light rays on the retina. Refractive error can often be corrected with glasses or contact lenses.

Accommodation Errors. Accommodation refers to the changing shape of the lens in focusing light rays. To clearly focus on an object that is approximately 20 feet or more away, the lens becomes relatively long and flat. When focusing on objects closer than 20 feet, it assumes a progressively more spherical shape. Presbyopia is a condition that occurs when the lens is unable to change shape. As a result, a person may have increased difficulty focusing on near items, which is especially notable when reading print. Presbyopia often occurs after age 40. Reading glasses or bifocal lenses are often prescribed to correct this problem.

Muscle Imbalance. Muscle imbalance means that some of the six extraocular muscles are stronger than others, resulting in an unequal pull on the eye, a condition known as strabismus. The two eyes do not align; one will look forward while the other appears to look either inward (commonly called a cross eye), outward (commonly

Figure 11–5
Focusing of light rays in the normal, myopic, and hyperopic eye.

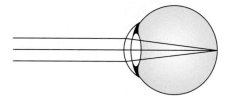

Normal Eye: Light rays focus on the retina

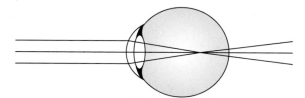

Myopic Eye: Light rays focus in front of the retina

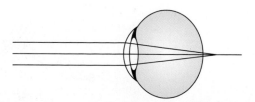

Hyperopic Eye: Light rays focus behind the retina

called a wall eye), upward, or downward. When the two eyes do not align, they each see a different image rather than focus on a single image. The result is double vision. Especially in young children, the brain attempts to repress the image from one eye to eliminate the double vision, eventually destroying that eye's ability to see perfectly. This later condition is known as amblyopia (commonly called lazy eye). An additional effect of strabismus (any condition in which the eyes do not focus together) is the loss of depth perception, which is important in doing such things as catching a ball and determining the height of descending stairs. If treated prior to age 5 or 6, strabismus can often be corrected surgically, or in some cases, by patching to tighten and strengthen weak eye muscles. Strabismus must be treated early, however, while the brain's ability to develop perception of binocularity is still developing.

Color Vision Problems.   Certain conditions affecting the cones in the retina result in diminished ability to discern certain colors. While impaired color vision does not cause a visual impairment directly, it can have a significant impact on learning, especially during the early years, when children are first learning the concept of colors and when color is used so extensively in the design of learning materials. The colors most often affected are red, blue, and green. Some conditions are genetic in nature and affect males most often; others are part of retinal conditions that affect both acuity and color vision. A total loss of color vision is rare.

Retinal Problems.   Problems with the retina can cause decreased acuity and/or field loss. Students with problems affecting the central retina have difficulty seeing small objects and distinguishing details. Also they may have impaired color vision. Students with problems affecting the peripheral retina experience difficulty seeing in dark areas and moving around the environment.

Common Conditions Affecting Vision

Teachers who work with students with visual impairments should be aware of the more common conditions causing visual impairment. Knowing these conditions helps teachers make needed modifications in teaching materials and instruction. For information about specific eye conditions and instructional modifications, regular teachers should work closely with a teacher of those who are visually impaired.

Cataracts.   Cataracts can be congenital (present at birth) or secondary to trauma to the eye. With this condition, the soft, clear lens of the eye hardens and becomes cloudy, blocking the entrance of light rays into the eye. Early effects of cataracts on vision include decreased acuity and sensitivity to glare. An analogy to cataracts would be to look through a dirty windshield. When headlights from an oncoming car shine on a dirty windshield, it momentarily becomes difficult to see past the dirt. Similarly, when bright light such as sunlight shines in the eye, it is difficult to see past the cataract. Further, because the lens is responsible for accommodation, a person with a hardened cataract or one that has been removed (a condition called aphakia) cannot read or see close objects easily. Cataracts can be removed surgically and artificial lenses implanted in the eye, or the person may be given special glasses to improve vision.

Glaucoma.   Glaucoma can be congenital, hereditary, or due to eye trauma. Excess pressure of aqueous humor builds up in the eye, causing decreased acuity and a progressive field loss. The field loss starts at the edges of the peripheral field of vision and works toward the center until vision is completely gone. When peripheral vision is impaired, persons have difficulty seeing in dimly lighted areas or at night. Sensitivity to glare is also a common problem. Medications and surgery can be effective in slowing or arresting the progression of glaucoma.

Nystagmus.   Nystagmus is a neurological disorder in which the eyes tend to rhythmically oscillate left and right or up and down. Because the eyes do not remain still, students may have difficulty focusing; thus, they experience problems reading and/or seeing small objects. The condition is not progressive.

Optic Nerve Disorders.   Congenital optic nerve disorders are usually not progressive and are characterized by reduced acuity and/or field loss. The loss can range from mild impairment to total blindness. *Optic nerve hypoplasia* is a common optic nerve disorder resulting from injury to the prenatal central nervous system. It may also be genetic or caused by trauma. This condition is commonly found in children who have fetal alcohol syndrome.

Retinopathy of Prematurity.   Retinopathy of prematurity (formerly called retrolental fibroplasia) is characterized by changes in retinal blood vessels and proliferations of vessels and scar tissue in the eye. It is thought to be due either to the immature development of the eye in premature infants or to be related to the administration of high oxygen concentrations to newborns of low birth weight. Although high concentrations of oxygen risk visual impairment, they are often necessary to prevent brain damage and to save the life of very premature infants. Vision may be mildly to severely impaired. Children who have moderate or severe cases often lose their vision later in life as scar tissue formed in the eye contracts and pulls the retina away from its blood supply (called retinal detachment).

Acquired Immune Deficiency Syndrome (AIDS).   To date, few cases of severe visual impairment among children with AIDS have been recorded, but several hospitals and organizations are reporting occasional visual impairment with differing etiologies in children who have AIDS. The fact that AIDS affects the central nervous system of children may, in part, account for this. The number of children with AIDS who are visually impaired is uncertain. This is due perhaps to lengthy incubation periods and the fact that many children with AIDS have died of other complications before their vision began to fail. With the use of drugs to prolong the life of people with AIDS, it is more likely that more cases of visual impairment will be identified in the future (Kiester, 1990).

Optic Albinism.   Genetically transmitted, optic albinism is characterized by lack of pigment in the eye. Albinism may affect the entire body, or it may be confined to the eyes. Visual acuity is generally diminished, and nystagmus may be present. Because the eye lacks pigment, persons with albinism are highly sensitive to bright light and glare. They must often wear sunglasses to protect their eyes when outdoors.

Retinitis Pigmentosa.   This condition is genetically transmitted and most often characterized by a slowly progressive loss of visual field, beginning at the periphery and progressing to the center. The onset of visual problems can begin in early youth or in teenage years. Early symptoms include a progressive loss of night vision and difficulty seeing in dimly lighted areas. Impairment of acuity occurs in the late stages.

Retinoblastoma.   Retinoblastoma is a malignant tumor of the eye. It generally necessitates that the eye be removed surgically to prevent spread of the malignancy, although in some cases it may be treated with radiation or other means. It generally occurs bilaterally and usually before 3 years of age.

Diabetic Retinopathy.   The major cause of blindness in the United States, diabetes mellitus causes damage to the retina as a consequence of impaired circulation. Visual acuity is initially affected. The condition may eventually result in total blindness. Diabetic retinopathy (pathology of the retina due to diabetes) can be treated with laser therapy, but progression of the disease cannot be halted altogether. Persons with diabetes often suffer from additional health problems secondary to impaired circulation, such as kidney impairment; progressive loss of feeling in the fingers, hands, and/or feet; and poor healing ability. The onset of visual impairment generally comes after the person has had diabetes for a number of years.

Leber's Congenital Amaurosis.   Genetically transmitted (autosomal recessive), Leber's congenital amaurosis is a form of retinitis pigmentosa that occurs at or shortly after birth. It is characterized by a progressive loss of central vision. Peripheral vision can also be affected and nystagmus may be present.

Congenital Macular Disease.   This disease causes degeneration of the central retina. Children with this disorder can have reduced acuity, photophobia (extreme sensitivity to bright light), and decreased color vision. Peripheral vision remains unimpaired.

Cortical Visual Insufficiency.   This condition results from damage to the visual cortex or the brain or the posterior visual pathways leading from the eyes to the brain. It is most commonly seen in children who have other neurological disorders such as cerebral palsy, epilepsy, or hydrocephalus. Children who have cortical visual insufficiency may demonstrate fluctuations in visual functioning, varying levels of inattention to visual stimuli, and difficulty discriminating figure-ground. Students may bring objects close to their eyes to see them, effectively blocking out visual clutter in the background. Some students may use touch more than vision as their preferred learning medium.

CHARACTERISTICS

Children who are blind or visually impaired are children first. Each is different, with unique needs and special learning styles. Blindness or limited visual abilities may cause delays in cognitive, language, motor, and social development (Sacks, Kekelis, & Gaylord-Ross, 1992; Santin & Nesker Simmons, 1977; Warren, 1984) because much of early learning is accomplished through imitation, primarily visual imitation (Skellenger, Hill, & Hill, 1992). Children with visual impairments miss out on many opportunities for incidental and imitative learning.

Factors that can affect the development of a child with a visual impairment include the etiology and age of onset of the visual impairment, the type and degree of visual impairment, and the presence of additional impairments. Children who lose their vision before age 5 are considered to be congenitally visually impaired for educational purposes because they often retain little visual imagery on which to draw in learning (Lowenfeld, 1980). The majority of students with visual impairments are in this category.

Even without the influence of additional disabilities, no two students with visual impairments are alike. One may excel in reading, another in mathematics, still another in music. One may be friendly and assertive, another shy and passive. There are only two generalizations that can be made: (1) they function with limited or no sight and (2) the way they develop and acquire skills may be very different from their sighted peers. Regardless of the age of the student with a visual impairment, an understanding of how visual impairment affects specific development is essential in order to understand each student's unique educational needs.

DEVELOPMENT

Motor Development

During the first few months of life when children are learning head control, sitting upright, and rolling, infants with visual impairment are not significantly different from their sighted peers. In later months, when their peers move from stationary to dynamic motor skills, the development of children who are visually impaired tends to fall behind (Palazesi, 1986; Pogrund, Fazzi, & Lampert, 1992; Schneekloth, 1989; Skellenger et al., 1992). It is not the visual impairment in and of itself that delays physical growth and development, but rather the lack of visual stimulation to encourage movement (Hill, Rosen, Correa, & Langley, 1984) and limited opportunities for imitative learning (Scholl, 1986). Environmental factors such as a lack of opportunity for a variety of motor activities and psychosocial factors such as overprotectiveness may also contribute to delayed motor development in children who are visually impaired (Schneekloth, 1989). Other factors that may contribute to delayed motor development are low muscle tone and poor proprioception (sensory awareness of the body's position in space). These conditions are particularly evident in children who are congenitally blind (Hill et al., 1984).

Such physical and environmental factors are believed to contribute to the development of problems in posture, coordination, and gait (walking) patterns characteristic of many children who are visually impaired, especially those who are totally blind. Early intervention, with cooperation between parents, teachers, physical education instructors, and occupational and physical therapists helps children with visual impairments develop fine and gross motor skills comparable to those demonstrated by their sighted peers.

Cognitive Development

Blindness does not itself impair a person's ability to process or manage sensory information intellectually. The limiting factor is the extent to which the child's interaction with the environment is impoverished, thus limiting his or her ability to gain the sensory information essential to cognitive development (Tuttle, 1986). If formulation of the initial object concept is delayed, acquisition of other concepts such as object permanence, causality, and spatial relationships will also be delayed, as will acquisition of higher-order skills such as classification and conservation. Further, there are certain concepts such as color that the child who is totally blind or color-blind may never grasp. Children who are totally blind also have difficulty acquiring concepts of spatial distance and relationships. Hearing and touch, although indispensable in learning, cannot compensate for lack of vision. Auditory and tactile cues do not always provide the same stimulus as vision. It is simply impossible to grasp fully the understanding of the height of a skyscraper, a cloud, or the flicker of a candle flame without vision.

Information conveyed by touch and hearing is largely sequential compared to the simultaneous presentation of information that is possible through vision. Vision enables a child to perceive the whole of an object and its parts, noting the relationship of parts to each other and to the whole. Touch and hearing, on the other hand, require that the child examine the parts and then integrate them into a whole through mental imagery. This latter conceptualization process is less efficient and much more susceptible to the formation of incomplete or erroneous concepts. It is critical to provide students with visual impairments with opportunities to learn about the world around them and to help them develop abstract concepts through opportunities for hands-on experiences.

There are two important points to remember concerning cognitive development. First is that many children with visual impairments are not delayed in concept development (e.g., those who have usable residual vision and those who are adventitiously blind) (Progrund, Fazzi, & Lampert, 1992). Low-vision children should be encouraged to use their functional vision along with other sensory modalities to form concepts and integrate the world around them. Second, the increased emphasis on early intervention programming means that children who do experience delays in concept development during the preschool years can catch up and enter school functioning at or near the same level as their sighted classmates.

Social Development

The social development of persons who are blind and visually impaired does not always parallel that of sighted individuals. Social learning is highly dependent on visual modeling and imitation. This poses a major problem for young children with severe visual impairments. Their ability to interact effectively with age-mates, parents, siblings, and other adults may be limited, causing isolation, negative attitudes, and an inability to mediate social encounters (e.g., initiations, turn taking, nonverbal cues).

There is a growing body of research relating to the social development of children with severe visual impairments. Studies of early social development suggest that parents may react negatively to their child because the child gives little or no evidence of eye contact or smiling (Fraiberg, 1977; Warren, 1984).

Another problem is that young children with visual impairments may be limited in their ability to move about and explore their social environment. Thus, they are dependent on others (parents, teachers, and siblings) to interpret social situations or play encounters. In a qualitative study of social interactions between children who were blind and peers who were sighted, Kekelis and Sacks (1992) and MacCuspie (1992) found that the play behavior of young children with visual impairments lacks imagination and expansion. In this study, conversations between those who were blind and their peers who were sighted were brief. The students with visual impairments were unable to hold their age-mates' interest. Their encounters were egocentric and reflected situations experienced only in the home environment. Their knowledge of an array of social (play) experiences was not commensurate with that of their sighted counterparts. As a result, the children were treated negatively or ignored by peers.

The development of age-appropriate social skills may be limited in range and variety because the opportunities to emulate social role models and to participate in social situations are often restricted (Sacks & Wolffe, 1992; Scott, 1969). The problem of limited social skills can be rectified. Teachers of those who are visually impaired and other professionals now realize that specific social skills (e.g., eye gaze, body space, positive initiations, joining groups) need to be taught and monitored. It is now recognized that simply placing a child who is visually impaired in an environment with sighted peers will not result in acquisition of appropriate social behaviors. There must be specific training with appropriate feedback to ensure learning, use, and generalization of social skills (Sacks & Gaylord-Ross, 1989; Sacks et al., 1992; Sisson, Van Hasselt, Hersen, & Strain, 1985; Van Hasselt, 1983).

Finally, the nature of social development for a child who is visually impaired is influenced greatly by the expectations that other people hold for him or her. If significant others expect the child to behave with certain limitations that they believe are inherent in visual impairment, then those limitations will become part of the child's self-concept. On the other hand, if significant others accept the visual impairment and acknowledge its impact on the child without setting limited expectations, the child will perceive his or her social abilities and attributes in a positive manner, which facilitate attainment of additional skills and social growth.

Language Development

The process of acquiring speech and language is the same for sighted children as for children with visual impairments. In general, the early vocabulary of children who are visually impaired parallels that of their sighted peers of the same age. Where there are differences in language patterns, they can be attributed to the influences of visual cuing and early social experiences (Bigelow, 1987, 1990).

Difficulties in acquiring certain concepts such as color or an understanding about objects that cannot be touched were discussed earlier. A secondary effect of these difficulties is evident in language development: too heavy reliance on verbal descriptions by others as a means of developing concepts about the environment and the world may result in what is termed "verbalism" or verbal unreality (Andersen, Dunlea, & Kekelis, 1984). Verbalism occurs when the child who is visually impaired uses concepts of which he or she has no firsthand experience. For example, a child who is blind may talk about the white, billowy clouds and yet have no real understanding of the words *white, billowy,* or *cloud.* When teaching a child who is blind, educators should be aware of verbalisms and verify through demonstration that the child truly understands the meanings being expressed.

Research by Dunlea and Andersen (1992) also suggests that young children with visual impairments tend to ask many more questions and verbally make more demands on peers and adults than do their sighted peers. They tend to focus on their own interests and actions rather than recognizing the needs of others.

ASSESSMENT

Assessing students with visual impairments is a coordinated effort of the teacher of those who are visually impaired, the school psychologist, the speech and language clinician, physical and occupational therapists, the orientation and mobility instructor, other educational specialists, the regular classroom teacher, and the family. Decisions regarding educational placement need to be made carefully.

Educational assessment is a multifaceted process of gathering information by using appropriate tools and techniques (Ysseldyke, 1979). Until recently, educational decisions for students with visual impairments typically were based on findings from instruments that yielded a standardized score or were normed for sighted children. These scores provided little useful information for educational planning and placement. Another problem was that assessments were often done in isolation with little regard for other team members' expertise and knowledge. Today, the assessment process emphasizes sharing of information among team members from various disciplines. The resulting information is more accurate and meaningful.

Comprehensive educational assessment for students with visual impairments is broad-based. Concerns include: (1) the developmental history of the student; (2) prognosis of visual functioning; (3) family status; (4) cultural attitudes; (5) other physical or emotional anomalies on the part of the student affecting educational functioning; and (6) the student's cognitive, social, and motor development. School programs typically use a combination of standardized educational assessments, observational procedures, and ecological information collected through interviews. Decisions should not be based on standardized test results alone. For example, the performance of a student who is visually impaired on the quantitative portion of the WISC-R (Wechsler Intelligence Scale for Children, Revised) will not give a true picture of his or her quantitative abilities because many of the questions require good visual and visual-perceptual abilities. It is also important to recognize that timed tasks place a student with a visual impairment at a disadvantage.

The areas generally covered in a comprehensive educational assessment for those with visual impairments are functional vision, intellectual and cognitive development, concept development, psychomotor skills, academic achievement, social and daily living skills, and career and prevocational skills. Many of these assessments are administered by the teacher and/or by the orientation and mobility specialist. Tests of intelligence are usually administered by a trained psychologist who has expertise in testing and interpreting the educational needs of students with visual impairments. Table 11–2 provides a summary of each component of a comprehensive *educational* assessment for students with visual impairments. Other assessment areas include speech and language development, orientation and mobility skills, listening skills, and tactile readiness skills.

Age-Level Distinctions

Early Childhood.   Early assessment of children who are blind and visually impaired provides valuable information for the educational team. The information obtained through a comprehensive assessment helps the team establish specific goals for intervention. Generally, assessment of infants, toddlers, and preschool students with visual impairments focuses on the child's relationships with his or her family, social develop-

Table 11–2

Components of a comprehensive educational assessment for students with visual impairments

Assessment	Purpose	Administered by
Functional Vision	Determines how the student uses vision in a variety of environments and tasks, such as daily living, orientation and mobility, vocational, and academics	Teacher, O&M specialist
Intelligence	Provides a standardized measure of innate abilities and experiences	School psychologist
Conceptual Skills	Closely related to cognitive development Provides information about abstract and concrete thinking, spatial awareness, and directionality	VI teacher and O&M specialist, speech and language clinician, regular education teacher
Psychomotor Skills	Provides information about the ability to use fine and gross motor skills in daily and academic tasks	VI teacher and O&M specialist, regular education teacher
Academic Achievement	Provides a measure of mastery in specific content areas such as reading, math, spelling, and language arts	VI teacher, regular education teacher
Social and Daily Living Skills	Provides information about affective skills, behavior control, peer relations, and ability to care for personal and living needs	VI teacher, O&M specialist, activities for daily living specialist, family members
Career and Vocational	Provides information about the student's understanding of the world of work, job options, and specific skill strengths or weaknesses	VI teacher, vocational specialist, family members

Note: VI = teacher of those who are visually impaired; O&M = orientation and mobility specialist.

ment, acquisition and use of language, motor development, concept development, and attainment of play skills.

Several assessment scales are designed specifically for young children with visual impairments. They include the Maxfield-Buchholz Social Maturity Scale for Blind Preschool Children (Maxfield & Buchholz, 1957), the Reynell-Zinkin Scales (the Parent Observation Protocol [POP] Parent Assessment; Reynell, 1983), and the Oregon Project. Each of these tasks is standardized to account for the unique developmental differences in young children with visual impairments. Other assessment tools evaluate readiness skills for braille reading and writing, motor development, visual functioning, and spatial orientation. These include the Mangold Development Program of Tactile Perception and Braille Letter Recognition (Mangold, 1977), the Revised Peabody Mobility Scale (Harley, Wood, & Merbler, 1981), and the Bailey-Hall Cereal Test (Bailey & Hall, 1986).

School Age.   Assessment of students with visual impairments in school settings is done by the teacher of those who are visually impaired, usually in conjunction with support personnel. It is important for the teacher of those who are visually impaired to assess students' use of functional vision in a variety of school and community environments.

Secondary/Transition.   Assessment of students preparing for transition from school to adult life incorporates academic skills, independent living skills, orientation and mobility skills, and career development skills. Students who wish to pursue a college track program should demonstrate skills in interpersonal relationships, assertion and self-advocacy skills, organization and study skills, and basic vocational skills. Assessment of vocational readiness skills provides information about a student's performance on a series of job tasks and behaviors over a period of time, specifically information about an individual's stamina, attention span, fatigue, and accuracy with regard to visual functioning.

Students with Multiple Disabilities.   Assessment of students with multiple impairments who are visually impaired should consider functional skills. The AAMD Adaptive Behavior Scales and other similar behavioral checklists can provide useful information about students' independent living skills, job skills, and social skills.

PROGRAM MODELS AND INTERVENTION

Before specific curriculum content areas are described for students who are blind and visually impaired within a variety of educational settings, it is important to discuss the range of available educational placement and intervention options. The "most appropriate placement" for students with visual impairments depends on the unique educational needs of the student, and the intensity of services required for the student to achieve success in an integrated school environment (Hatlen & Curry, 1987). The following program models provide a continuum of services for persons with visual impairments who are of school age. These placement models may also be appropriate for students who are multiply impaired.

Effective mainstreaming for a deaf-blind high school student involves cooperation from the classroom teacher and the VH specialist.

The Residential School Model

Residential school programs emphasize the attainment of academic skills while teaching specialized skills such as use of braille, slate and stylus, typing, and abacus. Intensive instruction in specialized skills, however, can be provided at residential schools. Community-based programs that include independent living skills, work experiences in real job settings, and recreational activities within the community are being incorporated into more traditionally oriented programs. It is not uncommon for students who have been mainstreamed into regular educational placements to receive intense, short-term services in a residential school program. This is often done through special summer programs where students receive intensive instruction in orientation and mobility, daily living skills, utilization of technological and adaptive devices, and vocational readiness training.

The Self-Contained Classroom Model

The self-contained classroom model is another traditional model that has been prevalent in public school programs throughout this century. Self-contained programs provide a specialized program for students who have disabilities in addition to visual impairment or who need constant support in a structured environment. Often, classes are housed on public school campuses that provide opportunities for mainstreaming or socialization with nondisabled peers.

The Resource Room Model

The resource room provides students with visual impairments with a less restrictive educational program than do the residential school and self-contained classroom models. The resource room is housed on a public school campus and staffed by a credentialed teacher of those who are visually impaired. Students are mainstreamed into regular education classes depending on their level of academic independence. A wide range of student abilities and needs are served within a resource room program. Many students use the resource room as a facility to receive training and assistance in adapting regular classroom materials for their use and learning to use assistive equipment and devices. The resource room program also lends itself to helping students acquire a set of essential nonacademic skills such as activities of daily living, career education, and social skills training. However, most students served in a resource room program must travel to a central geographic location instead of attending their local neighborhood school program.

The Itinerant or Teacher Consultant Model

The itinerant model allows students who are blind and visually impaired to attend their neighborhood school while receiving services from a teacher of those who are visually impaired. Usually, students are mainstreamed into the regular classroom setting for most of the school day. The itinerant teacher comes to the students' school and provides direct service on the school site. The amount and intensity of services depend on the students' academic and nonacademic needs. In some cases the teacher acts as a consultant to classroom teachers, program administrators, and specialized service personnel, but does not provide direct service to the student. This is often the arrangement for students served in programs for those who are severely disabled and are multiply impaired.

Early Childhood Models

Early intervention programs for infants and toddlers with visual impairments and their families are usually home-based. Services are provided by a specialist in visual impairment and early childhood. Visits are made to the home at least monthly, during which the educator and the parent or caregiver work together to facilitate the child's growth and development in language acquisition, motor development, concept formation, and social and self-help skills. The parent-infant educator provides useful support and assistance. In addition, the home counselor acts as a resource to assist the family in finding appropriate services. Sometimes, programs for young children (birth to 3 years) who are visually impaired incorporate both center-based services and home-based services.

Programs for toddlers and preschool children with visual impairments are usually center-based. They may be in a self-contained classroom on a public school campus or in another location where the children can be integrated into play groups and activities with sighted peers. Generally, programs are staffed by a teacher of those who are visually impaired, an orientation and mobility specialist, a speech and language clinician, and/or an occupational or physical therapist. These programs encourage and emphasize parent involvement.

Transition Models

Whether a student with a visual impairment is college bound or interested in vocational pursuits, the focus of secondary-level programs is on providing study skills, work skills, and independent living skills. Students often spend a portion of the school day working at a job site within the community. The educator, the rehabilitation counselor, the student, and the parent work together to plan for future job placement or training options, as well as to explore appropriate independent living programs. Greatest emphasis is placed on community work experiences. Many state agencies for those who are blind have begun to explore innovative models such as supported employment.

CURRICULUM IMPLICATIONS

Professionals in the field of education of those who are visually impaired have identified a set of unique educational needs and curriculum content areas for these students. Most important is that they achieve a positive self-concept and the independence necessary for adult functioning.

In order for effective instruction to occur, there needs to be a strong coordinated working relationship between the regular classroom teacher and the teacher of those who are visually impaired. This section describes curricula components of particular importance for the student with a visual impairment. Curriculum content areas are discussed according to age-level distinctions. They include strategies for working with students who exhibit visual impairments and those with multiple disabilities.

Age-Level Distinctions

Early Childhood. Early intervention programs for children who are blind and visually impaired attempt to facilitate their growth and development in cognitive and tactile skills, fine and gross motor skills, language and conversation skills, self-help skills, and social skills. Whether the program is center-based or integrated into a regular preschool environment, the teacher of those who are visually impaired works closely with the family to support their efforts at home.

Cognitive and language activities typically use real objects rather than plastic or toy models. The plastic representation of a food item such as an orange does not provide the child with a visual impairment with a complete realization of the object. A real orange has texture, smell, color, shape, and layering (an outside skin and an inside core). Firsthand experiences with real objects can help to promote children's awareness of concepts and functional use of language.

The acquisition of self-care skills is an integral part of any early intervention program for young children who are visually impaired. Dressing, grooming, and eating skills are a part of the daily curriculum, typically facilitated in the context of naturally occurring routines. Snack time, for example, provides opportunities to practice eating skills. Some children who are blind exhibit feeding problems, and they often find different textures or new foods distasteful. Incorporating simple food preparation activities with eating experiences help to motivate the student. Independent toileting and self-care skills such as hand washing, toothbrushing, and hair combing are encouraged and supported. Most important is for the young child with a visual impairment to develop a sense of responsibility for his or her own needs.

For many young children with visual impairments, exploration of the physical environment is limited and frightening. Young children may be fearful of new settings and of new objects in a familiar environment. Through play and toy manipulation, teachers of those who are visually impaired help children get a greater tactile and kinesthetic awareness of the world around them. The teacher of those who are visually impaired mediates and stimulates exploration by verbally describing activities, objects, or settings so that children become familiar with them and more willing to participate. Orientation and mobility training (discussed later in the chapter) help to improve posture, gait, spatial awareness, and general agility. Through such early experiences the young child with severe visual impairment is introduced to a cane, helped to refine gross motor skills, and taught to move confidently through the environment.

Preschoolers with visual impairments often exhibit weaknesses in hand and finger strength, which can be a problem because strength is important for reading braille. Braille users must be able to discriminate subtle tactile likenesses and differences. Teachers enhance fine motor skills through the use of clay, puzzles, formboards, block building, and cooking activities that require mixing, stirring, and opening of boxes or containers. Braille readiness activities, such as the Mangold Developmental Program of Tactile Perception and Braille Letter Recognition, provide additional opportunities to develop students' hand strength, searching techniques, hand placement, and symbol discrimination.

Finally, the integration of play skills and social skills into a comprehensive preschool program is essential. Like their sighted counterparts, children who are blind must learn to share and work effectively with others. Without a strong foundation in early social experiences, the child who is visually impaired is placed at risk for social isolation in later school experiences. It is important for the teacher of those who are visually impaired and the family to work together to provide realistic and consistent feedback regarding appropriate social behavior while fostering the students' positive self-image. Integration into play groups, preschool programs with sighted age-mates, and recreation activities such as swimming, gymnastics, and other preschool level activities helps to facilitate social growth.

School Age.　Many students with visual impairments can be effectively included in regular education classes given the appropriate materials, devices, and skills. Collaboration between the teacher of those who are visually impaired and the regular classroom teacher can effect the necessary adaptations, which are often as simple as front-row seating, lighting without glare, and presentation of information in a verbal rather than a written format.

Academic Skills

Utilization of Low Vision.　Simple adaptations in teaching often make it easier for low-vision students to use their vision more effectively. A significant education problem for these students is visual fatigue; they must put forth a great deal of effort to distinguish the details of print. Teachers can allow students to take frequent, short breaks and should mix visual activities with auditory and motor activities when possible. If the student has difficulty reading the board, the teacher may use thicker chalk to produce bolder lines. Photocopy materials with high contrast are more favorable than dittos.

Some students may use visual aids to help them see print and other images. Low-vision aids are classified as nonoptical or optical. Nonoptical aids do not require a special prescription or training in their use. The following are easy-to-use nonoptical aids:

1. *Acetate*. Yellow acetate can be placed over print to increase print darkness and contrast. (Acetate can be purchased in office supply stores.)
2. *Felt-tip pens*. Felt-tip pens increase the width of written lines and the contrast of the written material to the background. Black or dark blue pens in particular make written material easier to see.
3. *Bold-line paper*. Paper with bold, black lines helps students to write on the lines. (This paper can be purchased or it can be made by tracing preprinted lines on notebook paper with a felt-tip pen.)
4. *Bookstands*. Bookstands make it possible to elevate and/or angle to bring print closer. Use of a bookstand may reduce students' neck and back fatigue caused by bending over close to a book on a desk.
5. *Large-print textbooks*. Many students with visual impairments cannot read standard-size print. Large-print books usually contain letters that are 14 to 30 points high; 18-point type is most popular (see Figure 11–6). Large print can be produced by photoenlarging standard type or by specially typeset materials. Some children effectively enlarge print for themselves by holding printed material closer to their eyes. Students may use large print in combination with other aids such as tapes, magnifiers, and/or closed circuit television systems.

Optical aids consist of lenses placed between the eye and the object to be viewed. Examples include magnifiers that can be hand held or mounted on a stand, lenses mounted in spectacle frames, various forms of telescopes, and closed-circuit televisions (CCTVs) that project an enlarged image onto a television screen. The CCTV is far more expensive than the other low-vision aids; however, it allows for variable magnification, varied contrast, and illumination. In addition, some CCTV systems have adaptations that enable them to be used with typewriters, microfiche readers, and computer terminals. Optical low-vision aids are generally prescribed by a low-vision

---

This is a sample of 14-point print.

This is a sample of 18-point print.

This is a sample of

30-point print.

Figure 11–6
Samples of 14-, 18-, and 30-point print.

specialist (an ophthalmologist or optometrist who specializes in low vision). Instruction in the use of low-vision aids is provided by a qualified specialist such as the low-vision specialist or the teacher of those who are visually impaired.

Braille Reading and Writing.   In 19th century France, Louis Braille, himself blind, introduced the basic system of writing for people who are blind that is used today. The basic unit of braille is a quadrangular cell containing 1 to 6 dots arranged in 2 vertical columns of 3 dots each (see Figure 11–7). There are several different forms of braille, which vary primarily in the number of characters used. Grade 1 braille, for example, assigns a character to each letter of the alphabet, to each numeral 0 through 9, and to each punctuation mark. Words are spelled character by character exactly as they are in print. This system is relatively easy to use. However, because writing in braille is a much slower process than writing in print and because braille materials tend to be far bulkier than their print counterparts, Grade 1 braille has disadvantages. Grade 2 braille addresses these problems by substituting special contractions for common letter combinations. The letters *ing*, for example, can be represented by 1 braille character instead of 3 (see Figure 11–8). The majority of braille materials, including reading primers, are written using Grade 2 braille. There are higher grades of braille that incorporate even more shortcuts, but these are generally reserved for special purposes such as secretarial shorthand. In addition to the grade-level content taught their sighted peers, children with visual impairments typically receive instruction in Grade 2 braille. Braille instruction generally begins in kindergarten and is taught by the teacher of those who are visually impaired.

Competence in braille reading and writing is important to a successful mainstreaming program for a blind student.

The six dots of the Braille cell are arranged and numbered thus:

```
1 •• 4
2 •• 5
3 •• 6
```

The capital sign, dot 6, placed before a letter makes it a capital. The number sign, dots 3, 4, 5, 6, placed before a character, makes it a figure and not a letter.

1 a	2 b	3 c	4 d	5 e	6 f	7 g	8 h	9 i	0 j

k	l	m	n	o	p	q	r	s	t

u	v	w	x	y	z	Capital sign	Number sign	Period	Comma

Figure 11–7
Braille alphabet and numbers.
Source: From the Division for the Blind and Physically Handicapped, Library of Congress, Washington, DC 20542.

Braille is written using a 6-key machine called a braillewriter. Each of the 6 keys corresponds to one of the 6 dots in the braille cell. As the student presses the keys, braille characters are embossed onto special paper. Braille can also be written using a slate and stylus. A slate is a metal frame with openings through which braille dots are punched using a pointed stylus. Compared to the braillewriter, however, the slate and stylus require higher levels of manual dexterity and the ability to emboss letters in a mirror image. Thus, the slate and stylus are not usually introduced until the 5th grade.

Mathematical Aids.   A special braille code, known as Nemeth code, allows the students with visual impairments to perform the same mathematical computations as their sighted peers. In addition, students with visual impairments may use tactile and auditory math aids such as the Cranmer abacus and the talking calculator. The Cranmer abacus is a pocket-size adaptation of the Chinese abacus, with a special backing that prevents accidental movement of the beads. A talking calculator is similar to a standard calculator but with added voice output that repeats numbers as they are presented and voices the answer to calculations when completed. Given the accessibility and advances made through technology there is some debate among professionals serving students with visual impairments regarding the continuing use of the abacus as a viable mathematical aid.

Listening Skills and Auditory Training.   Because many children who are blind and visually impaired use a combination of print, braille, and taped material, it is essential that they develop refined listening skills. Although students with visual impairments may have a keen sense of hearing, they may not utilize it in a competent

Figure 11–8
Comparison of Grade 1 and Grade 2 braille.

i   n   g

Grade 1 braille

i n g

Grade 2 braille

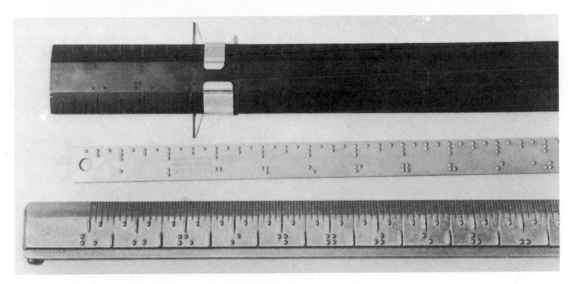

Braille rulers.

manner. It is important for them to learn to synthesize auditory information in an organized, concise way. Teachers work with students on following directions, auditory comprehension, summarizing information obtained through a lecture or a taped medium, and retaining information once presented (auditory memory). Students increase their listening abilities through sound localization experiences, environmental cuing, and exposure to new environments within the community.

Most Appropriate Reading Medium. Teachers of those who are visually impaired must decide what reading medium will be most effective for optimal learning (print, braille, taped format, or a combination of these modes) for each of their students. Recent concerns among professionals serving students with visual impairments regarding their students' level of literacy and competence in reading and writing have led to the development of guidelines and assessment criteria for determining the most appropriate learning medium (Koenig & Holbrook, 1989; Mangold & Mangold, 1989).

Organization and Study Skills. If a student with a visual impairment is to be mainstreamed effectively into a regular education classroom, the student must be able to obtain and complete classroom assignments independently. Further, the student must be responsible for keeping track of adaptive aids and devices that will assist in the mainstreaming process. Adaptive aids and devices that can enhance and mediate the student's acquisition of academic subjects include the following:

1. *Geographical aids.* Tactual maps and globes with raised surfaces and different textures are important aids for children with visual impairments. For children with low vision, the teacher can enlarge print maps and, if necessary, trace over the lines with a felt-tip pen.

2. *Scientific aids*. Many scientific aids that assist learning for students with visual impairments also enhance science education for sighted children. The Science Activities for the Visually Impaired (SAVI) materials produced by the Lawrence Hall of Science in Berkeley, California, are among the most innovative of science materials and include braille thermometers, spring-loaded balances, and materials for teaching science concepts about electricity, biology, earth science, and other scientific areas.

Utilization of Technology.   In the past, children with visual impairments had to rely on braille and braillewriters (or slate and stylus) to record class notes and do homework assignments. As noted before, braille—although a highly functional mechanism for written communication—is bulky (occupying several times the space of equivalent print material) and slow to write compared to handwriting. In conjunction with braille, and until recently the only alternative to braille, tapes and tape recorders are important tools used for taking class notes, recording homework, recording test answers, listening to assignments, and "reading" assigned books that have been recorded. Special tape players are available that have a compressed speech option, which allows speech to be accelerated from 150 to 175 words per minute of normal speech up to 275 words per minute of speech. Using compressed speech can be up to three times faster than using braille (Tuttle, 1974).

Computer and other technological advances, however, are greatly affecting education and employment options for persons with visual impairments. The following are a few examples of modern technological advances that provide easier and more independent access to print and computer terminals, and more efficient ways to use braille in the school setting:

1.   *Optacon (optical-to-tactual-converter)*. This electronic reading device transforms print into vibrating letter configurations that can be read tactually. The optacon con-

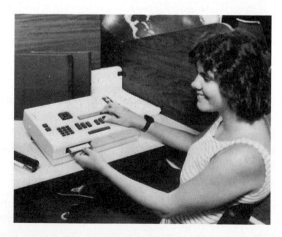 

Devices such as versabraille (left) and speech-activated computers (right) provide access to printed material.

sists of three parts: a camera, an electronics section, and a tactile array. The person who is visually impaired moves a miniature camera across a line of print with one hand while feeling a tactile representation of individual letters or numbers with the index finger of the other hand, which rests on a tactile array consisting of 144 vibrating pins. With the optacon, those who are totally blind finally have independent access to print media.

2. *Paperless braille.* With this equipment students can store information on audio-cassette tapes and then present it tactually in a braille display ranging from 12 to 32 cells in length. The reader can also produce and record his or her own braille writing and interface with an increasing variety of computers, typewriters, and calculators.

3. *Computer applications.* Rapid developments in computer technology are making a significant change in the accessibility of computers for individuals with visual impairments. Microcomputers, with appropriate peripherals and software, enable the child with a visual impairment to function alongside the sighted child in acquisition and manipulation of information. Those with low vision can use a large-print computer system or software that produces large print on the screen of a conventional computer system.

Microcomputers can also be used by braille users. They can type information in braille into the computer using a special keyboard that simulates a braille keyboard and, by means of a special printer, can obtain a hard copy in either braille or inkprint. Similarly, a teacher can input information in print and obtain a hard copy in braille or in large print for a student with a visual impairment. In addition, specialized speech output hardware or software enables the computer to read aloud selected passages of information entered into the computer.

4. *Optical scanning systems.* Optical scanners are small computers that convert print into speech. By placing material facedown on the scanner, the person with a visual impairment hears material being read by an electronic voice. The Kurzweil Personal Reader is an example of an optical scanning device. The Kurzweil is very expensive but is currently used in a large number of schools, colleges, libraries, and other locations (Orlansky & Rhyne, 1981).

Nonacademic Skills

There continues to be some disagreement as to whether the education of students with visual impairments should emphasize academic skills or functional skills. The excellence in education movement in regular education stresses the importance of providing all students with extensive education in basic academic skills and core curriculum subjects. For students with visual impairments, as for all students, there is another set of skills that are critical to successful living and adult independence: these are functional skills, the practical behaviors that enable a person to succeed and enjoy day-to-day living at work, in the community, and at home. Functional skills include personal/social skills, career and vocational skills, daily life skills, orientation and mobility skills, and recreation and leisure skills. Unlike their sighted peers who learn many of these skills through observation and imitative learning, students with visual impairments require specialized instruction in these areas. A comprehensive educational program for students with visual impairments must therefore strike a successful balance between academics and functional skills.

Daily Life Skills.   Daily life skills are the things we do each day as part of our normal routine. They can include dressing, hygiene, food preparation, cleaning, mending, and even home maintenance. For the sighted child many activities of daily living are learned through visual imitation. Once learned, they are often performed with a heavy reliance on visual feedback. For example, children rely on visual feedback to know that they have correctly placed the toothpaste on their toothbrush or that they have wiped the table completely clean after lunch. Children who are visually impaired do not have the benefit of visual feedback. They can, however, learn to perform the same daily life skills as their sighted peers by modifying items with auditory and tactile adaptations or by using techniques in which tactile and auditory feedback are substituted for visual feedback. For example, a student can use touch to verify that a table has been properly cleaned and can use listening to identify when water is boiling. Instruction on these techniques begins before the child reaches school age and continues throughout the child's school years. Numerous curricular materials are available to assist educators in developing age-appropriate living skills activities. For example, the Texas School for the Blind's Living Skills Curriculum (Loumiet & Levack, 1991) provides a comprehensive outline of activities that could be acquired by a student with a visual impairment (Figure 11–9).

Eshilian, Haney, and Falvey (1989) have advanced an appealing ecological inventory approach to selecting functional skills. It is a useful tool for looking at the environments (e.g., school, parent's home, own home, workplace, community sites) in which a student needs to function and for planning appropriate instruction in relevant daily life skills. After compiling such a tentative community-referenced list of functional skills, the teacher meets with the child's parents to elicit information about their expectations and priorities for the child's instruction. The community and home information is then synthesized into a list of specific instructional objectives.

Figure 11–9

Daily life skills—curricular areas.
Source: From *Independent Living: Self-Care and Maintenance of Personal Environment*, by R. Loumiet & N. Levack, 1991, Austin: Texas School for the Blind. Copyright 1991 by Texas School for the Blind and Visually Impaired.

Dressing
Clothing management
Personal hygiene and grooming
Eating
Eating in different settings
Food management
Housekeeping and home maintenance
Housing
Telephone use
Time concepts
Obtaining and using money
Health and safety
Self-advocacy

Learning to cook is only one aspect of an independent living program for a student who is visually impaired.

Orientation and Mobility. Orientation refers to knowing one's position in space and in relation to objects in the environment. Mobility is the ability to move around the environment safely and efficiently. Development of independent orientation and mobility skills is essential for children who are visually impaired. Not only does the level of independence in mobility have a direct relationship to the development of self-esteem (Tuttle, 1986), it is also a major factor in the ability of the child who is visually impaired to participate in social activities and later to obtain employment (Graves, 1983). Beginning during the preschool years, orientation and mobility training includes instruction in motor skills, optimal use of remaining senses, and learning about the physical environment and one's community. It also includes instruction in skills of independent travel, specifically the use of a long cane, the use of low-vision aids for reading signs, techniques for safely crossing streets, and other skills for safely and efficiently getting from point A to point B. Certified orientation and mobility specialists provide instruction in these four basic mobility systems:

1. *Human guides.* By holding onto the elbow of a person with sight, a child who is visually impaired can follow the movements of the guide's body and walk around obstacles, negotiate stairs, and travel safely in any environment.

2. *Basic skills and cane skills.* Using a variety of techniques, some involving the use of a long cane (often colored white), children learn to travel independently in school, at home, and in a variety of familiar and unfamiliar areas such as the residential area

in which a friend lives and downtown or business areas. Orientation and mobility instruction teaches the child the use of environmental cues; problem-solving techniques; use of a cane and other travel techniques; orientation skills; how to identify traffic patterns, cross streets, and take public transportation; and how to travel safely and efficiently in all environmental situations appropriate to one's age level.

3. *Dog guides*. Dog guides are used by only a small percentage of persons with visual impairments, and then only by individuals who have little or no vision usable for travel. Chosen for size, intelligence, and temperament German shepherds, labradors, and golden retrievers are the breeds most commonly trained for dog guide work. Dog guides are trained to obey a limited number of commands, including walk forward, stop, turn left, turn right, walk faster, walk slower, fetch a dropped object, sit, lie down, and locate a door. It is the responsibility of the person with visual impairment to direct the dog to a destination using orientation skills. The dog, in turn, leads the person around obstacles in the travel path, stops at street corners, and, when told to cross the street, leads the person directly to the opposite corner. In addition, dog guides are trained to disobey a command to cross the street if a vehicle is approaching, a behavior commonly called "intelligent disobedience."

Individuals who are visually impaired learn how to use a dog guide by participating in a 4-week residential training program at a dog guide school. Although not required, it is generally helpful for students to have received orientation and mobility instruction in the basic skills of independent travel before learning to travel with a dog guide. The use of a dog guide requires maturity, generally good physical health, and good orientation skills. Dog guide users generally must be over 16 years old.

4. *Electronic travel aids*. There are a number of sophisticated devices that are designed to be used either in conjunction with or in place of a long cane. These devices emit ultrasound or laser beams that are reflected by objects in the travel path and received by special transducers in the aid. The reflected signals are then transformed into auditory or tactile signals that inform the user as to the direction and distance of an object from his or her body. The most important feature of these aids is that they detect obstacles at head and chest height such as low-hanging branches, which are not detected by the long cane. Although new devices are being developed, the five most commonly used devices are the Mowat Sensor (a hand-held device that serves as a simple obstacle detector), Sonicguide (a spectacle-mounted device that serves as an obstacle detector and gives information about the roughness or smoothness of the object), the Russell Pathsounder (a simple obstacle detector), and the Laser Cane (an obstacle detector), and the Sensory-Six (an obstacle detector). Additional electronic aids that are currently being developed are the Pathfinder (an obstacle detector) and the Trisensor (an update of the Sonicguide that provides more precise information about the location of detected objects). Extensive training is required in the use of electronic travel aids and should be provided by a certified orientation and mobility specialist.

One of the newest trends in orientation and mobility is teaching cane skills to preschool children. Historically, cane skills were not taught until children entered 1st grade. Prior to 1st grade, they were taught to move around in the environment by feeling along a wall or other surface, or by walking through space using their hands and arms as "bumpers." Although this form of travel worked reasonably well for small children, it was not nearly as efficient and effective as a long cane.

Today, many orientation and mobility professionals provide cane instruction to children as soon as they are able to hold a cane and to walk independently with good balance (Progrund & Rosen, 1989). This early instruction seems to facilitate the earlier development of skills in environmental exploration in that it gives children a means of moving in the environment with less possibility of bumping into objects. It also gives them a means of "reaching" beyond their body to form concepts about the environment and the relative location of objects in space. Further, early cane skills have been linked to the development of self-confidence and self-esteem and the development of better posture and gait (through the increased movement and motor experience).

Innovations in orientation and mobility include the development of electronic orientation aids such as talking signs and the Verbal Landmark System. Designed to provide verbal or other directional information about the location of specific destinations in the environment, these aids operate using infrared beams or radio bands. When mounted on a street sign or above the doorway to a specific building, for example, these devices transmit information to a receiver that the traveler who is visually impaired carries in his or her pocket. When the receiver comes close enough to receive the transmissions, the person with the receiver hears helpful identifying information such as what street corner he or she is at or the presence of a specific building and the location of the nearest door.

Career Education.   Certain basic career skills, such as persistently working on tasks, can be taught in the earliest school years. Brolin (1982) has advanced a model

Orientation and mobility training prepares students for independent travel.

of career education that spans the primary through secondary to adult years. Brolin's life-span career education model has four phases: career awareness, career exploration, career preparation, and community classroom.

The *career awareness* phase begins in the elementary years and continues throughout a person's life. The main purpose of career awareness is to make the student knowledgeable of the wide variety of occupations in the world. Career awareness activities should involve both students with visual impairments and their parents. Activities include providing students with written and audiovisual materials describing different occupations and having students attend career fairs sponsored by businesses in the local community. Perhaps the most powerful vehicle for heightening career awareness is to have successfully employed adults with visual impairments share their experiences with students.

Finally, career awareness begins with instructing students in important general work behaviors, including stamina, following directions, grooming, and punctuality. Teachers can incidentally instruct these behaviors while students are working on academics, as well as on nonacademic activities. Research has shown that the absence of general work behaviors often results in the job termination of adults with disabilities (Rusch, 1979).

Career exploration, the second phase of Brolin's career education model, may begin in middle school (or at the end of the primary grades). Career exploration activities have the student with visual impairment come into contact with real jobs and work settings. For example, a class might take a field trip to a local factory to gain an understanding of how certain products are manufactured. A more active type of career exploration is job shadowing. Here, an individual student follows, or shadows, an actual employee while he or she is working. The goal is for the student to become aware of the rewards and demands of a particular occupation. By participating in a number of job-shadowing experiences, students may gain a more realistic understanding of whether they would like to work indoors or outdoors, manually or cerebrally, administratively or in direct contact with clients.

Minijobs is another important career exploration activity. Here, a student might informally work at school for short periods of time. For example, a student might do clerical tasks in the school office, work along with a janitor in cleaning up, or help out in the school cafeteria. Minijobs gives the student direct experience with the responsibility and joys of working. Also, the student can refine his or her vocational ability.

Career preparation is the third phase of career education and begins in secondary school. The student should begin to focus on specific occupations or career tracks. A vocational assessment should be completed early in high school to determine the student's vocational interests and abilities. In addition, career counseling should be provided by teachers, psychologists, or counselors. Counseling should make the student aware of the range of occupational opportunities and the type of education and training needed to attain them.

Whether a student is on an academic or vocational track in high school, he or she should participate in a number of occupational courses (e.g., electronics, culinary arts) to explore career possibilities firsthand. The student should also engage in a series of on-the-job work experiences over the secondary years, going to an off-campus work site for a number of hours or days each week.

Finally, the student can participate in a supervised *community classroom* (Gaylord-Ross, Forte, & Gaylord-Ross, 1985), which is the fourth phase of career education. The community classroom has a special education instructor supervise two to four students at a work site. For more independent students, a work experience educator may only come by the work site intermittently to check on student progress. Information collected from work experiences can prove invaluable in assessing vocational skills and career possibilities (Gaylord-Ross, Forte, Storey, Gaylord-Ross, & Jameson, 1986). In some cases the last work experience during a student's senior year may turn into a permanent job upon graduation.

Social Skills.   Social skills are among the most important behaviors a person can acquire. Among the behaviors under the rubric of social skills are simple skills such as greeting others and complex skills such as social problem solving and sharing of play materials.

Recent research provides three major conclusions about the social skills of individuals with visual impairments: (1) they tend to be socially isolated (Hoben & Lindstrom, 1980; Sacks & Gaylord-Ross, 1989; Sacks & Wolffe, 1992; Van Hasselt, 1983); (2) they tend to interact with peers whose social skills are deficient (Kekelis & Sacks, 1992; MacCuspie, 1992); and (3) their physical appearance and social physique inhibit their successful interaction with nondisabled persons (Sacks et al., 1992). Moreover, they may have difficulty in acknowledging nonverbal cues used in conversations (body space, physical gestures) and in initiating, expanding, and terminating conversations.

The few social skills training techniques that have been initiated for students with visual impairments have been limited in presentation and long-term effectiveness. Van Hasselt, Hersen, Kazdin, Simon, and Mastanuono (1983) trained 4 adolescent females to improve eye gaze, body posture, positive initiations, and overall social competence by using verbal and physical modeling, role plays, behavior rehearsal, and feedback. Training was initiated by an adult model and yielded positive gains from baseline to training. However, observations of the students in natural environments and on follow-up observations indicated a decline in their use of the trained social skills. Sacks and Gaylord-Ross (1989) examined the effectiveness of using nondisabled peers as social skill trainers for elementary-age students who are visually impaired. Using targeted behaviors similar to those in the Van Hasselt study, Sacks and Gaylord-Ross found that students with visual impairments not only learned the social behaviors within the training context, but also generalized and maintained the skills to other settings and peers.

Relationship interventions offer another way to promote social skills through friendship development. A number of schools have instituted relationship programs such as special friends and peer tutoring. In a special friends program a student who is blind and a student who is not disabled pair up for regular meetings at school or off-campus. The students engage in leisure activities such as bowling, board games, hanging out, or listening to music. Over time, it is hoped that a friendship will develop and that the students may then introduce each other to their own friends, thus expanding the social network of both students. In peer tutoring, the student who is not disabled usually teaches the student with a visual impairment either academic or nonacademic skills. The students routinely meet in the regular or special education classroom.

The Santa Clara County Regionalization Project in Visual Impairment, implemented in the spring of 1992, seeks to coordinate the service delivery for students with visual impairments across seven Special Education Local Planning Agencies in the San Jose/Santa Clara Valley in northern California. The program for students with visual impairments provides comprehensive services from infancy through adulthood. Infants and preschoolers are served by a parent-infant educator in the home and in center-based programs. School-age children are served by qualified teachers of those who are visually impaired in a variety of settings: in self-contained classrooms, in resource rooms, in regular education placements. These teachers work together with specialists in career/vocational training, orientation and mobility trainers, and regular classroom teachers to provide a broad-based educational program. The program is supervised by an administrator who has extensive knowledge and expertise in educational programming for students who are visually impaired. Further, this experimental model has allowed the program staff to design and implement innovative programs, such in assessment of those who are visually impaired and development of curricula specifically for this population.

Although the emphasis in the Santa Clara Program is to provide quality mainstreamed school experiences, the educational team works together to ensure a successful outcome in adult life. It is anticipated that students with visual impairments will be assessed by a diagnostic team whose members have particular expertise in visual impairment. The school psychologist, speech and language clinician, orientation and mobility specialist, adaptive physical education teacher, program administrator, and functional vision specialist will provide valuable information about a student's academic, social, emotional, and visual functioning abilities. This information will assist parents and teachers in adapting materials and initiating programs that will facilitate children's social growth and enhance their learning.

An experimental program is being undertaken to train parents and teachers in the implementation of a model social skills curriculum for students with visual impairments. The overall goal of this program is to help students feel good about themselves while they learn to maximize social encounters with sighted peers and adults. Also, it is felt that through effective parent education, the carryover of skills to the home and into the community will occur in an efficient manner.

The Santa Clara County Regionalization Project is also committed to providing quality transition experiences for students. A special transition project within the regional program has established community work experiences for students with visual impairments, working closely with the local department of vocational rehabilitation, and has linked efforts of the student, the teacher of those who are visually impaired, and the parents in establishing a plan of action for future life experiences. Also, a career immersion program is being designed so that students with visual impairments will have greater access to employment opportunities and independent living endeavors.

Recreation and Leisure Skills.   Students with visual impairments can participate in most of the same recreational and leisure activities as their sighted peers with minor or no modifications. With the assistance of audible balls and goal finders that produce sounds to indicate their location, students with visual impairments can participate in outdoor games and sports. Many students compete alongside their sighted peers in swimming, track, and cross-country skiing using guide ropes or sighted guides. Students with visual impairments also enjoy caring for pets, playing videogames, listening to music, going to concerts or movies, doing arts and crafts, and participating in community activities as do their sighted peers.

Some of these leisure skills may take special assistance to learn, and many teachers of those who are visually impaired facilitate their acquisition through dramatic play, by modeling the operation and function of a play object such as a doll or an action figure, by teaching students a variety of board games adapted with braille or large print labels, and by inviting sighted peers to participate with students who are visually impaired in social activities. In addition, special programs exist to teach those who are visually impaired and other individuals with disabilities how to participate in sports such as bowling, cross-country skiing, downhill skiing, river rafting, and sea kayaking.

Secondary/Adult Transition.   In recent years a great deal of attention has been given to planning for postsecondary school transition (Halpern, 1985; Sacks & Pruett, 1992). Federal transition initiatives focus on employment because of the deplorable rates of unemployment among adults who are disabled. There is consensus (e.g., Close & Keating, 1988; Halpern, 1985) about the need to expand nonsheltered employment options and expand transition models to include social and community living skills programs. While there have been substantial improvements in the quality of special educational services in the past several decades, there are still relatively few programs for adults who are visually impaired. Only 30% of adults with visual impairments without multiple impairments are employed in competitive settings, and many individuals are underemployed, that is, work in jobs that are not commensurate with their abilities (Kirchner & Peterson, 1989).

The transition process should begin during the early secondary years with preparation of Individualized Transition Plans (ITPs). The ITP, which overlaps the Individualized Educational Plan (IEP), contains specific goals and activities that are keyed to successful adult living. For example, the ITP might set goals for the acquisition of vocational skills through a specific work experience (e.g., entering data in a word processor). As the student approaches graduation, the ITP would provide for involvement of adult service agencies, such as the local department of vocational rehabilitation, to plan for future jobs, programs, and living accommodations. In optimal transition, a student might be placed in a permanent job by the school vocational team. Upon students' graduation, the vocational staff of an adult agency for persons who are severely visually impaired would provide job follow-up, retraining, and counseling as needed so that there would be no gap or falling between the cracks in service delivery.

A new breed of transition specialists is emerging (Sacks & Pruett, 1992). The transition specialists are housed in the school district or in the local department of rehabilitation, and many have specific skills in working with persons who are blind and visually impaired. The transition specialist makes sure that the ITP is fulfilled with respect to establishing linkages for the student with adult agencies, placement in an enhancing job, job follow-up, career counseling, and referral into continuing education and other intensive services (Sacks & Reardon, 1988; Siegel, Greener, Prieuer, Robert, & Gaylord-Ross, 1989). Sacks and Pruett (1992) are providing specialized training in transition for professionals who work with adolescents and young adults with visual impairments. The training incorporates didactic information and hands-on experiences in teaching students specific transition skills (e.g., job readiness skills, interviewing techniques, funding sources, legislative implications, supported work and community work experience models).

INNOVATION AND DEVELOPMENT

Much new technology for students who are blind or who have low vision is emerging. Advances in computer technology and electronics now give the student with a visual impairment access to both the printed page and computer screens. Persons who are sighted and persons who are visually impaired can share braille and print information. This accessibility plays a large role in education. It also opens the door to many jobs (e.g., reservation clerk, computer programmer) that were once closed to persons with visual impairments. In addition, technology facilitates the ease of travel through the use of electronic orientation and travel aids.

Audio description is an emerging technology that promises to enable people with visual impairment to receive information shown visually in films and videos. A verbal narration, which describes visual actions and scenes in films and videos, is inserted between sections of dialogue. Audio description is designed for use in both educational and entertainment films and videos. Analogous to closed-captioning for people with hearing impairments, it provides people with visual impairments access to a previously unavailable source of information.

Advances are also taking place in biomedicine. The effectiveness of low-vision aids is constantly being improved; research on vision substitution technology, in which visual stimuli are transformed into tactile stimuli, is continuing. Similarly, research on artificial sight, in which electrodes implanted in the brain connect to a small camera in an artificial eye, is being conducted.

There are also advances in the field of medicine that hold great promise for the future. Successful removal of cataracts and implantation of artificial lenses are a reality. Glaucoma and many other eye disorders are now successfully treated with medication and surgery. Improved methods for treating diabetes, the leading cause of blindness in the United States, are being tested. Efforts to stimulate the regrowth of damaged retina cells and to transplant retinal tissue are in the experimental stages.

Among the issues in special education for children with visual impairments the focus is on the questions of (1) when to begin cane instruction and (2) how to determine whether print or braille should be the primary learning for a child with a visual impairment (or even whether to teach both). Initial evidence suggests that providing cane instruction to preschool children rather than waiting until they reach school age may facilitate the earlier development of a variety of motor, conceptual, and independent travel skills in children with visual impairments. Similarly, criteria for determining the optimal learning medium for students with visual impairments are being refined, and instruction in print reading and braille reading are no longer being seen as mutually exclusive.

Changes in special education legislation will also greatly affect children who are visually impaired. The Individuals with Disabilities Education Act (IDEA), emphasizes the need to address specialized needs such as transition for students from the ages 16 to 22 and the provision of orientation and mobility services to preschool children with visual impairments in special education. Part H of IDEA addresses the need for early intervention for infants and their families. Through early intervention children with visual impairments can receive help in motor, cognitive, and other areas of development prior to entering preschool or kindergarten programs.

SUMMARY Formal education for children with visual impairments in the United States began in the 1830s, after Samuel Gridley Howe established the first residential school for persons who were blind, now known as the Perkins School for the Blind. Several other schools emerged across the nation; however, it was not until the early 1900s that the first day school program for students with visual impairments was initiated in Chicago. Despite the movement toward integration, only about 15% of all school-age children with visual impairments were mainstreamed into public school programs during the first half of the 20th century. The influx of students with severe visual impairments into public education programs was the direct result of the retinopathy of prematurity and rubella epidemics.

To qualify for educational services, a person who is visually impaired must be considered legally blind (a visual acuity of 20/200 in the better eye with the best correction or a visual field no greater than 20 degrees). More recently, placement of students in educational programs for those who are visually impaired has been contingent on the severity of visual functioning and on individual educational needs rather than on the more traditional legal or rehabilitative criteria. Visual impairment is a low-incidence disability, making up only about 0.1% of the school-age population. Generally, visual impairment in children is caused by prenatal influences, genetic anomalies, or trauma.

Educational assessment for students who are blind and visually impaired provides valuable information regarding their visual functioning abilities, academic and cognitive skills, and nonacademic skill pursuits. The information gained through a comprehensive educational assessment can help in appropriate placement and educational planning. Educational assessment, particularly vision screening and classroom observations, is an effective way to determine whether a student may require services and what type of special services he or she will need.

Recent research has demonstrated that there may be differences in the development of students with visual impairments and their sighted counterparts. Delays in cognitive, language, motor, and social development have been shown to affect the performance of students who are blind or visually impaired. However, early intervention programs, service delivery models that foster the acquisition of these skills, and a positive social environment can help bring about changes in a child's functioning.

Several delivery systems are used by teachers of those who are visually impaired to provide services for a wide range of students. Infants and preschoolers who are blind and visually impaired and their families are generally served in center-based or home-based models. School-age students receive disability-specific services accord-

TIPS FOR HELPING

1. Encourage the student who is visually impaired to assume responsibility for classroom assignments and age-appropriate behaviors.

2. Have realistic expectations for the students you serve.

3. Structure your classroom environment so that the student with a visual impairment can readily participate in activities.

4. When using the blackboard or overhead projector for instruction, try to verbalize written materials.

5. Present worksheets in dark-ink or photocopy format to help the student with a visual impairment function with greater success.

6. Allow the student with a visual impairment to experiment with seating to find the one in which he or she works most effectively. Front-row seating with good illumination that does not produce glare is preferable for students with low vision.

7. Provide opportunities and structured learning activities that help the student with a visual impairment become socially integrated within the mainstream classroom.

8. Communicate regularly with the teacher of those who are visually impaired to help facilitate a positive experience for the child who is visually impaired.

9. Present materials in a hands-on or manipulatable manner rather than in an abstract format to assist the student with a visual impairment acquire important concepts and skills.

10. Participate in inservice training and provide training to the classmates of the student with a visual impairment on an ongoing basis to ensure a positive educational experience for all involved.

11. Include the student with a visual impairment in all classroom activities. Facilitate group strategies such as cooperative learning, mapping, and tribes to help the student with a visual impairment become a "true" member of the classroom community.

ing to their unique educational needs. These services may be provided in residential schools, day schools, self-contained classrooms, and resource rooms. The trend is toward inclusion of students with visual impairments in mainstream environments. Services may be provided on an itinerant basis. The teacher of those who are visually impaired may provide consultation services to students who exhibit multiple impairments, within day school programs or in mainstreamed classrooms. Students with visual impairments who are in transition from school to adult life may spend a portion of their school day involved in community-based vocational experiences and independent living training. Collaborative efforts of the teacher of those who are visually impaired and the rehabilitation counselor help to promote successful outcomes in adult life.

Although a number of adaptations can be made within the regular classroom setting to help the student who is visually impaired function successfully, the acquisition of specific skills is critical. These skill areas include utilization of low vision, listening skills, concept and motor development, organization and study skills, activities of daily living, career education, and social skills. Further, advances in technology, medicine, and rehabilitation engineering will provide new opportunities in education, employment, and independent functioning for persons with visual impairments.

STUDY QUESTIONS

1. What two medical events influenced the growth of mainstreamed educational programs for students with visual impairments? Describe the service delivery models designed to aid in the integration of these students.

2. Describe the various ways blindness can be defined. What is the legal definition of blindness?

3. What are some specific visual impairments common to children? How do they affect learning?

4. Why is blindness considered a low-incidence disability? Why are exact demographics difficult to obtain?

5. How does the lack of vision affect development of the child who is visually impaired? What are some differences in development between those who are blind and those who are sighted?

6. Describe some specific intervention strategies designed for young children who are visually impaired. What role do parents play in skill attainment?

7. What are some specific skills that must be taught to ensure the effective mainstreaming of a student with visual impairment? What is the role of the teacher of those who are visually impaired? What is the role of the regular education teacher?

8. How has technology assisted students with visual impairments in becoming more independent in school and in the community?

9. Why is it important for children with visual impairments to be introduced to nonacademic skills? Identify and describe some nonacademic skills curricular content areas.

10. Describe how secondary/transition programs have changed for students who are visually impaired. What are some specific programs that can be implemented for these students?

12

The Gifted and Talented

Joan S. Wolf
University of Utah

 In this chapter you will learn about

- the major historical events related to educating gifted children and youth in the context of social, economic, and political forces

- major theories of intelligence and creativity

- the common characteristics of gifted children and youth and those who are highly creative

- the major methods of identification and assessment of gifted children, including those in special populations such as highly gifted, culturally different gifted, gifted who are disabled, gifted females, and gifted underachievers

- a list of important characteristics for teachers of the gifted

- various curriculum modifications, intervention methods, and administrative arrangements for gifted students

Eleven-year-old Carrie is in the 5th grade. She has always performed well in school. She is very conscientious about her schoolwork and grades are important to her. Her particular strengths emerge in math and science; from the age of 4, she has had perennial science projects going at home. Individual psychoeducational testing completed one year ago indicated that Carrie is in the superior range of intellectual ability at the 97th percentile. She performs consistently above grade level academically. Carrie is a youngster who is very anxious to please others, especially adults—teachers and parents. She has participated in a part-time gifted program since 2nd grade and, in the past, expressed many positive feelings about being part of this program. Carrie is scheduled to go to Middle School next year. When she brought her course scheduling materials home, she indicated that she didn't want to sign up for the accelerated math program. She is vague when asked her reasons for not wanting to participate in this program, saying only that "I need to be part of the group" and "I don't want to be a scientist any more."[1]

Gifted children and youth are so smart that they will make it on their own, say many. Certainly, some do manage to get the best a system has to offer. But others may not. Many gifted students who are denied opportunities for challenging and stimulating learning experiences fail to realize their potential. Some become dropouts or deviants in a society that has ignored or even abused them. There are varying estimates of the number of gifted students among high school dropouts. Lajoie and Shore (1981) reported that 19% of high school dropouts in New York state would be classified as gifted. Many experts attribute these failures and problems with underachievement to the social and academic environments of the classroom (Whitmore, 1980) and to an anti-intellectual atmosphere, which is very negative for the gifted (Gallagher, 1991a). Consider the example of Max.

By the age of 1, Max was speaking in sentences. He showed early interest in books and asked questions constantly: Why? How? What if? His need to explore and lack of fear sometimes got him into trouble. He was not a child who sat on the edge of the sandbox or who held onto the skating-rink railing; rather he would forge ahead, not always understanding the danger but eager to experience—to taste, smell, hear, see, and touch! His words sometimes spilled forth faster than his tongue could manage. Physically, he was a bit awkward with a tendency to fall and bang himself as he rushed about, eager to experience his world. He taught himself to read by age 4. His favorite magazine was *National Geographic.* His years in preschool were wonderful thanks to a caring, gifted teacher.

The school years were difficult and often painful for this child who was out of sync with peers. While other children were reading primers, he was devouring biographies of Clarence Darrow and other famous people. Eager to learn, he had little tolerance for activities that he did not see as meaningful. When encouraged to conform, he protested, often feeling misunderstood. He couldn't understand why his world of school didn't work better. "I think logically," he would say, "if my teacher can't think logically, then that's her problem." Ah, but in 1st grade, it was already his problem. In 3rd grade, he was punished for inattention and misbehavior by being banished for hours to the library, a place where he found refuge and solace in books. In 4th grade, he brought his own books to school, which he held in his lap while giving minimal attention and care to the daily schoolwork. Because his intellectual peers were not his age mates, he had difficulty finding acceptance from other children. At the recommendation of school personnel, he skipped 5th grade. Although he was small physically, it was clear that he needed some acceleration in order to increase his chances of survival.

---

[1]Adapted from M. McCormick & J. S. Wolf (in press).

Here's how Max looks back on his secondary school experiences:

At the time I attended junior and senior high school, I was still attempting to establish a distinct identity, and I felt very threatened by the pressure to conform. I had a strong desire to make progress academically, but the opportunities seemed very limited. I did not have a great deal of respect for many of my teachers, who seemed more interested in passing the time than in teaching anything of significance. The combination of academic frustration and my desire not to conform created a very negative pattern of interaction between me and the school. I did much of my assigned work very haphazardly, if at all. This was easy for me to rationalize because teachers often assigned work that was hard to take seriously: word searches, crossword puzzle games, coloring maps. Then I would become upset when my grade was lowered, feeling that I had learned all that was possible from such a poor class. I did not make many friends in school until my junior year. I always felt more comfortable with my parents and their friends than with kids my own age. Although I scorned the kind of personal style necessary for social success in the school environment, I nevertheless found my lack of such success distressing. This added to my dislike of school in general. The worst year was 10th grade. I stopped attending many of my classes altogether and spent most of my time getting stoned. In my junior year, fears about getting into college modified my behavior somewhat, and when I was a senior I actually had several stimulating placement classes and became a much better student.

Max continued:

When I am a parent, I hope not to subject my children to the same sort of public education which I received. In looking back on my experiences, I feel that the values of individuality, creativity, tolerance, and sincerity which I would hope to pass on to my children were actively discouraged by my school environment. Conformity was the key to success both academically and socially, and the standards to which one was expected to conform were often contrary to both my values and my personality.

Concern for the gifted has waxed and waned throughout our history. Jefferson and his followers believed that trained leadership from the best minds was essential to the survival of a free world. Andrew Jackson's era was noted for its anti-intellectualism, and the attitudes of Jacksonian democracy seemed to prevail in the United States in the 1960s, when gifted education was at a low ebb (Huntington, 1975). Interest in the gifted has come with changing political and economic priorities, reflected in funding support at both state and national levels (Gallagher, 1991b). Gallagher (1985) has suggested that athletic programs represent a prototype for one kind of gifted education. Enjoying wide support in urban and rural settings in both small and large districts, they have high acceptance in our schools and are rarely subjected to criticism for exclusionary policies for elitism. Yet they do provide special opportunities for the physically talented—far better opportunities than exist for students whose talents lie elsewhere. Certainly those who are talented physically should continue to be encouraged, but much more commitment to those with other talents is greatly needed.

HISTORY

In the United States there have been three major movements in the education of gifted children and youth. Terman's studies, begun in the twenties, focused on the intellectually gifted. His definition of giftedness (1925–1959) was limited, based solely on IQ scores from individual intelligence tests. Although the methodology he used has been questioned, his work served to dispel or at least to diminish many of the stereotypes of gifted children prevalent at the time. The image of the physically frail, socially timid, emotionally retarded but intellectually able youngster did not stand up under his scrutiny. The Terman studies were continued by his associates and have been the source of a great deal of information about the gifted.

Programs for the gifted enjoyed increased interest and attention in the *Sputnik* era of the late fifties. The space race was on, and talented scientists and technologists were in great demand. As a consequence, science and math programs for the gifted were upgraded. Yet with the advent of the sixties, the focus in education turned to civil rights, the war on poverty, and education of persons with disabilities.

Interest in the gifted was reawakened in the early seventies. In 1972 Sidney Marland, the U.S. Commissioner of Education, reported to Congress that many of the estimated 2.5 million gifted students in our elementary and secondary schools were not being served and that more than half of the school administrators surveyed reported that there were no gifted students in their schools. Few could disagree with Marland's description of the gifted as our "most neglected and potentially productive group" (p. ix). As a result of his report, the U.S. Department of Education created the Office of Gifted and Talented, and attention again turned to programs for the gifted.

Legislation and Policy

In 1976 the Special Projects Act provided $2.56 million to fund state and local proposals for service to gifted and talented students, and that amount has continued to rise. State and federal funds now support a wide variety of programs, and an increasing number of teachers are receiving preservice and inservice training (Sisk, 1978). Public Law 95–561, the Gifted and Talented Children's Act, was signed in 1978, authorizing a minimum appropriation of $50,000 to each state education agency "to assist them in planning, development, operation and improvement of programs designed to meet the educational needs of gifted and talented children" (*Congressional Record*, 1978). Various advocacy groups, including the Council for Exceptional Children (CEC) and the Gifted Advocacy Information Network (GAIN), have been working to obtain increases in the actual level of federal appropriations for services to the gifted so that they more nearly approach the $25 million maximum authorized by Congress. Many states have their own local parent and professional advocacy groups, which provide information about and support for gifted programs in their communities.

Two important issues shaped programs for the gifted in the seventies: the use of intelligence tests and the segregation of exceptional children in special classes (Tannenbaum, 1979). The equal rights movement has had a major effect on attitudes toward intelligence tests, especially as their use affected minority students. In some states abuses of IQ tests and reaction against them have resulted in laws barring their use (Tannenbaum, 1979). Grouping practices in schools have also come into question; programs that provided for gifted students by clustering them together have become suspect, and the trend has been toward mainstreaming special students.

For gifted programs to continue to develop, state and local education agencies must recognize their importance. Since 1984, 48 states have established definitions for children who are exceptional by virtue of giftedness either in statute or in state education department regulations as a basis for providing programs. Several states require the development of the same formal Individualized Educational Plan (IEP) for the gifted that is mandated for students with disabilities in Public Law 94–142. Factors that seem to influence growth and maintenance of state funding for gifted programs are the existence of a full-time consultant in state government, the availability of state funds for local program development, and the existence of teacher training programs. Renzulli and Reis (1991) identify the following factors as important to the growth and maintenance of support for gifted programs: longevity, administrative support, gifted program leadership, existing policy, program design and organization, ownership, evaluation, and sustained public relations efforts. According to a recent report by Karnes and Whorton (1991), 21 states reported specific certification and/or endorsement requirements for teachers of the gifted. However, 25 states indicated that they had no specific certification requirements for working with gifted and talented students in specialized programs.

In 1981, when the federal government merged 30 separate educational programs into a $471 million block grant, programs for the gifted were among them. The U.S. Department of Education abolished the Office of Gifted and Talented, and federal funding for the gifted and talented was reduced as a result, leaving many states struggling to maintain their programs. Professional and parent advocacy groups mobilized to promote more attention for the gifted. These advocacy groups paralleled the many commissions on the status of education in the nation, which called attention to the neglect of gifted and talented students as a major educational issue. These advocacy groups included the Coalition for the Advancement of Gifted Education and the Alliance of State Associations. In recent years the CEC, the professional special education association, has increased its advocacy for gifted education.

In August 1988 a measure entitled the Jacob K. Javits Gifted and Talented Student Education Act was funded by Congress as part of the Elementary and Secondary Education Bill, S. 373. This bill provided $8 million for identification and service for gifted and talented students, training and professional development for teachers of the gifted, and creation of a National Center for the Education of the Gifted. The Javits funding has continued from 1988 on with nearly $10 million in funding for 1990 and similar funding for 1991 (Harrington, Harrington, & Karns, 1991).

DEFINITION   In the past, *gifted* was a term applied to those individuals who, according to intelligence tests, were far above average. The meaning it conveys today has changed somewhat, yet no universally accepted definition has been formulated. Several central issues regarding the nature of giftedness remain unresolved:

- What is intelligence, and what role does it play in giftedness?
- What is creativity, and what role does it play in giftedness?
- Should giftedness be defined in terms of performance or potential?
- What is talent, and how does it pertain to giftedness?

Intelligence

The first problem is the nature of intelligence. Assuming that we decide to define giftedness as intelligence far above average, we must then find valid instruments for assessing intelligence across all ages and populations. For years educators have relied on traditional, standardized intelligence tests to evaluate intellectual ability. One of these educators, who has had an enormous impact on programs for the gifted, Lewis Terman, thinks that intelligence is manifested essentially in the ability to acquire and manipulate concepts (1954). Terman defines the gifted as those individuals who score at the upper end of the normal distribution of intelligence—the top 1%. Although the majority of subjects in the Terman study had IQ scores of 140 or above, a Binet score of 132 (2 standard deviations above the mean) was actually the cutoff. Terman's definition of giftedness is rooted in the assumption that intelligence can be measured, an assumption of great significance because it establishes a basis for valid prediction—but it is an assumption that is open to question. Terman carefully distinguishes giftedness from talent and creativity. He views talent as a promise of unusual achievement but only when combined with high IQ scores. Creativity, he believes, is a personality factor different from both giftedness and talent.

Guilford later developed a different approach to the concept of intelligence (1967). He analyzed intelligence in terms of the specific abilities and arrived at a model that divides intellectual performance into three dimensions:

1. *Operation.* The categories included are cognition (discovering or recognizing data), memory (retaining newly gained information), divergent production (generating logical alternatives from given information), convergent production (generating logical conclusions with emphasis on best response), and evaluation (comparing data to make judgments).
2. *Content.* The content forms in the Guilford model are figural (concrete forms), symbolic (symbols such as letters, numbers, or musical notes), semantic (concepts or ideas), and behavioral (information involving human interaction).
3. *Product.* The possibilities in the model are units (individual units of information), classes (sets of items grouped by common properties), relations (connections between items of information), systems (organized aggregates of information), transformations (changes or modifications in existing information), and implications (expected or predicted connections between items of information).

This model, shown in Figure 12–1, is known as the Structure of Intellect Model.

Spirited discussion among psychologists has revolved on new definitions of intelligence. Sternberg (1985) suggests that intelligence tests are limited in their ability to predict school and job performance. He maintains that there is a need to find measures that go beyond the scope of intelligence tests and that are more closely linked to behavior in the real world. He views intelligence as consisting of three major types of behaviors: problem-solving ability, verbal ability, and social competence. Conventional tests, he believes, do not measure these behaviors adequately.

Gardner (1984) claims that there is no general smartness: instead, people possess "several intellectual competencies of 'intelligences'" (p. 699). He proposes seven basic intelligences: linguistic, logical-mathematical, musical, spatial, body-kinesthetic, interpersonal, and intrapersonal. People will vary both in potential and in achievement in these domains. Sternberg (1985) suggests that intelligence should be considered in terms of the internal world of the individual, the external world of the individual, and the interaction between these two worlds as it unfolds through experience.

Figure 12–1
Guilford's Structure of Intellect Model.
Source: From *The Nature of Human Intelligence* (p. 63) by J. P. Guilford, 1967, New York: McGraw-Hill. Copyright 1967 by McGraw-Hill. Reprinted by permission.

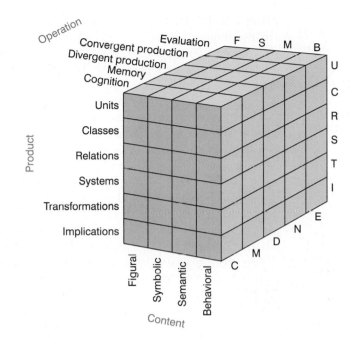

Creativity

Definitions of giftedness have expanded to encompass creativity in addition to superior intellectual potential or performance. Creativity is generally defined as the process of bringing a new, different, and unexpected response to a situation. However, there is a lack of agreement concerning this definition. Defining the term limits the very notion of creativity, and people can be creative in many different ways. One useful definition of creativity emerges from Guilford's concept of divergent thinking, which he sees as the ability to produce many alternative ideas in problem-solving situations (Guilford, 1977). The abilities that Guilford sees as most relevant to creative thinking are in his categories of divergent production and transformation. Khatena's (1976) notion of creativity as "the power of the imagination to break away from perceptual set so as to restructure ideas, thoughts, and feelings into novel and meaningful associate bonds" (p. 316) is also useful. Both Guilford and Khatena focus on the person who brings new, different, and unexpected responses to a situation and is a productive thinker and problem solver.

Torrance (1969) stresses creative thinking ability as a criterion for giftedness and identifies some of the appropriate characteristics:

- Fluency of ideas (the number of responses produced by a stimulus)
- Flexibility (shifts in thinking from one category to another)
- Originality (unusual or clever responses)
- Elaboration (adding details to basic ideas or thoughts)

According to Torrance, measurement of these qualities is an effective means of identifying gifted children and youth in culturally different or disadvantaged populations. He points out that IQ scores fail to identify large numbers of students in the top 20% of creative thinking ability.

There has been much discussion about the relationship of giftedness and creativity. Research suggests that most creative people are gifted, but not all gifted people are creative (Getzels & Jackson, 1962). Recent interest requires a distinction between academic giftedness and creativity. Studies of creativity and intelligence have revealed low correlations between creativity and the intelligence measured by an intelligence test. In one study, correlations between the rated creativity of 60 eminent architects and their scores on an adult intelligence test were reported to be low (MacKinnon, 1962). In another, correlations between intelligence test scores and creativity as measured by divergent thinking tests were low (Getzels & Jackson, 1962). Still another investigation that attempted to correlate intelligence test and creativity scores supported these results (Torrance, 1966). A review of the literature reveals that most studies report positive but low correlations between the two factors for the general population but little or no correlation at the higher ability levels (Taylor & Holland, 1962).

Support for distinctions between intelligence and creativity come from a study of young children by Moore and Sawyers (1987) in which they report that original thinking is distinct from intelligence. Runco and Albert (1986) found a nonlinear, positive relationship between intelligence and creativity test scores. And Treffinger and Renzulli (1986) argue that "IQ scores emphasize 'school house' giftedness rather than creative, productive giftedness" (p. 152). They argue that test scores do not provide information about creativity.

Performance Versus Potential

Opinions differ as to whether above-average performance or the apparent ability to perform exceptionally well should be the criterion in determining giftedness. The 1958 yearbook of the National Society for the Study of Education defined a talented or gifted individual as "one who shows consistently remarkable performance in any worthwhile line of endeavor" (p. 19). This widely accepted definition relies heavily on performance rather than on potential. Some authorities, however, insist that potential should be a significant factor in identifying gifted individuals. Fliegler and Bish (1959), for instance, propose potential as an identifying characteristic of the gifted and maintain, too, that students whose ability is in the top 15% to 20% of the school population are gifted.

There are, of course, advantages and disadvantages to excluding potential from the definition. It is far simpler to evaluate performance—in intelligence as well as in other areas. From an administrative viewpoint, therefore, it is more efficient to limit the definition to performance. On the other hand, by excluding those who perform poorly but seem to have high ability, we may deny educational services to those very young people who need them most—those whose exceptionality causes them difficulty in adjusting to regular educational and other environments. Thus, including potential in the definition encourages attention to gifted underachievers and bright youngsters from culturally different populations, as well as to those who may be late bloomers whose school performance lags behind their ability.

Talent

The concept of talent as part of the definition of giftedness was added in the seventies and resulted in a broader definition (U.S. *Senate Report*, 1972). Some educators use the term *giftedness* to denote outstanding intellectual ability and the term *talent* to denote superlative skills in a specific area, particularly in the arts. However, the terms are frequently used interchangeably.

Concern for the many aspects of giftedness is reflected in the definition adopted by the U.S. Department of Education in 1978:

> Gifted and talented children means children, and whenever applicable, youth, who are identified at the preschool, elementary, or secondary level as possessing demonstrated or potential abilities that give evidence of high performance capability in areas such as intellectual, creative, specific academic, or leadership ability, or in the performing and visual arts, and who by reason thereof require services or activities not ordinarily provided by the school. (*Congressional Record*, 1978, H–12179)

The federal government's definition is important because it is applied in policy and funding decisions. However, individual states and school districts have developed their own definitions of giftedness within the relatively broad federal guidelines, and the resultant diversity contributes further to the uncertainty surrounding the current definition.

Definitions of giftedness reflect the attitude of the times, and no one definition will ever be correct for all times. Indeed, Renzulli (1978) identifies some problems with the 1978 definition. Several of the areas, such as intellectual or creative ability, merely describe processes that can be brought to bear on a specific performance area and are not observable in themselves. Also, the definition fails to include motivational factors, such as devotion to hard work, quality output, interest in learning—all of which may have a strong impact on performance. Renzulli bases his definition of giftedness on three basic traits:

1. Above-average ability in any area (intellectual ability or specific talent)
2. Task commitment as reflected in a willingness to work hard and to produce at a high level
3. Creativity as measured by the generation of ideas or products

Clearly, the trend is toward broader and more general concepts. Since Terman's work, definitions have not been based on data or theory. Instead, they have evolved out of political and social movements, revealing the relationship between giftedness and society's values at various times in its history.

PREVALENCE   Prevailing attitudes determine not only who is designated gifted and talented but also what proportion of the population this group represents at any one time. When IQ scores were used as the sole criterion for identifying the gifted, a smaller proportion of the population was identified. Thus, as definitions of giftedness vary, so do prevalence figures. There may be only one child in a million, for example, who is highly gifted—who has an IQ of 180 or higher (Hollingworth, 1942). But the broader definitions of today produce higher prevalence figures. In a 1972 study, prevalence was estimated at

3% to 5% (Marland), and that estimate was the one accepted by the Office of Gifted and Talented. However, when an IQ cutoff of 115 is used, 15% to 20% of the school population may be found to be gifted.

CAUSES

As a general rule, more gifted students are identified in programs that draw from higher socioeconomic groups and from preschool populations. Students from the dominant culture perform better on the paper-and-pencil tests often used to identify gifted individuals. In addition, the behavior and performance of gifted young children can often be seen as different from those of their young peers, thus facilitating identification.

Gifted and talented youngsters can be found at every economic level and in every stratum of society, in all cultural, ethnic, and racial groups. Although we have found no way to predict or perfectly explain the occurrence of giftedness and talent, three factors do seem to contribute: (1) heredity, (2) prenatal and perinatal care, and (3) early childhood environment. Various authorities have expressed the view that heredity—a purely biological factor—does play a role, although no perfect correlation exists between the intelligence of parent and the intelligence of their children. Prenatal and perinatal care often reflects the home environment of the family, with poor care more frequently reported at low socioeconomic levels. Storfer (1990) has noted and discussed the importance of early environmental stimulation. Environmental stimulation is particularly important during the first 2 years of life if optimum development is to occur, a fact underscored by the negative effects of deprivation of environmental stimuli during early childhood. The interaction of heredity and environment seems to be a key in the development and nurturing of giftedness (Tannenbaum, 1992).

CHARACTERISTICS

As the definitions of giftedness and talent have become broader, the number and variety of characteristics associated with this category of exceptionality have increased greatly. For the sake of simplicity, we will examine characteristics commonly found in individuals with high IQ scores, as well as traits often seen in highly creative persons.

Characteristics of Individuals with High IQs

In 1925 Terman began a study of approximately 1,000 children with IQs of 132 or higher, a study that is still in process. Not only did he endeavor to discover what traits these children had in common, but he also followed their development into adulthood. Terman and his associates (Oden, 1968; Terman, 1925–1959; Terman & Oden, 1959) observed some specific characteristics in these individuals:

- Fast learning ability
- Interest in reading biographies
- Scientific inclination
- Reading prior to entering school
- Enjoyment of learning
- Good abstract reasoning
- Good command of language

- Poor handwriting
- Only child
- Eldest child
- Born of older parents
- Good adjustment
- Good physical health
- High scores on achievement tests
- Imagination
- High energy level

Subsequent reports have confirmed most of Terman's findings (Gallagher, 1985). We should, however, be cautious in accepting some of his results, particularly those of his psychological measures indicating the above-average size, strength, and health of gifted children. In a 1964 study that compared 81 bright youngsters to their significantly less bright siblings, no significant differences were found in the physiques in each pair (Laycock & Caylor, 1964). It may well be that Terman's sample was skewed in favor of youngsters from higher socioeconomic levels whose superior physical development was a function of nutritional advantages. Of particular significance, however, were Terman's findings that gifted children tended to be superior intellectually, socially, emotionally, and morally, dispelling the traditional stereotype of the one-sided, socially withdrawn, and emotionally insecure "brain."

The gifted child is often curious.

More recently, other intellectual traits have been identified as characteristic of academically gifted children:

1. *Capacity for learning*: Accurate perception of social and natural situations; independent, rapid, efficient learning of fact and principle; fast, meaningful reading, with superior retention and recall
2. *Power and sensitivity of thought*: Ready grasp of principles underlying things as they are; sensitivity to interference in fact, consequence of proposition, application of idea; spontaneous elevation of immediate observations to higher planes of abstraction; imagination; original interpretations and conclusions; discriminatory power, quick detection of similarities and differences among things and ideas; able in analysis, synthesis, and organization of elements; critical of situations, self, and other people
3. *Curiosity and drive*: Mental endurance; tenacity of purpose; stubbornness, sometimes contrarily expressed as reluctance to do as directed; capacity for follow-through with extensive, but meaningful plans; curiosity about things and ideas; intrinsic interest in the challenging and difficult; versatile and vital interests; varied, numerous, and penetrating inquiries; boredom with routine and sameness (Ward, 1975)

Another approach defines five major categories of characteristics that distinguish the gifted: cognitive, affective, physical, intuitive, and societal (Clark, 1988). On the basis of the characteristics identified, related needs and possible problems can be deduced as a first step in assessment and program planning. For example, an unusual discrepancy between physical and intellectual development in the gifted may mean that gifted students need to be guided toward physical activities that they can find satisfying. Thus, it may be desirable to encourage physical activity in gifted students who stress mental activity to the detriment of physical development (Clark, 1988).

Characteristics of Highly Creative Individuals

The 1962 Getzels and Jackson study revealed some important differences between highly intelligent and highly creative youngsters. Highly creative children tend to be nonconforming; they question, challenge, and even psychologically threaten some teachers who do not tolerate high levels of nonconformity. The following characteristics of creative youngsters have been compiled from various checklists (Lucito, 1974; Renzulli & Hartman, 1971):

• Generate a large number of ideas or solutions to problems and questions
• Are uninhibited in expression of opinion, sometimes radical and spirited in disagreement, tenacious
• Display a good deal of intellectual playfulness, fantasize, imagine not conforming, accept disorder, are not interested in details, do not fear being different
• Rely more on own evaluations than on those of others
• Build a reputation for having wild or silly ideas
• Display humor, playfulness, and relaxation in their creative products

Thus, some characteristics commonly ascribed to gifted children may be seen by teachers as negative rather than positive attributes. Swassing's (1980) classification of characteristics with positive and negative valence is helpful. For example, children who have unusual abilities to see relationships may also have difficulty accepting what they view as illogical. Students who have long attention spans and display persistent goal-directed behavior may be seen as stubborn and resistant to interruption or change.

Heterogeneity in the Gifted and Talented Population

The characteristics described here are frequently found in gifted and talented individuals. However, not all gifted and talented children will exhibit all of these characteristics. Indeed, the gifted and talented are a heterogeneous group. In addition to a wide range of interindividual differences, they exhibit a high degree of variability within themselves (intraindividual differences). An understanding of the characteristics of gifted children is further complicated because it is difficult to identify certain types of gifted youngsters. Some gifted children whose ability and performance are widely disparate are difficult to identify (Seaberg, 1989). Redding (1990) discusses these under-achieving youngsters and points out that focusing on conventional characteristics will often exclude them from receiving any service. They are frequently seen as excessively aggressive or withdrawn and as having negative self-concepts.

There are gifted children in all ethnic groups and at all socio-economic levels.

Other special populations that contribute to the complexity of characteristics are those who are gifted and disabled and those who are gifted and culturally different. Because teachers tend to focus on deficits rather than strengths, students who are gifted and disabled are rarely identified. In addition, the disabling conditions of gifted children can interfere with their demonstration of superior ability (Suter & Wolf, 1987). The same situation exists for culturally different gifted children who may have been raised in an environment that rewards certain types of behavior not consonant with conventional notions of giftedness. For example, in some Hispanic families there may be less reinforcement of children who are highly verbal. These children may seem somewhat reticent when they enter school and might be easily overlooked in screening for a gifted program. Although much has been written urging educators to be sensitive to the special characteristics of these populations, most programs persist in using traditional methods of identification that rely on popular notions of gifted characteristics (Scott, Prior, Urbano, Hogan, & Gold, 1992).

ASSESSMENT   Many techniques have been used in identifying gifted and talented students. These include intelligence and achievement tests, tests of creativity, teacher nomination, and parent, peer, and self-nominations. Although none of these identification methods is adequate alone, each has a place in the identification process. When used in some logical combination, these approaches can strengthen our ability to identify gifted and talented students. Effective assessment techniques should differentiate those youngsters whose environments have been so enriched that they are very high achievers and those who are gifted.

Assessing Aptitude (Intelligence)

Identification measures have traditionally included aptitude and achievement tests. Aptitude, or intelligence, tests usually provide IQ or other standard scores. The two most frequently used intelligence tests that are individually administered are the Stanford-Binet (Terman & Merrill, 1973) and the Wechsler intelligence scales (Wechsler, 1967, 1974, 1981, 1991). A new revision of the Stanford-Binet has been recommended for use with gifted students, especially those below age 9, although there is disagreement as to whether the Stanford-Binet L-M or the newer Stanford-Binet IV should be used (Robinson, 1992; Silverman & Kearney, 1992). Another fairly recent addition to intelligence scales is the Kaufman Assessment Battery for Children (K-ABC) (Kaufman & Kaufman, 1983). An instrument with particular relevance for identifying culturally different gifted children is the System of Multicultural Pluralistic Assessment (SOMPA), developed by Jane Mercer (1978). The SOMPA is based on three assessment models— a medical model, a social system model, and a pluralistic model—each providing unique information about the individual. One strength of the SOMPA is that a child's performance is evaluated not only against standard norms but also in comparison to children the same age from a similar sociocultural background. These comparisons yield estimates of learning potential that account for cultural differences. Performance in academic and nonacademic settings is assessed through standardized tests (e.g., the Wechsler Intelligence Scale for Children and tests of physical and visual-motor functioning) and with the Adaptive Behavior Inventory for Children (ABIC), health history inventories, and sociocultural scales.

Early Childhood.   Formal intelligence tests are available for assessing giftedness in young children. These include the Stanford-Binet, the Wechsler Preschool and Primary Scale of Intelligence (WPPSI), and the K-ABC. The Peabody Picture Vocabulary Test can also be used.

However, because IQ scores of young children are not highly stable over time (Tannenbaum, 1992), other means of identifying this population are important. These include behavioral checklists, parent interviews, and direct observation (Moon, Feldhusen, & Kelly, 1991). These informal methods are particularly important for gifted who are culturally different or disabled. Some model programs for identifying and serving young children who are gifted and disabled have developed such approaches. The RAPYHT (Retrieval and Acceleration of Promising Young Handicapped and Talented) Project at the University of Illinois has outlined procedures for identifying gifted and talented preschoolers (ages 2½ to 5). These procedures, which are being replicated in many states across the country, involve initial screening using a Preschool Talent Checklist, followed by a Preschool Talent Assessment Guide. Follow-up studies of the population involved in the RAPYHT program indicate excellent progress for these children in their subsequent school settings (Karnes, Schwedel, & Lewis, 1983), suggesting valid prediction of academic ability.

School Age.   Intelligence tests measure a variety of abilities, including social, problem-solving, and abstract and concrete reasoning abilities. In addition, they give opportunities for both verbal and nonverbal responses. Not only do these tests provide valuable standardized information about a youngster's abilities and learning style, they also can provide significant nonstandardized information. For example, the Wechsler scales can yield a profile of a student's cognitive abilities, as shown in Table 12–1.

The K-ABC test, which measures intellectual ability and achievement was introduced in 1983. It is an individually administered measure for use with youngsters from 2½ to 12 years old; it included gifted children in the sample used to develop norms. The developers describe the K-ABC as a measure built on a theory of intelligence that is based on two major types of skills. The first is termed *sequential* and includes sequential, analytic, and temporal processing skills; the second is termed *simultaneous* and involves spatial abilities and a holistic response to tasks. The K-ABC is designed to measure intelligence apart from achievement, with language or verbal skills playing a minimal role. The test gives the child opportunities to learn how to solve tasks and assesses ability on the basis of the processing style used. Because language or verbal skills play a minimal role in the assessment, the K-ABC has been proposed as a viable alternative for culturally diverse children (Haddad & Naglieri, 1984); it tends to identify more of this population than are found by traditional means.

Assessing Achievement

Sometimes special placement requires evaluation of achievement, as well as of aptitude. Tests that measure academic achievement are often group administered; performance is

Table 12–1

The Wechsler intelligence scales: A useful instrument for obtaining a profile of cognitive abilities

Test Category	Item Type	Example	Ability/Knowledge Tested
Verbal	Vocabulary	Define the word	Understanding of verbal concepts, quality and quantity of verbal expression
	Information	Who was the first U.S. president?	General information gained from environment
	Similarities	In what way are an accordion and a guitar alike?	Logical and abstract thinking, ability to recognize relationships between objects or ideas
	Comprehension	What should you do in a fire drill?	Practical knowledge, social judgment
Attention and Concentration	Digit span*	Student repeats numbers forward and backward.	Rote memory, ability to attend
	Arithmetic	If I have x books and lose y . . .	Ability to manipulate number concepts
Visual Organization	Picture arrangement	Student arranges a group of pictures in logical sequence.	Perception, visual comprehension, understanding of social situations
	Picture completion	Student identifies missing elements of pictures.	Ability to determine essential details, attention, and concentration
Visual-Motor	Object assembly	Student assembles picture puzzles.	Ability to organize parts into meaningful whole, perception of relationships, visual-motor coordination
	Block design	Student reproduces 2-dimensional design with colored blocks.	Ability to apply logic and reasoning to space relationships and to analyze and reproduce a geometric pattern
	Coding	Student matches and copies symbols using simple shapes and numerals.	Visual-motor dexterity, ability to absorb new material
	Symbol search*	Student scans for a target symbol in a row of presented symbols.	Visual-motor dexterity and perception
	Mazes*	Student solves a series of increasingly difficult mazes.	Visual-motor and planning skills

*Not included in scoring, but provide useful clinical information

usually interpreted in terms of grade placement and/or percentiles. When placement is an issue, achievement measures should be directly related to the program's requirements. The structure of most achievement tests makes it possible to evaluate only specific areas in question. When standardized tests are used, specimen copies could be reviewed prior to purchase; reviews describing the instruments and their development and citing related research can be found in the *Mental Measurement Yearbook* (Kramer &

Murphy, 1992). In addition to formal, standardized instruments, comprehensive test data from teachers can be valuable in assessing school achievement.

Assessing Performance in Nonacademic Areas

Talent in performance areas other than academic can sometimes be evaluated with standardized tests, but direct observation is a more valuable assessment technique. Methods of direct and daily observation of classroom performance have been systematized (Cooper, 1981). Often, permanent products, a student's work, and other readily identifiable outcomes of performance are the best indicators of talent. These outcomes—for instance, drawings, creative writing, music performance, or a gymnastic feat—usually can be evaluated with relative objectivity by a committee of experts. There is a great deal of interest in the use of student portfolios as a tool for assessing abilities and accomplishments (Reis & Renzulli, 1991).

Assessing Creativity

If we view divergent response as a major aspect of creativity, we are faced with the difficult task of finding an objective measure. Measurement of divergence is, in several respects, contradictory to the notion of standardized testing, which is based on convergence—supply the right answer. Nonetheless, several tests do exist that are purported to assess creativity. Perhaps best known are the Torrance Tests of Creative Thinking (TTCT) (Torrance, 1966), which were designed to measure four characteristics associated with creativity: fluency, flexibility, originality, and elaboration. A major issue related to tests of creativity is the lack of data on their validity and reliability (Silverman, 1986).

Some gifted children exhibit unusual interest and ability in intellectually demanding activities.

Other Procedures for Identifying the Gifted and Talented

One widely used procedure for locating potentially gifted and talented students is teacher nomination, even though the ability of teachers to pick out the gifted in their classes has been open to question for some time. Early research in teacher nomination revealed that junior high school teachers did not locate gifted children well enough to place much reliance on their screening (Pegnato & Birch, 1959). These studies of teacher identification, however, required teachers to make global assessments of students' abilities. Such assessments were general and related more to good behavior, high grades, and the value systems of the teachers than to the students' abilities. More recent studies have shown that when teachers are given specific criteria, they are more accurate in identifying gifted children. Borland (1978) found positive correlations between teacher ratings and IQ but also found that teachers were more accurate in identifying gifted girls than gifted boys and gifted underachievers than gifted achievers. Borland's results confirm those of Jacobs (1971), who demonstrated that training teachers to identify gifted children increased their accuracy. In addition, instruments that focus on observable characteristics are now available for teachers to use in selecting gifted students and seem to be more reliable than teacher judgment alone.

One such behavioral checklist dealing with observable characteristics is the Scale for Rating the Behavioral Characteristics of Superior Students (Renzulli & Hartman, 1971), designed to obtain teacher estimates of students' characteristics in the areas of learning, motivation, creativity, leadership, communication, and the arts. Separate, weighted scores are obtained for each dimension, permitting emphasis on different areas. Some sample items from the Renzulli scale are included here:

- Is a keen observer; usually "sees more" or "gets more" out of a story, film, etc.
- Has unusually advanced vocabulary for age or grade level; uses terms in a meaningful way
- Has a large storehouse of information about a variety of topics
- Is easily bored with routine tasks
- Is interested in many "adult" problems, such as religion, politics, sex, race—more than usual for age level
- Displays a great deal of curiosity about many things; is constantly asking questions about anything and everything
- Is a high risk taker; is adventurous and speculative
- Displays a keen sense of humor and sees humor in situations that may not appear to be humorous to others

Care must be taken when using multiple criteria to identify the gifted. When weighted scores are assigned to the various criteria, it is important that the method reflect the relative importance of each category so that the identification system represents the identification philosophy (Moore & Betts, 1987).

Other methods for identifying gifted children include parent, peer, and self-nomination. Parents are an excellent source of information about the strengths and weaknesses of their children. In a 1974 study, parents who responded to a questionnaire asking whether their kindergarten children were gifted, according to stated criteria, correctly nominated 39 of a total of 58 children, for a 76% accuracy rate as compared to 22% for teachers (Ciha, Harris, Hoffman, & Potter, 1974; Louis & Lewis, 1992). Classmates, too, can often provide significant information to aid in identifying the gifted and talented; even gifted and talented individuals themselves may be willing and able to identify their own special abilities and achievements. This may be particularly important in alternative learning centers, where it is necessary to look beyond the traditional identification methods in targeting gifted students (Osborne & Byrnes, 1990).

Special Problems in Identifying the Gifted

Conventional methods of identifying gifted children often miss some special populations. Among these are the culturally different gifted, gifted females, the gifted who are disabled, and gifted underachievers.

Culturally Different Gifted. Even though gifted children may be found in every socioeconomic and cultural group, schools have been more successful in identifying those in the majority or dominant culture. Indeed, the educational needs of many gifted children have not been well met because these children are more difficult to teach as well as to recognize. Now, at last, there is an increasing emphasis on identifying and serving culturally different gifted children (Frasier, 1980; Rhodes, 1992). Some difficulties in finding the culturally different gifted arose when concepts of giftedness were more limited and emphasized intellectual ability to the exclusion of broader concepts (Bernal, 1975). With current, broader definitions of giftedness and the new willingness of school personnel to use a variety of screening and evaluation techniques and instruments, more children from minority cultural groups are now being identified. Some early studies of the K-ABC (McCallum, Karnes, & Edwards, 1984) indicate that the culturally different gifted are likely to score higher on this instrument than on the Stanford-Binet or Wechsler scales, which depend more on verbal skills.

Dissatisfaction with conventional procedures for identifying gifted students has led to the development of alternative methods. Renzulli, for instance, designed the Subcultural Indices of Academic Potential (1973), a test that requires students to assess their reactions to everyday situations and thereby produces a profile of their preferences, learning styles, and ways of approaching tasks. Another researcher attempted to identify and test for specific types of giftedness using Guilford's Structure of Intellect Model (Meeker, 1969)—an important step because it relates traditional intelligence to the nontraditional structure of intellect. Specific items on the Stanford-Binet Intelligence Test, for example, can be looked at in terms of the Structure of Intellect Model, and student strengths and weaknesses can be analyzed (See Figure 12–1.) Does the child do well on items requiring understanding of abstract words? Such a skill involves cognition, semantic content, and units. Does the child have trouble explaining why certain statements are foolish? Such a task involves evaluation, semantic content, and systems. In this way a child's performance can be analyzed for specific patterns of ability and weakness, and teaching activities can be planned accordingly.

Another instrument for identifying the gifted is the Kranz Talent Identification Instrument (Kranz, 1982). This instrument is designed to raise awareness of the multiple criteria of giftedness in order to assist teachers in screening for talented children in their classes. Kranz uses a three-stage procedure in which teachers and administrators are prepared for the tasks of rating, screening, and selecting gifted and talented students. Input from parents is also a part of the process. The instrument trains professionals to focus on frequency, intensity, and quality of specific behaviors and aims at identifying children from all ethnic and sociological backgrounds. Additional efforts include Bernal's (1979) development of a means for identifying giftedness among Hispanic students in Texas, Baldwin's (1984) development of an identification matrix that includes data from both objective and subjective identification instruments, and Bruch's (1972) use of an abbreviated form of the Stanford-Binet to identify disadvantaged black youngsters. Frasier (1987) presents new perspectives on the current status of identifying gifted black students and recommends early identification, the use of multiple sources, and a focus on diversity.

Recent research indicates that one key factor in successful identification of culturally different gifted youngsters is teacher attitude (High & Udall, 1983; Rhodes, 1992). Both articles reported that culturally different students were not referred to gifted programs in the same proportion as Anglo students and that this lack of referrals may be related to negative teacher attitudes and lack of teacher awareness. In addition, the social and cultural milieu of a school seems to influence the way teachers evaluate students. In the High and Udall study, negative teacher attitudes seemed to be intensified in schools with large numbers of minority students. One conclusion is that teacher training is a key factor in the successful identification of gifted minority students. Another variable influencing the low referral rate is the close relationship between learning characteristics on the behavioral checklists used and the majority culture's idea of positive school behavior. Attempts to develop alternative methods for identifying gifted students will undoubtedly continue to receive increased attention.

Gifted Females.   Social expectations for women during the early decades of this century restricted them to the traditional roles of homemaking and teaching. In fact, Terman's study following a gifted sample into adulthood gathered data on the careers of the men only, because few women were expected to become professionals (Terman & Oden, 1959). Even today, women make up approximately one half of our nation's gifted and talented population but are conspicuously underrepresented in leadership roles (Fox & Tobin, 1978). Influenced by the civil rights movement of the sixties, attitudes have changed, and more options have opened up for women who want to assume nontraditional roles. Nonetheless, there remains a tendency among teachers to select different learning experiences for boys and girls (Reis, 1987). It appears that in our culture, even today, women are not expected to succeed. For gifted women this is a serious problem. Their motivation to achieve conflicts with their fear that they will be rejected or considered unfeminine if they do. This conflict can result in ambivalence or even anxiety, which, in turn, impedes success (Kerr, 1985; Reis, 1991).

There is little information available on assessing gifted females. However, some specific problems in identifying gifted females have been identified. They are related to differential treatment of males and females, as well as to different expectations on the part of adults and the gifted females themselves (Gilligan, 1990). The key to better assessment of gifted females may lie in counseling and career development programs. Hollinger (1991) recommends some specific strategies:

1. *Increasing awareness of barriers*: Exploring the impact of sex role socialization on the adolescent's self-belief system can be facilitated through a self-assessment process followed by comparison of identified self-perceptions with objective data and discussion of identified discrepancies.
2. *Broadening career exploration*: The gifted adolescent needs to be encouraged to explore occupations that are congruent with her talents and abilities. Information regarding such occupations must be complemented by interactions with individuals in these career areas and on-site visits to the workplace if occupational stereotypes and misconceptions are to be overcome.
3. *Helping gifted girls integrate multiple life roles*: ". . . the message that combining multiple life roles is indeed possible needs to be accompanied by the information and skills essential for coping successfully with multiple role demands." (pp. 136–137)

Grau (1985) identifies eight psychosocial barriers to the career achievement of gifted females: (1) the conflict between femininity and achievement, (2) women's self-hatred, (3) a socialized need for affiliation, (4) conflict created by the motherhood mandate, (5) conflict created by the expectations associated with homemaking, (6) a reliance on external sources of control and praise, (7) occupations and professional stereotypes, and (8) the lack of nontraditional female role models. A concerted effort to identify female role models in the school and community is recommended by Grau, thereby encouraging gifted and talented females to explore and refine their abilities. Formation of support groups may also help to provide settings in which gifted females feel free to show their particular abilities and talents.

Silverman (1991) identifies eight essential ingredients in developing the potential of gifted girls. These are parent education, early identification, gifted peers, early entrance, teacher inservice, special programs, career counseling, and conferences for gifted girls. McCormick and Wolf (in press) review a number of intervention programs that incorporate many of these essential ingredients in addressing the needs of gifted females.

Gifted Who Are Disabled. Identification of the gifted who are disabled depends on a willingness to focus on strengths rather than weaknesses. Wolf and Gygi (1981) reviewed some methods of identifying gifted students with learning disabilities, such as the use of individual intelligence tests (Hokansen & Jospe, 1976). Subtest scores can then be examined so that areas of high ability can be identified. Such an approach is useful, but it is not realistic to assume that it can be available to all those who need it.

Another method of assessing gifted students who are disabled is direct observation. Such observation in natural settings may indicate variability in performance. Parent reports and self-evaluation may also be used. The learning disability would probably have to be fairly severe or the giftedness fairly extreme for teachers to become aware of performance discrepancies in the classroom. In addition, because teachers are often reluctant to refer gifted students with learning disabilities to gifted programs (Minner, 1990), it is important to provide training to teachers so that they examine their own stereotypes and understand the special needs of this population.

Maker (1977) suggests three techniques to use in identifying gifted students who are disabled. The first is a focus on potential rather than on demonstrated ability alone. The second is a comparison of the student with other students who are disabled rather than with the general population. The third is observation of the student's skills in compensating for the disability. Observations of superior ability in reasoning and recognizing relationships (Given, 1977), intellectual curiosity, wide-ranging interests, and effective independent work can also be helpful in the assessment process. Such data can be good sources of information both for assessment purposes and for help in programming. For gifted students who are learning disabled, it is important to provide instruction in compensation strategies, exposure to higher-level concepts and materials, and support through counseling (Suter & Wolf, 1987).

Baum and Owen (1988) describe the limitations of programs for gifted students with learning disabilities that focus only on their areas of weakness, and they emphasize the importance of broad identification procedures to include potentially gifted students who are learning disabled.

Gifted Underachievers.   Another group of gifted students often missed in the assessment process is the gifted underachiever. Early studies attributed the problem to personality characteristics and/or family problems. There is some recent support for the premise that classroom conditions often contribute to the development of gifted underachievers. The maladjustment seen in this population is thought to be related to the interaction between the child, his or her personality and behavior, and the social environment of home and school (Gallagher, 1991a; Rimm, 1986). It is clear that there are difficulties in identifying this population in a setting that may be contributing to the problem. Common procedures for finding these youngsters involve a comparison of performance on individual and/or group tests with academic achievement. Although this method will successfully identify many gifted underachievers, some will still be missed because of depressed test scores—especially gifted youngsters with emotional problems. Identification of these students must combine standardized test performance and a profile of achievement with teacher evaluation of social, emotional, and physical status. The use of behavior checklists is also useful, and parent and student interviews can be extremely valuable. Whitmore (1986) states that the parents and teachers need to understand the causes of underachievement so that they can be effective in helping underachieving gifted students.

Redding (1990) found differences in learning styles between junior high age gifted underachievers and achievers. These differences may be attributable to poor coping skills. DeLisle (1990) indicated that underachievement is a behavior and can be changed over time, that it is content and situation specific, that it is in the eyes of the beholder, and that it is tied intimately to self-concept. Laffoon, Jerkins-Friedman, and Tollefson (1989) report that underachieving gifted students were more likely to attribute their lack of success to bad luck, fate, or other factors than were achieving gifted who attribute their success to effort.

INTERVENTION   All schools have some gifted and talented students; many, however, make no special provisions for them. In those schools that do, services may be provided on an individual basis or through various administrative arrangements. Whatever the model of service delivery selected, gifted children will profit greatly from early intervention because they require more and qualitatively different experiences than other children of the same ages. It has been demonstrated that gifted children benefit specifically from early instruction in academic areas (Bloom, 1985). According to Clark (1988), stimulation during the early years is a necessary requisite for the gifted child's optimal intellectual growth. Early nurturing of abilities can also bring forth latent talents, such as musical and mathematical aptitudes, which must be discovered and cultivated early. The majority of great talents are manifested before age 30, even though some great achievements, particularly in politics and historical research, do occur after age 45 (Lehman, 1953).

We should remember that for the gifted and talented, as for other exceptional students, it is important to individualize educational programs (Wolf, 1979). Individualization does not require having each 25 gifted and talented students studying a different subject area. It does require dynamic and fluid grouping, a recognition that individuals learn at different rates, and an expectation that students will assume some responsibility for their own learning (Wolf, 1979; Wolf & Stephens, 1979). Individualization of programs is not limited to special programs. It can and must take place in the regular classroom—frequently the place where gifted children spend the majority of their school day.

Direct Services. Direct services are those the student receives through personal contact with service providers. They may be offered in the regular classroom, in the student's home school, or elsewhere. In the regular classroom the teacher may provide special attention, more challenging assignments, and enriched experiences. Outside the regular classroom gifted and talented students may be given part of their instruction by a resource teacher or by individuals in the community with specific expertise, in accelerated classes, or in college or university courses.

Special counseling, tutoring, and interest development are other direct services that gifted and talented students may receive outside the regular classroom. Bright students typically need career counseling to be aware of the variety of career options open to them (Alexander & Muia, 1982; Kerr, 1985). Guidance should begin early and extend throughout the school experience. It is essential that it be objective; the counselor's role should be to inform students about qualifications for specific careers, not to encourage or discourage early career commitments. Special tutoring can extend the subject matter range or depth normally available to students. Regular teachers or outside personnel can serve as tutors. Gifted students are frequently curious and do, with encouragement, develop a wide range of interests, which can be stimulated and developed through after-school clubs or groups that meet during school hours. Sometimes community resources can be tapped.

Indirect Services. Assistance in meeting the needs of gifted students may come from individuals who have no direct contact with the students themselves; these services are thus referred to as indirect. Consultants who provide teachers with suggestions, conduct or coordinate inservice training, and locate resources outside the schools are a common resource. Concerned and supportive principals and central district administrators can underscore the importance of programs for the gifted and talented and can help consultants gain access to teachers and parents. It is the job of administrators, too, to provide incentives for school personnel to identify and provide special programming for bright students—additional funds for enrichment materials or special field trips, for example. Special bulletins and journals on the education of the gifted and talented are another form of indirect service.

Independent Study Contracting

Independent study may involve the use of contracts established and agreed upon by the teacher, the student, and the parents when appropriate. Some contracts will not involve outside resources, while others may draw from the entire school system or even the community. Outlined here is an example of an independent contract arranged for Scott Martin in an attempt to meet some specialized needs in reading.

As a first step, Scotty's teacher, Mrs. Webb, wanted to determine that he had indeed mastered with 95% accuracy all the basic skills that were part of the 6th-grade reading program. With a mastery test, Mrs. Webb could be assured that there were no gaps in Scotty's reading skills background or could assist Scotty in filling any gaps that were disclosed.

Independent study projects should culminate in a final product developed by the student.

Next, after assessing Scotty's reading interests, a decision was made to focus on modern science fiction writers. The various elements of the independent study contract were then worked out in the format shown in Figure 12–2. For this particular contract Scotty needed to examine the university course reading requirements before compiling his reading list. He then made a commitment to the contract as it was written. In fact, he was a major drafter of the contract, negotiating with his teacher the deadlines, methods of presenting the material, and evaluation criteria. The plan required the local university's permission for Scotty to enroll in a course in the English department and agreement from Scotty's parents to provide the necessary transportation.

Not all independent study contracts are so complex. Many can be carried out within the confines of the classroom and may simply involve a student's in-depth study of a topic studied less fully by the class. A student might contract to use different media and materials as part of his or her in-depth study, to develop a useful product, or in some special way to accomplish other specific objectives.

Bibliotherapy

Bibliotherapy, a counseling approach, particularly suited to gifted children, is a technique of providing reading material on ways of dealing with problems (Wolf & Penrod, 1980). Because many gifted children are avid readers, teachers or counselors can often help them resolve personal crises by directing them to appropriate books or articles. This method is also useful with young gifted children. For example, a child may be having difficulty getting along with peers. Her teacher can use a source such as The Bookfinder (Dryer, 1977) to identify fiction at an appropriate level that deals with peer relations. The child can then identify with the book's character in dealing with his or her problem. Full resolution can be facilitated by discussion of the book and opportunities to express feelings.

Mentor Programs

In some programs, arrangements are made for gifted and talented students to pursue a particular area of interest with an expert in the community. The goals and objectives as well as the particular learning activities are carefully delineated, and a time is set aside during the school day for the student to be with the mentor. Accountability is built in so that accomplishment of specific goals can be documented. An independent study contract or some other agreed-upon means can be used.

Colson, Borman, and Nash (1978) have described one program in which students have opportunities to examine career fields and then to work directly with a mentor in a chosen area. Activity logs are kept, and seminars are held in which students share experiences. Participating students have reported gaining insight into the life-styles of those in their chosen fields as well as into their own needs and interests. Other populations have been identified from which mentors can be drawn. These include college students, particularly teacher trainees (Harris, 1984), as well as college professors (McCleary & Hines, 1983), parents and other adults in the community (Bridges, 1980), and older students with a particular area of expertise (Mattson, 1983).

```
┌─────────────────────────────────────────────────────────────────────┐
│                      Independent Study Contract                       │
│                                                                       │
│  Student: Scott Martin                    Title of Study: Modern Science │
│  Estimated Completion Date: March 5, 1990                Fiction Writers │
│  MAIN QUESTIONS I PLAN TO EXPLORE:                                     │
│   A consideration of modern science fiction writers with focus on Heinlein, Asimov, Clarke, Herbert, Leguin │
│   Comparison and contrast of these authors                            │
│  MAIN SOURCES OF INFORMATION I PLAN TO USE:                           │
│            University course on Modern Science Fiction Writers         │
│            Fall quarter M – W 8:00 – 9:30 am Dr. Jones                 │
│  Primary Sources:                                                     │
│  Clarke:   Tales from the White Heart, 2001: A Space Odyssey          │
│  Heinlein:  Paths Through Tomorrow                                     │
│  Asimov:   The Foundation Trilogy                                      │
│  Herbert:  Stand on Zanzibar, The Sheep Look Up                       │
│  Leguin:  The Left Hand of Darkness, The Earth Sea Trilogy            │
│                                                                       │
│  Place and Format for Presenting My Study:                           │
│  1.  Written paper: Critique of Modern Science Fiction               │
│  2.  One-week seminar on modern science fiction for fifth-sixth graders at Snowbird School │
│                                                                       │
│             I would like to have my study evaluated by this set of criteria │
│  Written                            Oral                             │
│  Paper on critique of modern science fiction as   Presentation of one-week seminar on modern │
│  seen in writings of Asimov, Heinlein, Clarke,    science fiction for fifth-sixth graders of │
│  Herbert, Leguin                     Snowbird                         │
│                                                                       │
│  Course outline for one-week seminar             Teacher evaluation  │
│                                     Student evaluation               │
│                                                                       │
│                                     _____  │
│                                     Student's Signature              │
│                                                                       │
│  Date _____      _____  │
│                                     Teacher's Signature             │
│                                                                       │
│                                     _____  │
│                                     Parent's Signature              │
└─────────────────────────────────────────────────────────────────────┘
```

Figure 12–2

Example of an independent study contract.

Source: From "Individualized Educational Planning for the Gifted" by J. S. Wolf and T. M. Stephens, 1979, *Roeper Review*, 2(2), p. 12. Copyright 1979 by *Roeper Review*. Reprinted by permission.

Beck (1989) examined the effects of a mentorship program, finding that participants received significant personal, academic, and career-choice benefits. She recommended that programs that incorporate both classroom and mentorship experiences should be made available, with special attention to identifying female mentors for gifted girls. McGreevy's work (1990) suggests that mentorships are most successful when they are based on strong interests that are shared. She postulates that the mentor experience in the sciences are of critical importance.

Group Interaction with Peers

Even though independent study is a valuable educational tool for teaching the gifted and talented, opportunities for interaction with peers are equally important. The excitement of sharing knowledge and interests is both stimulating and motivating. The group setting allows opportunities for gifted students to learn from one another in an environment where unusual ideas are accepted and exciting discussions are plentiful. The group may include students of several ages or grades and may thus provide role models for younger gifted students. Emphasis should be on the topics or subjects studied and on the group process. Personal and social adjustment are enhanced by positive group experiences with gifted peers (Feldhusen, Sayler, Nielsen, & Kolloff, 1990).

Early Admission and Concurrent Enrollment

Interaction with gifted peers may be enhanced through alternative programs that go beyond the walls of the classroom. For secondary students who are significantly advanced academically and who have social and emotional stability, settings beyond the high school environment may be particularly suitable. Early admission programs allow high school students, most commonly seniors, to enter college early without earning a high school diploma. Decisions are made on an individual basis. An early prototype of the early admission program was the Ford Foundation effort in the sixties, in which selected youngsters throughout the country entered college at young ages. Results revealed that, as a group, these students were as successful as older students in their university work and participated in extracurricular activities as well.

A decision to admit some highly gifted youngsters to college may be made while they are still at an elementary age. Periodically, we read about such youngsters: Mike Grost is one example (Grost, 1970). He entered college at 12, received his B.S. degree at 15, and developed an original mathematical theorem as a college senior. A *New York Times* article reported a decision for a 7-year-old girl to enter high school because of her exceptional abilities ("High School," 1984). Reports of Coleman Miller's graduating from college at 15 and entering the California Institute of Technology as a graduate student in physics reveal another example of early admission policies. Although these youngsters represent extreme abilities, various modes of acceleration can be beneficial for the gifted.

One option of early admission programs is concurrent enrollment, in which high school students enroll in college classes for regular credit. These programs have been popular since the sixties and are quite common today. Many institutions have reported that this select group of high school students has successfully completed college level courses taught by regular college faculty and containing regular college students (Wolf & Geiger, 1986) and have earned good to excellent grade point averages. Such a program allows gifted students intellectual stimulation and challenge and provides opportunities for them to interact with intellectual peers who may not be age-mates.

Teachers of the Gifted

An important key to effective intervention for the gifted rests in the teacher. Practically all teachers prefer students who learn quickly and are interested in their studies. However, even though gifted and talented students are eager learners, they also present teachers with frequent challenges that require tolerance and maturity. Teachers of the gifted must be personally secure; they must be able to accept the fact that their students may be more knowledgeable in certain areas and encourage them to seek even higher levels of learning.

There is little agreement on the specific qualities that teachers of the gifted should have. We know generally that teachers who are excited about what they teach foster interest among bright students. At upper grade levels teachers must be knowledgeable in subject matter, willing to learn with their students, and capable of providing guidance and direction as students explore their intellectual interests. There is

Hands-on experiences can foster lifetime hobbies and careers.

some evidence that successful teachers of gifted high school students are mature, experienced, emotionally well adjusted, and highly intelligent (Newland, 1962; Ward, 1961). In addition, they typically are knowledgeable about giftedness and express support for special attention to the gifted (Bishop, 1968).

According to Story (1985), successful teachers of the gifted have certain behavioral characteristics that include the following: provide positive, close physical relationships with their gifted students; are flexible in scheduling their time; are process oriented; and demonstrate high quality and quantity in their verbal interactions. Using videotapes and observations, Wendel and Heiser (1989) found that effective teachers of the gifted demonstrated care and respect for their students and demanded high quality work. They also mentioned that effective teachers maintained a close physical presence.

In an examination of competencies of teachers of the gifted using an interview technique, Whitlock and DuCette (1989) found that outstanding teachers of the gifted differed from average teachers of the gifted in enthusiasm, self-confidence, serving as a facilitator, having a strong orientation to achievement, commitment to the role of gifted educator, and developing support for the gifted program.

Certain qualities seem to be characteristic of creative teachers at all levels: sensitivity and flexibility in their relationships with students, openness in thinking and activities, and respect and support for the individuality of each student. Wyatt (1982) further addresses the important behaviors of supportive classroom teachers of the gifted: (1) providing an enriched classroom environment and differentiated curriculum; (2) involving students in independent investigations; (3) teaching process skills, the scientific method, and research skills; (4) providing options to accommodate learning styles; and (5) demonstrating knowledge about the gifted child. Some recent work regarding the relationship of the teaching style of teachers and the learning style of gifted students has been reported (Griggs, 1984; Howell & Bressler, 1988). (See Figure 12–3.) Rogers (1989) presented a teacher training model that takes into account both the type of teacher and the setting in which the gifted students will be served.

Does it make any difference if special provisions are made for the gifted? There are a few studies that indicate that gifted students do indeed benefit from special programs. Tremaine (1979) compared the achievements and attitudes of gifted high school graduates who had participated in special programs with those of gifted graduates who had not. He found that those enrolled in gifted programs had significantly more scholarships and awards, tended to elect difficult courses in high school, enrolled in college in higher numbers, and were involved in more school activities. No evidence was found of negative attitudes either toward or from those in special programs. Feldhusen et al. (1990) reported positive gains in self-concept for gifted students who participated in a pullout enrichment program. In another study, Vaughn, Feldhusen, and Asher (1991) reported that pullout programs for gifted students had significant positive effects on achievement, critical thinking, and creativity with no decrease in self-concept.

CURRICULUM
IMPLICATIONS

Sound instructional practices are necessary, regardless of any special provisions made for gifted and talented students. Terman believed that bright students should receive systematically differentiated instruction throughout their school experience because they learn differently. There is, in fact, general agreement that both the nature of the

Personal Characteristics: The teacher is to present evidence of successful achievement(s) in each area prior to acceptance into the practicum.

Intellectual achievement: Is knowledgeable about a wide range of subjects and topics

Interpersonal skills: Is able to successfully establish a comfortable working relationship with both adults and students

Personal success: Has achieved success as a teacher or as a professional in some other field

Secure personality: Is at ease in most settings including those which are new and/or unknown

Intellectual curiosity: Is constantly seeking new solutions through continued learning

Organization: Has organized his personal life and maintains control over it

Leadership ability: Has demonstrated skills in leading people, especially young people, to successful accomplishment of a major undertaking

Professional Characteristics: The teacher is to demonstrate successful attainment in each area.

Subject matter knowledge: In-depth command of one subject area and familiarity with several others

Information-handling skills: Ability to organize information into units for teaching gifted students

Classroom teaching skills: The ability to relate to gifted students within a classroom and to create an environment within which learning takes place

Diagnostic skills: The ability to use diagnostic tests and other tools to determine student educational needs

Prescriptive teaching skills: The ability to design specific learning packages for students and to carry them out successfully

Program development skills: The ability to conceptualize a program for gifted students and to identify and organize the key elements related to its success

Program leadership skills: The ability to convince a wide variety of persons about the appropriateness of a program for the gifted

Figure 12–3

Characteristics of a teacher for the gifted.

Source: From "A Collaborative Program for Developing Teachers of Gifted and Talented Students" by J. D. Mulhern and M. Ward, 1983, *Gifted Child Quarterly,* 27(4), p. 155. Copyright 1983 by *Gifted Child Quarterly.* Reprinted by permission.

material and the rate of presentation may need modifying for gifted students. Although the objectives of instruction for the gifted are similar to those for other students, the approaches may differ. Emphasis should be on creativity, intellectual initiative, critical thinking, social adjustment, responsibility, and leadership. A common characteristic of academically gifted youngsters is their ability to grasp complex concepts and to master them easily. Their need for drill and practice is significantly less than that of average students. They should be taught concepts and principles rather than concrete facts, which are typically a natural part of their learning. The gifted learn inductively, too, responding to logic and reason (Tannenbaum, 1983). In short, bright students thrive on many new ideas and profit from moving through subject matter quickly in order to pursue interests in related areas, learning in depth and breadth.

Age-Level Distinctions

Many techniques that are appropriate for school-age gifted students can be applied in early childhood programs. Activities that promote inquiry and problem solving and encourage higher cognitive processes are particularly suitable. Opportunities for creative exploration are also important. Quattrocki (1974) describes an atmosphere in which young children can be creative as one that allows a child to be free from inhibition, to make novel combinations of ideas, and to express curiosity and imagination. Because gifted preschool children have a strong need to explore, a wide variety of materials should be available as well as time to explore them. Some support the Montessori method for the young gifted child (Tittle, 1984) because it encourages unlimited exploration with new materials.

The young gifted child may present some unique challenges to parents prior to school entry. The early talker, the precocious reader, the child who seems to absorb new ideas and concepts at a rapid rate can create problems in a household not prepared to provide needed stimulation. A variety of books and toys, opportunities for learning in informal situations, and interaction with other children to build social skills are important factors, along with parental willingness to respond to the child's interests and questions. One helpful approach brings gifted children together in a preschool program that responds to their needs and works with parents in understanding the nature and needs of a young gifted child.

Parke and Ness (1988) recommend attention to special learning needs through a fast-paced program that focuses on exploration, manipulation, and play. The program should be based on the interests and involvement of young gifted children so that they are involved in the curriculum decision-making process.

For elementary and secondary gifted students subject matter is often modified in the same ways that instructional methods are. For instance, principles and concepts are emphasized, and students are encouraged to use deductive and inductive logic as well as other scientific tools, such as observation. Because most bright students are steeped in information, they are often taught the scientific method early, as a means of evaluating rather than merely assimilating knowledge.

Curriculum Enrichment Modifications

The curriculum for the gifted needs to be qualitatively different from that designed for normal children. Gallagher (1985) suggests that curriculum modification be addressed by considering content, process, and product. Maker (1982) has developed a model for use in curriculum development for gifted students that is related to the characteristics of gifted students and includes content, process, product, and learning environment modification. To provide opportunities for gifted students to engage in appropriate learning activities, curriculum compacting can be used. Curriculum compacting ensures that the basic knowledge in a given subject area is mastered (Renzulli, Smith, & Reis, 1982), allowing gifted students to move on to more appropriate and challenging activities. As stated earlier, gifted students need less drill and practice than the typical youngster, and they need opportunities to use higher-level thinking skills as they deal with broad generalizations and solve real-world problems. Kaplan (1986) suggests the following guidelines for developing a differentiated curriculum for gifted and talented students:

- Curriculum content should focus on broad-based issues, themes, and problems.
- An area of study should be approached from the perspective of different disciplines.
- Experiences within an area of study should be comprehensive, related, and mutually reinforcing.
- Development of self-directed study and research skills and complex, abstract thinking skills should be stressed.
- Development of new and/or expanded ideas and products should be encouraged.
- Curriculum activities should prompt students to recognize and use their abilities, become self-directed, and appreciate similarities and differences between themselves and others.
- Evaluation procedures should include self-ratings as well as standardized instruments.

Instructional Models

In this section we will examine four models useful in teaching segments of the gifted student population. The first, Bloom's taxonomy (1956), is designed to encourage thinking on higher levels. The second, the Enrichment Triad Model (1986), is applicable for teaching the gifted within regular groups with a wide range of abilities. The third, the Sequence for Academic Skills and Concepts, is a generic model that we propose for teaching potentially gifted preschoolers (Stephens & Wolf, 1981), and the fourth is the Autonomous Learner Model, which is becoming widely used for gifted secondary students (Betts, 1985).

Bloom's Taxonomy.   Bloom's taxonomy (1956) is valuable both for the teacher, in designing appropriate learning activities, and for the students, in their own direct learning. It is divided into cognitive and affective domains. The cognitive domain, which is applicable to the instruction of intellectually gifted students, consists of a hierarchy of skill areas, proceeding from the simple to the complex: knowledge, comprehension, application, analysis, synthesis, and evaluation. Table 12–2 clarifies the nature of each of these skill areas.

Most learning activities in a regular classroom focus on knowledge and comprehension. For gifted students, however, it is important to promote use of the higher-level skills—application, analysis, synthesis, and evaluation. Figure 12–4 presents the taxonomy ladder of Bloom's cognitive domain and illustrates by the size of each piece in the triangles the appropriate emphasis on the specific skill areas for gifted and nongifted students. Often students are taught the Bloom model itself so that they can understand the higher cognitive processes involved in learning and make decisions about how they want to acquire information.

Table 12–2
Behaviors and sample items from the skill areas in Bloom's cognitive domain

Skill Area	Behavior	Sample Items
Knowledge	Recall facts, definitions, observations	Define the word *cosmos*. Who spoke first? Where was the building located? What did the boys want? When did Columbus discover America?
Comprehension	State main ideas, describe, match items, compare and contrast	What happened during the experiment? What is the major theme of the play? How are the climates alike? How are they different?
Application	Apply rules and techniques to solve problems	What is the area of the social hall? Classify the short stories as comedy, tragedy, etc.
Analysis	Make inferences, find evidence to support generalizations, identify causes or motives	What can you conclude about the effect of communism on the economic life of the people? How would you characterize the platform of the Republican party on women's rights?
Synthesis	Make predictions, produce original material, solve problems	Give a title to this paragraph. What might happen if gold replaced the dollar as the economic standard?
Evaluation	Give opinions, judge quality of products, validity of ideas, and merit of solutions	Do you agree or disagree with this conclusion? What is your opinion? How would you improve . . .? Do you think capital punishment is just?

Enrichment Triad Model. This model is particularly suited for teaching the gifted with a wide ability range in a regular classroom (Renzulli & Reis, 1986), but it can also be adapted for use in pullout programs for the gifted. It prescribes three types of enrichment: general exploratory activities, group training activities, and individual and small-group investigation of real problems.

General exploratory activities are designed to expose all students in the class to new subjects, topics, and/or experiences. They should serve as strong motivators permitting discovery and exploration on various levels and extending beyond the regular content areas of the curriculum. Examples are going on a field trip, listening to a guest speaker, and watching a film or TV program on a new topic.

Group training activities are especially appropriate for students who show a high degree of interest and involvement during general exploratory activities. Students can usually work in groups, cooperating and learning from each other and building on the information gathered in exploratory activities as they learn research techniques and develop advanced mental processes. Thought processes that might be emphasized are brainstorming, classifying, and evaluating. Students might be asked first to think of all the possible ways their school could be improved (brainstorm), then to categorize their ideas according to function or some other criterion (classify), and finally to suggest ways of improving the traffic pattern around the school building (evaluate). Two

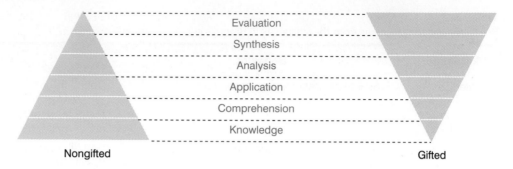

Figure 12–4
Bloom's taxonomy ladder for the cognitive domain.
Source: Reprinted with the permission of Macmillan Publishing Company from *Growing Up Gifted: Developing the Potential of Children at Home and at School,* Fourth Edition by Barbara Clark. Copyright ©1992 by Macmillan Publishing Company.

particularly important aspects of group training activities are a focus on higher-level cognitive and affective processes and a wide range of response options. Communication and interaction skills, cooperation, and appreciation of other students' contributions are emphasized.

Individual and small-group investigation of real problems is the culmination of earlier activities: student learning takes shape as a final product. The emphasis is on investigative or creative work that is of the real world, not a contrived classroom activity; it is particularly suited for gifted children, requiring not only the skills of exploration and communication already developed but also the skills of organization and analysis needed to process the raw data meaningfully. A possible follow-up to earlier activities might question how traffic patterns around the school could be improved. The student would gather data in a real-life situation and then organize a campaign to modify traffic patterns. In the course of the campaign the student would need to communicate with significant community leaders, perhaps by submitting a letter to the editor in the local newspaper or appearing before the city council.

A Sequence for Academic Skills and Concepts. Children with high academic potential typically show an interest in language acquisition, books, advanced ideas, and mathematics at an early age. These children can profit from systematic exposure to formal learning before they enter school. A Sequence for Academic Skills and Concepts is a model for use by parents, teachers, and other child care personnel in helping potentially gifted preschoolers acquire concepts and skills in an efficient and correct manner (Stephens & Wolf, 1981). It permits teachers and parents to determine the level of mastery that a young child has achieved on a specific skill or concept and provides a natural sequence for guiding the child toward total mastery.

Developmental learning theory suggests a natural sequence for the acquisition of early academic skills and concepts. The sequence, as shown in Table 12–3, specifies six phases in learning these beginning skills and concepts (Stephens & Wolf, 1981). This model provides a widely applicable teaching format that can be employed in natural environments as well as in school programs for the very young gifted.

Instruction should begin at whatever phase has not been mastered and progress to the most advanced phase. For example, the manipulation of printed symbols through reading and writing often will not require passing through phases 1 and 2 and aspects of phase 3 because proper names and basic meanings for symbols will already have been acquired naturally. But when these symbols take on more complex meanings—for instance, when they must be understood in the context of printed passages—instruction may be necessary to achieve mastery. In this case instruction would begin within phase 3.

These six phases do not always occur in the given sequence; learners can in some cases perform more advanced tasks prior to mastering easier ones. For example, children can sometimes copy or imitate responses (phase 3) without having acquired correct labels (phase 2). The extent to which the sequence is followed varies with the content learner and the learner's prior experiences.

The Autonomous Learner Model.   This model is designed to address the cognitive, social, and emotional needs of the gifted with the goal of helping them develop into independent learners. As an active participant, the child reaches the following goals (Goertz & Betts, 1989):

- Learning how to read
- Learning new knowledge
- Thinking independently

Table 12–3
A sequence for academic skills and concepts

Phase	Behaviors	Examples
1. Discriminating and differentiating	Attend to details, match stimuli, see and hear similarities and differences	Identify common root words with suffixes
2. Labeling	Use names and other language symbols to identify stimuli, forms, and concepts	Name root words and suffixes
3. Copying and imitating	Copy, trace, or imitate responses in the presence of stimuli or immediately following exposure	Tell meaning of root words and words after suffixes are added
4. Reproducing to mastery	Respond from memory or in presence of visual, auditory, or other sensory cues; receive feedback in form of correction and/or encouragement	Tell meaning of root words before and after addition of suffixes
5. Practicing	Practice newly acquired skill and/or concept	Practice identifying root words before and after suffixes are added
6. Applying	Use mastered skill under direction of instructional agent	Demonstrate knowledge of root words, apply suffixes appropriately in oral and/or written speech

Source: From "Instructional Models" by T. M. Stephens and J. S. Wolf, 1981, *Directive Teacher*, 3(3), p. 5.
Copyright 1981 by *Directive Teacher*. Reprinted by permission.

- Making choices
- Planning the activities
- Participating in a student-created, teacher-created, and/or parent-created center (p. 37)

The Autonomous Learner Model involves orientation to help gifted students understand their giftedness and learn to work effectively in groups, as well as understand themselves. The other components include individual development, enrichment activities, seminars, and in-depth study. Figure 12–5 shows the various components of the Autonomous Learner Model. Advantages cited by developers of this model are the encouragement of independent thinking and opportunities for the student to become involved in topics of intrinsic interest.

MAINSTREAMING   Many gifted youngsters are served in the regular classroom for a significant portion of their school day. The intervention strategies described can be used in this setting, as well as in classes for gifted individuals. Clark (1986) describes a responsive learning environment that could be created in a regular or special class. Students can learn at their own pace with material that is appropriate and can assume some responsibility for their own learning.

Because gifted children have a wide variety of educational, social, emotional, and physical needs, it is important to have varied service options. The guide in selecting a

Figure 12–5
The Autonomous Learner Model for the gifted and talented.
Source: From *The Autonomous Learner Model for the Gifted and Talented* (p. 1) by G. Betts and J. Knapp, 1986, Greeley, CO: Autonomous Learning Publications & Specialists. Copyright by Autonomous Learning Publications & Specialists. Reprinted by permission.

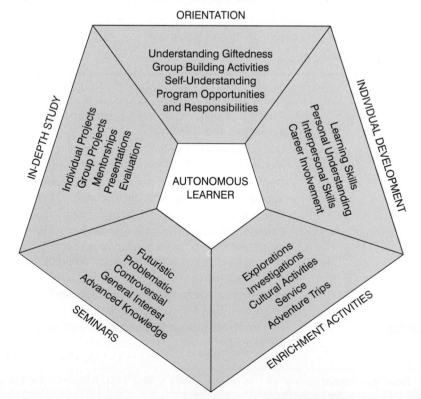

service delivery pattern for any youngster should be "goodness of fit." For gifted students, as for other exceptional children, the advantages and disadvantages of any arrangement should be considered in light of the particular needs of the student and his or her parents. Within the regular school system, a continuum of services can be designed to accommodate the educational needs of exceptionally able students. Special grouping, early school admission and grade acceleration, and advanced placement are three such arrangements.

Special Grouping

In relatively large schools, grouping may simply mean assigning all the gifted students of a particular age or grade level to one class. In smaller schools it is often necessary to include several age groups in special classes. A resource room, in which the gifted can spend part of their school day working with special teachers, represents another type of grouping. It is important to provide options or a continuum of services, which range from part-time to full-time programs, in order to meet the needs of all gifted students.

At the junior and senior high school levels special grouping is often achieved through tracking, which clusters students in classes on the basis of expected performance. Past achievement or potential ability may be used to determine placement. A gifted or talented student may be in different tracks for different classes. In programs of this type, self-selection often operates—students opt for those classes and tracks in which they are interested and for which they have prerequisite skills. Additional placement flexibility allows gifted individuals to receive advanced placement through proficiency exams and move through a given sequence of courses more rapidly. This is a particularly important option for gifted students. Special grouping arrangements are also useful for students with particular talents. Orchestra and band programs and advanced art classes, within the school and in the community—which go beyond academics—serve the needs of some students.

Early School Admission and Grade Acceleration

Some schools permit gifted students to enroll at earlier-than-usual ages, depending on psychological testing and trial placements. In some programs bright students can skip kindergarten or begin kindergarten early. In the primary grades students are seldom permitted to skip more than one grade because of the possible effect on social adjustment. Grade skipping can also be done in later years, although careful study of the individual student and parental approval are prerequisites. When a grade is skipped, the student should be provided with any supplemental instruction and personal assistance necessary to make the transition a smooth one. Research indicates that acceleration—a controversial issue for many years—is, in fact, an extremely viable option for many gifted students. It enables them not only to move through school at a faster pace but also to have increased opportunities for needed interaction with older classmates (Brody, Assouline, & Stanley, 1990; Proctor, Black, & Feldhusen, 1988). Studies indicate that programs that allow gifted students to accelerate their academic program have been highly successful in terms of academic achieve-

MODEL PROGRAM

The Johns Hopkins University Center for the Advancement of Academically Talented Youth is a program that has its roots in a study from the early seventies of mathematically precocious youth (SMPY). In 1971, 250 youngsters born between 1955 and 1961 were identified by their math performance on the Scholastic Achievement Test. They were selected for their strong mathematical reasoning ability (upper 1.5% of their age group in mathematical aptitude) and were encouraged to accelerate their educational programs, particularly in math and physical science. The Johns Hopkins program was initially limited to mathematically gifted students in Maryland but has been expanded over the years to serve youngsters gifted in verbal ability and those located in other geographic areas. The Johns Hopkins program and some other program types are described here.

The Johns Hopkins University Center for the Advancement of Academically Talented Youth operates in Baltimore; Washington, D.C.; Philadel-phia; Los Angeles; and four cities in New Jersey. Programs are offered throughout the year with residential summer programs also available at Dickinson College and Franklin and Marshall College in Pennsylvania. Twelve-year-olds are screened for this program in 7th grade; those who score in the top 3% on standard achievement tests, such as the Iowa Test of Basic Skills or the California Achievement Test, then take the Scholastic Achievement Test (SAT). To qualify for the Johns Hopkins program, they must score above the mean of college-bound seniors (430 out of 800 for the verbal section and/or 500 out of 800 in math). Since 1972, 3,400 gifted adolescents have participated in the program.

The Talent Identification Program (TIP) is a summer program initiated in 1980 and located at Duke University in Durham, North Carolina. It includes 12- to 16-year-olds who score at least 550 in math and 500 in the verbal on the SAT. TIP makes special efforts to identify ethnic and racial minorities and offers financial aid to economically disadvantaged students. Participants also become eligible for special programs developed by TIP, such as courses by mail on subjects ranging from literature, history, and Latin to chemistry, physics, and calculus. In addition, TIP produces the *Educa-*

ments, extracurricular activities, and social and emotional adjustment, with no discernible negative effects reported (Brody & Benbow, 1987; Stanley, 1985). The Model Program box provides brief descriptions of several different approaches for acceleration and special instruction in math.

Advanced Placement

Advanced placement generally refers to college credit obtained by high school students. Some high schools offer advanced placement courses, for which students can receive credit at certain colleges. Other high schools allow gifted students to take courses at nearby colleges in addition to their high school work. Still other systems *tional Opportunity Guide,* which lists 100 summer programs throughout 16 states in which these students may enroll.

The Rocky Mountain Talent Search operates at the University of Denver. It includes 7th- and 8th-graders, 12 to 14 years of age, who have scored at the 95th percentile on total math or total verbal portions of standardized aptitude or achievement tests with national norms or who have received math scores of at least 450 or verbal scores of at least 430 on the SAT. A variety of courses are offered, ranging from math and computer science to philosophy and global issues. Cultural, recreational, and social events are scheduled for residential students. Some financial aid is available.

The largest centers are located at private universities—Denver, Duke, Johns Hopkins and Northwestern. However, several other states have joined the Talent Search Program, like Iowa and Utah. Summer programs have been developed to bring gifted adolescents together for academic and social experiences.

In a look back at the SMPY program, Stanley (1989) discusses the impressive growth of this program. The growth from a handful of students to over 100,000 youngsters has been remarkable. Stanley makes a plea for more of a grass-roots movement in both public and private secondary education that would enable more students with exceptional math and/or verbal abilities to access supplemental academic programs.

Much of the research on acceleration has come from the SMPY program and its satellites. Founder of the program, Julian Stanley, is a strong proponent of educational acceleration (1978). The intent of the SMPY program and others based on it has been to foster as much educational acceleration as is deemed appropriate, with major input from the students themselves. Not only is such an approach cost effective for public education (Proctor et al., 1988), but it is also beneficial to capable students who are eager to move quickly through the educational system to earlier creative accomplishment. Examination of the effects of acceleration on social and emotional adjustment indicates that students who participated in the SMPY program had enhanced feelings of self-worth and accomplishment, retained a more positive attitude toward education, displayed less egotism and arrogance, and had more time to explore hobbies and career options (Stanley, 1976). Follow-up of gifted students who have participated in the SMPY program continues (Brody & Benbow, 1987; Stanley, 1985).

permit exceptionally bright students to skip one or more years of high school entirely and enter college early (Brody et al., 1990).

INNOVATION AND DEVELOPMENT	Asked in a recent interview to identify some significant events in gifted education in the last decade, Gallagher cited Guilford's Structure of Intellect Model and innovations in curriculum development spawned by the National Science Foundation—both contributions of the sixties. "The field of gifted," he noted, "has been running on the intellectual capital that was produced 20 years ago or more and what we're looking for now is some set of new discoveries or ideas or concepts that will be fit for the 1980s" (Wolf, 1981, p. 26). Unfortunately, we still lack definitive answers for many questions.

What Are the Most Effective Delivery Patterns for Serving the Gifted?

There is a need to examine the wide variety of program modes for the gifted and identify those patterns that are most successful for various types of gifted students. Should efforts be made to develop more self-contained programs? Is acceleration an option that should be more widely used? What are the variables to consider when planning programs? Can we relate the level of achievement of gifted students to the special services they received? What are the attitudes and perceptions of students in special programs? There are few studies examining these important questions. One interesting work is the survey of Cox, Daniel, and Boston (1985) of programs for the gifted.

What Is Appropriate Education for the Highly Gifted?

Early studies indicated more adjustment problems for the highly gifted, a finding confirmed in recent studies that point to some social and/or emotional problems among highly gifted youngsters (Dahlberg, 1992; Webb, Meckstroth, & Tolan, 1983). Longitudinal studies are needed that will examine the educational needs of this population so that alternatives can be provided within the public and private sectors. It seems certain that computer technology will play an increasingly significant role in meeting the educational needs of the gifted.

What Are the Critical Components of Effective Teacher Training for Those Working with Gifted Students?

More information is needed about teacher characteristics and appropriate training experiences for those who work with the gifted. Mulhern and Ward (1983) and Rogers (1989) have made attempts to identify important characteristics of the teacher for the gifted and to develop a list of appropriate training experiences. Much more remains to be done.

What Are the Prospects for Long-Term Continuous Support for Gifted Programs?

There is strong national momentum for providing educational services for the gifted (Cox, Daniel, & Boston, 1985). Part-time and full-time programs for the gifted abound. The number of teacher training programs is increasing. Professional and advocacy groups are better organized than ever. The future will be significantly affected by prospects for national funding to help support leadership training, systematic inservice training, research and development, and demonstration programs. The importance of monitoring federal funding for such projects cannot be overstated.

Future Directions

There are many significant developments that will influence the direction of this field. Prominent among them are the role of technology, the need for counseling of the gifted, and the role of parents.

Counseling the Gifted.   Counseling services in the schools are typically devoted to problem children or those who need support services to succeed. Yet gifted children have a great need for guidance also. They may face difficult career and occupational decisions, a lack of adult models, and uneven personal development and social mobility (Webb et al., 1983). School counselors should involve them in both individual and group counseling activities in order to attend to their concerns (Landrum, 1987). School counselors can also serve as an information source for teachers, administrators, and parents; and they can contribute to the field of gifted education through research and program evaluation.

In addition, teachers of the gifted should be competent in basic counseling skills. They are in a central position to focus on affective development and to provide supportive counseling, career information, and referrals to professionals for more extensive help. Buescher (1987) recommends a proactive approach to counsel and support the growth of gifted adolescents, and Silverman (1986) emphasizes the importance of career counseling for the gifted, especially gifted girls. With increasing efforts to provide appropriate education to the gifted and talented, counseling that is more specifically oriented to the unique needs of this population should become more widely available.

Parents of the Gifted.   In recent years parents of the gifted have become more active and involved in their children's education. Their involvement has been on two levels—organizing parent groups to be advocates for all gifted children and participating in the education of their own children.

There are growing numbers of parent advocacy groups around the country (Dettmer, 1991; Schatz, 1991). Many have become advocates for gifted education in general, as well as for their own gifted children. Parent activism has been a major factor in increasing funding, promoting local programs, and encouraging state consultants for the gifted to assume more active roles. Increasingly, parents are recognizing their role as agents of change in the school and community and are becoming concerned about improving their advocacy skills. Assistance has been provided in some regions through parent leadership groups, which cooperate with state consultants to offer education in advocacy techniques (Schatz, 1991). Workshops in which parents role-play to become sensitized to the complexities of decision making have been particularly successful (Wolf, 1987; Wolf & Stephens, 1984).

In addition, an examination of current journals of gifted education reveals many examples of parent involvement in the educational process (Wolf & Stephens, 1984). Parents seem to be interested in working as team members with educators in order to meet their children's unique needs. Teachers are sometimes reluctant to view parents as resources; a common cry is, "All parents think their children are gifted." However, as noted earlier, studies have indicated that parents are an excellent and fairly accurate source of information, and parent identification of gifted children has proved to be more accurate than that of teachers (Ciha et al., 1974; Wolf, 1989).

Nonetheless, many parents of gifted children are bewildered and frustrated about issues at home and school and want to develop basic parenting skills, as well as specific strategies for encouraging learning at home and making good use of community resources. They often feel inadequate in their management of their children and uncertain about what is appropriate programming or how to stimulate and challenge their children in and out of school. Just as schools have become more involved in educating parents of children with disabilities, there is a need for them to establish educational programs for parents of the gifted. There are, in fact, increasing numbers of such programs (Wolf & Stephens, 1984) under the sponsorship of parent groups, school districts, and universities. There is actually much to be learned from the advocacy models used to involve parents of children with disabilities in the educational process (Wolf & Stephens, 1990). Some help is also available in written form; an examination of the literature yields several current works for parents (Alvino, 1985; Webb et al., 1983). To meet the expanding role of the educator in parent education, there is also a need for increased training of professionals to deal with parents' concerns.

SUMMARY

Support of programs for the gifted has varied in response to social, political, and economic conditions. Although all gifted children are not yet identified and appropriately served, there is currently a high level of interest in meeting the needs of this population, and a wide variety of programs can be found nationwide. Professionals acknowledge some critical problems in identifying the gifted, especially those from culturally different environments, the gifted who are disabled, and gifted underachievers.

No precise definition of giftedness is widely accepted. A major problem is deciding what intelligence is. Terman defined intelligence as the ability to acquire and manipulate concepts. Guilford analyzed it in terms of three dimensions of performance: operation, content, and product. He included intelligence as measured by tests and divergent thinking. Torrance, on the other hand, stressed creative thinking ability as a criterion for giftedness and attributed to it fluency of ideas, flexibility, originality, and elaboration. The federal government's current definition says the gifted and talented possess "demonstrated or potential abilities that give evidence of high performance capability in areas such as intellectual, creative, specific academic, leadership ability, or in the performing and visual arts." Renzulli has identified some problems with this definition; he defines giftedness as a combination of three factors—above-average ability, task commitment, and creativity.

Many factors contribute to giftedness; they include heredity, prenatal and perinatal care, and early childhood environment. The gifted and talented exhibit individual as well as group differences; the highly creative may be very different from the highly intelligent, for example, and the highly gifted may present unique problems and needs.

Major assessment techniques used to identify the gifted and talented include intelligence and achievement tests; creativity tests; and teacher, parent, peer, and self-evaluation. Talent in an academic area can be evaluated with standardized tests and/or direct observation. Two instruments used to assess creativity and giftedness are the Torrance Tests of Creative Thinking and the Renzulli-Hartman Scales. Special efforts are being made to identify the culturally different gifted. Similar efforts need to be made to identify gifted females, the gifted who are disabled, and gifted underachievers.

The range of services to broaden the learning opportunities for the gifted should include community resources and extracurricular activities. Some services need to be

1. Provide a wide variety and level of instructional materials.

2. Emphasize ideas, concepts, theories, principles, relationships, and generalizations.

3. Provide opportunities for elementary-age students to learn and use research methods.

4. Provide learning experiences that go beyond the basic curriculum and beyond the classroom walls by using mentors in the community.

5. Provide access to computers and encourage students to learn to do their own programming.

6. Develop an affective curriculum to help gifted students understand themselves.

7. Provide training and support for teachers and parents of the gifted.

8. Encourage participation in enrichment and extension activities such as debate, chess, Future Problem Solving, Invent America, etc.

9. Use high-level questioning that encourages gifted students to organize, synthesize, evaluate, and transform their knowledge.

10. Provide many opportunities for interaction with intellectual peers across ages.

TIPS FOR HELPING

provided outside the scope of the regular school program. Within the school system various arrangements exist for serving the gifted: special grouping and tracking, early school admission and grade acceleration programs, advanced placement classes, and concurrent enrollment programs.

There is no firm agreement on the characteristics that make teachers successful with the gifted. However, there are some personal characteristics that seem to be critical: a high level of intellectual achievement, good interpersonal skills, a secure personality, intellectual curiosity, and leadership ability. Additional professional characteristics needed are a strong command of subject matter, good information handling skills, diagnostic and prescriptive teaching skills, and program development and leadership skills.

The curriculum for students who are gifted should stress conceptual, creative, and critical thinking, as well as social adjustment, responsibility, and leadership. Bloom's taxonomy and Renzulli's Enrichment Triad Model provide frameworks for teaching the gifted. Other options include independent study contracting, the use of bibliotherapy, mentor programs, and group work with peers. Attention needs to be paid to counseling the gifted, encouraging career decisions, and involving parents in gifted programs.

STUDY QUESTIONS

1. Describe briefly the three major historical movements in the education of children and youth who are gifted, and relate each to the social, economic, and political forces existing at the time.

2. "Giftedness is relative to a given society's values at certain times in its history." Explain this statement and describe its effect on the accepted definition of giftedness.

3. Contrast commonly accepted views of intelligence and creativity. Consider the positions of Terman, Guilford, Gardner, Khatena, and Torrance.

4. What three factors seem to interact in contributing to giftedness?

5. Based on your reading here, generate a comprehensive list of characteristics of the gifted. Consider the opening vignettes of Carrie and Max as you generate your list.

6. Based on the literature, what are some characteristics of individuals who are highly creative?

7. Discuss the interindividaul and intraindividual differences of children who are gifted.

8. What are some problems in the assessment of giftedness in very young children? What alternatives to traditional intelligence tests might be used?

9. What are some problems in the assessment of culturally different gifted children? of gifted children who are disabled? of gifted females? of gifted underachievers?

10. Contrast direct and indirect service provisions for the gifted.

11. Identify and discuss briefly the following intervention methods for the gifted: independent study contracting, bibliotherapy, mentor programs, group interaction techniques, early admission, and concurrent enrollment.

12. Based on your reading about the personal and professional characteristics of successful teachers of the gifted, develop and defend your own list of important characteristics for teachers of the gifted.

13. Why is a differential curriculum important for gifted students? Base your answer on the learning characteristics of the gifted.

14. Clark argues that instruction for the gifted should emphasize the higher levels of Bloom's taxonomy (analysis, synthesis, evaluation). Explain and defend or refute this position.

15. Identify the various administrative arrangements commonly used in serving the gifted, and cite some advantages and disadvantages of each.

13

Pamela J. Winton
Frank Porter Graham Child
Development Center
University of North Carolina
at Chapel Hill

Families of Children with Disabilities

In this chapter you will learn about

- the shifting perspectives on families of children with disabilities

- a rationale for working with these families

- the family components of Public Law 94–142, the Education for All Handicapped Children Act, and Public Law 99–457, which amended the act

- key concepts and theories about families of children with disabilities

- ways in which family needs vary according to the age of the child with disabilities

- skills needed by professionals to work in collaboration with families

Life for Susan and Jerry Price is the best that it has been in six years. Susan attributes the current state of affairs to several factors, the major one being that Mark, their 6-year-old son born with spina bifida, has not been hospitalized in the last 2 years for emergency surgery. He now is happily attending preschool 5 days a week.

But, Susan laments, why can't time stand still? As soon as everything is set, it is time to make a change. Mark has turned 6 and will begin his public school education in a few months. The question is, In which classroom and in which school? Susan is sold on mainstreaming as it operates in Mark's preschool and on the concept of mainstreaming in general, but mainstreaming in the public schools is an entirely different matter. Because the Prices' neighborhood school is not accessible to children with handicaps, Mark would have to ride a bus to a newer elementary school. Susan has visited this school and was not pleased with what she found—a principal who seemed lukewarm to the idea of having his school function as a repository for children in wheelchairs and a resource room teacher overwhelmed by children from impoverished homes. Mark definitely would need the assistance of a resource teacher, and Susan feels she and Mark need the kind of support she received from Mark's preschool teachers. Could they possibly get such support in that school?

Old fears have resurfaced as the transition to public school draws close. How will the other children react to Mark? Susan remembers how difficult it was for them both when Mark started at his preschool. The other children had been afraid of his wheelchair and his braces. Susan remembers how quickly and sensitively the staff dealt with the situation, letting Mark explain how his equipment worked and talk about his many stays in the hospital. How would Mark's adjustment to a public school classroom be handled? The principal hadn't mentioned even planning for this.

All of these things frighten Susan. She is distressed that her options are so limited. She has not given up; she plans to meet with the director of special education for the school district, if possible, to express her concerns. She plans to investigate her neighborhood school to see just how inaccessible it would be for Mark. She would consider special class placement, she says, if this seemed most appropriate. It does not matter what they call it—TMR, EMR, mainstreaming. Susan is looking for the best for Mark, and she plans to fight if necessary to get what she feels is the most appropriate public school placement.

Families who have a child with a disability report numerous challenges and triumphs associated with the unique status of their child. Each family's story is different, yet one of the common themes is the inevitable relationship with schools and other public service agencies that provide assistance to their child and family. Sometimes the family-professional relationship is collaborative and mutually supportive; in other cases it is adversarial. Never before in the history of special education has this relationship received as much attention.

We are standing at an important crossroads, with opportunities to create stronger ties between schools, communities, and families. Recent legislative and policy initiatives provide states and communities with incentives and support to reconceptualize the traditional family-professional relationship. Educators will play an important leadership role in defining this new relationship. Families like the Prices stand to benefit from these new directions.

This is not the first time that education has spearheaded new initiatives related to working with families. In the late seventies, Bronfenbrenner (1979) focused our attention on the importance of providing educational services to children with disabilities within an ecological framework, which includes family as a significant component. The translation of that concept into actual practice is now evident in the innovative approaches (i.e., functional assessment, community-based programs, and integrated therapy) described in this volume. The key to the success of these practices is the participation and collaboration of families. This means that skills related to working with families have become more important than ever for educators. It also means replacing traditional approaches to parent involvement with approaches that are in keeping with current knowledge and research.

The purpose of this chapter is to describe the redefinition of practices for working with families of exceptional children. The chapter consists of two major sections: (1) an examination of how special educators have approached families in the recent past and the factors that are bringing about a shift in professional assumptions and practices and (2) an overview of the knowledge, attitudes, and skills that special educators need to work effectively with families.

A HISTORICAL PERSPECTIVE

Today, most children with disabilities live at home with their families. This is a radical departure from the past when placement of persons with disabilities in residential institutions was common. Families need support from local communities to meet the needs of their children. Some consensus as to how best to support children and families has evolved over the last 20 years. Where we have been and where we are now is the subject of this section of this chapter.

Public Law 94–142: A Legal Mandate for Parent Involvement

One of the essential factors to a family's being able to adequately care for their child with a disability in the home is access to comprehensive educational services. In 1975 all families of school-aged children were guaranteed that right through the passage of the Education for All Handicapped Children Act, Public Law 94–142. Not only did this legislation mandate a free and appropriate education for all children, but the law also empowered parents of children with disabilities to decide what constituted a uniquely appropriate education for their child. (In 1990, P.L. 94-142 was reauthorized in the form of Public Law 101-476, the Individuals with Disabilities Education Act, or IDEA, and with further reauthorization in 1991 as Public Law 102–119).

Unfortunately, despite the intent of P.L. 94–142 to promote an active, decision-making role for parents in defining their child's Individualized Educational Plan (IEP), generally speaking, parent involvement has not been encouraged or practiced. Research suggests that most IEPs are written prior to the IEP meeting, giving parents little chance to contribute to their development meaningfully (Brinckerhoff & Vincent, 1986). Research related to professionals' attitudes toward parent participation in team decision making suggests that professionals promote and encourage passive, rather than active, roles for parents (Turnbull & Turnbull, 1990). Despite due process procedures that provide parents who are dissatisfied with the IEP process with a mechanism for challenging professionals, the outcomes are mixed. There is no doubt that due process has resulted in school systems' becoming more responsive to students' needs; however, it has costs for both schools and families. These include the financial costs related to legal and consultation fees and staff and family time, and emotional costs related to anxiety and escalation of conflictual school-family relationships (Turnbull & Turnbull, 1990).

The intent of the law was for parents to be active and empowered agents working in partnerships with professionals to ensure the best possible education for children with disabilities; however, the law's promise has not been fulfilled. What has developed in many situations is an adversarial relationship between families and schools. For many parents, involvement has been severely limited. When, like the Prices in the opening vignette, families pushed for different and more active roles, they were seen as troublemakers. As one administrator put it, "When a parent makes an appointment at the central office, we make sure we have our lawyer there." This state of affairs raises questions about the nature of change and to what extent a "top down" approach to policy implementation is adequate, as opposed to a "street level" approach, which involves active decision-making roles for traditionally powerless individuals such as local administrators, and families (Peck, 1992). As one parent put it, "You cannot mandate sensitivity, and that is what working with families is all about."

Recent Policy and Legislative Initiatives

The opportunity to create a different type of relationship with families has presented itself through several recent federal policy and legislative initiatives. Special education restructuring, school reform initiatives that provide parents with opportunities for increased decision-making authority, and the passage of Public Law 99–457 in 1986 (provision of services to children aged 3 to 5) have all contributed to the new direction. There are several features of these recent initiatives that are especially significant.

Family Support as a Legitimate Emphasis.　There is a growing acceptance that the conditions of children's lives and their futures rest on the well-being of families and that community institutions such as schools have an important role in supporting families (National Commission on Children, 1991). It is now recognized that without the support and collaboration of families, schools cannot have a substantial effect on the futures of children, especially those whose families have limited resources and multiple unmet needs. To build collaborative relationships with families, schools must support families' efforts to provide a stable and nurturing learning environment for their children. Sometimes this means addressing priorities of families that go beyond the typical educational goals created for children.

For the first time in history, broad-based support for families is considered a legitimate emphasis for public schools. In some places, schools are being restructured to include comprehensive community-based health clinics to serve families who otherwise cannot obtain health care (Melaville & Blank, 1991). In general, there are increasing efforts to create school environments where families feel welcomed, empowered, and supported through a variety of programs that meet family needs. This is in contrast to the limited roles traditionally available to parents as classroom volunteers, fund-raisers, and participants in twice yearly parent-teacher conferences. It is recognized that when schools support and recognize family goals, then families are more likely to support school efforts because these efforts reflect joint priorities.

Family Empowerment and Local Autonomy. As mentioned earlier, the intended empowerment of families by P.L. 94-142 did not fully materialize. Recent initiatives provide an opportunity for families to assume a more active decision-making role at both policy and program levels within schools and at an individual level related to the needs of their own child and family. There are two distinct initiatives that promote this role for families. One is the emphasis on site-based management that has emerged from the school reform movement. Site-based management (sometimes called school-based management) gives parents and school staff an important role in the governance and day-to-day operations of local schools, through membership on school management teams. Decisions made by these teams affect school budgets, curriculum, staffing patterns, and other areas that in the past were independent of parent input (David, 1989). As site-based management becomes more widespread, it is critical to ensure that parents of children with disabilities are adequately represented on such school management teams so that decisions made are in the best interests of *all* children (Strain & Smith, 1992).

The second initiative is the 1986 legislation (P.L. 99–457) mentioned earlier. There are two parts to this legislation. It expanded Part B of P.L. 94–142, which covers children with disabilities defined as school-aged (for most states 3-21 years); and it added a new part, Part H (see chapter 3). Part H provides states with incentives for extending services to infants and toddlers with disabilities and their families.

Public Law 99–457 is based on certain assumptions related to family support (Dunst, Trivette, & Deal, 1988; McGonigel, Kaufmann, & Johnson, 1991; Shelton, Jeppson, & Johnson, 1987). The key points underlying these assumptions are as follows (Winton & Bailey, in press).

- *Family-centered*: The family is the constant in the child's life while the service systems and personnel within those systems may be involved only episodically.
- *Ecologically based*: The interrelatedness of the various contexts that surround the child and family need to be considered when providing services.

- *Culturally sensitive*: Families have different cultural and ethnic backgrounds and traditions. Families reflect diversity in their views and expectations of themselves, of their children, and of professionals. Services should be provided in ways that are sensitive to these variations and consistent with family values and beliefs.
- *Enabling and empowering*: Services should foster a family's independence, skills, and sense of competence and worth.
- *Priority-based*: A "priority-based" philosophy starts with a family's expressed concerns and helps families identify and obtain assistance according to their priorities.
- *Coordinated service delivery*: Resources from a variety of informal and formal community sources should be coordinated, and information about those resources should be easily accessible to families.
- *Normalized*: Programs work to promote the integration of the child and the family within the community.
- *Collaborative*: Services should be planned, implemented, and evaluated through collaboration between parents and professionals.

One of the ways that the family-centered and interagency coordination principles have been made concrete for infants/toddlers and their families is through the Individualized Family Service Plan (IFSP). The Part H regulations state that the intervention plan developed through the IFSP process should be based on family resources and priorities, with families having the ultimate decision-making authority regarding services deemed appropriate for their child. Each family has the right to the services of a service coordinator to assist the family in accessing services and information. An additional feature of this law is the fact that much discretion is left to each state in terms of precisely how the law is implemented. State and local interagency coordinating councils, which include family representatives, plan for implementation of the legislation.

Although Part H applies only to infants and toddlers with disabilities and their families, the principles underlying the family support and empowerment movement apply to all service professionals who work with families across the life span. Resistance to these new approaches, which is sometimes evident in public school settings, is likely to be significantly challenged by families like the Prices who have been supported and empowered in the early intervention system. They are not likely to accept limited options for involvement in their children's programming.

NEW ROLES FOR SPECIAL EDUCATORS

The new approaches that broaden the definition of parent involvement also redefine the special educator's role in respect to families and other professionals. Rather than being experts who tell parents what they should do to further educational goals decided by professionals, special educators now have a collaborative role: they are expected to listen and understand the family's priorities and concerns. Also, as integrated and mainstreamed programs become more prevalent means of service delivery, special educators are expected to form partnerships with those in other disciplines. Thus, consultation skills become a necessary part of the expertise of special educators. Finally, many of the new initiatives emphasize a "street level" approach to policy implementation, with expanded opportunities for direct service providers to assume leadership positions whether through membership on a school-based management team or a local interagency coordinating council. As a result, special educators are expected to have skills in group dynamics and communication. Collaboration with families requires knowledge that extends beyond that which is required for working with children with special needs. This section will describe the following areas related to working with families in which special educators should demonstrate knowledge:

1. Concepts and theories related to family functioning and development
2. Parental rights under the law
3. Community resources and services for children and families
4. Attitudes and skills related to developing collaborative relationships with families

Understanding Concepts and Theories About Families

A frequent complaint expressed by families is that professionals do not understand what life is like for them, and thus, have only a vague idea as to what families need and want. Theories and models of family functioning posited by psychiatrists (Minuchin, 1974), sociologists (McCubbin & Patterson, 1983; Olson, Russell, & Sprenkle, 1983), and family therapists (Selvini, Boscolo, Cecchin, & Prata, 1980) help us understand the complexity of families and the many ways in which families function. Appreciation of these many variations is important to developing a collaborative relationship with a variety of families.

Families Vary in Membership.   What is a family? This deceptively simple question raises significant issues for professionals. Demographic information reported in Hanson and Lynch (1992) indicates that the "traditional" two-parent family represents a minority in our country. Alternative family structures—including single parent, step, blended, adoptive, foster, grandparent, and same-sex partners rearing children—are increasing. Perhaps the most helpful way of defining families is to rely on each family's own definition of the persons who are committed to providing support and care for one another. The implication of family variability for special educators is the importance of thinking broadly when considering who might be included in decision-making and support activities related to the child.

Each Family Fulfills Certain Functions in Unique Ways.   Every family has certain basic functions that it must fulfill. Turnbull, Summers, and Brotherson (1984) describe nine basic family functions: economic, physical, rest and recuperation, socialization, self-definition, affection, guidance, educational, and vocational. These functions are assumed to be essential for every family. What varies is how each family addresses the functions. For instance, every family needs some source of income. The way economic resources are secured, however, varies considerably across families. Some families rely on food stamps and public housing, some will earn money in jobs, and others live on family money or income from investments. By seeking to understand how a family typically meets its needs, professionals come to understand what is important for individual families and how to provide services that fit within the family's context.

The family is the constant in the child's life.

In addition, recognition that there are multiple family functions helps professionals realize that if parents are asked to spend too much time on any one function, they will have less time for the others. For example, asking a father to spend an hour a day in home follow-up of school goals and objectives (an educational function) means he will have less time to spend on other functions such as rest and recuperation or recreation.

Families Vary in Needs and Resources.   Families also differ in their needs for support, how much they want support, and their resources to solve problems. Some families want information, while others need financial assistance or help in teaching their child at home. Some want to be heavily involved in working with their child, while others prefer not to be so involved. Some families have many resources; others have few. By seeking to determine individual family needs and the extent to which families want to be involved in services, professionals are more likely to develop a trusting and collaborative relationship with families and to provide services that are individualized. By building on existing resources within the family, professionals help families see that they can solve problems themselves, rather than relying totally on professionals.

Families Define Events in Different Ways.   "One man's ceiling is another man's floor" is one way of expressing the variations in how a single event may be perceived and defined by different people. Some of the original research on this topic was conducted by the sociologist Reuben Hill (1958). He was interested in the differences between families in their responses to natural disasters. He found that some families were able to recover from a disaster and in fact were stronger than before, while other families were devastated beyond recovery. What was significant about his findings was the role that perceptions played in a family's adaptation to crisis.

Recent research by Affleck and associates adds to our understanding of differences in coping strategies (Affleck & Tennen, 1991; Affleck, Tennen, & Rowe, 1991). In research with families of very sick, premature infants, they found that babies whose mothers, on their hospital discharge, were more optimistic about their baby's future outcome were healthier at follow-up two years later than babies whose mothers were less optimistic (Affleck & Tennen, in press). This finding could not be explained by differences in the groups in terms of the babies' risk status measured before discharge. What is interesting about this finding is the implications for the professional stance toward "denial." In the interests of making sure that families face reality, educators

Some families are able to provide substantial support and encouragement for their child's efforts.

have been known to counter parents' hopes with warnings about not expecting too much or being unrealistic about what is possible. We now have a better understanding of the importance of listening to and respecting families' hopes and dreams. Using the family's vision for their child's future as a starting point for planning interventions is a powerful strategy for engaging families in the educational process.

Families Differ in Cultural Style and Values.   Values frame much of what we say and do, and they shape the decisions we make in all aspects of our lives. Based in the culture within which we are reared, values constitute one of the most fundamental dimensions of family functioning. Understanding the variety in cultural style and personal value systems is essential for any practicing professional. Professionals who do not understand a family's values may recommend strategies or provide services that are inconsistent with family beliefs and priorities. When goals and services are matched with family values, parents are more likely to trust professionals.

Families Across the Life Span

In seeking to understand families, it is important to recognize that a child with a disability is a lifelong responsibility. Several theorists have developed models of the stages or phases through which families pass in rearing a child with disabilities. Others have addressed the difficulties associated with transitions between phases or stages.

Families use different coping strategies at different life stages.

Tseng and McDermott (1979) describe 5 stages in the life of a family: the primary family (early stages of marriage), the childbearing family, the child-rearing family, the maturing family (children in adolescence and young adulthood), and the contracting family (adult children, aging spouses, declining health, loss of a family member). One way to look at the stages in family life is as a series of relatively calm plateaus punctuated by transition events that are frequently a source of family stress. These events require the family to make certain modifications in their established routines and to renegotiate roles in order to adapt to the new stage.

Transitions are even more difficult when there is a family member with a disability. Wikler, Wasow, and Hatfield (1981) identify 10 critical periods in the development of families with children with mental retardation. Five of these represent landmarks in normal development (walking, talking, beginning of school, onset of puberty, and 21st birthday). These periods are crises because they often draw attention to ways that the development of the child with disabilities differs from that of other children. The other 5 critical periods may occur at any age. They include the following: when the child is identified as having disabilities, whenever placement decisions occur, when younger siblings surpass the skills of the child with disabilities, when unusual behavior or health crises occur, and when guardianship and long-term care are decided. What follows is a discussion of the unique needs of families of children with disabilities at three stages of child development.

The Family with an Infant or Preschooler with Disabilities.

Childbearing years are exciting times for almost every family. Parents build up tremendous expectations of what their children will be like, even before their birth. The early childhood years are the time when children accomplish major developmental landmarks. In the space of 5 or 6 years, they go from a seemingly helpless newborn to a being who walks, controls a complex symbol system known as language, and manages almost every self-help task.

The early childhood years are the time when many children with moderate to severe disabling conditions are identified. Some children are identified at birth, particularly those with obvious physical impairments or chromosomal disorders. Others are identified in the early years when they show delays in attaining developmental landmarks.

One of the greatest needs of families with infants or preschoolers with disabilities is support in coping with the realization that their child has a disabling condition. Another important need is assistance in identifying appropriate services for their children. Parents of school-age children deal primarily with one agency—the public schools. Services for younger children, however, are more diverse and fragmented. Although IDEA mandates services for preschoolers, the way that services are provided varies considerably from state to state. For parents of infants, the situation is more complex. Families interact with many different service providers: mental health agencies, social service agencies, public schools, physicians, therapists, private programs, church-sponsored programs, and organizations such as the Association for Retarded Citizens or cerebral palsy hospitals.

When parents can find an agency to meet all of their needs, they themselves must serve as advocates and decision makers for their children, as the Price family did. The problem is that many families may not know how to evaluate the options: Should we keep our infant at home, or should he be in a program of some sort? Is mainstreaming an appropriate option for our child? Our therapist says she needs to see our child twice a week, but is it worth the expense? These questions are always difficult to answer. They are particularly difficult when there are a myriad of agencies with little communication among themselves, and no one to take a leadership role as advocate and "broker" for families. The stipulation in the Part H legislation that families should be assisted by a service coordinator addresses this problem.

The Family with a School-Age Child.   Families of school-age children with disabilities continue to need social-emotional, instrumental, and informational support, although the nature, form, and direction of that support generally change over time. There are also some needs that are unique to the school years. As opposed to the early childhood years, when parents had to deal with a multitude of agencies and programs, services at this age are generally provided by the public schools. Schools are mandated to provide almost all necessary services, with the exception of health care, for children with disabilities. This situation is both a blessing and a curse. When school systems are appropriate advocates for families and provide a comprehensive program of services for children, it is a blessing. It is a curse when school systems resist providing comprehensive or appropriate services, because families generally have nowhere else to go. Their options are to accept the services offered, fight for what they and their child need, or pay for private services. The Price family is struggling with these issues as Mark makes the transition to the public schools.

The school years are particularly difficult for some parents whose children are not formally identified or labeled as having a disability until they are 5 or older. Most children with moderate or severe disabilities have been identified before they enter public school, but the majority of children with mild disabilities are not identified until they enter school and are unable to meet customary age-level expectations. Included in this group are many children labeled as educable mentally handicapped, learning disabled, or emotional disabled. Also, many children with mild hearing or visual problems are not identified until their teachers realize that these children cannot see the chalkboard or follow directions adequately.

Very often, parents suspect a problem prior to their child entering school. Although the diagnostic and labeling process may be a difficult one for these parents, it may be a relief for them to have documentation of what they suspected. Other families have no idea that their child cannot perform up to expectations. For these parents the identification and labeling process is very difficult.

The diagnostic and labeling period is a time when parents need considerable support. Unfortunately, most school systems are not prepared to offer this support. In contrast, agencies and systems that serve younger children with disabilities are more sensitive to family needs for support and counseling, and they often have staff members responsible for facilitating that support. Public schools are typically more child focused than family focused. The process of informing and supporting parents often is left either to special education teachers, who may not be trained in working with families, or to a school psychologist, who may not have expertise in the area of children with disabilities. Thus, families of school-age children often have to seek out and establish their own support systems.

During the school-age years, parents of children with disabilities are often faced with reframing their expectations for their child. For example, during this period many families become aware that their children will not be able to succeed in college or that they have difficulties that cannot be "cured" by the schools. It becomes apparent that the child will have to cope with a disability throughout adult life.

Although it can happen at any age, it is during the school-age years that the self-concept of many children with disabilities is eroded. It may be during this period that a younger sibling matches or exceeds the academic performance of the child with disabilities. It is during the school-age years, when children's peer relations are so critical, that children with disabilities experience rejection or overt teasing or hostility from their typically developing peers, particularly during the late elementary and early junior high school years. Thus, parents of school-age children with disabilities bear the extra responsibility of helping their child develop and maintain a positive self-concept.

Finally, it is during the school-age years that most children reach puberty. This developmental milestone is challenging for all parents. For many parents of children with disabilities, it is a traumatic period. Puberty is a clear sign that the child is becoming an adult in a physical sense. Maturity accentuates any delays in academic or social development. Many parents have not viewed their children with disabilities as sexual beings. Puberty forces them to address a host of important issues regarding their child's sexual development as well as related concerns about the future, such as vocational and independent living possibilities for their child.

The Family with a Handicapped Adult.   The transition from childhood to adulthood is a time of mixed emotions for almost all families. A person's 21st birthday is generally celebrated in symbolic recognition of the passage to independence. Even parents who are happy to see their children reach adulthood have feelings of sadness and loss.

For families with children with disabilities, this transition can be especially difficult. First of all, parents find themselves in the same situation as when their child was very young: they must deal with a variety of service providers and no one will take a leadership or advocacy role for their child. Since public schools are no longer responsible after age 21, parents with adult sons or daughters who have disabilities must deal with groups such as social service agencies and vocational rehabilitation centers on their own.

The specific problems encountered during this phase depend upon the level of disabling condition. However, most families' concerns center on employment, independent living, social/recreational outlets, and planning for the future. Since adults in our society are generally expected to work and contribute to the economy, one responsibility of parents is to help their children seek and secure appropriate opportunities for employment. Many parents have mixed feelings about what is best for their child with disabilities. Typical of the questions asked during this stage is this: Should my child, who is moderately retarded, work in a sheltered workshop with other persons with disabilities, or should our goal be competitive employment? In many ways a sheltered workshop seems safer in that the person with disabilities will be accepted by peers and staff and receives training and work assignments commensurate with skill level. However, there will be fewer opportunities to make a decent salary and interact with nondisabled peers. Competitive employment provides an opportunity for the young adult to participate in normal work experiences and to earn competitive wages. However, it also involves competition (with other workers), and employers may not provide adequate training. Moreover, co-workers may not readily accept the employee with disabilities, and so social interactions may be less frequent.

Another major concern for families is living arrangements. Many individuals with disabilities live alone and care for themselves, but for others, placement in a public facility, such as a local group home, may be the best alternative. A third, smaller group of individuals with significant health and physical management problems will require lifelong care in a restrictive environment.

Parents are also concerned about their child's long-term social development. Dating, marriage, and childbearing are transitions that often pose difficulties for the family of an adolescent or young adult with a disabling condition. One problem is the individual's judgment or ability to accept responsibility. Appropriate use of free time is another problem: many persons with disabilities have not learned to participate in enjoyable and age-appropriate recreational activities. Recreational opportunities available in the community may need to be sought out and/or developed.

Finally, there is the problem of long-term care and guardianship. Many adults with disabilities are capable of making their own decisions and seeking out their own resources, but others will never be able to accept this level of responsibility. As parents begin to realize that their child with disabilities will probably outlive them, they are faced with the issue of who will be responsible. This anxiety is particularly traumatic for parents who have had to take an active and involved role in the care of their child. Their fundamental concern is whether anyone else will devote the time and energy necessary to ensure a life of as high a quality for their child. Parents imagine their child living on the back ward of an institution or in some cold and lonely apartment with no one to love and care for him or her. They realize that service agencies do not have an emotional investment—that only individuals make emotional and enduring commitments. However, unless a family member volunteers to assume this role, parents are often hesitant to ask anyone to accept such a lifelong responsibility. Thus, this decision is a very difficult one for parents. It calls for much support and assistance.

Implications for Special Educators.   An understanding of the theories of family functioning and family life cycle help special educators recognize that different families have different needs, and the same family has different needs at different times. Research with families with nondisabled family members (Olson et al., 1983) suggests that families use different coping strategies at different life stages. Although research of this type with exceptional populations has not been carried out, one can assume that they, too, utilize different ways of coping with different transition events. The task for special educators is to support or strengthen each family's unique way of coping, offering services or programs in areas of identified need.

Understanding and Communicating Parental Rights Under Law

The legislation (P.L. 94–142 and P.L. 99–457) contains a number of requirements that reinforce the family's role in the planning and provision of services for children.

To Be Informed and Give Consent. Parents are the key persons ensuring that children receive an appropriate education. Professionals must be knowledgeable about parental rights in order to inform families of their rights. First, families have a right to be informed before schools initiate any preplacement evaluation procedures. (A complete and fair evaluation must be conducted prior to designing an individual program for a child and placing the child in a specialized classroom or program.) Parents must be informed as to what the evaluation will consist of and give their written consent before any testing can begin.

Consent as defined in Part B and Part H of IDEA means that (Turnbull & Turnbull, 1990): (1) parents have been fully informed in their native language, or in another suitable manner of communication, of all information relevant to the activity (e.g., evaluation) for which consent was sought; (2) the parents understand and agree in writing that the activity may be conducted; (3) parents understand what records (if any) that will be released and to whom; and (4) parents understand that they may revoke consent at any time. Further, parents have the right to obtain an outside evaluation by a private consultant if they are not satisfied with the evaluation provided by the school.

Confidentiality and Privacy. Parents have the right (1) to see all records related to their child, (2) to challenge the content of the records, and (3) to prevent the records from being released to anyone other than the officials authorized to collect and use the information. In addition, parents should be assured of the confidentiality of information that they share verbally and should be provided with explanations about who else and under what circumstances this information would be shared with others.

Program Planning and Due Process. As discussed in chapter 1 and mentioned earlier in this chapter, the law mandates that an IEP be written and implemented for each child with disabilities. For eligible infants and toddlers, the law mandates an IFSP. Parent participation in the development of this plan and their approval of the final plan are fundamental rights guaranteed under Part B and Part H of IDEA. If parents feel that the plan does not adequately reflect their perspectives, they have a right to appeal to another authority to serve as mediator.

Under Part B, there are a series of steps for resolving disagreements. These are known as due process. They include filing a complaint with the school agency, which leads to a formal hearing conducted by an impartial hearing officer. The law guarantees that both the school system and the family (1) may have an attorney or an educational agent present, (2) may prepare evidence and cross-examine witnesses, and (3) may obtain a verbatim record of the hearing and a written finding of facts and decisions. The hearing officer weighs all of the evidence and makes a decision. If dissatisfied, either party may request review by the state education agency. If the review is not acceptable, either party may file a civil action in either a state or a federal district court.

Under Part H, where eligible infants and toddlers and their families are concerned, states may adopt the due process procedures outlined above or develop new procedures for resolving disagreements. In addition, the Part H regulations require that states establish procedures for resolving complaints about the Part H system itself and how it is implemented in the state.

Implications for Special Educators.   There are several implications of the parental rights provisions for special educators. First, they must be informed concerning parental rights. They should be aware of the mandatory federal and state requirements and guidelines for an appropriate evaluation, as described in chapters 1 and 3 and other literature (Turnbull & Turnbull, 1990). In addition, they should be thoroughly familiar with their agency's consent forms and all state and federal requirements and procedures for resolving disputes about implementation. Simply providing written information to parents may not fulfill the intent of parental rights as guaranteed under law. Research suggests that families often are not fully aware of their rights and responsibilities under law. A study by Roit and Pfohl (1984) investigating the readability of written materials on P.L. 94–142 provided to parents in 25 states, found that the reading level is often such that the information may not be comprehensible to a large number of parents. Educators should be prepared to explain this information to parents in clear, understandable language.

Knowing Community Resources

Most families who have a child with special needs have a strong desire for information. Families tell us that getting the information they need is not easy (Winton, Turnbull, & Blacher, 1984). Programs that would help their children are here today and gone tomorrow (as grant money, administrations, and priorities change). Even the professionals in a community often have difficulty keeping abreast of current programs and services. With the current emphasis on service coordination and broad-based community support, it is more important than ever for special educators to be knowledgeable about the resources in communities.

Community service/resource listings should not be restricted to specialized programs and services. Families should be assisted and supported to become fully integrated into all community activities and programs, including art, music, after-school care, gymnastics, scouts, and other programs available for nondisabled children. It often means that YMCAs, community centers, and churches must become better informed about disabilities. One mother describes what happened when professionals did not encourage or support her in the direction of full inclusion:

> When Brian was born and we were told he had Down syndrome, we were immediately channeled into special programs. These programs were not in our neighborhood and in fact were miles from where we lived. We wanted to do what was best for Brian so we essentially dropped out of most of the neighborhood kinds of things that we had started when our older daughter had come along. Brian did not go to the neighborhood preschool, the YMCA programs, etc. When he was about four years old, we realized that we had become

totally isolated from what had been a very supportive group of neighbors and friends because of our reliance on special programs for Brian. We did an "about-face" and realized that we needed to reestablish contact with our "normal" life.

Unknowingly, the professionals encouraged us down a road that in the end was not very supportive of our entire family. (A. Wagner, personal communication, 1992)

Special educators also need to be knowledgeable about other disciplines and other educational settings. Most of the innovative approaches, such as integrated therapy, functional assessments, and transition planning, that are described in this text require collaboration across disciplines and across agencies. Special educators now perform many functions that, in the past, were considered to be the exclusive domain of another specialist. In order to assist children and families with transitions from one setting to another, special educators must be knowledgeable concerning other settings and able to converse with the professionals in those settings. In addition, special educators need to be able to explain clearly what their own expertise entails and what approach they take to intervention in order to facilitate coordination with other programs and professionals.

Families often tell us that the professionals who work with their child do not communicate with one another; therefore, the information these professionals provide to families is often contradictory and confusing. For relationships with families to work effectively, we must improve our professional relationships. The children and families we seek to serve suffer when we do not collaborate and communicate with one another at the professional level.

Developing Collaborative Relationships with Families

The amount and complexity of information this chapter has presented suggest the challenges faced by special educators who want to broaden their expertise in working with families. There are no cookbook or step-by-step procedures to ensure the development of a collaborative relationship with families. Knowledge is helpful, but the attitudes and skills discussed below are important to engaging families in a trusting, respectful, and collaborative relationship that will best serve the child's needs for an appropriate education.

Encouraging More Active Involvement of Parents. It is one thing to inform parents of their rights to be partners in the educational process; it is quite another to actively facilitate growth and development of the partnership. The first step is to truly believe that the relationship is important and worth the expenditure of time and energy. The second step is to reexamine some of the traditional structures and options that have defined parent involvement and consider alternatives. The third step is to implement some of the guidelines and strategies identified in the literature as effective in facilitating family-professional collaboration.

Informal Opportunities for Involvement. One strategy to promote development of collaborative relationships is to create informal but frequent opportunities for exchanging information between home and classroom (Winton & Turnbull, 1981). Drop-off and pickup times provide one opportunity. In instances where parents are rarely physically present, logbooks or notebooks that can be passed between home and school are effective. The positive accomplishments of children are more likely to be passed on to families when there is a frequent exchange of information. When families are only contacted at conference time or when there are problems, they are not likely to feel positive about contacts with professionals.

Formal Opportunities for Involvement.   Because many contacts with parents take place in formal meetings or during formal events such as assessments or planning conferences, it is important to consider strategies for facilitating positive family participation in those events. One strategy is to enlist parents' participation in planning the assessment and/or the planning meeting. This strategy contrasts with past procedures that warned professionals against involving parents in child assessment activities and cautioned them to distrust assessment information provided by parents. The general feeling was that parents overestimate their child's abilities and that they are not able to accurately recall details of their child's development.

A completely different approach and attitude toward parents' contributions to the assessment process has emerged in the current professional literature (Gradel, Thompson, & Sheehan, 1981). It is now recognized that involving families in the process of assessing their child is beneficial to all parties involved. As noted by Gradel and associates (1981), parents can provide information about their child's functioning in everyday life that is otherwise not available to professionals. Parents have expanded opportunities to observe their child and thus are more likely to notice newly developing skills.

If they are involved in the assessment process, families are more likely to subsequently contribute to the development of a service plan. Brinckerhoff and Vincent (1986) involved some families in assessing their child prior to the IEP meeting. In addition, the parents met with a professional, who described the IEP process and discussed ways in which the family's information could be contributed during the meeting. Compared to parents who had not participated in these preparatory activities, experimental families contribute more in the IEP meeting, made more decisions, and generated more of the final goals. More decisions were characterized as joint decisions, and more home programming suggestions evolved.

Examples of a checklist and an inventory, designed to assist professionals in actively involving parents in planning assessments or conferences, are provided in Tables 13–1 and 13–2. The Preassessment Planning questions in Table 13–1 were developed by Project Dakota, an early intervention program, to facilitate parental involvement in child assessment. The Inventory of Family Preferences (Turnbull & Turnbull, 1990) in Table 13–2 was designed to facilitate parental involvement in the IEP conference.

Arena assessment is an example of an integrated assessment and planning process where families can be present and actively involved. With arena assessment, as described in the early intervention literature (Wolery & Dyk, 1984), parents and an interdisciplinary group of professionals observe and participate together in joint assessment and planning. Parents' concerns and priorities direct the assessment process. They provide information, administer items if necessary, and validate the

Table 13–1
Preassessment planning

1. What questions or concerns do others have (e.g., baby-sitter, clinic, preschool)?

2. Are there other places where we should observe your child?
    Place:
    Contact Person:
    What to Observe:

3. How does your child do around other children?

4. Where would you like the assessment to take place?

5. What time of day? (The best time is when your child is alert and when working parents can be present.)

6. Are there others who should be there in addition to parents and staff?

7. What are your child's favorite toys or activities that help him or her become focused, motivated, and comfortable?

8. Which roles would you find comfortable during assessment?
    ____ a. sit beside your child
    ____ b. help with activities to explore his or her abilities
    ____ c. offer comfort and support to your child
    ____ d. exchange ideas with the facilitator
    ____ e. carry out activities to explore your child's abilities
    ____ f. prefer facilitator to handle and carry out activities with your child
    ____ g. other

Source: Project Dakota Outreach, Dakota, Inc., Eagan, MN.

child's performance by comparing it to behaviors observed at home and in other settings. A facilitator, who might be the parent if the parent chooses, engages the child using a variety of play materials and in a variety of other ways so that the professionals can observe the child's skills across different tasks and activities. The professionals and parents then develop an intervention plan based on the child's observed skills and family and child needs.

Another strategy for actively involving family members and the school-age student with disabilities in the IEP conference is provided in the McGill Acting Planning System (MAPS) (Vandercook, York, & Forest, 1989). This system provides questions that could be asked of participants in the conference. The questions are designed to stimulate everyone's contribution to setting goals and outcomes based on a family's hopes and aspirations. Questions include the following:

- What is the individual's history?
- What is your dream for the individual?
- What is your nightmare?
- Who is the individual?
- What are the individual's strengths, gifts, and abilities?

Table 13–2
Inventory of family preferences

This form is designed to be administered orally—either in person or over the phone—to a parent or guardian of the student with an exceptionality.

1. **Who would you like to have attend the meeting?** (Suggest as possibilities both parents, stepparents, grandparents, the student with the exceptionality, brothers and sisters, other family members, friends, and/or other parental and student advocates. Remind parents to choose people who are close to the student and who can help develop the IEP.)

   NAME   POSITION
   _____
   _____
   _____

2. **What school personnel do you want to attend?** (Ask if they would feel more comfortable if a small number of professionals would attend or whether they want to have feedback from several different professionals. Tell them that by law one teacher and a person responsible for providing special education services must attend. Suggest as possibilities current teachers, paraprofessionals, next year's teachers, psychologist, school social worker, counselor, occupational therapist, speech therapist, physical therapist, adaptive physical education teacher, principal, director of special education, or staff from adult programs.)

   NAME   POSITION
   _____
   _____
   _____

3. **What day of the week would be most convenient for you (and your spouse)?**
   _____

4. **What time of day should we meet?**
   _____

5. **Where would be the best place for us to have the conference?** (Suggest as possibilities the school, their home, or a community building.)
   _____

6. **How can we help with transportation and child care or is our assistance needed?**
   _____
   _____

7. **Some people like to have information about their child's educational program before the conference. Others prefer to wait until the conference to receive information. What is your preference?**

_____

_____

(If parents say they want information before the conference, ask the following; if not, go on to Number 8.)

Which of the following types of information would you like to have? (Read list.)

_____ **Evaluation reports of performance on formal tests**

_____ **Checklist that you can fill out to describe for the other participants your son or daughter's strengths and needs**

_____ **List of subjects the school personnel plan to cover on the IEP**

_____ **Summary of your child's strengths and weaknesses in each subject area**

_____ **List of the goals and objectives school personnel plan to suggest at the meeting**

_____ **Information on your legal rights**

_____ **Information on placement options**

_____ **Information on available related services**

_____ **Other:** _____

_____

_____

How would you like to receive this information?
(Suggest letters, phone calls, conferences, brochures.)

_____

_____

8. **Do you have some information that might be helpful to share with school personnel?** _____ (If they say yes, ask the following; if not, go to Number 9.)
What information do you have and how would you like to share it?

_____

_____

9. (Close by expressing your appreciation to the family, assuring them of your support and interest, and telling them that you look forward to their participation in the conference.)

1. Each family has its own unique values, beliefs, ethnic and cultural background, and its own structure. Respect and accept this diversity.

2. Individualize programs and services for families according to each family's needs, resources, and desires.

3. Respect individual family differences by allowing families to choose the level and type of involvement they have in their children's educational programs.

4. Legislative changes, policy changes, and shifting perspectives on best practice are bringing about changes in how special educators define their roles. Reexamine traditional practices and assumptions and develop skills in areas such as communication in order to work effectively with families.

- What are the individual's needs?
- What would the individual's ideal day at school look like and what must be done to make it happen?

Accepting and Respecting Individual Family Differences. The strategies described above require a willingness on the part of the professional to value and respect the family's point of view and to accept that their priorities and concerns are valid ones that should be pursued in a collaborative fashion. This contrasts with professional-driven procedures where professional expertise and knowledge of child development and disability direct the educational planning process.

However, professionals are sometimes confused about how to proceed especially in situations where family priorities seem to be in direct conflict with traditional professional values. To address this challenging topic, it is necessary to return to the assumptions discussed earlier. If we truly believe that the best way to reach children is by supporting their families, then we must try to understand the values and adaptations that families make in order to accommodate their child's disability. If we do not acknowledge and provide support at basic levels, efforts at other levels may well be in vain. Economic circumstances is one of many variables that affects family decisions. A case example from a study by Gallimore and his associates (Gallimore, Wiesner, Kaufman, & Bernheimer, 1989) illustrates the impact of desperate economic circumstances on parenting:

> A mother called the project field worker in despair because her developmentally delayed son's child-care center could no longer keep him due to his destructiveness, and she could find no other center or baby-sitter that would take him. This state of affairs put at risk the mother's effort to complete a training course that would lead to a guaranteed civil service job. The job not only meant an improved income, it also would get her off public assistance and, most importantly, provide generous medical and other employee benefits. It was not that the mother was uninterested in the cognitive development of her child; in her priorities it merely assumed a lower importance than finding a safe, inexpensive caretaking arrangement so that her job training could continue. The subsistence pressures were such she was willing to entertain temporary placement of the child in a foster home, if that was the only way she could continue her job training program. (Case 312)

If our goal is to help each child reach his or her maximum potential as a contributing member of the community, then we must understand the community context and how the child can be supported outside and beyond the school setting. Most important, we must incorporate what family members think is important into our classroom routines and intervention planning efforts (McWilliam, 1992).

SUMMARY

Working with families of children with disabilities has become increasingly important for special educators and other human services professionals. Shifting assumptions and new laws are causing professionals to become more aware of family needs and to reexamine traditional approaches to working with families. The emerging relationship is best characterized as a "partnership" involving both parents and professionals (Turnbull & Turnbull, 1990).

This chapter has provided a brief overview of the emerging partnership philosophy, giving descriptions of the knowledge and skills that professionals need to facilitate successful partnerships. Fundamental to a family-centered approach is recognition of the individuality of families and the importance of working with families as collaborators both in the design of children's services and in the identification of resources for the family. In this task, families, like the Prices described in the vignette, can be powerful allies as we work together to help children, like Mark, reach their fullest potential.

STUDY QUESTIONS

1. What factors argue for individualization of services to families?

2. Assume that you have been given the responsibility of designing a brochure and training activities to ensure that parents of children with disabilities are aware of their legal rights. What information would be included? What else could be done to help parents actively strive to achieve those rights?

3. Assume that you have been given the responsibility of helping prepare parents for participating in IEP and IFSP meetings. What information would you give?

4. Provide a rationale for providing services to families. Make sure that your rationale extends beyond legal rights.

5. What are the critical skills that a teacher of children with disabilities should develop in the area of working collaboratively with families?

14

Sharon Field
Wayne State University

Norris G. Haring
University of Washington

Transition to Work and Community Living

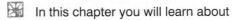   In this chapter you will learn about

- three legislative developments that have contributed significantly to preparing students with disabilities for the transition from school to work and community

- the concept of transition from school to work and community

- procedures for assessing student skills for employment and independent living

- strategies for intervention with students who have mild or moderate disabilities

- strategies for intervention with students who are severely disabled

- the rationale for instructing students who have disabilities in natural environments

Donna graduated from high school last year at the age of 19. She was referred for special education classes in the 4th grade because she was not keeping up with the rest of the class. While she was performing reasonably well in math, her reading skills were far below average. Donna had few friends and was increasingly becoming more withdrawn. Donna qualified for special education services under the learning disabilities category. She was placed in a self-contained special education classroom for students with learning disabilities, mild mental impairments, and behavior disorders.

When Donna entered junior high, she was placed in special education for reading and for one hour of resource help for her general education classes. Her general education classes included math, history, language arts, physical education, and electives such as art and chorus. Donna was quiet and still had few friends. Her grades were mostly C's and D's with an occasional F.

When she entered high school, she continued with 2 hours of resource room each day in a general education schedule. Resource room services focused on basic academic skills and tutorial assistance for her general education classes. Donna found the large high school to be overwhelming. She knew few people and she became increasingly withdrawn in class. She had difficulty completing all of the reading that was required in her social studies and language arts classes. Her parents hired a private tutor to help her. During her first semester, she received a failing grade in biology, earned a D and a C in social studies and language arts respectively, and received B's in her remaining three classes (i.e., art and her two special education classes).

Throughout high school, she continued to earn low grades and sometimes fail academic classes. She had to attend school for an extra year to earn the credits required for graduation, and so she graduated one year behind her class.

Donna has been at home for 7 months now. She has applied and interviewed for several jobs, but has never been called back after the first interview. Donna's mother claims that she is becoming increasingly argumentative. Her mother insists that Donna needs to get some help, but neither she nor Donna knows where to turn.

Unfortunately, Donna's story is not atypical of young adults with disabilities. A 1985 Lou Harris poll found that 62% of all Americans with disabilities between the ages of 16 and 64 are not working (Harris & Associates, 1986). The authors of the study concluded that "no other demographic group under age 65 of any size has such a small proportion working" (p. 47). Follow-up studies of graduates of special education programs also indicate that students with disabilities have lower employment levels, higher dropout rates, and do not pursue college as much as those without disabilities (Peraino, 1992). According to Peraino, the follow-up studies indicate that approximately 40% of graduates of special education programs are employed and approximately 25% attend postsecondary education after they leave the school program. This is compared to a 62% employment rate and a 56% rate of participation in postsecondary education programs for nondisabled graduates. The follow-up studies indicate considerable variation in educational outcomes among differing disability groups. For example, special education graduates with learning disabilities tend to have the highest rate of employment (71%), followed by persons with behavior disorders, mild mental retardation, or speech impairments. These groups have employment rates in the 50th to 60th percentiles. The next highest rate of employment was for graduates with physical or sensory (i.e., hearing or visual) impairments (approximately 40%). The groups with lowest rates of employment were those with most severe disabilities (e.g., multiple disabilities, deaf/blind, severe mental retardation). The average rate of employment for these groups after completion of special education programs was 12%. Because of the recognition of the tremendous problems that young adults with disabilities face in employment and adult living, the transition from school to work has recently become a major emphasis in special education.

HISTORY

Although the national focus on transition from school to work began in the early eighties, there were earlier efforts aimed at helping students with disabilities gain skills that would help them to become employed and live as independent adults. However, until recently, the development of programs to facilitate the transition from school to work for persons with disabilities has been a slow and fragmented process.

Formal vocational training for persons with disabilities can be traced back to England, where in 1791 Henry Dannett opened a school in Liverpool for persons who were blind. The training, which consisted of mechanical arts and music, was considered to have vocational value. Most students learned trades and returned to their homes to seek work. These methods for rehabilitating individuals who were blind are believed to have formed the basis for rehabilitation training programs in the United States (Wright, 1980).

Similar efforts aimed at vocational preparation for persons who were mentally retarded occurred at a slower rate. St. Vincent de Paul (1581–1660) established a facility in Paris that later became the Bicêtre, an important hospital and rehabilitation center for persons with disabilities. Jean-Jacques Rousseau (1712–1778) stipulated basic principles of learning that were applicable to children with mental retardation and also proposed direct teaching strategies. Both Jean-Marc-Gaspard Itard (1775–1838) and Édouard Séguin (1812–1880) were students of Rousseau and applied his principles to teaching children with retardation. Institutions in Europe for persons with disabilities emphasized occupational training. However, in practice, students were often isolated in segregated facilities where the general level of instruction was so poor that the instruction was only minimally effective (Wright, 1980). In 1848 Séguin brought the principles and methods developed in Europe to the United States, where he was appointed superintendent of a Massachusetts school for persons with mental retardation.

The first special schools in the United States were for children with deafness (e.g., Baltimore in 1812; Hartford, Connecticut, in 1817). During most of the early part of the 19th century, persons with mental retardation were relegated to insane asylums, poorhouses, or even local jails. By the middle of the century, however, there were some notable efforts to remedy this situation. In 1848 Dr. Samuel Gridley Howe (1801–1876) received $2,500 from the Massachusetts state legislature to set up an experimental school for training 10 paupers who were mentally retarded. The school was considered to be a success and in 1851 became a permanently functioning institution. Similar schools were established in Pennsylvania (1853), Ohio (1857), Connecticut (1857), and Kentucky (1860). Educators at these schools were initially optimistic and were able to demonstrate that some persons with mental retardation could learn to function well in the community. However, concepts and methods in these schools were less effective for people with more severe disabilities, who became increasingly dependent on the new institutions. The problem of what to do with individuals who could not respond to the treatment and training available became an urgent one at the time, and the schools consequently assumed more of a custodial role.

During the first quarter of the 20th century much of the occupational training for persons with disabilities occurred in these state residential institutions. Although some trainees became skilled at various trades and jobs within the walls of the institution, they had no opportunity to apply these skills in the outside world because they were considered to be an essential component of the institution's labor force. Comprehensive, systematic programs for transition from state institutions to the community were not to appear until much later, during the seventies and eighties.

One early effort to provide work in the community for persons with disabilities was undertaken by Goodwill Industries, which was founded in 1902 by Edgar James Helms (1863–1942), a Methodist minister from Boston. The basic program of Goodwill Industries consisted of gathering discarded clothing and household items, repairing them, and reselling them to the public. At first, persons who were poor were the primary workers of Goodwill, but as time went on, persons with disabilities also became a major part of the work force.

Channing's (1932) studies of the occupational status of adults with mental disabilities found that many of them held unskilled jobs. At the time, the study was interpreted to mean that, rather than train the individuals for specific occupations, they should be taught the work habits and attitudes that would help them keep the unskilled and semiskilled jobs they would later have.

In the early forties, high school classes for individuals with mild mental retardation were organized in many of the larger cities. Occupational education and work experience were the main focus of the secondary school curriculum in these special classes. During this period a group developed a series of learning activities based on the common requirements for obtaining, keeping, and advancing in a job. Douglas

(1944) specified the major objectives of occupational education: (1) to emphasize wage earning as a privilege that requires steady performance, (2) to build an understanding of the relationship between employer and employee with rights and privileges for each, and (3) to stress financial management and independence.

Hungerford (Hungerford, DeProspero, & Rosensweig, 1948) strengthened and broadened the occupational education curriculum for students with mental retardation by emphasizing the processes involved in achieving both vocational and social competence. The essentials of the Hungerford occupational education program were (1) developing student abilities for self-support by teaching students occupational and social skills that lead to successful adaptation in society; (2) providing information about jobs; (3) offering vocational guidance to match the student's abilities and interests with available jobs; (4) providing training in the manual skills and in general habits, attitudes, and skills necessary for successful socialization; (5) assisting in job placements; and (6) counseling in adjusting to the job and the community.

Recent legislative and public policy developments at the national level have provided the framework and impetus for a more comprehensive vocational special education. The Vocational Education Act of 1963 emphasized the creation of training programs that would be more responsive both to the diverse needs of youth and adults and to the demands of the rapidly changing labor market. In addition, the legislation authorized states to develop programs to assist persons with academic, social, or other handicaps. However, at the time the legislation was enacted, few states responded to this challenge, and in 1968 the U.S. Congress made several important amendments to the act. These amendments directed states to spend a minimum of 10% of their federal vocational educational funds annually for the excess costs of educating students with disabilities in vocational programs and 15% on programs for students who were academically, economically, and/or socially disadvantaged. These federal funds required a match of local funds on a 50% match basis (Phelps & Frasier, 1988).

The Rehabilitation Act of 1973 (Public Law 93–112) was another important legislative milestone. The purpose of this act was to ensure a broad array of services that would enable individuals with disabilities to secure gainful employment. The act also included provisions for removing all barriers to employment, not just those that are physical or architectural. Thus, according to the act, employers who are federal contractors or who receive federal funds must make reasonable accommodation for otherwise qualified workers with disabilities, unless the employers can show that these accommodations would create an undue hardship on the business. Examples of reasonable accommodation are extra rest breaks or flexible work hours for individuals with health impairments, sign language interpreters or amplified telephones for workers who are hearing impaired, or extra training time for employees who are mentally impaired. This act was amended in 1986 (Rehabilitation Act Amendments of 1986 [Public Law 99–506]). The amendments emphasize the importance of transition services and supported employment.

The Education for All Handicapped Children Act of 1975 (Public Law 94–142) opened up opportunities for both the general schooling and the vocational preparation of young people with disabilities, from early childhood to young adulthood. This piece of landmark legislation guaranteed the right to a free, appropriate public education for students with disabilities in the least restrictive environment. The least restrictive environment provisions of the law have particularly important implications for transition programming since they guaranteed the right of students with disabilities to participate in vocational education classes.

In 1984 Madeleine Will, assistant secretary of education, established as a national priority improving the transition from school to working life for all individuals with disabilities (Will, 1984b). This priority was set approximately one school generation after the guarantee of the right to a free, appropriate public education for all children with disabilities, with the realization that "joblessness, rather than employment, is the norm among persons who have disabilities" (Will, 1984a, p. 15). Students with disabilities, who for the first time have had guaranteed access to the public education system for 12 or more years, were completing school programs to find a confusing and inadequate system of adult services and few employment opportunities. Sobsey and McDonald (1988) provide the following explanation of the political factors underlying the transition movement:

> When services were unavailable throughout childhood, they were unexpected in adulthood. The new availability of educational programs vastly raised expectations. As the children who were served in these programs reached adulthood, they, their families, friends, and advocates expected services to continue. Unfortunately, the limited availability of adult services provided a sharp contrast, which made the need for these services and smooth transitions into their use painfully evident. (p. 27)

Continuing the thrust toward more community-oriented, real-world occupational preparation, the Education of the Handicapped Act amendments of 1983 (Public Law 98–199) authorized grants for demonstration projects that would assist youth with disabilities in the transition from school to postsecondary education, vocational training, competitive employment, and adult services. These demonstration projects have provided many excellent models of strategies, materials, and techniques that promote successful transition from school to work and community for students with disabilities.

In 1990 P.L. 94–142 was reauthorized and amended by the Individuals with Disabilities Education Act (IDEA), Public Law 101–476. This new act has had extremely important implications for the provision of transition services for students with disabilities. For the first time, transition services are mandated by law. IDEA requires a statement of transition services to be included in students' annual Individualized Education Plans (IEPs) beginning no later than age 16, or 14 if appropriate. The act defines transition services as

> A coordinated set of activities for a student, designed within an outcome oriented process, which promotes movement from school to postschool activities, including postsecondary education, vocational training, integrated employment, including supported employment, continuing adult education, adult services, independent living or community participation. The coordinated set of activities shall be based upon the individual student's needs taking into account the student's preferences and interests and shall include instruction, community experiences, employment development and other postschool adult living objectives, and when appropriate, acquisition of daily living skills and functional vocational evaluation. (P.L. 101–476, 20 U.S.C. § 1401 |a||19|)

The law also maintains the requirement that students with disabilities be provided with a free and appropriate public education in the least restrictive environment, i.e., the most appropriate educational environment with the greatest opportunity for interaction with nondisabled peers.

Successful transition for students with disabilities is also supported by the recent enactment of the Americans with Disabilities Act of 1990 (ADA). This act guarantees equal access for individuals with disabilities in employment, public accommodations (e.g., restaurants, theaters), state and local government services, transportation, and telecommunications. According to the employment provisions of the law, employers must make reasonable accommodations for persons with disabilities who are able to perform the essential functions of the job. This act has been described as the most comprehensive civil rights legislation for persons with disabilities ever enacted. This law should help to promote successful transition for students with disabilities by decreasing discrimination on the basis of disability.

In addition to legislative influences, several major developments beginning in the fifties helped to lay the groundwork for the emphasis on transition (Halpern, 1992b). These developments occurred in three major areas: (1) special education work experience programs, (2) vocational education, and (3) top-down approaches to special education curricular development such as career education.

Special education work experience programs originated in model projects of the fifties and sixties. These projects demonstrated that students with mental retardation who participate in work experiences during their school years are more likely to find employment after completing school programs than those who complete a predominantly academic course of study. According to Rusch, Mithaug, and Flexer (1986), the curriculum for special education work experience programs "combines part-time instruction by the school and work placements of varying length in which the primary emphasis is on learning how to work through exposure rather than instruction" (p. 13). Work experience programs incorporate part-time work placements of varying length as part of the total school program. Jobs performed in work experience programs may be paid or unpaid and may occur in the public or the private sector.

Flynn (1982) reports on additional studies conducted in the seventies that also found that participation in work experience programs significantly enhances the possibility that an individual with mental retardation will obtain employment after completing school programs. Rusch et al. (1986) note several weaknesses in the special education work experience model, including inconsistent implementation, a short-term emphasis on rehabilitation, and a lack of specificity from a standard industry training approach. However, these authors also note some positive benefits cited by Bellamy, Rose, Wilson, and Clarke (1982); they include the opportunity for students with mild disabilities to practice work support behaviors in a number of work environments and the opportunity for contact with nondisabled peers and locally available work.

Vocational education (i.e., training aimed at preparing individuals for gainful employment as semiskilled or skilled workers in jobs that do not require a baccalaureate or higher degree) has been available to students within the general education program since the enactment of the Smith-Hughes Act in 1917. There have been many efforts to ensure that students with disabilities have access to these job skills training programs. Legislation has been enacted that guarantees the right of access for students with disabilities to vocational education programs. Through the least restrictive environment provisions of P.L. 94–142, the right of access to federally funded programs guaranteed under Section 504 of P.L. 93–112, and various pieces of vocational education legislation, the right of students with disabilities to participate in vocational education classes has been well established. Federal funding to support the excess cost of educating students who are disabled in vocational education was first made available in 1968 with passage of amendments to the Vocational Education Act of 1963. Federal support for educating learners with disabilities in vocational education continued through the passage of the 1976 amendments (Public Law 94–482) and the Carl Perkins Act of 1984. The right of students with disabilities to participate in vocational education was reaffirmed with Public Law 101–392, the Carl D. Perkins Vocational Education and Technology Act of 1990. This act requires educators to provide curriculum, equipment and classroom modification, supportive personnel, and instructional aids and devices in vocational education classes for students who are members of special populations, including students with disabilities. It also requires that counseling and instructional services designed to facilitate the transition from school to postschool employment and career opportunities be provided.

Although the federal government has affirmed the right of students with disabilities to participate in vocational education, state and local education agencies have also played a significant role in adapting vocational education for these students. For example, many local districts have made efforts to accommodate these students by providing inservice training for vocational and special educators and furnishing adaptive devices, modified textbooks, and instructional aids.

Another major trend that influenced the development of the transition emphasis involved several major curricular efforts aimed at developing the functional skills of students. *Career education* was instituted within general education in the early seventies in response to a demand for more practical and relevant education (Brolin, 1982; White & Biller, 1988); the development of career education philosophy and curricula within special education paralleled this movement in general education.

There is no universally accepted definition of career education. However, most of the definitions that have evolved in special education take a broad view of career education. For example, Kokaska and Brolin (1985) define career education as

> the process of systematically coordinating all school, family and community components together to facilitate each individual's potential for economic, social, and personal fulfillment and participation in productive work activities that benefit the individual or others. (p. 43)

Although it is commonly assumed that career education and vocational education define essentially the same curricular activity, career education is actually considerably broader than vocational education. By defining work as "activities that benefit the individual or others," it is much broader than the specific skills orientation of vocational education and includes competencies such as leisure activities, daily living skills (e.g., budgeting, cooking, caring for clothing), and interpersonal skills.

The federal emphasis on career education within general education reached its peak in the middle to late seventies. However, the career education concept has continued to have a significant impact on special education and can be seen to be a forerunner of the current emphasis on equipping students who are disabled with the skills necessary to make a successful transition from school to work and independent living.

Career education is an example of a *top-down approach* to curriculum development. The seventies saw a steadily increasing growth of top-down approaches, which focus on identifying student goals on the basis of what will be expected of the student in the next environment.

According to Sobsey and McDonald (1988), two top-down models that received wide recognition during the late seventies and early eighties were the criteria of ultimate functioning (Brown, Nietupski, & Hamre-Nietupski, 1976) and the criteria of the next educational environment (Vincent et al., 1980). The criteria of ultimate functioning model states that goals should be included in a curriculum only if their accomplishment will lead to skills that aid individuals to function independently as adults. The criteria of the next educational environment model are that goals should be selected on the basis of what will be required of students in the next environment in which they will participate.

Clearly, the emphasis on functional skills in special education grew during the seventies and continued through the eighties. Combined with the normalization concept, which emphasizes the need to make available to individuals with disabilities "the patterns of mainstream society" (Nirje, 1970, p. 181), the emphasis on functional skills in special education curricula paved the way for the current focus on preparation for the real-life skills in transition programming.

Another factor contributing to the current emphasis on transition in special education was the development of interest among the general population in adult developmental stages, lifelong learning, and transitions that occur throughout the life span. Beginning in the late sixties numerous works published in academic journals and in the popular press addressed the effect of transitions that occur for all adults, not just for those with disabilities. Books such as *Passages: Predictable Crises of Adult Life* (Sheehy, 1976) and *The Seasons of a Man's Life* (Levinson, 1978) that described the transitions faced by adolescents and adults were popular with the baby-boom generation. This interest in lifelong learning, successful negotiations of a life's career, and personal transitions for all adults was likely a factor in the concern for transition programming for youth and adults with disabilities.

As transition programs and research have evolved, several important issues have emerged, most notably (1) the role of the student in transition, (2) low income levels and lack of job promotions for persons with disabilities who are employed, and (3) the relationship between meeting curriculum needs and serving students with disabilities in the least restrictive environment.

The concept of self-determination has recently taken on increased importance in the transition from school to work and community movement. Many have begun to question the lack of opportunity students with disabilities often have to make determinations about their futures. According to Ward (1992), "self-determination, which includes self-actualization, assertiveness, creativity, pride and self-advocacy, must be part of the career development process that begins in early childhood and continues throughout adult life" (p. 389). Developing strategies that encourage self-determination is currently a major thrust in school-to-work and school-to-community transition programs

Another major issue is the recognition that many persons with disabilities who are employed earn wages below the poverty level. Many people with disabilities are leaving the ranks of the unemployed to become part of the "working class poor." A 1985 Harris poll found that 50% of households headed by a person with a disability earned less than $15,000 per year, compared to 29% of nondisabled households (Harris & Associates, 1986). Peraino (1992) reports that special education graduates generally earn less than their nondisabled peers. If transition efforts help persons with disabilities to become employed, but the employment does not allow them to earn enough to live independently, a serious question must be raised about the effectiveness of transition programs.

An additional major issue is the adequacy of the secondary curriculum to meet the transition needs of the students with disabilities. Because of the least restrictive environment provisions of P.L. 94–142, instruction for students with disabilities is provided within the general education program to the greatest extent possible. Academic skills are highly stressed in the general education program, with functional skills often receiving much less attention. Serious questions have emerged about the degree to which students with disabilities can be adequately prepared for adult life within a general education program that stresses academic skills (Clark, 1991; Edgar, 1992). Meeting the need for developing functional skills while at the same time providing for maximum integration with nondisabled peers is a pressing issue in the transition field.

DEFINITION

There are several definitions of the term *transition*. As it applies to adult developmental psychology within the general population, Aslanian and Brickell (1980) define transition as "moving from one status in life to another" (p. 34). Even within the field of special education, several different definitions of transition have evolved. The transition movement emerged in 1984 with the following definition by Will (1984b):

> Transition is a period that includes high school, the point of graduation, additional post-secondary education or adult services, and the initial years in employment. Transition is a bridge between the security and structure offered by the school and the opportunities and risks of adult life. Any bridge requires both a solid span and a secure foundation at either end. The transition from school to work and adult life requires sound preparation in the secondary school, adequate support at the point of school leaving, and secure opportunities and services, if needed, in adult situations. (p. 3)

It is noteworthy that Will's definition includes the importance of providing quality secondary-school and adult services, as well as linkage services, within the scope of transition programming.

Even though Will's definition includes both secondary and adult services, it is often considered to be a more narrow view of transition because of its emphasis on employment (Blalock, 1988; Halpern, 1992a). Several authors have advocated taking a broader approach to the concept of transition—one that includes adult adjustment factors in the home and community, as well as in employment (Halpern, 1992a). The IDEA legislation sets forth the following broader definition of transition services:

> Transition services means a coordinated set of activities for a student, designed within an outcome-oriented process, which promotes movement from school to post-school activities, including postsecondary education, vocational training, integrated employment

(including supported employment), continuing and adult education, adult services, independent living or community participation. (P.L. 101–476, 20 U.S.C., § 300.18).

Although definitions of transition may vary in the degree of emphasis placed on employment, all of them address the importance of the relationship between school programs and successful adult functioning. This direction is seen by many as a long-overdue recognition that children with disabilities do grow up.

PREVALENCE Current estimates place the incidence of children with disabilities in the public schools at approximately 12% of the total school-age population. Because the need for transition programming is not limited to any one category of exceptionality, it can be assumed that there is a need for transition programs for all of the students in this 12%.

Further, advocates for youth who are gifted and talented (who constitute anywhere from 3% to 20% of the school-age population) have stressed the need for transition planning for this population as well. For example, a joint position paper was adopted by two divisions of the Council for Exceptional Children (the Association for the Gifted and the Division on Career Development) on career development for gifted and talented youth (Delisle & Squires, 1988). Youth who are gifted and talented have often been omitted from career education and transition efforts. According to Delisle and Squires, this omission has resulted in various problems among students who are gifted and talented, including premature career selection based on stereotypical notions associated with the label "gifted and talented," extended delay in career selection because of a lack of information, a perceived inability to change career paths after investments have been made in inappropriate career preparation programs, and the selection of a career that is beneath the individual's ability level. The authors claim that some of these difficulties can be avoided by the development of programs for youth who are gifted and talented that help the students learn how to (1) deal with multiple areas of strength in interest and ability, (2) cope with societal expectations, and (3) deal with career decisions that may require extensive investments of time, effort, and money.

Finally, an argument could be made that transition planning is important for all students in our public schools, not just those with exceptional needs. Certainly, the flood of interest in adult developmental stages and lifelong learning cited earlier in this chapter points to a need for bridging strategies between school and adult life that is not limited to individuals who are disabled or gifted.

ASSESSMENT The purpose of assessment in transition is to gather information that will help design instruction and services to facilitate the student's movement into adult life. Therefore, assessment for transition should take a very functional approach (West, Mast, Cosel, & Cosel, 1992). Variables typically assessed in transition planning include communication skills; work habits; occupational or vocational interests and preferences; preferred learning styles; abilities in specific technical, industrial, or other skills required in actual jobs; and life skills needed to address personal and independent living problems such as transportation, financial and housing management, and social skills (e.g., Rothenbacher & Leconte, 1990; Sarkees & Scott, 1990).

Most of these factors can best be assessed through interview or observational methods in real settings. Strategies frequently used in assessment for transition planning include (1) interviews, (2) ecological assessment, (3) curriculum-based assessment, (4) personal futures planning, and (5) comprehensive vocational assessment.

1. *Interviews.* It is important that the student be involved in the assessment planning process to help ensure that the most pertinent information is being collected and to reinforce the importance of self-determination. An interview with the student helps to establish the purpose and goals of the evaluation and to collect data regarding interest, strengths, and weaknesses from the student's perspective. The purpose of both vocational and career assessment is to gather information that can be used to help individuals function as independently as possible. Therefore, it is crucial that assessment be approached as a process that empowers the individual. Valuable information to guide assessment can be collected through such an interview process. This information can support and enhance data collected from other sources.

2. *Ecological assessment.* Ecological assessment involves analyzing activities that take place in a natural environment and then determining those skills the particular student may still need to perform the activity successfully. The first step in conducting an ecological assessment is to determine, through observation and actual performance, the steps involved in performing the activity. This list of steps then serves as an inventory of the skills a student must be able to perform to complete the activity. It is important that each step in the inventory be described in behavioral terms, that the skills are ordered in the appropriate sequence, and that the inventory includes all steps that are needed to initiate, prepare for, participate in, and terminate the activity (Black & Ford, 1989, p. 300).

After the inventory has been developed, student assessment is conducted at the actual site where the activity is typically performed. An observer then uses the inventory as a checklist to match the student's skills against the steps in the inventories, noting any discrepancies. According to the National Information Center for Children and Youth with Disabilities (1993),

> ecological assessment is one of the most appropriate means of determining what skills and components of skills a student needs to develop in order to address the many domains of post-school life. Its emphasis upon breaking tasks down into their component steps ensures that students are, indeed, focused upon learning to perform those tasks they will actually need in adult life. (p. 16)

3. *Curriculum-based assessment.* Curriculum-based vocational assessment emphasizes procedures that are tied directly to the vocational education curriculum in a given school. It is developed and conducted by vocational and special education teachers in the local setting and is used throughout the planning and implementation phases of a student's vocational program. The information gathered helps those who are concerned with the student's program to plan most effectively. According to West, Corbey, Boyer-Stephens, Jones, Miller, and Sarkees-Wircenski (1992), the primary strength of curriculum-based vocational assessment is "its direct relevance to existing curricula and its direct applicability to ongoing curriculum and instruction activities within a variety of settings."

4. *Personal futures planning.* There are three main components to personal futures planning: a personal profile, a planning meeting, and the futures plan document (Mount & Zwernik, 1988).

The personal profile is constructed through a group interview process involving the individual with disabilities, a few other people who care about and know the person well, and a facilitator. The purpose of the profile is to discover and document

a. the person's background including positive and negative experiences, major moves, critical events, and current dynamics that affect the person's immediate future, family issues, general health, and ethnic and community ties
b. the person's accomplishments in the areas of community participation, community presence, choices/rights, respect, and competence
c. the person's preferences and desires

The information gathered through this profile is then used to develop a personal futures plan. The personal futures plan is usually constructed by the same group of people who met to develop the profile. The plan is generally developed at a second meeting that occurs several days after the profile session.

A strength of this process is that it focuses on individuals' strengths rather than deficits (Nisbet, Covert, & Schuh, 1992). Furthermore, the process does not limit the individual by where he or she is now or by what services are currently available. Finally, the process supports self-determination by including the individual with a disability at the center of the process.

5. *Comprehensive vocational assessment* generally takes place in a vocational assessment center and is conducted by a trained vocational evaluator. Work—real or simulated—is at the focal point in the assessment process. Comprehensive vocational assessment was developed in the field of vocational rehabilitation for adults with disabilities. However, some school districts have used this type of assessment and have developed vocational evaluation centers or have contracted with outside agencies for such services.

INTERVENTION

The first issue in intervention for transition is planning. As stated earlier in this chapter, the Individuals with Disabilities Education Act requires that a plan for transition services be included in the IEP for each student who is at least 16 years of age, or at age 14 if appropriate. Schalock (1986) defines the transition planning process as an activity in which significant people in the individual's current and future life secure meaningful information about environments for which the individual needs to be prepared and analyzes services the individual should obtain to enhance the probability of a smooth adjustment to such settings. Transition plans are focused on identifying the preparation and resources needed for meeting targeted adult outcomes. According to West, Corbey, et al. (1992), "targeted outcomes should be based not on what is currently available in the community but on the needs and desires of the individual and family involved. Resources and services can be developed to meet the desired adult outcomes" (p. 18).

IDEA requires that, in addition to the usual participants at the IEP meeting (i.e., the student's teacher and a school representative), the students, the students' families, and representatives of any other agency that is likely to be responsible for providing or paying for transition services must be included as participants.

Individuals for whom transition plans are being written should be directly involved in the transition planning process. First, they are the best source of information for developing transition plans. Further, if students are to be prepared for adult decision making, they must be treated as adults or efforts to create a successful transition will be undermined. Ultimately, individual students will successfully, or unsuccessfully, make the transition from school to work through their own efforts, and they have the right to participate in the planning process.

Parent involvement is also a critical factor in the development of effective transition plans. IDEA mandates that parents be involved in the educational planning process; parent involvement takes on additional importance in transition planning. Often, parents are the only adults who are consistently involved with students over time. As a result, parents often assume primary responsibility for ensuring that their children receive the services they need as they move from school to adult services or employment. A follow-up study of special education program graduates conducted by Mithaug, Horiuchi, and Fanning (1985) found that 76% of the former students viewed their parents or relatives as being the most helpful persons in preparing them for the future. Parents often assume the roles of advocate and case manager for their children who are in the process of transition: their knowledge of, and commitment to, the transition plan is critical (Patton & Browder, 1988).

As Patton and Browder (1988) note, transition planning is conducted with parents, not *for* them. Parents know their children best and have their own perspective concerning the human quality of support or assistance as opposed to its technology (Bradley, 1988). Parents are thus well qualified to serve as advocates as these children become adults. In addition, parents can receive information and learn the skills they need to fill their roles by participating on the transition team. Through collaboration with service providers, parents can be supported in developing life goals with their children, learning about adult service options, and receiving support whenever they encounter problems.

In working with parents on transition issues, educators need to become sensitive to parental expectations for their children, work cooperatively to identify problems and come up with solutions, and be prepared to negotiate differences and revise plans (Carney & Orelove, 1988). Traditionally, the family was the important social institution that prepared children to become adults. Even in this fragmented, postindustrial age, the family still plays an important role in this respect, especially in the case of persons with disabilities. Educators and other service providers must always take into account parents and other family members, enlisting their participation in the transition process, which is no less crucial than their involvement in the schooling experience that preceded it.

Various adult service agency representatives who will be providing services to students after they complete school programs, such as vocational rehabilitation counselors and developmental disabilities caseworkers, should also be involved in the transition planning process. The importance of interagency cooperation is stressed throughout the transition literature. Hasazi and Clark (1988) advocate for the development of agreements between vocational education, special education, vocational rehabilitation, developmental disabilities, and employment and training agencies. Many states have adopted interagency agreements between education agencies and adult service agencies at the state level (Wehman, Kregal, Barcus, & Schalock, 1986).

However, if interagency cooperation is going to actually benefit students on the local level, the commitment of individual professionals in each community to the interagency collaborative process is required.

According to Patton and Browder (1988), there are four steps to making interagency cooperation a reality. First, there must be a commitment to collaboration by each of the diverse educational system and agency representatives. Second, within each organization the barriers to interagency cooperation must be removed. Third, individual representatives must negotiate the scope, parameters, responsibilities, and funding of collaboration at the policy-making, management, and direct service levels. Fourth, an implementation plan must be agreed upon.

Although formal transition plans are generally not created until students are in secondary programs, there is a strong emphasis in transition planning on the importance of early experiences. According to Sobsey and McDonald (1988), "the role of the preschool in the transition process is to lay the groundwork for the gradual movement towards successful adult functioning in the community" (p. 39). West, Corbey, et al. (1992) advocate that planning for transition should begin early so that students will have opportunities and experiences during their school years to prepare for postschool environments, as well as redesign strategies as necessary. Many of the attitudes and habits that affect successful adult adjustment in employment and in the community are formed in the preschool and elementary years. Clearly, preparation for employment and independent living for individuals with disabilities needs to begin early in a child's school program. Programs that wait until the secondary years to teach functional skills will meet with limited success.

A final factor in transition planning is working with employers and other community members to create receptive environments for persons with disabilities. The classic model of transition provided by Will (1984b) uses a bridge analogy to illustrate that effective transition programs must have a solid foundation in both the school and adult environments, as well as a strong span linking the two settings. Creating receptive community environments is a critical component of developing successful transitions for students with disabilities. Public awareness factors, such as employer attitudes, are often cited as deterrents to successful independent living for persons with disabilities (e.g., Mithaug, 1979; Pati, Adkins, & Morrison, 1981; Rochlin, 1987). In response, some transition programs have included employer awareness programs as a part of their transition efforts (e.g., Field & Allen, 1987). These programs focus on helping employers to become more comfortable and more skilled in supervising employees with disabilities. The development of accepting, respectful attitudes among employers and community members toward persons with disabilities is a critical factor in the success or failure of these persons' transition from school to adult settings.

Some employers have also initiated programs to promote disability awareness and employment of persons with disabilities. These programs have come about primarily through increased awareness fostered by the Americans with Disabilities Act and by a need to expand the labor market pool of qualified workers. The McDonald's and Marriott corporations have both made notable efforts in this area.

The McJobs program sponsored by the McDonald's corporation is an employment program designed to provide skill training and job placement for individuals with mental and physical disabilities. Trainees are referred to the program from vocational education programs and state vocational rehabilitation agencies. Training is provided by a job coach who is also a McDonald's manager. Using a combination of classroom activities, video instruction, demonstration and supervised practice, each job coach instructs and supervises 4 or 5 trainees for 15 hours a week over a 2- to 3-month period at a McDonald's Restaurant. Job coaches attend a 2-week course to prepare them for teaching persons with disabilities. Following successful completion of the training program "graduates" continue employment at the restaurant where they were trained.

The Marriott Corporation has also taken a proactive approach to training and employing persons with disabilities. The original impetus for the effort to employ persons with disabilities was the need to find workers to fill a critical labor market shortage. After the program was begun, however, Marriott managers found additional benefits arising from the exceptionally strong performance and work habits of the persons with disabilities who were hired (e.g., commitment, loyalty, motivation).

Marriott maintains a Community Employment and Training Programs Department, which, as part of its function, provides assistance to local Marriott managers who want to increase their efforts to promote the employment of persons with disabilities. The programs developed and implemented at each site are tailored to meet needs in the local community. In addition, the Marriott Foundation for People with Disabilities has created the Bridges Youth Internship Program to help students with disabilities develop job skills in competitive employment settings.

Cooperative learning through peer tutoring.

Transition for Students with Severe Disabilities

The preparation for transition for students with severe disabilities differs from that for students who are mildly disabled in at least two ways (Bellamy et al., 1982). First, preparation for students who are severely disabled becomes more complicated by their need for continuing services in addition to employment. Successful community living calls for much more than the ability to hold a job. Second, greater precision and sophistication are needed to train and maintain these individuals in employment.

Education for students who are severely disabled must provide the basic skills and knowledge for them to live as independently as possible in an integrated community throughout their lives. They must have the problem-solving skills and supporting knowledge needed to function successfully in society and to take advantage of the services necessary for effective living. According to Turnbull and Turnbull (1988), "creating great expectations for vocational opportunities requires a *revolution* in assumptions. . . . It means recognizing that the potential for independent living is maximized when adults with mental retardation have friends and live and work in typical community settings across their entire lives" (p. 338).

Of major concern are the gaps between school experience and adult life (Wilcox & Bellamy, 1982) and the wide variability in adult services. For adults who are severely disabled, service deficits create serious problems in making transitions.

Society, still oriented toward the segregation of persons who are severely disabled, has been slow to provide a full range of coordinated services. Although there has been some progress, efforts must be strengthened toward providing vocational settings that offer individuals with disabilities full contact with nondisabled co-workers, business customers, and neighbors. Individuals who are severely disabled also need increased opportunities to develop friendships. Services need to provide age-appropriate work, residential facilities, and leisure activities.

The quality and completeness of adult services may vary greatly from one community to the next. It is axiomatic that the quality of services affects the success of transition from school to adult life. In addition, continuity in the provision of services is extremely important for any individual with severe disabilities. Successful transition and good mental health require the cooperation and coordination of responsible state and local agencies—vocational education, vocational rehabilitation, and developmental disabilities agencies. Individuals with severe disabling conditions must have the problem-solving skills needed to make decisions about life and work and to take advantage of available support services.

Although preparation for transition should begin in the elementary years, the most critical period for preparing students with severe disabilities for transition occurs during the last 2 years of high school. Teachers and others responsible for the transition of a student must identify and contact the providers of services available in the community. In addition to student counseling and evaluation, planning is necessary to avoid problems resulting from delays in services, long periods on waiting lists, and lack of coordination between agencies. In short, case management, on an individualized basis, is especially important for the successful transition of a youth with severe disabilities. Without such attention to planning, the student's family must assume the burden of seeking out services piecemeal. Moreover, there must be an effective coordination among services for employment, housing, and recreation, all of which are essential for a rewarding life.

Thus, if we expect young adults who are severely disabled to have a long-term community placement, we must select work situations that have the potential both for training the individual and for increasing their job productivity. At the same time, they must have a home in the community that ensures maximum independence, as well as places for leisure activities that offer opportunities for contact with persons who are disabled. Attention must be directed toward the ongoing process of income support and health care. Finally, a successful long-term placement means a comprehensive plan to deal with such matters as guardianship and the administration of wills and trusts.

There must be a designated advocate to monitor the implementation of this long-term plan (Wilcox & Bellamy, 1982). An advocate is a person who represents the present and future interests of an individual with disabilities and tries to overcome barriers that may arise in the coordination and delivery of services. The person who is disabled may be referred to the wrong program, condemned to a long waiting list, or denied services altogether. On the other hand, a particular agency may be plagued by a poorly trained staff, inadequate funding, confusion over objectives, lack of coordination with other agencies, or failure to apply existing technology. Professionals who assume the role of advocate in facing problems like these need considerable patience and tact while working in the best long-term interests of persons with severe disabilities.

The transition from school to adult life also makes demands on the family of the individual who is disabled. Through the IEP process, parents should have been involved in the ongoing education of their children all along; their participation in the transition to adult life in the community is simply a natural outgrowth of their earlier involvement (Wilcox & Bellamy, 1982).

A major concern related to transition for persons with severe disabilities is the segregation that this group of individuals has often experienced.

CURRICULUM IMPLICATIONS

What kind of curriculum should be adopted to prepare individuals for transition from school to work and community? Regardless of its specific content or structure, any transition curriculum for persons with disabilities must be functional in the sense that it prepares students to participate to the fullest extent possible in community life. A functional curriculum is organized around goals and objectives that relate to the demands of adult life in a variety of settings, including leisure and recreational environments. These goals and objectives should be congruent with those on each student's IEP. Wilcox and Bellamy (1982) suggest that curriculum objectives reflect the activities that students need to master in order to take advantage of community opportunities and that instructional programs help the student to develop the relevant skills to perform these activities successfully.

Ideally, preparation for transition should begin at the elementary school level and become an integral part of a child's IEP (Wehman, Moon, Everson, Wood, & Barcus, 1988). In the earliest school years this training would concentrate on survival skills essential for the workplace and community in general, such as eating, toileting, dressing, grooming, communication, mobility, and time and money management. In addition, students should begin to learn in the early years the importance of factors such as work quality and work rate that are imparted in such simple tasks as washing and drying dishes. They should also have opportunities to observe and learn about work opportunities that will be available to them when they grow up.

During the middle school years the training of self-help skills should intensify, and the use of the skills should occur within the context of job training whenever possible. Wehman et al. (1988) recommend that this training take place in community job sites, although at this level it may be more realistic to begin training in a variety of school sites such as the cafeteria, office, and school grounds. Training should emphasize general work habits such as neatness, promptness, and responding to criticism within the context of specific work tasks. Information obtained about student interests and skills during this exploratory stage may help identify areas for more specific skill training during the high school years.

The high school years are the time when the transition team becomes operational for planning the student's vocational placement (Wehman et al., 1988). This team includes the student, parents or guardians, teacher, rehabilitation counselor, case manager, and other appropriate professionals. Its purpose is to facilitate the student's movement from school to community living, including an appropriate job or postschool training programs. The team should draw up a formal, written plan that lists the steps for training and placing the student upon graduation. The plan specifies who is responsible for completing each step and should also identify existing and potential job opportunities in the community. This kind of systematic attention to the transition process is essential for the eventual successful transition of the student. In all cases there should be continued monitoring of the student after placement to identify any needs for further training or additional services.

A curriculum oriented toward transition from school to work should include training skills in integrated community settings. By the last two years of high school it is recommended that students spend a majority of their time receiving training in a natural setting. Job training stations are one form of naturalistic training. These stations are sites located in industries or commercial enterprises that provide training for students with disabilities in real job environments. The stations should be specific to the local job market and include instructors who are not regular employees of the firm, such as special education trainers or aides. Ideally, the student should experience a number of stations as he or she progresses through school, gaining a variety of skills and being exposed to different kinds of work tasks. According to Hasazi and Clark (1988), difficulties that may occur on the job cannot be duplicated in a classroom and can best be addressed at an actual job site. Experience at job training stations should also help the student and other members of the transition team decide the most appropriate placement after graduation (Wehman et al., 1988).

Secondary transition programs that are considered to be exemplary use curricula that focus on community-based instructional programming. An increasing number of community-based instructional programs have documented their effectiveness in the acquisition of new skills as a result of instruction occurring in natural settings (Falvey, 1989). These skills include boarding and riding a bus, eating in public restaurants, and shopping in stores. Providing learning opportunities in integrated situations in the community creates opportunities for learning that are not available and cannot be reciprocated in segregated settings. The main goals for community-based instruction are (1) to promote the teaching of functional skills in a natural, integrated setting; (2) to provide a variety of natural situations as opportunities to facilitate generalization of skills to new situations; and (3) to provide experiences and opportunities for social interaction with adults who are not disabled.

Gaylord-Ross, Forte, and Gaylord-Ross (1986) recommend providing vocational training in numerous community settings during the secondary years, with each experience lasting for up to 9 months. The training experience in each setting (e.g., office, restaurant, factory) should be quite different in both the nature of the work and the skills required. In addition to providing the students opportunities to generalize skills, training in a number of settings exposes students to a variety of work experiences to help them make decisions about job preference. Support from the community, parents, and school administration is essential to the success of a community vocational training program.

Recent follow-up studies have found that both paid work experience and participation in vocational education are associated with greater success in the workplace after graduation. Hasazi et al. (1985) found that students with disabilities who participated in paid employment while still in high school were more likely to be employed after graduation than those who were not employed. They also found that students

General case strategy facilitates generalization.

who participated in in-school vocational training were employed in jobs that paid higher wages than those students who did not enroll in vocational education.

Preparing students with disabilities for successful work placement requires the careful selection of specific job skills, systematic methods of behavior management, individualized instruction, and programming for generalization. Even though all of these factors are important, the last one is crucial, because students must be able to function in a variety of social, residential, work, and leisure settings. Thus, effective high school transition programs must be directed toward building functional communication, social, and vocational skills that allow students to exercise their skills both in the training setting and in the community.

Skill generalization is concerned with the performance of responses to stimuli that can occur outside the training setting, that is, how well a student applies skills to new situations. There are several kinds of skill generalization, all of which are essential for successful transition. When the student responds appropriately to instances, objects, or cues that were not part of the original training setting, he or she has demonstrated generalization across stimuli. Generalization across settings occurs when the student adapts successfully to an office, for example, that differs significantly from the environment in which he or she was trained. When the student continues to respond appropriately after training has ceased, there is generalization across time (Haring, Liberty, & White, 1988).

Special educators need to teach behaviors using methods that increase the probability that skills will generalize in all three ways to new stimuli, new settings, and different times. They must select materials and objects that most closely approximate (if they are not actually identical to) the things people encounter in everyday environments. Even more important, students should ideally learn in the natural settings; teachers should not assume that successful performance of tasks in a school building will automatically lead to the same sort of performance in a work or residential setting (Belmore & Brown, 1976).

Natural environments may be more difficult to set up and manage than simulated environments, but they are the only environments that contain the full range of stimuli to which students must learn to respond (Wilcox & Bellamy, 1987). However, simulation is important in training, either as an initial stage or as a substitute for teaching in a community setting that is potentially dangerous (e.g., a street crossing) or is expensive or embarrassing to the participants (e.g., checkout counter in a supermarket). In these cases simulation is justified to make training easier and more efficient. However, teachers must make sure that the simulation reliably represents the targeted activity. They must also retain control of all the relevant situational characteristics (which would be "uncontrolled" in the real-life world) (Wilcox & Bellamy, 1982). Teachers need to give attention to planned variations of the simulation. According to Wilcox and Bellamy, simulation is most appropriate when teachers provide students with opportunities to practice the difficult steps of an activity, to receive training in alternative performance strategies, to practice responses to natural variations and low-probability events, and to rehearse proper ways of conducting oneself in the community.

Methods used in classroom or training settings must be applicable to the natural setting of residence or workplace as well. In short, teachers must know how to control the training environment effectively in order to ensure their students' abilities to generalize learned skills and behavior. Teachers must also become managers of the classroom and other instructional settings (simulated or real), combining the skills of planning, staffing, organizing, training, supervising, and evaluating (Wilcox & Bellamy, 1982). Such management is a form of active intervention that consists of designing objectives, collecting data to determine the relationship between these objectives and actual performance, and making changes in training to maintain or achieve the desired levels of performance.

In summary, the following steps designated by Wehman et al. (1988) can help to ensure the most effective preparation of students for transition into the world of work. First, educators must identify the most appropriate community and school-based training sites. On the basis of an ecological analysis of these sites, they identify training goals and related behavioral objectives and arrange them into a logical training sequence (the curriculum). Then they formulate skill sequences and task analyses that break activities into relevant, teachable units. They must choose the most appropriate instruction techniques and data collection procedures for each unit. The same kinds of procedures are also important for teaching related social or community survival skills. Most important for ensuring a genuine transition, teachers must determine methods to phase themselves out of students' lives so that supervision at a training site can be transferred to real employers and supervisors (see Figure 14–1).

INNOVATION AND DEVELOPMENT

Self-Determination

Self-determination is rapidly gaining attention and acceptance within the disability field. Self-determination has been defined as one's ability to define and achieve goals based on a foundation of knowing and valuing oneself (Field & Hoffman, 1992a). The importance of self-determination for persons with disabilities is receiving special attention within the transition from school to adulthood movement. This is occurring as persons with disabilities, their families, educators, and service providers are questioning the passive stereotypes and roles often assigned to persons with disabilities. These stereotypes are in direct conflict with typical expectations of adult behaviors.

The Individuals with Disabilities Education Act places an important emphasis on self-determination in transition planning. IDEA requires that students' preferences and

---

1. Identify the student's short-term and long-term occupational goals.
2. Gather current assessment data on all relevant skills and abilities.
3. Identify training goals and behavioral objectives.
4. Arrange goals and objectives into a logical training sequence.
5. Identify the most appropriate training sites in the community.
6. Analyze tasks and organize skill sequences into relevant, teachable units.
7. Choose appropriate instruction and data collection techniques.
8. Phase out teacher involvement so that the student will learn to relate to his or her supervisor or employer.

Figure 14–1
Steps in creating a community-based curriculum.

interests be taken into account in the planning of transition services. As mentioned earlier, this legislation also requires that school districts include students as participants in their transition planning meetings.

This increased focus on student self-determination in the IDEA legislation is mirrored in the disability and special education literature. According to Wehman (1992), a number of professionals, parents, and advocates are writing with increasing frequency about the importance of choice, self-determination, self-advancement, and freedom for students with disabilities. Wehman elaborates on this point:

> This philosophy is a very important aspect of planning for transition because the focus of control shifts from services providers to the person who is receiving the service and who should be making decisions. This is more than an initiative, priority, or theme. Instead, it will become the only way to provide services. If services providers do not honor this need for a student- or client-focused way of planning services, they will be out of business. (p. 15)

There are many ways teachers can help to promote self-determination. Curriculum and other materials to promote self-determination are increasingly becoming available as a result of the increased emphasis on self-determination for students with disabilities (e.g., Field & Hoffman, 1992b; Martin, Marshall, Maxson, & Jerman, 1993). Teachers can also promote self-determination by offering and respecting students' choices. Self-awareness, an important component of self-determination, can be further developed through assessment that occurs as part of the transition planning process. Per-

Computer technology is applied in academic and vocational training.

The Career Ladder Program (CLP) is a set of principles for facilitating challenged youths' transition from school to adult life. It operated as a program in San Francisco from 1984 to 1990, and the 127 graduates of the program experienced a 92% success rate during those years—that is, 92% of the participants worked, attended college, or some combination of the two (Siegel, Robert, Waxman, & Gaylord-Ross, 1992; Siegel, Robert, Avoke, Paul, & Gaylord-Ross, 1991). From 1991 to 1994, the Office of Special Education and Rehabilitative Services (OSERS) funded a multidistrict outreach grant to replicate the model.

The CLP model bases its practice on the premise that many challenged youths during and beyond high school cannot be "inoculated" against the likelihood of underemployment by a time-limited educational intervention or "cookbook" approach to career education. The only authentic solution for youths who are at risk of being outside the mainstream is to bring them into the community; program staff shape services to the youths' needs and make an authentic, long-term effort to be the liaison with the community and usher willing and motivated youths through a successful transition. How does the CLP accomplish this?

Services are shaped to meet the needs of the youth according to the six overarching principles of the program: (1) individualized responses to personality and learning styles, (2) employment skills, (3) family involvement, (4) benefactor relationships, (5) membership in a legitimate peer group, and (6) the ongoing availability of services. See Siegel et al. (1993) for a full discussion of the six principles of effective transition programming.

The six underlying principles are manifested in the three program components: (1) the community classroom, (2) the employment skills workshop, and (3) the continuous availability of services.

The community classroom is a semester-long supervised work experience for 5 to 15 high school juniors or seniors, where a single large company or several small businesses in a single neighborhood, agree to hire the students (CLP interns) for 3 hours a day, 4 days a week. The school supplies a trained paraprofessional, not unlike a job coach, who is able to provide support for the interns. The feature that distinguishes the CLP from other job programs is that the monitoring paraprofessional is never more than 10 minutes from any of the interns during work hours. That paraprofessional is thus enabled to nurture the work experience, guarantee that learning and real work are occurring, protect the interns from exploitation, and avoid the "putting out fires" reality that plagues all too many youth employment programs.

The second component is the employment skills workshop, a weekly seminar where interns

sonal futures planning, discussed earlier in this chapter, is an excellent assessment and planning tool that places students in a central, proactive position in their own planning process. Finally, students need to be reinforced for efforts to make personal decisions and to take risks.

Supported Employment

Supported employment has become a positive alternative to more segregated types of vocational training and work for persons with severe disabilities. Wehman (1988) claims that "this movement has evolved as a direct function of a favorable business meet to discuss the work experience and share the struggles of adolescence and their impending exit from public schools. This feature of bringing students into a safe setting where they can develop a support group, enhance their skills, operate in an atmosphere of trust, and face adulthood serves to help turn the work experience into a step on a real career ladder. The curriculum strands of the employment skills workshop include job skills, job keeping, job search, personal (peer counseling), and interpersonal (social) skills. The coordination of these strands builds momentum and an atmosphere of success.

The community classroom and the employment skills workshop are orientation events that *initiate* the transition process; they build basic employability skills, develop a group culture, and generate trust between staff and interns. These program components can get the graduates off to a good start, but by themselves they will have only a very limited effect on the youths' employment and engagement rates. The true building of community accelerates as interns graduate high school and begin to receive services through the third CLP component, continuous availability of services.

During this phase, the staff, with whom the graduates are already familiar, deliver an eclectic array of transition services designed to foster the ongoing career development of the graduates. These services include transition planning, independent living and social skills training, counsel-ing, resource referral, supported employment, vocational rehabilitation casework, job search assistance, college enrollment and tutoring, and intervention in the individuals' ecosystem. All services are delivered to facilitate the individuals' empowerment, with the understanding that services fade out as the likelihood of success without them exceeds 50%. However, the continuous *availability* of such services makes them exponentially more effective; graduates have the assurance that they have not been "cut loose" from the program and that their case is never really closed, because that is the nature of authentic community.

This is ultimately an effective and cost-effective means of delivering transition services. The high employment rates (and above-average wages and benefits) experienced by the CLP graduates are a by-product of a program that is based on a true commitment to community and the legitimate place of challenged youths in that community. Because the staff has the liberty to address issues above and beyond vocational outcomes, the level of those vocational outcomes was very substantially and very positively affected.

(For more information about the Career Ladder Program, contact Shep Siegel, Puget Sound Educational Service District, 400 SW 152nd St., Burien, WA 98166-2209, or order *Career Ladders for Challenged Youths in Transition from School to Adult Life from PRO-ED,* 8700 Shoal Creek Boulevard, Austin, TX 78758.)

environment for entry-level service positions, positive government initiatives toward employment of persons with severe disabilities, and advocacy on the part of families and consumers" (p. 357).

According to the Developmental Disabilities Act of 1984, supported employment must meet three conditions. First, it is paid employment for persons with developmental disabilities for whom competitive employment at or above the minimum wage is unlikely and who, because of their disabilities, need ongoing assistance to perform in a work setting. Second, this employment occurs in a variety of settings, particularly work sites where persons without disabilities are employed. Third, support is any activity needed to sustain paid work by persons with disabilities, including supervision, training, and transportation (*Federal Register,* 1984).

According to Bellamy, Rhodes, Mank, and Albin (1988), these three conditions are essential for supported employment to exist as an effective form of transition. First of all, individuals in supported employment work for pay and other benefits. Work performance, rather than skill development, is the objective of supported employment. The U.S. Department of Education in 1985 established 20 hours of paid work per week as the minimum standard, regardless of productivity or wage level.

The second essential feature is integration in the workplace. Supported employment is a step beyond more traditional vocational facilities that separate persons with disabilities from others in the community. Regular workplaces provide opportunities for persons with severe disabilities to meet people who are not paid caregivers. Depending on the type of work and job location, persons with severe disabilities can meet co-workers, customers, and supervisors who are not disabled, and can share mealtimes, breaks, and perhaps even commuting with others.

The third crucial factor is continued support. Despite the most careful and conscientious vocational preparation, many persons with severe disabilities will not immediately fit in with the demands of most workplaces. The discrepancy between these demands and the behavior of persons with severe disabilities requires ongoing support in the work setting. Support can take the form of periodic supervision, supervised transportation, assistance in personal care, or even retraining.

Various program models are used in supported employment. One common approach is the supported job program that locates full- or part-time job slots in private sector companies: these jobs are then filled by persons with severe disabilities. New employees receive continuous on-site training until they can competently do the job. Support from the trainer is never totally withdrawn but assumes a variety of forms depending on the circumstances: retraining as job assignments or requirements change, periodic consultation with co-workers and employers, regular evaluations of productivity, or orientation and training of co-workers. Supported jobs in community businesses are considered an attractive option by many professionals and advocates because they resemble normal patterns of work in most communities and, of great importance, effectively fulfill all three conditions for supported employment.

SUMMARY In 1984 Madeleine Will, assistant secretary of education, established improving the transition from school to work for all individuals with disabilities as a national priority. Since then, the transition from school to community life and full employment has become a major emphasis in special education.

In 1990 P.L. 94-142 was reauthorized and amended by the Individuals with Disabilities Education Act (IDEA), P.L. 101-476. For the first time, through IDEA, transition services for students with disabilities were mandated by law. IDEA requires that a statement of transition services be included in students' annual Individualized Educational Plans (IEP) beginning no later than age 16, or 14 if appropriate. Successful transition for students with disabilities is also supported by the Americans with Disabilities Act of 1990 (ADA). This act guarantees equal access for individuals with disabilities in employment, public accommodations (e.g., restaurants, theaters), state and local government services, transportation, and telecommunications.

1. Here are some basic steps in developing a program to help students learn functional skills. First, through discussions with students, generate a list of real-life activities appropriate for their community, work, and recreational environments. Include activities available to individuals with disabilities and activities available to people who are not disabled.

2. Record observations of activities in the immediate school community; identify behaviors of those engaged in the activities, including peers and adults who are not disabled, as well as of peers who are disabled.

3. Conduct interviews with individuals who are knowledgeable about the community. Include descriptions of all important social activities relevant to facilitating independent living. The analyses of skills necessary for performing these activities across environments serve as a base for curriculum development.

4. Choose one generic functional activity from the environmental activity list and provide an opportunity for students to perform the activity satisfactorily without instruction. Those who stumble in their attempt will need teaching, modeling, practice, and feedback. When the student's behavior reaches the goal, make sure a positive consequence follows.

5. Give additional assistance or prompting to students still having difficulty performing the activity.

6. When students make errors (and errors are inevitable), institute error correction procedures unemotionally by interrupting the incorrect response, immediately following the error with a positive form of assistance and providing additional opportunities to perform the activity.

7. Arrange it so that all activities performed by students in the training setting are also performed in the natural environment (the environment in which the behavior normally occurs). Keep a record of the error responses made in the natural environment and, if possible, provide positive correction and assistance immediately. If correction must be delayed, include the error responses as a target for teaching in the training setting.

8. In many instances a simulated environment may be established in the training setting. This may be necessary in cases of so-called low-probability events. Set up the environment so that students can practice responding appropriately to such events.

9. Provide students with choices and opportunities to make decisions.

10. The most critical stage of learning for students in transition programs is the generalization stage. Arrange for all learned responses to be performed across environments, persons, objects and cues, and times.

The purpose of assessment in transition is to gather information that will help design instruction and services to facilitate students' movement into adult life. Assessment for transition should take a very functional approach. Some variables typically assessed to aid in students' transition planning include communication skills; work habits; occupational or vocational interests and preferences; preferred learning styles; abilities in specific technical, industrial, or other skills required in actual jobs; and life skills needed to address personal and independent living problems such as transportation, financial and housing management, and social situations.

Most of these functional variables can best be assessed through interview or through observation in real settings. Strategies frequently used are interviews, ecological assessment, curriculum-based assessment, and personal futures planning.

The importance of self-determination for persons with disabilities is receiving special attention within the transition from school to adulthood movement. The IDEA places an important emphasis on self-determination in transition planning by requiring that students' preferences and interests be taken into account when planning transition services. This legislation also requires that school districts include students as participants in their transition planning meetings. Teachers can help to promote self-determination through direct instruction of skills associated with self-determination, by offering students choices and respecting the choices that they make, and by reinforcing students' efforts to make personal decisions.

Individuals for whom Individualized Transition Plans are being written and their families should be directly involved in the process. Ultimately, the individual students will successfully, or unsuccessfully, make the transition from school to work, and they have the right to participate in the planning program. Parent involvement is also a critical factor in the development of effective transition plans.

Transition planning for students with severe disabilities has some special characteristics. Plans for students who are severely disabled are more complicated as a result of the students' need for continuing services in addition to employment. Successful community living calls for much more than merely the ability to hold a job. In addition, precision in analysis and sophistication in implementation are needed to train these individuals for employment and help them continually improve and expand their employment-related skills.

A functional curriculum is organized around goals and objectives that relate to the demands of adult life in a variety of settings, including leisure and recreational environments. These goals and objectives should be congruent with those on the student's IEP.

The main goals for a curriculum involving community-based training are (1) to promote the teaching of functional skills in a natural, integrated setting; (2) to provide a variety of natural situations and circumstances as opportunities to perform skills that facilitate generalization; and (3) to provide experiences and opportunities for social interaction with nondisabled adults that will promote positive attitudes toward persons with disabilities.

STUDY QUESTIONS

1. What percentage of all Americans with disabilities between the ages of 16 and 64 are unemployed?

2. Describe the requirements of the Individuals with Disabilities Education Act as they relate to transition services.

3. Describe what is meant by a top-down model or approach to curriculum development.

4. Define transition as it is applied in special education.

5. Describe the following assessment strategies: ecological assessment, curriculum-based assessment, personal futures planning.

6. Give an example of a typical curriculum-based vocational assessment.

7. What is a transition plan, and what does it include?

8. Give the three main goals for community-based instruction.

9. Define skill generalization and discuss two strategies that can facilitate generalization.

10. What are the advantages of teaching in natural environments?

11. Identify three conditions of supported employment.

12. Why is self-determination important in transition from school to work and community? Identify three ways teachers can help promote self-determination.

References

PREFACE

National Association of State Boards of Education. (1992). *Winners all: A call for inclusive schools*. Alexandria, VA: Author.

Oberti v. Borough of Clementon School District, WL 178480 (3rd Cir. N.J. 1993).

CHAPTER ONE

Blackard, K., Hazel, L., Livingston, S., Ryan, T., Soltman, S., & Stade, C. (1977). The interdisciplinary educational team. In N. G. Haring (Ed.), *The exceptional education training program*: Vol. II. *Support services* (pp. 5–21). Seattle: University of Washington.

Blatt, B., & Morris, R. J. (Eds.). (1984). *Perspectives in special education*: *Personal orientations*. Glenview, IL: Scott, Foresman.

Brown, S. A., & Johnson, K. L. (1993, February–March). The impact of federal legislation on life after special education. FOCUS: *A Review of Special Education and the Law*, pp. 1–7.

Brown v. Board of Education of Topeka, Kansas, 347 U.S. 483, 493 (1954).

Campbell, P. (Ed.). (1986). Use of aversive procedures with persons who are disabled: An historical review and critical analysis. *Monographs of the Association for Persons with Severe Handicaps*, 2(1), 1–68.

Comptroller General of the United States. (1976, September 28). *Training educators for the handicapped*: A need to redirect federal programs. Report to the Congress.

Deno, E. (1970). Special education as developmental capital. *Exceptional Children*, 37, 229–237.

De Vault, G., & Haring, N. (1992). NewSHARE: *Collaborative training, collaborative teaming*. Seattle: University of Washington.

Dunn, L. (1968). Special education for the mildly retarded: Is much of it justifiable? *Exceptional Children*, 35, 5–22.

Erickson, M. (1976). *Assessment and management of developmental changes in children*. St. Louis: Mosby.

Federal Register. (1976, February 10). 41, 5692.

Federal Register. (1993, May 20). 58, 29422.

Friend, M., & Cook, L. (1992). *Interactions: Collaboration skills for school professionals*. White Plains, NY: Longman.

Fuchs, D., & Fuchs, L. S. (1988). Evaluation of the Adaptive Learning Environments Model. *Exceptional Children*, 55, 115–127.

Gartner, A., & Lipsky, D. K. (1987). Beyond special education: Toward a quality system for all students. *Harvard Educational Review*, 57, 367–395.

Gaylord-Ross, R., & Pitts-Conway, V. (1984). Social behavior development in integrated secondary autistic programs. In N. Certo, N. Haring, & R. York (Eds.), *Public school integration of severely handicapped students* (pp. 197–219). Baltimore: Paul H. Brookes.

Gelheizer, L. M. (1987). Reducing the number of students labeled as learning disabled: A question of practice, philosophy, or policy? *Exceptional Children*, 54, 145–150.

Gettinger, M. (1984). Measuring time needed for learning to predict learning outcomes. *Exceptional Children*, 51, 244–248.

Goldstein, A. P., Sprafkin, R. P., Gershaw, N. J., & Klein, P. (1980). *Skillstreaming the adolescent*. Champaign, IL: Research Press.

Gould, S. J. (1981). *The mismeasure of man*. New York: Norton.

Greenberg, M. T., Kusche, C. A., Gustafson, R. N., & Calderson, R. (1992). *The PATHS (Providing Alternative Thinking Strategies) Curriculum*. Seattle: University of Washington.

Grosenick, J., & Huntze, S. (1980). *National needs analysis in behavior disorders*: *Adolescent behavior disorders*. Columbia: University of Missouri, Department of Special Education.

Guess, D., Helmstetter, E., Turnbull, R., III, & Knowlton, S. (1986). Use of aversive procedures with persons who are disabled: An historical review and critical analysis. *Monographs of the Association for Persons with Severe Handicaps*, 2(1), 1–68.

Guess, D., & Siegel-Causey, E. (1985). Behavioral control and education of severely handicapped students: Who's doing what to whom? and why? In D. Bricker & J. Triler (Eds.), *Severe mental retardation from theory to practice* (pp. 230–244). Lancaster, PA: Lancaster Press, Division of Mental Retardation, The Council for Exceptional Children.

Gustafson, R. N., & Haring, N. G. (1992). Social competence issues in the integration of students with handicaps. In K. A. Haring, D. L. Lovett, & N. G. Haring (Eds.), *Integrated lifecycle services for persons with disabilities* (pp. 20–58). New York: Springer.

Hagerty, G. L., & Abramson, M. (1987). Impediments to implementing national policy change for mildly handicapped students. *Exceptional Children*, 53, 315–323.

Hales, R. M., & Carlson, L. B. (1992). *Issues and trends in special education*. Lexington, KY: Federal Resource Center for Special Education.

Haring, N. G., Jewell, J., Lehning, T., Williams, G., & White, O. R. (1987). Research on severe behavior disorders: A study of statewide identification and service delivery to children and youth. In N. G. Haring (Ed.), *Assessing and managing behavior disabilities* (pp. 39–104). Seattle: University of Washington Press.

Haring, T. G., & Breen, C. (in press). Social relationships between students with deaf-blindness and their age-peers in inclusive settings. In N. G. Haring & L. T. Romer (Eds.), *Including students with deaf-blindness in typical educational settings*. Baltimore: Paul H. Brookes.

Hayden, M. F., & Abery, B. H. (Eds.). (1993). *Challenges for a service system in transition: Ensuring quality community experiences for persons with developmental disabilities*. Baltimore: Paul H. Brookes.

Heward, W. L., & Orlansky, M. D. (1992). *Exceptional children: An introductory survey of special education* (4th ed.). New York: Merrill/Macmillan.

Kauffman, J. (1982). Social policy issues in special education and related services for emotionally disturbed children and youth. In M. Noel & N. Haring (Eds.), *Progress or change: Issues in educating the emotionally disturbed: Vol. 1. Identification and program planning* (pp. 1–10). Seattle: University of Washington Press.

Lakin, C. (1992). Improving the quality of community living to empower people with mental retardation. *OSERS News in Print*, 5(2), 30–35.

Larson, K. (1988). *Social Thinking Skills Program*. Santa Barbara: University of California Press.

Lilly, M. S. (1988). The Regular Education Initiative: A force for change in general and special education. *Education and Training in Mental Retardation*, 23, 253–260.

Lynch, V., & Haring, N. (1991). *Educational teaming trainer's kit*. Seattle: University of Washington, Experimental Education Unit.

McGinnis, E., & Goldstein, A. P. (1984). *Skillstreaming the elementary school child*. Champaign, IL: Research Press.

Meyer, L., & Evans, F. (1989). *Nonaversive intervention for behavior problems: A manual for home and community*. Baltimore: Paul H. Brookes.

Minner, S., & Knutson, B. (1980). Improving vocational educators' attitudes toward mainstreaming. *Career Development for Exceptional Individuals*, 3, 93–100.

Minner, S., Knutson, B., & Aloia, G. (1979). *Concerns of vocational and special education teachers*. Unpublished manuscript. (Available from Project EMPLOY, Amphitheater School District, Tucson, Arizona)

National Association of State Boards of Education. (1992). *Winners all: A call for inclusive schools*. Alexandria, VA: Author.

Nelson, R. (1980). The role of guidance in career education for handicapped students. In G. M. Clark & W. J. White (Eds.), *Career education for the handicapped: Current perspectives for teachers* (pp. 114–122). Bootwyn, PA: Educational Resources Center.

Neufeld, G. R. (1977). Deinstitutionalization procedures. *American Association for the Education of the Severely/Profoundly Handicapped Review*, 2(1), 15–23.

Oberti v. Borough of Clementon School District, WL 178480 (3rd Cir. N.J. 1993).

O'Neill, R. E., Horner R. H., Albin, R. W., Storey, K., & Sprague, J. R. (1990). *Functional analysis of problem behavior*. Sycamore, IL: Sycamore Press.

Pasanella, J. (1980). A team approach to educational decision making. *Exceptional Teacher*, 1, 1–2, 8–9.

Position Statement: Advocacy for appropriate educational services for all children. (1986). Boston: National Coalition of Advocates for Students and the National Association of School Psychologists.

Regan, M., & Deshler, D. (1980). Inservice training for vocational educators. *Career Development for Exceptional Individuals*, 1, 44–52.

Reschly, D. J. (1988). Learning characteristics of mildly handicapped students: Implications for classification, placement, and programming. In M. C. Wang, M. C. Reynolds, & H. J. Walberg (Eds.), *The handbook of special education: Research and practice: Vol. 1. Learner characteristics and adaptive education* (pp. 35-58). Oxford, England: Pergamon Press.

Reynolds, M. C., & Birch, J. W. (1977). *Teaching exceptional children in all America's schools*. Reston, VA: Council for Exceptional Children.

Reynolds, M. C., Wang, M. C., & Walberg, H. J. (1987). The necessary restructuring of special and regular education. *Exceptional Children*, 53, 391–398.

Sailor, W., & Haring, N. G. (1977). Some current directions in education of the severely/multiply handicapped. *American Association for the Education of the Severely/Profoundly Handicapped Review*, 2(2), 67–87.

Sartain, H. W. (1976). Instruction of disabled learners: A reading perspective. *Journal of Learning Disabilities*, 9, 489–497.

Scranton, T. R., Hajicek, J. O., Wolcott, G. J. (1978). Assessing the effects of medication: The physician and teacher team. *Journal of Learning Disabilities*, 11, 205–209.

Séguin, E. (1866). *Idiocy and its treatment by the physiological method*. New York: Brandow.

Shirey, M. L. (Ed.). (1991). *Family involvement trainer's kit*. Seattle: University of Washington, Experimental Education Unit.

Skrtic, T. M. (1988). An organizational analysis of special education reform. *Counterpoint*, 8(2), 15–19.

Sontag, E., Burke, P. J., & York, R. (1973). Considerations for serving the severely handicapped in the public schools. *Education and Training of the Mentally Retarded*, 8, 20–26.

Stainback, S., & Stainback, W. (1987). Integration versus cooperation: A commentary on "Educating children with learning problems: A shared responsibility." *Exceptional Children*, 54, 66–68.

Stainback, S., & Stainback, W. (1992). *Curriculum considerations in inclusive classrooms: Facilitating learning for all students*. Baltimore: Paul H. Brookes.

Stedman's medical dictionary (25th ed.). (1990). Boston: Williams and Wilkins.

Stick, S. (1976). The speech pathologist and handicapped learners. *Journal of Learning Disabilities*, 9, 509–519.

Stowitschek, J. (1993). *Progressive career placement for youth with disabilities through cooperatively developed apprenticeships and internship programs: A business interests orientation in postsecondary education*. Seattle: University of Washington, Experimental Education Unit.

Tawney, J., & Gast, D. (1984). *Single subject research in special education*. Baltimore: Paul H. Brookes.

Taylor, S. J. (1988). Caught in the continuum: A critical analysis of the principle of the least restrictive environment. *Journal of the Association for Persons with Severe Handicaps*, 13(1), 41–53.

Tucker, D., & Horner, R. (1977). Competency-based training of paraprofessional teaching associates for education of the severely and profoundly handicapped. In E. Sontag, J. Smith, & N. Certo (Eds.), *Educational programming for the severely and profoundly handicapped* (pp. 65–75). Reston, VA: Council for Exceptional Children, Division on Mental Retardation.

Turnbull, A. P., Blue-Banning, M., Beher, S., & Kerns, G. (1986). Family research and intervention: A value and ethical examination. In P. C. Dokecki & R. M. Zaner (Eds.), *Ethics of dealing with persons with severe handicaps* (pp. 273–282). Baltimore: Paul H. Brookes.

U.S. Department of Education. (1988). *Tenth annual report to Congress on the implementation of the Education of the Handicapped Act*. Washington, DC: Author.

U.S. Department of Education. (1992). *Fourteenth annual report to Congress on the implementation of the Individuals with Disabilities Education Act*. Washington, DC: Author.

Voeltz, L. (1984). Program and curriculum innovations to prepare children for integration. In N. Certo, N. Haring, & R. York (Eds.), *Public school integration of severely handicapped students* (pp. 155-183). Baltimore: Paul H. Brookes.

Walker, J. L., & Goldenn, N. (1983). *A Curriculum for Children's Effective Peer and Teacher Skills* (ACCEPTS). Austin, TX: Pro-Ed.

Wallace, G., & McLoughlin, J. (1988). *Learning disabilities: Concepts and characteristics* (3rd ed.). New York: Merrill/Macmillan.

Wang, M. C., & Stiles, B. (1976). An investigation of children's concept of self-responsibility for their school learning. *American Education Research Journal*, 13, 159–179.

Wang, M. C., & Walberg, H. J. (1988). Four fallacies of segregationism. *Exceptional Children*, 55, 128–137.

Weintraub, F. J., & Ballard, J. (1982). Introduction: Bridging the decades. In J. Ballard, B. A. Ramirez, & F. J. Weintraub (Eds.), *Special education in America: Its legal and governmental foundations* (pp. 1–10). Reston, VA: Council for Exceptional Children.

White, O. R., & Haring, N. G. (1980). *Exceptional teaching* (2nd ed.). Columbus, OH: Merrill.

Will, M. C. (1986). Educating children with learning problems: A shared responsibility. *Exceptional Children*, 52, 411–415.

Wilson, D. L. (1992, July 15). A blind professor discovers computers, and his life is changed profoundly. *Chronicle of Higher Education*, p. A18.

Wright, G. N. (1980). *Total rehabilitation*. Boston: Little, Brown.

York, J. (1991). Toward a shared agenda for general and special education. IMPACT, 4(3) [Feature issue on inclusive education], 2–3. Minneapolis: University of Minnesota.

Zelder, E. Y. (1953). Public opinion and public education for exceptional children: Congressional intent and judicial interpretation. *Remedial and Special Education, 7*(2), 49–53.

CHAPTER TWO

American Speech-Language-Hearing Association. (1982). Position statement on language learning disorders. *Asha, 24,* 937–944.

Baca, L. M., & Cervantes, H. T. (Eds.). (1989). *The bilingual special education interface* (2nd ed.). New York: Merrill/Macmillan.

Brown v. Board of Education of Topeka, Kansas, 347 U.S. 483, 493 (1954).

Campbell, J., Gersten, R., & Kolar, C. (1992). *Quality of instruction provided to language minority students with learning disabilities: Five findings from micro-ethnographics* (Technical Report 92–5). Eugene, OR: Eugene Research Institute.

Chan, S. (1992). Families with Asian roots. In E. W. Lynch & M. J. Hanson (Eds.), *Developing cross-cultural competence* (pp. 181–257). Baltimore: Paul H. Brookes.

Coles, R. (1977). Growing up Chicano. In R. Coles (Ed.), *Eskimos, Chicanos, Indians* (pp. 110–142). Boston: Little, Brown.

Deno, S. L. (1985). Curriculum-based measurement: The emerging alternative. *Exceptional Children, 52,* 219–232.

Diana v. State Board of Education, C.A. No. C–70–37, RFP (N.D. Cal. 1970).

DuBray, W. H. (1985). American Indian values: Critical factor in casework. *Social Casework, 66,* 30–37.

Dunn, L. M. (1968). Special education for the mildly retarded: Is much of it justifiable? *Exceptional Children, 35,* 5–22.

Dyricia S. v. New York City Board of Education, 79 Civ. 2562 (E.D. N.Y. 1979).

Echevarria-Ratleff, I., & Graf, V. L. (1988). California bilingual special model sites (1984–1986): Programs and research. In A. A. Ortiz & B. A. Ramirez (Eds.), *Schools and the culturally diverse exceptional student: Promising practices and future directions* (pp. 104–111). Reston, VA: Council for Exceptional Children.

Erickson, J. G. (1985). How many languages do you speak? An overview of bilingual education. *Topics in Language Disorders, 5*(4), 1–14.

Feuerstein, R. F. (1979). *The dynamic assessment of retarded performers: The learning potential assessment device, theory, instruments, and techniques.* Baltimore: University Park Press.

Figueroa, R. A., Fradd, S. H., & Correa, V. I. (1989). Bilingual special education and this special issue. *Exceptional Children, 56,* 174–178.

Fradd, S. H., & Correa, V. I. (1989). Hispanic students at risk: Do we abdicate or advocate? *Exceptional Children, 56,* 105–110.

Fuchigami, R. Y. (1980). Teacher education for culturally diverse children. *Exceptional Children, 46,* 634–641.

Gersten, R., Morvant, M., George, N., & Woodward, J. (1992). *Inner city teachers' perceptions of special education* (Technical Report 92–4). Eugene, OR: Eugene Research Institute.

Gersten, R., & Woodward, J. (1992). *The language minority student and special education* (Technical Report 92087). Eugene, OR: Eugene Research Institute.

Greenleaf, W. (1980, February). *Work with SOMPA.* Paper presented at the Bureau of Education for the Handicapped–National Institute of Education conference entitled Toward Equity in the Evaluation of Children Suspected of Educational Handicaps, Washington, DC.

Grossman, H. J. (Ed.). (1983). *Manual on terminology and classification in mental retardation* (rev. ed.). Washington, DC: American Association on Mental Deficiency.

Hanson, M. J. (1992). Families with Anglo-European roots. In E. W. Lynch & M. J. Hanson (Eds.), *Developing cross-cultural competence* (pp. 65–87). Baltimore: Paul H. Brookes.

Harris, C. R. (1991). Identifying and serving the gifted new immigrant. *Teaching Exceptional Children, 23*(4), 26–41.

Harry, B. (1992). Making sense of disability: Low-income, Puerto Rican parents' theories of the problem. *Exceptional Children, 59,* 27–40.

Howell, K. W., & Morehead, M. K. (1987). *Curriculum-based evaluation for special and remedial education.* Columbus, OH: Merrill.

Joe, J. R., & Malach, R. S. (1992). Families with Native American roots. In E. W. Lynch & M. J. Hanson (Eds.), *Developing cross-cultural competence* (pp. 89–120). Baltimore: Paul H. Brookes.

Kaufman, A. S., & Kaufman, N. L. (1983). *Kaufman Assessment Battery for Children.* Circle Pines, MN: American Guidance Service.

Kelley, T., Bullock, L., & Dykes, M. (1977). Behavioral disorders: Teachers' perceptions. *Exceptional Children, 43,* 316–318.

Larry P. v. Riles, 343 F. Supp. 1306, C–71–2270 (N.D. Cal. 1972).

Lau v. Nichols, 414 U.S. 563 (1974).

Leung, E. K. (1990). Early risk: Transition from culturally/linguistically diverse homes to formal schooling. *Educational Issues of Language Minority Students, 7,* 35–52.

Lora v. New York City Board of Education, 587 F. Supp. 1572 (E.D. N.Y. 1984).

Lynch, E. W., & Hanson, M. J. (1992). Steps in the right direction: Implications for interventionists. In E. W. Lynch & M. J. Hanson (Eds.), *Developing cross-cultural competence* (pp. 355–371). Baltimore: Paul H. Brookes.

MacMillan, D. L., Hendrick, I. G., & Watkins, A. V. (1988). Impact of Diana, Larry P., and P.L. 94–142 on minority students. *Exceptional Children, 54,* 426–432.

Mercer, J. R. (1979). SOMPA: *System of Multicultural Pluralistic Assessment: Concepts and technical manual.* New York: Psychological Corporation.

Mokuau, N., & Tauili'ili, P. (1992). Families with native Hawaiian and Pacific Island roots. In E. W. Lynch & M. J. Hanson (Eds.), *Developing cross-cultural competence* (pp. 301–318). Baltimore: Paul H. Brookes.

Ortiz, A. A. (1986). Characteristics of limited English proficient Hispanic students served in programs of the learning disabled: Implications for policy and practice (Pt. 2). *Bilingual Special Education Newsletter, 4,* 3–5. Austin: University of Texas.

Ortiz, A. A., & Garcia, S. B. (1988). A prereferral process for preventing inappropriate referrals of Hispanic students to special education. In A. A. Ortiz & B. A. Ramirez (Eds.), *Schools and the culturally diverse exceptional student: Promising practices and future directions* (pp. 6–18). Reston, VA: Council for Exceptional Children.

Ortiz, A. A., & Yates, J. R. (1982). Teacher training associated with serving bilingual exceptional students. *Teacher Education and Special Education, 5,* 61–68.

Rodriguez, F. (1982). Mainstreaming a multicultural concept into special education: Guidelines for teacher trainers. *Exceptional Children, 49,* 220–227.

Sharifzadeh, V. (1992). Families with Middle Eastern roots. In E. W. Lynch & M. J. Hanson (Eds.), *Developing cross-cultural competence* (pp. 319–351). Baltimore: Paul H. Brookes.

Spring, C., Blunden, D., Greenberg, L., & Yellin, A. (1977). Validity and norms of a hyperactivity rating scale. *Journal of Special Education, 11,* 313–321.

Tobias, S., Cole, C., Zibrin, M., & Bodlakova, V. (1981, November). *Bias in the referral of children to special services.* Paper presented at the meeting of the American Psychological Association, Los Angeles.

Trueba, H. T. (1989). *Raising silent voices.* New York: Newbury House.

U.S. Bureau of the Census. (1991). *Census of population: Chapter D. Detailed population characteristics: Part I. U.S. summary.* Washington, DC: U.S. Government Printing Office.

Willis, W. (1992). Families with African American roots. In E. W. Lynch & M. J. Hanson (Eds.), *Developing cross-cultural competence* (pp. 121–150). Baltimore: Paul H. Brookes.

Yates, J. R., & Ortiz, A. A. (1991). Professional development needs of teachers who serve exceptional language minorities in today's schools. *Teacher Education and Special Education, 14,* 11–18.

Ysseldyke, J. E. (1979). Issues in psychoeducational assessment. In D. J. Reschly & G. Phye (Eds.), *School psychology: Methods and roles* (pp. 247–260). New York: Academic Press.

Ysseldyke, J. E., & Algozzine, B. (1984). *Introduction to special education.* Boston: Houghton Mifflin.

Ysseldyke, J. E., Algozzine, B., & Allen, D. (1981). Participation of regular teachers in special education team decision making: A naturalistic investigation. *Elementary School Journal, 82,* 160–165.

Ysseldyke, J. E., Algozzine, B., Regan, R., Richey, L., & Thurlow, M. (1980). *Psychoeducational assessment and decision making: A computer simulated investigation.* Minneapolis: University of Minnesota, Institute for Research in Learning Disabilities.

Zuniga, M. E. (1992). Families with Latin roots. In E. W. Lynch & M. J. Hanson (Eds.), *Developing cross-cultural competence* (pp. 151–179). Baltimore: Paul H. Brookes.

CHAPTER THREE

Bayley, N. (1984). *Bayley Scales of Infant Development.* New York: Psychological Corporation.

Bloom, B. S. (1964). *Stability and change in human characteristics.* New York: Wiley.

Bredekamp, S. (Ed.). (1987). *Developmentally appropriate practice in early childhood programs serving children from birth through age 8.* Washington, DC: National Association for the Education of Young Children.

Bricker, D. (1986). *Early education of at-risk and handicapped infants, toddlers, and preschool children.* Glenview, IL: Scott, Foresman.

Brown, L., Branston, M. B., Hamre-Nietupski, S., Pumpian, I., Certo, N., & Gruenewald, L. (1979). A strategy for developing chronological-age-appropriate and functional curricular content for severely handicapped adolescents and young adults. *Journal of Special Education, 13,* 81–90.

Chandler, L. (1993). Steps in preparing for transition. *Teaching Exceptional Children, 25*(4), 52–55.

Cooke, T. P., Ruskus, J. A., Apolloni, T. A., & Peck, C. A. (1981). Handicapped preschool children in the mainstream: Background, outcomes, and clinical suggestions. *Topics in Early Childhood Special Education*, 1, 73–83.

Dunn, L. (1981). *Peabody Picture Vocabulary Test—Revised edition*. Circle Pines, MN: American Guidance Service.

Guess, D., Sailor, W., & Baer, D. M. (1977). A behavioral remedial approach to language training for the severely handicapped. In E. Sontag (Ed.), *Educational programming for the severely and profoundly handicapped* (pp. 97–120). Reston, VA: Council for Exceptional Children.

Guralnick, M. J. (1981). Programmatic factors affecting child-child social interactions in mainstream preschool programs. *Exceptional Education Quarterly*, 1(4), 71–92.

Guralnick, M. J. (1990). Major accomplishments and future directions in early childhood mainstreaming. *Topics in Early Childhood Special Education*, 10, 1–18.

Guralnick, M. J., & Groom, J. M. (1988). Peer interactions in mainstreamed and specialized classrooms: A comparative analysis. *Exceptional Children*, 5, 415–425.

Haring, K. A., Lovett, D. L., Haney, K. F., Algozzine, B., Smith, D. D., & Clarke, J. (1992). Labeling preschoolers as learning disabled: A cautionary position. *Topics in Early Childhood Special Education*, 12, 151–173.

Hunt, J. McV. (1961). *Intelligence and experience*. New York: Ronald.

Huntinger, P. L. (1986). ACTT *Starter Kit*. Macomb: Western Illinois University, College of Education.

Katoff, L., Reuter, J., & Dunn, V. (1978). *Kent Infant Development Scale*. Kent, OH: Kent State University.

Kennedy, M. D., Sheridan, M. K., Radlinski, S. H., & Beeghly, M. (1991). Play-language relationships in young children with developmental delays: Implications for assessment. *Journal of Speech and Hearing Research*, 34, 112–122.

Kirk, S. A. (1958). *Early education of the mentally retarded: An experimental study*. Urbana: University of Illinois Press.

Lynch, E. W., & Hanson, M. J. (1992). *Developing cross-cultural competence*. Baltimore: Paul H. Brookes.

McCormick, L., & Kawate, J. (1982). Kindergarten survival skills: New directions for preschool special education. *Education and Training of the Mentally Retarded*, 17, 247–251.

Noonan, M. J., & McCormick, L. (1993). *Early intervention in natural environments: Methods and procedures*. Pacific Grove, CA: Brooks/Cole.

Odom, S. L., & Strain, P. S. (1984). Peer-mediated approaches to increasing children's social interactions: A review. *American Journal of Orthopsychiatry*, 54, 544–557.

Odom, S. L., & Warren, S. F. (1988). Early childhood special education in the year 2000. *Journal of the Division for Early Childhood*, 12, 263–273.

Peterson, N. L. (1987). *Early intervention for handicapped and at-risk children*. Denver: Love.

Piaget, J. (1952). *The origins of intelligence in children*. New York: Norton.

Piaget, J. (1971). Piaget's theory. In P. H. Mussen (Ed.), *Carmichael's manual of child psychology* (Vol. 1, 3rd ed., pp. 319–347). New York: Wiley.

Ramey, C. T., & Ramey, S. L. (1992). *At risk does not mean doomed*. National Health/Education Consortium Occasional Paper #4, National Commission to Prevent Infant Mortality, 330 C Street SW, Switzer Building, Room 2014, Washington, DC 20201.

Skeels, H. (1966). Adult status of children with contrasting early life experiences: A follow-up study. *Monographs of the Society for Research in Child Development*, 31 (Serial No. 105).

Skeels, H., & Dye, H. (1939). A study of the effects of differential stimulation on mentally retarded children. *Proceedings and Addresses of the American Association on Mental Deficiency*, 44, 114–136.

Strain, P. S., & Odom, S. L. (1986). Peer social initiations: Effective interventions for social skills development of exceptional children. *Exceptional Children*, 52, 543–551.

Tjossem, T. D. (1976). *Intervention strategies for high risk infants and young children*. Baltimore: University Park Press.

Turnbull, A. P., & Turnbull, H. R. (1986). Stepping back from early intervention: An ethical perspective. *Journal of the Division for Early Childhood*, 10, 106–117.

U.S. Department of Education. (1990). *Twelfth Annual Report to Congress on the Implementation of the Education of the Handicapped Act*. Washington, DC: Author.

CHAPTER FOUR

Adelman, H. S., & Taylor, L. (1983a). Enhancing motivation for overcoming learning and behavior problems. *Journal of Learning Disabilities*, 16, 384–392.

Adelman, H. S., & Taylor, L. (1983b). *Learning disabilities in perspective*. Glenview, IL: Scott, Foresman.

Affleck, J. Q., Madge, S., Adams, A., & Lowenbraun, S. (1988). Integrated classroom versus resource model: Academic viability and effectiveness. *Exceptional Children*, 54, 339–348.

Alberto, P. A., & Troutman, A. C. (1990). *Applied behavior analysis for teachers* (3rd ed.). New York: Merrill/Macmillan.

Alley, G., & Deshler, D. (1979). *Teaching the learning disabled adolescent: Strategies and methods*. Denver: Love.

Allington, R. L. (1984). So what is the problem? Whose problem is it? *Topics in Learning and Learning Disabilities*, 3(4), 91–99.

American Psychiatric Association. (1982). *Diagnostic and statistical manual of mental disorders* (3rd ed.). Washington, DC: Author.

American Psychiatric Association. (1987). *Diagnostic and statistical manual of mental disorders* (3rd ed., rev.). Washington, DC: Author.

Arter, J. A., & Jenkins, J. R. (1979). Differential diagnosis-prescriptive teaching: A critical appraisal. *Review of Educational Research, 49,* 517–555.

Association for Children with Learning Disabilities. (1986, July 25). ACLD description: Specific learning disabilities. *ACLD Newsbriefs,* pp. 15–16.

Ausubel, D. P. (1960). The use of advance organizers in the learning and retention of meaningful verbal material. *Journal of Educational Psychology, 51,* 267–272.

Bachara, G. H., & Zaba, J. N. (1978). Learning disabilities and juvenile delinquency. *Journal of Learning Disabilities, 11,* 242–246.

Baker, L. (1982). An evaluation of the role of metacognitive deficits in learning disabilities. *Topics in Learning and Learning Disabilities, 2,* 27–35.

Bartel, N. R. (1990). Problems in mathematics achievement. In D. D. Hammill & N. R. Bartel (Eds.), *Teaching students with learning and behavior problems* (5th ed., pp. 289–343). Boston: Allyn and Bacon.

Bateman, B. D. (1964). Learning disabilities: Yesterday, today, and tomorrow. *Exceptional Children, 31,* 167.

Baum, D. D., Duffelmeyer, F., & Geelan, M. (1988). Resource teacher perceptions of the prevalence of social dysfunction among students with learning disabilities. *Journal of Learning Disabilities, 21,* 380–381.

Bender, W. N., & Golden, L. B. (1990). Subtypes of students with learning disabilities as derived from cognitive, academic, behavioral, and self-concept measures. *Learning Disability Quarterly, 13,* 183–194.

Bender, W. N., & Ukeje, I. C. (1989). Instructional strategies in mainstream classrooms: Prediction of the strategies teachers select. *Remedial and Special Education, 10(2),* 23–30.

Bigler, E. D. (1987). Acquired cerebral trauma: An introduction to the special series. *Journal of Learning Disabilities, 20,* 454–457.

Blankenship, C., & Lilly, M. S. (1981). *Mainstreaming students with learning and behavior problems: Techniques for the classroom teacher.* New York: Holt, Rinehart and Winston.

Bley, N. S., & Thornton, C. A. (1989). *Teaching mathematics to the learning disabled* (2nd ed.). Austin, TX: Pro-Ed.

Brackbill, Y., McManus, K., & Woodward, L. (1985). *Medication in maternity: Infant exposure and maternal information.* Ann Arbor: University of Michigan Press.

Brophy, J., & Good, T. (1986). Teacher behavior and student achievement. In M. C. Wittrock (Ed.), *Third handbook of research on teaching* (3rd ed., pp. 328–375). New York: Macmillan.

Brown, A. L., Day, J. D., & Jones, R. S. (1983). The development of plans for summarizing texts. *Child Development, 54,* 968–979.

Bryan, T. (1977). Learning disabled children's comprehension of nonverbal communication. *Journal of Learning Disabilities, 10,* 501–506.

Bryan, T. (1991). Social problems and learning disabilities. In B. Y. L. Wong (Ed.), *Learning about learning disabilities* (pp. 195–229). San Diego: Academic Press.

Bryan, T. H., & Bryan, J. H. (1986). *Understanding learning disabilities* (3rd ed.). Palo Alto, CA: Mayfield.

Bulgren, J. A., Schumaker, J. B., & Deshler, D. D. (1988). Effectiveness of a concept teaching routine in enhancing the performance of LD students in secondary-level mainstream classes. *Learning Disability Quarterly, 11,* 3–17.

Carlberg, C., & Kavale, K. (1980). The efficacy of special versus regular class placement for exceptional children: A meta-analysis. *Journal of Special Education, 14,* 295–309.

Carnine, D. (1989). Teaching complex content to learning disabled students: The role of technology. *Exceptional Children, 55,* 524–533.

Carnine, D. (1990). Beyond technique: Direct instruction and higher-order skills. *Direct Instruction News, 9(3),* 1–13.

Carnine, D., Silbert, J., & Kameenui, E. J. (1990). *Direct instruction reading* (2nd ed.). New York: Merrill/Macmillan.

Carpenter, R. L. (1985). Mathematics instruction in resource rooms: Instruction time and teacher competence. *Learning Disability Quarterly, 8,* 95–100.

Cawley, J. F. (1984). *Developmental teaching of mathematics for the learning disabled.* Austin, TX: Pro-Ed.

Cawley, J. F. (1985). Cognition and the learning disabled. In J. Cawley (Ed.), *Cognitive strategies and mathematics for the learning disabled* (pp. 1–32). Austin, TX: Pro-Ed.

Cawley, J. F., & Miller, J. H. (1989). Cross-sectional comparisons of the mathematical performance of children with learning disabilities: Are we on the right track toward comprehensive programming? *Journal of Learning Disabilities, 23,* 250–254, 259.

Chalfant, J. C. (1985). Identifying learning disabled students: A summary of the National Task Force report. *Learning Disabilities Focus, 1,* 9–20.

Chelser, B. (1982, September 8). ACLD vocational committee completes survey on LD adult. *ACLD Newsbriefs,* pp. 5, 20–23.

Coleman, J. M., Pullis, M. E., & Minnett, A. M. (1987). Studying mildly handicapped children's adjustment to mainstreaming: A systematic approach. *Remedial and Special Education*, 8(6), 19–30.

Coles, G. S. (1980). Evaluation of genetic explanations of reading and learning problems. *Journal of Special Education*, 14, 365–383.

Cone, T. E., & Wilson, L. R. (1981). Quantifying a severe discrepancy: A critical analysis. *Learning Disability Quarterly*, 4, 359–371.

Cordoni, B. (1982). A directory of college LD services. *Journal of Learning Disabilities*, 15, 529–534.

Cosden, M. A., Gerber, M. M., Semmel, D. S., Goldman, S. R., & Semmel, M. I. (1987). Microcomputer use within micro-educational environments. *Exceptional Children*, 53, 399–409.

Cott, A. (1972). Megavitamins: The orthomolecular approach to behavior disorders and learning disabilities. *Academic Therapy*, 7, 245–259.

Council for Learning Disabilities Research Committee. (1992). Minimum standards for the description of participants in learning disabilities research. *Learning Disability Quarterly*, 15, 65–70.

Crawford, D. (1984). ACLD–R and D project summary: A study investigating the link between learning disabilities and juvenile delinquency. In W. Cruickshank & J. Kliebhan (Eds.), *Early adolescence to early adulthood: Vol. 5. The best of ACLD* (pp. 3–18). Syracuse, NY: Syracuse University Press.

Cronin, M. E., & Currie, P. S. (1984). Study skills: A resource guide for practitioners. *Remedial and Special Education*, 5(2), 61–69.

Deaton, A. V. (1987). Behavioral change strategies for children and adolescents with severe brain injury. *Journal of Learning Disabilities*, 20, 581–589.

DeFries, J., & Decker, S. (1982). Genetic aspects of reading disability: A family study. In R. N. Malatesha & P. G. Aaron (Eds.), *Reading disorders: Varieties and treatments* (pp. 255–279). New York: Academic Press.

Deshler, D. D., Alley, G. R., Warner, M. M., & Schumaker, J. B. (1981). Instructional practices for promoting skill acquisition and generalization in severely learning disabled adolescents. *Learning Disability Quarterly*, 4, 415–421.

Deshler, D. D., & Lenz, B. K. (1989). The strategies instructional approach. *International Journal of Disability, Development, and Education*, 36, 203–224.

Deshler, D. D., & Schumaker, J. B. (1983). Social skills of learning disabled adolescents: A review of characteristics and intervention. *Topics in Learning and Learning Disabilities*, 3, 15–23.

Deshler, D. D., & Schumaker, J. B. (1988). An instructional model for teaching students how to learn. In J. L. Graden, J. E. Zins, & M. J. Curtis (Eds.), *Alternative educa-tional delivery systems: Enhancing instructional options for all students* (pp. 124–141). Washington, DC: National Association of School Psychologists.

Deshler, D. D., Schumaker, J. B., & Lenz, B. K. (1984). Academic and cognitive interventions for LD adolescents: Part 1. *Journal of Learning Disabilities*, 17, 108–117.

Deshler, D. D., Schumaker, J. B., Lenz, B. K., & Ellis, E. (1984). Academic and cognitive interventions for LD adolescents: Part II. *Journal of Learning Disabilities*, 17, 170–179.

Ellis, E. S., Deshler, D. D., Lenz, B. K., Schumaker, J. B., & Clark, F. L. (1991). An instructional model for teaching learning strategies. *Focus on Exceptional Children*, 24(1), 1–14.

Ellis, E. S., & Sabornie, E. J. (1986). Effective instruction with microcomputers: Promises, practices, and preliminary findings. *Focus on Exceptional Children*, 19(4), 1–16.

Engelmann, S., & Carnine, D. (1982). *Corrective mathematics program*. Chicago: Science Research Associates.

Engelmann, S., & Osborn, J. (1976). DISTAR *language: An instructional system*. Chicago: Science Research Associates.

Englert, C. (1984). Effective direct instruction practices in special education settings. *Remedial and Special Education*, 5(2), 38–47.

Feagans, L. (1983). Current view of learning disabilities. *Journal of Pediatrics*, 102, 484–493.

Feingold, B. F. (1975). Hyperkinesis and learning disabilities linked to artificial food flavors and colors. *American Journal of Nursing*, 75, 797–803.

Feingold, B. F. (1976). Hyperkinesis and learning disabilities linked to the ingestion of artificial food colors and flavors. *Journal of Learning Disabilities*, 9, 551–559.

Fernald, G. (1943). *Remedial techniques in basic school subjects*. New York: McGraw-Hill.

Fernald, G. (1988). *Remedial techniques in basic school subjects*. Austin, TX: Pro-Ed.

Finlan, T. G. (1992). Do state methods of quantifying a severe discrepancy result in fewer students with learning disabilities? *Learning Disability Quarterly*, 15, 129–134.

Fitzgerald, G., Fick, L., & Milich, R. (1986). Computer-assisted instruction for students with attentional difficulties. *Journal of Learning Disabilities*, 6, 376–379.

Frankenberger, W., & Fronzaglio, K. (1991). A review of states' criteria and procedures for identifying children with learning disabilities. *Journal of Learning Disabilities*, 24, 495–500.

Fuchs, L. S., Fuchs, D., & Hamlett, C. L. (1989). Effects of alternative goal structures within curriculum-based measurement. *Exceptional Children*, 55, 429–438.

Fuchs, L. S., Wesson, C., Tindal, G., Mirkin, P., & Deno, S. (1981). *Teacher efficiency in continuous evaluation of* IEP *goals* (Research Report No. 53). Minneapolis: University of Minnesota, Institute for Research in Learning Disabilities.

Gersten, R., Carnine, D., & Woodward, J. (1987). Direct instruction research: The third decade. *Remedial and Special Education*, 8(6), 48–56.

Gersten, R., & Woodward, J. (1990). Rethinking the regular education initiative: Focus on the classroom teacher. *Remedial and Special Education*, 11(3), 7–16.

Gersten, R., Woodward, J., & Darch, C. (1986). Direct instruction: A research-based approach to curriculum design and teaching. *Exceptional Children*, 53, 17–31.

Gibbs, D. P., & Cooper, E. B. (1989). Prevalence of communication disorders in students with learning disabilities. *Journal of Learning Disabilities*, 22, 60–63.

Gillingham, A., & Stillman, B. (1970). *Remedial teaching for children with specific disability in reading, spelling, and penmanship* (7th ed.). Cambridge, MA: Educators Publishing Service.

Gold, S., & Sherry, L. (1984). Hyperactivity, learning disabilities, and alcohol. *Journal of Learning Disabilities*, 17, 3–6.

Gottlieb, J. (1981). Mainstreaming: Fulfilling the promise? *American Journal of Mental Deficiency*, 86, 115–126.

Graden, J. L., Casey, A., & Christenson, S. L. (1985). Implementing a prereferral intervention system: Part I. The model. *Exceptional Children*, 51, 377–384.

Gresham, F. M. (1982). Misguided mainstreaming: The case for social skills training with handicapped children. *Exceptional Children*, 48, 422–433.

Gresham, F. M. (1988). Social competence and motivational characteristics of learning disabled students. In M. Wang, M. Reynolds, & H. Walberg (Eds.), *The handbook of special education: Research and practice* (pp. 283–302). Oxford, England: Pergamon Press.

Gresham, F. M., & Elliott, S. N. (1989). Social skills deficits as a primary learning disability. *Journal of Learning Disabilities*, 22, 120–124.

Grimes, L. (1981). Computers are for kids: Designing software programs. *Teaching Exceptional Children*, 14, 48–53.

Grise, P. J. (1980). Florida's minimum competency testing program for handicapped students. *Exceptional Children*, 47, 186–191.

Hallahan, D. P., & Cruickshank, W. M. (1973). *Psychoeducational foundations of learning disabilities*. Englewood Cliffs, NJ: Prentice-Hall.

Hallahan, D. P., & Kauffman, J. M. (1988). *Exceptional children: Introduction to special education* (4th ed.). Englewood Cliffs, NJ: Prentice-Hall.

Hallahan, D. P., Kauffman, J. M., & Lloyd, J. W. (1985). *Introduction to learning disabilities* (2nd ed.). Englewood Cliffs, NJ: Prentice-Hall.

Hallahan, D. P., & Reeve, R. E. (1980). Selective attention and distractibility. In B. K. Keogh (Ed.), *Advances in special education: Vol. 1. Basic constructs and theoretical orientations* (pp. 141–181). Greenwich, CT: JAI Press.

Hallgren, B. (1950). Specific dyslexia: A clinical and genetic study. *Acta Psychiatrica Neurologica*, 65, 1–287.

Hammill, D. D. (1990). On defining learning disabilities: An emerging consensus. *Journal of Learning Disabilities*, 23, 74–84.

Hammill, D. D., Leigh, J. E., McNutt, G., & Larsen, S. C. (1981). A new definition of learning disabilities. *Learning Disability Quarterly*, 4, 336–342.

Haring, N. G., & Krug, D. A. (1975). Placement in regular programs: Procedures and results. *Exceptional Children*, 41, 413–417.

Haring, N. G., & Schiefelbusch, R. L. (Eds.). (1976). *Teaching special children*. New York: McGraw-Hill.

Hasselbring, T. S., Goin, L. I., & Bransford, J. D. (1988). Developing math automaticity in learning handicapped children: The role of computerized drill and practice. *Focus on Exceptional Children*, 20(6), 1–7.

Haynes, J. A., & Malouf, D. B. (1986). Computer assisted instruction needs help. *Academic Therapy*, 22, 157–164.

Hazel, J. S., & Schumaker, J. B. (1988). Social skills and learning disabilities: Current issues and recommendations for future research. In J. F. Kavanagh & T. J. Truss, Jr. (Eds.), *Learning disabilities: Proceedings of the national conference* (pp. 293–344). Parkton, MD: York Press.

Heckelman, R. G. (1969). The neurological impress method of remedial reading instruction. *Academic Therapy*, 4, 277–282.

Hofmeister, A. M. (1984). *Microcomputer applications in the classroom*. New York: Holt, Rinehart and Winston.

Horn, W. F., O'Donnell, J. P., & Vitulano, L. A. (1983). Long-term follow-up studies of learning-disabled persons. *Journal of Learning Disabilities*, 16, 542–555.

Horton, S. V., Lovitt, T. C., Givens, A., & Nelson, R. (1989). Teaching social studies to high school students with academic handicaps in a mainstreamed setting: Effects of a computerized study guide. *Journal of Learning Disabilities*, 22, 102–107.

Howell, K. W., Kaplan, J. S., & O'Connell, C. Y. (1979). *Evaluating exceptional children: A task analysis approach*. Columbus: Merrill.

Hresko, W. P., & Reid, D. K. (1981). Five faces of cognition: Theoretical influences on approaches to learning disabilities. *Learning Disability Quarterly*, 4, 238–243.

Hughes, C. A., Schumaker, J. B., Deshler, D. D., & Mercer, C. D. (1988). *The learning strategies curriculum: The test-taking strategy*. Lawrence, KS: Edge Enterprises.

Hughes, C. A., & Smith, J. (1990). Cognitive and academic performance of college students with learning disabilities: A synthesis of literature. *Learning Disability Quarterly, 13,* 66–79.

Interagency Committee on Learning Disabilities. (1987). *Learning disabilities: A report to the U.S. Congress.* Bethesda, MD: National Institutes of Health.

Kavale, K. A., & Forness, S. R. (1985). *The science of learning disabilities*. San Diego, CA: College Hill Press.

Kavale, K. A., & Forness, S. R. (1987). The far side of heterogeneity: A critical analysis of empirical subtyping research in learning disabilities. *Journal of Learning Disabilities, 20,* 374–382.

Keefe, C. H., & Candler, A. C. (1989). LD students and word processors: Questions and answers. *Learning Disabilities Focus, 4,* 78–83.

Keilitz, I., & Dunivant, N. (1986). The relationship between learning disability and juvenile delinquency: Current state of knowledge. *Remedial and Special Education, 7(3),* 18–26.

Keilitz, I., Zaremba, B. A., & Broder, P. K. (1979). The link between learning disabilities and juvenile delinquency: Some issues and answers. *Learning Disability Quarterly, 2(2),* 2–11.

Kelly, B., Gersten, R., & Carnine, D. (1990). Student error patterns as a function of curriculum design: Teaching fractions to remedial high school students and high school students with learning disabilities. *Journal of Learning Disabilities, 1,* 23–29.

Keogh, B. K. (1987). Learning disabilities: In defense of a construct. *Learning Disabilities Research, 3,* 4–9.

Keogh, B. K. (1990). Narrowing the gap between policy and practice. *Exceptional Children, 57,* 186–190.

Kerr, M. M., & Nelson, C. M. (1989). *Strategies for managing behavior problems in the classroom* (2nd ed.). New York: Merrill/Macmillan.

Kershner, J. F., Hawks, W., & Grekin, R. (1977). *Megavitamins and learning disorders: A controlled double-blind experiment.* Unpublished manuscript, Ontario Institute for Studies in Education, Toronto.

Kimball, W. H., & Heron, T. E. (1988). A behavioral commentary on Poplin's discussion of reductionistic fallacy and holistic/constructivist principles. *Journal of Learning Disabilities, 21,* 425–428.

Kirk, S. A., & Chalfant, J. C. (1984). *Academic and developmental learning disabilities*. Denver: Love.

Kirk, S. A., Gallagher, J. J., & Anastasiow, N. J. (1993). *Educating exceptional children* (7th ed.). Boston: Houghton Mifflin.

Kline, F., Schumaker, J. B., & Deshler, D. D. (1991). Development and validation of feedback routines for instructing students with learning disabilities. *Learning Disability Quarterly, 14,* 191–207.

Knowles, B. S., & Knowles, P. S. (1983). A model for identifying learning disabilities in college-bound students. *Journal of Learning Disabilities, 16,* 425–434.

Kolich, E. M. (1985). Microcomputer technology with the learning disabled: A review of the literature. *Journal of Learning Disabilities, 18,* 428–431.

Kulik, J. A., Kulik, C. C., & Bangert-Drowns, R. L. (1985). Effectiveness of computer-based education in elementary schools. *Computers in Human Behavior, 1,* 59–74.

Langford, K., Slade, K., & Barnett, A. (1974). An explanation of impress techniques in remedial reading. *Academic Therapy, 9,* 309–319.

Lenz, B. K. (1992). Cognitive approaches to teaching. In C. D. Mercer, *Students with learning disabilities* (4th ed., pp. 268–309). New York: Merrill/Macmillan.

Lenz, B. K., Alley, G. R., & Schumaker, J. B. (1987). Activating the inactive learner: Advance organizers in the secondary content classroom. *Learning Disability Quarterly, 10,* 53–67.

Lenz, B. K., Bulgren, J., & Hudson, P. (1990). Content enhancement: A model for promoting the acquisition of content by individuals with learning disabilities. In T. E. Scruggs & B. Y. L. Wong (Eds.), *Intervention research in learning disabilities* (pp. 122–165). New York: Springer.

Lenz, B. K., & Hughes, C. A. (1990). A word identification strategy for adolescents with learning disabilities. *Journal of Learning Disabilities, 23,* 149–158, 163.

Lenz, B. K., Schumaker, J. B., Deshler, D. D., & Beals, V. L. (1984). *The learning strategies curriculum: The word identification strategy*. Lawrence: University of Kansas, Institute for Research in Learning Disabilities.

Lerner, J. W. (1993). *Learning disabilities: Theories, diagnosis, and teaching strategies*. Boston: Houghton Mifflin.

Licht, B. G. (1984). Cognitive-motivational factors that contribute to the achievement of learning-disabled children. *Annual Review of Learning Disabilities, 2,* 119–126.

Lindsey, J. D. (1987). *Computers and exceptional individuals*. Columbus: Merrill.

Lloyd, J. (1980). Academic instruction and cognitive techniques: The need for attack strategy training. *Exceptional Education Quarterly, 1,* 53–63.

Loper, A. B. (1980). Metacognitive development: Implications for cognitive training of exceptional children. *Exceptional Education Quarterly, 1,* 1–8.

Loucks-Horsley, S., & Roody, D. S. (1990). Using what is known about change to inform the Regular Education Initiative. *Remedial and Special Education, 11(3),* 51–56.

Lovitt, T. C. (1975). Applied behavior analysis and learning disabilities: Part II. Specific research recommendations and suggestions for practitioners. *Journal of Learning Disabilities, 8,* 514–518.

Lyon, G. R. (1985). Educational validation studies. In B. P. Rourke (Ed.), *Neuropsychology of learning disabilities* (pp. 228–253). New York: Guilford.

Macy, D. J., & Carter, J. L. (1978). Comparison of a mainstream and self-contained special education program. *Journal of Special Education, 12,* 303–313.

Majsterek, D. J., & Wilson, R. (1989). Computer-assisted instruction for students with learning disabilities: Considerations for practitioners. *Learning Disabilities Focus, 5,* 18–27.

Mayer, R. E. (1983). *Thinking, problem solving, cognition.* New York: Freeman.

Mayer, R. E. (1987). *Educational psychology: A cognitive approach.* Boston: Little, Brown.

McKinney, J. D. (1984). The search for subtypes of specific learning disability. *Journal of Learning Disabilities, 17,* 43–50.

McKinney, J. D. (1989). Longitudinal research on the behavioral characteristics of children with learning disabilities. *Journal of Learning Disabilities, 22,* 141–150, 165.

McLoughlin, J. A., & Lewis, R. B. (1990). *Assessing special students* (3rd ed.). New York: Merrill/Macmillan.

Mellard, D. (1990). The eligibility process: Identifying students with learning disabilities in California's community colleges. *Learning Disabilities Focus, 5,* 75–90.

Meltzer, L. J., Levine, M. D., Karniski, W., Palfrey, J. S., & Clarke, S. (1984). An analysis of the learning styles of adolescent delinquents. *Journal of Learning Disabilities, 17,* 600–608.

Mercer, C. D. (1992). *Students with learning disabilities* (4th ed.). New York: Merrill/Macmillan.

Mercer, C. D., Forgnone, C., & Wolking, W. D. (1976). Definitions of learning disabilities used in the United States. *Journal of Learning Disabilities, 9,* 376–386.

Mercer, C. D., Hughes, C., & Mercer, A. R. (1985). Learning disabilities definitions used by state education departments. *Learning Disability Quarterly, 8,* 45–55.

Mercer, C. D., King-Sears, P., & Mercer, A. R. (1990). Learning disabilities definitions and criteria used by state education departments. *Learning Disabilities Quarterly, 13,* 141–152.

Mercer, C. D., & Mercer, A. R. (1993). *Teaching students with learning problems* (4th ed.). New York: Merrill/Macmillan.

Mercer, C. D., Peterson, S. K., & Ross, J. J. (1988). A university-based model of multidisciplinary services to exceptional students and related professionals. *Focus on Exceptional Children, 21*(2), 1–12.

Miller, L. (1990). The Regular Education Initiative and school reform: Lessons from the mainstream. *Remedial and Special Education, 11*(3), 17–22, 28.

Murphy, M. L. (1976). *Idaho study of learning disabilities: Definition, eligibility criteria, and evaluation procedures.* Unpublished manuscript, State of Idaho Department of Education, Boise.

Myers, P. I., & Hammill, D. D. (1990). *Learning disabilities: Basic concepts, assessment practices, and instructional strategies* (4th ed.). Austin, TX: Pro-Ed.

National Council of Teachers of Mathematics. (1989). *Curriculum and evaluation standards for school mathematics.* Reston, VA: Author.

National Governors Association. (1990). *National education goals for the year 2000.* U.S. Presidential and Governors Summit.

National Joint Committee on Learning Disabilities. (1985, February). *Adults with learning disabilities: A call to action* [Position paper of the National Joint Committee on Learning Disabilities]. Baltimore: The Orton Dyslexia Society.

National Joint Committee on Learning Disabilities. (1988). [Letter to NJCLD member organizations].

National Joint Committee on Learning Disabilities and the Preschool Child. (1985, February). *A position paper of the National Joint Committee on Learning Disabilities.* Baltimore: The Orton Dyslexia Society.

Orton, S. (1937). *Reading, writing and speech problems in children.* New York: Norton.

Palincsar, A. S., & Brown, A. L. (1984). Reciprocal teaching of comprehension fostering and comprehension monitoring activities. *Cognition and Instruction, 1,* 117–175.

Rapp, D. J. (1978). Does diet affect hyperactivity? *Journal of Learning Disabilities, 11,* 383–389.

Rappaport, S. (1975). Ego development in learning disabled children. In W. M. Cruickshank & D. P. Hallahan (Eds.), *Perceptual and learning disabilities in children: Vol 1. Psychological practices* (pp. 355–376). Syracuse, NY: Syracuse University Press.

Reynolds, M. C. (1989). An historical perspective: The delivery of special education to mildly disabled and at-risk students. *Remedial and Special Education, 10*(6), 7–11.

Riegel, R. H., & Mathey, J. P. (Eds.). (1980). *Mainstreaming at the secondary level: Seven models that work.* Plymouth, MI: Wayne County Intermediate School District.

Rooney, K. J., & Hallahan, D. P. (1988). The effects of self-monitoring on adult behavior and student independence. *Learning Disabilities Research, 3,* 88–93.

Rosenshine, G. (1978). The third cycle of research on teacher effects: Content covered, academic engaged time, and quality of instruction. In National Society for the Study of Education, *78th yearbook* (pp. 272–290). Chicago: University of Chicago Press.

Salvia, J., & Ysseldyke, J. E. (1991). *Assessment in special and remedial education* (5th ed.). Boston: Houghton Mifflin.

Schumaker, J. B., & Deshler, D. D. (1984). Setting demand variables: A major factor in program planning for the LD adolescent. *Topics in Language Disorders*, 4(2), 22–40.

Schumaker, J. B., Deshler, D. D., Alley, G. R., & Warner, M. M. (1983). Toward the development of an intervention model for learning disabled adolescents: The University of Kansas Institute. *Exceptional Education Quarterly*, 4, 45–74.

Schumaker, J. B., & Hazel, J. S. (1984). Social skills assessment and training for the learning disabled: Who's on first and what's on second? Part I. *Journal of Learning Disabilities*, 17, 422–431.

Schumaker, J. B., Hazel, J. S., & Pederson, C. S. (1988). *Special skills for daily living*. Circle Pines, MN: American Guidance Service.

Schumaker, J. B., Hazel, J. S., Sherman, J. A., & Sheldon, J. (1982). *Social skill performance of learning disabled, non-learning disabled, and delinquent adolescents* (Research Report No. 60). Lawrence: University of Kansas, Institute for Research in Learning Disabilities.

Semel, E., & Wiig, E. (1982). *Clinical language intervention program*. San Antonio, TX: Psychological Corporation.

Shaywitz, B. (1987). Hyperactivity/attention deficit disorder. In Interagency Committee on Learning Disabilities, *Learning disabilities: A report to the U.S. Congress* (pp. 194–218). Bethesda, MD: National Institutes of Health.

Showers, B. (1990). Aiming for superior classroom instruction for all children: A comprehensive staff development model. *Remedial and Special Education*, 11(3), 35–39.

Shuell, T. J., & Schueckler, L. M. (1988, April). *Toward evaluating software according to principles of learning and teaching*. Paper presented at the meeting of the American Educational Research Association, New Orleans.

Silbert, J., Carnine, D., & Stein, M. (1990). *Direct instruction mathematics* (2nd ed.). New York: Merrill/Macmillan.

Silver, L. B. (1987). The "magic cure": A review of current controversial approaches for treating learning disabilities. *Journal of Learning Disabilities*, 20, 498–504, 512.

Silver, L. B. (1988). A review of the federal government's Interagency Committee on Learning Disabilities report to the U.S. Congress. *Learning Disabilities Focus*, 35, 73–80.

Silver, L. B. (1990). Attention deficit-hyperactivity disorder: Is it a learning disability or a related disorder? *Journal of Learning Disabilities*, 23, 394–397.

Silverman, R., Zigmond, N., & Sansone, J. (1981). Teaching coping skills to adolescents with learning problems. *Focus on Exceptional Children*, 13(6), 1–20.

Sitlington, P. L., & Frank, A. R. (1990). Are adolescents with learning disabilities successfully crossing the bridge into adult life? *Learning Disability Quarterly*, 13, 97–111.

Slavin, R. E. (1990). General education under the Regular Education Initiative: How must it change? *Remedial and Special Education*, 11(3), 40–50.

Slingerland, B. G. (1971). *A multisensory approach to language arts for specific language disability children: A guide for primary teachers*. Cambridge, MA: Educators Publishing Service.

Smith, C. R. (1983). *Learning disabilities: The interaction of learner, task, and setting*. Boston: Little, Brown.

Spekman, N. J., Goldberg, R. J., & Herman, K. L. (1992). Learning disabled children grow up: A search for factors related to success in the young adult years. *Learning Disabilities Research and Practice*, 7, 161–170.

Spivak, M. P. (1986). Advocacy and legislative action for head-injured children and their families. *Journal of Head Trauma Rehabilitation*, 1, 41–47.

Stainback, S., & Stainback, W. (1987). Integration versus cooperation: A commentary on "Educating children with learning problems: A shared responsibility." *Exceptional Children*, 54, 66–68.

Stephens, T. M. (1977). *Teaching skills to children with learning and behavior disorders*. Columbus: Merrill.

Stowitschek, J. J., & Stowitschek, C. E. (1984). Once more with feeling: The absence of research on teacher use of microcomputers. *Exceptional Education Quarterly*, 4(4), 23–39.

Strain, P. S., & Odom, S. L. (1986). Peer social initiation: Effective intervention for social skills development of exceptional children. *Exceptional Children*, 52, 543–551.

Strauss, A. A., & Lehtinen, L. E. (1947). *Psychopathology and education of the brain-injured child* (Vol. 1). New York: Grune and Stratton.

Swanson, H. L. (1988). Memory subtypes in learning disabled readers. *Learning Disability Quarterly*, 11, 342–357.

Swanson, H. L. (1991). Operational definitions and learning disabilities: An overview. *Learning Disability Quarterly*, 14, 242–254.

Swanson, H. L., Cochran, K. F., & Ewers, C. A. (1990). Can learning disabilities be determined from working memory performance? *Journal of Learning Disabilities*, 23, 59–67.

Telzrow, C. F. (1987). Management of academic and educational problems in head injury. *Journal of Learning Disabilities*, 20, 536–545.

Thornton, C. (1989). "Look ahead" activities spark success in addition and subtraction number fact learning. *The Arithmetic Teacher, 36,* 8–11.

Thornton, C. A., & Toohey, M. A. (1985). Basic math facts: Guidelines for teaching and learning. *Learning Disabilities Focus, 1,* 44–57.

Tindal, G. A., & Marston, D. B. (1990). *Classroom-based assessment: Evaluating instructional outcomes.* New York: Merrill/Macmillan.

Torgesen, J. K. (1977). The role of nonspecific factors in the task performance of learning disabled children: A theoretical assessment. *Journal of Learning Disabilities, 10,* 27–34.

Torgesen, J. K. (1988). Studies of children with learning disabilities who perform poorly on memory span tasks. *Journal of Learning Disabilities, 21,* 605–612.

Torgesen, J. K., & Kail, R. V. (1980). Memory processes in exceptional children. In B. K. Keogh (Ed.), *Advances in special education: Vol. 1. Basic constructs and theoretical orientations* (pp. 16–26). Greenwich, CT: JAI Press.

Torgesen, J. K., Waters, M. D., Cohen, A. L., & Torgesen, J. L. (1988). Improving sight-word recognition skills in LD children: An evaluation of three computer program variations. *Learning Disability Quarterly, 11,* 125–132.

Torgesen, J. K., & Young, K. A. (1983). Priorities for the use of microcomputers with learning disabled children. *Journal of Learning Disabilities, 16,* 234–237.

Treiber, F. A., & Lahey, B. B. (1983). Toward a behavioral model of academic remediation with learning disabled children. *Journal of Learning Disabilities, 16,* 111–116.

Turnure, J. E. (1985). Communication and cues in the functional cognition of the mentally retarded. In N. R. Ellis & N. W. Bray (Eds.), *International review of research in mental retardation* (pp. 161–180). New York: Academic Press.

Turnure, J. E. (1986). Instruction and cognitive development: Coordinating communication and cues. *Exceptional Children, 53,* 109–117.

Unger, K. (1978). Learning disabilities and juvenile delinquency. *Journal of Juvenile and Family Courts, 29*(1), 25–30.

U.S. Department of Education. (1990). *Twelfth annual report to Congress on the implementation of the Education of the Handicapped Act.* Washington, DC: Department of Education, Office of Special Education and Rehabilitative Services.

U.S. Department of Education. (1991). *Thirteenth annual report to Congress on the implementation of the Individuals with Disabilities Education Act.* Washington, DC: Department of Education, Office of Special Education and Rehabilitative Services.

U.S. Office of Education. (1977). Assistance to states for education of handicapped children: Procedures for evaluating specific learning disabilities. *Federal Register, 42,* 65082–65085.

Van Reusen, A. K., Bos, C. S., Schumaker, J. B., & Deshler, D. D. (1987). *The learning strategies curriculum: The educational planning strategy.* Lawrence, KS: Edge Enterprises.

Vogel, S. A. (1975). *Syntactic abilities in normal and dyslexic children.* Baltimore: University Park Press.

Vygotsky, L. S. (1978). *Mind in society: The development of higher psychological processes.* Cambridge, MA: Harvard University Press.

Wang, M. C., & Baker, E. T. (1985–1986). Mainstreaming programs: Design features and effects. *Journal of Special Education, 19,* 503–521.

Wang, M. C., Reynolds, M. C., & Walberg, H. J. (1986). Rethinking special education. *Educational Leadership, 44*(1), 26–31.

Watkins, M. W., & Webb, C. (1981, September/October). Computer assisted instruction with learning disabled students. *Educational Computer Magazine,* pp. 24–27.

Waxman, H. C., Wang, M. C., Anderson, K. A., & Walberg, H. J. (1985). Adaptive education and student outcomes: A quantitative synthesis. *Journal of Educational Research, 78,* 228–236.

Weisberg, R. (1988). 1980s: A change in focus on reading comprehension research: A review of reading/learning disabilities research based on an interactive model of reading. *Learning Disability Quarterly, 11,* 149–159.

Weller, C. (1980). Discrepancy and severity in the learning disabled: A consolidated perspective. *Learning Disability Quarterly, 3,* 84–90.

Wesson, C. L., King, R. P., & Deno, S. L. (1984). Direct and frequent measurement of student performance: If it's good for us, why don't we do it? *Learning Disability Quarterly, 7,* 45–48.

West, J. F., & Idol, L. (1990). Collaborative consultation in the education of mildly handicapped and at-risk students. *Remedial and Special Education, 11*(1), 22–31.

White, O. R. (1986). Precision teaching—Precision learning. *Exceptional Children, 52,* 522–534.

Wiederholt, J. L. (1974). Historical perspectives on the education of the learning disabled. In L. Mann & D. Sabatino (Eds.), *The second review of special education* (pp. 103–152). Philadelphia: Journal of Special Education Press.

Wiig, E. (1982). *Let's talk: Developing pro-social communication skills.* San Antonio, TX: Psychological Corporation.

Wiig, E. H., & Semel, E. M. (1984). *Language assessment and intervention for the learning disabled* (2nd ed.). Columbus: Merrill.

Will, M. C. (1986). Educating children with learning problems: A shared responsibility. *Exceptional Children*, *52*, 411–415.

Wong, B. Y. L. (1987). How do the results of metacognitive research impact on the learning disabled individual? *Learning Disability Quarterly*, *10*, 189–195.

Wong, B. Y. L. (1991). The relevance of metacognition to learning disabilities. In B. Y. L. Wong (Ed.), *Learning about learning disabilities* (pp. 231–258). San Diego: Academic Press.

Woodward, J., & Carnine, D. (1988). Antecedent knowledge and intelligent computer-assisted instruction. *Journal of Learning Disabilities*, *21*, 131–139.

Woodward, J., Carnine, D., & Gersten, R. (1988). Teaching problem solving through a computer simulation. *American Educational Research Journal*, *25*, 72–86.

Ysseldyke, J. E., Thurlow, M., Graden, J., Wesson, C., Algozzine, B., & Deno, S. (1983). Generalizations from five years of research on assessment and decision making: The University of Minnesota Institute. *Exceptional Education Quarterly*, *4*(1), 75–93.

Zigmond, N., & Brownlee, J. (1980). Social skills training for adolescents with learning disabilities. *Exceptional Education Quarterly*, *1*(2), 77–83.

CHAPTER FIVE

Achenbach, T. M. (1982). *Developmental psychopathology* (2nd ed.). New York: Wiley.

Achenbach, T. M., & Edelbrock, C. (1989). Diagnostic, taxonomic, and assessment issues. In T. H. Ollendick & M. Hersen (Eds.), *Handbook of child psychopathology* (2nd ed., pp. 53–73). New York: Plenum Press.

Algarin, A., & Friedman, R. M. (Eds.). (1991). *Third annual research conference proceedings of the Research and Training Center for Children's Mental Health: A system of care for children's mental health: Building a research base*. Tampa: Florida Mental Health Institute.

Algarin, A., Friedman, R. M., Duchnowski, A. J., Kutash, K. M., Silver, S. E., & Johnson, M. K. (Eds.). (1990). *Second annual conference proceedings of the Research and Training Center for Children's Mental Health: Children's mental health services and policy: Building a research base*. Tampa: Florida Mental Health Institute.

American Psychiatric Association. (1987). *Diagnostic and statistical manual of mental disorders* (3rd ed., rev.). Washington, DC: Author.

Anderson-Inman, L. (1986). Bridging the gap: Student-centered strategies for promoting the transfer of learning. *Exceptional Children*, *52*, 562–572.

Anderson-Inman, L., Walker, H. M., & Purcell, J. (1984). Promoting the transfer of skills across settings: Transenvironmental programming for handicapped students in the mainstream. In W. L. Heward, T. E. Heron, D. S. Hill, & J. Trap-Porter (Eds.), *Focus on behavior analysis in education* (pp. 16–36). New York: Merrill/Macmillan.

Apter, S. J. (1982). *Troubled children/troubled systems*. New York: Pergamon Press.

Arizona Department of Health Services. (1991). *State of Arizona children's behavioral health services needs and resources assessment* (A.R.S. Section 36–3421 and A.R.S. Section 36–3431–35). Phoenix: Author.

Axline, V. M. (1969). *Play therapy* (2nd ed.). New York: Ballantine Books.

Baer, D. M., & Fowler, S. A. (1984). How should we measure the potential of self-control procedures for generalized educational outcomes? In W. L. Heward, T. E. Heron, D. S. Hill, & J. Trap-Porter (Eds.), *Focus on behavior analysis in education* (pp. 145–161). New York: Merrill/Macmillan.

Baker, K. (1985). Research evidence of a school discipline problem. *Phi Delta Kappan*, *66*, 482–488.

Bandura, A. (1978). The self system in reciprocal determinism. *American Psychologist*, *33*, 344–358.

Bandura, A. (1986). *Social foundations of thought and action*. Englewood Cliffs, NJ: Prentice-Hall.

Baum, C. G. (1989). Conduct disorders. In T. H. Ollendick & M. Hersen (Eds.), *Handbook of child psychopathology* (2nd ed., pp. 171–196). New York: Plenum Press.

Beachler, M. B. (1990). The mental health services program for youth. *Journal of Mental Health Administration*, *17*, 115–121.

Behar, L. (1984, April). *An integrated system of services for seriously disturbed children*. Paper presented at the State of the Art Research Conference on Juvenile Offenders with Serious Alcohol, Drug Abuse, and Mental Health Problems, Rockville, MD.

Behar, L. (1985). Changing patterns of state responsibility: A case study of North Carolina. *Journal of Clinical Psychology*, *14*, 188–195.

Berne, E. (1964). *Games people play*. New York: Macmillan.

Bornstein, P. H. (1985). Self-instructional training: A commentary and state-of-the-art. *Journal of Applied Science Behavior Analysis*, *18*, 69–72.

Botvin, G. J. (1986). Substance abuse prevention: Recent developments and future directions. *Journal of School Health*, *56*, 369–374.

Botvin, G. J., & Tortu, S. T. (1988). Preventing adolescent substance abuse through Life Skills Training. In R. H. Price, E. L. Cowen, R. P. Lorion, & J. Ramos-McKay (Eds.), *Fourteen ounces of prevention: A casebook for practitioners* (pp. 98–110). Washington, DC: American Psychological Association.

Bower, E. M. (1969). *The early identification of emotionally handicapped children in school* (2nd ed.). Springfield, IL: Charles C Thomas.

Braaten, S., Kauffman, J. M., Braaten, B., Polsgrove, L., & Nelson, C. M. (1988). The Regular Education Initiative: Patent medicine for behavioral disorders. *Exceptional Children*, 55, 21–27.

Burchard, J. D., & Clarke, R. T. (1990). The role of individualized care in a service delivery system for children and adolescents with severely maladjusted behavior. *Journal of Mental Health Administration*, 17, 148–154.

Burchard, J. D., Schaefer, M., Harrington, N., Rogers, J., Welkowitz, J., & Tighe, T. (1991). *An evaluation of the community integration demonstration project.* Unpublished manuscript, University of Vermont, School of Psychology, Burlington.

Burns, B. J., & Friedman, R. M. (1990). Examining the research base for children's mental health services and policy. *Journal of Mental Health Administration*, 17, 87–99.

Camp, B. W., & Bash, M. A. (1981). *Think aloud: Increasing social and cognitive skills: A problem-solving program for children (Primary level).* Champaign, IL: Research Press.

Camp, B. W., & Ray, R. S. (1984). Aggression. In A. W. Meyers & W. E. Craighead (Eds.), *Cognitive behavior therapy with children* (pp. 315–350). New York: Plenum Press.

Campbell, S. B., & Werry, J. S. (1986). Attention deficit disorder (hyperactivity). In H. C. Quay & J. S. Werry (Eds.), *Psychopathological disorders of childhood* (3rd ed., pp. 111–155). New York: Wiley.

Canter, A. S. (1991). Effective psychological services for all students: A data-based model of service delivery. In G. Stoner, M. R. Shinn, & H. M. Walker (Eds.), *Interventions for achievement and behavior problems* (pp. 49–78). Silver Spring, MD: National Association of School Psychologists.

Cantor, S. (1989). Schizophrenia. In C. G. Last & M. Hersen (Eds.), *Handbook of child psychiatric diagnosis* (pp. 279–298). New York: Wiley.

Cantrell, M. L., & Cantrell, R. P. (1985). Assessment of the natural environment. *Education and Treatment of Children*, 8, 275–295.

Cartledge, G., & Milburn, J. F. (Eds.). (1986). *Teaching social skills to children* (2nd ed.). New York: Pergamon Press.

Catania, A. C. (1975). The myth of self-reinforcement. *Behaviorism*, 3, 192–199.

Center, D. B. (1990). Social maladjustment: An interpretation. *Behavioral Disorders*, 15, 141–148.

Chan, K. S., & Rueda, R. (1979). Poverty and culture in education: Separate but equal. *Exceptional Children*, 45, 422–431.

Cooper, J. O., Heron, J. E., & Heward, W. L. (1987). *Applied behavior analysis.* New York: Merrill/Macmillan.

Costello, E. J. (1989). The status of epidemiologic research on psychiatric disorders of childhood and adolescence. In A. Algarin, R. M. Friedman, A. J. Duchnowski, K. M. Kutash, S. E. Silver, & M. K. Johnson (Eds.), *Second annual conference proceedings of the Research and Training Center for Children's Mental Health: Children's mental health services and policy: Building a research base* (pp. 304–316). Tampa: Florida Mental Health Institute.

Council for Children with Behavioral Disorders. (1987). *Position paper on identification of students with behavioral disorders.* Reston, VA: Council for Exceptional Children.

Cowen, E. L., & Hightower, A. D. (1990). The primary mental health project: Alternative approaches in school-based preventive intervention. In T. B. Gutkin & C. R. Reynolds (Eds.), *The handbook of school psychology* (pp. 775–795). New York: Wiley.

Cullinan, D., Epstein, M. H., & Kauffman, J. M. (1982). The behavioral model and children's behavior disorders: Foundations and evaluations. In R. McDowell, F. Wood, & G. Adamson (Eds.), *Teaching emotionally disturbed children* (pp. 15–46). Boston: Little, Brown.

Cullinan, D., Epstein, M. H., & Lloyd, J. (1983). *Behavior disorders of children and adolescents.* Englewood Cliffs, NJ: Prentice-Hall.

Cullinan, D., Epstein, M. H., & Lloyd, J. W. (1991). Evaluation of conceptual models of behavior disorders. *Behavioral Disorders*, 16, 148–157.

Cullinan, D., Epstein, M. H., & Sabornie, E. J. (1992). Selected characteristics of a national sample of seriously emotionally disturbed adolescents. *Behavioral Disorders*, 17, 273–280.

Cullinan, D., & Root, H. (1985). Assessment of behavior disorders. In A. F. Rotatori & R. Fox (Eds.), *Assessment for regular and special education teachers: A case study approach* (pp. 279–310). Austin, TX: Pro-Ed.

Deitz, D. E. D., & Repp, A. C. (1983). Reducing behavior through reinforcement. *Exceptional Education Quarterly*, 3, 34–46.

Denton, D. L., & McIntyre, C. W. (1978). Span of apprehension in hyperactive boys. *Journal of Abnormal Child Psychology*, 6, 19–24.

Donnellan, A. M., & Neel, R. S. (1986). New directions in educating students with autism. In R. H. Horner, L. H. Meyer, & H. D. "Bud" Fredericks (Eds.), *Education of learners with severe handicaps: Exemplary service strategies* (pp. 99–124). Baltimore: Paul H. Brookes.

Dozier, M. (1988). Rejected children's processing of interpersonal information. *Journal of Abnormal Child Psychology*, 16, 141–149.

Duchnowski, A. J., & Friedman, R. M. (1990). Children's mental health: Challenges for the nineties. *Journal of Mental Health Administration*, 17, 3–12.

DuPaul, G. J., Guevremont, D. C., & Barkley, R. A. (1991). Attention-deficit hyperactivity disorder. In T. R. Kratochwill & R. J. Morris (Eds.), *The practice of child therapy* (2nd ed., pp. 115–144). New York: Pergamon Press.

Epstein, M. H., Kauffman, J. M., & Cullinan, D. (1985). Patterns of maladjustment among the behaviorally disordered: 2. Boys aged 6–11, boys aged 12–18, girls aged 6–11, and girls aged 12–18. *Behavioral Disorders*, 11, 125–135.

Epstein, M. H., Kinder, D., & Bursuck, B. (1989). The academic status of adolescents with behavior disorders. *Behavioral Disorders*, 14, 157–165.

Executive Committee of the Council for Children with Behavioral Disorders. (1987). Position paper on definition and identification of students with behavioral disorders. *Behavioral Disorders*, 13, 9–19.

Fagen, S. A., Long, D. J., & Stevens, D. J. (1975). *Teaching children self-control*. Columbus, OH: Merrill.

Federal Register. (1992). 57, 44801.

Feldman, R. A., Caplinger, T. E., & Wodarski, J. S. (1983). *The St. Louis conundrum: The effective treatment of antisocial youths*. Englewood Cliffs, NJ: Prentice-Hall.

Fernandez, G. A. (1987). *Demographic and behavioral characteristics of certified "Willie M." class members*. Unpublished manuscript.

Ferster, C. B., & Culbertson, S. A. (1982). *Behavior principles* (3rd ed.). Englewood Cliffs, NJ: Prentice-Hall.

Firestone, P., & Martin, J. E. (1979). An analysis of the hyperactive syndrome: A comparison of hyperactive, behavior problem, asthmatic, and normal children. *Journal of Abnormal Child Psychology*, 7, 261–274.

Foley, R. M., Cullinan, D., & Epstein, M. H. (1990). Academic and related functioning of mainstreamed and nonmainstreamed seriously emotionally disturbed students. In R. B. Rutherford & J. W. Maag (Eds.), *Monographs in behavioral disorders* (Vol. 13, pp. 80–89). Reston, VA: Council for Children with Behavioral Disorders.

Forness, S. R., & Knitzer, J. (1990). A *new proposed definition and terminology to replace "Serious Emotional Disturbance" in the Education of the Handicapped Act* (Report of the Workgroup on Definition, National Mental Health and Special Education Coalition). Alexandria, VA: National Mental Health Association.

Friedman, R. (1988). Strategies for conducting needs assessments based on system of care models. In P. Greenbaum, R. Friedman, A. Duchnowski, K. Kutash, & S. Silver (Eds.), *Children's mental health services and policy: Building a research base* (pp. 52–58). Tampa: Florida Mental Health Institute.

Gadow, K., & Sprafkin, P. (1993). Television "violence" and children with emotional and behavioral disorders. *Journal of Emotional and Behavioral Disorders*, 1, 54–63.

Garrison, W. T., & Earls, F. J. (1987). *Temperament and child psychopathology*. Newbury Park, CA: Sage.

Gersten, J. C., Langner, T. S., Eisenberg, J. B., Simcha-Fagen, O., & McCarthy, E. D. (1976). Stability and change in types of behavioral disturbance of children and adolescents. *Journal of Abnormal Child Psychology*, 4, 111–127.

Glasser, W. (1969). *Schools without failure*. New York: Harper and Row.

Goldstein, A. P., Sprafkin, R. P., Gershaw, N. S., & Klein, P. (1980). *Skillstreaming the adolescent*. Champaign, IL: Research Press.

Graham, P. J. (1979). Epidemiological studies. In H. C. Quay & J. S. Werry (Eds.), *Psychopathological disorders of childhood* (2nd ed., pp. 185–209). New York: Wiley.

Gray, J. W., & Raymond, D. S. (1990). Implications of neuropsychological research for school psychology. In T. B. Gutkin & C. R. Reynolds (Eds.), *The handbook of school psychology* (pp. 269–286). New York: Wiley.

Greenwood, C. R., Walker, H. M., & Hops, H. (1977). Issues in social interaction/withdrawal assessment. *Exceptional Children*, 43, 490–501.

Gresham, F. M. (1988). Social skills: Conceptual and applied aspects of assessment, training, and social validation. In J. C. Witt, S. N. Elliott, & F. M. Gresham (Eds.), *Handbook of behavior therapy in education* (pp. 523–546). New York: Plenum Press.

Hammill, D. D., Brown, L., & Bryant, B. R. (1989). A *consumer's guide to tests in print*. Austin, TX: Pro-Ed.

Haring, N. G., & Phillips, E. L. (1962). *Educating emotionally disturbed children*. New York: McGraw-Hill.

Harris, T. (1976). *I'm OK, you're OK*. New York: Avon.

Henggeler, S. W. (1989). *Delinquency in adolescence*. Newbury Park, CA: Sage.

Hetherington, E. M., & Martin, B. (1986). Family factors and psychopathology in children. In H. C. Quay & J. S. Werry (Eds.), *Psychopathological disorders of childhood* (3rd ed., pp. 332–390). New York: Wiley.

Heward, W. L., & Orlansky, M. D. (1992). *Exceptional children: An introductory survey of special education* (4th ed.). New York: Merrill/Macmillan.

Hewett, F. M. (1968). *The emotionally disturbed child in the classroom.* Boston: Allyn and Bacon.

Hightower, A. D., & Braden, J. (1991). Prevention. In T. R. Kratochwill & R. J. Morris (Eds.), *The practice of child therapy* (2nd ed., pp. 410–440). New York: Pergamon Press.

Howell, K. W., & Morehead, M. K. (1987). *Curriculum-based evaluation for special and remedial education: A handbook for deciding what to teach.* Columbus, OH: Merrill.

Hresko, W. L., & Brown, L. (1984). *Test of early socioemotional development.* Austin, TX: Pro-Ed.

Illback, R. (1991). *Formative evaluation of the Kentucky IMPACT program for children and youth with severe emotional disabilities.* Unpublished manuscript, Kentucky Department of Mental Health.

Institute of Medicine. (1989). *Research on children and adolescents with mental, behavioral and developmental disorders: Mobilizing a national initiative.* Rockville, MD: National Institute of Mental Health.

Johnson, J. H. (1986). *Life events as stressors in childhood and adolescence.* Beverly Hills, CA: Sage.

Jordan, D. D., & Hernandez, M. (1990). The Ventura planning model: A proposal for mental health reform. *Journal of Mental Health Administration, 17,* 26–47.

Kaslow, N. J., & Rehm, L. P. (1991). Childhood depression. In T. R. Kratochwill & R. J. Morris (Eds.), *The practice of child therapy* (2nd ed., pp. 43–75). New York: Pergamon Press.

Kauffman, J. M. (1993). *Characteristics of emotional and behavior disorders of children and youth* (5th ed.). New York: Merrill/Macmillan.

Kauffman, J. M., Cullinan, D., & Epstein, M. H. (1987). Characteristics of students placed in special programs for the seriously emotionally disturbed. *Behavioral Disorders, 12,* 175–184.

Kazdin, A. E. (1977). Assessing the clinical or applied significance of behavior change through social validation. *Behavior Modification, 1,* 427–452.

Kazdin, A. E. (1985). *Treatment of antisocial behavior in children and adolescents.* Homewood, IL: Dorsey.

Kazdin, A. E. (1989). Conduct and oppositional disorders. In C. G. Last & M. Hersen (Eds.), *Handbook of child psychiatric diagnosis* (pp. 129–155). New York: Wiley.

Kazdin, A. E. (1991). Aggressive behavior and conduct disorders. In T. R. Kratochwill & R. J. Morris (Eds.), *The practice of child therapy* (2nd ed., pp. 174–221). New York: Pergamon Press.

Kazdin, A. E., & Wilson, G. T. (1978). *Evaluation of behavior therapy: Issues, evidence, and research strategies.* Cambridge, MA: Ballinger.

Kerr, M. M., & Nelson, C. M. (1989). *Strategies for managing behavior problems in the classroom* (2nd ed.). New York: Merrill/Macmillan.

Khanna, M., Singh, N. N., Nemil, M., Best, A., & Ellis, C. (1992). Homeless women and their families: Characteristics, life circumstances, and needs. *Journal of Child and Family Studies, 1,* 155–166.

Knitzer, J. (1993). Children's mental health policy: Challenging the future. *Journal of Emotional and Behavioral Disorders, 1,* 8–16.

Knitzer, J., Steinberg, Z., & Fleisch, B. (1990). *At the school house door.* New York: Bank Street College of Education.

Koegel, R. L. (1981). *How to integrate autistic and other severely handicapped children into a classroom.* Austin, TX: Pro-Ed.

Koegel, R. L., Russo, D. C., & Rincover, A. (1977). Assessing and training teachers in the generalized use of behavior modification with autistic children. *Journal of Applied Behavior Analysis, 10,* 197–205.

Koegel, R. L., & Schreibman, L. (1981). *How to teach autistic and other severely handicapped children.* Austin, TX: Pro-Ed.

Kohlberg, L., LaCrosse, J., & Ricks, D. (1972). The predictability of adult mental health from childhood behavior. In B. B. Wolman (Ed.), *Manual of child psychopathology* (pp. 1217–1284). New York: Wiley.

Kopp, C. B. (1983). Risk factors in development. In P. H. Mussen (Ed.), *Handbook of child psychology* (pp. 1081–1188). New York: Wiley.

Kozol, J. (1988). *Rachel and her children: Homeless families in America.* New York: Fawcett.

Kozol, J. (1992). *Savage inequalities: Children in America's schools.* New York: Harper/Collins.

Last, C. G. (1989). Anxiety disorders of childhood or adolescence. In C. G. Last & M. Hersen (Eds.), *Handbook of child psychiatric diagnosis* (pp. 156–169). New York: Wiley.

Leone, P. E. (1991). *Alcohol and other drugs: Use, abuse, and disabilities.* Reston, VA: Council for Exceptional Children.

Litow, L., & Pumroy, D. K. (1975). A brief review of classroom group-oriented contingencies. *Journal of Applied Behavior Analysis, 8,* 341–347.

Lloyd, J. W., Kauffman, J. M., & Kupersmidt, J. B. (1990). Integration of students with behavior disorders in regular education environments. In K. D. Gadow (Ed.), *Advances in learning and behavioral disabilities* (Vol. 6, pp. 225–264). Greenwich, CT: JAI Press.

Long, N. J. (1974). Nicholas J. Long. In J. M. Kauffman & C. D. Lewis (Eds.), *Teaching children with behavior disorders: Personal perspectives* (pp. 171–196). Columbus, OH: Merrill.

Long, N. J., & Newman, R. G. (1976). Managing surface behavior of children in school. In N. J. Long, W. C. Morse, & R. G. Newman (Eds.), *Conflict in the classroom* (3rd ed., pp. 308–317). Belmont, CA: Wadsworth.

Lovaas, O. I. (1987). Behavioral treatment and normal educational and intellectual functioning in young autistic children. *Journal of Consulting and Clinical Psychology, 55,* 3–9.

Lovaas, O. I., Ackerman, A. B., Alexander, D., Firestone, P., Perkins, J., & Young, D. (1980). *Teaching developmentally disabled children: The me book.* Austin, TX: Pro-Ed.

Lovaas, O. I., & Newsom, C. D. (1976). Behavior modification with psychotic children. In H. Leitenberg (Ed.), *Handbook of behavior modification and behavior therapy* (pp. 303–360). Englewood Cliffs, NJ: Prentice-Hall.

Mace, F. C., & Kratochwill, T. R. (1988). Self-monitoring. In J. C. Witt, S. N. Elliott, & F. M. Gresham (Eds.), *Handbook of behavior therapy in education* (pp. 489–522). New York: Plenum Press.

Magrab, P. R., Young, T., & Waddell, A. (1985). *A community workbook for: Developing collaborative services for the seriously emotionally disturbed.* Washington, DC: Georgetown University Child Development Center.

Mattison, R. E., Morales, J., & Bauer, M. A. (1992). Distinguishing characteristics of elementary schoolboys recommended for SED placement. *Behavioral Disorders, 17,* 107–114.

Moore, D. R., & Arthur, J. L. (1989). Juvenile delinquency. In T. H. Ollendick & M. Hersen (Eds.), *Handbook of child psychopathology* (2nd ed., pp. 197–217). New York: Plenum Press.

Morgan, D. P. (1992). *Substance use prevention and students with behavioral disorders: Guidelines for school professionals.* Logan: Utah State University, Department of Special Education.

Morgan, D. P., & Jenson, W. R. (1988). *Teaching behaviorally disordered students: Preferred practices.* New York: Merrill/Macmillan.

Morris, R. J., & Kratochwill, T. R. (1991). Childhood fears and phobias. In T. R. Kratochwill & R. J. Morris (Eds.), *The practice of child therapy* (2nd ed., pp. 76–114). New York: Pergamon Press.

Morse, W. C. (1965). The crisis teacher. In N. J. Long, W. C. Morse, & R. G. Newman (Eds.), *Conflict in the classroom* (pp. 251–254). Belmont, CA: Wadsworth.

Neel, R. S., Billingsley, F. F., & Lambert, C. (1983, Summer). IMPACT: A functional curriculum for educating autistic youth in natural environments. In R. B. Rutherford (Ed.), *Monograph in severe behavior disorders* (pp. 40–50). Reston, VA: Council for Children with Behavioral Disorders.

Neel, R. S., Meadows, N., Levine, P., & Edgar, E. B. (1988). What happens after special education: A statewide follow-up study of secondary students who have behavioral disorders. *Behavioral Disorders, 13,* 209–216.

Nelson, C. M., & Pearson, C. A. (1991). *Integrating services for children and youth with emotional and behavioral disorders.* Reston, VA: Council for Exceptional Children.

Nelson, J. R., Smith, D. J., Young, R. K., & Dodd, J. (1991). A review of self-management outcome research conducted with students who exhibit behavioral disorders. *Behavioral Disorders, 16,* 169–179.

Nye, R., Short, J., & Olson, V. (1958). Socio-economic status and delinquent behavior. *American Journal of Sociology, 63,* 381–389.

Olinger, E., & Epstein, M. H. (1991). The behavioral model and adolescents with behavioral model disorders: A review of selected treatment studies. In M. Hersen, R. M. Eisler, & P. M. Miller (Eds.), *Progress in behavior modification* (Vol. 27, pp. 122–156). Newbury Park, CA: Sage.

Ornitz, E. M. (1989). Autism. In C. G. Last & M. Hersen (Eds.), *Handbook of child psychiatric diagnosis* (pp. 233–278). New York: Wiley.

Paternite, C. E., & Loney, J. (1980). Childhood hyperkinesis: Relationship between symptomatology and home environment. In C. K. Whalen & B. Henker (Eds.), *Hyperactive children: The social ecology of identification and treatment.* New York: Academic Press.

Patterson, C. J., Kupersmidt, J. B., & Vaden, N. A. (1990). Income level, gender, ethnicity, and household composition as predictors of children's school-based competence. *Child Development, 61,* 485–494.

Patterson, G. R., DeBarsyshe, B. D., & Ramsey, E. (1989). A developmental perspective on antisocial behavior. *American Psychologist, 44,* 329–335.

Peacock Hill Working Group. (1991). Problems and promises in special education and related services for children and youth with emotional or behavioral disorders. *Behavioral Disorders, 16,* 299–313.

Prior, M., & Werry, J. S. (1986). Autism, schizophrenia, and allied disorders. In H. C. Quay & J. S. Werry (Eds.), *Psychopathological disorders of childhood* (3rd ed., pp. 156–210). New York: Wiley.

Quay, H. C. (1986). Classification. In H. C. Quay & J. S. Werry (Eds.), *Psychopathological disorders of childhood* (3rd ed., pp. 1–34). New York: Wiley.

Quay, H. C., Glavin, J. P., Annesley, F. R., & Werry, J. S. (1972). The modification of problem behavior and academic achievement in a resource room. *Journal of School Psychology, 10,* 187–198.

Quay, H. C., & LaGreca, A. M. (1986). Disorders of anxiety, withdrawal, and dysphoria. In H. C. Quay & J. S. Werry (Eds.), *Psychopathological disorders of childhood* (3rd ed., pp. 73–110). New York: Wiley.

Ramsey, E., & Walker, H. M. (1988). Family management correlates of antisocial behavior among middle school boys. *Behavioral Disorders, 13,* 187–201.

Redl, F., & Wineman, D. (1951). *Children who hate.* New York: Free Press.

Rezmierski, V. E., Knoblock, P., & Bloom, R. B. (1982). The psychoeducational model: Theory and historical perspective. In R. L. McDowell, G. W. Adamson, & F. H. Wood (Eds.), *Teaching emotionally disturbed children* (pp. 47–69). Boston: Little, Brown.

Rhode, G., Morgan, D. P., & Young, K. R. (1983). Generalization and maintenance of treatment gains of behaviorally handicapped students from resource rooms to regular classrooms using self-evaluation procedures. *Journal of Applied Behavior Analysis, 16*, 171–188.

Rhodes, W. C. (1970). A community participation analysis of emotional disturbance. *Exceptional Children, 37*, 309–314.

Rogers-Warren, A. K. (1984). Ecobehavioral analysis. *Education and Treatment of Children, 7*, 283–303.

Sailor, W., & Guess, D. (1983). *Severely handicapped students: An instructional design.* Hopewell, NJ: Houghton-Mifflin.

Schinke, S. P., Botvin, G. J., & Orlandi, M. A. (1991). *Substance abuse in children and adolescents.* Newbury Park, CA: Sage.

Schreibman, L., & Charlop, M. H. (1989). Infantile autism. In T. H. Ollendick & M. Hersen (Eds.), *Handbook of child psychopathology* (2nd ed., pp. 105–129). New York: Plenum Press.

Schreibman, L., & Mills, J. I. (1983). Infantile autism. In T. H. Ollendick & M. Hersen (Eds.), *Handbook of child psychopathology* (pp. 123–149). New York: Plenum Press.

Select Committee on Children, Youth, and Family. (1989). *Where are our children?* Washington, DC: U.S. Government Printing Office.

Seymour, F. W., & Stokes, T. F. (1976). Self-recording in training girls to increase work and evoke staff praise in institutions for offenders. *Journal of Applied Behavior Analysis, 9*, 41–54.

Shapiro, E. S., & Kratochwill, T. R. (1988). *Behavioral assessment in schools: Conceptual foundations and practical applications.* New York: Guilford Press.

Siegel, L. J., & Ridley-Johnson, R. (1985). Anxiety disorders of childhood and adolescence. In P. H. Bornstein & A. E. Kazdin (Eds.), *Handbook of clinical behavior therapy with children* (pp. 266–308). Homewood, IL: Dorsey.

Skinner, B. F. (1957). *Verbal behavior.* New York: Appleton-Century-Crofts.

Skinner, B. F. (1968). *The technology of teaching.* New York: Knopf.

Smith, C. R., Wood, F. H., & Grimes, J. (1987). Issues in the identification and placement of behaviorally disordered students. In M. C. Wang, M. C. Reynolds, & H. J. Walberg (Eds.), *Handbook of special education research and practice: Vol. 2. Mildly handicapped conditions* (pp. 95–123). New York: Pergamon Press.

Smith, D. J., Young, K. R., West, R. P., Morgan, D. P., & Rhode, G. (1988). Reducing the disruptive behavior of junior high school students: A classroom self-management procedure. *Behavior Disorders, 13*, 231–239.

Stokes, F., & Baer, D. M. (1977). An implicit technology of generalization. *Journal of Applied Behavior Analysis, 10*, 349–367.

Stroul, B. A., & Friedman, R. M. (1986). *A system of care for severely emotionally disturbed children and youth.* Washington, DC: Georgetown University, Child and Adolescent Service System Program Technical Assistance Center.

Swap, S. M., Prieto, A. G., & Harth, R. (1982). *Ecological perspectives of the emotionally disturbed child.* In R. L. McDowell, G. W. Adamson, & F. H. Wood (Eds.), *Teaching emotionally disturbed children* (pp. 70–98). Boston: Little, Brown.

Thomas, A., & Chess, S. (1977). *Temperament and development.* New York: Brunner/Mazel.

Tindal, G. A., & Marston, D. B. (1990). *Classroom-based assessment.* New York: Merrill/Macmillan.

Tindal, G. A., Wesson, C., Deno, S., German, G., & Mirkin, P. K. (1985). The Pine County Model for special education delivery: A data-based system. In T. R. Kratochwill (Ed.), *Advances in school psychology* (Vol. 4, pp. 223–250). Hillsdale, NJ: Erlbaum.

Tolan, P. H. (1987). Implications of age of onset for delinquency risk. *Journal of Abnormal Child Psychology, 15*, 47–65.

U.S. Department of Education. (1992). *Fourteenth annual report to Congress on the implementation of the Individuals with Disabilities Education Act.* Washington, DC: Author.

VanDenBerg, J. (1989). *The Alaska youth initiative.* Anchorage: Department of Mental Health.

Walker, H. M., & Fabre, T. R. (1987). Assessment of behavior disorders in the school setting: Issues, problems, and strategies revisited. In N. G. Haring (Ed.), *Assessing and managing behavior disabilities* (pp. 198–243). Seattle: University of Washington Press.

Walker, H. M., Hops, H., & Greenwood, C. R. (1984). The CORBEH research and development model: Programmatic issues and strategies. In S. C. Paine, T. C. Bellamy, & B. Wilcox (Eds.), *Human services that work* (pp. 57–77). Baltimore: Paul H. Brookes.

Walker, H. M., McConnell, S., Holmes, D., Todis, B., Walker, J., & Golden, N. (1983). *The Walker social skills curriculum: The ACCEPTS program.* Austin, TX: Pro-Ed.

Walker, H. M., Severson, H., Stiller, B., Williams, G., Haring, N., Shinn, M., & Todis, B. (1988). Systematic screening of pupils in the elementary age range at risk for behavior disorders: Development and trial testing of a multiple gating model. *Remedial and Special Education, 9*, 8–14.

Werry, J. S. (1986). Biological factors. In H. C. Quay & J. S. Werry (Eds.), *Psychopathological disorders of childhood* (3rd ed., pp. 294–331). New York: Wiley.

Whalen, C. K. (1989). Attention deficit and hyperactivity disorders. In T. H. Ollendick & M. Hersen (Eds.), *Handbook of child psychopathology* (2nd ed., pp. 131–169). New York: Plenum Press.

Willis, D. J., & Walker, C. E. (1989). Etiology. In T. H. Ollendick & M. Hersen (Eds.), *Handbook of child psychopathology* (2nd ed., pp. 29–51). New York: Plenum Press.

Wirt, J. (1989). The invisible homeless: Women and children. *Virginia Commonwealth University Voice*, 18, 1–2.

Wolery, M., Bailey, D. B., & Sugai, G. M. (1988). *Effective teaching: Principles and procedures of applied behavior analysis with exceptional students.* Boston: Allyn and Bacon.

Wolfe, D. A. (1987). *Child abuse: Implications for child development and psychopathology.* Newbury Park, CA: Sage.

Wood, M. M., Combs, C., Gunn, A., & Weller, D. (1986). *Developmental therapy in the classroom: Methods for teaching students with social, emotional, and behavioral handicaps* (2nd ed.). Austin, TX: Pro-Ed.

Wood, M. M., & Long, N. J. (1991). *Life space intervention: Talking with children and youth in crisis.* Austin, TX: Pro-Ed.

CHAPTER SIX

Adams, G. L. (1984). *Comprehensive Test of Adaptive Behavior.* Columbus, OH: Merrill.

Affleck, J., Edgar, E., Levine, P., & Kortering, L. (1990). Postschool status of students classified as mildly mentally retarded: Does it get better with time? *Education and Training in Mental Retardation*, 25, 315–324.

Alabiso, F. (1977). Inhibitory functions of attention in reducing hyperactive behavior. *American Journal of Mental Deficiency*, 77, 259–282.

American Association on Mental Retardation. (1992). *Mental retardation: Definition, classification, and systems of supports* (9th ed.). Washington, DC: Author.

Baird, P. A., & Sadovnick, A. D. (1985). Mental retardation in over half-a-million consecutive live births: An epidemiological study. *American Journal of Mental Deficiency*, 89, 323–330.

Balla, D., & Zigler, E. (1979). Personality development in retarded persons. In N. R. Ellis (Ed.), *Handbook of mental deficiency: Psychological theory and research* (2nd ed., pp. 143–168). Hillside, NJ: Erlbaum.

Baumeister, A. A., & Brooks, P. H. (1981). Cognitive deficits in mental retardation. In J. M. Kauffman & D. P. Hallahan (Eds.), *Handbook of special education* (pp. 87–107). Englewood Cliffs, NJ: Prentice-Hall.

Becker, C. W., & Carnine, D. W. (1980). Direct instruction: An effective approach to educational intervention with disadvantaged and low performers. In B. B. Lahey & A. E. Kazdin (Eds.), *Advances in clinical child psychology* (Vol. 3, pp. 429–473). New York: Plenum Press.

Begab, M. J. (1981). Issues in the prevention of psychosocial retardation. In M. J. Begab, H. C. Haywood, & H. L. Garber (Eds.), *Psychosocial influences in retarded performance* (pp. 3–19). Baltimore: University Park Press.

Beirne-Smith, M., Patton, J. R., & Ittenbach, R. F. (1994). *Mental retardation* (4th ed.). New York: Merrill/Macmillan.

Bellamy, G. T., Rhodes, L. E., Mank, D. M., & Albin, J. M. (1988). *Supported employment: A community implementation guide.* Baltimore: Paul H. Brookes.

Belmont, J. M. (1966). Long-term memory in mental retardation. In N. R. Ellis (Ed.), *International review of research in mental retardation* (Vol. 1, pp. 219–255). New York: Academic Press.

Blatt, B. (1987). *The conquest of mental retardation.* Austin, TX: Pro-Ed.

Borkowski, J. G., & Cavanaugh, J. C. (1979). Maintenance and generalization of skills and strategies by the retarded. In N. R. Ellis (Ed.), *Handbook of mental deficiency: Psychological theory and research* (2nd ed., pp. 569–617). Hillside, NJ: Erlbaum.

Bray, N. W. (1979). Strategy production in the retarded. In N. R. Ellis (Ed.), *Handbook of mental deficiency: Psychological theory and research* (2nd ed., pp. 699–737). Hillside, NJ: Erlbaum.

Bruininks, R. H. (1977). *Bruininks-Osretsky Test of Motor Proficiency.* Circle Pines, MN: American Guidance Service.

Bruininks, R. H., Warfield, G., & Stealey, D. S. (1978). The mentally retarded. In E. L. Meyen (Ed.), *Exceptional children and youth: An introduction* (pp. 196–261). Denver: Love.

Cegelka, W. J., & Tyler, J. L. (1970). The efficacy of special class placement for the mentally retarded in proper perspective. *Training School Bulletin*, 67(1), 33–67.

Chasey, W. C., & Wyrick, W. (1971). Effects of a physical development program on psychomotor ability of retarded children. *American Journal of Mental Deficiency*, 75, 566–570.

Clark, G. M., Carlson, B. C., Fisher, S., Cook, I. D., & D'Alonzo, B. J. (1991). Career development for students with disabilities in elementary schools: A position statement of the Division on Career Development. *Career Development for Exceptional Individuals*, 14, 109–120.

Cohen, R. L. (1982). Individual differences in short-term memory. In N. R. Ellis (Ed.), *International review of research in mental retardation* (Vol. 11, pp. 43–77). New York: Academic Press.

Connis, R. T. (1979). The effects of sequential pictorial cues, self-recording, and praise on the job-task sequencing of retarded adults. *Journal of Applied Behavior Analysis, 12,* 355–361.

Corman, L., & Gottlieb, J. (1978). Mainstreaming mentally retarded children: A review of research. In N. R. Ellis (Ed.), *International review of research in mental retardation* (Vol. 9, pp. 251–275). New York: Academic Press.

Coulter, W. A., & Morrow, H. W. (1978). The future of adaptive behavior: Issues surrounding the refinement of the concepts and its measurement. In W. A. Coulter & H. W. Morrow (Eds.), *Adaptive behavior: Concepts and measurement* (pp. 215–225). New York: Grune and Stratton.

Crain, E. J. (1980). Socioeconomic status of educable mentally retarded graduates of special education. *Education and Training of the Mentally Retarded, 15,* 90–94.

Cronin, M. E., & Patton, J. R. (1993). *Life skills instruction for all students with special needs: A practical guide for integrating real life content into the curriculum.* Austin, TX: Pro-Ed.

Diana v. State Board of Education, C.A. No. C–70–37, RFP (N.D. Cal. 1970).

Division on Mental Retardation. (1992). Education program design. *MR Express, 3*(1), 4.

Dunn, L. M. (1968). Special education for the mildly retarded—Is much of it justifiable? *Exceptional Children, 35,* 5–22.

Dunn, L. M. (1973). Children with mild general learning disabilities. In L. M. Dunn (Ed.), *Exceptional children in the schools: Special education in transition* (pp. 127–188). New York: Holt, Rinehart and Winston.

Edgar, C. L., Ball, T. S., McIntyre, R. R., & Shotwell, A. M. (1969). Effects of sensory-motor training on adaptive behavior. *American Journal of Mental Deficiency, 73,* 713–720.

Edgar, E. (1987). Secondary programs in special education: Are many of them justifiable? *Exceptional Children, 53,* 555-561.

Epstein, M. H., Polloway, E. A., Patton, J. R., & Foley, R. (1989). Mild retardation: Student characteristics and services. *Education and Training in Mental Retardation, 24,* 7–16.

Forness, S. R., & Polloway, E. A. (1987). Physical and psychiatric diagnoses of pupils with mild mental retardation currently being referred for related services. *Education and Training in Mental Retardation, 22,* 221–228.

Francis, R. J., & Rarick, G. L. (1959). Motor characteristics of the mentally retarded. *American Journal of Mental Deficiency, 63,* 792–811.

Gottlieb, J. (1982). Mainstreaming. *Education and Training of the Mentally Retarded, 17,* 79–82.

Gottlieb, J., & Budoff, M. (1973). Social acceptability of retarded children in nongraded schools differing in architecture. *American Journal of Mental Deficiency, 78,* 15–19.

Gottlieb, J., Gottlieb, B. W., Schmelkin, L. P., & Curci, R. (1983). Low- and high-IQ learning disabled children in the mainstream. *Analysis and Intervention in Developmental Disabilities, 3,* 59–69.

Gottlieb, J., & Leyser, Y. (1981). Facilitating the social mainstreaming of retarded children. *Exceptional Education Quarterly, 1*(4), 57–69.

Gottlieb, J., Semmel, M. I., & Veldman, D. J. (1978). Correlates of social status among mainstreamed mentally retarded children. *Journal of Educational Psychology, 70,* 396–405.

Grossman, H. J. (Ed.). (1973). *Manual on terminology and classification in mental retardation.* Washington, DC: American Association on Mental Deficiency.

Grossman, H. J. (Ed.). (1983). *Classification of mental retardation.* Washington, DC: American Association on Mental Deficiency.

Grossman, H. J., & Tarjan, G. (1987). AMA *handbook on mental retardation.* Chicago: American Medical Association, Division of Clinical Science.

Halpern, A. S., & Benz, M. R. (1987). A statewide examination of secondary special education for students with mild disabilities: Implications for high school curriculum. *Exceptional Children, 54,* 122–129.

Haywood, H. C. (1979). What happened to mild and moderate mental retardation? *American Journal of Mental Deficiency, 83,* 429–431.

Hewett, F. M., & Forness, S. R. (1977). *Education of exceptional learners.* Boston: Allyn and Bacon.

Howell, K. W., Rueda, R., & Rutherford, R. B. (1983). A procedure for teaching self-recording to moderately retarded students. *Psychology in the Schools, 20,* 202–209.

Johnson, N. M., & Chamberlin, H. R. (1983). Early intervention: The state of the art. In *Developmental handicaps: Prevention and treatment* (pp. 1–23a). Washington, DC: American Association of University Affiliated Programs for Persons with Developmental Disabilities.

Kaufman, A. S., & Kaufman, N. L. (1982). *Kaufman Assessment Battery for Children.* Circle Pines, MN: American Guidance Service.

Kehle, T. J., & Guidubaldi, J. (1978). Effect of EMR placement models of affective and social development. *Psychology in the Schools, 15,* 275–282.

Keilitz, I., & Miller, S. L. (1980). Handicapped adolescents and young adults in the justice system. *Exceptional Education Quarterly, 1*(2), 117–126.

Keogh, B. K., & Daley, S. E. (1983). Early identification: One component of comprehensive services for at-risk children. *Topics in Early Childhood Special Education, 3*(3), 7–16.

Kneedler, R. D., & Hallahan, D. P. (1981). Self-monitoring of on-task behavior with learning disabled children: Current studies and directions. *Exceptional Education Quarterly*, 2(3), 73–82.

Kolstoe, O. P. (1976). *Teaching educable mentally retarded children* (2nd ed.). New York: Holt, Rinehart and Winston.

Kral, P. A. (1972). Motor characteristics and development of retarded children: Success experience. *Education and Training of the Mentally Retarded*, 7, 14–21.

Larry P. v. Riles, 343 F. Supp. 1306, C–71–2270 (N.D. Cal. 1972).

Lawrence, E. A., & Winschel, J. F. (1975). Locus of control: Implications for special education. *Exceptional Children*, 41, 483–490.

Lazar, I., & Darlington, R. (1982). Lasting effects of early education: A report from the Consortium for Longitudinal Studies. *Monographs of the Society for Research in Child Development*, 47(2–3, Serial No. 195).

Leinhardt, G., Bickel, W., & Pallay, A. (1982). Unlabeled but still entitled: Toward more effective remediation. *Teachers College Record*, 84, 391–422.

Logan, D. R., & Rose, R. (1982). Characteristics of the mildly mentally retarded. In P. T. Cegelka & H. J. Prehm (Eds.), *Mental retardation: From categories to people* (pp. 149–185), Columbus, OH: Merrill.

Luftig, R. L. (1980, April). *The effect of differential education placements on the self-concept of retarded pupils*. Paper presented at the meeting of the American Educational Research Association. (ERIC Document Reproduction Service No. ED 196 198).

MacMillan, D. L. (1982). *Mental retardation in school and society* (2nd ed.). Boston: Little, Brown.

MacMillan, D. L. (1988). "New" EMRS. In G. A. Robinson, J. R. Patton, E. A. Polloway, & L. R. Sargent (Eds.), *Best practices in mental disabilities* (Vol. 2, pp. 1–24). Des Moines: Iowa Department of Education.

MacMillan, D. L. (1989). Mild mental retardation: Emerging issues. In G. A. Robinson, J. R. Patton, E. A. Polloway, & L. R. Sargent (Eds.), *Best practices in mild mental retardation* (pp. 1–20). Reston, VA: Division on Mental Retardation, Council for Exceptional Children.

MacMillan, D. L., & Borthwick, S. (1980). The new educable mentally retarded population: Can they be mainstreamed? *Mental Retardation*, 18, 155–158.

MacMillan, D. L., Meyers, C. E., & Morrison, G. M. (1980). System-identification of mildly mentally retarded children: Implications for interpreting and conducting research. *American Journal of Mental Deficiency*, 85, 108–115.

MacMillan, D. L., Meyers, C. E., & Yoshida, R. K. (1978). Regular class teachers' perceptions of transition pro-grams for EMR students and their impact on the students. *Psychology in the Schools*, 15, 99–103.

Marsh, R. L., Friel, C. M., & Eissler, V. (1975). The adult MR in the criminal justice system. *Mental Retardation*, 13(2), 21–25.

Mascari, B. G., & Forgnone, C. (1982). A follow-up study of EMR students four years after dismissal from the program. *Education and Training of the Mentally Retarded*, 17, 288–292.

Matson, J. L., & Breuning, S. E. (Eds.). (1983). *Assessing the mentally retarded*. New York: Grune and Stratton.

McLaren, J., & Bryson, S. E. (1987). Review of recent epidemiological studies of mental retardation: Prevalence, associated disorders, and etiology. *American Journal of Mental Retardation*, 92, 243–254.

Mercer, J. R., & Lewis, J. P. (1977). *System of Multicultural Pluralistic Assessment: Parent interview manual*. New York: Psychological Corporation.

Meyen, E. L., & Moran, M. R. (1979). A perspective on the unserved mildly handicapped. *Exceptional Children*, 45, 526–530.

Morgan, D. I. (1979). Prevalence and types of handicapping conditions found in juvenile correctional institutions: A national survey. *Journal of Special Education*, 13, 283–295.

Nihira, K., Lambert, N., & Leland, H. (1993a). AAMR *Adaptive Behavior Scales: School* (2nd ed.). Austin, TX: Pro-Ed.

Nihira, K., Leland, H., & Lambert, N. (1993b). AAMR *Adaptive Behavior Scales: Residential and community* (2nd ed.). Austin, TX: Pro-Ed.

Patrick, J. L., & Reschly, D. J. (1982). Relationship of state educational criteria and demographic variables to school-system prevalence of mental retardation. *American Journal of Mental Deficiency*, 86, 351–360.

Patton, J. R., & Browder, P. M. (1988). Transitions into the future. In B. Ludlow, R. Luckasson, & A. Turnbull (Eds.), *Transitions to adult life for persons with mental retardation: Principles and practices* (pp. 293–311). Baltimore: Paul H. Brookes.

Patton, J. R., Kauffman, J. M., Blackbourn, J. M., & Brown, G. B. (1991). *Exceptional children in focus* (5th ed.). New York: Merrill/Macmillan.

Polloway, E. A., Epstein, M. H., & Cullinan, D. (1985). Prevalence of behavior problems among educable mentally retarded students. *Education and Training of the Mentally Retarded*, 20, 3–13.

Polloway, E. A., Epstein, M. H., Patton, J. R., Cullinan, D., & Luebke, J. (1986). Demographic, social, and behavioral characteristics of students with educable mental retardation. *Education and Training of the Mentally Retarded*, 21, 27–34.

Polloway, E. A., & Patton, J. R. (1986). Social integration: The goal and the process. AAMD *Education Newsletter*, 2(1), 1–2.

Polloway, E. A., & Patton, J. R. (1993). *Strategies for teaching learners with special needs* (5th ed.). New York: Merrill/Macmillan.

Polloway, E. A., Patton, J. R., Epstein, M. H., & Smith, T. (1989). Comprehensive curriculum for students with mild handicaps. *Focus on Exceptional Children*, 21(8), 1–12.

Polloway, E. A., Patton, J. R., Smith, J. D., & Roderique, T. W. (1991). Issues in program design for elementary students with mild retardation. *Education and Training in Mental Retardation*, 26, 142–150.

Polloway, E. A., & Smith, J. D. (1982). *Teaching language skills to exceptional learners* (2nd ed.). Denver: Love.

Polloway, E. A., & Smith, J. D. (1983). Changes in mild mental retardation: Population, programs, and perspectives. *Exceptional Children*, 50, 149–159.

Polloway, E. A., & Smith, J. D. (1988). Current status of the mild mental retardation construct: Identification, placement, and programs. In M. C. Wang, M. C. Reynolds, & H. J. Walberg (Eds.), *The handbook of special education: Research and practice* (pp. 1-22). Oxford, England: Pergamon Press.

Polloway, E. A., & Smith, J. D. (1994). Causes of mental retardation. In M. Beirne-Smith, J. R. Patton, & R. F. Ittenbach (Ed.), *Mental retardation*. New York: Merrill/Macmillan.

Prehm, H. J. (1985, January). *Education and training of the mentally retarded: Mid-year report to the board of directors*. Washington, DC: Division on Mental Retardation of the Council for Exceptional Children.

President's Committee on Mental Retardation. (1976). *Mental retardation: Century of decision*. Washington, DC: U.S. Government Printing Office.

Ramey, C. T., & Campbell, F. A. (1984). Preventive education for high-risk children: Cognitive consequences of the Carolina Abecedarian project. *American Journal of Mental Deficiency*, 88, 515–523.

Ramey, C. T., & Finkelstein, N. W. (1981). Psychosocial mental retardation: A biological and social coalescence. In M. J. Begab, H. C. Haywood, & H. L. Garber (Eds.), *Psychosocial influences in retarded performance: Issues and theories in development* (Vol. 1, pp. 65–92). Baltimore: University Park Press.

Rantalkallio, P., & Von Wendt, L. (1986). Mental retardation and subnormality in a birth cohort of 12,000 children in northern Finland. *American Journal of Mental Deficiency*, 90, 380–387.

Reschly, D. J. (1988). Assessment issues, placement litigation, and the future of mild mental retardation classifi

cation and programming. *Education and Training in Mental Retardation*, 23, 285–301.

Reschly, D. J., Robinson, G., Volmer, L., & Wilson, L. (1988). *Iowa mental disabilities research project: Final report and executive summary*. Des Moines: State of Iowa, Department of Education.

Robinson, N. M., & Robinson, H. B. (1976). *The mentally retarded child* (2nd ed.). New York: McGraw-Hill.

Rogers-Warren, A. K., & Poulson, C. L. (1984). Perspectives on early childhood education. In E. L. Meyen (Ed.), *Mental retardation: Topics of today—issues of tomorrow* (pp. 67–87). Washington, DC: Division on Mental Retardation, Council for Exceptional Children.

Sarason, S. B. (1985). *Psychology and mental retardation: Perspectives in change*. Austin, TX: Pro-Ed.

Schweinhart, L. J., Berrueta-Clement, J. R., Barnett, W. S., Epstein, A. S., & Weikart, D. P. (1985). Effects of the Perry preschool programs on youths through age 19: A summary. *Topics in Early Childhood Special Education*, 5(2), 26–35.

Seiter, M. M. (1992). *Mental retardation: Definition, classification, and systems of supports: Workbook*. Washington, DC: American Association on Mental Retardation.

Seligman, M. E. (1975). *Helplessness: On depression, development, and death*. San Francisco: Freeman.

Simeonsson, R. J. (1978). Social competence. In J. Wortis (Ed.), *Mental retardation and developmental disabilities: An annual review* (Vol. 10, pp. 130–171). New York: Brunner/Mazel.

Smith, J. D. (1985). *Minds made feeble: The myth and legacy of the Kallikaks*. Austin, TX: Pro-Ed.

Smith, J. D. (1989). *The sterilization of Carrie Buck*. New York: New Horizons.

Smith, J. D., & Polloway, E. A. (1993). Institutionalization, involuntary sterilization, and retardation: Profiles from the practice. *Mental Retardation*, 31, 208–214.

Smith, T. E. C., Polloway, E. A., Patton, J. R., & Dowdy, C. (in press). *Teaching students with special needs in inclusive settings*. Boston: Allyn and Bacon.

Sparrow, S. S., Balla, D. A., & Cicchetti, D. V. (1985a). *Vineland Adaptive Behavior Scales: Classroom edition*. Circle Pines, MN: American Guidance Service.

Sparrow, S. S., Balla, D. A., & Cicchetti, D. V. (1985b). *Vineland Adaptive Behavior Scales: Interview edition, expanded form*. Circle Pines, MN: American Guidance Service.

Spitz, H. H. (1966). The role of input organization in the learning and memory of mental retardates. In N. R. Ellis (Ed.), *International review of research in mental retardation* (Vol. 2, pp. 29–56). New York: Academic Press.

Spradlin, J. E. (1963). Language and communication of mental defectives. In N. R. Ellis (Ed.), *Handbook of mental deficiency* (pp. 512–555). New York: McGraw-Hill.

Spradlin, J. E. (1968). Environmental factors and the language development of retarded children. In S. Rosenberg & J. H. Koplin (Eds.), *Developments in applied psycholinguistic research* (pp. 261–290). New York: Macmillan.

Stebbins, L. B., St. Pierre, R. G., Proper, E. C., Anderson, R. B., & Cerva, T. R. (1977). *Education as experimentation: A planned variation model: An evaluation of Follow Through* (Vol. 4). Cambridge, MA: ABT.

Stephens, W. E. (1972). Equivalence formation by retarded and nonretarded children at different mental ages. *American Journal of Mental Deficiency, 77*, 311–313.

Stevenson, H. W. (1972). *Children's learning.* Englewood Cliffs, NJ: Prentice-Hall.

Strichart, S. S., & Gottlieb, J. (1982). Characteristics of mild mental retardation. In T. L. Miller & E. Davis (Eds.), *The mildly handicapped student* (pp. 37–65). New York: Grune and Stratton.

Tarjan, G., Wright, S. W., Eyman, R. K., & Kerran, D. V. (1973). Natural history of mental retardation: Some aspects of epidemiology. *American Journal of Mental Deficiency, 77*, 369–379.

Thorndike, R. L., Hagan, E. P., & Sattler, J. M. (1986). *The Stanford-Binet Intelligence Scale* (4th ed.). Chicago: Riverside.

Tucker, J. (1980). Ethnic proportions in classes for the learning disabled: Issues in nonbiased assessment. *Journal of Special Education, 14*, 93–105.

Turnbull, H. R., & Barber, P. (1984). Perspectives on public policy. In E. L. Meyen (Ed.), *Mental retardation: Topics of today—issues of tomorrow* (pp. 5–24). Washington, DC: Division on Mental Retardation, Council for Exceptional Children.

U.S. Department of Education. (1992). *Fourteenth annual report to Congress on the implementation of the Individuals with Disabilities Education Act.* Washington, DC: Author.

Utley, C. A., Lowitzer, A. C., & Baumeister, A. A. (1987). A comparison of the AAMD's definition, eligibility criteria, and classification schemes with state departments of education guidelines. *Education and Training in Mental Retardation, 22*, 35–43.

Wallace, G., Cohen, S. B., & Polloway, E. A. (1987). *Language arts: Teaching exceptional students.* Austin, TX: Pro-Ed.

Wechsler, D. (1992). *Wechsler Intelligence Scale for Children* (3rd ed.). New York: Psychological Corporation.

Wehman, P. (1992). *Life beyond the classroom: Transition strategies for young people with disabilities.* Baltimore: Paul H. Brookes.

Wehman, P., & Kregel, J. (1985). A supported-work approach to competitive employment of individuals with moderate and severe handicaps. *Journal of the Association for Persons with Severe Handicaps, 10*, 3–11.

Wolfensberger, W. (1983). Social role valorization: A proposed new term for the principle of normalization. *Mental Retardation, 21*, 234–239.

Woodcock, R. W., & Johnson, M. B. (1989). *Woodcock-Johnson Psychoeducational Battery* (rev. ed.). Hingham, MA: Teaching Resources.

Zeaman, D., & House, B. J. (1979). A review of attention theory. In N. R. Ellis (Ed.), *Handbook of mental deficiency: Psychological theory and research* (2nd ed., pp. 63–120). Hillsdale, NJ: Erlbaum.

Zigler, E. (1966). Research on personality structure in the retardate. In N. R. Ellis (Ed.), *International review of research in mental retardation* (Vol. 1, pp. 77–108). New York: Academic Press.

Zigler, E. (1973). The retarded child as a whole person. In D. K. Routh (Ed.), *The experimental psychology of mental retardation* (pp. 231–322). Chicago: Aldine.

Zirpoli, T. (1986). Child abuse and children with handicaps. *Remedial and Special Education, 7*(2), 39–48.

CHAPTER SEVEN

Abramowicz, H. K., & Richardson, S. A. (1975). Epidemiology of severe mental retardation in children: Community studies. *American Journal of Mental Deficiency, 80*, 18–39.

Alberto, P. A., Sharpton, W. R., Briggs, A., & Straight, M. H. (1986). Facilitating task acquisition through the use of a self-operated auditory prompting system. *Journal of the Association for Persons with Severe Handicaps, 11*, 85–91.

American Association on Mental Retardation. (1992). *Mental retardation: Definition, classification, and systems of supports* (9th ed.). Washington, DC: Author.

Baer, D. B. (1981). A hung jury and a Scottish verdict: "No proven." *Analysis and Intervention in Developmental Disabilities, 1*(1), 91–97.

Bailey, D. B. (in press). Working with families of children with special needs. In M. Wolery & J. S. Wilbers (Eds.), *Including children with special needs in preschool programs: Research and implications for practice.* Washington, DC: National Association for the Education of Young Children.

Bailey, D. B., McWilliam, P. J., Winton, P. J., & Simeonsson, R. J. (1992). *Implementing family-centered services in early intervention: A team-based model for change.* Cambridge, MA: Brookline Books.

Bailey, D. B., Simeonsson, R. J., Yoder, D. E., & Huntington, G. S. (1990). Preparing professionals to serve infants and toddlers with handicaps and their families: An integrative analysis across eight disciplines. *Exceptional Children*, 57, 26–53.

Bailey, D. B., & Wolery, M. (1992). *Teaching infants and preschoolers with disabilities* (2nd ed.). New York: Merrill/Macmillan.

Banks, R., & Aveno, A. (1986). Adapted miniature golf: A community leisure program for students with severe physical disabilities. *Journal of the Association for Persons with Severe Handicaps*, 11, 209–215.

Barnett, D. W., Macmann, G. M., & Carey, K. T. (1992). Early intervention and the assessment of developmental skills: Challenges and directions. *Topics in Early Childhood Special Education*, 12, 21–43.

Baumeister, A. A., Kupstas, F., & Klindworth, L. M. (1990). New morbidity: Implications for prevention and children's disabilities. *Exceptionality*, 1, 1–16.

Baumgart, D., Filler, J., & Askvig, B. (1991). Perceived importance of social skills: A survey of teachers, parents, and other professionals. *Journal of Special Education*, 25, 236–251.

Baumgart, D., Johnson, J., & Helmstetter, E. (1990). *Augmentative and alternative communication systems for persons with moderate and severe disabilities*. Baltimore: Paul H. Brookes.

Belfiore, P. J., & Browder, D. M. (1992). The effects of self-monitoring on teacher's data-based decisions and on the progress of adults with severe mental retardation. *Education and Training in Mental Retardation*, 27, 60–67.

Bellamy, G. T. (1986). View point: Severe disability in adulthood. *Newsletter, TASH: The Association for Persons with Severe Handicaps*, 11(6), 1, 6.

Bellamy, G. T., Rhodes, L. E., Wilcox, B., Albin, J., Mank, D. M., Boles, S. M., Horner, R. H., Collins, M., & Turner, J. (1984). Quality and equality in employment services for adults with severe disabilities. *Journal of the Association for Persons with Severe Handicaps*, 9, 270–277.

Billingsley, F. F., Burgess, D., Lynch, V. W., & Matlock, B. L. (1991). Toward generalized outcomes: Considerations and guidelines for writing instructional objectives. *Education and Training in Mental Retardation*, 26, 351–360.

Blum, R. E. (1985). Outcome-based schools: A definition. *Outcomes*, 5(1), 1–5.

Breen, C., & Haring, T. G. (1991). Effects of contextual competence on social initiations. *Journal of Applied Behavior Analysis*, 24, 337–347.

Breen, C., Haring, T. G., Pitts-Conway, V., & Gaylord-Ross, R. (1985). The training and generalization of social interaction during breaktime at two job sites in the natural environment. *Journal of the Association for Persons with Severe Handicaps*, 10, 41–50.

Brigance, A. H. (1978). *Brigance Diagnostic Inventory of Early Development*. Worcester, MA: Curriculum Associates.

Browder, D. B. (1991). *Assessment of individuals with severe disabilities: An applied behavior approach to life skills assessment* (2nd ed.). Baltimore: Paul H. Brookes.

Brown, F. (1991). Creative daily scheduling: A nonintrusive approach to challenging behaviors in community residences. *Journal of the Association for Persons with Severe Handicaps*, 16, 75–84.

Brown, L., Branston, M. B., Hamre-Nietupski, S., Pumpian, I., Certo, N., & Gruenewald, L. (1979). A strategy for developing chronological-age-appropriate and functional curricular content for severely handicapped adolescents and young adults. *Journal of Special Education*, 13, 81–90.

Brown, L., Long, E., Udvari-Solner, A., Davis, L., VanDeventer, P., Ahlgren, C., Johnson, F., Gruenewald, L., & Jorgensen, J. (1989). The home school: Why students with severe intellectual disabilities must attend the schools of their brothers, sisters, friends, and neighbors. *Journal of the Association for Persons with Severe Handicaps*, 14, 1–7.

Brown, L., Long, E., Udvari-Solner, A., Schwarz, P., VanDeventer, P., Ahlgren, C., Johnson, F., Gruenewald, L., & Jorgensen, J. (1989). Should students with severe intellectual disabilities be based in regular or in special education classrooms in home schools? *Journal of the Association for Persons with Severe Handicaps*, 14, 8–12.

Brown, L., Nisbet, J., Ford, A., Sweet, M., Shiraga, B., York, J., & Loomis, R. (1983). The critical need for nonschool instruction in educational programs for severely handicapped students. *Journal of the Association for Persons with Severe Handicaps*, 8, 71–77.

Brown, L., Schwarz, P., Udvari-Solner, A., Kampschroer, E. F., Johnson, F., Jorgensen, J., & Gruenewald, L. (1991). How much time should students with severe intellectual disabilities spend in regular education classrooms and elsewhere? *Journal of the Association for Persons with Severe Handicaps*, 16, 39–47.

Brown, L., Shirage, B., York, J., Kessler, K., Strohm, B., Rogan, P., Sweet, M., Zanella, K., VanDeventer, P., & Loomis, R. (1984). Integrated work opportunities for adults with severe handicaps: The extended training option. *Journal of the Association for Persons with Severe Handicaps*, 9, 262–269.

Bruder, M. B. (in press). Working with members of other disciplines: Collaborations for success. In M. Wolery & J. S. Wilbers (Eds.), *Including children with special needs in preschool programs: Research and implications for practice*. Washington, DC: National Association for the Education of Young Children.

Bruininks, R. H., Woodcock, R. W., Weatherman, R. F., & Hill, B. K. (1984). *Scales of independent behavior: Woodcock-Johnson*

Psychoeducational Battery. Allen, TX: Developmental Learning Materials.

Buysse, V., & Bailey, D. B. (1993). Behavioral and developmental outcomes in young children with disabilities in integrated and segregated settings: A review of comparative studies. *Journal of Special Education, 26,* 434–461.

Carta, J. J., Sainato, D. M., & Greenwood, C. R. (1988). Advances in the ecological assessment of classroom instruction for young children with handicaps. In S. L. Odom & M. B. Karnes (Eds.), *Early intervention for infants and children with handicaps: An empirical base* (pp. 217–239). Baltimore: Paul H. Brookes.

Collins, B. C., Gast, D. L., Ault, M. J., & Wolery, M. (1991). Small group instruction: Guidelines for teachers of students with moderate to severe handicaps. *Education and Training in Mental Retardation, 26,* 18–32.

Consortium on Adaptive Performance Evaluation. (1980). *Adaptive Performance Instrument.* Moscow, ID: Department of Special Education.

Cooper, J. O., Heron, T. E., & Heward, W. L. (1987). *Applied behavior analysis.* New York: Merrill/Macmillan.

Cosden, M. A., & Haring, T. G. (1992). Cooperative learning in the classroom: Contingencies, group interactions, and students with special needs. *Journal of Behavior Education, 2,* 53–71.

Covert, S. B. (1992). Supporting families. In J. Nisbet (Ed.), *Natural supports in school, at work, and in the community for people with severe disabilities* (pp. 121–163). Baltimore: Paul H. Brookes.

Crocker, A. C. (1992a). Data collection for the evaluation of mental retardation prevention activities: The fateful forty-three. *Mental Retardation, 30,* 303–317.

Crocker, A. C. (1992b). Introduction: Where is the prevention movement? *Mental Retardation, 30,* iii–v.

Cronin, K. A., & Cuvo, A. J. (1979). Teaching mending skills to mentally retarded adolescents. *Journal of Applied Behavior Analysis, 12,* 401–406.

Crump, I. (1987). *Nutrition and feeding of the handicapped child.* Boston: College Hill Press.

Cutler, B. C. (1993). *You, your child, and "special" education: A guide to making the system work.* Baltimore: Paul H. Brookes.

Doyle, P. M., Wolery, M., Ault, M. J., & Gast, D. L. (1988). System of least prompts: A review of procedural parameters. *Journal of the Association for Persons with Severe Handicaps, 13,* 28–40.

Dunlap, G., Kern-Dunlap, L., Clarke, S., & Robbins, F. R. (1991). Functional assessment, curricular revision, and severe behavior problems. *Journal of Applied Behavior Analysis, 24,* 387–397.

Dunst, C. J., Trivette, C. M., & Deal, A. G. (1988). *Enabling and empowering families: Principles and guidelines for practice.* Cambridge, MA: Brookline Books.

Ellis, D. (1986). The epidemiology of visual impairment in people with mental handicaps. In D. Ellis (Ed.), *Sensory impairments in mentally handicapped people* (pp. 3–34). San Diego, CA: College Hill Press.

Falvey, M. A. (1989). *Community-based curriculum: Instructional strategies for students with severe handicaps* (2nd ed.). Baltimore: Paul H. Brookes.

Farlow, L. J., & Snell, M. E. (1989). Teacher use of student performance data to make instructional decisions: Practices in programs for students with moderate to profound disabilities. *Journal of the Association for Persons with Severe Handicaps, 14,* 13–22.

Federal Register. (1988). *Code of federal regulations: 34: Education: Parts 300–399,* revised as of July 1, 1988. Washington, DC: U.S. Government Printing Office.

Ferguson, D. L., & Baumgart, D. (1991). Partial participation revisited. *Journal of the Association for Persons with Severe Handicaps, 16,* 218–227.

Forest, M., & Pearpoint, J. (1992). Families, friends, and circles. In J. Nisbet (Ed.), *Natural supports in school, at work, and in the community for people with severe disabilities* (pp. 65–86). Baltimore: Paul H. Brookes.

Foxx, R. M., & Azrin, N. H. (1973). *Toilet training the retarded: A rapid program for day and nighttime independent toileting.* Champaign, IL: Research Press.

Frankenberger, W., & Fronzagilo, K. (1991). States' definitions and procedures for identifying children with mental retardation: Comparison over nine years. *Mental Retardation, 29,* 315–321.

Fredericks, H. D., Baldwin, V. L., Grove, D. N., & Moore, W. G. (1975). *Toilet training the handicapped child.* Monmouth, OR: Instructional Development Corporation.

Gallagher, J. J., Trohanis, P. L., & Clifford, R. M. (1989). *Policy implementation and PL 99–457: Planning for young children with special needs.* Baltimore: Paul H. Brookes.

Gast, D. L., Collins, B. C., Wolery, M., & Jones, R. (1993). Teaching preschool children with disabilities to respond to the lures of strangers. *Exceptional Children, 59,* 301–311.

Gast, D. L., Winterling, V., Wolery, M., & Farmer, J. A. (1992). Teaching first-aid skills to students with moderate handicaps in small group instruction. *Education and Treatment of Children, 15,* 101–124.

Gaylord-Ross, R., Forte, J., Storey, K., Gaylord-Ross, C., & Jameson, D. (1987). Community-referenced instruction in technological work settings. *Exceptional Children, 54,* 112–120.

Gaylord-Ross, R., Haring, T. G., Breen, C., & Pitts-Conway, V. (1984). The training and generalization of social interaction skills with autistic youth. *Journal of Applied Behavior Analysis*, 17, 229–247.

Gee, K., Graham, N., Goetz, L., Oshima, G., & Yoshioka, K. (1991). Teaching students to request the continuation of routine activities by using time delay and decreasing physical assistance in the context of chain interruption. *Journal of the Association for Persons with Severe Handicaps*, 16, 154–167.

Goldstein, H., & Ferrell, D. R. (1987). Augmenting communicative interactions between handicapped and non-handicapped preschool children. *Journal of Speech and Hearing Disorders*, 52, 200–211.

Goldstein, H., & Gallagher, T. M. (1992). Strategies for promoting the social-communicative competence of young children with specific language impairment. In S. L. Odom, S. R. McConnell, & M. A. McEvoy (Eds.), *Social competence of young children with disabilities: Issues and strategies for intervention* (pp. 189–213). Baltimore: Paul H. Brookes.

Gould, S. J. (1981). *The mismeasure of man*. New York: Norton.

Griffen, A. K., Wolery, M., & Schuster, J. W. (1992). Triadic instruction of chained food preparation responses: Acquisition and observational learning. *Journal of Applied Behavior Analysis*, 25, 193–204.

Grigg, N. C., Snell, M. E., & Loyd, B. (1989). Visual analysis of student evaluation data: A qualitative analysis of teacher decision making. *Journal of the Association for Persons with Severe Handicaps*, 14, 23–32.

Grossman, H. J. (1983). *Classification in mental retardation*. Washington, DC: American Association on Mental Deficiency.

Guess, D., & Helmstetter, E. (1986). Skill cluster instruction and the individualized curriculum sequencing model. In R. H. Horner, L. Meyer, & H. D. Fredericks (Eds.), *Education of learners with severe handicaps: Exemplary service strategies* (pp. 221–248). Baltimore: Paul H. Brookes.

Guess, D., Roberts, S., Siegel-Causey, E., Ault, M. M., Guy, B., Thompson, B., Rules, J., & Siegel-Causey, D. (1991). *Investigations into the state behaviors of students with severe and profound handicapping conditions* (Monograph No. 1). Lawrence: University of Kansas, Special Education Department, Severely Handicapped Area.

Hamre-Nietupski, S., Nietupski, J., & Strathe, M. (1992). Functional life skills, academic skills, and friendship/social relationship development: What do parents of students with moderate/severe/profound disabilities value? *Journal of the Association for Persons with Severe Handicaps*, 17, 53–58.

Haring, K., Farron-Davis, F., Goetz, L., Karasoff, P., Sailor, W., & Zeph, L. (1992). LRE and the placement of students with severe disabilities. *Journal of the Association for Persons with Severe Handicaps*, 17, 145–153.

Haring, N. G. (1987). *Investigating the problem of skill generalization: Literature review III*. Seattle: University of Washington Press. (ERIC Document Reproduction Service No. ED 287 270)

Haring, N. G. (1988). *Generalization for students with severe handicaps: Strategies and solutions*. Seattle: University of Washington Press.

Haring, N. G., Liberty, K. A., & White, O. R. (1980). Rules for data-based strategy decisions in instructional programs: Current research and instructional implications. In W. Sailor, B. Wilcox, & L. Brown (Eds.), *Methods of instruction for severely handicapped learners* (pp. 159–192). Baltimore: Paul H. Brookes.

Haring, N. G., White, O. R., Edgar, E., Affleck, J., & Hayden, A. (1982). *Uniform Performance Assessment System*. Columbus, OH: Merrill.

Haring, T. G. (1992). The context of social competence: Relations, relationships, and generalization. In S. L. Odom, S. R. McConnell, & M. A. McEvoy (Eds.), *Social competence of young children with disabilities: Issues and strategies for intervention* (pp. 307–320). Baltimore: Paul H. Brookes.

Haring, T. G., Breen, C., Pitts-Conway, V., Lee, M., & Gaylord-Ross, R. (1987). Adolescent peer tutoring and special friend experiences. *Journal of the Association for Persons with Severe Handicaps*, 12, 280–286.

Haring, T. G., Breen, C. G., Weiner, J., Kennedy, C. H., & Bednersh, F. (in press). Using videotape modeling to facilitate generalized purchasing skills. *Journal of Behavioral Education*.

Haring, T. G., & Kennedy, C. H. (1990). Contextual control of problem behavior in students with severe disabilities. *Journal of Applied Behavior Analysis*, 23, 235–243.

Haring, T. G., Kennedy, C. H., Adams, M. J., & Pitts-Conway, V. (1987). Teaching generalization of purchasing skills across community settings to autistic youth using videotape modeling. *Journal of Applied Behavior Analysis*, 20, 89–96.

Haring, T. G., & Lovinger, L. (1989). Promoting social interaction through teaching generalized play initiation responses to children with autism. *Journal of the Association for Persons with Severe Handicaps*, 14, 58–67.

Haring, T. G., Neetz, J. A., Lovinger, L., Peck, C. A., & Semmel, M. I. (1987). Effects of four modified incidental teaching procedures to create opportunities for communication. *Journal of the Association for Persons with Severe Handicaps*, 12, 218–226.

Harris, K. C. (1990). Meeting diverse needs through collaborative consultation. In W. Stainback & S. Stainback (Eds.), *Support networks for inclusive schooling: Interdependent and integrated education* (pp. 139–150). Baltimore: Paul H. Brookes.

Haseltine, B., & Miltenberger, R. G. (1990). Teaching self-protection skills to persons with mental retardation. *American Journal on Mental Retardation, 95*, 188–197.

Hayden, M. F., & DePaepe, P. A. (1991). Medical conditions, level of care needs, and health-related outcomes of persons with mental retardation: A review. *Journal of the Association for Persons with Severe Handicaps, 16*, 188–206.

Helmstetter, E., & Guess, D. (1987). Application of the individualized curriculum sequencing model to learners with severe sensory impairments. In L. Goetz, D. Guess, & K. Stremel-Campbell (Eds.), *Innovative program design for individuals with dual sensory impairments* (pp. 255–282). Baltimore: Paul H. Brookes.

Hill, M. L., Wehman, P. H., Kregel, J., Banks, D., & Metzler, H. M. D. (1987). Employment outcomes for people with moderate and severe disabilities: An eight-year longitudinal analysis of supported employment. *Journal of the Association for Persons with Severe Handicaps, 12*, 182–189.

Hilton, A., & Liberty, K. (1992). The challenge of ensuring educational gains for students with severe disabilities who are placed in more integrated settings. *Education and Training in Mental Retardation, 27*, 167–175.

Hofmeister, A. M., & Ferrara, J. M. (1986). Expert systems and special education. *Exceptional Children, 53*, 235–239.

Holmes, L. (1987). Epidemiology of Down syndrome. In S. M. Pueschel, C. Tingey, J. E. Rynders, A. C. Crocker, & D. M. Crutcher (Eds.), *New perspectives on Down syndrome* (pp. 97–104). Baltimore: Paul H. Brookes.

Horn, E. M., Jones, H. A., & Hamlett, C. (1991). An investigation of the feasibility of a video game system for developing scanning and selection skills. *Journal of the Association for Persons with Severe Handicaps, 16*, 108–115.

Horn, E. M., Warren, S. F., & Reith, H. J. (1992). Effects of a small group microcomputer-mediated motor skills instruction package. *Journal of the Association for Persons with Severe Handicaps, 17*, 133–144.

Horner, R. H., Albin, R. W., & Ralph, G. (1986). Generalization with precision: The role of negative teaching examples in the instruction of generalized grocery item selection. *Journal of the Association for Persons with Severe Handicaps, 11*, 300–308.

Horner, R. H., & Day, H. M. (1991). The effects of response efficiency on functionally equivalent competing behaviors. *Journal of Applied Behavior Analysis, 24*, 719–732.

Horner, R. H., Dunlap, G., & Koegel, R. L. (1988). *Generalization and maintenance: Life-style changes in applied settings.* Baltimore: Paul H. Brookes.

Horner, R. H., Sprague, J. R., O'Brien, M., & Heathfield, L. T. (1990). The role of response efficiency in the reduction of problem behaviors through functional equivalence training. *Journal of the Association for Persons with Severe Handicaps, 15*, 91–97.

Hughes, C. (1992). Teaching self-instruction utilizing multiple exemplars to produce generalized problem-solving among individuals with severe mental retardation. *Journal of the Association on Mental Retardation, 97*, 302–314.

Hunt, P., Alwell, M., & Goetz, L. (1991). Establishing conversational exchanges with family and friends: Moving from training to meaningful communications. *Journal of Special Education, 25*, 305–319.

Izen, C. L., & Brown, F. (1991). Education and treatment needs of students with profound, multiply handicapping, and medically fragile conditions: A survey of teachers' perceptions. *Journal of the Association for Persons with Severe Handicaps, 16*, 94–103.

Jones, K. L. (1988). *Smith's recognizable patterns of human malformation* (4th ed.). Philadelphia: Saunders.

Kaiser, A., Yoder, P. J., & Keetz, A. (1992). Evaluating milieu teaching. In S. F. Warren & J. Reichle (Eds.), *Causes and effects in communication and language intervention* (pp. 9–47). Baltimore: Paul H. Brookes.

Karsh, K. G., & Repp, A. C. (1992). The Task Demonstration Model: A concurrent model for teaching groups of students with severe disabilities. *Exceptional Children, 59*, 54–67.

Kauffman, J. M., & Krouse, J. (1981). The cult of educability: Searching for the substance of things hoped for, the evidence of things not seen. *Analysis and Intervention in Developmental Disabilities, 1*, 53–60.

Kinney, P., Ouellette, T., & Wolery, M. (1989). Screening and assessing sensory functioning. In D. B. Bailey & M. Wolery (Eds.), *Assessing infants and preschoolers with handicaps* (pp. 144–165). New York: Merrill/Macmillan.

Lambert, N., Windmiller, M., Tharinger, D., & Cole, L. (1981). *Administration and instructional planning manual, AAMD Adaptive Behavior Scale: School edition.* Monterey, CA: CTB/McGraw-Hill.

Lane, H. (1979). *The wild boy of Aveyron.* Cambridge, MA: Harvard University Press.

Marchetti, A. G., McCartney, J. R., Drain, S., Hooper, M., & Dix, J. (1983). Pedestrian skills training for mentally retarded adults: Comparison of training in two settings. *Mental Retardation, 21*, 107–110.

Marfo, K. (1988). *Parent-child interaction and developmental disabilities: Theory, research, and intervention*. New York: Praeger.

Mason, S. A., McGee, G. G., Farmer-Dougan, V., & Risley, T. R. (1989). A practical strategy for ongoing reinforcer assessment. *Journal of Applied Behavior Analysis*, 22, 171–179.

McCartney, J. R. (1990). Toilet training. In J. L. Matson (Ed.), *Handbook of behavior modification with the mentally retarded* (2nd ed.). New York: Plenum Press.

McDonnell, J. (1987). The effects of time delay and increasing prompt hierarchy strategies on the acquisition of purchasing skills by students with severe handicaps. *Journal of the Association for Persons with Severe Handicaps*, 12, 227–236.

McDonnell, J., & Ferguson, B. (1988). A comparison of general case in vivo and general case simulation plus in vivo training. *Journal of the Association for Persons with Severe Handicaps*, 13, 116–124.

McEvoy, M. A., Twardosz, S., & Bishop, N. (1990). Affection activities: Procedures for encouraging young children with handicaps to interact with their peers. *Education and Treatment of Children*, 13, 159–167.

McLaren, J., & Bryson, S. E. (1987). Review of recent epidemiological studies of mental retardation: Prevalence, associated disorders, and etiology. *American Journal of Mental Retardation*, 92, 243–254.

Meyer, L. H. (1991). Guest editorial: Why meaningful outcomes? *Journal of Special Education*, 25, 287–290.

Mulligan-Ault, M., Guess, D., Struth, L., & Thompson, B. (1988). The implementation of health-related procedures in classrooms for students with severe multiple impairments. *Journal of the Association for Persons with Severe Handicaps*, 13, 100–109.

Musselwhite, C. R. (1986). *Adaptive play for special needs children: Strategies to enhance communication and learning*. Boston: College Hill Press.

Neel, R. S., & Billingsley, F. F. (1989). *IMPACT: A functional curriculum handbook for students with moderate to severe disabilities*. Baltimore: Paul H. Brookes.

Nietupski, J. A., Clancey, C., & Christiansen, P. (1984). Acquisition, maintenance, and generalization of vending machine purchasing skills in moderately handicapped students. *Education and Treatment of the Mentally Retarded*, 22, 91–96.

Nietupski, J. A., & Hamre-Nietupski, S. M. (1987). An ecological approach to curriculum development. In L. Goetz, D. Guess, & K. Stremel-Campbell (Eds.), *Innovative program design for individuals with dual sensory impairments* (pp. 225–250). Baltimore: Paul H. Brookes.

Nietupski, J. A., Hamre-Nietupski, S. M., Clancy, P., & Veerhusen, L. (1986). Guidelines for making simulation an effective adjunct to in vivo community instruction. *Journal of the Association for Persons with Severe Handicaps*, 11, 12–18.

Odom, S. L., McConnell, S. R., & McEvoy, M. A. (Eds.). (1992). *Social competence of young children with disabilities: Issues and strategies for intervention*. Baltimore: Paul H. Brookes.

Odom, S. L., & McEvoy, M. A. (1988). Integration of young children with handicaps and normally developing children. In S. L. Odom & M. B. Karnes (Eds.), *Early intervention for infants and children with handicaps: An empirical base* (pp. 241–267). Baltimore: Paul H. Brookes.

O'Neill, R. E., Horner, R. H., Albin, R. W., Storey, K., & Sprague, J. R. (1990). *Functional analysis of problem behavior: A practical assessment guide*. Sycamore, IL: Sycamore Publishing.

Orelove, F. P., & Sobsey, D. (1991). *Educating children with multiple disabilities: A transdisciplinary approach* (2nd ed.). Baltimore: Paul H. Brookes.

Park, H. S., & Gaylord-Ross, R. (1989). A problem-solving approach to social skills training in employment settings with mentally retarded youth. *Journal of Applied Behavior Analysis*, 22, 373–380.

Pennsylvania Association for Retarded Citizens (PARC) v. Commonwealth of Pennsylvania, 334 F. Supp. 1253 (1972).

Pope, A. M. (1992). Preventing secondary conditions. *Mental Retardation*, 30, 347–354.

Prizant, B., & Bailey, D. B. (1992). Facilitating the acquisition and use of communication skills. In D. B. Bailey & M. Wolery (Eds.), *Teaching infants and preschoolers with disabilities* (2nd ed., pp. 299–361). New York: Merrill/Macmillan.

Pugach, M. C., & Johnson, L. J. (1990). Meeting diverse needs through professional peer collaboration. In W. Stainback & S. Stainback (Eds.), *Support networks for inclusive schooling: Interdependent and integrated education* (pp. 123–137). Baltimore: Paul H. Brookes.

Purkey, S. D., & Smith, M. S. (1983). Effective schools: A review. *Elementary School Journal*, 83, 417–452.

Rainforth, B., York, J., & Macdonald, C. (1992). *Collaborative teams for students with severe disabilities: Integrating therapy and educational services*. Baltimore: Paul H. Brookes.

Repp, A. C., & Singh, N. N. (1990). *Perspectives on the use of nonaversive and aversive interventions for persons with developmental disabilities*. Sycamore, IL: Sycamore Publishing.

Robinson, D., Griffith, J., McComish, L., & Swasbrook, K. (1984). Bus training for developmentally disabled adults. *American Journal of Mental Deficiency*, 89, 37–43.

Rosenberg, S. A., & Robinson, C. C. (1988). Interactions of parents with their young handicapped children. In S. L. Odom & M. B. Karnes (Eds.), *Early intervention for infants and children with handicaps: An empirical base* (pp. 159–177). Baltimore: Paul H. Brookes.

Rusch, F. (Ed.). (1986). *Competitive employment issues and strategies*. Baltimore: Paul H. Brookes.

Rusch, F., & Hughes, C. (1989). Overview of supported employment. *Journal of Applied Behavior Analysis, 22,* 351–363.

Sailor, W., Gee, K., Goetz, L., & Graham, N. (1988). Progress in educating students with the most severe disabilities: Is there any? *Journal of the Association for Persons with Severe Handicaps, 13,* 87–99.

Sailor, W., & Guess, D. (1983). *Severely handicapped students: An instructional design*. Boston: Houghton Mifflin.

Sainato, D. M., & Carta, J. J. (1992). Classroom influences on the development of social competence in young children with disabilities. In S. L. Odom, S. R. McConnell, & M. A. McEvoy (Eds.), *Social competence of young children with disabilities: Issues and strategies for intervention* (pp. 93–109). Baltimore: Paul H. Brookes.

Salisbury, C. L. (1989). *Translating commitment into practice: Evolution of the SUNY Binghamton-Johnson City Collaborative Education Project.* Paper presented at the Office of Special Education Programs Project Officer's meeting on Integration Education: State of Implementation and Future Directions, Washington, DC.

Salisbury, C. L. (1991). Mainstreaming during the early childhood years. *Exceptional Children, 58,* 146–155.

Salisbury, C. L. (1992). Parents as team members: Inclusive teams, collaborative outcomes. In B. Rainforth, J. York, & C. Macdonald (Eds.), *Collaborative teams for students with severe disabilities: Integrating therapy and educational services* (pp. 43–66). Baltimore: Paul H. Brookes.

Salisbury, C. L., Mangino, M., Petrigala, M., Rainforth, B., Syryca, S., & Palombaro, M. M. (1993). *Promoting the inclusion of young children with disabilities in the primary grades: A curriculum adaptation process.* Manuscript submitted for publication.

Salisbury, C. L., Palombaro, M. M., & Hollowood, T. M. (1993). On the nature and change of an inclusive elementary school. *Journal of the Association for Persons with Severe Handicaps, 18,* 75–84.

Salvia, J., & Ysseldyke, J. E. (1991). *Assessment* (5th ed.). Boston: Houghton Mifflin.

Sandknop, P. A., Schuster, J. W., Wolery, M., & Cross, D. P. (1992). The use of an adaptive device to teach students with moderate mental retardation to select lower priced grocery items. *Education and Training in Mental Retardation, 27,* 219–229.

Santarcangelo, S., Dyer, K., & Luce, S. C. (1987). Generalized reduction of disruptive behavior in unsupervised settings through specific toy training. *Journal of the Association for Persons with Severe Handicaps, 12,* 38–44.

Schuster, J. W., Gast, D. L., Wolery, M., & Guiltinan, S. (1988). The effectiveness of a constant time-delay procedure to teach chained responses to adolescents with mental retardation. *Journal of Applied Behavior Analysis, 21,* 169–178.

Schuster, J. W., & Griffen, A. K. (1991). Using constant time delay to teach recipe following skills. *Education and Training in Mental Retardation, 26,* 411–419.

Schwartz, I. S., Anderson, S. R., & Halle, J. W. (1989). Training teachers to use naturalistic time delay: Effects of teacher behavior on the language use of students. *Journal of the Association for Persons with Severe Handicaps, 14,* 48–57.

Sobsey, D., & Wolf-Schein, E. G. (1991). Sensory impairments. In F. P. Orelove & D. Sobsey (Eds.), *Educating children with multiple disabilities: A transdisciplinary approach* (2nd ed., pp. 119–153). Baltimore: Paul H. Brookes.

Sparrow, S. S., Balla, D. A., & Cicchetti, D. V. (1984). *Vineland Adaptive Behavior Scale: Classroom edition.* Circle Pines, MN: American Guidance Service.

Stainback, W., & Stainback, S. (1990). *Support networks for inclusive schooling: Interdependent and integrated education.* Baltimore: Paul H. Brookes.

Strain, P. S., & Odom, S. L. (1986). Peer social initiations: Effective intervention for social skills development of exceptional children. *Exceptional Children, 52,* 543–551.

Strain, P. S., & Sainato, D. M. (1987). Preventive discipline in early childhood. *Teaching Exceptional Children, 19,* 26–30.

Strully, J. L., & Strully, C. F. (1992). The struggle toward inclusion and the fulfillment of friendship. In J. Nisbet (Ed.), *Natural supports in school, at work, and in the community for people with severe disabilities* (pp. 165–177). Baltimore: Paul H. Brookes.

Swenson-Pierce, A., Kohl, F. L., & Egel, A. (1987). Siblings as home trainers: A strategy for teaching domestic skills to children. *Journal of the Association for Persons with Severe Handicaps, 12,* 53–60.

Taras, M. E., & Matese, M. (1990). Acquisition of self-help skills. In J. L. Matson (Ed.), *Handbook of behavior modification with the mentally retarded* (2nd ed., pp. 273–303). New York: Plenum Press.

Thousand, J. S., & Villa, R. A. (1990). Sharing expertise and responsibilities through teaching teams. In W. Stainback

& S. Stainback (Eds.), *Support networks for inclusive schooling: Interdependent and integrated education* (pp. 151–166). Baltimore: Paul H. Brookes.

Turnbull, J. R. (1990). *Free appropriate public education: The law and children with disabilities* (3rd ed.). Denver: Love.

Vandercook, T. (1991). Leisure instruction outcomes: Criterion performance, positive interactions, and acceptance by typical high school peers. *Journal of Special Education, 25*, 320–339.

Venn, M. L., Holcombe, M. A., & Wolery, M. (1992). Feeding and nutritional issues. In D. B. Bailey & M. Wolery (Eds.), *Teaching infants and preschoolers with disabilities* (2nd ed., pp. 441–480). New York: Merrill/Macmillan.

Venn, M. L., Wolery, M., Fleming, L. A., DeCesare, L. D., Morris, A., Sigesmund, M. H. (1993). Effects of teaching preschool peers to use the mand-model procedure during snack activities. *American Journal of Speech-Language Pathology, 2*(1), 38–46.

Venn, M. L., Wolery, M., Werts, M. G., Morris, A., DeCesare, L. D., & Cuffs, M. S. (1993). *Embedding instruction in art activities to teach preschoolers with disabilities to imitate their peers.* Manuscript submitted for publication.

Voeltz, L. M. (1982). Effects of structured interactions with severely handicapped peers on children's attitudes. *American Journal of Mental Deficiency, 86*, 380–390.

Warren, S. F., & Reichle, J. (Eds.). (1992). *Causes and effects in communication and language intervention.* Baltimore: Paul H. Brookes.

Weisz, J. R., & Zigler, E. (1979). Cognitive development in retarded and non-retarded persons: Piagetian tests of the similar sequence hypothesis. *Psychological Bulletin, 86*, 831–851.

Wilcox, B., & Bellamy, G. T. (1987). *The activities catalog: An alternative curriculum for youth and adults with severe disabilities.* Baltimore: Paul H. Brookes.

Winterling, V., Gast, D. L., Wolery, M., & Farmer, J. A. (1992). Teaching safe skills to high school students with moderate disabilities. *Journal of Applied Behavior Analysis, 25*, 217–227.

Winton, P. J. (1988). The family-focused interview: An assessment measure and goal-setting mechanism. In D. B. Bailey & R. J. Simeonsson (Eds.), *Family assessment in early intervention* (pp. 185–205). New York: Merrill/Macmillan.

Winton, P. J., & Bailey, D. B. (1993). Communicating with families: Examining practices and facilitating change. In J. Paul & R. Simeonsson (Eds.), *Children with special needs: Family, culture, and society* (pp. 210–230). Orlando, FL: Harcourt Brace Jovanovich.

Wolery, M. (1989). Using direct observation in assessment. In D. B. Bailey & M. Wolery (Eds.), *Assessing infants and preschoolers with disabilities* (2nd ed., pp. 64-96). New York: Merrill/Macmillan.

Wolery, M., Ault, M. J., & Doyle, P. M. (1992). *Teaching students with moderate and severe disabilities: Use of response prompting strategies.* White Plains, NY: Longman.

Wolery, M., Ault, M. J., Gast, D. L., Doyle, P. M., & Griffen, A. K. (1991). Teaching chained tasks in dyads: Acquisition of target and observational behaviors. *Journal of Special Education, 25*, 198–220.

Wolery, M., Holcombe, A., Brookfield, J., Huffman, K., Schroeder, C., Martin, C. G., Venn, M. L., Werts, M. G., & Fleming, L. A. (in press). The extent and nature of preschool mainstreaming: A survey of general early educators. *Journal of Special Education.*

Wolery, M., Holcombe, A., Cybriwsky, C. A., Doyle, P. M., Schuster, J. W., Ault, M. J., & Gast, D. L. (1992). Constant time delay with discrete responses: A review of effectiveness and demographic, procedural, and methodological parameters. *Research in Developmental Disabilities, 13*, 239–266.

Wolery, M., & Smith, P. D. (1989). Assessing self-care skills. In D. B. Bailey & M. Wolery (Eds.), *Assessing infants and preschoolers with handicaps* (pp. 447–477). New York: Merrill/Macmillan.

Wolfensberger, W. (1972). *The principle of normalization in human services.* Toronto: National Institute on Mental Retardation.

York, J., & Rainforth, B. (1991). Developing instructional adaptations. In F. P. Orelove & D. Sobsey (Eds.), *Educating children with multiple disabilities: A transdisciplinary approach* (2nd ed., pp. 259–295). Baltimore: Paul H. Brookes.

Ysseldyke, J. E., Algozzine, B., & Thurlow, M. L. (1992). *Critical issues in special education* (2nd ed.). Boston: Houghton Mifflin.

CHAPTER EIGHT

Alexander, M. A., & Bauer, R. E. (1988). Cerebral palsy. In V. B. Van Hasselt, P. S. Strain, & M. Hersen (Eds.), *Handbook of developmental and physical disabilities* (pp. 215–226). New York: Pergamon Press.

Anderson, J., Hinojosa, J., Bedell, G., & Kaplan, M. T. (1990). Occupational therapy for children with perinatal HIV infection. *The American Journal of Occupational Therapy, 44*, 249–255.

Angelo, J. (1992). Comparison of three computer scanning modes as an interface method for persons with cerebral palsy. *The American Journal of Occupational Therapy, 46,* 217–222.

Annual directory of national organizations, 1992–1993. (1993). *Exceptional Parent, 22,* D1–D28.

Ballard, J. K., & Calhoun, M. L. (1991). Special Olympics: Opportunity to learn. *Teaching Exceptional Children, 24*(1), 20–23.

Batshaw, M. L., & Perret, Y. M. (Eds.). (1986). *Children with handicaps: A medical primer.* Baltimore: Paul H. Brookes.

Behrmann, M. (Ed.). (1984). *Handbook of microcomputers in special education.* San Diego, CA: College Hill Press.

Behrmann, M., & Lahm, L. (1984). Babies and robots: Technology to assist learning of young multiply disabled children. *Rehabilitation Literature, 45,* 194–201.

Best, S. J. (1991). People with health impairments. In S. Schwartz (Ed.), *Exceptional people: A guide for understanding* (pp. 1007–1011). New York: McGraw-Hill.

Best, S. J. (1992). Orthopedic handicaps and handicapping conditions. In M. Alkin (Ed.), *Encyclopedia of educational research* (Vol. 6, pp. 129–141). New York: Macmillan.

Best, S. J., Carpignano, J. L., Sirvis, B., & Bigge, J. L. (1991). Psychosocial aspects of physical disability. In J. L. Bigge (Ed.), *Teaching individuals with physical and multiple disabilities* (3rd ed., pp. 102–131). New York: Merrill/Macmillan.

Bigge, J. L. (1988). *Curriculum based instruction for special education students.* Palo Alto, CA: Mayfield.

Bigge, J. L. (1991). *Teaching individuals with physical and multiple disabilities* (3rd ed.). New York: Merrill/Macmillan.

Blackburn, J. A. (1987). Cerebral palsy. In M. L. Wolraich (Ed.), *The practical assessment of and management of children with disorders of development and learning* (pp. 164–193). Chicago: Yearbook Publishers.

Blackstone, S. (Ed.). (1986). *Augmentative communication: An introduction.* Rockville, MD: American Speech-Language-Hearing Association.

Bleck, E. E. (1982a). Cerebral palsy. In E. E. Bleck & D. A. Nagel (Eds.), *Physically handicapped children: A medical atlas for teachers* (2nd ed., pp. 59–143). New York: Grune and Stratton.

Bleck, E. E. (1982b). Spina bifida. In E. E. Bleck & D. A. Nagel (Eds.), *Physically handicapped children: A medical atlas for teachers* (2nd ed., pp. 345–362). New York: Grune and Stratton.

Bobath, K. (1980). *A neurophysiological basis for the treatment of cerebral palsy* (Clinics in Developmental Medicine No. 75). Philadelphia: Lippincott.

Bowman, O. J., & Marzouk, D. K. (1991). Implementing the Americans with Disabilities Act of 1990 in higher education. *The American Journal of Occupational Therapy, 46,* 521–533.

Brolin, D. E. (1982). *Vocational preparation for persons with handicaps* (2nd ed.). Columbus, OH: Merrill.

Brown, M., & Gordon, W. A. (1987). Impact of impairment on activity patterns of children. *Archives of Physical Medicine and Rehabilitation, 68,* 828–832.

Burkhart, L. J. (1987). *Using computers and speech synthesis to facilitate communication interaction with young and/or severely handicapped children.* Santa Barbara, CA: Special Needs Project.

Burkhead, E. J., Sampson, J. P., & McMahon, B. T. (1986). The liberation of disabled persons in a technological society: Access to computer technology. *Rehabilitation Literature, 47,* 162–168.

Buzolich, M. J., & Wiemann, J. M. (1988). Turn taking in atypical conversations: The case of the speaker/augmented-communicator dyad. *Journal of Speech and Hearing Research, 31,* 3–18.

Byrne, K., Abbeduto, L., & Brooks, P. (1990). The language of children with spina bifida and hydrocephalus: Meeting task demands and mastering syntax. *Journal of Speech and Hearing Disorders, 55,* 118–123.

Calculator, S. N. (1988). Promoting the acquisition and generalization of conversational skills by individuals with severe disabilities. *Augmentative and Alternative Communication, 4,* 94–103.

California State Department of Education (1990). Guidelines and procedures for meeting the health care needs of chronically ill pupils including specialized physical health care. Sacramento, CA: Author.

Campbell, P. (1989). Dysfunction in posture and movement in individuals with profound disabilities. In F. Brown & D. Lehr (Eds.), *Persons with profound disabilities: Issues and practices* (pp. 163–189). Baltimore: Paul H. Brookes.

Carney, N. C. (1990). The Americans with Disabilities Act: Civil rights for an emerging minority. *American Rehabilitation, 16*(4), 2–4.

Carr, G. S., & Gee, G. (1986). AIDS and AIDS-related conditions: Screening for populations at risk. *Nurse Practitioner, 11*(10), 25–46.

Christiansen, R. O., & Hintz, R. L. (1982). Juvenile diabetes mellitus. In E. E. Bleck & D. A. Nagel (Eds.), *Physically handicapped children: A medical atlas for teachers* (2nd ed., pp. 269–277). New York: Grune and Stratton.

Church, G., & Glennen, S. (1992). *The handbook of assistive technology.* San Diego, CA: Singular Publishing Group.

Chutorian, A. M., & Engel, M. (1982). Diseases of the muscle. In J. A. Downey & N. L. Low (Eds.), *The child with a disabling illness: Principles of rehabilitation* (2nd ed., pp. 291–347). New York: Raven Press.

Coleman, M., & Apts, S. (1991). Home-alone risk factors. *Teaching Exceptional Children*, 23(3), 36–39.

Collins, B. C., Wolery, M., & Gast, D. L. (1992). A national survey of safety concerns for students with special needs. *Journal of Developmental and Physical Disabilities*, 4, 263–276.

Connor, F. P., Scandary, J., & Tulloch, D. (1988). Education of physically handicapped and health impaired individuals: A commitment to the future. DPH *Journal*, 10(1), 5–24.

Corrigan, J. J., & Damiano, M. L. (1983). Blood diseases. In J. Umbreit (Ed.), *Physical disabilities and health impairments: An introduction* (pp. 167–174). New York: Merrill/Macmillan.

Crain, L. S. (1984). Prenatal causes of atypical development. In M. J. Hanson (Ed.), *Atypical infant development* (pp. 27–55). Baltimore: University Park Press.

Creer, T. L., Marion, R. J., & Harm, D. L. (1988). Childhood asthma. In V. B. Van Hasselt, P. S. Strain, & M. Hersen (Eds.), *Handbook of developmental and physical disabilities* (pp. 177–194). New York: Pergamon Press.

Decker, B. (1992). A comparison of the Individual Education Plan and the Individual Family Service Plan. *The American Journal of Occupational Therapy*, 46, 247–252.

DeVivo, M. J., Rutt, R. D., Black, K. J., Go, B. K., & Stover, S. L. (1992). Trends in spinal cord demographics and treatment outcomes between 1973 and 1986. *Archives of Physical Medicine and Rehabilitation*, 73, 424–430.

Doyle, K. (1989). The physically challenged: A continuum of services. DPH *Journal*, 11(1), 9–18.

Drotar, D. (1981). Psychological perspectives in chronic childhood illness. *Journal of Pediatric Psychology*, 6, 211–228.

Fenton, J. (Ed.). (1981). *Research directory of rehabilitation research and training centers: Fiscal year 1980*. Washington, DC: U.S. Department of Education.

Finnie, N. R. (1975). *Handling the young cerebral palsied child at home* (2nd ed.). New York: Dutton.

Foulds, R. (1982). Applications of microcomputers in the education of the physically disabled child. *Exceptional Children*, 49, 155–162.

Franks, C., Palisano, R. J., & Darbee, J. C. (1991). The effect of walking with an assistive device and using a wheelchair on school performance in students with myelomeningocele. *Physical Therapy*, 71, 570–577.

Fraser, B. A., Hensinger, R. N., & Phelps, J. A. (1990). *Physical management of multiple handicaps: A professional's guide* (2nd ed.). Baltimore: Paul H. Brookes.

Gortmacher, S., & Sappenfield, W. (1984). Chronic childhood disorders: Prevalence and impact. *Pediatric Clinics of North America*, 31, 3–18.

Hall, D. M. B. (1984). *The child with a handicap*. Boston: Blackwell Scientific.

Hanline, M. F., Hanson, M., Veltman, M., & Spaeth, D. (1986). Electromagnetic teaching toys for infants and toddlers with disabilities. *Teaching Exceptional Children*, 18, 20–21.

Hanson, M. J. (Ed.). (1984). *Atypical infant development*. Baltimore: University Park Press.

Hanson, V. (1983). Juvenile rheumatoid arthritis. In J. Umbreit (Ed.), *Physical disabilities and health impairments: An introduction* (pp. 240–249). New York: Merrill/Macmillan.

Hart, V. (1988). Multiply disabled children. In V. B. Van Hasselt, P. S. Strain, & M. Hersen (Eds.), *Handbook of developmental and physical disabilities* (pp. 370–383). New York: Pergamon Press.

Harvey, B. (1982). Cystic fibrosis. In E. E. Bleck & D. A. Nagel (Eds.), *Physically handicapped children: A medical atlas for teachers* (2nd ed., pp. 255–263). New York: Grune and Stratton.

Hermann, B. P., Desai, B. T., & Whitman, S. (1988). Epilepsy. In V. B. Van Hasselt, P. S. Strain, & M. Hersen (Eds.), *Handbook of developmental and physical disabilities* (pp. 247–270). New York: Pergamon Press.

Hilgartner, M. (Ed.). (1990). *Hemophilia in the child and adult*. New York: Raven Press.

Holm, V. (1982). The causes of cerebral palsy. *Journal of the American Medical Association*, 247, 1473–1477.

Holvoet, J., & Helmstetter, E. (1989). *Medical problems of students with special needs: A guide for educators*. Boston: College Hill Press.

Hooper, E. H., & Hasselbring, T. S. (1985). Electronic augmentative communication aids for the nonreading student: Selection criteria. *Journal of Special Education Technology*, 8(2), 39–49.

Hulme, J. B., Bain, B., Hardin, M., McKinnon, A., & Waldron, D. (1989). The influence of adaptive seating devices on vocalization. *Journal of Communication Disorders*, 22, 137–145.

Hulme, J. B., Gallacher, K., Walsh, J., Nielson, S., & Waldron, D. (1987). Behavioral and postural changes observed with use of adaptive seating by multihandicapped clients. *Physical Therapy*, 67, 1060–1067.

Inge, K. A. (1987). Atypical motor development and cerebral palsy. In F. P. Orelove & D. Sobsey, *Educating children with multiple disabilities: A transdisciplinary approach* (pp. 43–65). Baltimore: Paul H. Brookes.

Jacobs, I. B. (1983). Epilepsy. In G. H. Thompson, I. L. Rubin, & R. M. Bilenker (Eds.), *Comprehensive management of cerebral palsy* (pp. 131–137). New York: Grune and Stratton.

Jaffe, K. M., Fay, G. C., Polissar, N. L., Martin, K. M., Shurtleff, H., Rivara, J. B., & Winn, H. R. (1992). Severity of pediatric traumatic brain injury on early neurobehavioral outcome: A cohort study. *Archives of Physical Medicine and Rehabilitation*, 73, 540–548.

Jewell, K. H. (1989). A custom-made head pointer for children. *The American Journal of Occupational Therapy*, 43, 456–460.

Johnsen, S. K., & Corn, A. (1989). The past, present, and future of education for gifted children with sensory and/or physical disabilities. *Roeper Review*, 12, 13–22.

Jubala, J. A., & Brenes, G. (1988). Spinal cord injuries. In V. B. Van Hasselt, P. S. Strain, & M. Hersen (Eds.), *Handbook of developmental and physical disabilities* (pp. 423–438). New York: Pergamon Press.

Kalscher, J. A. (1991). Benefits of the Americans with Disabilities Act of 1990 for children and adolescents with disabilities. *The American Journal of Occupational Therapy*, 46, 419–426.

Kannenberg, P., Marquardt, T. P., & Larson, J. (1988). Speech intelligibility and two voice output communication aids. *Journal of Communication Disorders*, 21, 11–20.

Koblinsky, S. A., & Todd, C. M. (1991). Teaching self-care skills. *Teaching Exceptional Children*, 23(3), 40–44.

Koehler, J. (1982). Spinal muscular atrophy. In E. E. Bleck & D. A. Nagel (Eds.), *Physically handicapped children: A medical atlas for teachers* (2nd ed., pp. 477–481). New York: Grune and Stratton.

Kokaska, C. J., & Brolin, D. E. (1985). *Career education for handicapped individuals* (2nd ed.). New York: Merrill/Macmillan.

Krauss, M. (1990). New precedent in family policy: Individualized Family Service Plans. *Exceptional Children*, 56, 388–395.

Kübler-Ross, E. (1969). *Death and dying*. New York: Macmillan.

Lian, M. J., & Goyette, A. L. (1988). Adapted aquatics for people with severe multiple disabilities. *American Rehabilitation*, 14(3), 12–14.

Link, M. P. (1982). Cancer in childhood. In E. E. Bleck & D. A. Nagel (Eds.), *Physically handicapped children: A medical atlas for teachers* (2nd ed., pp. 43–58). New York: Grune and Stratton.

Low, N. L. (1982). Seizure disorders in children. In J. A. Downey & N. L. Low (Eds.), *The child with a disabling illness: Principles of rehabilitation* (2nd ed., pp. 121–144). New York: Raven Press.

Lyle, R. R., & Obringer, S. J. (1983). Muscular dystrophy. In J. Umbreit (Ed.), *Physical disabilities and health impairments: An introduction* (pp. 100–107). New York: Merrill/Macmillan.

MacNeela, J. (1987). An overview of therapeutic positioning for multiply handicapped persons, including augmentative communication users. *Physical and Occupational Therapy in Pediatrics*, 7(2), 39–60.

Male, M. (1988). *Special magic: Computers, classroom strategies, and exceptional students*. Mountain View, CA: Mayfield.

Mangos, J. A. (1983). Cystic fibrosis. In J. Umbreit (Ed.), *Physical disabilities and health impairments: An introduction* (pp. 206–213). New York: Merrill/Macmillan.

Marquardt, E. G. (1983). A holistic approach to rehabilitation for the limb-deficient child. *Archives of Physical Medicine and Rehabilitation*, 64, 237–242.

May, D. C., & Marozas, D. S. (1989). Electronic devices in the classroom: Are they effective? *DPH Journal*, 10(2), 88–93.

McEwen, I., & Karlan, G. (1989). Assessment of effects of position on communication board access by individuals with cerebral palsy. *Augmentative and Alternative Communication*, 5, 235–242.

McInerney, W. F. (1989). The instruction of students with Acquired Immune Deficiency Syndrome (AIDS). *DPH Journal*, 10(2), 43–57.

Mills, J., & Higgins, J. (1984). *The assessment for non-speech communication*. San Diego, CA: California Publications.

Mira, M. P., Tucker, B. F., & Tyler, J. S. (1992). *Traumatic brain injury in children and adults: A sourcebook for teachers and other school personnel*. Austin, TX: Pro-Ed.

Mirenda, P., & Iacono, T. (1990). Communication options for persons with severe and profound disabilities: State of the art and future directions. *Journal of the Association for Persons with Severe Handicaps*, 15, 3–21.

Molnar, G. E. (1983). Musculoskeletal disorders. In J. Umbreit (Ed.), *Physical disabilities and health impairments: An introduction* (pp. 108–116). New York: Merrill/Macmillan.

Morrissey, P. A., & Silverstein, R. (1989). The Technology Act of 1989. *American Rehabilitation*, 15(2), 4–7.

Mullins, J. B. (1985). Events influencing physically handicapped and health impaired people in the United States. *DPH Journal*, 9(1), 27–39.

National Information Center for Children and Youth with Disabilities. (1991). The education of children and youth with special needs: What do the laws say? *NICHCY News Digest*, 1, 1–15.

National Institute on Disability and Rehabilitation Research. (1989). *Chartbook on disability in the United States*. Washington, DC: U.S. Department of Education.

Nelson, C. M. (1988). Social skills training for handicapped children. *Teaching Exceptional Children*, 20(4), 19–23.

Nissen, S. J., & Newman, W. P. (1992). Factors influencing reintegration of normal living after amputation. *Archives of Physical Medicine and Rehabilitation*, 73, 548–551.

O'Connell, D. G., Barnhart, R., & Park, L. (1992). Muscular endurance and wheelchair propulsion in children with cerebral palsy and myelomeningocele. *Archives of Physical Medicine and Rehabilitation*, 73, 709–711.

Orelove, F. P., & Sobsey, D. (1987). *Educating children with multiple disabilities: A transdisciplinary approach*. Baltimore: Paul H. Brookes.

Peterson, C. A., & Gunn, S. L. (1984). *Therapeutic recreation program design: Principles and procedures* (2nd ed.). Englewood Cliffs, NJ: Prentice-Hall.

Platt, J. M., & Janeczko, D. (1991). Adapting art instruction for students with disabilities. *Teaching Exceptional Children*, 24(1), 10–12.

Rando, T. A. (1984). *Grief, death, and dying: Clinical interventions for caregivers*. Champaign, IL: Research Press.

Raschke, D. B., Dedrick, C. V. L., & Hanus, K. (1991). Adapting playgrounds for all children. *Teaching Exceptional Children*, 24(1), 25–28.

Reed, K. L. (1991). History of federal legislation for persons with disabilities. *The American Journal of Occupational Therapy*, 46, 397–408.

Rowland, B. H., & Robinson, B. E. (1991). Latchkey kids with special needs. *Teaching Exceptional Children*, 23(3), 34–35.

Sirvis, B. (1978). Developing IEPs for physically handicapped students: A transdisciplinary approach. *Teaching Exceptional Children*, 10(3), 78–82.

Sirvis, B. (1980). Career education for the severely handicapped. In G. M. Clark & W. J. White (Eds.), *Educating the physically handicapped: Current perspectives for teachers* (pp. 86–110). Boothwyn, PA: Educational Resources Center.

Sirvis, B. (1988). Students with special health care needs. *Teaching Exceptional Children*, 20(4), 40–44.

Smith, A. K., Thurston, S., Light, J., Parnes, P., & O'Keefe, B. (1989). The form and use of written communication produced by physically disabled individuals using microcomputers. *Augmentative and Alternative Communication*, 5, 115–124.

Smith, P., & Nwaobi, O. (1985). Seating children who have cerebral palsy: Therapeutic and technical considerations. *Alabama CEC Journal*, 6, 20–29.

Sowers, J. A., & Powers, L. (1991). *Vocational preparation and employment of students with physical and multiple disabilities*. Baltimore: Paul H. Brookes.

Thompson, G. H., Rubin, I. L., & Bilenker, R. M. (Eds.). (1983). *Comprehensive management of cerebral palsy*. New York: Grune and Stratton.

Turner, K., Snart, F., & McCarthy, C. (1992). Promoting integration and cooperation: The Friendship Games. *Teaching Exceptional Children*, 24(3), 34–37.

U.S. Department of Education. (1990). *Twelfth annual report to Congress on the implementation of the Education of the Handicapped Act*. Washington, DC: Author.

U.S. Department of Health and Human Services. (1988). *Understanding AIDS*. Rockville, MD: Centers for Disease Control.

U.S. Department of Labor/Department of Health and Human Services. (1987). *Joint advisory notice: Protection against occupational exposure to hepatitis B virus (HBV) and human immunodeficiency virus (HIV)*. Rockville, MD: Centers for Disease Control.

Viscardi, H. (1972). *But not on our block*. New York: Eriksson.

Ward, D. E. (1984). *Positioning the handicapped child for function: A guide to evaluate and prescribe equipment for the child with central nervous system dysfunction*. Chicago: Phoenix Press.

Williamson, G. G. (1978). The Individualized Education Program: An interdisciplinary endeavor. In B. Sirvis, J. W. Baken, & G. G. Williamson (Eds.), *Unique aspects of the IEP for the physically handicapped, homebound, and hospitalized* (pp. 280–312). Reston, VA: Council for Exceptional Children.

Williamson, G. G. (1987). *Children with spina bifida: Early intervention and programming*. Baltimore: Paul H. Brookes.

Wright, B. A. (1983). *Physical disability: A psychosocial approach*. New York: Harper and Row.

Wright, K. C., & Nicholas, J. J. (1988). Musculoskeletal disorders. In V. B. Van Hasselt, P. S. Strain, & M. Hersen (Eds.), *Handbook of developmental and physical disabilities* (pp. 384–394). New York: Pergamon Press.

Yuker, H. E. (1988). Perceptions of severely and multiply disabled persons. *Journal of the Multihandicapped Person*, 1, 5–16.

Zangari, C., Kangas, K. A., & Lloyd, L. L. (1988). Augmentative and alternative communication: A field in transition. *Augmentative and Alternative Communication*, 4, 60–64.

CHAPTER NINE

Abbeduto, L. (1991). Development of verbal communication in persons with moderate to mild mental retardation. In N. Bray (Ed.), *International review of research in mental retardation* (Vol. 17, pp. 91–151). New York: Academic Press.

American Speech-Language-Hearing Association. (1980). Definitions: Communicative disorders and variations. *Asha, 22,* 949-950.

American Speech-Language-Hearing Association. (1985). Clinical management of communicatively handicapped minority language populations. *Asha, 27,* 29–32.

Aram, D. M., & Nation, J. E. (1980). Preschool language disorders and subsequent language and academic difficulties. *Journal of Communication Disorders, 13,* 159–170.

Baker, H., & Leland, B. (1967). *Detroit Tests of Learning Aptitudes.* Indianapolis: Bobbs-Merrill.

Bates, E. (1976). *Language and context: The acquisition of pragmatics.* New York: Academic Press.

Biklen, D. (1992). Typing to talk: Facilitated communication. *American Journal of Speech-Language Pathology, 1*(2), 15–17.

Bloom, L. (1970). *Language development: Form and function in emerging grammars.* Cambridge, MA: MIT Press.

Bloom, L., & Lahey, M. (1978). *Language development and language disorders.* New York: Wiley.

Bowerman, M. (1976). Semantic factors in the acquisition of rules for word use and sentence construction. In D. Morehead & A. Morehead (Eds.), *Normal and deficient child language* (pp. 99–179). Baltimore: University Park Press.

Brown, R. (1973). *A first language: The early stages.* Cambridge, MA: Harvard University Press.

Bruner, J. (1975). The ontogenesis of speech acts. *Journal of Child Language, 2,* 1–19.

Ceci, J. J. (Ed.). (1986). *Handbook of cognitive social and neuropsychological aspects of learning disabilities.* Hillsdale, NJ: Erlbaum.

Chomsky, N. (1957). *Syntactic structures.* The Hague: Mouton.

Chomsky, N. (1981). *Lectures on government and binding.* Dordrecht, Holland: Doris.

Cromer, R. (1974). The development of language and cognition: The cognitive hypothesis. In B. Foss (Ed.), *New perspectives in child development* (pp. 184–252). New York: Penguin Education.

Donahue, M., & Bryan, T. (1984). Communicative skills and peer relations of learning disabled adolescents. *Topics in Language Disorders, 4*(2), 10–20.

Donahue, M., Pearl, R., & Bryan, T. (1983). Learning disabled children's syntactic proficiency during a communicative task. *Journal of Speech and Hearing Disorders, 47,* 397–403.

Frith, U. (1989). *Autism: Explaining the enigma.* Cambridge: MIT Press.

Hammill, D. D., Brown, V. L., Larsen, S. C., & Wiederholt, J. L. (1980). *Test of Adolescent Language: A multidimensional approach to assessment.* Austin, TX: Pro-Ed.

Hammill, D. D., & Larsen, S. (1974). The relationship of selected auditory perceptual skills and reading ability. *Journal of Learning Disabilities, 7,* 429–435.

Hammill, D. D., & Wiederholt, J. L. (1973). Review of the Frostig Visual Perception Test and the related training program. In L. Mann & D. Sabatino (Eds.), *The first review of special education* (Vol. 1, pp. 33–48). Philadelphia: Grune and Stratton.

Hart, B., & Risley, T. R. (1968). Establishing the use of descriptive adjectives in the spontaneous speech of disadvantaged preschool children. *Journal of Applied Behavior Analysis, 1,* 109–120.

Hart, B., & Risley, T. (1975). Incidental teaching of language in the preschool. *Journal of Applied Behavior Analysis, 7,* 243–256.

Hart, B., & Risley, T. R. (1982). *How to use incidental teaching for elaborating language.* Lawrence, KS: H & H Enterprises.

Hart, B., & Rogers-Warren, A. (1978). Milieu approach to teaching language. In R. L. Schiefelbusch (Ed.), *Language intervention strategies* (pp. 193–235). Baltimore: University Park Press.

Holland, A. L. (1980). *Communicative activities of daily living.* Baltimore: University Park Press.

Hymes, D. (1971). Competence and performance in linguistic theory. In R. Huxley & E. Ingram (Eds.), *Language acquisition: Models and methods* (pp. 3–28). New York: Academic Press.

Kamhi, A. G., Catts, H. W., Mauer, D., Apel, K., & Gentry, B. F. (1988). Phonological and spatial processing abilities in language- and reading-impaired children. *Journal of Speech and Hearing Disorders, 53,* 140–148.

Kirk, S., McCarthy, J., & Kirk, W. (1968). *The Illinois Test of Psycholinguistic Abilities* (rev. ed.). Urbana: University of Illinois Press.

Leonard, L. B. (1987). Is specific language impairment a useful construct? In S. Rosenberg (Ed.), *Advances in applied psycholinguistics: Vol. 1. Disorders of first language acquisition* (pp. 1–39). New York: Cambridge University Press.

Leonard, L. B. (1990). Language disorders in preschool children. In G. H. Shames & E. H. Wiig (Eds.), *Human communication disorders* (3rd ed., pp. 159–192). New York: Merrill/Macmillan.

Liberman, I. Y., & Liberman, A. M. (1990). Whole language vs. code emphasis? Underlying assumptions and their implications for reading instruction. *Annals of Dyslexia, 40,* 51–76.

McCormick, L. (1987). Comparison of the effects of a microcomputer activity and toy play on social and communication behaviors of young children. *Journal of the Division for Early Childhood, 11,* 195–205.

McCormick, L. (1990). Sequence of language and communication development. In L. McCormick & R. L. Schiefelbusch (Eds.), *Early language intervention: An introduction* (2nd ed., pp. 71–105). New York: Merrill/Macmillan.

McCormick, L., & Schiefelbusch, R. L. (1990). *Early language intervention: An introduction* (2nd ed.). New York: Merrill/Macmillan.

McWilliams, B. J. (1990). Cleft palate. In G. H. Shames & E. H. Wiig (Eds.), *Human communication disorders* (3rd ed., pp. 320–415). New York: Merrill/Macmillan.

Miller, J. F. (1983). Identifying children with language disorders and describing their language performance. In J. F. Miller, D. E. Yoder, & R. Schiefelbusch (Eds.), *Contemporary issues in language intervention* (pp. 61–74). Rockville, MD: American Speech-Language-Hearing Association.

Nelson, K. (1977). The conceptual basis for naming. In J. MacNamara (Ed.), *Language learning and thought* (pp. 117–136). New York: Academic Press.

Owens, R. E. (1988). *Language development: An introduction* (2nd ed.). New York: Merrill/Macmillan.

Piaget, J. (1952). *The origins of intelligence in children* (M. Cock, Trans.). New York: International Universities Press.

Piaget, J. (1954). *The construction of reality in the child*. New York: Basic Books.

Piaget, J. (1962). *Play, dreams, and imitation in childhood*. New York: Norton.

Raver, S. A. (1987). Practical procedures for increasing spontaneous language in language-delayed preschoolers. *Journal of the Division for Early Childhood*, 11, 226–232.

Schlesinger, I. (1971). Production of utterances and language acquisition. In D. Slobin (Ed.), *The ontogenesis of grammar* (pp. 63–101). New York: Academic Press.

Schory, M. E. (1990). Whole language and the speech-language pathologist. *Language, Speech, and Hearing Services in the Schools*, 21, 206–211.

Schumaker, J. B., & Deshler, D. D. (1984). Setting demand variables: A major factor in program planning for the LD adolescent. *Topics in Language Disorders*, 4(2), 22–40.

Semel, E. M., & Wiig, E. H. (1980). *Clinical evaluation of language functions*. San Antonio, TX: Psychological Corporation.

Skinner, B. F. (1957). *Verbal behavior*. New York: Appleton-Century-Crofts.

Slobin, D. I. (1970). Universals in grammatical development in children. In G. B. Flores d'Arcais & W. J. M. Levelt (Eds.), *Advances in psycholinguistics* (pp. 237–280). New York: American Elsevier.

Taylor, J. S. (1980). Public school speech-language certification standards: Are they standard? *Asha*, 22, 159–165.

U.S. Department of Education. (1992). *Fourteenth annual report to Congress on the implementation of the Individuals with Disabilities Education Act*. Washington, DC: Author.

Van Riper, C. (1978). *Speech correction: Principles and methods* (6th ed.). Englewood Cliffs, NJ: Prentice-Hall.

Westby, C., & Erickson, J. (1992). Prologue. *Topics in Language Disorders*, 12(3), v–viii.

Westby, E. C., & Rouse, G. R. (1985). Culture in education and the instruction of language-learning disabled students. *Topics in Language Disorders*, 5(4), 15–28.

Wiig, E. H. (1982). Communication disorders. In N. G. Haring (Ed.), *Exceptional children and youth* (3rd ed., pp. 81–109). New York: Merrill/Macmillan.

Wiig, E. H. (1990). Language disabilities in school-age children and youth. In G. H. Shames & E. H. Wiig (Eds.), *Human communication disorders* (3rd ed., pp. 193–222). New York: Merrill/Macmillan.

CHAPTER TEN

Adler, S. (1988). Cytomegalovirus transmission among children in day care, their mothers and caretakers. *Pediatric Infectious Disorders Journal*, 7, 279–285.

Anderson, R. J., & Sisco, F. H. (1977). *Standardization of the WISC–R performance scale for deaf children*. Washington, DC: Gallaudet College, Office of Demographic Studies.

Bayley, N. (1969). *Bayley Scales of Infant Development*. New York: Psychological Corporation.

Berko Gleason, J. (1985). Studying language development. In J. Berko Gleason (Ed.), *The development of language* (pp. 1–36). New York: Merrill/Macmillan.

Brown, S. C., & Karchmer, M. A. (1987). Who will be served? *Gallaudet Today*, 18, 4–7.

Commission on Education of the Deaf. (1988, February). *Toward equality: Education of the deaf*. Report to the President and the Congress.

Conference of Executives of American Schools for the Deaf. (1975).

Davis, J., Elfenbein, J., Schum, R., & Bentler, R. (1986). Effects of mild and moderate hearing impairments on language, educational, and psychological behavior of children. *Journal of Speech and Hearing Disorders*, 51, 53–62.

Decker, T. (1992). Otoacoustic emissions. *Seminars in Hearing*, 13, 1–104.

Eimas, P. D., Miller, J., & Jusczyk, P. (1987). On infant speech and the acquisition of language. In S. Harnad (Ed.), *Categorical perception* (pp. 161–195). Cambridge, England: Cambridge University Press.

Evans, L. (1980). WISC Performance Scale and coloured progressive matrices with deaf children. *British Journal of Educational Psychology*, 50, 216–222.

Friedlander, B., & Cyrulik, A. (1970, November). *Automated home measurement of infants' preferential discrimination and loudness levels*. Paper presented at the meeting of the American Speech and Hearing Association, Chicago.

Garretson, M. D. (1976). Total communication. *Volta Review*, 78(4), 88–95.

Gustason, G., Pfetzing, D., & Zawolkow, E. (1972). *Signing exact English*. Rosemoor, CA: Modern Sign Press.

Harkins, J. (Ed.). (1985, Winter). H.I. children and youth: A demographic and academic profile. *Newsletter, Gallaudet Research Institute* (R. Trybus, Director), pp. 1–4.

Hiskey, M. S. (1966). *Nebraska Test of Learning Aptitude*. Lincoln, NE: Union College Press.

Johnson, J. O., & Boyd, H. F. (1981). *Nonverbal Test of Cognitive Skills*. Columbus, OH: Merrill.

Johnson, K., Daniel, M., & Chmiel, R. (1991). Management of hearing disorder resulting from cytomegalovirus. *Hearing Instruments, 42*, 20–22.

Kaufman, A. S., & Kaufman, N. L. (1982). *Kaufman Assessment Battery for Children*. Circle Pines, MN: American Guidance Service.

Kluwin, T. N. (1981). The grammaticality of manual representations of English in classroom settings. *American Annals of the Deaf, 126*, 417–421.

Kuhl, P. (1987). Perception of speech and sound in early infancy. In P. Salapatek & L. B. Cohen (Eds.), *Handbook of infant perception* (pp. 398–410). New York: Academic Press.

Leiter, R. (1948). *The Leiter International Performance Scale*. Chicago: Stoelting.

Madden, R. G., Gardner, E. F., Rudman, H. C., Karlsen, B., & Merwin, J. C. (1972). *Stanford Achievement Test special edition for hearing-impaired children*. Washington, DC: Gallaudet College Press.

Marmor, G. S., & Petitto, L. (1979). Simultaneous communication in the classroom: How well is English grammar represented? *Sign Language Studies, 23*, 99–136.

Martin, F. (1991). *Introduction to audiology* (4th ed.). Englewood Cliffs, NJ: Prentice-Hall.

Matkin, A., & Matkin, N. (1985). Benefits of total communication as perceived by parents of hearing-impaired children. *Language Speech and Hearing Services in the Schools, 16*, 64–74.

McFarland, W., & Simmons, B. (1980). The importance of early intervention with severe childhood deafness. *Pediatric Annals, 9*, 13–19.

Northern, J., & Downs, M. (1991). *Hearing in children* (4th ed.). Baltimore: Williams and Wilkins.

Owens, R. (1988). *Language development: An introduction* (2nd ed.). New York: Merrill/Macmillan.

Phelps, L., & Branyan, B. J. (1990). Academic achievement and non-verbal intelligence in public school hearing impaired children. *Psychology in the Schools, 27*, 210–217.

Salvia, J., & Ysseldyke, J. (1991). *Assessment* (5th ed.). Boston: Houghton Mifflin.

Schlesinger, H., & Meadow, K. (1972). *Sound and sign: Childhood defense and mental health*. Berkeley: University of California Press.

Shafer, D., & Lynch, J. (1981). Emergent language of six prelingually deaf children. *Journal of the British Association of Teachers of the Deaf, 5*, 94–111.

Smith, A. J., & Johnson, R. E. (1977). *Smith-Johnson Nonverbal Performance Scale*. Los Angeles: Western Psychological Service.

Sullivan, P., & McCay, V. (1979). Psychological assessment of hearing-impaired children. *School Psychology Digest, 8*, 271–291.

Swisher, M. W., & Thompson, M. D. (1985). Mothers learning simultaneous communication: The dimensions of the task. *American Annals of the Deaf, 130*, 212–217.

Thompson, M., & Thompson, G. (1991). Early identification of hearing loss: Listen to parents! *Clinical Pediatrics, 30*, 77–78.

Trybus, R., & Karchmer, M. (1977). School achievement scores of hearing impaired children: National data on achievement status and growth patterns. *American Annals of the Deaf, 122*, 62–69.

U.S. Department of Education. (1992). *Fourteenth annual report to Congress on the implementation of the Individuals with Disabilities Education Act*. Washington, DC: Author.

Uzgiris, I. V., & Hunt, J. M. (1978). *Assessment in infancy: Ordinal scales of psychological development*. Urbana: University of Illinois Press.

Vernon, M. (1968). Fifty years of research on the intelligence of hard of hearing children: A review of the literature and discussion of implications. *Journal of Rehabilitation of the Deaf, 1*(4), 1–12.

Watkins, S. (1987). Long term effects of home intervention with hearing-impaired children. *American Annals of the Deaf, 132*, 267–271.

Wechsler, D. (1974). *Wechsler Intelligence Scale for Children—Revised*. New York: Psychological Corporation.

Williams, W. D., Murdina, M. D., LaFeuers, N., Taber, L., Catlin, F. I., & Weaver, T. G. (1982). Symptomatic congenital cytomegalovirus. *American Journal of the Disabled Child, 138*, 902–905.

CHAPTER ELEVEN

American Printing House for the Blind. (1987). *Distribution of federal quota based on the January 1987 registration of eligible students* (Research Report). Louisville, KY: Author.

American Printing House for the Blind. (1992). *Distribution of federal quota based on the January 1992 registration of eligible students* (Research Report). Louisville, KY: Author.

Andersen, E. S., Dunlea, A., & Kekelis, L. (1984). Blind children's language development: Resolving some differences. *Journal of Child Language, 11*, 645–664.

Bailey, I., & Hall, A. P. (1986). *Bailey-Hall Cereal Test.* Berkeley: University of California, School of Optometry, Instructional Materials Center.

Bailey, I., & Hall, A. (1990). *Visual impairment: An overview.* New York: American Foundation for the Blind.

Barraga, N. (1983). *Visual handicaps and learning* (rev. ed.). Austin, TX: Exceptional Resources.

Bigelow, A. (1987). Early words of blind children. *Journal of Child Language, 14*, 47–56

Bigelow, A. (1990). Relationship between the development of language and thought in young blind children. *Journal of Visual Impairment and Blindness, 84*, 414–418.

Brolin, D. (1982). *Vocational preparation of persons with handicaps* (2nd ed.). Columbus, OH: Merrill.

Caton, H. (1981). Visual impairments. In A. E. Blackhurst & W. H. Berdine (Eds.), *An introduction to special education* (pp. 205–253). Boston: Little, Brown.

Close, D., & Keating, T. (1988). Community living and work. In R. Gaylord-Ross (Ed.), *Vocational education for persons with handicaps* (pp. 87–108). Mountain View, CA: Mayfield.

Corn, A. (1980). *Development and assessment of an inservice training program for teachers of the visually handicapped: Optical aids in the classroom.* Unpublished doctoral dissertation, Teachers College, Columbia University, New York.

Dunlea, A., & Andersen, E. S. (1992). The emergence process: Conceptual and linguistic influences on morphological development. *First Language, 12, 95 115.*

Eshilian, L., Haney, M., & Falvey, M. (1989). Domestic skills. In M. Falvey (Ed.), *Community-based curriculum: Instructional strategies for students with severe handicaps* (2nd ed., pp. 115–140). Baltimore: Paul H. Brookes.

Fraiberg, S. (1977). *Insights from the blind: Comparative studies of blind and sighted infants.* New York: New American Library.

Gaylord-Ross, C., Forte, J., & Gaylord-Ross, R. (1985). The community classroom: Technological vocational training for students with serious handicaps. *Career Development for Exceptional Individuals, 9*, 24–33.

Gaylord-Ross, R., Forte, J., Storcy, K., Gaylord-Ross, C., & Jameson, D. (1986). Community-referenced instruction in technological work settings. *Exceptional Children, 53*, 112–120.

Graves, W. (1983). Rehabilitation research and educational services for blind and visually impaired individuals. *Education of the Visually Handicapped, 14*, 126–132.

Halpern, A. (1985). Transition: A look at the foundations. *Exceptional Children, 51*, 479–486.

Harley, R., Wood, T., & Merbler, J. (1981). *Peabody Mobility Scale.* Chicago: Stoelting.

Hatlen, P., & Curry, S. (1987). In support of specialized programs for blind and visually impaired children: The impact of vision loss on learning. *Journal of Visual Impairment and Blindness, 81*, 7–13.

Hill, E., Rosen, S., Correa, V., & Langley, M. (1984). Preschool orientation and mobility: An expanded definition. *Education of the Visually Handicapped, 16*, 58–72.

Hoben, M., & Lindstrom, V. (1980). Evidence of isolation in the mainstream. *Journal of Visual Impairment and Blindness, 74*, 289–292.

Irwin, R. (1955). *As I saw it.* New York: American Foundation for the Blind.

Kekelis, L., & Sacks, S. Z. (1992). The effects of visual impairment on children's social interactions in regular education programs. In S. Z. Sacks, L. Kekelis, & R. J. Gaylord-Ross (Eds.), *The development of social skills by blind and visually impaired students: Exploratory studies and strategies* (pp. 59–82). New York: American Foundation for the Blind.

Kiester, E. (1990). *AIDS and vision loss.* New York: American Foundation for the Blind.

Kirchner, C. (1990). Trends in the prevalence rates and numbers of blind and visually impaired schoolchildren. *Journal of Visual Impairment and Blindness, 84*, 478–479.

Kirchner, C., & Peterson, R. (1989). Employment: Selected characteristics. In C. Kirchner (Ed.), *Blindness and visual impairment in the US* (pp. 1690-1770). New York: American Foundation for the Blind.

Koenig, A. J., & Holbrook, M. C. (1989). Determining the reading medium for students with visual impairments: A diagnostic teaching approach. *Journal of Visual Impairment and Blindness, 83*, 296–302.

Loumiet, R., & Levack, N. (1991). *Independent living: Self-care and maintenance of personal environment.* Austin: Texas School for the Blind.

Lowenfeld, B. (1980). Psychological problems of children with severely impaired vision. In W. M. Cruickshank (Ed.), *Psychology of exceptional children and youth* (4th ed., pp. 255–341). Englewood Cliffs, NJ: Prentice-Hall.

MacCuspie, A. P. (1992). The social acceptance and interaction of visually impaired children in integrated settings. In S. Z. Sacks, L. Kekelis, & R. J. Gaylord-Ross (Eds.), *The development of social skills by blind and visually impaired students: Exploratory studies and strategies* (pp. 83–102). New York: American Foundation for the Blind.

Mangold, S. (1977). *The Mangold Developmental Program of Tactile Perception and Braille Letter Recognition.* Castro Valley, CA: Exceptional Teaching Aids.

Mangold, S., & Mangold, P. (1989). Selecting the most appropriate primary learning medium for students with functional vision. *Journal of Visual Impairment and Blindness, 83*, 294–296.

Maxfield, K., & Buchholz, F. (1957). *Social Maturity Scale for Blind Children*: A *guide to its use*. New York: American Foundation for the Blind.

O'Donnell, L., & Livingston, R. (1991). Active exploration of the environment by young children with low vision: A review of the literature. *Journal of Visual Impairment and Blindness, 85,* 287–291.

Orlansky, J., & Rhyne, J. (1981). Special adaptations necessitated by visual impairments. In J. M. Kauffman & D. P. Hallahan (Eds.), *Handbook of special education* (pp. 552–575). Englewood Cliffs, NJ: Prentice-Hall.

Palazesi, M. (1986). The need for motor development programs for visually impaired preschoolers. *Journal of Visual Impairment and Blindness, 80,* 574–576.

Progrund, R. L., Fazzi, D., & Lampert, J. S. (1992). *Early focus: Working with young blind and visually impaired children and their families.* New York: American Foundation for the Blind.

Progrund, R. L., & Rosen, S. (1989). The preschool blind child CAN be a cane user. *Journal of Visual Impairment and Blindness, 83,* 431–439.

Reynell, J. (1983). *Manual for the Reynell-Zinkin Scales.* New Windsor, Berkshire, United Kingdom: NFER-NELSON.

Rusch, F. R. (1979). Toward the validation of social/vocational survival skills. *Mental Retardation, 17,* 143–145.

Sacks, S. Z., & Gaylord-Ross, R. (1989). Peer-mediated and teacher-directed social skills training for visually impaired students. *Behavior Therapy, 20,* 619–638.

Sacks, S. Z., Kekelis, L., & Gaylord-Ross, R. J. (1992). *The development of social skills by blind and visually impaired students: Exploratory studies and strategies.* New York: American Foundation for the Blind.

Sacks, S. Z., & Pruett, K. M. (1992). Summer transition training project for professionals who work with adolescents and young adults. *Journal of Visual Impairment and Blindness, 86,* 211–214.

Sacks, S. Z., & Reardon, M. (1988). Maximizing social integration for visually handicapped students. In R. J. Gaylord-Ross (Ed.), *Integration strategies for students with handicaps* (pp. 77–104). Baltimore: Paul H. Brookes.

Sacks, S. Z., & Wolffe, K. (1992). The importance of social skills training in the transition process for students with visual impairments. *Journal of Vocational Rehabilitation, 2*(1), 46–55.

Santin, S., & Nesker Simmons, J. (1977). Problems in the construction of reality in congenitally blind children. *Journal of Visual Impairment and Blindness, 71,* 425–429.

Schneekloth, L. (1989). Play environments for visually impaired children. *Journal of Visual Impairment and Blindness, 83,* 196–211.

Scholl, G. (1986). Visual impairment and other exceptionalities. In G. Scholl (Ed.), *Foundations of education for blind and visually handicapped children and youth* (pp. 137–144). New York: American Foundation for the Blind.

Schulz, P. (1980). *How does it feel to be blind?* Van Nuys, CA: Muse-Ed.

Scott, R. (1969). Socialization of blind children. In D. Goslin (Ed.), *Handbook of socialization theory and research* (pp. 1025–1046). New York: Rand McNally.

Siegel, S., Greener, K., Prieuer, J., Robert, M., & Gaylord-Ross, R. (1989). The community vocational training program. *Career Development for Exceptional Individuals, 12,* 48–64.

Sisson, L., Van Hasselt, V., Hersen, M., & Strain, P. (1985). Peer interventions: Increasing social behaviors in multihandicapped children. *Behavior Modification, 9,* 293–321.

Skellinger, A. C., Hill, M. M., & Hill, E. (1992). The social functioning of children with visual impairments. In S. L. Odom, S. M. McConnell, & M. A. McEvoy (Eds.), *Social competence of children with disabilities: Issues and strategies for intervention* (pp. 165–188). Baltimore: Paul H. Brookes.

Tuttle, D. (1974). Comparison of three reading media for the blind: Braille, normal recording, and compressed speech. *American Foundation for the Blind Research Bulletin, 27,* 217–230.

Tuttle, D. (1986). *Self-esteem and adjusting to blindness.* Springfield, IL: Charles C Thomas.

Van Hasselt, V. (1983). Social adaptation in the blind. *Clinical Psychology Review, 3,* 87–102.

Van Hasselt, V., Hersen, M., Kazdin, A., Simon, J., & Mastanuono, A. (1983). Social skills training for blind adolescents. *Journal of Visual Impairment and Blindness, 77,* 99–103.

Warren, D. (1984). *Blindness and early childhood development* (2nd ed.). New York: American Foundation for the Blind.

Ysseldyke, J. (1979). Issues in psychoeducational assessment. In G. Phye & D. J. Reschly (Eds.), *School psychology: Perspectives and issues* (pp. 87–121). New York: Academic Press.

CHAPTER TWELVE

Alexander, P. A., & Muia, J. A. (1982). *Gifted education:* A *comprehensive roadmap.* Rockville, MD: Aspen.

Alvino, J. (Ed.). (1985). *Parents' guide to raising a gifted child.* Boston: Little, Brown.

Baldwin, A. (1984). *The Baldwin Identification Matrix 2 for the identification of the gifted and talented: A handbook for its use.* New York: Trillium Press.

Baum, S., & Owen, S. (1988). High ability/learning disabled students: How are they different? *Gifted Child Quarterly*, 32, 321–326.

Beck, L. Mentorship: Benefits and effects in career development. *Gifted Child Quarterly*, 33(1), 22–28.

Bernal, E. (1975). A response to the educational uses of tests with disadvantaged subjects. *American Psychologist*, 30, 93–95.

Bernal, E. (1979). The education of the culturally different gifted. In A. H. Passow (Ed.), *The gifted and the talented: Their education and development* (78th Yearbook of the National Society for the Study of Education, Pt. 1, pp. 24–80). Chicago: University of Chicago Press.

Betts, G. (1985). *The autonomous learner model*. Greeley, CO: Autonomous Learning Publications and Specialists.

Betts, G., & Knapp, J. (1986). *The autonomous learner model for the gifted and talented*. Greeley, CO: Autonomous Learning Publications and Specialists.

Bishop, W. (1968). Successful teachers of the gifted. *Exceptional Children*, 34, 317–325.

Bloom, B. S. (Ed.). (1956). *Taxonomy of educational objectives: Handbook I. Cognitive domain*. New York: McKay.

Bloom, B. S. (Ed.). (1985). *Developing talent in young people*. New York: Ballantine Books.

Borland, J. (1978). Teacher identification of the gifted: A new look. *Journal for the Education of the Gifted*, 2, 22–32.

Bridges, R. D. (1980). Mentors open new careers and hobby vistas for youth. *Phi Delta Kappan*, 62, 199.

Brody, L. E., Assouline, S. G., & Stanley, J. C. (1990). Five years of early entrants: Predicting successful achievement in college. *Gifted Child Quarterly*, 34, 138–142.

Brody, L. E., & Benbow, C. P. (1987). Accelerative strategies: How effective are they for the gifted? *Gifted Child Quarterly*, 31, 105–110.

Bruch, C. (1972). ABDA: *Making the Stanford-Binet culturally unbiased for disadvantaged black children*. Paper presented at the Southeastern Invitational Conference on Testing Problems, University of Georgia, Athens.

Buescher, T. M. (1987). Counseling gifted adolescents: A curriculum model for students, parents and professionals. *Gifted Child Quarterly*, 31, 90–94.

Ciha, I., Harris, R., Hoffman, C., & Potter, M. W. (1974). Parents as identifiers of giftedness, ignored but accurate. *Gifted Child Quarterly*, 18, 191–195.

Clark, B. (1986). *Optimizing learning: The integrative education model in the classroom*. New York: Merrill/Macmillan.

Clark, B. (1988). *Growing up gifted* (3rd ed.). New York: Merrill/Macmillan.

Colson, S., Borman, C., & Nash, W. R. (1978). A unique learning opportunity for talented high school seniors. *Phi Delta Kappan*, 59, 542–543.

Congressional Record. (1978, October 10). H–12179.

Cooper, J. O. (1981). *Measuring behavior* (2nd ed.). Columbus, OH: Merrill.

Cox, J., Daniel, N., & Boston, B. O. (1985). *Educating able learners: Promising programs and practices*. Austin: University of Texas Press.

Dahlberg, W. (1992). Brilliance: The childhood dilemma of unusual intellect. *Roeper Review*, 15, 7.

Dale, E. (1987). Computers and gifted and talented individuals. In J. D. Lindsey (Ed.), *Computers and exceptional individuals* (pp. 147–168). Columbus, OH: Merrill.

DeLisle, J. (1990). *Underachieving gifted students* (ERIC Digest #E478). Reston, VA: Clearinghouse on Handicapped and Gifted Children, Council for Exceptional Children.

Dettmer, P. (1991). Gifted program advocacy: Overhauling bandwagons to build support. *Gifted Child Quarterly*, 35, 165–171.

Dryer, S. S. (1977). *The bookfinder*. Circle Pines, MN: American Guidance Service.

Feldhusen, J. F., Sayler, M. F., Nielsen, M. E., & Kolloff, P. B. (1990). Self-concepts of gifted children in enrichment programs. *Journal for the Education of the Gifted*, 13, 380–387.

Fliegler, L., & Bish, C. (1959). Summary of research on the academically talented student. *Review of Educational Research*, 29, 408–450.

Fox, L., & Tobin, D. (1978). Broadening career horizons for gifted girls. *Gifted/Creative/Talented*, 4, 18, 22.

Frasier, M. M. (1980). Screening and identification of gifted students. In J. B. Jordan & J. A. Grossi (Eds.), *An administrative handbook on developing programs for the gifted and talented* (pp. 23–40). Reston, VA: Council for Exceptional Children.

Frasier, M. M. (1987). The identification of gifted black students: Developing new perspectives. *Journal for the Education of the Gifted*, 10, 155–180.

Gallagher, J. (1985). *Teaching the gifted child* (3rd ed.). Boston: Allyn and Bacon.

Gallagher, J. J. (1991a). Educational reform, values, and gifted students. *Gifted Child Quarterly*, 35, 12–19.

Gallagher, J. J. (1991b). Personal patterns of underachievement. *Journal for the Education of the Gifted*, 14, 221–233.

Gardner, H. (1984). Assessing intelligence: A comment on testing intelligence without IQ tests. *Phi Delta Kappan*, 65, 699–700.

Getzels, I., & Jackson, P. (1962). *Creativity and intelligence*. New York: Wiley.

Gilligan, C. (1990). Teaching Shakespeare's sister: Notes from the underground of female adolescence. In C. Gilligan, N. P. Lyon, & T. J. Hanmer (Eds.), *Making connections: The relational world of adolescent girls at Emma Willard School* (pp. 6–29). Cambridge, MA: Harvard University Press.

Given, B. K. (1977). Reaching the learning disabled gifted. In J. H. Orloff (Ed.), *Creativity and the gifted/talented child* (pp. 187–213). Falls Church, VA: Northern Virginia Conference on Gifted Talented Education.

Goertz, J., & Betts, G. (1989). Center for autonomous learning. *Gifted/Creative/Talented*, 12(5), 37–40.

Grau, P. N. (1985). Counseling the gifted girl. *Gifted/Creative/Talented*, 38, 8–11.

Griggs, S. A. (1984). Counseling the gifted and talented based on learning styles. *Exceptional Children*, 50, 429–432.

Grost, A. (1970). *Genius in residence*. Englewood Cliffs, NJ: Prentice-Hall.

Guilford, J. P. (1967). *The nature of human intelligence*. New York: McGraw-Hill.

Guilford, J. P. (1977). *Way beyond the IQ*. Buffalo, NY: Creative Education Foundation.

Haddad, F. A., & Naglieri, J. A. (1984). The Kaufman Assessment Battery for Children: An alternative to present approaches. *Directive Teacher*, 6(1), 12–13.

Harrington, J., Harrington, C., & Karns, E. (1991). The Marland Report: Twenty years later. *Journal for the Education of the Gifted*, 15, 31–43.

Harris, R. A. (1984). Mentorship for the gifted. *Gifted/Creative/Talented*, 33, 8–9.

High, M. H., & Udall, A. J. (1983). Teacher ratings of students in relation to ethnicity of students and school ethnic balance. *Journal for the Education of the Gifted*, 6, 154–166.

High school classes set for a 7-year-old. (1984, May 7). *The New York Times*, p. A4.

Hokansen, D. T., & Jospe, M. (1976). *The search for cognitive giftedness in exceptional children*. New Haven, CT: Project SEARCH.

Hollinger, C. L. (1991). Facilitating the career development of gifted young women. *Roeper Review*, 13, 135–139.

Hollingworth, L. (1942). *Children with above 180 IQ*. Yonkers-on-Hudson, NY: World.

Howell, H., & Bressler, J. (1988). Research on teaching styles of teachers of the gifted. *Roeper Review*, 10, 144–146.

Huntington, S. (1975). The United States. In M. Croziers, S. Huntington, & I. Watanuki (Eds.), *The crisis of democracy: Report on the governability of democracies to the Trilateral Commission*. New York: New York University Press.

Jacobs, J. C. (1971). Effectiveness of teacher and parent identification of gifted children as a function of school level. *Psychology in the Schools*, 8, 140–142.

Kaplan, S. N. (1986). The grid: A model to construct differentiated curriculum for the gifted. In J. Renzulli (Ed.), *Systems and models for developing programs for the gifted and talented* (pp. 182–193). Mansfield Center, CT: Creative Learning Press.

Karnes, F. A., & Whorton, J. E. (1991). Teacher certification and endorsement in gifted education: Past, present and future. *Gifted Child Quarterly*, 35, 148–150.

Karnes, M. B., Schwedel, A. M., & Lewis, G. F. (1983). Long term effects of early programming for the gifted/talented handicapped. *Journal for the Education of the Gifted*, 6, 266–278.

Kaufman, A. S., & Kaufman, N. L. (1983). *Kaufman Assessment Battery for Children*. Circle Pines, MN: American Guidance Service.

Kerr, B. A. (1985). *Smart girls, gifted women*. Columbus, OH: Ohio Psychology Publishing.

Khatena, J. (1976). Major directions of creativity research. In J. Gowan, J. Khatena, & P. Torrance (Eds.), *Educating the ablest*. Itasca, IL: Peacock.

Kramer, J. J., & Murphy, L. L. (Eds.). (1992). *The eleventh Mental Measurements Yearbook*. Lincoln: University of Nebraska Press.

Kranz, B. (1982). *Kranz Talent Identification Instrument*. Moorehead: University of Minnesota Press.

Laffoon, K. S., Jerkins-Friedman, R., & Tollefson, N. (1989). Causal attributions of underachieving gifted, achieving gifted, and nongifted students. *Journal for the Education of the Gifted*, 13, 4–21.

Lajoie, S. P., & Shore, B. M. (1981). Three myths: The over-representation of the gifted among dropouts, delinquents, and suicides. *Gifted Child Quarterly*, 25, 138–141.

Landrum, M. S. (1987). Guidelines for implementing a guidance/counseling program for gifted and talented students. *Roeper Review*, 10, 103–106.

Laycock, F., & Caylor, J. S. (1964). Physiques of gifted children and their less gifted siblings. *Child Development*, 35, 63–74.

Lehman, H. (1953). *Age and achievement*. Princeton, NJ: Princeton University Press.

Louis, B., & Lewis, M. (1992). Parental beliefs about giftedness in young children and their relation to actual ability level. *Gifted Child Quarterly*, 36, 27–31.

Lucito, L. (1974). The creative. In R. Martinson (Ed.), *Identification of the gifted and talented* (pp. 14–72). Ventura, CA: Office of the Ventura County Superintendent of Schools.

MacKinnon, D. (1962). The nature and nurture of creative talent. *American Psychologist*, 17, 484–495.

Maker, J. C. (1977). *Providing programs for the gifted handicapped*. Reston, VA: Council for Exceptional Children.

Maker, J. C. (1982). *Curriculum development for the gifted*. Rockville, MD: Aspen.

Marland, S. (1972). *Education of the gifted and talented* (Report to Congress by the U.S. Commissioner of Education). Washington, DC: U.S. Government Printing Office.

Mattson, B. D. (1983). Mentors for the gifted and talented: Whom to seek and where to look. *Gifted/Creative/Talented*, 27, 10–19.

McCallum, R. S., Karnes, F. A., & Edwards, R. P. (1984). The test of choice for assessment of gifted children: A comparison of the K–ABC, WISC–R, and Stanford-Binet. *Journal of Psychoeducational Assessment*, 2, 57–63.

McCleary, I. D., & Hines, S. (1983). Expanding horizons: University professors serve as mentors for gifted middle-graders. *Phi Delta Kappan*, 64, 661–662.

McCormick, M. E., & Wolf, J. S. (in press). Intervention programs for gifted girls. *Roeper Review.*

McGreevy, A. (1990). Darwin and teacher: An analysis of the mentorship between Charles Darwin and Professor John Henslow. *Gifted Child Quarterly*, 34, 5–9.

Meeker, M. (1969). *The structure of intellect: Its interpretation and use.* Columbus, OH: Merrill.

Mercer, J. (1978). SOMPA: *System of Multicultural Pluralistic Assessment.* New York: Psychological Corporation.

Minner, S. (1990). Teacher evaluations of case descriptions of LD gifted children. *Gifted Child Quarterly*, 34, 37–39.

Moon, S. M., Feldhusen, J. F., & Kelly, K. W. (1991). Identification procedures: Bridging theory and practice. *Gifted Child Today*, 14, 30–36.

Moore, A. D., & Betts, G. T. (1987). Using judgment analysis in the identification of gifted and talented children. *Gifted Child Quarterly*, 31, 30–33.

Moore, L. C., & Sawyers, J. K. (1987). The stability of original thinking in young children. *Gifted Child Quarterly*, 31, 126–129.

Mulhern, J. D., & Ward, M. (1983). A collaborative program for developing teachers of gifted and talented students. *Gifted Child Quarterly*, 27, 152–156.

National Society for the Study of Education. (1958). *Education for the gifted* (57th Yearbook of the National Society for the Study of Education, Pt. 2). Chicago: University of Chicago Press.

Newland, T. (1962). Some observations on essential qualifications of teachers of the mentally superior. *Exceptional Children*, 29, 111–114.

Oden, M. (1968). The fulfillment of promise: 40-year follow-up of the Terman gifted group. *Genetic Psychology Monographs*, 77, 3–93.

Osborne, J. K., & Byrnes, D. A. (1990). Identifying gifted and talented students in an alternative learning center. *Gifted Child Quarterly*, 34, 143–146.

Parke, B. N., & Ness, P. S. (1988). Curricular decision-making for the education of young gifted children. *Gifted Child Quarterly*, 32, 196–199.

Pegnato, C. W., & Birch, J. W. (1959). Locating gifted children in junior high schools: A comparison of methods. *Exceptional Children*, 25, 300–304.

Proctor, T. B., Black, K. N., & Feldhusen, J. F. (1988). Early admission to elementary school: Barriers versus benefits. *Roeper Review*, 11, 85–87.

Quattrocki, C. G. (1974). Recognizing creative potential in preschool children. *Gifted Child Quarterly*, 18, 74–80.

Redding, R. (1990). Learning preferences and skill patterns among underachieving gifted adolescents. *Gifted Child Quarterly*, 34, 72–75.

Reis, S. (1987). We can't change what we don't recognize: Understanding the special needs of gifted females. *Gifted Child Quarterly*, 31, 83–89.

Reis, S. M. (1991). The need for clarification in research designed to examine gender differences in achievement and accomplishment. *Roeper Review*, 13, 193–197.

Reis, S. M., & Renzulli, J. S. (1991). The assessment of creative products in programs for gifted and talented students. *Gifted Child Quarterly*, 35, 128–134.

Renzulli, J. S. (1973). Talent potential in minority group students. *Exceptional Children*, 39, 437–444.

Renzulli, J. S. (1978). What makes giftedness? Reexamining a definition. *Phi Delta Kappan*, 60, 180–184, 261.

Renzulli, J. S., & Hartman, R. K. (1971). Scale for rating behavioral characteristics of superior students. *Exceptional Children*, 38, 243–248.

Renzulli, J. S., & Reis, S. (1986). The enrichment triad/revolving door model: A schoolwide plan for the development of creative productivity. In J. Renzulli (Ed.), *Systems and models for developing programs for the gifted and talented* (pp. 216–266). Mansfield Center, CT: Creative Learning Press.

Renzulli, J. S., & Reis, S. M. (1991). Building advocacy through program design, student productivity and public relations. *Gifted Child Quarterly*, 35, 182–187.

Renzulli, J. S., Smith, L., & Reis, S. (1982). Curriculum compacting: An essential strategy for working with gifted students. *Elementary School Journal*, 82, 185–194.

Rhodes, L. (1992). Focusing attention on the individual in identification of gifted black students. *Roeper Review*, 14, 108–110.

Rimm, S. B. (1986). *Underachievement syndrome: Causes and cures.* Watertown, WI: Apple.

Robinson, N. (1992). Which Stanford-Binet for the brightest? Stanford-Binet IV of course: Time marches on. *Roeper Review*, 15, 32–34.

Rogers, K. B. (1989). Training teachers of the gifted: What do they need to know? *Roeper Review*, 11, 145–150.

Runco, M., & Albert, R. S. (1986). The threshold theory regarding creativity and intelligence. *Creative Child and Adult Quarterly*, 11, 212–218.

Schatz, E. (1991). Dissemination by design: A tool for advancing gifted education. *Gifted Child Quarterly*, 35, 188–195.

Scott, M. S., Prior, R., Urbano, R., Hogan, A., & Gold, S. (1992). The identification of giftedness: A comparison of white, Hispanic and black families. *Gifted Child Quarterly*, 36, 131–139.

Seaberg, V. (1989). *State of the State's Gifted and Talented Education Program*. Augusta: Maine Department of Education and Cultural Services.

Silverman, L. K. (1986). An interview with Elizabeth Hagen: Giftedness, intelligence, and the new Stanford-Binet. *Roeper Review*, 8, 168–171.

Silverman, L. K. (1991). Helping gifted girls reach their potential. *Roeper Review*, 13, 122–123.

Silverman, L. K., & Kearney, K. (1992). The case for the Stanford-Binet L–M as a supplemental test. *Roeper Review*, 15, 34–37.

Sisk, D. (1978). Education for the gifted and talented: A national perspective. *Journal for the Education of the Gifted*, 1, 5–24.

Stanley, J. C. (1976). The study of mathematically precocious youth. *Gifted Child Quarterly*, 20, 246–283.

Stanley, J. C. (1978). Educational non-acceleration: An international tragedy. *Gifted/Creative/Talented*, 3, 3–5, 53–57, 60–63.

Stanley, J. C. (1985). How did six highly accelerated gifted students fare in graduate school? *Gifted Child Quarterly*, 29, 180.

Stanley, J. C. (1989). A look back at educational non-acceleration: An international tragedy. *Gifted/Creative/Talented*, 12(4), 60–61.

Stephens, T. M., & Wolf, J. S. (1981). Instructional models. *Directive Teacher*, 3(3), 5–6.

Sternberg, R. J. (1985). *Beyond IQ: A triarchic theory of human intelligence*. New York: Cambridge University Press.

Storfer, M. D. (1990). *Intelligence and giftedness: The contributions of heredity and early environment*. San Francisco: Jossey-Bass.

Story, C. (1985). Facilitator of learning: A microethnographic study of the teacher of the gifted. *Gifted Child Quarterly*, 29, 155–159.

Suter, D. P., & Wolf, J. S. (1987). Issues in the identification and programming of the gifted/learning disabled child. *Journal for the Education of the Gifted*, 10, 227–237.

Swassing, R. H. (1980). Gifted and talented children. In W. L. Heward & M. D. Orlansky (Eds.), *Exceptional children* (pp. 149–200). New York: Merrill/Macmillan.

Tannenbaum, A. J. (1979). Pre-Sputnik to post-Watergate concern about the gifted. In A. H. Passow (Ed.), *The gifted and the talented: Their education and development* (78th Yearbook of the National Society for the Study of Education, Pt. 1, pp. 382–410). Chicago: University of Chicago Press.

Tannenbaum, A. J. (1983). *Gifted children: Psychological and educational perspectives*. New York: Macmillan.

Tannenbaum, A. J. (1992). Early signs of giftedness: Research and commentary. *Journal for the Education of the Gifted*, 15, 104–133.

Taylor, C., & Holland, J. (1962). Development and application of tests of creativity. *Review of Educational Research*, 32, 91–102.

Terman, L. M. (Ed.). (1925–1959). *Genetic studies of genius* (Vols. 1–5). Stanford, CA: Stanford University Press.

Terman, L. M. (1954). The discovery and encouragement of exceptional talent. *American Psychologist*, 9, 221–230.

Terman, L. M., & Merrill, M. A. (1973). *Stanford-Binet Intelligence Scale* (3rd rev.). Boston: Houghton Mifflin.

Terman, L. M., & Oden, M. (1959). The gifted group at midlife: Thirty-five years' follow-up of the superior child. In L. M. Terman (Ed.), *Genetic studies of genius* (Vol. 5). Stanford, CA: Stanford University Press.

Tittle, B. M. (1984). Why Montessori for the gifted? *Gifted/Creative/Talented*, 33, 3–7.

Torrance, E. P. (1966). *Torrance Tests of Creative Thinking*. Princeton, NJ: Personnel Press.

Torrance, E. P. (1969). Creative positives of disadvantaged children and youth. *Gifted Child Quarterly*, 13, 71–81.

Treffinger, D. J., & Renzulli, J. S. (1986). Giftedness as potential for creative productivity: Transcending IQ scores. *Roeper Review*, 8, 150–159.

Tremaine, C. D. (1979). Do gifted programs make a difference? *Gifted Child Quarterly*, 23, 500–517.

U.S. *Senate report of the Gifted and Talented Subcommittee on Labor and Public Welfare*. (1972, March). Washington, DC: U.S. Department of Health, Education and Welfare.

Vaughn, V. L., Feldhusen, J. F., & Asher, W. J. (1991). Meta-analyses and review of research on pull-out programs in gifted education. *Gifted Child Quarterly*, 35, 92–98.

Ward, V. (1961). *Educating the gifted*. Columbus, OH: Merrill.

Ward, V. (1975). Basic concepts. In W. Barbe & I. Renzulli (Eds.), *Psychology and education of the gifted* (pp. 214–253). New York: Irvington.

Webb, I., Meckstroth, E., & Tolan, S. (1983). *Guiding the gifted child*. Columbus, OH: Ohio Psychology Publishing.

Wechsler, D. (1967). *Wechsler Preschool and Primary Scale of Intelligence*. New York: Psychological Corporation.

Wechsler, D. (1974). *Wechsler Intelligence Scale for Children—Revised*. New York: Psychological Corporation.

Wechsler, D. (1981). *Wechsler Adult Intelligence Scale—Revised.* New York: Psychological Corporation.

Wechsler, D. (1991). *Wechsler Intelligence Scale for Children* (3rd ed.). New York: Psychological Corporation.

Wendel, R., & Heiser, S. (1989). Effective instructional characteristics of teachers of junior high school gifted students. *Roeper Review, 11,* 151–153.

Whitlock, M. S., & DuCette, J. P. (1989). Outstanding and average teachers of the gifted: A comparative study. *Gifted Child Quarterly, 33,* 15–21.

Whitmore, J. R. (1980). *Giftedness, conflict, and underachievement.* Boston: Allyn and Bacon.

Whitmore, J. R. (1986). Understanding a lack of motivation to excel. *Gifted Child Quarterly, 30,* 66–69.

Wolf, J. S. (1979). Education of the gifted: Some critical issues. *Insight: A Forum for Leaders and Policy Makers in Western Education, 2,* 15–20.

Wolf, J. S. (1981). An interview with James Gallagher. *Directive Teacher, 3*(1), 25–27.

Wolf, J. S. (1987). Workshops for parents of the gifted. *Roeper Review, 9,* 243–246.

Wolf, J. S. (1989). Consultation for parents of young gifted children. *Roeper Review, 11,* 219–221.

Wolf, J. S., & Geiger, J. (1986). Concurrent enrollment: A program to foster educational excellence. *High School Journal, 69,* 218–221.

Wolf, J., & Gygi, J. (1981). Learning disabled and gifted: Success or failure? *Journal for the Education of the Gifted, 4,* 199–206.

Wolf, J., & Penrod, D. (1980). Bibliotherapy: A classroom approach to sensitive problems. *Gifted/Creative/Talented, 15,* 52–54.

Wolf, J., & Stephens, T. M. (1979). Individualized educational planning for the gifted. *Roeper Review, 2*(2), 11–12.

Wolf, J., & Stephens, T. M. (1984). Training models for parents of the gifted. *Journal for the Education of the Gifted, 7,* 120–129.

Wolf, J. S., & Stephens, T. M. (1990). Friends of special education: A parent training model. *Journal of Educational and Psychological Consultation, 1,* 343–356.

Wyatt, F. (1982). Responsibility for gifted learners: A plea for the encouragement of classroom teacher support. *Gifted Child Quarterly, 26,* 140–143.

CHAPTER THIRTEEN

Affleck, G., & Tennen, H. (1991). Social comparison and coping with major medical problems. In J. Suls & T. Wills (Eds.), *Social comparison: Contemporary theory and research* (pp. 369–394). Hillsdale, NJ: Erlbaum.

Affleck, G., & Tennen, H. (in press). Cognitive adaptation to adversity: Insights from parents of medically fragile infants. In A. Turnbull, J. Patterson, S. Behr, D. Murphy, J. Marquis, & M. Blue-Banning (Eds.), *Cognitive coping, families and disability: Participatory research in action.* Baltimore: Paul H. Brookes.

Affleck, G., Tennen, H., & Rowe, J. (1991). *Infants in crisis: How parents cope with newborn intensive care and its aftermath.* New York: Springer.

Brinckerhoff, J., & Vincent, L. (1986). Increasing parental decision-making at the individualized educational program meeting. *Journal of the Division for Early Childhood, 11,* 46–58.

Bronfenbrenner, U. (1979). *The ecology of human development.* Cambridge, MA: Harvard University Press.

David, J. L. (1989). Synthesis of research on school-based management. *Educational Leadership, 45,* 45–53.

Dunst, C. J., Trivette, C. M., & Deal, A. G. (1988). *Enabling and empowering families: Principles and guidelines for practice.* Cambridge, MA: Brookline Books.

Gallimore, R., Wiesner, T. S., Kaufman, S. Z., & Bernheimer, L. P. (1989). The social construction of ecocultural niches: Family accommodation of developmentally delayed children. *American Journal on Mental Retardation, 94,* 216–230.

Gradel, K., Thompson, M., & Sheehan, R. (1981). Parental and professional agreement in early childhood assessment. *Topics in Early Childhood Special Education, 1*(2), 31–39.

Hanson, M. J., & Lynch, E. W. (1992). Family diversity: Implications for policy and practice. *Topics in Early Childhood Special Education, 12,* 283–303.

Hill, R. (1958). Social stresses on the family. *Social Casework, 19,* 139–150.

McCubbin, H., & Patterson, J. (1983). The family stress process: The double ABCX model of family adjustment and adaptation. In H. McCubbin, M. Sassman, & J. Patterson (Eds.), *Advances and developments in family stress theory and research* (pp. 213–241). New York: Haworth Press.

McGonigel, M. J., Kaufmann, R. K., & Johnson, B. H. (Eds.). (1991). *Guidelines and recommended practices for the individualized family service plan* (2nd ed.). Bethesda, MD: Association for the Care of Children's Health.

McWilliam, R. (1992). *Family-centered intervention planning: A routines-based approach.* Tucson, AZ: Communication Skill Builders.

Melaville, A. I., & Blank, M. J. (1991). *What it takes: Structuring interagency partnerships to connect children and families with comprehensive services.* Washington, DC: Education and Human Services Consortium.

Minuchin, S. (1974). *Families and family therapy.* Cambridge, MA: Harvard University Press.

National Commission on Children. (1991). *Beyond rhetoric: A new American agenda for children and families* (A final report of the National Commission on Children). Washington, DC: U.S. Government Printing Office.

Olson, D., Russell, C., & Sprenkle, D. (1983). Circumplex model of marital and family systems: Vol. I. Theoretical update. *Family Process, 22*, 69–83.

Peck, C. (1992). Ecological perspectives on the implementation of integrated early childhood programs. In C. Peck, S. Odom, & D. Bricker (Eds.), *Integrating young children with disabilities into community programs* (pp. 3–15). Baltimore: Paul H. Brookes.

Roit, M., & Pfohl, W. (1984). The readability of P.L. 94–142 parent materials: Are parents truly informed? *Exceptional Children, 50*, 496–505.

Selvini, M. P., Boscolo, L., Cecchin, G., & Prata, G. (1980). Hypothesizing–circularity–neutrality: Three guidelines for the conductor of the session. *Family Process, 19*, 3–12.

Shelton, T., Jeppson, E., & Johnson, B. (1987). *Family-centered care for children with special care needs.* Washington, DC: Association for the Care of Children's Health.

Strain, P., & Smith, B. (1992). Comprehensive educational, social, and policy forces. In C. Peck, S. Odom, & D. Bricker (Eds.), *Integrating young children with disabilities into community programs* (pp. 209–222). Baltimore: Paul H. Brookes.

Tseng, W. S., & McDermott, J. F. (1979). Triaxial family classification. *Journal of the American Academy of Child Psychiatry, 18*, 22–43.

Turnbull, A. P., Summers, J. A., & Brotherson, M. J. (1984). *Working with families with disabled members: A family systems approach.* Lawrence: Kansas University Affiliated Facility.

Turnbull, A. P., & Turnbull, R. (1990). *Families, professionals, and exceptionality: A special partnership* (2nd ed.). New York: Merrill/Macmillan.

Vandercook, T., York, J., & Forest, M. (1989). MAPS: A *strategy for building the vision.* Minneapolis: University of Minnesota, Institute on Community Integration.

Wikler, L., Wasow, M., & Hatfield, E. (1981). Chronic sorrow revisited: Parent vs. professional depiction of the adjustment of parents of mentally retarded children. *American Journal of Orthopsychiatry, 51*, 63–70.

Winton, P., & Bailey, D. (in press). Family-centered practices in early intervention for children with hearing loss: Strategies for self-examination. In J. Roush & N. Matkin (Eds.), *Infants and toddlers with hearing loss: Identification and family-centered intervention.* Parkton, MD: York Press.

Winton, P. J., & Turnbull, A. P. (1981). Parent involvement as viewed by parents of preschool handicapped children. *Topics in Early Childhood Special Education, 1*(3), 11–19.

Winton, P. J., Turnbull, A. P., & Blacher, J. (1984). *Selecting a preschool: A guide for parents of handicapped children.* Dallas, TX: Pro-Ed.

Wolery, M., & Dyk, L. (1984). Arena assessment: Description and preliminary social validity data. *Journal of the Association for the Severely Handicapped, 3*, 231–235.

CHAPTER FOURTEEN

Aslanian, C. B., & Brickell, H. M. (1980). *Americans in transition: Life changes as reasons for learning.* New York: College Entrance Examination Board.

Bellamy, G. T., Rhodes, L. E., Mank, D. M., & Albin, J. M. (1988). *Supported employment: A community implementation guide.* Baltimore: Paul H. Brookes.

Bellamy, G. T., Rose, H., Wilson, D. J., & Clarke, J. Y. (1982). Strategies for vocational preparation. In B. Wilcox & G. T. Bellamy (Eds.), *Design of high school programs for severely handicapped students* (pp. 139–152). Baltimore: Paul H. Brookes.

Belmore, K., & Brown, L. (1976). A job skill inventory strategy for use in a public school vocational training program for severely handicapped potential workers. In L. Brown, N. Certo, K. Volmar, & T. Crowner (Eds.), *Madison's alternative for zero exclusion* (Vol. 6). Madison, WI: Madison Public Schools.

Black, J., & Ford, A. D. (1989). Planning and implementing activity-based lessons. In A. Ford, R. Schnorr, L. Meyer, L. Davern, J. Black, & P. Dempsey (Eds.), *The Syracuse community-referenced curriculum guide for students with moderate and severe disabilities.* Baltimore: Paul H. Brookes.

Blalock, G. (1988). Transitions across the lifespan. In B. L. Ludlow, A. P. Turnbull, & R. Luckasson (Eds.), *Transitions to adult life for people with mental retardation: Principles and practices* (pp. 3–20). Baltimore: Paul H. Brookes.

Bradley, V. (1988). Ensuring the quality of services for persons with mental retardation. In B. L. Ludlow, A. P. Turnbull, & R. Luckasson (Eds.), *Transitions to adult life for people with mental retardation: Principles and practices* (pp. 275–292). Baltimore: Paul H. Brookes.

Brolin, D. E. (1982). *Vocational preparation of persons with handicaps* (2nd ed.). Columbus, OH: Merrill.

Brown, L., Nietupski, J., & Hamre-Nietupski, S. (1976). The criterion of ultimate functioning. In M. A. Thomas (Ed.), *Hey, don't forget about me!* (pp. 2–15). Reston, VA: Council for Exceptional Children.

Carney, I., & Orelove, F. (1988). Implementing transition programs for community participation. In B. L. Ludlow, A. P. Turnbull, & R. Luckasson (Eds.), *Transitions to adult life for people with mental retardation: Principles and practices* (pp. 137–158). Baltimore: Paul H. Brookes.

Channing, A. (1932). *Employment of mentally deficient boys and girls* (U.S. Department of Labor Children's Bureau Publication No. 210). Washington, DC: U.S. Government Printing Office.

Clark, G. M. (1991, October). *Functional curriculum and its place in the Regular Education Initiative.* Paper presented at the Seventh International Conference of the Division on Career Development, Council for Exceptional Children, Kansas City, MO.

Delisle, L., & Squires, S. (1988). *Career development for gifted and talented youth.* Reston, VA: Council for Exceptional Children.

Douglas, M. C. (1944). Some concrete contributions to occupational education in the academic classroom. *American Journal of Mental Deficiency, 48,* 288.

Edgar, E. (1992). Secondary options for students with mild intellectual disabilities: Facing the issue of tracking. *Education and Training in Mental Retardation, 27,* 101–111.

Falvey, M. A. (1989). *Community-based curriculum: Instructional strategies for students with severe handicaps* (2nd ed.). Baltimore: Paul H. Brookes.

Federal Register. (1984). 98 1074, Sec. 102, (11)F.

Field, S., & Allen, M. (1987). *Managing diversity: Maximizing employee strengths and minimizing limitation.* Seattle: University of Washington Press.

Field, S., & Hoffman, A. (1992a). *Skills and knowledge for self-determination.* Paper presented at the 70th Annual Convention of the Council for Exceptional Children, Baltimore.

Field, S., & Hoffman, A. (1992b). *Steps to self-determination* (Field-test version). Detroit, MI: Wayne State University.

Flynn, R. J. (1982). Effectiveness of conventional and alternative vocational education with handicapped and disadvantaged youth: A research review. In K. P. Lynch, W. E. Kiernan, & J. A. Stark (Eds.), *Prevocational and vocational education for special needs youth* (pp. 35–62). Baltimore: Paul H. Brookes.

Gaylord-Ross, C., Forte, J., & Gaylord-Ross, R. (1986). The community classroom: Technological vocational training for students with serious handicaps. *Career Development for Exceptional Children, 9,* 24–33.

Halpern, A. S. (1992a). Quality of life as a conceptual framework for evaluating transition outcomes: Excerpts from a keynote speech. *Interchange, 12*(2), 1–6.

Halpern, A. S. (1992b). Transition: Old wine in new bottles. *Exceptional Children, 58,* 202–211.

Haring, N., Liberty, K., & White, O. R. (1988). *Generalization for students with severe handicaps: Strategies and solutions.* Seattle: University of Washington Press.

Harris, L., & Associates. (1986). *Disabled Americans' self perceptions: Bringing disabled Americans into the mainstream* (Study No. 854009). New York: Author.

Hasazi, S., & Clark, G. (1988). Vocational preparation for high school students labeled mentally retarded: Employment as a graduation goal. *Mental Retardation, 26,* 343–349.

Hasazi, S., Gordon, L. R., Roe, C. A., Hull, M., Finck, K., & Salembrer, G. (1985). A statewide follow-up on post high school employment and residential status of students labeled "mentally retarded." *Education and Training of the Mentally Retarded, 20,* 222–234.

Hungerford, R. H., DeProspero, C. J., & Rosensweig, L. E. (1948). The non-academic pupil. In *Philosophy of occupational education.* New York: Association for the New York City Teachers of Special Education.

Kokaska, C. J., & Brolin, D. E. (1985). *Career education for handicapped individuals* (2nd ed.). New York: Merrill/Macmillan.

Levinson, D. J. (1978). *The seasons of a man's life.* New York: Knopf.

Martin, J., Marshall, L. H., Maxson, L., & Jerman, P. (1993). *Self-directed IEP.* Colorado Springs: University of Colorado.

Mithaug, D. E. (1979). Negative employer attitudes toward hiring the handicapped: Fact or fiction? *Journal of Contemporary Business, 8*(4), 19–26.

Mithaug, D. E., Horiuchi, C. N., & Fanning, P. N. (1985). A report on the Colorado statewide follow-up survey of special education students. *Exceptional Children, 51,* 397–404.

Mount, B., & Zwernik, K. (1988). *It's never too early, it's never too late: A book about personal futures planning.* St. Paul, MN: Metropolitan Council.

National Information Center for Children and Youth with Disabilities. (1993). Transition services in the IEP. *Newsletter, 3*(1), 1–19.

Nirje, B. (1970). The normalization principle and its human management implications. *Journal of Subnormality, 16,* 62–70.

Nisbet, J., Covert, S., & Schuh, M. (1992). Family involvement in the transition from school to adult life. In F. R. Rusch, L. Destefano, J. Chadsey-Rusch, L. A. Phelps, & E. Szymanski (Eds.), *Transition from school to adult life.* Sycamore, IL: Sycamore Press.

Pati, G. C., Adkins, J. I., & Morrison, G. M. (1981). *Managing and employing the handicapped: The untapped potential.* Lake Forest, IL: Brace-Park.

Patton, J., & Browder, P. (1988). Transitions into the future. In B. L. Ludlow, A. P. Turnbull, & R. Luckasson (Eds.),

Transitions to adult life for people with mental retardation: Principles and practices (pp. 293–311). Baltimore: Paul H. Brookes.

Peraino, J. M. (1992). Post-21 follow-up studies: How do special education graduates fare? In P. Wehman (Ed.), *Life beyond the classroom: Transition strategies for young people with disabilities*. Baltimore: Paul H. Brookes.

Phelps, L. A., & Frasier, J. R. (1988). Legislative and policy aspects of vocational special education. In R. Gaylord-Ross (Ed.), *Vocational education for persons with handicaps* (pp. 3–29). Mountain View, CA: Mayfield.

Rochlin, J. (1987, May 1). *Promoting employment opportunities for persons with disabilities*. Keynote address presented at the Young Adult Institute, New York.

Rothenbacher, C., & Leconte, P. (1990). Vocational assessment: A guide for parents and professionals. *Transition Summary, 6*, 1–24. (Newsletter of the National Information Center for Handicapped Children and Youth, Washington, DC)

Rusch, F., Mithaug, D., & Flexer, R. (1986). Obstacles to competitive employment and traditional program options for overcoming them. In F. R. Rusch (Ed.), *Competitive employment issues and strategies* (pp. 471–490). Baltimore: Paul H. Brookes.

Sarkees, M. D., & Scott, J. L. (1990). *Vocational special needs*. Alsip, IL: American Technical.

Schalock, R. L. (1986). Service delivery coordination. In F. R. Rusch (Ed.), *Competitive employment issues and strategies* (pp. 115–127). Baltimore: Paul H. Brookes.

Sheehy, G. (1976). *Passages: Predictable crises of adult life*. New York: Dutton.

Siegel, S., Robert, M., Avoke, S. K., Paul, P., & Gaylord-Ross, R. (1991). A second look at the adult lives of participants in the Career Ladder Program. *Journal of Vocational Rehabilitation, 1*(4), 9–23.

Siegel, S., Robert, M., Greener, K., Meyer, G., Halloran, W., & Gaylord-Ross, R. (1993). *Career ladders for challenged youths in transition from school to adult life*. Austin, TX: Pro-Ed.

Siegel, S., Robert, M., Waxman, M., & Gaylord-Ross, R. (1992). A follow-along study of participants in a longitudinal transition program for youths with mild disabilities. *Exceptional Children, 58*, 346-356.

Sobsey, D., & McDonald, L. (1988). Special education: Coming of age. In B. L. Ludlow, A. P. Turnbull, & R. Luckasson (Eds.), *Transitions to adult life for people with mental retardation: Principles and practices* (pp. 20–44). Baltimore: Paul H. Brookes.

Turnbull, A. P., & Turnbull, H. R. (1988). Toward great expectations for vocational opportunities: Family-professional partnerships. *Mental Retardation, 26*, 337–342.

Vincent, L. J., Salisbury, C., Walter, G., Brown, P., Gruenwald, L. J., & Powers, M. (1980). Program evaluation and curriculum development in early childhood/special education: Criteria for the next environment. In W. Sailor, B. Wilcox, & L. Brown (Eds.), *Methods of instruction for severely handicapped students* (pp. 303–328). Baltimore: Paul H. Brookes.

Ward, M. J. (1992). Self-determination revisited: Going beyond expectations. *Transition Summary, 7*, 2–4, 12. (Newsletter of the National Information Center for Handicapped Children and Youth, Washington, DC)

Wehman, P. (1988). Supported employment: Toward equal employment opportunity for persons with severe disabilities. *Mental Retardation, 26*, 357–361.

Wehman, P. (Ed.). (1992). *Life beyond the classroom: Transition strategies for young people with disabilities*. Baltimore: Paul H. Brookes.

Wehman, P. H., Kregal, J., Barcus, J. M., & Schalock, R. L. (1986). Vocational training for students with developmental disabilities. In W. E. Kiernan & J. A. Stark (Eds.), *Pathways to employment for adults with developmental disabilities* (pp. 113–127). Baltimore: Paul H. Brookes.

Wehman, P., Moon, M., Everson, J., Wood, W., & Barcus, J. (1988). *Transition from school to work: New challenges for youth with severe disabilities*. Baltimore: Paul H. Brookes.

West, L., Corbey, S., Boyer-Stephens, A., Jones, B., Miller, R. J., & Sarkees-Wircenski, M. (1992). *Integrating transition planning into the IEP process*. Reston, VA: Council for Exceptional Children.

West, M., Mast, M., Cosel, R., & Cosel, M. (1992). Applications for youth with orthopedic and other health impairments. In P. Wehman (Ed.), *Life beyond the classroom: Transition strategies for young people with disabilities* (pp. 373–393). Baltimore: Paul H. Brookes.

White, W., & Biller, E. (1988). Career education for students with handicaps. In R. Gaylord-Ross (Ed.), *Vocational education for persons with handicaps* (pp. 30–64). Mountain View, CA: Mayfield.

Wilcox, B., & Bellamy, G. T. (Eds.). (1982). *Design of high school programs for severely handicapped students*. Baltimore: Paul H. Brookes.

Wilcox, B., & Bellamy, G. T. (1987). *The activities catalog: An alternative curriculum for youth and adults with severe disabilities*. Baltimore: Paul H. Brookes.

Will, M. (1984a). Let us pause and reflect—but not too long. *Exceptional Children, 51*, 11–16.

Will, M. (1984b). OSERS *programming for the transition of youth with disabilities: Bridges from school to working life*. Washington, DC: Office of Special Education and Rehabilitative Services.

Wright, G. N. (1980). *Total rehabilitation*. Boston: Little, Brown.

Glossary

acuity   keenness of the senses; reception of external stimuli

adaptive behavior   behavior that meets standards of personal-occupational independence consistent with one's age and culture

advanced placement   option available to high school students by which they may complete college-level courses and receive college credit through examination

advocacy   the act of providing support

amblyopia ex anopsia (lazy eye)   inability to focus both eyes on same object (strabismus), sometimes resulting in the brain's repression of an image received from one eye; can eventually destroy that eye's ability to function

American Sign Language (ASL)   the language of deaf culture in the United States; a visual-gestural language with its own rules of syntax, semantics, and pragmatics that do not correspond to written or spoken English

amniocentesis   the drawing of amniotic fluid from the uterus of a pregnant woman to determine the presence of genetic and chromosomal abnormalities in the fetus. The sex of the fetus can also be determined.

anoxia   lack of oxygen severe enough to cause tissue damage; can cause permanent brain damage and mental retardation

anticonvulsant   medication used to control convulsions

apgar assessment   observation of a newborn at 1 minute and 5 minutes after birth scoring heart rate, respiratory condition, muscle tone, reflexes, and color. Each condition counts 2 points with a total score of 10 points.

aphasia   severe language disorder affecting use of symbols; results from damage to central nervous system

apnea   failure to breathe readily during or immediately after birth

applied behavior analysis   application and experimental evaluation of procedures for modifying significant human behaviors in practical situations

appropriate education   as used in P.L. 94–142, "education sufficient to confer benefit upon the handicapped child"

apraxia   impaired ability to organize motor commands to speech musculature, which results in improper sequencing of sounds in word production

aqueous humor   fluid between the lens and cornea of the eye

ARC (the)   acronym for the Association for Retarded Citizens, a national organization on mental retardation

articulation disorders   speech production problems including omissions, substitutions, additions, and distortions

asphyxia   impaired or absent exchange of oxygen and carbon dioxide; usually caused by interruption in breathing

assistive communication   communication forms, such as computer aids, that supplement or replace verbal speech

asthma   chronic respiratory condition characterized by wheezing, coughing, and difficulty breathing

astigmatism   defect of vision usually caused by irregularities in the cornea. It results in blurred vision and difficulties in focusing and can usually be corrected by lenses.

at-risk infants   infants who, for socioeconomic, health, physiological, or genetic reasons, face likely developmental delay

ataxia poor sense of balance and body position and lack of coordination of the voluntary muscles; characteristic of one type of cerebral palsy

athetosis type of cerebral palsy characterized by large, irregular, uncontrollable twisting motions, often accompanied by difficulty with oral language

atonia condition characterized by lack of muscle tone

attention deficit disorder (ADD) See *attention deficit-hyperactivity disorder* (ADHD).

attention deficit-hyperactivity disorder (ADHD) diagnostic category of the American Psychiatric Association DSMIII for a condition in which a child exhibits developmentally inappropriate inattention and impulsivity

audiogram a graph of the level of sound a person can hear in each ear at least 50% of the time at each of several frequencies, covering the range of normal speech

audiologist person who is certified in identification, measurement, and study of hearing and hearing impairments and who can recommend rehabilitative procedures

audiometry various methods for assessing hearing acuity

auditory canal part of the ear that slightly amplifies and transports sound waves from the external ear to the middle ear

auditory training training in listening skills to teach persons who are hearing impaired to make as much use as possible of their residual hearing

augmentative communication nonspeech communication used to supplement whatever naturally acquired speech may be present; includes computer-based speaking systems or signing and gestures

autism severe disorder of childhood, usually appearing by age 2½, characterized by lack of social participation, noncommunication, stereotypic behavior, and lowered cognitive and language abilities

aversive consequences consequences characterized by obvious signs of physical pain experienced by the individual and potential or actual physical side effects

behavior overt response to a stimulus emitted voluntarily or elicited involuntarily

behavior disorders behavior characteristics that (1) deviate from educators' standards of normality and (2) impair the functioning of that student and/or others. They are manifested as environmental conflicts and/or personal disturbances and typically accompanied by learning disorders.

behavior modification systematic arrangement of environmental events (antecedent and consequent events) to produce specific changes in observable behavior; may include positive reinforcement, negative reinforcement, time-out, response cost, modeling, and so on

behavioral model model based on the assumption that many forms of abnormal behavior are learned responses. Operant conditioning, respondent conditioning, and modeling are some of the mechanisms through which behaviors are acquired and regulated. Treatment involves environmental modifications of antecedent or consequent events.

bibliotherapy use of reading to help solve emotional problems and to promote mental health

Bilingual Education Act law providing that non-English-speaking students are entitled to educational opportunities in their native language

blind totally without vision, or having light perception only

bonding process by which infants and parents become attached to each other through a series of reciprocal and rhythmical interactions

braille system of reading and writing for the blind that uses embossed dots, named after its developer, Louis Braille

Brown v. Board of Education case in which the U.S. Supreme Court ruled that states may not provide "separate but equal" educational facilities; beginning of racial integration in U.S. schools and foundation for integration of students with disabilities into regular classrooms

CAI computer-assisted instruction; includes drill and practice, tutorials, games, simulations, problem solving, and word processing

career education process of facilitating an individual's potential for economic, social, and personal fulfillment and participation in productive work activities by systematically coordinating all school, family, and community efforts and programs

case management process of planning, implementing, and monitoring an individual's program(s) from assessment through intervention; used in social and educational programs

cataract a reduction or loss of vision that occurs when the crystalline lens of the eye becomes cloudy or opaque

categorical descriptors labels that classify learning and behavior disabilities according to traditional categories (e.g., mental retardation, behavior disorders, and learning disabilities)

catheter a tube inserted into the body to allow injections or withdrawal of fluids or to keep a passageway open; often refers to a tube inserted into the bladder to remove urine from a person who does not have effective bladder control

central visual acuity sharpness or clarity of vision at the center or focal point of the visual field

cerebral palsy disorder resulting from damage to, or maldevelopment of, the brain

child find system used within a state or local area to identify all children who are disabled or at risk and make referrals for appropriate support services

childhood schizophrenia severe disorder of childhood, probably distinguishable from autism; characterized by bizarre behavior patterns, distortions of thinking, and abnormal perceptions

chorion villus sampling (CVS) procedure for prenatal diagnosis of chromosomal abnormalities; conducted during the first 8 to 10 weeks of pregnancy. Fetal cells are removed from tissue that surrounds the fetus and are directly analyzed.

chromosomal abnormalities deviations in chromosomes, the threadlike materials that carry genes and therefore play a central role in heredity

cleft palate a congenital split in the palate often causing an excessive nasal quality of the voice; can often be repaired by surgery or dental appliance

cluttering rapid, garbled speech with extra or mispronounced sounds and sometimes mixed-up sentence structure

CMI computer-managed instruction; system using computers for planning, for documenting student needs and progress, and for data-processing functions

cochlea main receptor organ for hearing located in the inner ear; tiny hairlike cells within the cochlea transform energy into neural impulses that then travel through the auditory nerve to the brain

cognitive disability disorder in the formation or use of symbols and concepts during thinking, reasoning, planning, and problem solving

cognitive functioning ability to think and process information and knowledge

cognitive strategies techniques that involve one in the self-control of one's own behaviors; may include elements of self-instruction, self-monitoring, and self-reinforcement

cognitive-behavioral training approach in which the individual is taught to use internalized speech strategies to respond to problem situations

collaboration process of working together to attain a common goal; sometimes referred to as professional partnerships

communication whole spectrum of visual and auditory stimuli—facial expression, gestures, sounds, words, phrases—used to convey interpersonal messages

community-based instruction approach that focuses on the individual's learning and applying skills in community settings

complex partial seizure a type of epileptic seizure in which an individual goes through a period of inappropriate activity but is not aware of that activity

compulsory education education required by state and/or federal law

conditioning technique that uses new objects or situations to elicit responses that were previously elicited by other stimuli

conduct disorder behavior disorder manifested by disobedience, disruptiveness, fighting, or tantrums

conductive hearing loss impairment in the mechanical transmission of sound waves through the outer and middle ear

congenital present at or arising from birth

contingency contracting contracting, usually written, that stipulates conditions for certain desired behaviors. Conditions typically include precise behaviors desired, stated in clear and objective terms; the time period within which the behaviors are to be performed; and the consequences contingent upon successful performance.

continuum of services range of placement and instructional options that a school district can use to serve children with disabilities; typically depicted as a pyramid, ranging from the least restrictive placement (regular classroom) at the bottom to the most restrictive placement (institution or hospital) at the top

contributory conditions situations that increase the risk of occurrence of a disability or disorder

cooperative learning instructional approach in which students work together to achieve group goals or rewards

cornea the transparent part of the eyeball that admits light to the interior

creativity process of bringing a new, different, and unexpected response to a situation

cri-du-chat syndrome a chromosomal abnormality resulting from deletion of material from the fifth pair of chromosomes and often causing severe retardation. Its name is

French for "cat cry," named for the high-pitched crying of the child as the result of a related larynx dysfunction.

cultural assimilation relates to the "melting pot" concept whereby the entire American population is considered to be assimilated into a single group of people with similar life-styles, values, language, and cultural patterns

cultural bias inaccurate and/or distorted judgment based on cultural differences

cultural pluralism appreciation of cultural differences in which unique contributions of various cultural groups in strengthening and enriching society are recognized

cultural-familial mental retardation any case of mental retardation for which no known organic cause can be found; suggests that retardation can be caused by a poor social and cultural environment

curriculum-based assessment evaluation of a student's progress in terms of performance on the skills that compose the curriculum of his or her local school

cystic fibrosis inherited disorder that causes dysfunction of the pancreas, mucus, salivary, and sweat glands with no known cure; causes severe, long-term respiratory difficulties

deaf-blind describes the condition of an individual having simultaneous vision and hearing deficiencies

deafness hearing disability that prevents processing of linguistic information through audition, with or without a hearing aid

decibels (dB) units of sound intensity perceived as loudness or softness

deinstitutionalization effort to bring individuals in institutions into the closest possible contact with the mainstream of normal society, either by removing them from institutions and placing them in alternative settings in the community or by changing the institution to permit more interaction with the outside community

developmental disability severe, chronic disability attributable to a mental or physical impairment or combination of the two, which manifests itself before the age of 22 and results in substantial functional limitations

diabetic retinopathy type of vision impairment caused by hemorrhages on the retina and other disorders of blood circulation in people with diabetes

differential reinforcement of other behavior behavior modification technique in which any behavior except the targeted maladaptive response is reinforced. Its goal is the reduction of the inappropriate behavior.

diplegia paralysis that affects the legs more often than the arms

direct instruction criterion-referenced, systematic instruction based on a scope and sequence skills list; begins with lowest-level skill not mastered

disability reduced function or loss of a particular body part or organ

disabled having reduced functioning as a result of a physical deficit or a significant problem in learning or social adjustment; sometimes used more narrowly to refer to physical deficits or crippling conditions

disordered having reduced functioning, particularly in academic achievement (e.g., learning disorders), social adjustment (e.g., behavior disorders), or oral language use (e.g., speech or language disorders)

double hemiplegia paralysis of the arms, with less severe involvement of the legs

Down syndrome chromosomal disorder characterized by an extra chromosome in each somatic cell; syndrome associated with characteristic flat facial features, mental retardation, and other congenital defects; also called *mongolism*

drug therapy major treatment for behavior and learning disorders, based on constellation of stimulant drugs such as amphetamines

due process right of a citizen to protest before any government acts to deprive him or her of the rights to life, liberty, or property

dyslexia disorder characterized by failure to attain adequate reading skills

early intervention approach in which comprehensive services are provided both for infants and toddlers with disabilities or at risk of eventually developing disabilities and for their families. Services may include education, health care, and/or social-psychological assistance.

eating disorders conditions characterized by serious disturbances in eating behaviors (e.g., anorexia nervosa, bulimia)

echolalia condition characterized by meaningless repetition or imitation of speech

ecological model model in which behavior disorders are viewed as disturbances in interchanges between the individual and the social environment. Treatment is directed toward modifying the total ecological system.

educable mentally retarded (EMR) description for individuals who have mild mental retardation, achieve academically about 2 years slower than normal children during school age, and have a high probability of vocational independence

electroacoustic aids electronic devices that assist an individual in hearing; types include body and behind-the-ear hearing aids

electroencephalograph (EEG) device that detects and records brain wave patterns

eligibility determination as to whether a child qualifies for special educational and related services

emotional disturbance See *behavior disorders*.

endogenous describing conditions that originate from within an organism

enrichment approach offering a child extra learning experiences that the standard curriculum would not normally provide; most often used with gifted and talented children

epilepsy seizure disorder caused by abnormal, excessive electrical brain discharges

etiology origins or causes, whether organic or environmental, of a disease or condition

evoked-response audiometry a method of testing hearing by measuring the electrical activity generated by the auditory nerve in response to stimulation; often used to measure the hearing of infants and children considered difficult to test

exceptional describing deviation from the norm, either by higher-than-average or lower-than-average performance or ability

exclusion component one part of the P.L. 94–142's definition of *specific learning disability*, which excludes children whose learning problems are a result of physical or sensory handicap; mental retardation; emotional disturbance; or environmental, cultural, or economic disadvantages

exogenous describing conditions that originate outside an organism

extinction procedure to weaken or eliminate problem behaviors by contingently withholding attention after a problem behavior occurs

facilitative communication communication techniques that facilitate or augment general communication ability (e.g., prompting). See also *augmentative communication*.

fetal alcohol syndrome (FAS) condition sometimes found in the infants of alcoholic mothers; can involve low birth weight; developmental delay; and cardiac, limb, and other physical defects

fine motor skills small muscle actions such as those involved in eye-hand coordination, reaching, grasping, and object manipulation

fluency disorders interruptions of natural, smooth flow of speech by inappropriate hesitations, pauses, and/or repetitions

fragile-X syndrome a chromosomal abnormality associated with mild to severe mental retardation; thought to be the most common known cause of inherited mental retardation; affects males more often and more severely than females. Behavioral characteristics resemble autism; diagnosis can be confirmed by studies of the X chromosome.

full inclusion placement option in which students who are disabled or at risk receive all instruction in a regular classroom setting in their home or neighborhood school and in which support services come to the students

functional life/compensatory approach instructional approach in which only practical skills facilitating a student's accommodation to natural settings—whether the classroom, home, or neighborhood—are taught. Typically taught are self-care, personal/social skills, and occupational/vocational skills.

functional skills tasks and activities most often required in routine settings

galactosemia condition characterized by a metabolic problem in which an infant has difficulty processing lactose; may cause mental retardation and other problems

gene specific segment of a DNA molecule that mediates transmission of inherited characteristics that influence an individual's development

gifted describing individuals who exhibit high levels of intellectual ability or who show potential for such development as demonstrated by their ability to think abstractly, solve complex problems, see relationships, and make generalizations

glaucoma eye disease characterized by abnormally high pressure inside the eyeball. If left untreated, it can cause total blindness, but if detected early, most cases can be arrested.

grammatical method method of teaching language to children with hearing impairments by presenting them with specific grammatical rules for putting sentences together and then having them construct sentences using those rules

grand mal seizure severe type of epileptic seizure in which the individual has convulsions and loses consciousness

grant-in-aid　law that provides federal money to state and local governments to be spent for specific purposes in accordance with federal regulations

gross motor skills　large muscle actions such as sitting, crawling, standing, and walking

habilitation　provision of education and training opportunities that enable an individual to attain a level of independence commensurate with his or her potential

handicapped　describing reduced functioning as a result of difficulty in responding or adjusting to the environment because of intellectual, physical, or emotional problems

hard-of-hearing　having sufficient residual hearing to process linguistic information through audition, usually with a hearing aid

hearing impairment　hearing disability ranging from mildly to profoundly severe; includes *deafness* and *hard-of-hearing*

hemiplegia　paralysis of both the arm and the leg on the same side of the body

hemophilia　inherited deficiency in the ability of blood to clot, which can cause serious internal bleeding

hertz (Hz)　a unit of sound frequency equal to one cycle per second; used to measure pitch

human immunodeficiency virus (HIV)　the virus that causes acquired immune deficiency syndrome (AIDS)

hydrocephalus　abnormal blockage of cerebrospinal fluid in the cranial cavity. If not corrected, spinal fluid accumulates in the cranial cavity, enlarging the head and damaging the brain, usually causing mental retardation.

hyperactivity　behavior disorder characterized by excessive, nonpurposeful movement, restlessness, inattentiveness, and impulsivity

hyperopia　farsightedness; results in blurred vision for near objects

hypertonia　muscle tone that is too high; tense, contracted muscles

hypoactivity　unnatural inactivity; passivity

hypotonia　muscle tone that is too low; weak, floppy muscles

IDEA　See *Public Law* 101-476.

idiopathic　of unknown origin

imitation　act of matching a modeled behavior, or behaving similarly to what is observed

impaired　describing reduced functioning, often as a result of a sensory deficit (e.g., loss of hearing or sight)

impedance audiometry　procedure for testing middle ear functioning by inserting a small probe and pump to detect sound reflected by the eardrum

in utero　means "in the uterus" and used to describe fetal development; may be used to describe abnormalities or accidents that occur before birth (e.g., in utero infection)

incidence　Incidence estimates include the occurrences of the condition that are reported over a period of time. See *prevalence*.

incoordination　lack of muscular control

independent study　arrangement whereby a student works independently on a project or unit of study using methods, materials, and evaluation criteria agreed on by the student and teacher

Individualized Educational Plan (IEP)　educational plan mandated by federal legislation in P.L. 94–142 for children with disabilities, which is designed and signed by parents, teachers, sometimes the child, and any additional professionals needed to implement the plan. The plan reflects short- and long-term goals for the child for a year, and process is designed to ensure confidentiality; placement in the least restrictive environment; and appropriate, individualized education.

Individualized Family Service Plan (IFSP)　a requirement of P.L. 99–457, Education of the Handicapped Act Amendments of 1986, for the coordination of early intervention services for infants and toddlers with disabilities; similar to the IEP that is required for all school-age children deemed eligible for special education

Individualized Transition Plan (ITP)　plan providing for services for an individual's transition to adult life; mandated by IDEA for students 16 years of age or older

infantile autism　See *autism*.

institutionalization　placement in a collective, residential facility, usually administered by the state and housing individuals labeled as mentally retarded or emotionally disturbed

integration　mixing of students with disabilities and those without disabilities in education and community environments

interindividual differences　differences between two or more individuals in a particular area; comparison of one person to another

intervention　design for changing an individual's behavioral, medical, or health status, or a program itself

intraindividual differences　differences within one individual on different measures—indicate strengths and weaknesses

IQ (intelligence quotient) quantity derived in some systems by dividing chronological age into mental age and multiplying by 100 (MA/CA x 100)

kinesthetic describing neuromuscular sensing of the position of body parts in space

Kurzweil Personal Readers reading devices for individuals who are blind that convert printed material into synthetic speech

labeling categorizing individuals by some group of like characteristics

language arbitrary system of vocal symbols providing people with a way to interact and communicate, as well as nonverbal language that involves signing, use of physical symbols, and body language

language use the pragmatic, functional, or social interaction aspects of language; the why, when, and where of language

learning disability generic term referring to a heterogeneous group of disorders that are most evident as problems with the acquisition and use of listening, speaking, reading, writing, reasoning, or mathematical abilities; presumed to be due to central nervous system dysfunction

least restrictive environment educational setting that is closest to full participation in the regular classroom but that still meets the exceptional student's special needs

legally blind condition in which central visual acuity is 20/200 or less in the better eye after correction or in which peripheral vision is reduced to an angle of 20 degrees or less in the better eye

limb deficiency absence of one or more limbs, as the result either of postnatal disease or injury or of a congenital problem

longitudinal study a research project that follows one subject or group of subjects over an extended period of time, usually several years

low vision vision limited to seeing objects and materials within a few inches or feet away

low-incidence disability a disability that occurs relatively infrequently in the general population (e.g., vision and hearing impairments, severe mental retardation, severe behavior disorders such as autism, and multiple handicaps)

mainstreaming system for integrating students with disabilities into regular classes, providing for their special needs through individualized instruction, tutoring, or their spending a portion of their day with a resource or special education teacher

maladaptive behavior inappropriate behavior or behavior judged as significantly below expectation for a specific age and cultural group

meningitis inflammation of the membranes covering the brain and spinal cord; can cause problems with sight and hearing and/or mental retardation

meningocele type of spina bifida in which the covering of the spinal cord protrudes through an opening in the vertebrae, but the cord itself and the nerve roots are enclosed

mental retardation subaverage general functioning with impairment of adaptive behavior, manifested during the developmental period. It is classified by etiology and severity; classifications by intellectual functioning are mild, moderate, severe, and profound.

metacognition refers to knowledge about, and regulation of, thinking processes

microcephalus condition characterized by an abnormally small skull with resulting brain damage and mental retardation

minimum competency testing trend among some states to ensure that student promotions and graduations are based on mastery of certain basic skills

misarticulation abnormal production of phonemes

mobility ability to move safely through the environment

mobility training instruction to help persons with visual impairments learn to travel independently in their home and community environments

modeling behavior that is learned or modified by observing and imitating the actions of others

motor disorders broad term for disabilities related to controlling muscles and maintaining a straight and normal skeletal and muscular state

multicultural education education that supports and encourages cultural pluralism. See also *cultural pluralism*.

multidisciplinary team group of professionals from various disciplines (e.g., educators, psychologists, and social workers) who work together for a common goal; required by P.L. 101-476 (IDEA) for developing an Individualized Educational Plan (involving parents, as well). See also *Individualized Educational Plan (IEP)*.

multifactored assessment evaluation of a child with a variety of test instruments and observational procedures; required by P.L. 94–142 when assessment is for educational placement of a child who is to receive special education services; prevents the misdiagnosing and misplacing a student as the result of considering only one test score

multihandicapped demonstrating two or more disabling conditions

muscular dystrophy a group of diseases that gradually weakens muscle tissue; usually becomes evident by the age of 4 or 5

myopia nearsightedness; results in blurred vision for objects at a distance

natural method system of teaching language to children who are hearing impaired in carefully structured situations so that they can learn through the process of hypothesis formulation and testing in sequences that closely follow language development of normal children

nature vs. nurture issue of whether behavior can be attributed to hereditary or environmental causes

negative reinforcement process of strengthening a response by removal of an aversive event contingent upon the response being produced

neurological pertaining to functioning of the central nervous system

normalization principle stating that care, education, and services for persons with disabilities be available to permit them to function in a manner that approximates or equals what is normal in society

nystagmus a rapid, involuntary, rhythmic movement of the eyes that may cause difficulty in reading or fixating on an object

observational learning learning that occurs from watching the behavior of others (models)

occupational therapist a professional person trained and/or licensed to provide training in functional skills. The training is designed to help an individual integrate neuromuscular activity in order to attain and maintain maximum functioning in daily living activities.

operant conditioning control of environmental stimuli so as to modify behavior

ophthalmologist physician who specializes in the care and treatment of the eyes

optacon device for translating print into tactile letters

optic atrophy condition characterized by deterioration of the nerve fibers connecting the retina to the brain

orientation ability to locate oneself in relationship to the environment or objects in the environment

otitis media an infection or inflammation of the middle ear that can cause a conductive hearing loss

overcorrection a behavior modification procedure in which the learner must make restitution for, or repair, the effects of his or her undesirable behavior and then put the environment in even better condition than it was prior to the misbehavior

paraplegia paralysis of the lower part of the body, including both legs; usually results from injury to, or disease of, the spinal cord

paraprofessionals (in education) trained classroom aides (instructional assistants) who assist teachers (e.g., parents and occupational and physical therapy aides)

partially sighted describing central visual acuity between 20/70 and 20/200 in the better eye after correction

perceptual disorder disorder resulting from inability to use one or more of the senses to recognize, discriminate, and interpret stimuli

perinatal beginning with birth and extending through the first 3 or 4 weeks of life. Perinatal factors influencing child health include disorders of delivery, infections, prematurity, hypoglycemia, asphyxia, cardiac irregularities, respiratory difficulties, and factors that originated during the prenatal period

peripherals devices attached to a computer that are not part of the central processing unit

peripheral vision ability to perceive objects outside the direct line of vision

phenylketonuria (PKU) an inherited metabolic disease that can cause severe retardation; can now be detected at birth and the detrimental effects prevented with a special diet

phoneme smallest unit of sound that can be identified in a spoken language. There are 45 phonemes in the English language.

physical therapist person registered or licensed to apply knowledge of neurodevelopmental techniques to problems of feeding, positioning, ambulation, and development of other gross motor and fine motor skills

pinpoint specify an observable behavior

play therapy treatment approach in which play activities are used to establish rapport and communication between the child and therapist

positive reinforcement refers to the increased probability of a response resulting from the application of a positive event

postlingual occurring after the development of language; usually used to classify hearing losses that begin after a person has learned to speak

postnatal pertaining to or occurring after birth

pragmatics study of the rules that govern how language is actually used

precision teaching instructional procedure involving (1) pinpointing behaviors to be changed, (2) measuring frequency of behaviors, (3) designing an instructional plan or intervention procedure, (4) measuring performance continuously and directly, and (5) graphing data to analyze trends and ensure that aims are met

prelingual describes a hearing impairment that develops before a child has acquired speech and language

prenatal pertaining to or occurring before birth

prevalence reported occurrence of a condition, usually expressed as a percentage of the total population. See *incidence*.

prosthesis artificial device replacing a body part that was absent at birth or later removed

psychodynamic psychology theories and therapies about behavior disorders, originally conceived by Sigmund Freud and revised by his many followers; emphasizes the importance of mental conflicts as causes of behavior disorders

psychoeducational model adaptation of psychodynamic concepts for use with students with behavior disorders in educational settings. Emphasis is on educational factors—abilities, interpersonal relations, skill level—in understanding and treating behavior disorders.

psycholinguistic approach approach that emphasizes the development of reception, association, and memory skills in the visual and auditory channels to alleviate learning problems

psycholinguistics psychological study of language and its effect on how the individual receives, processes, and expresses information

psychoses profound behavior disorders of childhood; includes autism and childhood schizophrenia

Public Law (P.L.) 94-142 Education for All Handicapped Children Act, originally passed in 1975, requiring that all children with disabilities receive "a free, appropriate public education which emphasizes special education and related services designed to meet their unique needs." Its name was later changed to the Education of the Handicapped Act.

Public Law (P.L.) 101-476 Individuals with Disabilities Education Act (IDEA), a reauthorization in 1990 of the Education of the Handicapped Act. It added new eligibility categories and services to P.L. 94–142.

public policy law made or carried out by federal, state, and local governments

punishment any event that immediately follows a behavior and is intended to result in the reduction or elimination of that behavior

quadriplegia paralysis of all four limbs

refraction the bending or deflection of light rays from a straight path as they pass from one medium (e.g., air) into another (e.g., the eye); used by eye specialists in assessing and correcting vision

Regular Education Initiative (REI) a perspective that all students with mild disabilities, as well as some with moderate disabilities, can and should be educated in regular classrooms under the primary responsibility of general education rather than special education

rehabilitation a social service program designed to teach a person newly identified as having disabilities the basic skills needed for independence

reinforcement any event or procedure that results in strengthening an existing behavior or teaching a new one

related services supportive services required for a child with disabilities to benefit from special education; include special transportation services, speech and language pathology, audiology, psychological services, physical and occupational therapy, school health services, counseling and medical services for diagnostic and evaluation purposes, rehabilitation counseling, social work services, and parent counseling and training

residential school a school, usually self-contained, where students live, going home only for major holidays or vacation. Many provide programs for preschool or elementary grades through secondary level.

residual hearing the remaining hearing, however slight, of a person with a hearing impairment

residual vision vision that remains despite an impairment

resource room a place where a teacher is available to work with individuals or small groups of students who have specific learning difficulties

response behavior that follows and results from a presented stimulus

retina a sheet of nerve tissue at the back of the eye on which an image is focused

retinitis pigmentosa (RP) an eye disease in which the retina gradually degenerates and atrophies, causing the field of vision to become progressively more narrow

retinopathy of prematurity (ROP) a condition characterized by an abnormally dense growth of blood vessels and scar tissue in the eye, often causing visual field loss and retinal detachment; usually caused by high levels of oxygen administered to premature infants in incubators; also called retrolental fibroplasia (RLF)

rigidity a type of cerebral palsy characterized by increased muscle tone, minimal muscle elasticity, and little or no stretch reflex

rubella mild viral infection (German measles). If a mother contracts this infection during pregnancy, especially in the first trimester, the infant may be born with hearing loss and/or defective vision and heart and nervous system anomalies.

screening process of identifying—provisionally—those children that require more complete assessment

self-contained day class class composed entirely of exceptional children, usually all categorized under the same label (e.g., educable mentally retarded, learning disabled), who therefore do not participate in regular academic programs with their other peers

sensorineural hearing loss impairment of the inner ear or the eighth cranial nerve; reduces intensity of signal and may also distort sounds received

sensory modality systematic way of sensing the environment by use of hearing, vision, touch, and so on (each is a sensory modality)

serious emotional disturbance an eligibility category under P.L. 101–476 (IDEA) that defines children whose mental, emotional, or behavioral disorders limit functioning in the educational setting

sheltered workshops segregated vocational settings for people with severe disabilities

shunt tube inserted in the body to divert fluid from one body part to another; often implanted in people with hydrocephalus to remove extra cerebrospinal fluid from the head and send it directly into the heart or intestines

social maladjustment behavior that violates laws or community standards but conforms to standards of some social subgroup

social validity desirable outcome of instruction, indicating its appropriateness for the learner (e.g., the goal of riding a bus independently would have social validity for learners residing in most cities, but not for those in small towns or rural areas)

spasticity excessive tension of muscles and resistance to extension or flexion, as in cerebral palsy

speech vocal transmission of language

speech pathology applied discipline made up of professionals with expertise in remediation of verbal behavior disorders and/or delays

speech reception threshold (SRT) decibel level at which one can identify a speech stimulus 50% of the time

speechreading skill of understanding a spoken message by observing the speaker's lips in combination with information gained from facial expressions, gestures, and the context or situation

spina bifida disorder in which a portion of the spinal cord is not enclosed by vertebral arches; usually a distortion of the spinal cord and roots; results in a neurological disorder and related deformities

spinal cord injury traumatic injury to the spinal cord that may result in paraplegia or quadriplegia

standard error of measurement estimate of the standard deviation of the population on which a test was normed

standardized tests assessment instruments that meet certain reliability and validity criteria; include precise instructions for administration and scoring

stereotypic (stereotyped) behavior repetitive nonfunctional movements (e.g., hand flapping, rocking), characteristic of autism and other severe disabilities

stimulus anything that evokes a response (e.g., sound, light, shape, sight)

stimulus control a condition demonstrated when a behavior is emitted more often in the presence of a particular stimulus than it is in the absence of that stimulus

strabismus a condition in which one eye cannot attain binocular vision with the other eye because of imbalanced muscles

stuttering speech disorder characterized by severe nonfluency

supported employment paid employment for persons with disabilities that takes place in an integrated environment and where increased support (e.g., additional supervision, specialized training) is provided

syntax the system of rules governing the meaningful arrangement of words in a language

systematic instruction process of instruction characterized by (1) systematic arrangement of conditions for learning, (2) initial assessment, (3) specification of objectives, (4) continuous measurement of performance, (5) instructional decisions based on performance measured, and (6) evaluation of overall effects of instructional conditions

tactile receiving meaning from stimuli by using touch

talented describing individuals who display superlative skills in a specific area as evidenced by outstanding performance or products

task analysis act of breaking down a skill into its behavioral components

Tay-Sachs disease a progressive nervous system disorder causing profound mental retardation, deafness, blindness, paralysis, and seizures; usually fatal by age 5; caused by a recessive gene. A blood test can identify carrier; an analysis of enzymes in fetal cells can provide a prenatal diagnosis.

teaching family model community-based group home program developed by behavioral psychologists to help predelinquent youths learn socially adaptive skills

time-out behavior management technique that involves removing the opportunity for reinforcement for a specific period of time following an inappropriate behavior. Its goal is a reduction of the inappropriate behavior.

token economy system of reinforcing various behaviors by delivering tokens (e.g., stars, points, poker chips) when specified behaviors are emitted; tokens are accumulated and turned in for the individual's choice of items on a "menu" of backup reinforcers (e.g., a sticker, hall monitor for a day)

topography (of behavior) physical shape or form of a response

total communication approach to teaching language to children with hearing impairments that combines the aural-oral approach with manual communication

tracking systems special grouping arrangements in which students of like ability or interest in a particular area are grouped together

trainable mentally retarded (TMR) description (no longer widely used) for people who generally have an IQ of 25 to 50; indicates low rate of development; semidependence throughout life; potential for learning self-care and adjusting socially to family and neighborhood; not capable of profiting from a program for educable mentally retarded; may have physical and/or motor impairments and sensory deficits

transition period that includes high school, point of graduation, additional postsecondary education or adult services, and initial years in employment; generally refers to transition from school to adult/work life

traumatic brain injury an eligibility category under P.L. 101-476 that defines children injured by forceful impact or open wound to the head, causing long-term learning and behavioral problems. Common symptoms are memory deficits, distractibility, and confusion in directionality.

tremor a type of cerebral palsy characterized by regular, strong, uncontrolled movements; may cause less overall difficulty in movement than other types of cerebral palsy

trial placement placing a student in a particular grade or grouping arrangement subject to evaluating its effectiveness; often used for children given early admission to school or for acceleration (grade skipping)

tymphonic membrane (eardrum) membrane located in the middle ear. The eardrum moves in and out to variations in sound pressure, changing acoustical energy to sound energy.

Usher syndrome an inherited combination of visual and hearing impairments in which a person is born with a profound hearing loss and then loses vision gradually in adulthood because of retinitis pigmentosa, which affects the visual field

visual acuity the ability to distinguish forms or discriminate details at a specified distance

visually limited describing vision that is limited under average circumstances. With aids, materials, or assistance the person can function visually.

vocational assessment multidisciplinary process of identifying characteristics and skills of an individual as they relate to vocational training and employment

vocational education training in specific skills, designed to prepare individuals for gainful employment as skilled or semiskilled workers or technicians for jobs that require less than a baccalaureate degree

vocational rehabilitation a program designed to help youth and adults with disabilities obtain and hold employment

voice disorders (voicing) inappropriate intensity, pitch, and/or quality of vocal tone produced at the larynx and resonated in the pharynx, oral cavity, and sometimes nasal cavity

work activity center a sheltered work and activity site for persons with severe disabilities. Individuals are taught concentration and persistence, along with basic life skills, for little or no pay.

Contributors

Norris G. Haring is currently professor of education/special education at the University of Washington and principal investigator of the Washington Research Organization (UWRO) and Program Development Services (PDS), funded by the U.S. Department of Education, Office of Special Education and Rehabilitation. Both UWRO and PDS projects are based at the University of Washington. Presently UWRO's focus is on research in education and technical assistance to promote development of friendships and inclusion of students with deaf-blindness in general education settings. PDS projects provide technical assistance, inservice training, and systems change for educators within Washington State.

As an educator, Dr. Haring has served as instructor in education at Syracuse University from 1954 to 1956; director of special education for the Arlington County Public Schools in Arlington, Virginia, from 1956 to 1957; associate professor and coordinator of special education at the University of Maryland from 1957 to 1960;; professor of education, associate professor of pediatrics, and educational director of the Children's Rehabilitation Unit at the University of Kansas Medical Center from 1960 to 1965; and adjunct professor in the Department of Pediatrics at the University of Washington from 1966 to 1978.

Dr. Haring served as founding president of the Association for Severely Handicapped (TASH—now the Association for Persons with Severe Handicaps) from 1975 to 1978. He has special interests in research in systematic instruction with children who are mildly or severely disabled.

Linda McCormick is a professor of special education at the University of Hawaii and coordinator of the Personnel Preparation Program for Infant Specialists and Preschool Interventionists. She received her Ph.D. in 1973 from George Peabody College of Vanderbilt University. Her primary commitments are to the areas of early intervention and language and communication disorders. She has authored and co-authored numerous articles and several texts, including *Early Language Intervention: An Introduction* and *Early Intervention in Natural Environments.* Current research interests are related to innovative personnel preparation and increasing and evaluating inclusion options for young children with disabilities.

Thomas G. Haring received a B.A. from the University of Washington, majoring in microbiology. He was awarded a master's degree in special education at the University of Kansas with a major in behavior disorders. He completed his special education training in the combined Ph.D. program of the University of California, Berkeley and San Francisco State University. At the time of his death in January, 1993, Tom was professor of educational psychology at the University of California, Santa Barbara.

Dr. Haring served on the editorial boards of the *Journal of Behavioral Education*, the *Journal of the Association for Persons with Severe Handicaps*, and the *Journal of Applied Behavior Analysis*. He received the Distinguished Professional Award from the Association for Persons with Severe Handicaps.

During the 15 years that Tom was active in research, he contributed more than 50 scholarly articles. His areas of interest included social interactions, nonaversive approaches to managing problem behavior, and the development of friendship networks between students with severe disabilities and nondisabled peers. His research was distinguished by his defining the variables that constitute friendships. His last project, which is yet to be published, is a culmination of his research on facilitating social relationships.

Sherwood J. Best is an assistant professor in the Division of Special Education at California State University, Los Angeles, and was previously the coordinator of special education credential programs at the University of California, Riverside. She received a B.A. in psychology from Pitzer College in 1973 and her M.A. in special education from California State University, Los Angeles, in 1980. She plans to complete her Ph.D. in educational psychology/special education at the University of California, Riverside, in 1994.

Before she began her university career, Sherwood taught children with physical and health impairments in a special day class on an integrated elementary campus. Prior to public school teaching, she implemented behavior management and self-care programs for students with severe and profound developmental disabilities at the Lanterman Developmental Center.

Sherwood J. Best is an active member of The Council for Exceptional Children and has served as editor and secretary of DPHD (the Division for Physical and Health Disabilities). She is 1993-94 president of the California Trainers of Teachers of the Physi-

cally Handicapped. She has made numerous conference and workshop presentations, is the author of several articles, and has co-authored a chapter in the third edition of *Teaching Individuals with Physical and Multiple Disabilities* by June L. Bigge.

June L. Bigge is Professor Emerita of special education at San Francisco State University. She received the Ed.D. with honors from the University of Oregon. Before she began university teaching, she taught regular first grade, classes of children with physical and multiple disabilities in a special education schools, individuals with severe learning disabilities in regular classes, and students with physical disabilities who received most of their education in regular classes. She was among the first in her field to include students with physical and multiple disabilities in regular classes with their nondisabled peers.

Dr. Bigge is a past president of DOPH (Division of the Physically Handicapped) of The Council for Exceptional Children. Her publications include *Teaching Individuals with Physical and Multiple Disabilities* and *Curriculum-Based Instruction for Special Education Students*.

Douglas Cullinan is a professor at North Carolina State University. He has taught students with behavioral, learning, and emotional disabilities in public schools and in a correction institution. He received the doctorate in special education from the University of Virginia. As a faculty member in special education since 1973, Cullinan has taught and advised persons receiving professional training in special education and related fields at the bachelor's, master's and doctoral degree levels. He has served on the editorial boards of *Behavioral Disorders*, *Exceptional Children*, *Journal of Special Education*, and several other professional journals; he currently serves as co-editor (with Michael H. Epstein) of the *Journal of Emotional and Behavioral Disorders*.

Dr. Cullinan served during 1992–93 as president of the Council for Children with Behavioral Disorders. His main professional interests are the nature, measurement, and improvement of behavioral and emotional problems of students. Studies in these areas are among the more than 100 publications he has authored or co-authored.

Michael H. Epstein received his doctoral degree in special education with an emphasis in emotional and behavioral disorders from the University of Virginia. He has been as a teacher of children with behavior disorders, a director of special education programs, and a university teacher. Currently, Dr. Epstein is a professor of special education at Northern Illinois University. Dr. Epstein has directed 12 U.S. Department of Education research and personnel preparation grants, published more than 130 professional papers, and served as a reviewer for numerous professional journals. He has also been a consultant to several state and local education agencies.

Sharon Field is an associate professor (research) at Wayne State University. She received her Ed.D. from the University of Washington in policy, governance, and administration. She taught high school classes for students who are mildly disabled for 6 years, and she was a work experience coordinator for a local school district for 3 years. Her local school district experience also includes coordinating secondary level special education programs.

Dr. Field is a past president of the Division on Career Development of The Council for Exceptional Children. Her research and writing focus on self-determination, employment, and life skills preparation for adolescents and adults with disabilities and workplace-related factors affecting the employment of persons who are disabled.

Sheila Lowenbraun is chair of the area of special education and associate dean for professional programs at the University of Washington. Until recently she directed the program for preparing teachers for working with children with hearing impairments. Dr. Lowenbraun's focus has now shifted to preparing regular educators to work effectively with children with disabilities (including children with hearing impairments) in integrated and inclusive classrooms. Her recent research has focused on model programs for integrated education.

Dr. Lowenbraun earned her undergraduate degree in zoology from Barnard College, and her master's in education of children who are hearing impaired from Teachers College, Columbia University.

She taught adolescents with hearing impairments and multiple disabilities at the New York School for the Deaf for several years prior to returning to Columbia for her Ph.D.

Cecil D. Mercer is a professor of special education at the University of Florida. Dr. Mercer is the author or co-author of 15 books, 6 curriculum materials, and numerous journal articles and book chapters in the field of special education. He specializes in learning disabilities, and his two major texts are *Students with Learning Disabilities* and *Teaching Students with Learning Problems*. Dr. Mercer's research and interests have focused on the areas of learning strategies, mathematics, effective teaching principles, and behavior management, and he currently is producing a math strategies curriculum. Dr. Mercer received his Ed.D. in special education from the University of Virginia.

James R. Patton is the executive editor at PRO-ED and adjunct associate professor at the University of Texas at Austin. He has taught students with special needs at the elementary, secondary, and postsecondary levels. His professional interests include curriculum development, lifelong learning, instructional methodology, and science education. Currently he is developing life skills programs and integrated curricula. He earned his B.S. from the University of Notre Dame and his M.Ed. and Ed.D. from the University of Virginia.

Edward A. Polloway is the dean of the School of Education and Human Development at Lynchburg College, Lynchburg, Virginia. His previous professional experience includes teaching elementary and special education public school classes. He has published numerous books and journal articles in special education, has twice been president of the Division on Mental Retardation of The Council for Exceptional Children, and served on the Terminology and Classification Committee of AAMR. He received his B.A. from Dickinson College and his M.Ed. and Ed.D. from the University of Virginia.

Sandra Rosen is director of the Orientation and Mobility Program at San Francisco State University.

She earned her Ph.D. in education and human development from Vanderbilt University in 1986. Dr. Rosen has published on such topics as orientation and mobility services for preschool children, distance education, and the sensorimotor development of children with visual impairments. Her research interests include the areas of motor development and the use of interactive videodisc technology in teacher preparation.

Sharon Sacks is an associate professor in the Division of Special Education and Rehabilitation Services at San Jose State University and San Francisco State University. She received her Ph.D. in special education from the University of California, Berkeley and San Francisco State University in 1987. She is currently the project director of a personnel training grant in rehabilitation that focuses on the transition needs of young adults who are blind or visually impaired. She was instrumental in the development and implementation of the Rehabilitation Teacher Training Program at San Francisco State University. In addition to her teaching responsibilities, Dr. Sacks has written extensively and given numerous presentations in the areas of social skills instruction and transition programming for students with visual impairments. Her most recent publication is a book entitled *The Development of Social Skills by Blind and Visually Impaired Students: Exploratory Studies and Strategies*.

Barbara Sirvis is the vice president for academic affairs at the State University of New York College at Brockport; she also holds the rank of professor in the Departments of Education and Human Development and Recreation and Leisure Studies. She began her career working as a classroom teacher of children with physical and multiple disabilities. She has taught in self-contained preschool classes, piloting a transdisciplinary approach, and in secondary resource programs. She has also worked in clinical and community-based therapeutic recreation programs. Prior to her current position, she was dean of the faculty of Applied Science and Education at SUNY College at Buffalo; she has held previous faculty and administrative appointments at the Univer-

sity of Washington, San Francisco State University, and the University of Illinois at Urbana-Champaign. She earned her doctorate at Teachers College, Columbia University. Dr. Sirvis has served as a consultant, external evaluator, and workshop presenter for programs in both special education and therapeutic recreation; her publications include numerous articles and book chapters in both of these disciplines.

Marie Thompson is a professor of early childhood special education, College of Education, and an adjunct professor in speech and hearing sciences at the University of Washington. She has directed a program for children from birth to age 3 who are hearing impaired and their families in western Washington for 20 years. She is the primary author for the curriculum that is used in this program and has received recognition from the Washington State legislature for the program's excellence. Dr. Thompson has worked with students who are hearing impaired or deaf-blind both in the public schools and at the state level. She currently teaches graduate students at the University of Washington about these populations. She has had numerous state and federal grants that support her interest in these children and their parents.

Pam Winton is a research investigator at the Frank Porter Graham Child Development Center and a clinical professor in the School of Education at the University of North Carolina at Chapel Hill. She received a master's degree in special education from Peabody College in 1971 and a Ph.D. from the University of North Carolina at Chapel Hill in 1981. Her teaching and research interests are early intervention, families, inclusion, and personnel preparation.

Mark Wolery is a senior research scientist at Allegheny-Singer Research Institute and professor of psychiatry at the Medical College of Pennsylvania-Allegheny Campus. He has been a teacher of preschool and school-aged children with severe disabilities. He received his Ph.D. in early childhood special education and education of children with severe disabilities from the University of Washington in 1980. He is co-author of *Teaching Infants and Preschoolers with Disabilities*, *Assessing Infants and Preschoolers with Handicaps*, and *Teaching Students with Moderate and Severe Disabilities: Use of Response Prompting Strategies*. Current research interests are evaluating the efficiency of instructional procedures and embedding effective strategies in ongoing activities in mainstreamed classrooms.

Joan Wolf is associate professor and coordinator of the Program in Gifted Education in the Department of Special Education at the University of Utah. She began her career as an elementary school teacher and then completed an M.A. in school psychology and a Ph.D. in special education. She has worked with learning disabled and gifted youth and has been active in gifted program development and in the area of home/school collaboration. She has written numerous articles and book chapters and has conducted many workshops for teachers and parents. Dr. Wolf is also president of Educational Consulting Services.

Name Index

Subject Index

ISBN 0-02-350093-X

9 780023 500930

90000>